CASE FORMULATION FOR PERSONALITY DISORDERS

CASE FORMULATION FOR PERSONALITY DISORDERS

TAILORING PSYCHOTHERAPY TO THE INDIVIDUAL CLIENT

Edited by

UELI KRAMER

Foreword by

MARY C. ZANARINI

ELSEVIER

ACADEMIC PRESS

An imprint of Elsevier

Academic Press is an imprint of Elsevier
125 London Wall, London EC2Y 5AS, United Kingdom
525 B Street, Suite 1650, San Diego, CA 92101, United States
50 Hampshire Street, 5th Floor, Cambridge, MA 02139, United States
The Boulevard, Langford Lane, Kidlington, Oxford OX5 1GB, United Kingdom

Library of Congress Cataloging-in-Publication Data
A catalog record for this book is available from the Library of Congress

British Library Cataloguing-in-Publication Data
A catalogue record for this book is available from the British Library

ISBN: 978-0-12-813521-1

Publisher: Nikki Levy
Acquisition Editor: Nikki Levy
Editorial Project Manager: Barbara Makinster
Production Project Manager: Vijayaraj Purushothaman
Cover Designer: Matthew Limbert

Typeset by TNQ Technologies

Contents

List of Contributors **xiii**
About the Editor **xv**
Foreword **xvii**

Introduction xix
Case Formulation: From the Theory to the Case xix
UELI KRAMER

What Is Case Formulation? xx
A Disorder-Specific Approach to Case Formulation xxi
Constraints to Case Formulation for Personality Disorders: Occasions to Learn from the Individual Client xxii
Integrative Approach to Case Formulation for Personality Disorders and the Role of Clinical Theory xxv
Case Formulation as a Means to Increase Therapist Effectiveness xxvi
The Present Volume xxvii
References xxviii

1. Case Formulation in Dialectical Behaviour Therapy
SHELLEY MCMAIN, MICHELLE LEYBMAN AND TALI BORITZ

Introduction 1
Theoretical Foundation of Dialectical Behaviour Therapy (DBT) 3
Step-By Step Approach to Developing a Dialectical Behaviour Therapy (DBT) Case Formulation 5
Concluding Remarks 17
Acknowledgements 17
References 17

2. Transference-Focused Psychotherapy: Structural Diagnosis as the Basis for Case Formulation
KENNETH N. LEVY, YOGEV KIVITY AND FRANK E. YEOMANS

Review of Object Relations Theory in Relation to an Understanding of Personality Disorders in Terms of Psychological Structure 19
The Structural Interview as a Clinical Instrument 21
Discussion of the Diagnostic Impression/Formulation With the Patient 28

Using the Diagnostic Impression/Case Formulation to Choose a Therapy 30
Case Example 31
Review of Research 37
Research on the Structural Interview 37
Concluding Remarks 38
Acknowledgements 39
References 39

3. Case Formulations in Mentalization-Based Treatment (MBT) for Patients With Borderline Personality Disorder

SIGMUND KARTERUD AND MICKEY T. KONGERSLEV

The Heterogeneity of Borderline Personality Disorder 41
The Theoretical Grid for Case Formulations for Borderline Patients 42
The Mentalization-Based Approach to Case Formulations 44
Needed Information 46
Working in Concert with the Psychoeducational Group 47
Technical Details 47
The Mental Activity of the Therapist While Constructing a Case Formulation 49
Case Formulations in Mentalization-Based Treatment (MBT) Training 50
Two Different Borderline Personality Disorder (BPD) Case Formulations 50
Minding the Difficult Patient 57
Implications and Consequences for Therapy 58
Summary and Conclusions 58
Acknowledgements 59
References 59

4. The Corrective Experience of Getting a Life: Case Formulation Using General Psychiatric Management as a Framework to Facilitate Remission and Recovery

LOIS W. CHOI-KAIN AND ELLEN F. FINCH

Introduction 61
Case Vignette 67
Conclusions 74
Acknowledgements 74
References 74

5. Case Formulation in Schema Therapy: Working With the Mode Model

EVA FASSBINDER, ODETTE BRAND-DE WILDE AND ARNOUD ARNTZ

Introduction 77
Case Formulation With the Mode Model 81
Illustration of Case Formulation With an Example of a Borderline Personality Disorder (BPD) Patient 91

Conclusion 93
Acknowledgements 93
References 93

6. Cognitive Analytic Therapy: A Relational Approach to Young People With Severe Personality Disorder

LOUISE K. MCCUTCHEON, IAN B. KERR AND ANDREW M. CHANEN

Introduction 95
What Unique Features Characterize Cognitive Analytic Therapy? 96
Cognitive Analytic Therapy (CAT) Model of Development and Psychopathology 98
The Attributes of Cognitive Analytic Therapy (CAT) Formulation of Personality Disorder 101
Cognitive Analytic Therapy (CAT) Model of Borderline Personality Disorder 102
The Process of Reformulation 102
Applying Cognitive Analytic Therapy (CAT) to a Case Example 103
Laura's Reformulation Letter 107
Remainder of the Therapy 108
Conclusions 110
Acknowledgements 110
References 111
Further Reading 111

7. Case Conceptualization in Clarification-Oriented Psychotherapy

RAINER SACHSE

What Is Clarification-Oriented Psychotherapy? 113
The Model of Dual-Action Regulation 117
What Characterizes Clients with Narcissistic Personality Disorder? 121
What Defines a Narcissist from the Perspective of Dual-Action Regulation Model? 123
Therapy 125
Case Conceptualization of Narcissistic Personality Disorder 125
Meaning of the Case Conceptualization 129
Conclusion 130
Acknowledgements 130
References 130

8. Formulation of Functioning for Avoidant Personality Disorder in Metacognitive Interpersonal Therapy

GIANCARLO DIMAGGIO, RAFFAELE POPOLO AND GIAMPAOLO SALVATORE

Underlying Theory 137
Maladaptive Schemas for Self and Others 139
Impaired Metacognition 142
Poor Autobiographical Memory 143
Maladaptive Emotional Regulation and Coping 143

A Metacognitive Interpersonal Therapy (MIT)-Based Case Formulation: Self-Sustaining Processes 146
Clinical Guide to Case Formulation 147
Metacognitive Interpersonal Therapy (MIT)-Based Case Formulation and Therapy Planning: Mario's Story 148
Conclusions 156
Acknowledgements 156
References 157
Further Reading 160

9. What Might Work When Nothing Seems to Work: Case Formulation in the Treatment of Antisocial Personality Disorder in a Forensic Mental Health Setting
I. FRANKE, ST. NIGEL AND M. DUDECK

Introduction 161
Antisocial Personality Disorder 163
Case Formulation Theories 167
Example of Case Formulation for Antisocial Personality Disorder (ASPD) 173
Conclusions 177
Acknowledgements 177
References 177

10. Formulating Key Psychosocial Mechanisms of Psychopathology and Change in Interpersonal Reconstructive Therapy
KENNETH L. CRITCHFIELD, MARIAFÉ T. PANIZO AND LORNA SMITH BENJAMIN

IRT Theory 182
Centrality of Attachment Mechanisms, Learning and Development 183
Distinguishing Between Adaptive and Maladaptive Patterns Using SASB 185
IRT Case Formulation Method in Four Steps 187
Step One: Outline Patterns in the Present 189
Step Two: Seek Copy Process Evidence to Identify Key Attachment Figures 189
Step Three: the Gift of Love (GOL) Hypothesis 190
Step Four: Identify Treatment Implications 190
Application of the IRT Formulation Method 191
Current Patterns 192
Developmental History and Copy Process Analysis 194
Copy Process-Based Diagnosis of Personality Disorder 195
Gift of Love 196
Treatment Implications 196
Outcome 197
Case Formulation Research in IRT 199
Conclusion 200
Acknowledgements 200
Conflict of Interest 200
References 200

11. Motives, Defences, and Conflicts in the Dynamic Formulation for Psychodynamic Psychotherapy Using the Idiographic Conflict Formulation Method

J. CHRISTOPHER PERRY, MEGAN KNOLL AND VIET TRAN

Steps in Constructing a Case Formulation 205
Case Example 209
Case Formulation of Zofia 209
Treatment and Outcome 215
Discussion 216
Acknowledgements 217
Appendix A 217
Appendix B 219
Appendix C 222
References 222
Further Reading 224

12. Case Formulation in Cognitive and Behavioural Therapy

PETER STURMEY AND MARY MCMURRAN

Introduction 225
Case Formulation 226
Application of Case Formulation to Personality Disorders 228
Case Formulation of Personality Disorder: Traits and Processes 231
The Case of Arthur 234
Training to Make Formulations of Personality Disorders 240
Conclusion 242
Acknowledgements 242
References 242
Further Reading 244

13. Conceptualizing Borderline Personality Disorder Within an Emotional Disorders Framework: Implications for Treatment With the Unified Protocol

SHANNON SAUER-ZAVALA, KATE H. BENTLEY AND JULIANNE G. WILNER

Borderline Personality Disorder (BPD) Is an Emotional Disorder 246
Unified, Transdiagnostic Case Conceptualization for Emotional Disorders 249
Treating Borderline Personality Disorder (BPD) With the Unified Protocol: A Conceptualization-Focused Case Presentation 252
Conclusions 258
Acknowledgements 259
References 259
Further Reading 262

14. Plan Analysis and the Motive-Oriented Therapeutic Relationship

FRANZ CASPAR

Underlying Concepts 265
Methodology 269
Clinical Case with Personality Disorder 282
Research 286
Training 286
Acknowledgements 288
References 288
Further Reading 290

15. Tailored Treatment Planning for Individuals With Personality Disorders: The Operationalized Psychodynamic Diagnosis (OPD) Approach

JOHANNES C. EHRENTHAL AND CORD BENECKE

The Operationalized Psychodynamic Diagnosis (OPD) System 291
Practical Applications of the Operationalized Psychodynamic Diagnosis (OPD) System 301
Using the Operationalized Psychodynamic Diagnosis (OPD) System as an Integrative Approach to Case Formulations and Treatment Planning: A Clinical Case Example 305
Discussion 310
Closing Remarks and Future Perspectives 311
Acknowledgements 311
References 311

16. Case Formulation in Interpersonal Defence Theory: A Process Model of Interpersonal Phenomena that Play Key Roles in Psychopathology and Psychotherapy

MICHAEL A. WESTERMAN

Interpersonal Defence Theory 316
Case Formulation 319
Case Example 322
Treatment Implications 331
Concluding Comments 334
Acknowledgements 334
References 334

17. Alliance-Focused Formulation: A Work in Process

CATHERINE F. EUBANKS

Defining Alliance Ruptures 338
Alliance-Focused Process Formulation Methodology 338

Case Example 343
Future Directions 352
Acknowledgements 353
References 353

18. Emotion-Based Case Formulation for Personality Disorders
MICHAEL A. STRATING AND ANTONIO PASCUAL-LEONE

Emotion-Based Case Conceptualization: Theory and Key Concepts 356
Mapping out Emotional Change 357
Using the Process Map to Guide Clinical Practice 361
Empirical Support for Emotion-Based Case Formulation 364
Conducting Emotion-Based Case Formulations 366
Summary and Conclusion 371
Acknowledgements 372
References 372

Individualizing Treatment for Clients With Personality Disorders 375
UELI KRAMER

Occasions To Learn From The Individual Client 375
A Common Pathway To Understanding A Disruptive Experience: The Symbolizing Process 378
Case Formulations and The Therapeutic Relationship 379
Individualizing Psychotherapy Research Paradigms 382
Acknowledgments 386
References 386

Index 391

List of Contributors

Michael A. Strating University of Windsor, Windsor, Ontario, Canada

Arnoud Arntz Department of Clinical Psychology, University of Amsterdam, Amsterdam, The Netherlands

Cord Benecke Department of Psychology, University of Kassel, Kassel, Germany

Lorna Smith Benjamin University of Utah Neuropsychiatric Institute, University of Utah, Salt Lake City, UT, United States

Kate H. Bentley Department of Psychiatry, Massachusetts General Hospital, Boston, MA, United States

Tali Boritz Centre for Addiction and Mental Health, Toronto, ON, Canada; Department of Psychiatry, University of Toronto, Toronto, ON, Canada

Odette Brand-de Wilde Department of Clinical Psychology, University of Amsterdam, Amsterdam, The Netherlands

Franz Caspar University of Bern, Department of Clinical Psychology and Psychotherapy, Bern, Switzerland

Andrew M. Chanen Orygen, The National Centre of Excellence in Youth Mental Health, Melbourne, Australia; Centre for Youth Mental Health, The University of Melbourne, Melbourne, Australia; Orygen Youth Health, Northwestern Mental Health, Melbourne, Australia

Lois W. Choi-Kain McLean Hospital, Belmont, MA, United States

Kenneth L. Critchfield Department of Graduate Psychology, James Madison University, Harrisonburg, VA, United States

Giancarlo Dimaggio Centro di Terapia Metacognitiva Interpersonale, Rome, Italy

M. Dudeck Department of Forensic Psychiatry and Psychotherapy, Ulm University, Germany

Johannes C. Ehrenthal Institute of Medical Psychology, Heidelberg University, Germany

Catherine F. Eubanks Ferkauf Graduate School of Psychology, Yeshiva University, New York, NY, United States

Eva Fassbinder Department of Psychiatry and Psychotherapy, University of Luebeck, Luebeck, Germany

Ellen F. Finch McLean Hospital, Belmont, MA, United States

I. Franke Department of Forensic Psychiatry and Psychotherapy, Ulm University, Germany

Sigmund Karterud Norwegian Institute for Mentalizing, Oslo, Norway

Ian B. Kerr Department of Psychotherapy, Coathill Hospital, Coatbridge, Scotland

Yogev Kivity Pennsylvania State University, University Park, PA, United States

Megan Knoll McGill University, Montreal, Quebec, Canada

Mickey T. Kongerslev Centre of Excellence on Personality Disorder, Region Zealand Psychiatry, Slagelse, Denmark; Psychiatric Research Unit, Region Zealand Psychiatry, Slagelse, Denmark; Psychiatric Clinic Roskilde, Region Zealand Psychiatry, Roskilde, Denmark; Department of Psychology, University of Southern Denmark, Odense, Denmark

Kenneth N. Levy Pennsylvania State University, University Park, PA, United States; Weill Medical College of Cornell University, New York, NY, United States

Michelle Leybman Centre for Addiction and Mental Health, Toronto, ON, Canada

Louise K. McCutcheon Orygen, The National Centre of Excellence in Youth Mental Health, Melbourne, Australia; Centre for Youth Mental Health, The University of Melbourne, Melbourne, Australia; Orygen Youth Health, Northwestern Mental Health, Melbourne, Australia

Shelley McMain Centre for Addiction and Mental Health, Toronto, ON, Canada; Department of Psychiatry, University of Toronto, Toronto, ON, Canada

Mary McMurran Institute of Mental Health, University of Nottingham, Nottingham, United Kingdom

St. Nigel Department of Forensic Psychiatry and Psychotherapy, Ulm University, Germany

Mariafé T. Panizo Department of Graduate Psychology, James Madison University, Harrisonburg, VA, United States

Antonio Pascual-Leone University of Windsor, Windsor, Ontario, Canada

J. Christopher Perry McGill University at the Jewish General Hospital, Montreal, Quebec, Canada

Raffaele Popolo Centro di Terapia Metacognitiva Interpersonale, Rome, Italy

Rainer Sachse IPP, Institut für Psychologische Psychotherapie, Bochum, Germany

Giampaolo Salvatore Centro di Terapia Metacognitiva Interpersonale, Rome, Italy

Shannon Sauer-Zavala Department of Psychological and Brain Sciences, Boston University, Boston, MA, United States

Peter Sturmey The Graduate Center and Department of Psychology, Queens College, City University of New York, Queens, NY, United States

Viet Tran McGill University, Montreal, Quebec, Canada

Michael A. Westerman New York University, New York, United States

Julianne G. Wilner Department of Psychological and Brain Sciences, Boston University, Boston, MA, United States

Frank E. Yeomans Weill Medical College of Cornell University, New York, NY, United States

About the Editor

Ueli Kramer, PhD, is Privat-Docent, psychotherapy researcher and clinical psychotherapist according to Federal Law, at the Department of Psychiatry (Institute of Psychotherapy and General Psychiatry Service), University of Lausanne, Switzerland. He holds an adjunct appointment at the Department of Psychology, University of Windsor, Canada. His research focuses on process and outcome in psychotherapy, in particular the mechanisms of change in treatments of personality disorders and case formulation in personality disorders. He is a broadly trained clinician, working from an integrative psychotherapy perspective. He serves on the editorial board of *Psychotherapy Research, Journal of Personality Disorders, Journal of Psychotherapy Integration and Pragmatic Case Studies in Psychotherapy,* among others. Dr. Kramer is the co-recipient of the 2015 Inger Salling Award, the recipient of the 2016 Outstanding Early Career Achievement Award of the Society for Psychotherapy Research, the 2016 Hamburg Award for Personality Disorders and the 2018 Marvin Goldfried New Researcher Award of the Society for the Exploration of Psychotherapy Integration.

Foreword

Dr. Kramer has a deep and abiding interest and expertise in the many forms of psychotherapy that have been developed for those with personality disorders or less than optimally mature ways of seeing themselves and others and functioning in the world. He has brought together in this book chapters written on each of the five major empirically based treatments for borderline personality disorder (BPD; Dialectical Behavior Therapy, Transference-focused Psychotherapy, Mentalization-based Treatment, General Psychiatric Management, and Schema-Focused Therapy) and two others that are widely used in their treatment (Cognitive Analytic Therapy and the Unified Protocol for Emotional Disorders that has been adapted for BPD). Other chapters pertain to therapies used with a variety of personality disorders.

Each chapter carefully describes a specific form of psychotherapy or a method for structuring a case formulation. Each type of therapy is somewhat different than the others. Each method for developing a case formulation if also different and even unique to that form of treatment.

Any clinician or trainee interested in working with patients with a personality disorder will benefit from reading this book. They will learn about the wide variety of therapies for these disorders that are available for their treatment. They will also learn about the content and method of case formulation for the many treatments described in this comprehensive book.

Some of these types of case formulation focus more on the past than others. Some focus more on a collaborative process than others. All aim to base a treatment on a written formulation of what is causing the suffering and impairment of a patient at a time in his or her life.

Some of the treatments described are psychodynamic in nature and others are more cognitive or behavioral. They offer a wide array of treatments to choose from based on the personality of the therapist and the presentation and problems of a patient.

This is an empirical age and one would hope that most clinicians working with this patient population will be trained in one or more of these evidence-based treatments. One would also hope that case formulations will be developed with the care and thought evidenced in this book.

Dr. Kramer who has been a valued colleague of mine for several years deserves credit for putting this worthwhile book together. His expertise is clear in the choices he has made for this comprehensive and compelling book.

Mary C. Zanarini

Introduction

CASE FORMULATION: FROM THE THEORY TO THE CASE

UELI KRAMER

Case formulation links the process of diagnosis with the treatment, psychopathology with psychotherapy, the clinical theory with the unique case, and the general with the particular. As such, it gives the therapist a unique opportunity for clinically appropriate decision making, personalizing the intervention and gaining insight into the client's subjective experience. Research has shown that experts in psychotherapy propose parsimonious, synthetic and clinically relevant case formulations. When comparing with less experienced psychotherapists, experts in psychotherapy seem to make 'better' – more precise and less erroneous – case formulations of their client's situations (Eells, Lombart, Kendjelic, Turner, & Lucas, 2005), and adopt a more cautious and hypothetical stance with regard to their own formulation (Dudley, Ingham, Sowerby, & Freeston, 2015). Despite these conclusions, psychotherapy models – and psychotherapy research – have not always used the potential of the idiographics contained in case formulations (Eells, 2013a,b; Persons, 1991, 2013).

Clients presenting with a personality disorder (PD) may particularly benefit from a therapy process informed by effective case formulation. Their symptoms and problematic processes often are manifold and multilayered, which may require a clinically relevant formulation; also, these processes have started to be empirically understood on the level of the distinct categories. This population presents with a large between-client heterogeneity, which challenges categorical systems of classification, and may fundamentally require an individualized approach to the understanding and the treatment. As noted by Livesley (2018), the heterogeneity of the PDs may be reflected in the plurality of theoretical perspectives the field currently characterizes. Case formulation may play a pivotal role in breaking multiple theories down to an individual case. What precision medicine is for the treatment of somatic disorders is case formulation for the treatment of mental disorders, and in particular, personality disorders: the missing link between nomothetic knowledge bases and the idiographic contents of the individual client's narrative, experience and self-presentation. It is so important that a recent biannual conference of the North American Chapter of the Society for Psychotherapy

Research (NA-SPR, at Berkeley, CA, USA, in November 2016) dedicated its theme to the personalization of psychotherapy. To acknowledge SPR as a source of inspiration of my work, this book borrows its subtitle from this conference.

WHAT IS CASE FORMULATION?

Case formulation may generally be defined as 'a hypothesis about the causes, precipitants, and maintaining influences of a person's psychological, interpersonal, and behavioral problems' (Eells, 2007, p. 4). Adopting a disorder-specific approach, as in the present volume, we understand under case formulation a set of idiosyncratic hypotheses, explaining observations through the lenses of both clinical theory and relevant knowledge bases, with the aiming of understanding a client. As such, it synthesizes information and integrates, differentiates and gives meaning to seemingly contradictory observations. The meaning constructed in this process may vary in focus, depth and differentiation. Whereas the observed behaviour may be similar across individuals, the symbolized meaning may be different for each of these: case formulation helps explaining these differences. It provides the therapist with a compass, which assists him/her to select an intervention, helps give meaning to emerging manifestations, helps shape the therapy planning and implementation, and the therapist relationship offer. Case formulation may help in clinically critical situations, to understand self-harming behaviour or an experience of interpersonal rage or deep grief, which may be specific interaction situations where an evidence-based therapy intervention does not always indicate what to do. An individualized case formulation is a blueprint for the therapy process, which should be critically and dynamically revised as the therapy progresses. As such, it implies the therapist is active meta-conceptualizing the ongoing process, according to the underlying clinical theory. There is a feedback loop incorporated in case formulation methodology (Eells, 2013a): the formulation contains predictions about the client's behaviour and experience which will then be monitored, tested and assessed throughout the entire psychotherapy, the result of this process is then fed back into the case formulation. Case conceptualization may be a therapist activity, which may help to study the development of expertise in psychotherapy (Chi, 2006; Dudley et al., 2015; Vollmer, Spada, Caspar, & Burri, 2013). Case formulation helps bridge a still present gap between science and practice. Closing such a gap was considered by Goldfried (2010) as one of the major tasks of psychotherapy integration in the 21st century.

Case formulation, in its present formats, is a modern – for some authors post-modern – component of psychological and psychotherapeutic intervention (Caspar, 2000; Eells, 2007; Ingram, 2016; Johnstone & Dallos, 2013;

Macneil, Hasty, Conus, & Berk, 2012; Persons, 1989; Sturmey, 2009). It has outgrown of the early practices of medical history taking, the examination of case history and psychiatric anamnesis. Whereas early – Hippocratic medical – practices of describing clinical features in a client, followed by the activities of inferring and concluding, are still of relevance in today's psychiatry and medicine in general (Eells, 2007), their empirical stance has inspired the development of many psychotherapy case formulation methods.

Case formulation methodology has not the same history in each of the traditional clinical theories. Psychoanalysis contributed to contemporary case formulation with its rich theoretical development gained from a series of case studies that were rigorously documented by the use of in-session information for the formulation (Eells, 2007; Gill, Newman, & Redlich, 1954). Early psychoanalytic formulations tended to use a quite high degree of inference, moving away from the actual observed facts. Cognitive-behavioural therapy did not develop case formulation methods nor conceptualize the need for assessment until the 1960s (Goldfried & Pomeranz, 1968; Kanfer & Saslow, 1965; Tarrier, 2006) with the emergence of functional analyses. The latter helped establish the links between symptoms, psychological processes and outcomes, as demonstrated by empirical research; the symbolic meaning of the client's experience was not modelled in these early approaches. Humanistic therapies have traditionally taken a radical approach to case formulation, deeming it as a tool impeding on the productive collaborative therapy process (Rogers, 1951). Modern theorists articulate an integrative position by focusing on facets of emotional experience to be formulated from an idiographic perspective (Goldman & Greenberg, 2015).

A DISORDER-SPECIFIC APPROACH TO CASE FORMULATION

Personality disorders (PDs) do not give the therapist free rein to formulate a case. Case formulation grounded in a group of disorder, specifically personality disorders, may be relevant facing clients which have been described as 'difficult'. Indeed, conclusions from nomothetic research on aetiology, psychopathology and treatment of PD may be available for translation into practice of formulation. To do this, we argue that case formulation is central: it is time to articulate – and individualize – the psychopathological *constraints* a therapist faces when starting a treatment with a client with personality pathology. Before we outline possible constraints to case formulation, one word on the notion of personality disorder or pathology. This is important in times when scholars raise serious doubts about categorical classifications, or specific diagnostic criteria related to a particular personality disorder, for example related to their lack of comprehensiveness and articulation with the underlying psychological features (Herpertz et al., 2017a,b; Livesley, 2018; Widiger, 2018). Dimensional approaches tend to provide a more fine-grained picture of the PD, but do not replace an individualized case formulation. In the present volume, a certain focus will be laid on the well-researched category of borderline personality disorder (BPD), but specific psychological and psychopathological constraints pertain also to many other categories of PDs, such as narcissistic, antisocial, dependent and avoidant, as well as to relevant personality traits.

We understand the so-called 'constraints' to case formulation in the weakest sense possible: these may be client's clinical features as described by (mainly nomothetic) research. These features may emerge at specific occasions – moments in therapy – enabling the therapist to reflect and test his/her formulated hypothesis facing the individual client and learn from him/her. It does not mean that each client must present the 'constraining' feature nor that each case formulation method must explain all these features for a given client. These constraints to case formulation may encompass (1) psychopathological and psychological processes, and (2) contextual knowledge. Both will be introduced below, with the aim of providing an integrative prism through which readers may discover the series of chapters in the present volume. An integrative and comparative approach will be adopted in the final chapter, discussing the main constraints, possible ways to address them and relationship implications discussed by the authors.

CONSTRAINTS TO CASE FORMULATION FOR PERSONALITY DISORDERS: OCCASIONS TO LEARN FROM THE INDIVIDUAL CLIENT

The following summarized knowledge base may be considered a possible starting point of occasions to learn from the individual client. We call this synthesis a preliminary, and certainly incomplete, list of psychological and psychopathological constraints related to personality disorders. It stands for an even larger, and continuously evolving, mostly nomothetic knowledge base a clinician may draw from when formulating a case, in articulation with clinical theory. In order to increase the links with current diagnostic conceptualizations of personality pathology, we link these constraints with the Alternative Model for Personality Disorders in the DSM-5 (APA, 2013).

Clients with PD may present with identity problems (DSM-5 Alternative Model impairment area identity). These may not only encompass the difficulty of knowing who they are, but also a more profound loss of the sense of direction, felt fragmentation and quick changes in the narrative and in the interpersonal coherence, along with highly conflictual self-images

(Westen & Cohen, 1993). Clients with PDs may present with vague and ill-defined episodic memories. This may be true for clients with BPD who tend to present with severe inconsistencies in the autobiographic memory, along with generalized and incomplete narratives (Startup et al., 2001).

Clients with PDs may present with high levels of motivational problems, or a conflictual motivational stance (DSM-5 Alternative Model impairment area self-direction). The experience of internal conflictuality and high ambivalence with regard to change was described in qualitative research on clients with BPD (e.g., Berthoud, Kramer, de Roten, Despland, & Caspar, 2013). Clients with PDs may present with low levels of self-esteem and self-value, and self-criticism in the elaboration of sensitive self-related information. This is particularly true for BPD (e.g., Beeney, Hallquist, Ellison, & Levy, 2016; Vater, Schröder-Abé, Weissgerber, Roepke, & Schütz, 2015) and narcissistic personality disorder (NPD; Vater et al., 2013).

Clients with PDs may fail in meta-cognitive tasks when they are asked to reflect upon their own experience, their own thoughts or the thoughts of others (DMS-5 Alternative Model impairment area empathy). Clients with BPD present with certain difficulties with theory of mind, or empathy, tasks (Dimaggio & Brüne, 2016; O'Neill et al., 2015), they lack the capacity to put oneself into the other person's experience, and understand their experience using this resonating experience. Clients with BPD may present with hypermentalizing in the context of significant relationships. When confronted with conflictual information, such a particularly harmful over-interpretative stance may emerge (Sharp et al., 2016). It is also more difficult for them to detect non-verbal signs and emotion expression in others. Specific abilities of empathy lack in clients with NPD (Roepke & Vater, 2014).

Clients with BPD may present with insecure attachments patterns (DSM-5 Alternative Model impairment area intimacy), when compared with healthy controls, in particular over-involved or anxious-avoidant attachment styles in a majority of the observed cases (Bo & Kongerslev, 2017; Fonagy et al., 1996). Clients with PDs may present with repetitive interpersonal patterns and may present with problematic relationship offers to other persons (Drapeau, Perry, & Koerner, 2012) and problematic attachment patterns (Eikenaes, Pederson, & Wilberg, 2016).

Clients with borderline personality disorder (BPD), as well as NPD, may present with emotion dysregulation when confronted with stressful stimuli (DSM-5 Alternative Model trait domain negative affectivity vs. emotional stability; Dixon-Gordon, Peters, Fertuck, & Yen, 2017; Ebner-Priemer et al., 2007; Koenigsberg et al., 2002; Ronningstam, 2016; Schmahl et al., 2014). Compared to healthy controls and certain other psychological disorders, they have a unique, at times particularly harmful, way of coping with stressful stimuli (Kramer, 2014). Emotion dysregulation has neurobiological underpinnings, at least for BPD (Schulze, Schmahl, & Niedtfeld, 2016). Clients with PDs were reported to lack emotion awareness. Also called alexithymia, the difficulty of putting words on one's experience was described in experimental (De Panfilis et al., 2015) and clinical studies (Nicolo et al., 2011; Ogrodniczuk, Piper, & Joyce, 2011). Clients with BPD may have an altered perception of pain, as compared to healthy controls. These clients may support higher levels of objectively painful stimuli, and may also use these sensations as means to regulate emotions (Schmahl et al., 2014); some of these manifestations have neurobiological correlates. Clients with PD may present with vague and shallow processing of emotional and cognitive contents; shallow verbal self-reports of worry mediated the relationship between PD pathology and the specificity of autobiographical memories (Spinhoven, Bamelis, Molendijk, Haringsma, & Arntz, 2009).

Clients with certain types of PD, in particular avoidant and obsessive-compulsive, may present with emotion restriction or overcontrol and inhibitory processes (DSM-5 Alternative Model trait domain detachment vs. extraversion; Popolo et al., 2014).

Clients with BPD, and probably other PDs, may present with low scores on interpersonal agreeableness (DSM-5 Alternative Model trait domain antagonism vs. agreeableness; Zanarini, 2005), and the presence of interpersonal hostility, a personality feature which was shown to be related to outcome in psychotherapy (Hirsh, Quilty, Bagby, & McMain, 2012; Zufferey, Caspar, & Kramer, 2018).

Clients with BPD, NPD and certain other PDs may present with inaccurate emotion expression, in particular the expression of anger (DSM-5 Alternative Model trait domain disinhibition vs. conscientiousness; Berenson, Downey, Rafaeli, Coifman, & Paquin, 2011). Male clients with BPD lack executive control and present difficulty in impulse control, when confronted with interpersonal rejection; this pattern may explain the oftentimes aggressive outbursts observed in these clients (Herpertz et al., 2017).

Clients with PDs present with overgeneralized thinking which are biases toward an overreliance on certain negative information, and with certain types of dichotomous thinking (DSM-5 Alternative Model trait domain psychoticism vs. lucidity; Kramer, Vaudroz, Ruggeri, & Drapeau, 2013; Veen & Arntz, 2000). Clients with PD may present with harmful assumptions about relationships, themselves and the world, compared with healthy controls (Arntz, Dietzel, & Dreessen, 1999).

In addition to these psychological and psychopathological constraints, there may be at least three contextual constraints, which are occasions for the therapist to reflect upon his/her practice of case formulation in its context: the role of culture, the legal obligation to treatment and client's age (and possibly other socio-demographic variables).

Cultural context is central when formulating a case, in particular with severe disorders, e.g., personality disorders. In general, clinicians working in specific contexts may be subject to biased over-rating of normal phenomena as being clinically relevant, as was shown by Rosenhan (1973). More specifically, culture as broad value system may impact – sometimes unwillingly – the therapist in the practice of case formulation and may impact the client in his/her clinical presentation. In addition, culture may impact both interaction partners on secondary levels, in the interpersonal encounter: the client anticipating or guessing 'cultural' specificities of the therapist and the therapist guessing 'cultural' specificities of the client. This may lead to two types of diagnostic, or case formulation, biases (Edwards, 1982): (1) type I (therapist considers a client behaviour as pathological while it is normal given the client's cultural context); (2) type II (therapist considers a client behaviour as normal, by invoking the client's 'culture', while it is pathological).

A context of legal, or otherwise more formal, constraint to treatment may affect case formulation on the contextual level. In these contexts, the therapists may be more aware of ethical dilemmas, which may occur in any case formulation (Hart, Sturmey, Logan, & McMurran, 2011). These contexts may affect the focus, the depth and the comprehensiveness of the case formulation.

Age of the client, gender and other socio-demographic variables may function as contextual factors potentially influencing the therapist activity of case formulation. In particular facing youth, the question is discussed whether the therapist's understanding of the presenting problems should be done by taking into account the context – or the opinion – of the actual family members and their sets of interactions (Kongerslev, Chanen, & Simonsen, 2015).

INTEGRATIVE APPROACH TO CASE FORMULATION FOR PERSONALITY DISORDERS AND THE ROLE OF CLINICAL THEORY

After this overview of some of the constraints related to a disorder-specific approach to case formulation – there are certainly others – it might now become a daunting experience to try to formulate a case. In clinical reality, the therapist may be confronted with a number of such constraints, and the function of case formulation may be used here as argument: case formulation aims at facilitating a synthesis of seemingly contradictory or overwhelming information, by creating clinically useful 'solution algorithms' (Eells et al., 2005) or heuristics for psychotherapeutic intervention aiming at bringing about change. As noted by Gigerenzer and Brighton (2011), not without some humour, therapists are human beings and part of the species of *homo heuristicus*. Human beings, as they practice a focused activity, use shortcuts and abbreviations to be effective. Expert psychotherapists, as they formulate an individual case, need effective conceptual and methodological tools which favour the therapist self- and other-reflexive processes and which may be directly used in practice. It may be argued that an effective case formulation is therefore only to a certain degree comprehensive and accurate, while at the same time being parsimonious and marked by clinical utility for the therapeutic process and outcome.

As such, the therapist activity of formulating a case may be considered a practice-infused theory-building process, based on a single case: the individual client. This process of theory-building is a generative and creative one where the actual content of the formulation is unknown at the moment of the initial client-therapist encounter. Case formulation becomes a central piece for a particular type of research that is case study research (Fishman & Edwards, 2017). While the clinical theory at hand is indispensable, the same theory may be challenged by empirical data. This makes the theoretical assumptions in each model of case formulation malleable to revision and transformation from within, by using the observed information from the clinical case, thus creating a feed-back loop. The theory, or explanation, formulated will need to fit the client, not the client the theory.

The present volume is therefore written for scientist-practitioners, and those about to become one, who pursue two objectives: (1) learn or differentiate at least one method of case formulation in depth, in order to optimally understand and treat clients with personality disorders; (2) become aware of the possible limitations this particular methodology pertains facing a client with PD and complete with alternative methodologies. As such, the leading descriptor of the present volume 'integrative' means a continual creative process marked by a 'sense of surprise and eagerness to learn' (Safran & Messer, 1997), as opposed to a finished product ready to be applied. Case formulation methodology is therefore a practice-based way of psychotherapy integration, while at the same time offering tools learnable for any practitioner who does not necessarily practice psychotherapy in the narrower sense. Understanding a client's disruptive experience may be a human endeavour independent from the fact whether or not the professional has a full training in an evidence-based psychotherapy for treating PD. Finally, this book is written for psychotherapy researchers who are willing to tackle complex problems of methodology, for example assessing the therapist responsiveness to clients' characteristics or studying the process of change in individualized treatments.

CASE FORMULATION AS A MEANS TO INCREASE THERAPIST EFFECTIVENESS

Case formulation may be part of the content of a variable which has been under-studied in psychotherapy research: the person of the therapist (Castonguay & Hill, 2017). The methodology used by a therapist to understand a client's situation might be an indispensable building block to understanding therapist effects in psychotherapy. Individualizing psychotherapy based on a rigorous, well thought-through, method, or treatment plan, may strengthen the therapist's technical and relational competencies in session, beyond an intuitive approach. From this perspective, the virtues of case formulation methodology are possibly (1) providing the therapist with a structure enabling to explain seemingly contradictory clinical (client and therapist) manifestations and experiences, (2) a systematic help to create a shared treatment focus, (3) a theory-building creative process aiming at integrative practice of psychotherapy, (4) its content can be used directly for the therapeutic interaction with the client (i.e., discuss the contents explicitly with the client) and (5) its content can be used for implicitly anticipating and adjusting relationship offer in a responsive manner (i.e., implicitly use the contents in the therapeutic interaction). All these virtues may be essential components for the quality of psychotherapy collaboration, the process and outcome. Case formulation appears as a specific process, or therapist activity, which takes place in interaction with technical and/or relationship manifestations in session. Case formulation appears to be central not only in the therapy hour, but also outside the therapy hour, as part of (1) the therapist reflective activity on the case, (2) the supervision process, (3) the accreditation process of therapists-in-training, (4) the legal and insurance context in which the treatment takes place, and (5) research (i.e., single case research).

The therapist activity of formulation takes place in an – emerging – dyadic relationship, the one between the client and the therapist, and specific contents of formulation may be affected by this relationship. Also, the therapist, by formulating a case, may be in an ethical dilemma between the aim of providing to the client a precise explanation of a problem – which inevitably includes inference – and the aim of transparent communication with the client. The higher the level of inference of the explanation, the stronger the therapist will be in this ethical dilemma. The therapist may consider to what extent it is ethically acceptable to shield the client off from information related to a case formulation? Which information from the case formulation can easily be shared and which information should be considered with more caution? Some of these questions may be addressed in the present volume.

THE PRESENT VOLUME

Each of the 18 chapter authors, and author groups, were asked to answer the following questions in their contribution: (1) What are the theoretical concepts that pertain to this case formulation method? (2) How does a scientist-practitioner go by to formulate a case according to this case formulation method? (3) How does this case formulation method plays out in a case with PD, and how did the case formulation affect the process and outcome in this treatment? The authors were also asked, if applicable, to review research carried out using this case formulation method and other additional topics which seemed relevant to them. The opening chapters concern the tailoring of brand-name, and to various extents evidence-based, psychotherapy approaches, to the individual client. Two chapters concern case formulation methods applied in specific contexts (i.e., contextual constraints): to youth and to the forensic context. The book ends with a focus on psychotherapy process variables used as information for case formulation.

I would like to ask for the reader's compassionate forgiveness: no volume can include it all, nor discuss all case formulation methods that exist for personality disorders. I would like to thank the 41 contributors for a truly inspiring cooperation and Barbara Makinster, Nikki Levy and Dennis McGonagle at Elsevier, Cambridge, MA, USA, for their proficient support through the process of publication. Special thanks to Mary C. Zanarini for writing the foreword to this book. Warm thank you to all – family, friends, colleagues and students – for being there, and for being a continuous source of inspiration of my work.

References

American Psychiatric Association. (2013). *Diagnostic and statistical manual of mental disorders. DSM-5*. Washington, D. C.: American Psychiatric Publishing.

Arntz, A., Dietzel, R., & Dreessen, L. (1999). Assumptions in borderline personality disorder: Specificity, stability and relationship with etiological factors. *Behaviour Research and Therapy*, *37*, 545–557.

Beeney, J. E., Hallquist, M. N., Ellison, W. D., & Levy, K. N. (2016). Self-other disturbance in borderline personality disorder: Neural, self-report and performance-based evidence. *Personality Disorders*, *7*(1), 28–39.

Berenson, K. R., Downey, G., Rafaeli, E., Coifman, K. G., & Paquin, N. L. (2011). The rejection-rage contingency in borderline personality disorder. *Journal of Abnormal Psychology*, *120*(3), 681.

Berthoud, L., Kramer, U., de Roten, Y., Despland, J.-N., & Caspar, F. (2013). Using plan analysis in psychotherapeutic case formulation of borderline personality disorder. *Clinical Psychology and Psychotherapy*, *20*, 1–9.

Bo, S., & Kongerslev, M. (2017). Self-reported patterns of impairments in mentalization, attachment and psychopathology among clinically referred adolescents with and without borderline personality pathology. *Borderline Personality Disorder and Emotion Dysregulation*, *4*(4).

Caspar, F. (2000). Therapeutisches Handeln als individueller Konstruktionsprozess. In J. Margraf (Ed.), *Lehrbuch der Verhaltenstherapie* (2nd ed.) (pp. 155–166). Berlin: Springer.

Castonguay, L. G., & Hill, C. E. (Eds.). (2017). *How and why are some therapists better than others? Understanding therapist effects*. Washington, D.C.: American Psychological Association.

Chi, M. T. H. (2006). Two approaches to the study of experts' characteristics. In K. A. Ericsson, N. Charness, P. J. Feltovich, & R. R. Hoffman (Eds.), *The Cambridge handbook of expertise and expert performance* (pp. 21–30). Cambridge: Cambridge University Press.

De Panfilis, C., Ossola, P., Tonna, P., Catania, L., & Marchesi, C. (2015). Finding words for feelings: The relationship between personality disorders and alexithymia. *Personality and Individual Differences*, *74*, 285–291.

Dimaggio, G., & Brüne, M. (2016). Dysfunctional understanding of mental states in personality disorders: What is the evidence? *Comprehensive Psychiatry*, *64*, 1–3.

Dixon-Gordon, K. L., Peters, J. R., Fertuck, E. A., & Yen, S. (2017). Emotional processes in borderline personality disorder: An update for clinical practice. *Journal of Psychotherapy Integration*, *27*(4), 425–438.

Drapeau, M., Perry, J. C., & Koerner, A. (2012). Intepersonal patterns in borderline personality disorder. *Journal of Personality Disorders*, *26*(4), 583–592.

Dudley, R., Ingham, B., Sowerby, K., & Freeston, M. (2015). The utility of case formulation in treatment decision making: The effect of experience and expertise. *Journal of Behavior Therapy and Experimental Psychiatry*, *48*, 66–74.

Ebner-Priemer, U. W., Kuo, J., Kleindienst, N., Welch, S. S., Reisch, T., Reinhard, I., et al. (2007). State affective instability in borderline personality disorder assessed by ambulatory monitoring. *Psychological Medicine*, *37*(7), 961–970.

Edwards, A. W. (1982). The consequences of error in selecting treatment for blacks. *Social Casework: The Journal of Contemporary Social Work*, *63*, 429–433.

Eells, T. D. (2007). History and current status of psychotherapy case formulation. In T. D. Eells (Ed.), *Handbook of psychotherapy case formulation* (2nd ed.) (pp. 3–32). New York: Guilford.

Eells, T. D. (2013a). The case formulation approach to psychotherapy research revisited. *Pragmatic Case Studies in Psychotherapy*, *9*, 426–447.

Eells, T. D. (2013b). In support of evidence-based case formulation in psychotherapy (from the perspective of a clinician). *Pragmatic Case Studies in Psychotherapy*, *9*(4), 457–467.

Eells, T. D., Lombart, K. G., Kendjelic, E. M., Turner, L. C., & Lucas, C. P. (2005). The quality of psychotherapy case formulations : A comparison of expert, experienced, and novice cognitive-behavioral and psychodynamic therapists. *Journal of Consulting and Clinical Psychology*, *73*(4), 579–589.

Eikenaes, I., Pederson, G., & Wilberg, T. (2016). Attachment styles in patients wit avoidant personality disorder compared with social phobia. *Psychology and Psychotherapy: Theory, Research and Practice*, *89*, 245–260.

Fishman, D. B., & Edwards, D. J. A. (2017). The terrain. In D. B. Fishman, S. B. Messer, D. J. A. Edwards, & F. M. Dattilio (Eds.), *Case Studies within Psychotherapy Trials* (pp. 3–25). New York: Oxford University Press.

Fonagy, P., Leigh, T., Steele, M., Steele, H., Kennedy, R., Mattoon, G., et al. (1996). The relation of attachment status, psychiatric classification, and response to psychotherapy. *Journal of Consulting and Clinical Psychology*, *64*(1), 22–31.

Gigerenzer, G., & Brighton, H. (2011). Homo heuristicus: Why biased minds make better inferences. In G. Gigerenzer, R. Hertwig, & T. Pachur (Eds.), *Heuristics. The foundations of adaptive behavior* (pp. 2–30). Oxford: Oxford University Press.

Gill, M., Newman, R., & Redlich, F. C. (1954). *The initial interview in psychiatric practice*. New York: International Universities Press.

Goldfried, M. R. (2010). The future of psychotherapy integration: Closing the gap between research and practice. *Journal of Psychotherapy Integration*, *20*, 386–396.

Goldfried, M. R., & Pomeranz, D. M. (1968). Role of assessment in behavior modification. *Psychological Reports*, *23*, 75–87.

Goldman, R., & Greenberg, L. S. (2015). *Case formulation in emotion-focused therapy. Co-creating clinical maps for change*. Washington, D.C.: American Psychological Association.

Hart, S., Sturmey, P., Logan, C., & McMurran, M. (2011). Forensic case formulation. *International Journal of Forensic Mental Health*, *10*(2), 118–126.

Herpertz, S. C., Huprich, S. K., Bohus, M., Chanen, A., Goodman, M., Mehlum, L., et al. (2017). The challenge of transforming the diagnostic system of personality disorders. *Journal of Personality Disorders*, *31*(5), 577–589.

Herpertz, S. C., Nagy, K., Ueltzhöffer, K., Schmitt, R., Mancke, F., Schmahl, C., et al. (2017). Brain mechanisms underlying aggression in borderline personality disorder – sex matters. *Biological Psychiatry*, *82*, 257–266.

Hirsh, J. B., Quilty, L., Bagby, M. R., & McMain, S. F. (2012). The relationship between agreeableness and the development of the working alliance in patients with borderline personality disorder. *Journal of Personality Disorders, 26*, 616–627.

Ingram, B. L. (2016). Case formulation and treatment planning. In J. C. Norcross, G. R. Vandenbos, D. K. Freedheim, & R. Krishnamurthy (Eds.), *APA handbook of clinical psychology: Applications and methods, Vol. 3* (pp. 233–249). Washington, D.C.: APA.

Johnstone, L., & Dallos, R. (2013). *Formulation in psychology and psychotherapy: Making sense of people's problems*. New York: Routledge.

Kanfer, F. H., & Saslow, G. (1965). Behavioral analysis: An alternative to diagnostic classification. *Archives of General Psychiatry, 12*, 529–538.

Koenigsberg, H. W., Harvey, P. D., Mitropoulou, V., Schmeidler, J., New, A. S., Goodman, M., et al. (2002). Characterizing affective instability in borderline personality disorder. *American Journal of Psychiatry, 159*(5), 784–788.

Kongerslev, M., Chanen, A. M., & Simonsen, E. (2015). Personality disorder in childhood and adolescence comes of age: A review of the current evidence and prospects for future research. *Scandinavian Journal of Child and Adolescent Psychiatry and Psychology, 3*(1), 31–48.

Kramer, U. (2014). Observer-rated coping associated with borderline personality disorder: An exploratory study. *Clinical Psychology and Psychotherapy, 21*(3), 242–251.

Kramer, U., Vaudroz, C., Ruggeri, O., & Drapeau, M. (2013). Biased thinking assessed by external observers in borderline personality disorder. *Psychology and Psychotherapy: Theory, Research and Practice, 86*, 183–196.

Livesley, W. J. (2018). Conceptual issues. In W. J. Livesley, & R. Larstone (Eds.), *Handbook of personality disorders* (2nd ed.) (pp. 3–24). New York: Guilford Press.

Macneil, C. A., Hasty, M. K., Conus, P., & Berk, M. (2012). Is diagnosis enough to guide interventions in mental health? Using case formulation in clinical practice. *BMC Medicine, 10*, 111–113.

Nicolo, G., Semerari, A., Lysaker, P. H., Dimaggio, G., Conti, L., d'Angerio, S., et al. (2011). Alexithymia in personality disorders. Correlations with symptoms and interpersonal functioning. *Psychiatry Research, 190*, 37–42.

Ogrodniczuk, J. S., Piper, W. E., & Joyce, A. S. (2011). Effect of alexithymia on the process and outcome of psychotherapy: A programmatic review. *Psychiatry Research, 190*(1), 43–48.

O'Neill, A., D'Souza, A., Samson, A. C., Carballedo, A., Kerskens, C., & Frodl, T. (2015). Dysregulation between emotion and theory of mind networks in borderline personality disorder. *Psychiatry Research: Neuroimaging, 231*, 25–32.

Person, J. B. (2013). Who needs a case formulation and why: Clinicians use the case formulation to guide decision-making. *Paragmatic Case Studies in Psychotherapy, 9*, 448–456.

Persons, J. B. (1989). *Cognitive therapy in practice: A case formulation approach*. New York: Norton.

Persons, J. B. (1991). Psychotherapy outcome studies do not accurately represent current models of psychotherapy: A proposed remedy. *American Psychologist, 46*, 99–106.

Popolo, R., Lysaker, P. H., Salvatore, G., Montano, A., Sirri, L., Buonocore, L., et al. (2014). Emotional inhibition in personality disorders. *Psychotherapy and Psychosomatics, 83*, 377–378.

Roepke, S., & Vater, A. (2014). Narcissistic personality disorder: An integrative review of recent empirical data and current definitions. *Current Psychiatry Report, 16*(5), 445.

Rogers, C. R. (1951). *Client-centered therapy: Its current practice, implications, and theory*. Boston: Houghton Mifflin.

Ronningstam, E. (2016). Pathological narcissism and narcissistic personality disorder. Recent research and clinical implications. *Current Behavior Neuroscience Reports, 3*, 34–42.

Rosenhan, D. L. (1973). On being sane in insane places. *Science, 179*, 250–258.

Safran, J. D., & Messer, S. B. (1997). Psychotherapy integration: A postmodern critique. *Clinical Psychology: Science and Practice, 4*, 140–152.

Schmahl, C., Herpertz, S. C., Bertsch, K., Ende, G., Flor, H., Kirsch, P., et al. (2014). Mechanisms of disturbed emotion processing and social interaction in borderline personality disorder: State of knowledge and research agenda of the German clinical research unit. *Borderline Personality Disorder and Emotion Dysregulation*, *1*, 12.

Schulze, L., Schmahl, C., & Niedtfeld, I. (2016). Neural correlates of disturbed emotion processing in borderline personality disorder: A multimodal meta-analysis. *Biological Psychiatry*, *79*(2), 97–106.

Sharp, C., Venta, A., Vanwoerden, S., Schramm, A., Ha, C., Newlin, E., et al. (2016). First empirical evaluation of the link between attachment, social cognition and borderline features in adolescents. *Comprehensive Psychiatry*, *64*, 4–11.

Spinhoven, P., Bamelis, L., Molendijk, M., Haringsma, R., & Arntz, A. (2009). Reduced specificity of autobiographical memory in Cluster C personality disorders and the role of depression, worry and experiential avoidance. *Journal of Abnormal Psychology*, *118*, 520–530. https://doi.org/10.1037/a00162393.

Startup, M., Heard, H., Swales, M., Jones, B., Williams, J. M., & Jones, R. S. (2001). Autobiographical memory and para-suicide in borderline personality disorder. *The British Journal of Clinical Psychology*, *40*, 113–120. https://doi.org/10.1348/014466501163535.

Sturmey, P. (2009). *Varieties of case formulation*. Chichester: Wiley.

Tarrier, N. (2006). An introduction to case formulation and its challenges. In N. Tarrier (Ed.), *Case formulation in cognitive behaviour therapy* (pp. 1–11). London: Routledge.

Vater, A., Ritter, K., Schröder-Abé, M., Schütz, A., Lammers, C. H., Bosson, J. K., et al. (2013). When grandiosity and vulnerability collide: Implicit and explicit self-esteem in patients with narcissistic personality disorder. *Journal of Behavior Therapy and Experimental Psychiatry*, *44*(1), 37–47.

Vater, A., Schröder-Abé, M., Weissgerber, S., Roepke, S., & Schütz, A. (2015). Self-concept structure and borderline personality disorder: Evidence for negative compartmentalization. *Journal of Behavior Therapy and Experimental Psychiatry*, *46*, 50–58.

Veen, G., & Arntz, A. (2000). Multidimensional dichotomous thinking characterizes borderline personality disorder. *Cognitive Therapy and Research*, *24*(1), 23–45.

Vollmer, S., Spada, H., Caspar, F., & Burri, S. (2013). Expertise in clinical psychology. The effects of university training and practical experience on expertise in clinical psychology. *Frontiers in Psychology*, *4*(141).

Westen, D., & Cohen, R. P. (1993). The self in borderline personality disorder: A psychodynamic perspective. In Z. V. Segal, & S. J. Blatt (Eds.), *The self in emotional distress. Cognitive and psychodynamic perspectives* (pp. 334–360). New York: Guilford.

Widiger, T. A. (2018). Official classification systems. In W. J. Livesley, & R. Larstone (Eds.), *Handbook of personality disorders* (2nd ed.) (pp. 47–71). New York: Guilford Press.

Zanarini, M. C. (2005). The subsyndromal phenomenology of borderline personality disorder. In M. C. Zanarini (Ed.), *Borderline personality disorder* (pp. 19–40). Boca Raton, FL: Taylor & Francis.

Zufferey, P., Caspar, F., & Kramer, U. (2018). The role of interactional agreeableness in responsive treatments for patients with borderline personality disorder. *Journal of Personality Disorders*.

CHAPTER

1

Case Formulation in Dialectical Behaviour Therapy

Shelley McMain[1,2], *Michelle Leybman*[1], *Tali Boritz*[1,2]

[1]Centre for Addiction and Mental Health, Toronto, ON, Canada; [2]Department of Psychiatry, University of Toronto, Toronto, ON, Canada

INTRODUCTION

Dialectical behaviour therapy (DBT) is an evidence-based form of psychotherapy that can be used to treat individuals with severe emotional and behavioural dysregulation. While it is widely implemented, DBT—like all psychotherapies—is not one-size-fits-all, and its effectiveness hinges on the ability of the clinician to tailor the treatment for each client. Case formulation, a method for personalizing psychotherapy, is considered essential for effective implementation of DBT, and is a core competency for DBT certification (see https://dbt-lbc.org/). In real-world settings, however, for a variety of reasons, many practitioners are neither well informed about case formulation, nor well trained in its implementation. It has been observed that clinicians often come to appreciate the value of this process once it becomes clear to them how it can be used to coordinate treatment and improve outcomes in complex cases (Davidson, 2006; Hart, Sturmey, Logan, & McMurran, 2011).

The preparation of a case formulation is especially important when working with clients with personality disorders (Davidson, 2006). First, such individuals often have multiple co-morbid problems, which makes it difficult for clinicians to know where to focus any interventions. Further, clients who are highly emotionally and behaviourally dysregulated are likely to become emotionally aroused and reactive in session, which can cause the clinician to feel confused or overwhelmed and may contribute to countertherapeutic reactions. A sound case formulation helps the

Case Formulation for Personality Disorders
https://doi.org/10.1016/B978-0-12-813521-1.00001-1

therapist understand the client better, thereby allowing for accurate empathy and validation, which in turn promotes collaboration and strengthens the therapeutic alliance. Finally, understanding a client's patterns of thinking, feeling, and acting improves the therapist's ability to anticipate challenges and to determine how and when to effectively intervene.

As with other therapeutic approaches, case formulation in DBT is both a process and a product. As a process, case formulation acts as a systematic method of organizing complex and diverse clinical information into clear and meaningful explanations which provide both therapist and client with an awareness and understanding of what and how to change. Like a GPS device, it provides information about the starting point (the target problems), the endpoint (the desired outcomes), and a suggested route (the treatment plan). It maps out the client's psychological condition, which issues to prioritize, hypotheses about how the client will respond to suitable interventions, and ideas on how to evaluate the impact of interventions (Logan, Nathan, & Brown, 2011). This map can then be turned into a product, such as a written document that can be referred to throughout treatment and shared with the client.

DBT case formulation integrates theory and research (i.e., what we understand broadly about a particular condition or a certain type of human behaviour) to create a specific and idiographic understanding of each client, including how to effectively navigate the therapeutic process. In keeping with the GPS metaphor, we may have in mind a route to get from Point A to Point B but will need to change course if we encounter unexpected road closures or particularly rough pavement. As with the practice of DBT overall, case formulation is a transparent and collaborative process between therapist and client, and is discussed explicitly throughout the course of treatment.

The process of generating a case formulation in DBT, which begins within the first few sessions, involves five essential steps (Koerner & Linehan, 1997). First, the therapist gathers information about the biological and environmental factors that have contributed to the development and maintenance of the client's mental state. Second, the client's goals are identified, and treatment targets are specified and prioritized. Third, the function of specific behaviours and the variables that control these behaviours are assessed, primarily through the method of behavioural chain analyses. Fourth, data collected from behavioural chain analyses are synthesized across behaviours to identify common themes relevant to the client's mental functioning. Finally, suitable interventions are selected to address these common problematic themes.

This chapter provides an overview of case formulation in DBT. It begins by describing the theories that underpin DBT, and then presents a detailed explanation of each of the five steps for generating a case formulation, using a case history to illustrate each step.

THEORETICAL FOUNDATION OF DIALECTICAL BEHAVIOUR THERAPY (DBT)

Learning Theory

An assumption in DBT is that all behaviours develop through a complex interplay of biological and environmental factors that are governed by the laws of learning: antecedent stimuli precede a behaviour (classical conditioning), and consequential stimuli follow it (operant conditioning). Modelling plays a role as well. The variables that control (i.e., cause or maintain) problematic behaviours therefore become the target of intervention. For a review of the behaviour therapy approach, see Goldfried and Davison (1994).

In keeping with the above, the development of a case formulation is based on a learning theory perspective, and involves a problem-solving approach to identify the stimulus-response relationship associated with problematic behaviours. Behavioural strategies are used to assess both the classical conditioning links in the sequence of events leading up to a behaviour (e.g., cognitions, actions, emotions) and the operant conditioning links that follow that behaviour (i.e., the contingencies that reinforce or punish it) (Swales & Heard, 2017). From a DBT perspective, the therapist is encouraged to contemplate the *function* of behaviours. For example, one common assumption is that dysfunctional behaviour is motivated by urges to achieve 'amelioration of unendurable pain' (Linehan, 1993a,b, p. 265).

Zen Philosophy

DBT focuses on both change and acceptance. The part of DBT that focuses on change is based on learning theory, whereas the emphasis on acceptance is anchored in Eastern mindfulness; specifically, Zen philosophy. The present moment is considered inevitable given the 'collective impact of all previous moments' (Swenson, 2016, p. 46). That is, all behaviour that happens *should* happen, and is understandable (Linehan, 1997). The DBT concept of 'wise mind' refers to a state of balance between viewing the world rationally and viewing it emotionally, sometimes experienced as a 'gut feeling' about the best course of action to take.

Following these Zen principles, a therapeutic stance of acceptance and nonjudgment guides the process of developing an explanatory theory of a client's problems, and the therapist seeks to discover how these problems are perfectly understandable in context of the client's biology, history, and current reality. The concept of wise mind informs the process through which the therapist seeks to clarify and identify the wisdom in the client's responses or behaviours.

Dialectical Philosophy

The dialectical perspective in DBT adopts a holistic understanding of the client. Dialectical philosophy posits that reality is composed of interrelated parts that cannot be defined without reference to the system as a whole. The system and its parts are in a constant state of flux, and changes in one part of the system influence changes in the others. Dialectical philosophy also emphasizes the understanding that reality consists of opposites or polarities. Tensions or polarizations in thinking, feeling, and acting are seen to naturally arise. This natural tension between opposites is resolved through a process of synthesis.

This perspective influences the development of a case formulation in several ways. We seek a systemic and contextual understanding of the client, taking both emotional aspects and the external environment into account. A DBT therapist considers how polarizations in thoughts, feelings, or actions contribute to problematic behaviour, and determines how to identify polarizations when these occur and how to target them for intervention. As the process of change involves the synthesis of opposites, when selecting interventions there is usually a focus on helping the client move either toward acceptance or toward change.

Biosocial Theory

The biosocial theory of DBT posits that the core dysfunction underlying borderline personality disorder and certain other clinical disorders is pervasive emotion dysregulation, which arises from the combination of a biological predisposition toward emotional vulnerability and an invalidating developmental environment (Linehan, 1993a). *Emotional vulnerability* refers to experiencing heightened sensitivity to emotions, heightened reactivity, and a slow return to baseline. An *invalidating environment* refers to an environment that minimizes, ignores, dismisses, or punishes the expression of emotion, thereby communicating to a person that his or her understanding of events and internal experiences are fundamentally wrong and are due to unacceptable and socially undesirable character traits.

When biological emotional vulnerability is combined with an invalidating interpersonal environment, people may fail to learn how to understand, label, modulate, and tolerate emotional distress, or how to solve the problems contributing to their emotional reactions (Linehan, 1993a,b; McMain, Korman, & Dimeff, 2001). Instead, they learn to manage their emotional vulnerabilities through maladaptive strategies. In case formulation, biosocial theory is used to construct a developmental explanation for emotion dysregulation and associated problems. Based on the information gathered when obtaining a developmental history, we are able to begin making hypotheses about how a particular client is coping with emotions in the present.

STEP-BY STEP APPROACH TO DEVELOPING A DIALECTICAL BEHAVIOUR THERAPY (DBT) CASE FORMULATION

The five steps involved in developing a case formulation are detailed below, using a case study to illustrate each step.

Step 1: Obtain a Developmental History

Starting at the first session, gather historical information to help understand how the client experiences, modulates, and expresses emotions. The types of information include relationships with significant family members (parents, siblings) as well as with peers. Assess for any events of childhood abuse, neglect, and bullying, as well as for the environmental response to any disclosures of traumatic experiences.

Assess for evidence of biologically based emotional vulnerability. Was the client a sensitive child, or described as such by others? Emotional vulnerability may include shyness, anxiety, temper tantrums, or other sensitivities to the environment. Assessing for family history of mental health and substance use disorders or other psychological difficulties can also provide valuable information.

Assess for evidence of invalidation in the developmental environment, with specific questions about what messages were received about emotion. For example, when the client became emotional in childhood, what were the responses from caregivers, teachers, and peers? Were normative emotional behaviours ignored or punished? Determine how the environment responded to signs of distress or struggle. For example, did parents, other family members, or teachers provide support, or did they oversimplify what was needed to solve the problem?

Identify the transactions between biologically based emotional vulnerability and the invalidating environment. How did the client regulate emotions as a child: i.e., what strategies did he or she learn in order to modulate and express emotions and to get emotional needs met? For example, some children who are punished for displays of emotion learn to mask their emotions or to isolate themselves when they are emotionally dysregulated, whereas others learn to intensify their emotional displays in order to elicit a desired response from caregivers.

The Case of Beth: Overview and Application to Step 1

Beth, a 35-year-old woman with a diagnosis of borderline personality disorder (BPD), self-referred to an outpatient BPD treatment programme clinic due to difficulties in several areas of her life, and received one year of standard DBT. Her presenting symptoms included frequent self-harm: she was engaging in cutting herself several times a week, would punch herself, and would overdose on pain medication. She also drank alcohol excessively, struggled to hold steady employment, and had frequent 'blowouts' with her partner, with whom she had been living for two years. She reported intense and chronic anxiety, extreme self-criticism, and strong feelings of self-hatred. In addition to being diagnosed with BPD, her pretreatment assessment identified co-morbid Major Depressive Disorder, Social Phobia, Generalized Anxiety Disorder, Alcohol Dependence, and Post-Traumatic Stress Disorder.

Assessment of the origins of Beth's emotional vulnerability began at the first orientation session. Invalidating experiences had been pervasive in her early interpersonal environment. Her biological father had left within the first year of her birth and was not in touch with anyone in the family thereafter. Beth said she often believed she was not good enough for him to stick around for. Her mother remarried when Beth was three, and when her stepfather and three stepsisters became part of the family, she had a strong feeling of being 'an outsider'. This was highlighted by her stepfather frequently requesting to take two sets of pictures at family gatherings; one that included her and one that did not. Of the four children, she was identified as 'the sensitive one in the bunch'. She described crying often, as well as losing her temper frequently both at school and at home. She remembered feeling 'out of control' much of the time and being ganged up upon by her siblings for being 'such a crybaby'. Beth received overt messages that her emotions were 'too much' for the rest of her family. For example, when she cried she would frequently be told something like 'suck it up, buttercup'. When she got angry, she was often sent to her room and told that she could rejoin the family when she got control of herself.

There was a significant interaction at play between Beth's biological sensitivity and her invalidating environment. Beth's sensitivity meant that she experienced a sense of intense abandonment and rejection much of the time, and any time that she expressed her thoughts about this, the invalidating reactions from her family created new reasons to feel even more of those intense feelings of hurt. Importantly, the only time that Beth ever felt any kind of reassurance or validation was when she had her biggest 'crying fits'. At these times, her mother, who herself was diagnosed with BPD, seemed to recognize herself in her daughter and would become more soothing than usual. This reinforced Beth's belief that getting visibly and highly upset about something was the best way to be heard by others.

Step 2: Identifying and Prioritizing Treatment Targets

A major challenge for most psychotherapists is to be able to appreciate the complexity of a client while simultaneously distilling what is occurring in a session moment-by-moment. To do so, they must alternate between a broad, macrolevel focus on treatment targets (e.g., abstinence from substances, improving relationships) and a more specific, microlevel focus on emotions and patterns of emotional processing (e.g., hint of frustration in tone of voice, eyes shimmering with tears, emotion inhibition).

Vision for Life

In DBT, treatment is geared toward helping people attain their life goals; thus, those goals are the foundations of the case formulation. Encouraging a conversation about what the client wants out of life may be an unexpected way to begin therapy, as many people enter therapy holding views of themselves as broken or damaged and feel hopeless about the prospect of life ever being different. Problems often dominate the landscape and can overshadow any positive aspirations. Probing about hopes and aspirations can help generate motivation to engage in treatment. Reminders about life goals are often returned to in therapy, especially when a client loses hope and motivation. Helping people hold onto a new vision of a new life can help anchor the treatment and mobilize them toward new possibilities.

To identify a client's life goals, the therapist may begin with a question such as, 'If treatment could help you build the life that you want, what would your life look like?' It may be helpful to use a metaphor of a paradise island, asking the client to describe as fully as possible what such an island would look like and what it would include.

Primary Treatment Targets: Macrolevel Behaviours

Once the client's aspirations are clarified, the next step is to sort out what is getting in the way of achieving them. Sometimes clients are well aware of their problematic behaviours; for example, knowing that anger outbursts are interfering with interpersonal relationships and with maintaining a job. Other problems may be less obvious, and may be uncovered over the course of treatment: for example, being unaware that problematic shame is underlying the anger outbursts. During the first few sessions of treatment, the clinician sifts through information and identifies the difficulties that the client is struggling with.

Next, the therapist works to convert the client's goals into specific problems to be addressed in treatment. Lists of such problems, referred to as treatment targets, are established early in therapy and become a focus of assessment and intervention. Clear and specific identification of behaviours that are to be eliminated and behaviours that are to be increased make the goals concrete and easier to move toward.

Treatment must match the client's motivation, as people are not necessarily motivated to address all the behaviours that are compromising their life goals. For example, someone engaging in self-destructive substance use may be unwilling to give this up. No matter how sincere the therapist's conviction about the path a client 'ought' to take and how strong the attempts to steer that person in a certain direction, it is ultimately the client's responsibility to make these choices. In the words of Dr. Seuss, 'You're on your own / And you know what you know / And *you* are the one who'll decide where to go'.

Finally, it is important to consider the timeframe of treatment and to focus on goals that can be reasonably addressed within a specific period of time. Establishing a timeframe helps to mobilize the client and decreases the likelihood of issues being avoided, and also helps to provide a metric to gauge progress toward goals.

Secondary Treatment Targets: Microlevel Behaviours

DBT is particularly concerned with emotions, so observable patterns of problematic emotion processes are a focus at a microlevel of analysis and intervention. Microlevel moment-by-moment changes in a client's in-session behaviours, including voice tone, facial expressions, body language, and respiratory rate, can reveal emotions and level of arousal. Markers of emotional processing problems are critical to consider when deciding where to focus and intervene.

Linehan identified three problematic patterns of emotion regulation characterized by an opposing tendency to over- and underregulate emotions. Referred to as secondary targets, these involve dialectical dilemmas across three dimensions: (1) modulation of emotions, (2) expression of emotional needs, and (3) avoidance of grief and pain. When developing a case formulation, it is critical to identify in-session markers of patterns of emotion processing difficulties that take one of these forms.

- Emotion modulation problems are characterized by the vacillation between emotion vulnerability and self-invalidation. *Emotion vulnerability* refers to an individual's sensitivity to emotional arousal, susceptibility to negative emotion, and challenges controlling intense emotional reactions. Behavioural markers include intense overwhelming emotions, often involving rage reactions. In contrast, *self-invalidation* refers to an individual's tendency to overcontrol emotions. Markers of self-invalidation include the suppression, inhibition, and dismissal of emotional experience such as self-criticism, self-attack, physical tightening and squeezing back bodily expressions, and dissociating.
- Difficulties around expressing emotional needs are characterized by a vacillation between active passivity and apparent competence. *Active passivity* is the tendency to approach life's problems helplessly with the expectation that others will solve one's problems. *Apparent competence* involves a masking of emotional distress in such a way that others do not perceive one's level of distress or need for assistance.

- Avoidance of grief or trauma is characterized by a vacillation between unrelenting crises and inhibited grieving. *Unrelenting crisis* refers to a constant stream of stressful life events or episodes of behavioural dyscontrol (e.g., suicide attempts, substance abuse, and other impulsive behaviours). This problem reflects a tendency to be controlled by aversive emotions and an inability to tolerate reactions to events, but also results when a persistent suppression of emotion erupts to the surface (Swenson, 2016). In contrast, *inhibited grieving* is the tendency to suppress or avoid painful emotions associated with grief and trauma. Markers of inhibited grieving may include an absence of emotional reactions to loss or ending (e.g., treatment termination, therapist vacation), and an avoidance of cues that trigger loss (e.g., premature withdrawal from treatment).

Treatment Focus

When treating a client with multidisorders, it can be challenging for the clinician to know what to focus on and how to prioritize problems. In developing a DBT case formulation, the first consideration is a macrolevel assessment of the client's level of severity and emotional capacities. Clients with significant behavioural dyscontrol, including suicidal and self-harm behaviours, substance use, anger outbursts, or eating disorders, are considered to be in Stage 1 of treatment, in which the main goal is to facilitate the development of basic emotional regulation capacities. Increasing the ability to modulate behaviours that are associated with intense emotions is the most critical target of this stage. Clients who are less behaviourally dysregulated are deemed to be in Stage 2. In Stage 2, the focus of intervention shifts to enhancing and processing deeper emotional experiences. Thus, an individual who is suicidal but capable of not acting on suicidal urges may be ready to begin focusing on emotional non-avoidance, including the treatment of trauma and post-traumatic stress reactions.

The hierarchy of treatment targets in DBT provides a map for determining the focus in each therapy session. While each session typically focuses on multiple problems, primary targets are organized in terms of a hierarchy of priority focus. Suicidal and life-threatening behaviours are prioritized over other behaviours for obvious reasons. Next are behaviours that interfere with receiving treatment, since these need to be overcome if treatment is to be maximally effective. Such behaviours include missing sessions, showing up late for sessions, and being intoxicated in session. They can also include problems on the part of the therapist, such as anger toward a client, fragilizing a client, or lateness to sessions. Next to be targeted are behaviours that comprise a client's quality of life, such as substance use, homelessness, eating disorders, and lack of productive activity.

Finally, the therapist must carefully observe the client's level of emotional arousal during sessions in order to determine the most optimal direction for intervention. For example, there may have been a plan to address the client's drug use, but while exploring the factors that led up to that problem, the client becomes emotionally aroused and angry due to being in a state of emotional vulnerability. At this point, it may be most productive to shift the focus away from the drug use and onto this emotional vulnerability to help the client reregulate. In other cases, the level of emotional arousal may be too low and may need to be heightened, such as when a client exhibits 'apparent competence' as described earlier.

The Case of Beth: Application to Step 2

Beth arrived at her first session with a list of vague goals such as 'I want to feel better' and 'I want to love myself'. In DBT, the first four sessions are typically considered a pretreatment phase in which the focus is on orienting the client to treatment, bolstering commitment and motivation, and identifying clear and specific goals, In Beth's case, much of the time was spent on specifying her goals and problems. In terms of aspirations, she expressed a desire for a career in childcare, a stable relationship and a family, ownership of a pet, and being a better model of emotion regulation for her future children than her mother had been for her.

Beth was highly motivated to improve her relationship with her partner and expressed fear and ambivalence about her ability to control her destructive behaviours. She was, however, afraid of discussing past traumatic experiences. The therapist agreed that at this stage, attempts to reprocess trauma would likely intensify Beth's emotions and possibly exacerbate further behavioural dysregulation. Accordingly, it was collaboratively decided to prioritize working on the self-harm behaviours, and to address the processing of trauma only once there was an improvement in behavioural control. Whenever Beth expressed ambivalence about treatment, the therapist would refocus on her desire to have a stable relationship and a family. In setting goals, these aspirations were used as a starting point for discussions around what Beth's behaviours would look like once her relationship had improved.

The discussion frequently came back to the problems getting in the way of Beth's having a career and a family, and it became apparent that avoidance played a significant role. The most common reason for her being fired from jobs was a failure to show up, a behaviour that was precipitated by emotional distress following a fight with her partner. While reducing anger outbursts with her partner was a goal, it was also important to increase Beth's ability to not 'drop everything' when conflicts did occur. It emerged that Beth frequently ate only one meal per day and slept only four to five hours per night, and it became evident that she was particularly prone to behavioural dysregulation when she was hungry and tired. Because her poor self-care was often prompting self-harm and anger outbursts, improvements in her sleeping and eating habits were identified as treatment targets.

By the end of the pretreatment orientation phase, Beth had established the following primary treatment targets: (1) eliminate self-harm behaviours; (2) eliminate angry outbursts; (3) limit alcoholic drinks to three in one sitting (no more than 1 oz per drink when it was a mixed drink); (4) sleep eight hours per night; (5) eat three meals per day; and (6) decrease avoidance of commitments. A diary card was developed so that she could track these primary targets and her emotions.

With respect to secondary targets, Beth exhibited clear markers for emotional vulnerability and self-invalidation. She presented as highly anxious in session, and frequently avoided eye contact with the therapist when discussing anything that triggered shame, which was almost everything. She apologized constantly while she was expressing being in distress, and used many phrases like 'I'm so stupid'. She also presented with the dialectical dilemma of apparent competence and active passivity, oscillating between stating that she didn't need help and that everything was fine, to indicating in the diary card that she was having anger outbursts at her partner almost every day. She typically avoided fully filling in the diary card on weeks when she self-harmed. Related to her secondary targets, treatment focused on increasing self-validation, letting go of self-criticism, and increasing direct communication about her need for help.

Step 3: Analyzing Factors Controlling Behaviours

An essential step in developing a case formulation entails identifying the issues controlling problematic behaviours so that suitable interventions can be selected. From a DBT perspective, all behaviours are considered to serve a function, so identifying the function of a behaviour is critical to changing it. An assessment of the function of a behaviour requires a behavioural assessment of the stimulus-response associations. The daily diary cards are reviewed at each treatment session and are used to identify relevant primary problems that warrant attention. The use of diary cards helps to increase a client's awareness of thoughts, emotions, and actions, and the interrelationships between these variables and patterns of behaviours.

Target behaviours, both primary and secondary, are analyzed using the technique of behavioural chain analysis, which involves a detailed assessment of a specific instance of a type of behaviour. Either the client attempts to vividly recall a particular event (whether recent or past), or an instance of this type of behaviour is examined in-session as it arises in the moment. Data on controlling stimuli are collected and examined in an effort to determine the interrelationship and temporal sequencing (from the beginning to the end) of the stimuli controlling the behaviour.

Rather than a 'cold' cognitive processing of the events associated with a behaviour, the therapist attempts to stimulate an emotionally evocative analysis of behaviour, since cognitive processing and memories are positively impacted by arousal.

Several critical elements are highlighted through the process of a chain analysis. First, a specific instance of the target behaviour is identified, or a precise description of it (details, intensity, and duration) is obtained. Following this, the event (whether internal or external) that prompted or set off the behaviour is uncovered. Next, the factors that made the person vulnerable to the behaviour occurring are considered. A detailed, temporal fine-grained analysis is conducted to assess the thoughts, emotions, actions, and environmental events leading up to the behaviour. Subsequently, the consequences of the behaviour are identified. Ultimately, all the variables controlling a problem are identified: these typically reflect a combination of skills deficit, contingency problems, cognitive dysfunction, and/or problematic emotions (Koerner, 2012).

The therapist must probe for information that is not disclosed or that may be outside of the client's conscious awareness. For example, a client who reports having had no feelings of hurt after receiving critical feedback might be asked whether there had been any experience of bodily sensations associated with emotions; or a client who has completed three months of skills training yet still reports engaging in self-harm behaviour in response to intense painful emotions might be asked what is getting in the way of using the acquired skills in distress tolerance.

A poorly constructed case formulation that is based on a limited understanding of the controlling variables can impede rather than advance treatment progress. Common problems in the analysis include the mistargeting of problems and overlooking important information about controlling variables. Another concern is the failure to identify the primary mechanism underlying the function of the problem behaviour. For example, if angry outbursts are providing an escape from inhibited grief, then helping the client accept and process the grief will be essential for resolving this behaviour. Focusing on the anger behaviours alone will be insufficient.

Case of Beth: Application to Step 3

Early in treatment with Beth, almost every session included a behavioural analysis (BA) to understand the functions of her target behaviours. Most often, the focus of these BAs were on analyzing self-harm incidents, excessive drinking, missing sessions, or avoiding filling in the diary card. The following describes a BA that focused on a self-harm incident.

According to Beth, the prompting event for this incident was that following an argument with her partner over the cleanliness of their apartment, he told her that he was unsure if he would be comfortable having children with her. This comment led her to a series of linked thoughts such as, 'I'm not good enough' and 'no one will ever want me', and her sense of shame skyrocketed and quickly turned into anger toward both him and herself. Importantly, when she became aware of her anger, she tried several strategies to address it, telling her partner that he shouldn't say things like that during a fight, and attempting to self-validate her feelings of anger. She did not, however, do anything to regulate her shame; on the contrary, she told herself that she deserved to feel ashamed because she was a 'terrible person'. She then went into the bathroom, took a pair of manicure scissors, and used them to cut both of her legs superficially. She did not tell her partner what she had done, but her feelings of shame decreased and she cleaned the wounds, thus providing herself with a small amount of compassion.

When first going over the BA, Beth was unaware of any other thoughts that had led her to this act of self-harm. The therapist urged her to consider that many people can have thoughts of being a 'terrible person' without proceeding to hurt themselves. Together with the therapist, Beth came to understand that she had also been having the thought that the shame was intolerable and she 'needed to get rid of it'. That was the link that led her to the bathroom, the place where she often cut herself, and once there she did not attempt to use any other coping skills. After determining the links in the chain, the therapist attempted to analyze whether anything had made Beth particularly vulnerable that day. Beth revealed that she had had only one meal, that her boss had criticized her at work, and that when she got home, to help herself feel better about her boss's comments, she drank five drinks, which she had not recorded in her diary card. Table 1.1 provides a summary of this BA.

Step 4: Observing Patterns Across Behaviours

As behavioural chain analyses are repeated across similar and different classes of behaviours, recurring patterns will become apparent. The therapist must isolate the recurring cognitions, emotions, and actions that set off problematic behaviours, and then map out the relationship between these variables. Typical problematic patterns may be tied to similar behaviours, whereas other problematic patterns may distinguish other behaviours. For example, self-harm behaviour may be triggered by critical feedback and shame, while suicidal behaviour may be triggered by perceived loss and panic related to a sense of being alone. It is important to observe and highlight the recurring patterns as they arise within the therapy and the therapeutic relationship.

Targeting common problematic patterns for intervention means that multiple symptoms can be addressed simultaneously. For example, a client with underlying maladaptive shame and an intense fear of

TABLE 1.1 Summary of a Chain Analysis of Beth's Self-Harm Episode

Vulnerability	Prompting Event	Links	Links	Behaviour	Consequence
Restricted eating. Criticized by boss.	Criticism from partner.	Thoughts about not being good enough. Shame.	Thoughts about not being able to tolerate shame. Self-invalidation of shame.	Cutting legs with manicure scissors.	Relief of shame. Took care of self by cleaning wounds.

abandonment may use drugs with his girlfriend because he is afraid that she will leave him. This same client may fail to complete therapy homework assignment and not fully engage in treatment because he views himself as incapable, and is also afraid that if he changes, the treatment will end and he will lose his relationship with his therapist. A therapist can identify maladaptive shame and avoidance of shame as a common link between the two problematic behaviours (drug use, failure to complete homework). Helping the client reduce his avoidance and decrease the intensity of shame will target both his drug use and his therapy-interfering behaviours.

Over time, a case formulation uncovers the recurring common patterns seen in repeated behavioural chains, and these recurring patterns are targeted for intervention. Some responses will need to be strengthened, while others will need to be modified or replaced. Metaphors are particularly useful of summarizing patterns of behaviour in a way that is easier for clients to understand, and can help create some distance from the problem (Koerner, 2012).

Case of Beth: Application to Step 4

A common pattern that emerged with Beth was her avoidance of emotions, particularly her maladaptive shame. For example, she once arrived at a session without her diary card, and the BA revealed that she had not wanted to complete it because she had self-harmed that week and due to shame could not bring herself to look at the 'yes' in the self-harm column. The BAs that analyzed her frequent absences from work revealed that these stemmed from her not wanting people at her workplace to think she was doing a bad job. The BAs that analyzed her overdrinking showed that this was almost always prompted by perceived criticism from either her partner or her boss. In short, an avoidance of shame held clear links to all of Beth's primary problems.

Importantly, along with this avoidance came an exquisite sensitivity to shame. Beth felt shame even in neutral situations: e.g., if a stranger on the street asked her for the time, she would think they felt sorry for her and only asked her out of pity. Shame arose automatically across many situations. Her thinking would then immediately shift to wanting to avoid shame and, depending on what was around, she would use varying destructive means to escape these feelings: avoiding the situation, drinking, or self-harming. While the behaviours and the specific prompting events were different, her primary maladaptive shame and the desire to avoid it were underlying many of them.

The therapist offered Beth the following metaphor to capture her sensitivity to shame: 'The harsh criticism that you received as a child has left you like a burn victim, and when anything touches your wounds, it leaves you feeling seething pain'. Describing her shame in this way was less threatening to Beth and captured the intensity of her feelings. In keeping with this metaphor, the DBT skills that she was learning were likened to a healing ointment that would heal her burns.

Step 5: Identifying Interventions and Solutions

The final task in the development of a case formulation involves specifying solutions to address specific behaviours. At this stage, the therapist needs to consider whether the client has the ability to engage in alternate behaviours. If the necessary skills seem to be present but the client is not implementing them, the obstacles to responding differently need to be determined. Usually, the impediment is coming from lack of commitment or motivation. The long-term and short-term benefits of different solutions must be considered so that the most effective alternate response can be selected. In the earlier example (see Step 2) of a client being unaware of problematic shame underlying explosive angry outbursts, the most effective short-term solution may be to help the client modulate this response and not act on anger urges; in the long term, the resolution of underlying maladaptive shame needs to be addressed. Ultimately, a case formulation links together several mini-treatment plans to address common problematic patterns of behaviour (Koerner, 2012).

When selecting techniques to solve problematic behaviours, the therapist should consider the following guidelines:

- In DBT, the focus is usually on helping clients move either toward acceptance or toward changing behaviour.
- It is usually most productive to target problematic patterns as they arise in session and hence are emotionally alive.
- It is important to monitor the client's motivation and find out which areas he or she is willing to work on.

- Severe or imminent behaviours are the most important to address. For example, if a client who wants to eliminate suicidal and self-harm behaviour reports to her therapist that she is holding on to her 'suicide kit' just in case things become very difficult, encouraging her to dispose of this kit is critical to the elimination of the behaviours.
- Brainstorming solutions together serves to strengthen the client's sense of mastery and active problem solving. The solutions selected should be considered in terms of both their short-term and long-term consequences.
- Finally, it is important to consider how solutions will be implemented by the client in the real world, and to identify the barriers to implementation.

Case of Beth: Application to Step 5

Several variables were found to control Beth's self-harm behaviours, drinking, and anger outbursts, including ones from the four general problem areas (e.g., skills deficit, contingency problems, cognitive dysfunction, and/or problematic emotions) With respect to skills deficits, Beth struggled to communicate effectively with her partner, and lacked both distress tolerance and emotion regulation skills. She attended a skills training group in order to learn these, and her therapist worked with her outside of the group, using role playing to further strengthen her ability to communicate more directly and effectively. Regarding contingencies or consequences of the behaviour, Beth's partner had a pattern of giving into her demands when she had an angry outburst, which only reinforced them. He attended a family support group and received help in learning how to validate Beth when she was able to express herself effectively and to avoid reinforcing her angry outbursts.

Beth also had several problematic cognitions that contributed to her behavioural dyscontrol. She would constantly think 'I'm so stupid' or 'I'm not good enough', and these thoughts were heightened in response to perceived criticism. She told herself frequently that she was a burden to others. The therapist used a variety of cognitive modification techniques to target these beliefs, such as mindfully observing her self-criticism and interrupting her judgements of herself. In addition, the therapist designed behavioural experiments that allowed Beth to check the facts related to her beliefs. For example, Beth's belief that she was a burden would stop her from using the clinic's pager system. The therapist encouraged her to experiment by using the pager service to see if the person who answered it acted in the ways that Beth would have predicted based on her belief.

Perhaps the most important controlling variable in Beth's case was her primary maladaptive shame. This was addressed using both formal and informal exposure procedures, paired with mindfulness of shame.

In-session work played an important role, as this was the time when Beth was most able to tolerate experiencing shame. When she would show markers of shame such as avoiding eye contact, the therapist would gently name it or ask whether a sense of shame was coming up and would guide Beth to describe the experience. Beth began to understand that her shame was not as dangerous to her as she had once thought.

CONCLUDING REMARKS

This chapter portrays the practice of case formulation in DBT, describing the underlying core theories (Zen philosophy, learning theory, dialectical philosophy, and biosocial theory) and summarizing the key steps involved. The development of a sound case formulation is essential to the effective implementation of DBT, and the hope is that the information here will serve as a practical guide to clinicians who are interested in learning how to tailor DBT therapy for each client.

A case formulation that is based on accurate and precise assessments serves to facilitate therapist empathy and compassion, description of problems, identification and targeting of relevant difficulties, and the selection of suitable interventions. It is important to recognize, however, that a case formulation is a dynamic entity constantly undergoing revisions based on new information. Invariably, there will be gaps in the analysis, and it is important to revise a case formulation and the associated treatment plan as needed, especially if a client is failing to make progress or is deteriorating. To date, no research has examined the impact of case formulation on the efficacy of DBT, and such studies are needed. In addition, future research is needed to investigate approaches to teaching case formulation skills, and on how to generalize these skills across diverse clients.

Acknowledgements

Some details of the case description (age, clinical symptoms) were changed so as to protect client privacy.

References

Davidson, K. (2006). Cognitive formulation in personality disorder. In *Case formulation in cognitive behaviour therapy: The treatment of challenging and complex cases* (pp. 216–237).

Goldfried, M. R., & Davison, G. C. (1994). *Clinical behaviour therapy - expanded edition*. New York: John Wiley and Sons, Inc.

Hart, S., Sturmey, P., Logan, C., & McMurran, M. (2011). Forensic case formulation. *International Journal of Forensic Mental Health, 10*(2), 118–126.

Koerner, K. (2012). *Doing dialectical behavior therapy: A practical guide*. New York: Guilford Press.

Koerner, K., & Linehan, M. M. (1997). Case formulation in dialectical behavior therapy for borderline personality disorder. In T. D. Eells (Ed.), *Handbook of psychotherapy case formulation* (pp. 340–367). New York: Guilford Press.

Linehan, M. (1993a). *Cognitive-behavioral treatment of borderline personality disorder*. New York, NY: Guilford Press.

Linehan, M. M. (1993b). *Skills training manual for treating borderline personality disorder*. New York, NY: Guilford Press.

Linehan, M. M. (1997). Validation and psychotherapy. In A. C. Bohart, & L. S. Greenberg (Eds.), *Empathy reconsidered: New directions in psychotherapy* (pp. 353–392).

Logan, C., Nathan, R., & Brown, A. (2011). Formulation in clinical risk assessment and management. In *Self-harm and violence: Towards best practice in managing risk in mental health services* (pp. 187–204).

McMain, S., Korman, L. M., & Dimeff, L. (2001). Dialectical behavior therapy and the treatment of emotion dysregulation. *Journal of Clinical Psychology*, *57*(2), 183–196.

Swales, M., & Heard, H. (2017). *Dialectical behaviour therapy: Distinctive features* (2nd ed.). Oxford: Routledge.

Swenson, C. R. (2016). *DBT® principles in action: Acceptance, change, and dialectics*. New York, NY: Guilford Press.

CHAPTER

2

Transference-Focused Psychotherapy: Structural Diagnosis as the Basis for Case Formulation

Kenneth N. Levy[1,2], *Yogev Kivity*[1], *Frank E. Yeomans*[2]

[1]Pennsylvania State University, University Park, PA, United States; [2]Weill Medical College of Cornell University, New York, NY, United States

Case formulation in transference-focused psychotherapy (TFP) is based on the severity of the patient's personality pathology, also referred to as Personality Organization, which is mainly determined by the patient's capacity for reality testing, predominant defence mechanisms, and consolidation of identity. In TFP, the patient's level of personality organization or structure is evaluated at the beginning of treatment using the structural interview, which is a clinical psychiatric/psychological interview developed and articulated by Otto Kernberg (1984). That evaluation then serves as the basis for case formulation and treatment planning. The structural interview, and TFP more broadly, are theoretically rooted in the psychodynamic object relations theory (Kernberg, 1984).

REVIEW OF OBJECT RELATIONS THEORY IN RELATION TO AN UNDERSTANDING OF PERSONALITY DISORDERS IN TERMS OF PSYCHOLOGICAL STRUCTURE

Central to our thinking about personality is how to understand identity and, in the case of severe personality disorder, identity diffusion. This latter term refers to an identity that is fragmented, without a clear and

https://doi.org/10.1016/B978-0-12-813521-1.00002-3

coherent sense of self. To better understand this fragmentation, we refer to the concept of the object relations dyad in the development of psychological structure. A dyad consists of a very specific and narrow mental image, or representation, of the self in relation to a corresponding very specific image, or representation, of another (the object of the self's emotion) linked by an intense affect. The object relations dyad thus brings together affects with cognitive representations. These cognitive/affective dyads are first internalized in the mind in the course of a person's early development but are also subject to continued modification throughout life. They become the building blocks of psychological structure, understood as the matrix through which the individual perceives self and the world.

In the course of early development, the newborn experiences both moments of total satisfaction when the caretaker responds perfectly to its needs and also moments of fear, abandonment, and suffering when the caretaker is not available or, even worse, is neglectful or abusive. In this early phase of development, before object constancy is achieved, the self and the world are perceived through equally extreme and unrealistic lenses of all-good or all-bad. Libidinal (loving and affectionate) and aggressive (hateful and destructive) affects become organized around these extreme representations of self and others. This split state is sometimes referred to as the 'paranoid-schizoid' organization: schizoid because it is split and paranoid because the part of the mind characterized by aggressive affects is not experienced as part of the self but is projected and experienced as coming from others. Individuals whose subjective experience is mainly organized in this way tend to experience anxiety in relations to others since closeness is associated with danger and the risk of abandonment or attack.

In most individuals, identity diffusion is an early stage of psychological development that resolves as they develop more complex and realistic images of self and others. However, identity diffusion persists in those with a borderline level of psychological organization and, in fact, defines that condition. In the state of identity diffusion, the dyads imbued with very specific affects (love, trust, hate, fear) are not brought together in a more coherent representation of a whole and complex self-characterized by nuanced emotions in relation to a complex sense of others. Instead of this, there is no ambivalence – one either totally loves or hates, one is totally fearful or trusting.

In terms of subjective experience, identity diffusion is characterized by rapid changes in the sense of self in relation to other that correspond to the activation of a specific dyad by a 'trigger event'. For example, a patient in a therapy session might abruptly shift from experiencing the therapist as a concerned caregiver to experiencing him as uncaring and hateful if the therapist glances at the clock. While a person with an integrated sense of self and others might think 'my therapist can be concerned about me and also need to know when to end the session', a person with identity diffusion might think 'If my therapist doesn't care for me totally and without limits, he hates me and wants to get rid of me'. A core feature of identity diffusion is the ongoing segregation of the cognitive and affective mental elements into a segment of purely positive affect and the opposing segment of exclusively negative affect. This split psychological structure is considered the basis of primitive defence mechanisms such as splitting itself, idealization/devaluation, and projective identification.

In successful psychological development, life experience and learning lead individuals to move beyond the split paranoid-schizoid position and to achieve a mature psychological organization in which, for example, they can continue to love someone even when frustrated by that person rather than believe that frustration equals total rejection and abandonment.

It is important to appreciate the impact of the level of psychological organization on: (1) the perception of oneself, (2) the perception of others, (3) the experience of affects/emotions, and (4) the expression of affects/emotions. A split internal world corresponds to extreme emotional states while an integrated self facilitates balance and modulation of emotions. Emotional complexity does not exist in the split internal world of identity diffusion; what the person experiences in the immediate moment determines their experience of *all* of reality at that moment, without taking into account what they may have experienced at other times. This has an impact on reality testing. Without experiencing a total break from reality testing, the extreme and simplistic internal representations that are projected onto everyday experiences can distort perception according to the exaggerated images of the internal world. The combination of these distortions and the projection of aggressive affects hinders an individual's capacity to adapt to the complexity of the world.

THE STRUCTURAL INTERVIEW AS A CLINICAL INSTRUMENT

Structural interviewing consists of a mental status examination that has been adapted for assessing personality disorders. Kernberg called the interview 'structural' because it tries to evaluate the basic structures of the mind. It is not structured in terms of a decision tree for interview like the SCID or the ADIS or even the IPDE. The structures that it tries to evaluate are, first, the presence or level of identity diffusion (sense of self, coherence and commitment to goals, representation of others); Second, the degree of reality testing (differentiation of self vs. non-self, distinguishing internal vs. external, and social tact and empathy for social criteria of reality), and third, in that context, also, a secondary element, the diagnosis of the dominant defensive operations that characterize the individual (splitting, projective identification vs. repression). The defensive operations in what we call neurotic personality organization (milder cases), usually don't show up in the interview, while defensive operations in severe personality disorder usually show up and reinforce diagnosis (particularly what we call primitive or immature defences, in contrast to neurotic or mature defences). Mature defences as articulated by Kernberg (1984), Vaillant (1994), and A. Freud (1965) include repression, intellectualization, isolation, rationalization, displacement, projection. Immature defences include splitting, primitive idealization, projective identification, omnipotent control, and denial. In the structural interview the therapist is assessing these areas in order to make a decision about the patient's level of personality organization. This task is of utmost importance because it will dictate how therapists proceed with treatment. However, it is important to note that case conceptualization in TFP, while occurring mostly during the structural interview, is almost always a dynamic process that continues and develops throughout treatment, as the therapist's understanding of the patient and their difficulties is modified based on information obtained in the process of therapy and becomes increasingly nuanced and accurate.

During the structural interview, the therapist observes and obtains information through three channels: (1) the patient's verbal communication; (2) the patient's nonverbal communication (e.g., behaviour, affect); and (3) the therapist's countertransference. Diagnoses and case formulation from the structural interview are based on an integration of clinical symptoms (both reported and observed), the assessment of intrapsychic structures (inferred from the patient's narrative and experienced through countertransference), and quality of the therapeutic relationship (observed and experienced through countertransference).

During the structural interview, therapists should get the following information: mental status, a complete symptom picture, the patients current functioning, and the patient's sense of self and others, and, toward the end of the interview, their response to trial interpretations. In addition, the therapist provides the patient with feedback regarding their initial formulations and uses this feedback to assess the patients' willingness to engage in treatment. Figure 2.1 illustrates how the therapist moves through the structural interview.

As the therapist carries out the structural interview, he is constantly aware of the attitude of both the clinician and the patient. The therapist's attitude should be one of concern but without siding with either side of the patient's conflicts. Kernberg referred to this attitude as technical neutrality. In referring to the attitude as technical neutrality he was trying to differentiate it from the more traditional psychoanalytic concept of neutrality. By technical neutrality, we do not mean taking a bland, cool, and aloof attitude but rather a nonjudgmental stance that allows for all aspects of the patient's experience to be considered.

It is also important to note the patient's attitude. Are they concerned? Are they cavalier?

It is very important for rapport building that the therapist convey their understanding of the patient's difficulties. This can be done without overt support, reassurance, or validation. Instead, a genuinely concerned attitude, an attentive stance, and staying close to the patient's phenomenological experience all convey understanding, especially when embedded in warmth. It is important to remember two things about validation: (1) It can be invalidating; and (2) it can support distortions. For instance, reassuring the patient that you are confident in their ability to do something or that you value them can be experienced as invalidating of their concerns even if the reassurance is authentic to the therapist. It is also important to remember that a good interpretation can have a holding quality and be experienced as both very accepting and validating of the patient. For example, when working with a patient that expresses doubts about his ability to complete college despite being very intelligent, instead of providing direct reassurance, the therapist could say: 'Despite being very smart and creative, it is difficult for you to imagine that you could achieve the goals you are aspiring toward. I, like others in your life, could tell you that I think you could complete college, but I imagine that at some level you might still doubt that it is possible'. Rather than overt reassurance this kind of comment captures the complexity of the patient's experience.

Also, maintaining technical neutrality can be very validating and filled with empathic regard. Nonjudgmental, noncritical stance provides patients with sense of safety that allows exploration of previously avoided memories, thoughts, and feelings. In TFP, empathy is defined as being able to connect with the entirety of the patient's internal experience – even parts that they are not aware of (Yeomans, Clarkin, & Kernberg, 2015).

By the end of the structural interview, the therapist should be able to provide the patient with their *initial* diagnostic impressions or understanding and be ready to move onto getting more history and to the contract-setting phase. The contract-setting phase sets the frame for the treatment. It makes explicit conditions for treatment and what the role and responsibilities are for both the patient and the therapist.

During the course of the interview, the therapist should also assess attitude, attention, orientation, consciousness, comprehension, judgement, memory, and intelligence. The therapist begins the interview by providing some context: what they know about the patient, the purpose of the meeting, and what they are interested in finding out. We usually begin with the following four questions, which both facilitates the collection of important information as well as mental status:

1. I would like to know what brings you here?
2. What is your understanding of the nature of your difficulties?
3. What do you expect from treatment?
4. Where are you now?

Often, after their initial answer, a patient will ask whether they answered all the questions and may state something like 'I don't know if that answers all of your questions'. This is a good opportunity to assess mental status. The therapist can say: 'Do you think you answered all the questions?'; 'What do think?'; 'What is your sense?' The therapist can follow by respectfully asking, 'Did you understand what I was asking?'

The four questions begin concretely and become more abstract. The first one is very concrete: What brought you here? The patient may answer concretely and say 'my mother brought me' or 'I came by bus'. What's the nature of your difficulties? That's somewhat more abstract. What do you expect from treatment? That's quite abstract. Where are you now? That's totally unstructured. These questions at the same time have a progressive degree of unstructured nature to test the reality testing.

The patient's answers to these questions provide some cursory evidence for their level of personality organization because, for example, schizophrenic patients usually cannot answer these questions. In addition, although formally assessed only later in the interview, with these first four questions, the therapist immediately tests the patient's sensorium: capacity for attention, degree of consciousness, intelligence and capacity to realistically provide appropriate answers.

1. The therapist challenges the patient's memory – whether they can remember those four questions.
2. The therapist tests intelligence – whether the patient can provide intelligent answers to the questions or not.
3. The therapist also observes the patient's behaviour with them.
4. The therapist observes the patient's affect.
5. The therapist observes the patient's thoughts, both regarding content and process.

Next, the therapist asks symptoms and very completely so, and whenever there is a symptom that needs a differential diagnosis, they go into it. It is our experience that therapists often do not pay sufficient attention to descriptive symptoms. Research suggests that there are a number of important comorbidities to assess for and differential diagnoses to make with regard to BPD. These include: psychotic disorders, mood disorders, anxiety disorders, stress related disorders, attentional disorders, substance use disorders and eating disorders, and other personality disorders. A full discussion of the shared characteristics and the differential diagnosis of these disorders is beyond the scope of this chapter (see Kernberg & Yeomans, 2013).

The next step is to assess the patient's present life. The therapist can say to the patient, 'I'd like to know about your present life, so to get to know you as you are, as a person. Can you tell me about your work, your studies, your family, your parents, your girlfriend or boyfriend, your children, what do you do in your free time?' The goal is to get a complete picture of the patient's present life circumstances. This allows the therapist to assess problems in the areas of: love and sex, in work and profession, in social life, in recreation, in creativity, in functioning.

Once information about the patient's current life has been obtained, the therapist asks about and assesses identity. There are two questions for assessing identity. First, the therapist selects one or two of individuals that the patient mentioned as important in their life and asks them to describe that person (s) to them, so that the therapist gets a live picture of them: 'What makes this person unique? What makes them different from everybody else?' With normal identity it is possible for a person to provide a live description and a sense of the person. It's not something easy to do, but it evokes a thought process by which the therapist can see how a person reconstructs what's essential. In contrast to a thoughtless, some kind of standard, canned, or stereotyped answer (e.g., 'Oh, that's a lovely person, great, very sensitive, lovely, beautiful person'.). The therapist obtained others' descriptions until they have a clear sense, and then asks the patient: 'Now that you've described somebody else to me, could you describe yourself? What makes you different from everybody else? What makes you a unique person?' Of course, by that point the therapist already has an impression of the person and can already contrast that description with what they are observing, but also can evaluate to what extent there is a capacity for an assessment in depth. The therapist assesses the capacity for an integrated view of significant others and of self, in which contradictions may exist, but are described in an integrated, satisfactory way. Identify diffusion is an important indicator of a severe personality disorder and strongly suggest further exploration of personality disorder features.

The next step is assessment of reality testing and is carried out only with patients who, during the interview, give the therapist a sense of something strange. The therapist focuses on those inappropriate aspects in the patient's affect, thought, or behaviour. The therapist describes these aspects to the patient and then asks: 'I noticed X – affect, thought, or behaviour – that seems strange to me. Can you see that?' If the patient provides a conceivable explanation, reality testing is maintained. If that question disorganizes the patient, it indicates impairments in reality testing, which likely suggest a psychotic disorder rather than a personality disorder. If strong evidence exists for impaired reality testing early in the interview (e.g., patient falls asleep while at the same time talking with the therapist; or patient is unable to remember the therapist's questions), the therapist can skip the previous parts and move immediately to evaluate the sensorium. If there are alterations of thought, affect, or behaviour, the therapist evaluated psychotic symptoms (hallucinations or delusions), that have to be distinguished from obsessive ideas, overvalued ideas, illusions, pseudohallucinations, hallucinosis, hypnogogic experiences, and faked hallucinations. If the therapist is unsure of the information obtained and how best to evaluate it, they can return again through the cycle in Fig. 2.1. If the patient seems confused and disoriented (i.e., an alteration of the sensorium), they may have acute organic mental illness that requires immediate psychiatric attention. If the sensorium is intact, the therapist moves to assessing alright memory, by ordinary memory tests, and intelligence. The similarities subtest of the WAIS is a very nice and easy way to get a gross assessment and compare it with the patient's educational background.

After that, the therapist obtains a thorough history from the patient. For example, 'What I would like to do now (or in our next meeting) is to get a very complete history about your parents, what they were like, your childhood, the major influences on you, your sexual history, your school and work history, your prior therapy (or therapies), and so forth. This will give me a context to understand what we talked about today and what we continue to discuss in therapy'.

After obtaining the history the therapist acknowledges that they have completed the task and asks the patient if there was anything that should have been asked that was not or if there is anything else that they feel the therapist should know in order to be helpful to them.

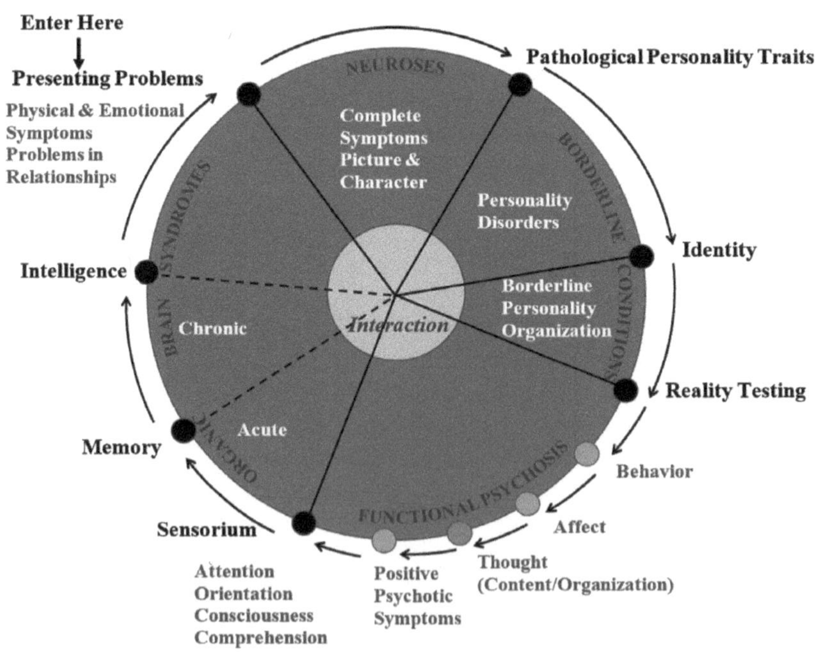

FIGURE 2.1 Cycling Through The Structural Interview

The therapist can conclude the interview when he/she feels he has adequate information to support to have a clear diagnostic impression and sufficient information to set the treatment frame with the patient. The patient's description of self and others, along with continuity or discontinuity/contradictions in his discourse and narrative, have provided the therapist with information about his level of identity diffusion versus integration. The patient's understanding of his condition and problems add to what has been learned about his level of defensive operations from the presence or absence of split views of self and others: a tendency to externalize responsibility for problems within seeing any contribution on his part supports the presence of projection as a primitive defence. The therapist's sense of the patient's capacity to have a nuanced and rich experience of others versus a superficial one is an indication of the degree to which the patient is unknowingly trapped in his own internal world of object representations in contrast to being engaged in deep and genuine relations with others. The structural interview will also have provided information about the consistency/inconsistency/lack of the patient's internal value system and about the level of aggressive affects and if they are egosyntonic or egodystonic. Finally, any questions about reality testing will have determined if the patient may be subject to distortions based on the power of simplistic internal representations or if the patient may be frankly psychotic.

If the structural interview has provided evidence of identity diffusion, primitive defence mechanisms, and shaky but intact reality testing, the therapist will consider the patient to have a psychological structure organized at the borderline level (BPO). The next question is whether the patient is situated at the higher or lower level of BPO; this is determined mostly with regard to whether aggressive drives and affects are stronger than affiliative ones and whether the patient has some degree of meaningful involvement with others and with life activities. This distinction is important to guide the therapist is establishing an adequate treatment contract and frame.

The next question is if the patient's identity diffusion is manifest as such, as in prototypic BPD, or whether it is masked by the pathological grandiose structure (PGS) that distinguishes patients with narcissistic personality disorder (NPD) from other personality disorders in the BPO range. The PGS is a brittle and fundamentally hollow self structure present in the mind of those with NPD that appropriates all that is good to the self and projects all that is negative onto others. This can be seen in self-descriptions that are relatively intact and differentiated compared to those with BPD but also characterized by pathological grandiosity. The description of others, in contrast to the description of self in those with narcissistic personality is characterized by a poverty of detail and richness. The presence of this structure requires certain modifications of the techniques of TFP (see Diamond et al., submitted; Diamond, Yeomans, & Levy, 2011; Levy, 2012).

Finally, the therapist decides if the patient falls within a more specific PD category (BPD proper, paranoid PD, schizoid PD, avoidant PD, etc.). The latter distinction has less bearing on the next step treatment (the discussion of diagnosis and of the treatment contract and frame) than the triage into the higher versus lower level of BPO and presence/absence of the PGS that subtends NPD. Fundamental to the discussion of the diagnostic impression is the explanation to the patient that his symptomatic picture, which, of course, must be addressed, is best understood and ultimately best treated by considered a fundamental underlying difficulty in the sense of self.

DISCUSSION OF THE DIAGNOSTIC IMPRESSION/ FORMULATION WITH THE PATIENT

The structural interview is not only important in establishing a diagnosis and case formulation with personality-disordered patients but it is useful in gathering information that can be shared with the patient when providing feedback and in developing collaborate goals for the psychotherapy. Often therapists are reluctant to provide diagnostic feedback/case formulation to the patient because of concerns such as upsetting or stigmatizing the patient. Some therapists view the diagnosis of a personality disorder as pejorative, stigmatizing, or are afraid of the patient's reaction. However, providing diagnostic feedback is important because patients have a right to know how the therapist conceptualizes their difficulties and importantly, one cannot begin the treatment in earnest if there is no explicit agreement about what the problems are that the patient is in treatment for (e.g., it makes no sense to propose a psychological treatment to a patient who insists his problems are exclusively biological). Additionally, the frame, its rationale, and the treatment approach and techniques are related to the diagnosis/case formulation. Patients often conceptualize their difficulties as depression, anxiety, bipolar disorder, PTSD, ADHD, substance abuse, or as the victim of other people's impositions and malevolence. Thus it is important to collect the necessary information to assess and make the differential diagnoses that will be helpful for the patient in understanding how the therapist understands their difficulties. A poorly conducted structural interview, will likely result in difficulty convincingly providing feedback to the patient. Having the information acquired in the structural interview allows the therapist to present feedback that can resonate with the patient's experience without unnecessarily stigmatizing or upsetting them. In doing so, the therapist should stay phenomenologically close to the patient's conscious experience and take their time in bringing disparate information into the patients awareness. Providing feedback obviously has to be done sensitively and rather than leaving the patient feeling labelled it should leave them feeling understood and hopeful. In sharing this information with the patient, they should feel understood and helped rather than stigmatized and judged. However, despite the best efforts, because the patient is identity diffused, they may have very disparate and unintegrated experiences of the feedback. On the one hand, they may feel the therapist is taking their concerns seriously, being thoughtful in their deliberations and phrasing, and on the other hand feel attacked and judged, not necessarily because of anything the therapist has said but because of their own judgements or experiences of others judgements. Also, this ambivalence can lead the patient to feel hopeful about the treatment with the therapist during the session, but afterwards, contradictory feelings may fester. It is important for the therapist to be vigilant for any ambivalence and gently address it.

Following the diagnostic feedback, the therapist sets the frame for treatment. When working with personality-disordered patients it is important to have a clear discussion of the treatment frame or what is called the treatment contract in a TFP model (Yeomans, Selzer, & Clarkin, 1992). As described earlier, the contract-setting phase has multiple purposes. First, it educates the patient to psychotherapy. This is important for not only the therapy naïve patients but also therapy experienced ones because even those patients who have been in multiple treatments may have only minimal understanding of this particular type of therapy, in part because they may have been in therapies that utilized very different stances (e.g., supportive treatment, medication management, or CBT) or because all too frequently therapists are not explicit with patients about the structure and rationale for a treatment.

A second goal of the contract-setting phase is to establish a clear treatment frame that allows the patient and therapist to address and reflect on the material that arises in treatment, including feelings both in and out of session. The treatment contract creates a safe environment for patients that allow their dynamics to unfold with the therapist. By providing structure and clear expectations, it also provides a safe environment for the therapist to work within. Having an explicit agreement of the tasks and responsibilities of each party also provides an avenue for discussing and understanding deviations from the frame or contract. As Diamond et al. (2013) outline more fully, the contract-setting phase is more difficult with narcissistic patients because the expectations and responsibilities confront and limit the patient's grandiosity and omnipotent control and often results in their perceiving the therapist as controlling and imposing. The frame or contract is often initially rejected or tested in ways that may threaten the treatment. It is important when setting the treatment frame with personality disorder patients that the therapist utilize patients' past treatment experiences and relationship patterns to predict the kind of difficulties they might experience in the treatment. It is also important for the therapist to examine a patient's responses to the treatment frame to ensure that he or she is not simply acquiescing to the goals proposed by the therapist but is making a true commitment. The frame is established before beginning the therapy per se through negotiation of the treatment contract. The process is a collaborative one in which the therapist presents the rationale for elements of the therapy and the patient discusses any concerns that they may have. The therapist's stance is collaborative not imposing, to avoid acquiescence of the patient. The therapist observes and monitors how the patient is responding and verbally checks-in with them about how they are feeling. The therapist combines flexibility and openness to discussion with adherence to essential aspects of the treatment. In addition to defining the responsibilities of patient and therapist, the structure provided by the contract protects the therapist's ability to think clearly and reflect, provides a safe place for the patient's dynamics to unfold, and sets the stage for exploring and interpreting the meaning of deviations from the contract. When there are deviations from the frame, referring back to the contract supports the patient's capacity to step outside of the moment and to view their behaviour from alternate perspectives. An implicit message in the establishment of the contract is that all feelings can be experienced and reflected on, in contrast to the patient's felt need to manage threatening aspects of affective experience through acting out and projection. This verbal agreement is often referred to as the treatment contract; it establishes the conditions or frame of the therapy in a way that emphasizes the experience of emotions within the therapy and curbs the expression of emotions in the form of acting out (cutting, taking overdoses, substance abuse, unsafe sex, etc.)

USING THE DIAGNOSTIC IMPRESSION/CASE FORMULATION TO CHOOSE A THERAPY

Ultimately the diagnostic data from the structural interview is used to choose and guide therapy. In the broadest sense, knowing if the patient is organized at the neurotic, borderline, or psychotic level allows the therapist to make a choice about treatment intervention. Neurotically organized individuals can utilize a range of therapies across cognitive-behavioural and psychodynamic treatments. The particular therapy is a function of the patient's difficulties and the patient's interests. Some patients are interested in working on specific concerns or symptoms whereas others on broader issues such as capacity for intimacy and self-actualization. For those with focal interests and/or needs, short-term treatments are appropriate, such as cognitive-behavioural therapy, interpersonal therapy, and short-term psychodynamic therapy, especially for those with depression. For patients with panic disorder, in addition, to a number of CBT based treatments, panic-focused psychodynamic psychotherapy can be used. When the patient is interested, psychoanalysis can be appropriate.

CASE EXAMPLE

The case below is adapted from Levy (2012).

Presenting Problem and Client Description

Anne was referred by a friend of hers in the field to a colleague who referred her to the therapist for treatment. Her chief complaints were feelings of chronic depression and diffuse anxiety. The colleague who referred her had also indicated that she was prone to angry outbursts, which a number of times resulted in having the police being called. These outbursts occurred in places of business, when travelling, with friends, family, lovers, and with neighbours.

Anne was a tall, attractive, married woman in her mid-thirties with three children, who looked slightly younger than her chronological age. She was the older of two children. Growing up, her father was an extremely successful businessman who had left her with a substantial inheritance. He was a self-made man who was 'all business', hostile and very derogating of her, and generally too busy for his children. After her father's death, her mother remarried. Her mother was both physically absent and emotionally distant while Anne was growing up; although she provided for basic and nonemotional needs, Anne's mother tended to use this support to coerce her children to do as she desired. This pattern of behaviour continued into her children's adulthood. Anne's mother often provided the patient with loans and helped her with her finances as much of her inheritance was unavailable (e.g., in the form of stocks). Because of the unavailability of these funds, Anne had difficulty managing her money and often relied on her mother to organize her finances. In return, her mother often put pressure on Anne about where to live, where the children should go to school, and other major decisions in her life.

Despite her overt perception that she had superior intelligence and abilities, Anne reported constant difficulties doing well in school and in sticking with any one of her multiple hobbies (e.g., horseback riding, acting, and singing). She generally blamed her parents for not encouraging her or helping her develop her talents. She perceived herself as having difficulty concentrating or at least following through on tasks. She felt easily bored or frustrated with whatever she was doing. Despite her difficulties with money, she tended to hire assistants to carry out the more mundane aspects of her work and hobbies (e.g., she hired someone to take her horseback riding for exercise because she found having to do so boring and an imposition). Her difficulties sticking with hobbies were sometimes made worse due to angry outbursts she would have with friends, colleagues, or others involved in these activities. She would frequently change her mind with regard to which hobbies were most important to and where she wanted to invest her time and efforts. She once sold a horse she owned because she had not ridden it in years, and then a few days later bought another after she saw a new horse she admired. The result of these patterns was that as she entered her 30s she had not yet developed expertise in any one area nor did she have a stable sense of what she wanted to do with her life.

To gain the approval of her parents, she married a man who, while supportive of her and tolerant of her rages, was unable to provide sufficiently for the family, in part because he was disproportionally responsible for the children, and in part because he was probably identity diffused himself. Her inheritance and support from her mother provided for the family and allowed both her and her husband to live comfortably but without steady career investments. She felt terribly put out by having children, found them to be quite a burden, yet needed them as an excuse for not having invested in a career path nor achieved tangible successes.

In addition to depressed mood and diffuse anxiety, the patient reported angry outbursts, significant alcohol and marijuana use, fleeting concerns about rapidly shifting interests, and unhappiness with the lack of success in her life. Upon detailed questioning the therapist determined that she was heavily involved with drinking and marijuana use. She felt considerably activated by routine situations and demands and saw the alcohol and drug use as ways of dampening her internal experience. She shared that her husband was concerned that she was too disconnected from the children and overly frustrated with them – frequently losing her temper with them over rather developmentally normal stresses. By all appearances, she was quite brittle and needed much support. In addition, to her mother's financial and logistical support, she had a housekeeper, gardener, au pair, and a number of babysitters to help her maintain the household and take care of the children. Additionally, her husband did not work regularly and was the primary caregiver who not only took care of the children's emotional needs but also brought them to all their lessons.

At times Anne believed that her children and 'unsupportive' husband were responsible for her 'not making it' or becoming famous and she had frequent fantasies of leaving her family and 'making it big'. She attended acting workshops and sang in a series of local bands, occasionally developing crushes on fellow actors or band members, particularly younger men. Sometimes these crushes resulted in affairs, sometimes in unrequited love relationships. She often fantasized about leaving her family and touring

Europe with a younger man who would produce her music and help her achieve fame and fortune.

Case Formulation

The case formulation for this patient was derived over a number of sessions using Kernberg's structural interview. From the data that emerged, it became clear that despite her complaints Anne did not meet criteria for any axis I disorder. Although there were some somatic symptoms, she did not have any of the neurovegetative symptoms of depression, nor did she report feelings of worthlessness or excessive or inappropriate guilt or recurrent thoughts about death. She did report depressed mood and occasional loss of interest in activities, but these states were variable, fleeting, and typically in response to a perceived interpersonal slight or some other failure. In fact, rather than being anhedonic, she was particularly self-indulgent and pleasure seeking. Likewise, she did not meet criteria for dysthymia or depressive personality disorder, bipolar disorder, or an anxiety disorder.

Although at times she displayed elevated, expansive, and irritable moods, they never lasted at least a week (or even four days for a hypomanic mood); instead, these symptoms tended to be quite labile, reactive to environmental triggers, quickly vacillating with depressed mood states or irritability as is more characteristic of personality disorders (Henry et al., 2001; Koenigsberg et al., 2002). This pattern was chronic as opposed to being present in discrete episodes as is the case with bipolar disorders. With regard to Generalized Anxiety Disorder (GAD), her anxiety was diffuse, free-floating, and variable. Her anxiety was also imbued with irritability and impulsivity and the GAD diagnosis was contradicted by a variable presence of anxiety and long periods of lack of any anxiety, even in the face of anxiety-provoking situations. Although she had described an occasional panic attack, she did not meet criteria for the disorder.

Her reality testing and sensorium were mostly intact, but as she discussed her functioning, she described situation after situation in which she flew into rages and made outrageous verbal attacks on those she was close to as well as strangers she encountered. She would fly into rages against her parents, her husband, her children, the au pair, her auto mechanic, her singing and acting coaches, lovers, and countless others. No one was safe from her wrath. On the section in which patients are asked to describe themselves and others, consistent with Kernberg's theory, Anne was able to provide a relatively intact and coherent, albeit grandiose, description of herself, whereas her descriptions of others were quite impoverished and in terms of need gratification and frustration. In terms of NPD, she clearly displayed a pervasive pattern of grandiosity in her fantasy and behaviour, a need for admiration, and described instances of clear lack of empathy for others. With regard to specific criteria, she (1) displayed a sense of self-importance that was exaggerated in terms of her achievements and talents and she certainly expected to be recognized as superior without commensurate achievements; (2) described being preoccupied with fantasies of unlimited success, power, beauty, and ideal love; (3) indicated that she considered herself to be special and should associate with other special or high-status people; (4) described a clear need for excessive admiration; (5) displayed a sense of entitlement; (6) periodically was interpersonally exploitive; (7) had difficulty recognizing feelings and needs of others; (8) was often envious of others and believed that others were envious of her; and (9) at times behaved or displayed an arrogant, haughty attitude.

Based on her symptom picture, her functioning in work and love, and inferred psychological organization based on the quality of the narrative descriptions of self and others as well as the quality of her relatedness to others, it was determined that the panoply of symptoms she presented with could best be understood as occurring in the context of an NPD diagnosis, with a borderline personality organization. This is a woman who aggressively defended against feeling small and inconsequential to her parents – one of whom was hostile and derogating and the other who was cold and disengaged. Understandably, she deeply wanted to be with her parents, to be valued by them, and to be nurtured by them. She was angry with them and others, sensitive to any indication that she was being devalued, and prone to distort benign situations so as to feel belittled. In these situations, she quickly responded with extreme rage that often resulted in her being removed from a situation and/or the dissolution of previously established relationships.

The therapist could tell from the onset that he was about to begin a challenging treatment. Anne's opening volley to the therapist showed both her aggression and her neediness. The very first thing she said to the therapist, referring to his office, was 'Gee, this is the nicest broom closet I have ever seen', which was quickly followed by reprimands for a series of perceived failures on his part: The therapist had no water cooler in his faculty office, his office was too far from where she had to park, the weather did not suit her. Each of these comments was embedded in an angry 'put-out' affect and resulted in the therapist feeling both criticized and sympathetic toward her. She was hostile but the therapist hypothesized that part of her wanted him to care for her. She wanted him to provide nourishment, intimacy, and atmospheric comfort. And even before the therapist said anything more than 'come in', she was angry at him for her own desires of wanting these things from him. Her comments invited interpretations but to do so would have been too early, too exposing, and too penetrating. Consistent with the therapist's countertransference, she would feel attacked without any good options. Immediately, the therapist had a sense of the link between her neediness and her feelings of abandonment with her aggressiveness and superiority. The therapist felt she wanted these things from him and she was sad that he could not provide them, but she was also angry at him that he had not provided them and that the therapist evoked such desire in her. The therapist also sensed that she took great pleasure in knowing that he was incapable of making a water cooler appear or move the parking garage. And, even if he could get her some water and find her a closer parking spot, he could not change the weather. Thus, it was the therapist who was incapable not her.

This dynamic continued, for as the therapist explained his practice to her, she dismissed everything he said as if he was telling her things she already knew (despite the fact that this was her first therapy). When the therapist told her his fee, she told him that he 'would never get rich charging so little'. She followed this comment with stories of all the people who wanted a piece of her financially as if she was made of money and others were corrupt users who wanted nothing more than to have what was rightfully hers. Infused in these comments were the therapists presumed greed (i.e., that he was using her for his financial gain) but also its opposite: that he was not charging as much as he could and therefore, maybe he was not a greedy money-hungry user. Additionally, she was scoffing at his fee as if it was inconsequential to someone with her money maintaining her superiority to him but at the same time expressing her concern that the therapist didn't really care about her besides the money. Early on, it was clear that her communications were complicated and represented a condensation of overt and covert narcissistic concerns.

Despite the therapist's experience of the patient as critical of him, she also spoke very glowingly about him and it became apparent that her experience of him was very different than the way she spoke to him. Anne described multiple situations in which she was hostile, disparaging, and rude toward others and the therapist experienced her as that way toward him too, despite the intermittent idealizations. However, she saw herself as someone others attacked, derogated, coerced, imposed upon, and controlled. She could not acknowledge it but it seemed to him from her affect and the content of what she was saying that she found him and his questions a terrible imposition. Someone was being imposed upon and controlled and someone was imposing and controlling, but it was unclear to her who had what roles. She and the therapist in the consultation room and others outside it vacillated back and forth in her scenarios.

As the therapist continued the structural interview and he gathered information about her relationships and experience of others, she frequently talked about people in her life that she thought were narcissists or had a personality disorder. She often spoke to the therapist as if the two of them were colleagues discussing her family members who were patients two colleagues might consult one another about. The therapist began to experience dread about sharing his diagnostic impressions with her. He fretted how she was going to take it and imagined that she might lash out at him and end the treatment (part fear, part wish upon reflection). This was an unusual feeling for the therapist. Although it can be difficult to share a personality disorder diagnosis with patients, it is important that therapists convey diagnostic impressions to collaboratively set the treatment frame. The therapist not only advocates the sharing of diagnoses with patients but usually feels quite at ease and skilled when doing so. Despite the therapist's apprehension, he knew what he needed to do and dutifully did so. The therapist did his best to be tactful and precise in his language and to utilize the material she shared in ways that he thought would resonate with her. To his surprise she initially took the news very well. His descriptions of her experience and the psychological rationales he described resonated with her but, most importantly, despite her disparagement of those she perceived as narcissistic in her circle of family and friends, she disclosed that she had long suspected that she herself could be diagnosed with NPD (in fact, she reported that she wondered about this for almost 10 years!). This was an important moment of both reflection and connection between them. They had a shared experience that the therapist could now refer back to as needed. It was not just the therapist who thought she was narcissistic; she too believed this.

The discussion of the treatment frame was easier now that both were on the same page about the problems and they discussed each of their roles and responsibilities in the treatment as well as the rationale behind them. She was less defensive but the therapist realized that this state was most likely only temporary. With Anne, the therapist stated that although she felt what they were suggesting was reasonable right now, we might predict that at some later time she might feel differently and that it would be important to discuss those feelings as they arise.

It is not uncommon for NPD patients to begin therapy with either a haughty devaluing attitude toward the therapist or conversely with an idealization of the therapist as one who can magically provide solutions to all problems. Both these stances result from the need to sustain the grandiose sense of self and from the envy the patient experiences in relation to others. In both cases the patient envies the therapist's functioning and psychological health. This conflict often leads the patient to devalue the therapist or aspects of the therapy and to either subtly or explicitly reject the therapist's interventions. In Anne's case, she prefaced every acceptance of what the therapist offered by stating 'Of course'. At other times, she made small tweaks to the therapist wording. At still other times, she would reject what the therapist said, only to come in the next week or sometime later and share with him her newfound understanding that was exactly what the therapist had offered earlier but which she had rejected.

REVIEW OF RESEARCH

Empirical support for the reliability, validity, and clinical utility of the structural interview comes from two main lines of research: studies on the traditional structural interview, and studies on the Structured Interview of Personality Organization (STIPO), a semistructured interview derived from the structural interview.

RESEARCH ON THE STRUCTURAL INTERVIEW

Reliability of the Structural Interview

Several studies have now established the interrater reliability of structural diagnosis based on the structural interview (e.g., Armelius, Sundbom, Fransson, & Kullgren, 1990; Bauer, Hunt, Gould, & Goldstein, 1980; Carr, Goldstein, Hunt, & Kernberg, 1979; Derksen, Hummelen, & Bouwens, 1994; Ingenhoven et al., 2009; Kullgren, 1987; Lewis & Harder, 1991). These studies show that, regardless of whether clinicians provide global impression or dimensional ratings, high rates of agreements are achieved on structural diagnosis using the structural interview.

Validity and Clinical Utility of the Structural Interview

The convergent validity of the structural diagnosis has been supported in studies that show that measures of the structural diagnosis from the structural interview are positively correlated with related constructs such as DSM personality disorders diagnoses, personality pathology, and use of primitive defence mechanisms, as assessed by a variety of methods, such as structured interviews, batteries of psychological testing and self-report questionnaires (Armelius et al., 1990; Bauer et al., 1980; Carr et al., 1979; Kernberg et al., 1981; Kullgren, 1987; Lewis & Harder, 1991; Reich & Frances, 1984).

Research on the Structured Interview of Personality Organization (STIPO)

The STIPO (Clarkin, Caligor, Stern, & Kernberg, 2004), and its revised version the STIPO-R (Clarkin, Caligor, Stern, & Kernberg, 2015) is a semistructured interview based on the structural interview that was developed for use in clinical and research settings. The 55-item STIPO-R consists of standard questions along with additional clarification probes. Ratings are then used to compute five subscales: identity; object relations; defences; aggression; and moral values. In addition, a narcissism dimension can be scored from items that are included in the other subscales. It is possible to also classify patients into categories of neurotic, high borderline and low borderline personality organization (Hörz et al., 2009).

Reliability of the Structured Interview of Personality Organization (STIPO)

The interrater reliability of the STIPO is well-established, with estimates of excellent intraclass correlations (ICCs) as well as good-to-excellent internal consistency coefficients, except for the reality testing subscale for which internal consistency is just short of satisfactory (0.69), possibly due to small number of items (Doering et al., 2013; Preti, Prunas, Sarno, & De Panfilis, 2012; Stern et al., 2010).

Validity and Clinical Utility of the Structured Interview of Personality Organization (STIPO)

The STIPO has been shown to differentiate between various DSM disorders in theoretically meaningful ways and to correlate with self-report measures of personality organization, as well as other theoretically relevant constructs such as attachment style, coping, anger, dissociation, and temperament (Doering et al., 2013; Stern et al., 2010).

Studies have also shown that the STIPO is sensitive to improvements in personality organization during successful treatments of borderline personality disorder, including TFP (Doering et al., 2010). In addition, higher STIPO scores also predicted greater likelihood of dropout among dual-diagnosis patients in a residential treatment for substance abuse (Preti et al., 2015).

In sum, research on the traditional and semistructured versions of the structural interview shows that trained clinicians can achieve adequate agreement on the structural diagnosis based on either a global clinical judgement or dimensional ratings. In addition, the structural interview is successful in capturing the construct of structural diagnosis, and, more broadly, various dimensions of personality pathology, in theoretically and clinically meaningful ways.

CONCLUDING REMARKS

The structural interview is a clinical psychiatric/psychological interview developed by Otto Kernberg (1984) that is central to the case formulation in TFP. Through structural interviewing the therapist is able to assess the severity of the patient's personality pathology conceptualized both in terms of personality organization and the specific PD diagnosis.

Assessment of personality organization provides an understanding of the patient's capacity for reality testing, predominant defence mechanisms employed, and the patients level of identity consolidation. Based on the structural interview, the therapist derives a complete picture of the patients presenting symptoms, pathological personality traits, identity, and mental status needed to make the differential between levels of personality organization and various diagnoses such as major depression, bipolar disorder, panic disorder and borderline and narcissistic personality disorders. The information gathered during the structural interview allows the therapist to confidently provide feedback to the patient that resonates with both parties and thus contributes to the collaborative development of a treatment frame and plan. Additionally, the information obtained allows the therapist to discuss threats to the treatment (e.g., coming late, missing sessions, etc) and how those threats can be protected against in advance and addressed if they arise.

Acknowledgements

Select details of the case description were changed so as to protect client privacy.

References

Armelius, B. Å., Sundbom, E., Fransson, P., & Kullgren, G. (1990). Personality organization defined by DMT and the structural interview. *Scandinavian Journal of Psychology*, *31*(2), 81–88.

Bauer, S. F., Hunt, H. F., Gould, M., & Goldstein, E. G. (1980). Borderline personality organization, structural diagnosis and the structural interview: A pilot study of interview analysis. *Psychiatry*, *43*(3), 224–233.

Carr, A. C., Goldstein, E. G., Hunt, H. F., & Kernberg, O. F. (1979). Psychological tests and borderline patients. *Journal of Personality Assessment*, *43*(6), 582–590.

Clarkin, J. F., Caligor, E., Stern, B. L., & Kernberg, O. F. (2004). *Structured Interview of Personality Organization (STIPO)*. New York: Personality Disorders Institute, Weill Medical College of Cornell University.

Clarkin, J. F., Caligor, E., Stern, B. L., & Kernberg, O. F. (2015). *Structured Interview for Personality Organization – Revised (STIPO-R)*. New York: Personality Disorders Institute, Weill Medical College of Cornell University.

Derksen, J. J., Hummelen, J. W., & Bouwens, P. J. (1994). Interrater reliability of the structural interview. *Journal of Personality Disorders*, *8*(2), 131–139.

Diamond, D., Yeomans, F. E., & Levy, K. (2011). Psychodynamic Psychotherapy for Narcissistic Personality Disorder. In K. Campbell, & J. Miller (Eds.), *The Handbook of Narcissism and Narcissistic Personality Disorder: Theoretical Approaches, Empirical Findings, and Treatment* (pp. 423–433). New York: Wiley.

Diamond, D., Yeomans, F., Stern, B. & Kernberg, O. *A Clinical Guide for Treating Narcissistic Disorder: A Transference Focused Psychotherapy*. (Guilford Press, *Submitted*).

Diamond, D., Yeomans, F. E., Stern, B., Levy, K. N., Hörz, S., Doering, S., et al. (2013). Transference focused psychotherapy for patients with comorbid narcissistic and borderline personality disorder. *Psychoanalytic Inquiry*, *33*(6), 527–551.

Doering, S., Burgmer, M., Heuft, G., Menke, D., Bäumer, B., Lübking, M., et al. (2013). Reliability and validity of the German version of the Structured Interview of Personality Organization (STIPO). *BMC Psychiatry*, *13*(1), 210.

Doering, S., Hörz, S., Rentrop, M., Fischer-Kern, M., Schuster, P., Benecke, C., et al. (2010). Transference-focused psychotherapy v. treatment by community psychotherapists for borderline personality disorder: Randomised controlled trial. *The British Journal of Psychiatry*, *196*(5), 389–395.

Freud, A. (1965). *Normality and pathology in childhood: Assessments of development*. Harmondsworth: Penguin.

Henry, C., Mitropoulou, V., New, A. S., Koenigsberg, H. W., Silverman, J., & Siever, L. J. (2001). Affective instability and impulsivity in borderline personality and bipolar II disorders: Similarities and differences. *Journal of Psychiatric Research*, *35*(6), 307–312.

Hörz, S., Stern, B., Caligor, E., Critchfield, K., Kernberg, O. F., Mertens, W., et al. (2009). A prototypical profile of borderline personality organization using the Structured Interview of Personality Organization (STIPO). *Journal of the American Psychoanalytic Association*, *57*(6), 1464–1468.

Ingenhoven, T. J., Duivenvoorden, H. J., Brogtrop, J., Lindenborn, A., van den Brink, W., & Passchier, J. (2009). Brief communications: Interrater reliability for Kernberg's structural interview for assessing personality organization. *Journal of Personality Disorders*, *23*(5), 528–534.

Kernberg, O. (1984). *Severe personality disorders: Psychotherapeutic strategies*. New Haven: Yale University Press.

Kernberg, O. F., Goldstein, E. G., Carr, A. C., Hunt, H. F., Bauer, S. F., & Blumenthal, R. (1981). Diagnosing borderline personality. A pilot study using multiple diagnostic methods. *The Journal of Nervous and Mental Disease*, *169*(4), 225–231.

Kernberg, O. F., & Yeomans, F. E. (2013). Borderline personality disorder, bipolar disorder, depression, attention deficit/hyperactivity disorder, and narcissistic personality disorder: Practical differential diagnosis. *Bulletin of the Menninger Clinic*, *77*(1), 1–22.

Koenigsberg, H. W., Harvey, P. D., Mitropoulou, V., Schmeidler, J., New, A. S., Goodman, M., et al. (2002). Characterizing affective instability in borderline personality disorder. *American Journal of Psychiatry*, *159*(5), 784–788.

Kullgren, G. (1987). An empirical comparison of three different borderline concepts. *Acta Psychiatrica Scandinavica*, *76*(3), 246–255.

Levy, K. N. (2012). Subtypes, dimensions, levels, and mental states in narcissism and narcissistic personality disorder. *Journal of Clinical Psychology*, *68*(8), 886–897.

Lewis, S. J., & Harder, D. W. (1991). A comparison of four measures to diagnose DSM-III-R borderline personality disorder in outpatients. *The Journal of Nervous and Mental Disease*, *179*(6), 320–337.

Preti, E., Prunas, A., Sarno, I., & De Panfilis, C. (2012). Proprietà psicometriche della STIPO [Psychometric properties of the STIPO]. In F. Madeddu, & E. Preti (Eds.), *La diagnosi strutturale di personalità secondo il modello di O.F. Kernberg. La versione italiana della Structured Interview of Personality Organization* (pp. 59–84). Milano: Raffaello Cortina.

Preti, E., Rottoli, C., Dainese, S., Di Pierro, R., Rancati, F., & Madeddu, F. (2015). Personality structure features associated with early dropout in patients with substance-related disorders and comorbid personality disorders. *International Journal of Mental Health and Addiction*, *13*(4), 536–547.

Reich, J., & Frances, A. (1984). The structural interview method for diagnosing borderline disorders: A critique. *Psychiatric Quarterly*, *56*(3), 229–235.

Stern, B. L., Caligor, E., Clarkin, J. F., Critchfield, K. L., Horz, S., MacCornack, V., et al. (2010). Structured Interview of Personality Organization (STIPO): Preliminary psychometrics in a clinical sample. *Journal of Personality Assessment*, *92*(1), 35–44.

Vaillant, G. E. (1994). Ego mechanisms of defense and personality psychopathology. *Journal of Abnormal Psychology*, *103*(1), 44–50.

Yeomans, F. E., Clarkin, J. F., & Kernberg, O. F. (2015). Transference-focused psychotherapy for borderline personality disorder: A clinical guide. American Psychiatric Publishing, Washington D.C.

Yeomans, F. E., Selzer, M. A., & Clarkin, J. F. (1992). *Treating the borderline patient: A contract-based approach*. New York: Basic Books.

CHAPTER

3

Case Formulations in Mentalization-Based Treatment (MBT) for Patients With Borderline Personality Disorder

Sigmund Karterud[1], *Mickey T. Kongerslev*[2,3,4,5]

[1]Norwegian Institute for Mentalizing, Oslo, Norway; [2]Centre of Excellence on Personality Disorder, Region Zealand Psychiatry, Slagelse, Denmark; [3]Psychiatric Research Unit, Region Zealand Psychiatry, Slagelse, Denmark; [4]Psychiatric Clinic Roskilde, Region Zealand Psychiatry, Roskilde, Denmark; [5]Department of Psychology, University of Southern Denmark, Odense, Denmark

THE HETEROGENEITY OF BORDERLINE PERSONALITY DISORDER

A mentalization-based case formulation is an integral part of mentalization-based treatment (MBT) (Bateman & Fonagy, 2016, p. 157–161), primarily targeted at borderline personality disorder (BPD). As a diagnostic category, BPD is very heterogeneous. Based upon the DSM-IV/DSM-5, there are 256 different possible combinations to meet criteria for BPD (Johansen, Karterud, Pedersen, Gude, & Falkum, 2004). In addition, most patients diagnosed with BPD have a range of other pathological personality traits. BPD comes in different combinations, e.g., with additional avoidant, narcissistic, histrionic, antisocial and/or paranoid traits. Then there are the concurrent symptom disorders, like anxiety, mood, eating and substance abuse disorders. Add to that the different levels of functioning (e.g., according to the global assessment of functioning scale (GAF), or the levels of personality functioning scale (LPFS) in the alternative DSM-5 model). BPD patients might also be at the brink of psychosis and in need

Case Formulation for Personality Disorders
https://doi.org/10.1016/B978-0-12-813521-1.00003-5

of hospital treatment, or they may be reasonably well adjusted but characterized by stormy relationships.

This palpable heterogeneity clearly indicates that treatment should be tailored to the individual patient. However, as we will discuss in the next section, the underlying pathological mechanisms in BPD are quite similar, or more correctly, they are variations of a limited set of dysfunctions which justifies some schemes in the construction of case formulations for these patients. In recent years, MBT has also been applied to the treatment of other personality and symptom disorders, e.g., antisocial PD (Bateman, O'Connell, Lorenzini, Gardner, & Fonagy, 2016), and eating and substance abuse disorders (Morken, Binder, Arefjord, & Karterud, 2017; Robinson et al., 2016). Case formulations in these conditions will naturally reflect these disorders' special personality traits and symptoms. However, they will also build upon the principles which have been developed for the more prototypical BPD patient that is candidate for the kind of intensive and concurrent outpatient treatment which constitutes a modern MBT treatment programme: i.e., a poorly functioning BPD patient who is unable to work or study properly, is isolated and alone or in stormy relationships, who is more or less chronic suicidal and often self-mutilating, is confused with respect to own identity, emotionally unstable and often resorts to drug or alcohol abuse. This is the typical patient we focus on in this chapter.

THE THEORETICAL GRID FOR CASE FORMULATIONS FOR BORDERLINE PATIENTS

The core constituent components of human personality are (1) temperament, (2) attachment pattern, and (3) capability for self-reflection (explicit mentalizing) (Karterud, 2017; Karterud, Wilberg, & Urnes, 2017). What we denote as BPD is a particular combination of features belonging to these components. These features undermine the individual's sense of self and self-stability and his/her capability of responsible social agency. In contrast to other theoretical formulations we do not regard BPD primarily as an emotion regulation disorder, but as a disorder of personality in the sense that all of the three major components are affected: temperament, attachment and mentalizing capability. The temperament, or primary emotional system liability of BPD concerns impulsivity as well as low threshold, high intensity and regulation problems, particularly of the primary emotions of RAGE and SEPARATION DISTRESS (written in bold in accordance with the style of J. Panksepp) (Karterud et al., 2016; Panksepp & Biven, 2012). The separation distress accounts for the profound dysphoria of being left alone and the desperate attempts at avoiding abandonment. The tragedy for BPD patients is that their proclivity for rage reactions enhances the risk of being left alone.

However, an intense temperament is not enough for a borderline condition. There also needs to be an insecure attachment in addition, and prototypically of an overinvolved or disorganized type (Karterud et al., 2017). However, all sorts of insecure attachment may be encountered in BPD patients, e.g., a dismissive pattern when there also are concurrent narcissistic and/or antisocial traits, an unresolved pattern with respect to trauma and loss, and not the least a disorganized pattern. It is particularly important to become aware of a disorganized pattern, since especially these patients will have great problems with the group part of MBT (Morken, Karterud, & Arefjord, 2014). They have no effective strategy for dealing with interpersonal closeness. Realizing that a disorganized attachment pattern is operative, makes it easier to understand the patient's reluctance to group involvement and their need for time and patience to approach fellow patients.

The mentalizing problems of BPD patients account for their poor sense of self. The problems are twofold. First, there is the general lowered capability of mentalizing which makes the person liable to misunderstanding of others and oneself and thereby exploitable and exploiting. In addition, there comes the liability for gross breakdowns of mentalizing abilities and the risk for (self-) destructive acting out. Both deficits affect the capability for self-understanding and experience of identity, coherence and agency. The deficits can be traced back to failures in the formative parent-child interaction, whereby the child's subjective experiences are victims of faulty mirroring and distorting intersubjective transaction (Fonagy, Gergely, Jurist, & Target, 2002).

One aspect of the triadic constellation described above is epistemic mistrust – one of the new theoretical developments within MBT (Bo, Sharp, Fonagy, & Kongerslev, 2017; Fonagy & Allison, 2014). Epistemic trust is defined as a person's trust in the authenticity and personal relevance of interpersonally transmitted knowledge (Bateman, Campbell, Luyten, & Fonagy, 2017). As such, epistemic trust is a prerequisite for being open to and learning from an ever-changing social environment. Put briefly, this theoretical reasoning, furthermore, argues that one of the most devastating developmental consequences of impoverished, insecure or traumatic parenting, is that it leaves the child in a state of epistemic mistrust. Attachment trauma (including incongruent and unmarked mirroring) undermines the child capacity for trust in others, and hence the individual's ability to learn from others, to learn in interpersonal contexts. This is a core feature of BPD, a widespread inability to learn from others, presumably based on a lack of epistemic trust. To address epistemic mistrust, therapists must use so-called ostensive cues, which are signals that communicate to the person, that the information presented are for *you*. In terms of babies and their psychosocial development, good-enough parenting is rich on ostensive cues in terms of eye-contact, motherese and so forth, though some recent studies calls the relative necessity or importance of ostensive cues into question (see, e.g., Szufnarowska, Rohlfing, Fawcett, & Gredebäck, 2014). Regarding psychotherapy, ostensive cues concern the 'marking' of personally relevant information to the patient. In this respect, the case formulation becomes highly important, inasmuch as it attempts to address how the general MBT model of BPD and psychotherapy is meaningful and makes sense, signalling to the patient that the model and therapy in question are of relevance not only to patients with BPD in general, but for him/her specifically. If a case formulation achieves this end, makes the patient feel understood and that the therapy makes sense to him/her, then it will help the patient to also become more motivated and less distrustful, enhancing the chance of successful outcome through making him/her more open to new interpersonal learning.

A case formulation for BPD patients should contain references to the individual's peculiar constellation of the earlier-mentioned personality constituents.

THE MENTALIZATION-BASED APPROACH TO CASE FORMULATIONS

Until the millennium shift, treatment of BPD was considered very difficult to perform and even more difficult to do research upon. High drop-out-rates was a major obstacle (Hummelen, Wilberg, & Karterud, 2007). It is highly problematic to do intention-to-treat analysis when 40%–60% of the patients drop out of treatment and do not respond to calls for follow-up investigations. Consequently, modern approaches to the treatment of BPD considers treatment retention and working alliance (as conceptualized by Bordin, 1979) as crucial factors for therapeutic success (Bateman & Fonagy, 2016; Weinberg et al., 2011). Therapists should invest continuous efforts in the establishment and maintenance of an alliance. In MBT, the case formulation is regarded as a major tool in this respect. *This pragmatic aspect of case formulations for BPD patients overrule all other considerations, e.g., extensiveness, completeness, complexity, etc.* This means that the case formulation should be highly individually tailored, and always aim, above all, to maximize the therapeutic alliance, treatment adherence and motivation.

Some authors have called for studies of reliability and validity for case formulations (Eells, 2009). However, traditional reliability and validity studies do not make sense with respect to case formulations in MBT. Rather, the overriding aims are: (1) Does the patient feel understood? (2) Does the case formulation help the patient to make sense of his/her problems and understand more of the forthcoming therapeutic project, including the tasks and goals of therapy? (3) Does the formulation help counteract dropout risk? Because BPD patients are so diverse and often in very unstable states of mind at the beginning of treatment, and may display periods of very low reflective functioning (RF; Fonagy, Target, Steele, & Steele, 1998), case formulations for some patients may be very brief, while others are more extensive and comprehensive. The mentalizing level of the patient is decisive in this respect. There is thus no objective position from which to judge if the case formulation is valid or reliable. The ultimate judge is the patient him/herself. *That* might be a topic for research, i.e., not validity in a traditional sense, but validity as experienced as meaningful and helpful from the perspective of the patient. These considerations are of course controversial. For example, Gunderson (2011) has commented upon an MBT case formulation on a difficult patient and writes 'it should not be prepared with concern for whether the patient shares or agrees with that understanding' (p. 91). There is a disagreement here, and the clinician has to choose his/her own priorities.

Another principle that derives from the same overall alliance view, is that a MBT case formulation should not be formulated from the position of the therapist being an expert on the patient's mind couched in a professional jargon which might please a supervisor or other colleagues, but a document written in plain common-sense language, preferably using the patient's own terms, aimed at this particular patient, and no one else. A MBT case formulation is a text directed towards a specific person. Indeed, too much professional jargon and references to general/abstract principles and concepts, could be considered iatrogenic in the sense that they might alienate the patient from the treatment project and/or stimulate pseudomentalizing rather than mentalizing proper (Bateman & Fonagy, 2004, p. 169–172).

The treatment context will also influence the content of the case formulation. Intensive outpatient MBT is the most common treatment format. That is a concurrent group-individual kind of psychotherapy and in this instance the case formulation should address challenges in both components, and ideally attempt to weave the different components together. However, treatment may also take place in a hospital setting where the case formulation is part of the milieu therapy (Skårderud & Sommerfeldt, 2015). Age will also influence the formulation, e.g., when applied to adolescents. And finally, there is the time aspect. Usually the case formulation is worked out and presented during the initial phase of treatment. However, it can and should be reformulated over the whole course of treatment, in light of new knowledge, changing aims, or lack of progress.

Overall, the aims of an MBT case formulation are to mutually organize the thinking for therapist and patient, model a mentalizing approach in a formal/explicit way and model humility about the nature of understanding minds (Bateman & Fonagy, 2004, 2016).

NEEDED INFORMATION

Patients diagnosed with BPD who are admitted to an MBT programme are usually assessed with a broad battery of tests. A personality profile according to SCID-5-PD (formerly SCID-II) is crucial. It displays the extensiveness of personality pathology (e.g., the total number of DSM-5 PD criteria fulfilled) and the particular combination of specific criteria. Is it mainly a combination of borderline and avoidant features (more common in women) or a combination of borderline and antisocial features (more common in men)? The GAF should also be rated. There is a huge difference between a BPD patient functioning at GAF = 40 compared to a patient at GAF = 65. Patients should be interviewed with respect to their awareness and tolerance of primary emotions. The interviewer should be very alert to different manifestations of separation distress. It does not only concern fear about being left alone in a physical sense, but also experiences of not being seen, heard, respected, being an outsider, an alien in the world, etc. Ideally one should have performed an Adult Attachment Interview (AAI; Hesse, 1999), but that is primarily a research instrument. It is too time-consuming for clinical practice. Alternatively, one can give the Experiences in Close Relationship questionnaire (ECR; Fraley, Waller, & Brennan, 2000). It will indicate if there is an overinvolved versus a dismissive attachment pattern. The clinician should decide on the question of attachment insecurity from the life history as told by the patient and from information recorded in accompanying professional documents and from results on attachment measures.

There is no quick and easy way to measure mentalizing ability. The clinician should explore interpersonal encounters and judge whether eventual mentalizing problems are typical for the patient's overall relational style and cognition. This might be done by the Interview on Mentalizing Failures (Karterud et al., 2017). This is a semistructured interview where the interviewer first explains how mentalizing failures might be experienced and then asks the patient to describe an event (or more) during the last 1–2 weeks where this may have happened to him/her. Usually patients go straight on to tell about recent difficult interpersonal encounters where they were overwhelmed by emotions, 'lost their mind', became confused, could not think clearly, etc. The primary task of the interviewer is to explore (1) the event in detail, (2) the patient's capacity for narrating the event and the intersubjective scenario therein, and (3) the patient's capability of reflecting upon the event from the more secure distance of the present moment. Finally, the interviewer asks if this event is typical for a range of situations in the patient's life. Most often it will be, and the interviewer might suggest that some of the details, which have been explored, could be pasted into the case formulation, as typical relational problems concerning emotions, attachment figures and mentalizing difficulties.

WORKING IN CONCERT WITH THE PSYCHOEDUCATIONAL GROUP

In contrast to many other variants of case formulations, the MBT case formulation has few references to theoretical explanatory principles of the psychopathology or the treatment rationale. This is the job of the psychoeducational group which is a component of the initial treatment package. This group is manualized (Karterud & Bateman, 2010) and consists of 12 1,5 hour sessions. Different techniques are utilized: Written handouts, small 'lectures', homework, roleplaying, vignette exercises, but above all the participants are encouraged to tell about their personal experiences with the themes covered in the sessions. The themes are: What is mentalizing? What is mentalizing failures? What are primary emotions? How do we regulate emotions? What is attachment? What is attachment conflict? What is the relation between primary emotions, anxiety and attachment? What is the relation between primary emotions, depression and attachment? What are personality disorders in general and BPD in particular? What is MBT? How does MBT work and what is my role in it? Patients are encouraged to discuss their personal experiences from this group with the individual therapist. The initial treatment package thus provides powerful means to 'socialize' with the treatment, i.e., to understand the therapist's words and procedures as meaningful expressions of a certain theory of personality and its disorders and how one's own particular problems fit into this scheme.

TECHNICAL DETAILS

The MBT case formulation is a cooperative text, i.e., worked out in open cooperation with the patient. The therapist should inform the patients early on during the assessment phase that a case formulation is to be constructed and that the therapist will present a first draft. During assessment, the therapist may suggest some content to be included, e.g., as revealed by the Interview on Mentalizing Failures. Most often patients accept the formulations that are suggested by the therapist, or just have minor corrections on faulty facts ('actually I lived in Oslo by that time and it was my sister who self-harmed, not my brother'). If therapist and patient disagree on content, one should explore the roots of the different viewpoints and find compromises if need be. For example, patient X had a paranoid personality disorder and felt easily slighted by other people. X considered the people whom he felt slighted by to be 'difficult persons'. He wanted this written explicitly in his formulation. The therapists thought that X himself often was the most difficult person in encounters with others. The compromise was that 'difficult' was written in brackets, marking that it was a formulation that was quoted from X.

There are somewhat divergent views if the case formulation should address the patient with the personal pronoun 'you' (Allen, Fonagy, & Bateman, 2008, p. 172–176; Bateman & Fonagy, 2016), or first name or surname, e.g., 'Rita' (Karterud et al., 2017). Should one start like 'You grew up in a large family in Oslo that sadly broke down when ...' or 'Rita grew up in a large family ...'? 'You' is more direct and personal. However, we prefer first names for various reasons. Above all we want to stimulate the person to regard him/herself from the outside, from a third-person perspective. That is an overall aim with MBT. Looking at oneself from the outside means that one is able to take a more common-sense perspective at oneself, e.g., 'look, this is how people in our culture usually regard such things'. When we label the person in the case formulation by first name, e.g., 'Rita', we present a narrative which is shared by the whole MBT team. We have constructed a fictive person, 'Rita', which hopefully may resemble the 'Rita' which is the narrative self-construct, but which is not identical with it. 'Rita' may be viewed in different ways. 'Here is the way we conceive you. Does it make sense? Here are the elements in your life story that we, at this point in time, regard as most crucial'. We do not indicate that the 'Rita' which we have constructed is the 'true Rita'. We indicate some perspectives that we regard as useful working hypotheses. We want to stimulate the person's curiosity to learn more about that person we have sketched in the case formulation.

Ideally, the text should not be identical to the person's prior self-understanding. It should add something more, be slightly ahead of it. We want to get at a point where the person will say, 'yes that is me, but I haven't quite thought of it that way before'.

For patients to reach such a realization, it is important that the text is formulated in a plain language. The text is directed to them, it is about them, from the MBT team. The text should not be too long. One should remember that the content is condensed and highly emotional and patients should not be overburdened. We usually recommend a length of approximately 1–1.5 pages, but again, this is a general recommendation and in the end, it always depends on the specific patient.

Although MBT case formulations might differ considerably, the usual format will be paragraphs that cover the following themes:

1. Family background. Very often this has been seriously disturbed, e.g., with neglect, violence, sexual traumas, chaos, misuse, lies, manipulations, psychotic parents, substance abusing parents and the like. This should shortly be described.
2. Early symptoms and traits and consequences for school attendance and peer relationships.
3. The most difficult emotions.
4. Adult relational pattern.

5. Self-destructive behaviour.
6. Consequences for education, work and intimate relations.
7. Typical mentalizing failures exemplified through interpersonal encounters – and sometimes also validating examples on situations where the patient manages well regarding mentalizing.
8. Previous treatment attempts.
9. What could possibly be difficult in MBT?
   a. In individual therapy?
   b. In group therapy?
10. Aims and means of the treatment. Concrete and specific short- and long-term treatment goals, as well as means to deliver them might also be briefly stated and thereby mutually agreed upon by both patient and therapist.

THE MENTAL ACTIVITY OF THE THERAPIST WHILE CONSTRUCTING A CASE FORMULATION

The mental activity of the therapists may be condensed to the slogan 'minding minds'. This fundamental capability is what distinguishes *Homo sapiens* from other animals. However, minding minds can be performed at different levels of sophistication. While constructing a case formulation, it should be at its peak, i.e., constructing an understanding of the other in terms of that individual's unique developmental history within a certain culture at a certain historical epoch. It calls for therapist personal skills that involve a combination of empathy with a good mastery of the theory of mentalizing and its relevance for personality development. Neither aspect is sufficient alone. Empathy without theory favours the destiny of being lost in emotions. This trap is always present when working with patients with a personality disorder. Strong emotions will spill over to the therapist by contagion, arousal of primary emotions (Karterud et al., 2016) and projective identification, and his/her power of mentalizing will suffer. In particular might the activation of care and fear in the mind of the therapist pull the treatment in an overly supportive direction that undermines the more fundamental aim of developing the patient's mentalizing ability. On the other hand, a merely theoretical understanding of the individual will miss the necessary ingredients that make the individual being felt understood. And furthermore, a different kind of theory will imply different conceptualizations and priorities which also might be useful in certain contexts, but it will not be MBT. That part should also be present in the therapist's mind, how the theory-driven and contextualized understanding of the patients might colour the interpersonal scenarios that most likely will be staged in the peculiar kind of combined group-individual treatment that characterizes MBT.

CASE FORMULATIONS IN MENTALIZATION-BASED TREATMENT (MBT) TRAINING

How to make an MBT case formulation is taught in the advanced course on MBT as practised in the Nordic countries. This course consists typically of 8 whole days distributed over 8–10 months. All participants are required to present video-recordings of an ongoing MBT. We start with the case formulations. The typical beginner's mistake is that the formulation is too much formulated as a text aimed at colleagues and that references to the forthcoming treatment is missing. Training candidates usually reformulate their case formulations several times. The example below we will illustrate how the formulations are evaluated.

TWO DIFFERENT BORDERLINE PERSONALITY DISORDER (BPD) CASE FORMULATIONS

In this section, we will present two different case formulations so that the reader can get an impression of what we are talking about. The contexts for these two patients are different. The first concerns a prototypical BPD patient in the initial phase of an intensive outpatient MBT programme (e.g., Kvarstein et al., 2015). The second example concerns an adolescent BPD patient who received a treatment programme consisting of mainly MBT group therapy and it reflects the growing recognition that BPD is indeed a highly prevalent and debilitating disorder amongst young people (Bo & Kongerslev, 2017; Kongerslev, Chanen, & Simonsen., 2015).

Borderline Personality Disorder (BPD) Case Formulation 1

Mary (30) was raised in a home where both mother and father drank excessively. She frequently experienced stormy parties and fierce quarrelling. The quarrels often turned quite dramatic and Mary harbours many painful memories from that time. As a child she was concerned to protect her younger brother from the turmoil at home. She describes her mother as being emotionally unstable and Mary was always alert to what kind of mood her mother was in and how she could adapt to that. She found it difficult to predict how mother would react: Would she be helpful and supportive or raging and scolding?

Mary came to develop symptoms of anxiety and depression at an early age. Around 16 she received medication, such as tranquilizers, sleeping pills and antidepressants. In the years after she joined her mother at her parties and drank accordingly. Nevertheless, she managed to complete high school with good results and started working as a nurse assistant. She gave up the work when addiction came to rule most of her life. Over the next 8–10 years, she was out of work for long periods, floating around without any home and dependent on a mixture of alcohol and different drugs. She had different boyfriends and lovers and was often dependent on them for practical life purposes which made it difficult to stand up against abuse and violence.

Mary was approached by outgoing team members from the local Youth and Young Adult Addiction Programme and reluctantly she engaged in (periods of) drug management treatments and rehabilitation. Over the last couple of years she has established a more enduring relationship and she now lives with her boyfriend and their two-year old daughter. Her motivation for change has increased, and she was referred to the local MBT programme.

In the initial assessments, Mary tells that she is not keen on spending too much time in therapy on her childhood and adolescent experiences. She has the opinion that the 'past is past' and that one cannot do anything about it. She wants to focus on the present. She wants help with her everyday problems of coping with people. Strictly speaking, she would have preferred no contact with other people at all since it always leads to trouble. Her choice would have been living on a remote island, alone with her boyfriend. However, after becoming a mother she realizes that she should get along with people she encounters, for the sake of her daughter. She hates the idea that her own problems should become a burden for her daughter.

Mary's therapist believes that childhood and youth experiences influence Mary's present days relational trouble, e.g., that an insecure upbringing has a significant share in her experiences of interpersonal insecurity as an adult. One example may be that she often relates to people in a suspicious way, that she is alert and sceptical as to their motives. She might easily judge people on beforehand and get a feeling of 'something wrong'. This might upset her, and she easily gets annoyed or angry and can yell at people and say things to hurt them. However, inside she experiences strong feelings of fear and insecurity as well. She is afraid of being left alone, particularly by her boyfriend, and to be cheated by other people.

When Mary gets this feeling that 'something is wrong', she most probably suffers what her therapist labels as 'mentalizing failure', i.e., that her emotions take over and blurs her ability to think clearly. However, Mary might look for 'proof'to validate her impression that 'something is wrong', and the intensity of her thoughts might then escalate in concert with overwhelming and scaring feelings. In such situations, she might say and do things, which she regrets in the aftermath. This pattern is a heavy burden for Mary, and she worries if she is turning more and more like her mother and that it will be harmful for her daughter and boyfriend if she keeps on in this way.

As for the current MBT, it is important that Mary reports on such events to the therapist so that they can explore them in detail. It is a challenge to find out if acts and utterances of other people concern other affairs than what Mary believes when she is in a suspicious mode. Since Mary often feels shameful after such incidences, and in the aftermath, tends to scold and blame herself fiercely, it is important to also explore what happens between her and other people, what we, in MBT treatment label interpersonal transactions, to avoid self-blaming – that 'everything is Mary's fault'.

So far, in the individual part of the treatment programme, 'Mary has done a good job. She has attended treatment sessions regularly, reported on significant events, explored these with the therapist and tried out new strategies in between sessions. Now, when it is time for her to attend the group part of the programme, it might be useful to focus her attention on situations where she becomes puzzled by thoughts and actions by other group members, trying to be more curious and open-minded and not judgemental on the reasons why other people think or do what they do. Such 'exercises' might be easier for her in the group than in the often-heated encounters with her boyfriend. This is in accordance with her overall aim of the treatment: To come to trust other people in a better way'.

When Mary received this case formulation, she was anxious about the content, but curious. After reading it, she was silent for a while before she spoke with a low voice: 'Yes, this is me. But it's tough to read. I feel pity for this person. How did you come to understand so much?'

This case formulation was presented by a participant at an MBT advanced training course. It was discussed by the training group of 12 candidates and their teacher. It was found quite good as it satisfied the criteria in the following way:

1. The length and narrative style seemed appropriate. The text contained two professional phrases, 'mentalizing failures' and 'interpersonal transactions', but they were explained and were believed to function appropriately as bridges to the psychoeducational part of the programme.
2. The family background was described in terms and references that makes it plausible that Mary developed an insecure attachment pattern of a mixed kind, alternating between overinvolvement (identification with mother, parentification, emotional overreaction) and distancing (longing for an isolated existence with an idealized object).
3. Early symptoms and traits and consequences for school attendance are described. Symptoms of anxiety and depression were recognized, but handled in a medicalized way, possibly reinforcing the family culture of coping with difficult feelings and emotions through chemicals.

4. The most difficult emotions are described, e.g., rage, separation distress, fear, shame and guilt feelings.
5. Adult relational pattern is described as being exploitable, suspicious and emotional.
6. Self-destructive behaviour is described as part of previous addictive lifestyle.
7. Consequences for education, work and intimate relations are described as: Completing high school, but cannot cope with ordinary work demands due to addictive lifestyle and interpersonal sensitivity. Intimate relations are coined by being dependent and exploitable and utterly sensitive for critical remarks.
8. Typical mentalizing failures are described including suspiciousness, often distorted views of other's intentions, being victim of unmentalized affects, loss of self-control and excessive self-blame.
9. Previous treatment attempts are mentioned shortly, being initiated by an outgoing team for youth addicts. After several attempts aiming at substance use reduction, she sobers up after childbirth and becomes motivated for doing something with her emotional, relational and mentalizing problems.
10. Treatment challenges are described, including that Mary should: (a) report on troublesome interpersonal events and (b) be aware of own reactions in the MBT group that resembles troublesome events in real life.
11. The major response from the patient was that she felt understood.

At MBT training courses, the case formulations are discussed and evaluated according to the criteria mentioned earlier in this section. Through these discussions, MBT training candidates usually learn the style and format quickly. Many candidates do considerable revisions of their initial drafts that often: (1) are too long, (2) have too many irrelevant details, (3) are written in a professional discourse style, more like a report to a colleague, (4) lacks some of the ingredients mentioned above, e.g., examples of emotional dysregulation or mentalizing failures and implications for current treatment.

There is often a palpable curiosity when the candidate, after having discussed the case formulation, presents the first video-recording of a therapy session with the patient. Most often the candidates are nodding, indicating that what they see corresponds with what they had expected. However, not so seldom they react with surprise, when the patient seems to function on a higher or lower mentalizing level than what was expected from the case formulation. If this is the case, we go back to the case formulation to find out where the discrepancy resides. Usually this is a most enlightening exercise for the therapist.

It is crucial for the learning process to discuss details of the therapist's video-recordings. This should be done differently than the practice of MBT (video-based) supervision. During training, the therapy process details are discussed from a theoretical perspective. How do we understand the constant flow of patient's speech acts and nonverbal communications as they unfold in the peculiar discourse conjointly developed by the therapy couple? How do we understand the therapist? And both of them, and their interaction, in terms of the theory of mentalizing and personality disorders? And most important, what we see, is that consonant with the case formulation? During this training group practice, therapists come to a more profound understanding of what mentalizing is all about. They become socialized to a certain way of understanding intersubjective transactions and, when internalized, it will affect the way they will construct their case formulations.

Borderline Personality Disorder (BPD) Case Formulation 2

Emily (17) is a young girl who lives with her mum and dad. Emily does not remember a lot about her early childhood, but she does remember that her mum and dad had many rows, and especially her dad's outburst of anger could make her feel scared. Emily, however, also remembers how she always, even as a child, had very intense temper tantrums – for example when she hit a teacher in first grade, which also meant that she got referred to a school psychologist. When Emily entered her teens, she began to feel different and as an outsider in her school class. The other pupils bullied her, so Emily began to skip school and hang around with somewhat older boys and girls. She had plenty of one-night stands as well as brief but stormy relationships, including some abusive ones. At the age of 14 Emily also began to smoke grass and occasionally take coke. She also developed an eating disorder, because she felt fat though she was thin in terms of BMI, and she began to cut herself regularly. When the other pupils in her class began high school, Emily dropped out and just stayed at home, spending her time looking for dates and boys on dating sites. Emily was also frequently admitted to emergency departments because of her self-harming behaviour. Often this was the results of rows with her boyfriends, which led her to become self-harming or suicidal.

Currently, Emily has a boyfriend who is six years older than her. Emily feels that he is good for her. But her boyfriend works, whilst Emily just stays at home. This creates troubles for Emily, because she panics when her boyfriend does not respond to her text messages or calls during the day. This makes Emily worry, thinking relentlessly and becoming angry, because she then feels she does not mean anything to him, that he really does not care about her. And then she feels sad and scared, and fears he will leave her, which often triggers feelings of emptiness or being unlovable, which in turn makes Emily cut herself or take an overdose of pills. This again, often results in Emily being admitted to emergency department and being hospitalized for a night or two. In the wake of her self-harm or suicide attempts, Emily experiences distressing feelings of shame and fear of her boyfriend leaving her, or her parents giving up on her, which becomes almost unbearable. In such a state Emily sometimes becomes self-harming again or aggressive when hospitalized, which often leads to her being restrained. Though Emily understands why staff at the hospital restrains her in such situations, she also feels ashamed and, in a way, abused.

Emily is now about to begin group therapy to help her with her interpersonal problems, fears of being unlovable and rejected by her boyfriend, her low self-esteem and tendency for self-harm and suicide attempts. She has especially three concerns regarding embarking on group therapy. First, she worries about being able to attend regularly. To help Emily attend, she has agreed to that mum will take her to therapy for the first 3 months, and also that the group therapists (Tine and Eric) may call her and/or her parents in case she misses a session without contacting the clinic. Second, Emily worries if she will fit into the group, because she feels that no one else would be interested in her. This could also make it difficult for Emily to speak out in the group. To help Emily, she has agreed that the group therapists might address her gently in the group in case she remains silent, but also that the group therapists must respect if she does not feel for talking when addressed. Lastly, Emily fears her own temper, that due to her tendency to becoming easily annoyed and provoked, she might react angrily towards other members in the group. To help Emily with this issue, the group therapists have promised Emily that they will help her, by monitoring her arousal. But because Emily is good at hiding her feelings right up to the moment when she explodes, Emily also needs to help the therapists with the monitoring – e.g., through saying it to them once she notices any annoyance or in case she feels she cannot speak, than just leaving the group and taking a moment by herself. Then one of the group therapists will come to her and help her calm down if necessary.

'Emily hopes that the treatment can help her get better control of herself and intense feelings of rage and being unlovable. To this end, Emily must bring episodes of self-harm and/or rows with her boyfriend to the group, so she can work on her problems in the group. Through this work Emily can get a better perspective on herself and her own reactions. Also, the group might stimulate some of the very feelings of anger or being different/unlovable/wrong as she struggles with in her private life. In that case it is important that Emily, once she feels safe in the group and with her therapists, is willing to explore this in the group'.

The above illustrates the use of MBT case formulation with an adolescent diagnosed with BPD embarking on MBT group therapy. The case formulation was developed in cooperation between the patient and one of the group therapists, in the sense that she knew that the first three sessions (of which mother also attended two) with the group therapist would result in a written formulation, which in the fourth sessions was discussed with Emily. Emily was happy with the formulation and did not suggest any changes. Adopting the general scheme for MBT case formulations outlined in this chapter, the example illustrates these in the following way:

1. Unnecessary jargon was avoided. Though Emily (and her mother) received some psychoeducation during the second session with one of the group therapists regarding MBT treatment and its theoretical model for BPD.
2. Her developmental history was sketched, in a condensed form, and included to highlight her temperament characterized by highly intense feelings of anger together with her separation anxiety and developmental experiences of trauma, and of being different and wrong.
3. Her difficult emotions and self-states are named, in terms of e.g., anger, rage, being wrong and unlovable, coupled with feelings of shame.
4. Attachment difficulties are also highlighted and exemplified in terms of current relationships, in terms of her desperate need for a fast response and in case the boyfriend did not, how this would lead her into self-destructive behaviours.
5. Mentalizing difficulties in terms of hypermentalizing are described, often highly prototypical for adolescents with BPD. How she begins to worry when her boyfriends do not react and gets stuck in this worry until she mentally collapses and begins to cut herself or gets suicidal to rid herself of the intense negative feelings.
6. Her concerns regarding the group therapy was addressed together with her aims for the therapy.

Both Emily and her therapists found the formulation regarding her concerns about group therapy especially helpful because the group therapist then could go back and refer to this written text, whenever Emily, during therapy, notably, in the beginning, missed sessions and was reluctant to return to the group claiming that the other group members disliked her. Over the course of her therapy, Emily in fact became a very popular member of the group, though it was only at the end of her therapy that she herself became able to see this. Moreover, when she on five occasions left the group in anger, slamming the door, the therapists used the case formulation to help her understand that her reaction was actually understandable, and that even though she felt ashamed in the aftermath, her reactions had been anticipated and accepted, and in this light, was indeed 'just' something to be worked upon.

MINDING THE DIFFICULT PATIENT

Some patients are more complicated than others. They may have frequent transient psychotic experiences of borderline type or have a regular comorbid psychotic disorder, substance use disorder, eating disorder or Asperger traits, have a low IQ or a personality profile with prominent narcissistic, antisocial or paranoid features. In these conditions, we find either a general and very low mentalizing ability or 'pockets' of mental functioning with very low mentalizing, or misuse of mentalizing. Simonsen, Nørgaard, Larsen, and Bjørnholm (2011) have discussed such a difficult patient diagnosed with borderline and antisocial PDs as well as substance use disorder (cannabis and amphetamine), and this case has been commented on by Gunderson (2011), Bateman (2011) and Skårderud (2011). The patient had previously been convicted for selling drugs and involved in several acts of violence, but she was now enrolled in an MBT day hospital programme in Denmark. According to Simonsen et al. (2011), it was clear from the outset that Ms X was difficult to integrate in the treatment programme: 'Irregularities and breach of rules persisted during the four and a half months she was treated at the Day Clinic including non-attendance, showing up late, walking out, verbal abuse, open cell phone and bringing her pets to the clinic' (p.74). In the group, she was often silent and commented seldom on the stories told by the other patients. When she responded, it was often perceived as insensitive and provoked anger. Her own stories concerned conflicts with friends and family where her emotions seemed to be constricted to those of anger and need for revenge. Empathy, whether in the here and now, or displayed towards her friends and family, did not seem to belong to the repertoire of Ms X. Her rude relational style also showed up in the relation towards her individual therapist who had to endure a lot of derogatory remarks and sometimes even be called an idiot. When she was presented with her case formulation that amounted to two pages, she spontaneously responded 'are you crazy?'

Both Skårderud (2011) and Bateman (2011) points to the *priority of process over content* in the construction of the case formulation and that this principle might be all the more important the more crippled the mentalizing ability is. In this case, Ms X *did not seem to experience the case formulation as hers.* Rather it seemed to be experienced as yet another document from more or less hostile authorities (e.g., 'you have been so and so – habitually braking so and so rules'). Skårderud calls for more explicit cooperative strategies which might have promoted an experience of there being *'two minds in the text'*. Patients need to feel their subjectivity being mirrored sensitively and accurately: 'Where am I in the text? I can hear the authorities, but where am I?' A take-home message from this is that when the MBT therapist writes a case formulation he/she should be aware of how hypersensitive patients with severe BPD pathology is towards being mentalized/mirrored in ways that does not resonate exactly with their own current mentalizing of themselves. Hence, though we ideally want the MBT case formulation to not only mirror the patients current self-understanding but also further it through being slightly ahead of it, it should be noted that with the most severe BPD patients, it is often wiser to stick to empathic formulations, to which both patient and therapist can agree, to avoid dysregulating the patient unnecessarily.

IMPLICATIONS AND CONSEQUENCES FOR THERAPY

How MBT case formulations might influence the therapeutic process, have been a theme for some recent studies (Folmo, Karterud, Kongerslev, Kvarstein, & Stänicke, 2018; Karterud, 2018; Morken et al., 2014). It is noteworthy that all of them focus on the transference (understood in a broad sense of the term), e.g., how to mentalize the patient's style of relating as it unfolds in the here and now, in relation to the therapist and/or the group. That is equal to 'mentalizing attachment relationships' which is particularly difficult for borderline patients. Confronted with this task, patients tend to give up the project which is sketched in their case formulation and turn to all kind of defensive manoeuvres. A typical scenario is trying to control and idealize the individual therapist by leaving certain topics unexplored and flee from the (devaluated) group. Folmo et al. (2018) compared two high quality MBT sessions from different therapists with two low quality MBT sessions by different therapists. In the two low-quality MBT sessions, the therapists had resigned from the task of doing MBT in accordance with the manuals and case formulations, while in the high-quality sessions, the therapists worked hard on alliance issues to reach a kind of therapeutic discourse where the relationship to the devalued group component could be explored, with reference to the patients' case formulations.

SUMMARY AND CONCLUSIONS

MBT is an empirically supported treatment tailored to target the core pathology of BPD. In MBT, the case formulation functions to tailor the general MBT treatment principles and model of BPD towards each individual patient. This is done, through a description of how each patient represents a unique variation on a general theoretical model, including an intense temperament (primary emotions), an insecure attachment pattern and mentalizing dysfunctions. The MBT case formulation is a cooperative text, developed through a process of cooperation between the patient and the therapist, to help them organizing their thinking and arrive at a shared understanding. The overriding aim of the formulation is to maximize the therapeutic alliance, treatment adherence and motivation – through making the patient feel understood and being a person whose problems and suffering makes sense as well as anticipating potential problems the patient might have with attending and benefitting from therapy. In general, the style of writing should be empathic, avoid jargon, and use the patient's own language and match the patient's current level of mentalizing capacities.

Acknowledgements

Some details of the case description, e.g., name, age, habilitation, identity markers, were changed so as to protect client privacy.

References

Allen, J. G., Fonagy, P., & Bateman, A. (2008). *Mentalizing in clinical practice*. Washington, DC: American Psychiatric Publishing.

Bateman, A. (2011). Commentary on "minding the difficult patient": Mentalizing and the use of formulation in patients with borderline personality disorder comorbid with antisocial personality disorder. *Personality and Mental Health*, *5*(1), 85–90.

Bateman, A., Campbell, C., Luyten, P., & Fonagy, P. (2017). A mentalization-based approach to common factors in the treatment of borderline personality disorder. *Current Opinion in Psychology*, *21*, 44–49.

Bateman, A., & Fonagy, P. (2004). *Psychotherapy for borderline personality disorder: Mentalization-based treatment*. Oxford: Oxford University Press.

Bateman, A., & Fonagy, P. (2016). *Mentalization-based treatment for personality disorders: A practical guide*. Oxford: Oxford University Press.

Bateman, A., O'Connell, J., Lorenzini, N., Gardner, T., & Fonagy, P. (2016). A randomised controlled trial of mentalization-based treatment versus structured clinical management for patients with comorbid borderline personality disorder and antisocial personality disorder. *BMC Psychiatry*, *16*, 304.

Bo, S., & Kongerslev, M. (2017). Self-reported patterns of impairments in mentalization, attachment, and psychopathology among clinically referred adolescents with and without borderline personality pathology. *Borderline Personality Disorder and Emotion Dysregulation*, *4*(4).

Bo, S., Sharp, C., Fonagy, P., & Kongerslev, M. (2017). Hypermentalizing, attachment, and epistemic trust in adolescent BPD: Clinical illustrations. *Personality Disorders*, *8*(2), 172–182.

Bordin, E. S. (1979). The generalizability of the psychoanalytic concept of the working alliance. *Psychotherapy: Theory, Research and Practice*, *16*(3), 252–260.

Eells, T. E. (2009). Contemporary themes in case formulations. In P. Sturmey (Ed.), *Clinical case formulation: Varieties of approaches* (pp. 293–316). Oxford: John Wiley & Sons.

Folmo, E. J., Karterud, S. W., Kongerslev, M., Kvarstein, E. H., & Stänicke, E. (2018). *Battles of the comfort zone: A model of therapeutic strategy, technique, alliance and epistemic trust Journal of Contemporary Psychotherapy*, (In revision).

Fonagy, P., & Allison, E. (2014). The role of mentalizing and epistemic trust in the therapeutic relationship. *Psychotherapy*, *51*(3), 372–380.

Fonagy, P., Gergely, G., Jurist, E. L., & Target, M. (2002). *Affect regulation, mentalization, and the development of the self*. New York: Other Press.

Fonagy, P., Target, M., Steele, H., & Steele, M. (1998). *Reflective-functioning manual for application to adult attachment interviews (version 5)*. London: University College London.

Fraley, R. C., Waller, N. G., & Brennan, K. A. (2000). An item response theory analysis of self-report measures of adult attachment. *Journal of Personality and Social Psychology*, *78*(2), 350–365.

Gunderson, J. (2011). Complex case: Mentalization-inspired case formulation: Minding the difficult patient. *Personality and Mental Health*, *51*(1), 91–92.

Hesse, E. (1999). The adult attachment interview: Historical and current perspectives. In J. Cassidy, & P. R. Shaver (Eds.), *Handbook of attachment: Theory, research, and clinical applications* (pp. 395–433). New York: Guilford Press.

Hummelen, B., Wilberg, T., & Karterud, S. (2007). Interviews of female patients with borderline personality disorder who dropped out of group psychotherapy. *International Journal of Group Psychotherapy*, *57*(1), 67–91.

Johansen, M., Karterud, S., Pedersen, G., Gude, T., & Falkum, E. (2004). An investigation of the prototype validity of the borderline DSM-IV construct. *Acta Psychiatrica Scandinavica*, *109*(4), 289–298.

Karterud, S. (2017). *Personlighet* [*Personality*]. Oslo: Gyldendal akademisk.

Karterud, S. (2018). A high quality mentalization-based group therapy session. *Group Analysis*, *51*(1).

Karterud, S., & Bateman, A. (2010). *Manual for mentaliseringsbasert psykoedukativ gruppeterapi (MBT-I)* [*Manual for mentalization-based group psychoeducation*]. Oslo: Gyldendal Akademisk.

Karterud, S., Pedersen, G., Johansen, M., Wilberg, T., Davis, K., & Panksepp, J. (2016). Primary emotional traits in patients with personality disorders. *Personality and Mental Health*, *10*(4), 261–273.

Karterud, S., Wilberg, T., & Urnes, Ø. (2017). *Personlighetspsykiatri* [*Personality psychiatry*]. (2nd ed.). Oslo: Gyldendal Akademisk.

Kongerslev, M. T., Chanen, A. M., & Simonsen, E. (2015). Personality disorder in childhood and adolescence comes of age: A review of the current evidence and prospects for future research. *Scandinavian Journal of Child and Adolescent Psychiatry and Psychology*, *3*(1), 31–48.

Kvarstein, E. H., Pedersen, G., Urnes, O., Hummelen, B., Wilberg, T., & Karterud, S. (2015). Changing from a traditional psychodynamic treatment programme to mentalization-based treatment for patients with borderline personality disorder - does it make a difference? *Psychology and Psychotherapy*, *88*(1), 71–86.

Morken, K., Karterud, S., & Arefjord, N. (2014). Transforming disorganized attachment through mentalization-based treatment. *Journal of Contemporary Psychotherapy*, *44*(2), 117–126.

Morken, K. T. E., Binder, P. E., Arefjord, N., & Karterud, S. (2017 May 17). Juggling thoughts and feelings: How do female patients with borderline symptomology and substance use disorder experience change in mentalization-based treatment? *Psychotherapy Research*, 1–16. https://doi.org/10.1080/10503307.2017.1325021. Advance online publication.

Panksepp, J., & Biven, L. (2012). *The archaeology of mind: Neuroevolutionary origins of human emotions*. New York: W.W Norton.

Robinson, P., Hellier, J., Barrett, B., Barzdaitiene, D., Bateman, A., Bogaardt, A., et al. (2016). The NOURISHED randomised controlled trial comparing mentalisation-based treatment for eating disorders (MBT-ED) with specialist supportive clinical management (SSCM-ED) for patients with eating disorders and symptoms of borderline personality disorder. *Trials*, *17*(1), 549.

Simonsen, S., Nørgaard, N. L., Larsen, K. A., & Bjørnholm, K. I. (2011). Mentalization-inspired case formulation: Minding the difficult patient. *Personality and Mental Health*, *5*, 73–79.

Skårderud, F. (2011). Two minds in the text: A commentary to sebastian simonsen, nana lund nørgaard, kirsten aaskov larsen and kraka ingeborg bjørnholm: Mentalization-inspired case formulation: Minding the difficult patient. *Personality and Mental Health*, *5*(1), 80–84.

Skårderud, F., & Sommerfeldt, B. (2015). *Miljøterapiboka* [*Milieu therapy book*]. Oslo: Gyldendal Akademisk.

Szufnarowska, J., Rohlfing, K. J., Fawcett, C., & Gredebäck, G. (2014). Is ostension any more than attention? *Scientific Reports*, *4*, 5304.

Weinberg, I., Ronningstam, E., Goldblatt, M. J., Schechter, M., & Maltsberger, J. T. (2011). Common factors in empirically supported treatments of borderline personality disorder. *Current Psychiatry Reports*, *13*(1), 60–68.

CHAPTER

4

The Corrective Experience of Getting a Life: Case Formulation Using General Psychiatric Management as a Framework to Facilitate Remission and Recovery

Lois W. Choi-Kain, Ellen F. Finch
McLean Hospital, Belmont, MA, United States

INTRODUCTION

Case formulation is a fundamental common ingredient in evidence-based treatments (EBTs) for borderline personality disorder (BPD). This book uniquely illustrates the way that different treatments for BPD outline specific formulations of how the disorder develops, thereby illuminating pathways for intervention or change. For both the patient and clinician, case formulation anchors a collaborative understanding of problems, basis for setting goals, and plan for the management of symptoms. The case formulation can in this way stabilize care and predict threats to the therapeutic alliance.

While psychodynamic formulations present a depth and refinement in conceptualization about how an individual's unique personal history influences the development of their psychological conflicts and difficulties, modern psychiatric formulation emphasizes the interface between biology and social factors (i.e., biopsychosocial considerations), perhaps with less depth and specificity than psychodynamic formulation, focusing

Case Formulation for Personality Disorders
https://doi.org/10.1016/B978-0-12-813521-1.00004-7

instead on neurobiology and disease process (Summers, 2003). The major EBTs for BPD – both psychodynamic and behavioural – incorporate a way of understanding BPD in biopsychosocial terms, considering 'nondynamic factors' such as genetics, temperament, and neurobiology as well as social cognitive differences. Considering the stigmatization of BPD patients as being 'treatment resistant', the medicalization of the case formulation provides a kind of objectivity that decreases blame and judgement and invokes a standard of care.

General Psychiatric Management (GPM; McMain et al., 2009; Gunderson & Links, 2014) entered the arena of evidence-based care when it proved to be similar to Dialectical Behavioural Therapy (DBT; Linehan, 1993; Linehan, Suarez, & Allmon, 1991) in effectiveness in all the major indicators of clinical improvement. A large one-year randomized control trial of BPD patients treated with either GPM (n=90) or DBT (n=90) found that both groups improved across outcomes, including frequency and severity of suicidal and nonsuicidal self-injury, health care utilization, and BPD symptoms (McMain et al., 2009). There were no significant differences between groups for any outcomes and improvements were sustained at a two-year follow up (McMain, Guimond, Streiner, Cardish, & Links, 2012). DBT is more intensive in its framework, with at least an additional 2–3h of treatment time per week. It, like other EBTs for BPD, requires more extensive training for its practitioners.

A meta-analysis of randomized controlled trials of psychotherapies for BPD concluded that effectiveness of treatment were not related to intensity and duration (Cristea et al., 2017). However, on review of these data, it appears that treatments with a coherent and consistent formulation of BPD have larger effects than CBT for personality disorders (Davidson, 2007), which takes a more transdiagnostic approach. One interpretation of these results may be that a major source of efficacy in the EBTs for BPD is the way the treatment content, focus, and techniques revolve around a formulation of BPD as the central clinical problem.

GPM distills experienced clinical wisdom about BPD in a straightforward, coherent framework for clinicians of any level of experience to implement. It may be that GPM boils down the essential ingredients of effective treatment for BPD in a more accessible, less complicated way than the more intensive evidence-based approaches available. Attending a one-day GPM workshop also improves clinicians' attitudes about treating BPD. For example, clinicians report feeling more hopeful, competent, and open to treat BPD (Keuroghlian et al., 2016; Masland et al., 2018). Unique to GPM are guidelines on how to prioritize common comorbidities as well as medication management. The clarity and empirical basis of these clinical guidelines may underpin the finding that patients with high Axis 1 comorbidity had significantly lower dropout rates in GPM than their DBT counterparts (Wnuk et al., 2013). These findings are particularly important given that BPD is a disorder for which significant stigma may introduce barriers to sustained consistent care. With more optimism and more clear directives in clinical management, founded in up-to-date knowledge about the disorder as well as a relatable case formulation, clinicians may sustain care with BPD patients consistently and effectively enough to have good outcomes.

It is arguable that what lends to GPM's effectiveness is its core formulation of BPD, rendering its symptoms as expectable and understandable. Compared to DBT, mentalization-based treatment (MBT; Bateman & Fonagy, 1999; Bateman & Fonagy, 2006), and transference-focused psychotherapy (TFP; Clarkin & Kernberg, 2015; Clarkin, Levy, Lenzenweger, & Kernberg, 2007), GPM is a less ambitious treatment with less detail in its content and technique. Explicitly, it does not rest on psychotherapeutic skills as much as it rests of understanding the psychopathology of BPD. While skilled therapists of either cognitive behavioural or psychodynamic stripes can easily convey the approach using their well-honed psychotherapeutic demeanour, clinicians who serve as a psychopharmacologist, nurse practitioner, or case manager can apply GPM with common sense and good clinical management. GPM's handbook (Gunderson & Links, 2014) is user friendly, briefly spanning under 70 pages of content plus an equal proportion illustrating the approach through case vignettes.

GPM provides a road map for both the clinician and patient to navigate expectable areas of chaos and tension in the treatment alliance related to safety, intersession contact, management of complex comorbidity, and medication management. It directs the clinician to start the treatment with diagnosis and psychoeducation about BPD. Included in GPM's psychoeducation is a review of BPD's biological basis and heritability, natural course, co-occurrence with other disorders, and greater responsiveness to treatments that are psychotherapeutic rather than pharmacological. The psychoeducational, rather than psychotherapeutic, vehicle of delivering this information presents clinical facts about the disorder in a way that diminishes blame on families, thereby increasing sources of support. This approach also increases optimism and accountability. Change is presented as both possible and expected, and like any clinical intervention, GPM's efficacy in any individual case is to be determined by progress in the patient's decreasing symptomatology and increasing effectiveness in managing their illness and vulnerabilities.

Within GPM's medicalized formulation of BPD, interpersonal hypersensitivity is centralized as the core of the disorder (Gunderson & Lyons-Ruth, 2008). Symptoms of BPD are understood as resulting from an emotional cascade that begins with a real or perceived interpersonal threat (e.g., separation, criticism). The clinician actively hypothesizes that any emotional instability, impulsivity, or self-destructive behaviour has resulted from an interpersonal problem. The clinician works with the

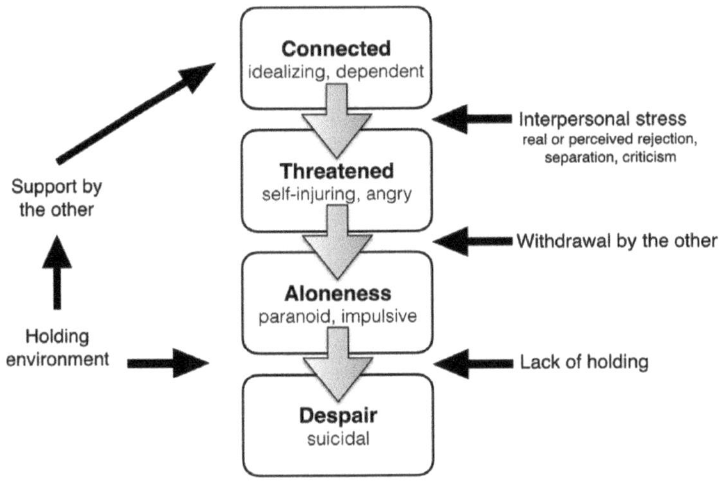

FIGURE 4.1 General Psychiatric Management's formulation of borderline personality disorder (BPD) as a disorder of interpersonal hypersensitivity (Gunderson & Links, 2014). *Note*: This diagram models the influence of interpersonal context on the *oscillation* of symptoms in patients with BPD. When caregivers show concern and responsiveness, the patient remains in a stable state of connectedness. In this state, he or she remains anxious and hypervigilant to real or perceived signs of rejection of imminent abandonment. Inevitably, when the patient perceives abandonment or rejection, he or she exhibits aggressive or self-injurious behaviours, which in turn elicits either rescuing or withdrawal from the caregiver. If the caregiver provides rescue, or increased involvement, the patient returns to a connected state. If the caregiver withdraws, the patient devolves into aloneness and despair. An external container (e.g., hospital, jail) may then provide containment that relieves the sense of loneliness, and this support can return the patient to the connected state. See Gunderson and Links (2014), pp. 13–14.

patient to better understand his or her sensitivities to interpersonal stress and the impact of his or her responses. The BPD patient's intolerance to aloneness is understood as the basis of frantic efforts to avoid abandonment, which paradoxically can ultimately push others away (Gunderson, 1996). It is in the withdrawal of others that the individual with BPD will shift into states of despair, suicidality, and paranoia. Here, interventions like hospitalization provide a form of holding and a grounds on which connection to others can be reestablished so the patient with BPD can reconstitute.

The interpersonal hypersensitivity model (Fig. 4.1) explains the common shifts between anxiety, anger, and despair that define the affective lability in BPD. Unlike the shifts between elation, depression, and euthymia characteristic of bipolar disorder, affective lability in BPD is uniquely characterized by intense and frequent shifts between euthymia, anger, depression, and anxiety (Reich, Zanarini, & Fitzmaurice, 2012). The interpersonal hypersensitivity model also incorporates an understanding of the rejection sensitivity inherent to BPD that can determine the shifts between anxiety in anticipation of rejection as well as anger in reaction to perceived rejection (Ayduk et al., 2000; Staebler, Helbing, Rosenbach, & Renneberg, 2011). Cognitive priming tasks and experience-sampling diary methods provide corroborating evidence that rage contingent upon feelings of rejection is elevated in those with BPD (Berenson, Downey, Rafaeli, Coifman, & Paquin, 2011). This model of interpersonal hypersensitivity integrates psychodynamically rooted notions of BPD with modern empirical findings in an explanatory framework that ties BPD's major affects – anxiety, anger, and despair – to interpersonal functioning.

While this model provides a basis for conceptualization of how different symptoms of BPD evolve and function, it is not a treatment plan and does not encourage clinicians and patients to rely on suicidal crisis as a compensatory measure to reinstate idealized dependent connections with others. Rather, it instructs clinicians and patients alike to understand anger in reaction to threats and aloneness. With this understanding, clinicians can learn to lean in and help the patient understand and more effectively express their feelings when threatened or alone. Interventions which occurs at this level, while the patients remain engaged but before self-destructive action is taken, is preferred over unilateral interventions taken by the clinician to ensure the patient's safety after destructive behavior (Fig. 4.2).

Importantly, GPM conceptualizes states of anger as an understandable reaction to the threat of aloneness. Problems of anger, as a specific criterion of BPD, is poorly conceptualized by most treatments other than TFP. By formulating an understanding of the anger, it can be contained within the patient's mind and also within the relationship, which potentially detoxifies it and renders it more approachable. If the clinician can then lean into the interaction during states of anger, when the patient is in fact seeking engagement and attempting, however, suboptimally, to communicate, the patient may feel more connected and less threatened, mitigating the descent into less workable, more mistrusting states of aloneness and suicidality. Over time, GPM aims to help the patient with BPD find different solutions to their problems of aloneness.

Clinicians portray an air of doubt in response to idealized dependency as an adequate solution to poor self-esteem and underdeveloped coping strategies. Imperatives to get a life, to both become more self-reliant and develop more self-esteem, are central to GPM. This manoeuvre is founded on the observation that the interpersonal hypersensitivity has the potential to encourage recurrent suicidality, hospitalization, and crisis, as a means to solve problems of aloneness. The forces that can render a BPD patient chronic and disabled are to be taken seriously, so that GPM evaluates the outcome on the basis of its progress is helping the BPD patient get a life. Herein lies its corrective influence that can counter the iatrogenic effects of unstructured, non-BPD informed treatments.

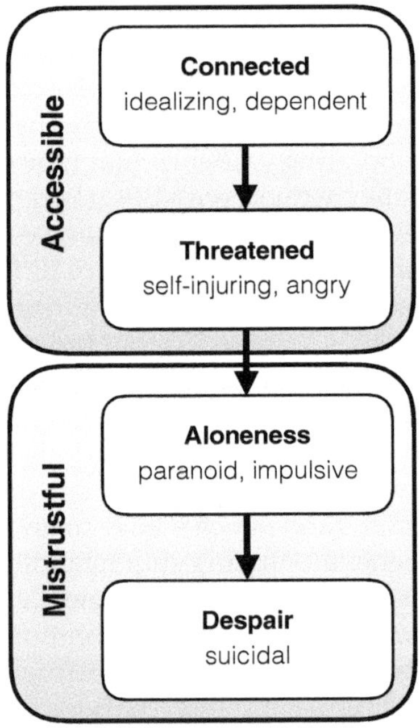

FIGURE 4.2 Accessibility of patient for intervention. *Note*: When the patient is connected or threatened (exhibiting anger or self-injurious behaviour), they are trusting and open to receiving intervention. It is optimal for clinicians to lean in when the patient is threatened, to help them understand and to resolve their current interpersonal dilemma. However, once the patient devolves to aloneness and despair, they become mistrustful and inaccessible. External interventions that rely less on the patient's collaboration may be necessary at this point. Hence to diminish dependency, intervening before unilateral manaeuvers are required is optimal.

GPM relies on a case-management model approach to retain focus on a life outside of therapy. GPM prioritizes the attainment of stable vocational functioning over romantic relationships, as well as improvement in social functioning over specific symptom improvement. This prioritization is informed by longitudinal studies that show 68.6% of borderline patients achieve symptomatic remission after six years, yet only 32.6% achieve good overall psychosocial functioning (Zanarini, Frankenburg, Hennen, Reich, & Silk, 2005; Zanarini, Frankenburg, Hennen, & Silk, 2003). Therefore, GPM's mechanism of change is to facilitate the natural course of the disorder's improvement with specific attention to promoting functioning in endeavours outside of treatment, instead of focusing solely on symptom reduction, which might happen over time without specified treatment. The interpersonal hypersensitivity model provides a means to understanding why patients with BPD cycle through a dysfunctional pattern of repeated hospitalization and unguided polypharmacy which promotes the identity of being a patient, and depending on the system. Informed by this formulation, clinicians in GPM offer a corrective experience of promoting a life outside of treatment to provide a source of identity, structure, and meaning, while conveying healthy scepticism about the benefits of treatment or any exclusive relationship as a solution to their interpersonal sensitivities.

The GPM case formulation is not one of detailed psychological insight but instead succinct and purposeful medical information. This focus aligns with findings from a study of case formulation in cognitive behavioural therapy (CBT): experienced clinicians developed more parsimonious and accurate formulations in comparison to their less experienced counterparts, who included more information and that led to errors in their formulation (Dudley, Ingham, Sowerby, & Freeston, 2015). Through focusing on medical knowledge about BPD and advising against initial diversions into exploration of personal histories, GPM keeps both clinician and client focused on key factors (i.e., psychoeducation, interpersonal hypersensitivity, getting a life) that lead to functional improvements.

We will present a psychotherapeutic process with rationale behind treatment management decisions key to the GPM approach. The following clinical example illustrates GPM based case formulation and how it is employed in the context of care.

CASE VIGNETTE

Emily is a 23-year-old single female, who is currently on her third medical leave from college. She is referred to Dr. G for a consultation after being discharged from her ninth hospitalization over the past three years. Emily has been treated for her depression and anxiety, with little relief and progressive functional decline.

Emily presents as a soft-spoken, underweight, sullen woman. In the first appointment, she does not hesitate to enumerate her long history of self-harm, which began at the age of 12 when she was struggling socially in a small, private middle school. Emily had few friends, and her parents, who are successful professionals, spent much of their time while at home doing work. Emily reports that cutting relieves her emotional pain. Her parents learned of Emily's consistent self-harm from a concerned school counsellor, and they promptly enrolled her in a different school and helped her find treatment. While her parents responded readily to crisis and showed support when she harmed herself, they generally shied away from talking about problems, as to not upset her more, fearing they would make things worse.

Emily's self-harm continued throughout high school, becoming more frequent and obvious when she began dating and disclosed to her parents that she was gay. Over the remainder of high school years, Emily was in multiple tumultuous relationships and began cutting more frequently. Despite her emotional difficulties, she performed well academically and was accepted to a prestigious small college in a rural setting.

In college, she began overdosing on medications as well. Emily reports that throughout college she did not care if she lived and felt a constant struggle with sadness, anxiety, and feeling unloved. She tells Dr. G that she would overdose on a 'handful' of tablets of her gabapentin, which she knew wouldn't kill her. She explains that if she had wanted to kill herself she could have.

After multiple hospitalizations for her overdoses, Emily has taken her third medical leave and moved back home with her parents. Though Emily held down various jobs at the local shopping centre, her self-harming behaviours and ambiguous suicidality did not subside. Emily's current therapist reported that Emily would not show up for appointments when she was most distressed and would not call the therapist before taking self-harming or suicidal actions. The therapist was no longer willing to work with Emily given the increase in both self-harming and suicidal behaviours. While Emily's therapist has told Dr. G that she believed Emily has BPD, she has not disclosed the diagnosis to either Emily or her family.

Emily: So Dr. G, are you going to take me on as a patient or not? I don't want to waste your time if you are not interested in working with me.

Dr. G: Before I answer that question, it is important for us to talk about how we understand the problems in your current treatment. If we can agree on an understanding of the problems and a way of working on them, then working together might make sense.

Emily: Well, just tell me what to do and I will do it. My therapist clearly does not know what she is doing.

Dr. G: I would agree with you that there is a problem in your treatment. The fact that you have been in the hospital nine times in three years is a sign that the treatment is not working.

Emily: Are you saying this is my fault?! I knew it. I knew you would blame me just like she does.

Dr. G: Let's take a step back. It will only be a good idea to work together if we can actually collaborate. That means we need to step away from whose fault or responsibility it is and communicate. The first item of business I want to communicate is how I understand your problems.

Emily: Okay, I'm listening.

Dr. G: The failure of your current treatment suggests to me that the underlying problems are not being addressed. Hospitalization is a temporary band-aid but does not provide any lasting relief to your problems. I think your problems are best explained by a diagnosis of borderline personality disorder. Have you ever heard of it?

Emily: Are you saying there is something wrong with my personality? That is pretty insulting.

Dr. G: Yes, I am saying the way you manage yourself at points of stress and in relationships is the central problem. I can see why this might be perceived as a criticism, but I look at it differently and see the diagnosis as good news. It is a disorder that improves in a majority of cases over time and has many effective treatments. The good news is that you likely have not had relief from your psychiatric problems because this has not been addressed.

Emily: Is that why the medications don't work? I thought it was just that I was doomed and unhelpable.

Dr. G goes on to provide basic psychoeducation about BPD, its natural course, and the expectation that with treatment, it can improve. Emily and Dr. G collaborate in thinking about how her history fits with the diagnosis. Dr. G notes that the pattern of either Emily taking matters into her own hands and self-harming or her therapist unilaterally hospitalizing her without discussions of what has happened is a sign of communication failures. Dr. G emphasizes the need for both Emily and Dr. G to contribute in the process. At the end of the session, Dr. G tells Emily to start by doing some homework on what her goals are for change.

Case Formulation

While there are many interesting and meaningful aspects of Emily's history that can be employed in a psychodynamic formulation of the case, the GPM clinician opts to keep the interaction focused on the diagnosis and psychoeducation to frame the treatment in terms of its aim to reduce symptoms (i.e., self-harm or hospitalization), increase collaboration between Emily and Dr. G through communication, and increase functioning outside treatment. Before making links or interpretations to how this might have developed from early childhood influences, the GPM clinician will want to prioritize a collaborative means of setting up the treatment rationale, goals, and roles in a way that promotes the patient's responsibility.

While the model of interpersonal hypersensitivity is not yet made explicit, Dr. G can both see in Emily's history and in her interactions with him that she is sensitive and quick to either blame herself or others when there is conflict. While he does not take this up right away, he does stay engaged when she becomes angry and clarifies his position through frank communication. Dr. G prioritizes building a shared focus on the problems of BPD and enlisting Emily's involvement in developing goals above any opportunities to make interpretations and discuss the meaning of her actions. He meets the request to 'tell her what to do' by setting the stage that the treatment will depend on Emily's activity in her life outside the sessions and builds an expectation of 'homework'.

In the next session, Emily arrives on time with her homework. She expresses feeling relieved she 'finally has a therapist who wants to accomplish something' and is receptive to Dr.G's feedback. She tells Dr. G she feels much more motivated to get better with his support and direction. Dr. G shows enthusiasm for Emily's goal of finishing school, pointing out how the recurrent hospitalizations interfere with that important task. Dr. G proposes that they work together to develop a better understanding of her suicide attempts as well as a plan for how Emily can manage differently.

Dr. G: It will help to look at your last hospitalization and why it happened. If we understand it better, we can be in a better position to avoid it next time.

Emily: I was doing okay during the last semester. My best friend Jane and I were spending a lot of time together doing homework. She made sure I woke up in time for classes, and brought me coffee and snacks when I was up late studying. I started to have more than a 'just friends' feelings for her and could not wait to hear from her or see her every day. After midterms, we were at a party and we both had too much to drink. I told her that I loved her and wanted to be more than just friends. After that, Jane started acting weird and stopped waking me up in the morning.

Dr. G: Oh? And how did you react to that?

Emily: I got really angry at Jane and called her all day long, sometimes telling her I needed her and other times telling her to never speak to me again since she was ruining my life. She then stopped talking to me altogether. I knew I fucked it up. I stopped going to class and just spent all my time in bed. My roommate also started avoiding me. I told my therapist I was feeling depressed, and she suggested

I talk to the doctor about starting new medications. I started an antidepressant and antianxiety medication and felt worse, like nauseous and sleepy. I just could not function anyways at that point. I started taking more of the anxiety medication so I could sleep all day.

Dr. G: It sounds like Jane's availability to you was very important to your mood and ability to function.

Emily: Yeah, my life pretty much revolved around her. I took it too far, as usual, and was left with nothing. I felt like my life was over and I would never get close to anyone again. I told my therapist I felt like it wasn't worth it anymore.

Dr. G: What do you mean, 'not worth it anymore?' Do you mean relationships, school, life?

Emily: I guess I meant relationships. The problem was I just did not feel I could function without Jane. I did not want to live anymore, but was not planning on killing myself. My therapist got worried about me right before finals and kept asking me if I was safe. I could not manage any of my work, and was falling behind so just felt it would be better to drop out. I didn't want to tell my parents that I was failing again. I could just see them saying 'you do the same thing every year.' They keep telling me to focus on my studies and I keep getting wrapped up in relationships. It was all in my head though, because when they saw me in the hospital, they were so worried and just told me everything would be okay.

Dr. G: What happened that you ended up in the hospital?

Emily: I didn't show up for my appointment with my therapist and she kept calling me. I didn't feel like talking to anyone, and knew if I talked to her she would want to talk about all the problems I was having. After the second missed appointment, she left a message to call her or she was going to hospitalize me. I didn't call her back and ended up having the campus police take me to the emergency room.

Dr. G: It helps me to hear the details of what happened so we can work on changing the way these things unfold. Last week, we discussed the diagnosis of borderline personality disorder. This week I want to review with you how this story you shared illustrates how vulnerable you can be around relationships.

Dr. G starts explaining to Emily the interpersonal hypersensitivity model of GPM by taking out the GPM Handbook and showing her the diagram.

Dr. G: When you are feeling connected in a relationship, like with Jane, you can feel better, receptive to encouragement and support, while somewhat anxious to see her. This sensitivity to her may develop into a dependency, in the absence of any stable way you feel you can manage on your own.

Emily: That's true. I do well at the start of relationships, but when they go downhill, I do too.

Dr. G: I'm glad you see that because learning to rely more on yourself, while difficult and perhaps lonely, may provide more stability. The problem is that when Jane is out of the picture, you feel threatened because you depend on her so much. If that scares her away or makes it hard for her to talk to you, then you are really out on your own. This might be when you start to really develop despair, feel no one cares, or even worse are out to get you, and that life is not worth it.

Emily: That is true. Once Jane stopped talking to me, I felt like nobody cared and that everyone was talking behind my back. I just couldn't face anyone or anything, and it seemed there was no way out. I was kind of relieved to go to the hospital, just to end the feeling that I was trapped.

Dr. G: That's understandable, but will get in the way of your goal of finishing school. Finishing school may make you feel better about yourself, so your self-esteem does not rise and fall so much with one relationship.

Emily: You make it sound easy. I can't do it. I can't cope on my own.

Dr. G: I understand that has been the case for you. My job is to help you find ways to build your ability to rely on yourself. It will take time. To start, let's first figure out a safety plan, that is, what you will do when you are starting to feel suicidal. Let's plan ahead for it, so that the lack of communication that we can predict based on what happened with your last therapist does not land you in the hospital. Have you ever made a safety plan before?

Emily: The doctors in the hospital sometimes would ask me to sign something saying I would not kill myself. Is that what you are asking?

Dr. G explains safety planning (GPM Handbook pages 37–4, 152) and asks Emily to fill out her own safety plan for the next appointment.

Emily comes to the third appointment having completed the safety plan. Dr. G explains he will be available during those times, but will rely on her ability to use her safety plan and community resources, including other supports, and the emergency room in case she cannot reach him.

Dr. G: I want to underline one more thing about this model of your sensitivities to relationships. We can predict that what happened with Jane in terms of your over-reliance on her and difficulty to communicate your needs, might happen here in this treatment.

Emily: Don't flatter yourself. I like women. No offense, I don't go for men so you don't need to worry about that.

Dr. G: What I am saying is that there will be times I can be helpful and you will feel comfortably supported in a way that makes you depend on me, until I somehow let you down. Then you may feel frantic and angry. It will be essential that you talk to me about that instead of cutting yourself or ending up in the hospital.

Emily: Okay, I don't think that will happen. As much as I don't go for men, I do trust you and think you are a much better doctor than my last therapist.

Dr. G: My effectiveness in your care will be determined by whether or not we see a change in this pattern.

Case Formulation

The GPM clinician, Dr. G, introduces the idea of reducing hospitalizations around the patient's stated goal of finishing school, establishing the idea that treatment itself can actually interfere with building life structures that enable a person to develop the self-confidence needed to rely on themselves rather than others. He also introduces the interpersonal hypersensitivity model to provide a shared understanding of 'suicidality', or in this case her despair and loneliness that fueled a process of dropping out of life and allowing treatment to take over. While Emily is not expected to simply change from this insight, it starts a conversation about how the safety plan can be constructed to understand that being alone is a situation that can be helped by using other supports. While the clinician will be available, Dr. G also warns that the safety plan cannot revolve around Dr. G completely, and that Emily will have a key role in keeping herself safe and managing her vulnerabilities. She will better be able to do so by understanding what happens to make her more self-destructive.

Notably, Emily is starting to feel buoyed up and optimistic due to the connection with Dr. G, not unlike her experience with Jane. GPM instructs clinicians to work against undue dependency and idealization of the clinicians, and Dr. G makes it clear Emily can do her part in the treatment to contribute to reaching its shared goal of her sustaining a life outside treatment. Dr. G uses the interpersonal hypersensitivity model to predict that what has happened in prior relationships, including in treatment, might recur in their treatment as well. He makes clear this is a part of her disorder and is expectable. It becomes the focus of the work, rather than a signal of Dr. G being a good or bad doctor. This is made distinct from whether or not the work they are doing is effective in terms of its goals.

Dr. G begins meeting with Emily weekly, offering combined psychopharmacology and psychotherapy. The treatment goes relatively well – Emily is actively engaged and thoughtful. Two months into treatment, Dr. G needs to reschedule an appointment due to another meeting. During the time of their usual appointment, Emily sends Dr. G a series emails stating that she cut herself, refuses to see the covering doctor, and really needs to talk to him and can't be safe without him.

Over the next week, Emily does not respond to Dr. G's emails or texts and does not come to the scheduled appointment. That night she calls Dr. G, sobbing, saying he is the only person who can help her. Dr. G says he looks forward to discussing this during their next session and she abruptly hangs up.

Emily ends up going to the emergency room that night and accepts voluntary admission in the hospital. She does not self-harm or overdose before her admission and Dr. G visits her in the hospital the next day.

Emily: Now you show up. Don't you have a more important meeting or something?

Dr. G: Ah, now that we are talking, I understand you are angry that I was not available at our usual time?

Emily: That's obvious. What kind of doctor are you? You are the one that keeps insisting I get a job, and right when I have an interview for a job I actually want you don't bother to keep our appointment.

Dr. G: I'm sorry that happened. It seems you really wanted to see me. I am encouraged by the fact you were invested in that job, but can also see your reliance on me for preparations failed you.

Emily: I really wanted to talk to you to plan for it, exactly what I would say, and role play maybe? I ended up being so anxious, I could not do it. I wasn't prepared so I didn't go.

Dr. G: I can see I failed you the week of the interview, but still don't understand why you did not come to see me for our next appointment.

Emily: What's the point? I failed and this is not working. You are not there when I need you most.

Dr. G: You are right. Our failure to collaborate has resulted in this hospitalization. We need to do a better job at talking about these feelings of anger before you start harming yourself and separating yourself from sources of support.

Dr. G discusses his dilemma about hospitalization, i.e., that on the one hand it makes her safe, but on the other it has become a regressive and life-interfering means of managing her emotional dilemmas. Implicating himself as part of the problem, Dr. G refers to 'our failure' to have a constructive conversation about this in appointments and how that reflects the fragility of the treatment vis-à-vis Emily's stated goals.

Dr. G and Emily look more in detail at the chain of events leading to the self-harm with an emphasis on how Emily can help herself when she is in situations or emotional states that lead her to self-harm or overdose. He focuses on problem-solving efforts to emphasize her agency to manage safety. Without shaming her, Dr. G notes that her panic about his absence is quite extraordinary. He reminds her about interpersonal hypersensitivity, rejection sensitivity, and the basic attachment dilemmas in BPD, followed by developing a plan with Emily about its management.

Lastly Dr. G suggests she tell her family about what happened. While Emily at first protests, she expresses willingness for them to join the next session to discuss Emily's problems in terms of the framework of interpersonal hypersensitivity. Her parents are relieved to be included and agree with the framework. Dr. G emphasizes the importance of inviting and tolerating discussions of difficulties, rather than walking on eggshells to only engage when hospitalizations happen. Parents are advised to provide support when Emily is more isolated from friends or feeling rejected and agree broadening her system of support is the goal, not an overreliance on parents.

Case Formulation

Despite the initial smooth sailing, recurrence of the patient's poor communication in the face of perceived rejection or deprioritization is to be expected. This opportunity is again utilized by Dr. G to underline Emily's interpersonal hypersensitivity as the focus on their work. Per the GPM framework, Dr. G remains engaged during Emily's angry expressions of disappointment, and instead of being put off or withdrawing he remains curious to know what has happened for Emily and how she understands it. The effort to become more engaged rather than withdraw can provide a sense of containment for Emily so she can be more willing and receptive to using the treatment to better problem solve around her sensitivity to the availability of others. When Emily expresses her disappointments in Dr. G, he affirms his failures to meet her idealized need for him, in the hope that the disappointing reality of his, and anyone else's, limited availability helps the patient develop a more realistic scepticism of their level of dependency on others.

Dr. G also starts to involve family to help them understand Emily's symptoms better, so they might cooperate with the aims of the treatment. Emily already demonstrated her interpersonal hypersensitivity to Dr. G, which he notices. In response, he advises she broaden her supports and enhances them by being more communicative and less reactive. In GPM, it is ideal to have families involved in the treatment for children with BPD. When safety issues are at hand, families benefit from having some education and can offer useful sources of support.

After she is discharged, Dr. G and Emily resume therapy as usual and reschedule the job interview she missed. She gets the job and does well, receiving recognition for her work from her supervisor. Emily sees consistent improvements in self-harm over the next six months and reports feeling better overall. She stays out of the hospital, stating she does not want to lose her job. Her parents want her to move out but Emily is staunchly opposed to this. Dr. G and Emily work together to help her get past this barrier and continue to take steps toward getting a life.

CONCLUSIONS

Emily's case illustrates the clinical management style of GPM, which rests heavily on both the interpersonal hypersensitivity model for formulating the problems of BPD paired with the imperatives to get a life, as a corrective manoeuvre away from unrealistic regressive dependencies on treatment systems. This medicalized focus allows the clinician to advise patients on how to best manage their inherent vulnerabilities to minimize handicaps and maximize functioning. While GPM's central formulation integrates both psychodynamic concepts and empirical findings on BPD, it relies on common sense problem solving rather than in depth exploration of past history or acquisition of an armamentarium of skills. Other intensive and more ambitious psychotherapies for BPD included in this book are highly effective, appealing, and interesting to patients and therapists as well. GPM might offer a basic approach that can be tried as a first line of treatment for generalist clinicians, not just therapists, can employ. Patients who fail GPM, might respond better to other more elaborate approaches (Choi-Kain, Albert, & Gunderson, 2016).

Acknowledgements

The case vignette is a composite of a number of clinical experiences that have been veiled to protect patient confidentiality.

References

Ayduk, O., Mendoza-Denton, R., Mischel, W., Downey, G., Peake, P. K., & Rodriguez, M. (2000). Regulating the interpersonal self: Strategic self-regulation for coping with rejection sensitivity. *Journal of Personality and Social Psychology, 79*(5), 776.

Bateman, A., & Fonagy, P. (1999). Effectiveness of partial hospitalization in the treatment of borderline personality disorder: A randomized controlled trial. *American Journal of Psychiatry, 156*(10), 1563–1569.

Bateman, A., & Fonagy, P. (2006). *Mentalization-based treatment for borderline personality disorder: A practical guide*. OUP Oxford.

Berenson, K. R., Downey, G., Rafaeli, E., Coifman, K. G., & Paquin, N. L. (2011). The rejection–rage contingency in borderline personality disorder. *Journal of Abnormal Psychology, 120*(3), 681.

Choi-Kain, L. W., Albert, E. B., & Gunderson, J. G. (2016). Evidence-based treatments for borderline personality disorder: Implementation, integration, and stepped care. *Harvard Review of Psychiatry, 24*(5), 342–356.

Clarkin, J. F., & Kernberg, O. F. (2015). *Transference-focused psychotherapy for borderline personality disorder: A clinical guide*. American Psychiatric Pub.

Clarkin, J. F., Levy, K. N., Lenzenweger, M. F., & Kernberg, O. F. (2007). Evaluating three treatments for borderline personality disorder: A multiwave study. *American Journal of Psychiatry, 164*(6), 922–928.

Cristea, I. A., Gentili, C., Cotet, C. D., Palomba, D., Barbui, C., & Cuijpers, P. (2017). Efficacy of psychotherapies for borderline personality disorder: A systematic review and meta-analysis. *JAMA Psychiatry, 74*(4), 319–328.

Davidson, K. (2007). *Cognitive therapy for personality disorders: A guide for clinicians*. Routledge.

Dudley, R., Ingham, B., Sowerby, K., & Freeston, M. (2015). The utility of case formulation in treatment decision making; the effect of experience and expertise. *Journal of Behavior Therapy and Experimental Psychiatry, 48*, 66–74.

Gunderson, J. G. (1996). The borderline patient's intolerance of aloneness: Insecure attachments and therapist availability. *American Journal of Psychiatry, 153*(6), 752.

Gunderson, J. G., & Links, P. (2014). *Handbook of good psychiatric management for borderline personality disorder*. American Psychiatric Pub.

Gunderson, J. G., & Lyons-Ruth, K. (2008). BPD's interpersonal hypersensitivity phenotype: A gene-environment-developmental model. *Journal of Personality Disorders, 22*(1), 22–41.

Keuroghlian, A. S., Palmer, B. A., Choi-Kain, L. W., Borba, C. P., Links, P. S., & Gunderson, J. G. (2016). The effect of attending good psychiatric management (GPM) workshops on attitudes toward patients with borderline personality disorder. *Journal of Personality Disorders, 30*(4), 567–576.

Linehan, M. (1993). *Cognitive-behavioral treatment of borderline personality disorder*. Guilford press.

Linehan, M. M., Suarez, A., & Allmon, D. (1991). Cognitive-behavioral treatment of chronically. *Archives of General Psychiatry, 48*, 1060–1064.

Masland, S. R., Price, D. G., MacDonald, J. M., Finch, E. F., Gunderson, J. G., & Choi-Kain, L. W. (2018). *The enduring effects of one-day training in General Psychiatric Management on clinician attitudes about borderline personality disorder*. Manuscript under review at *Journal of Nervous and Mental Disease*.

McMain, S. F., Guimond, T., Streiner, D. L., Cardish, R. J., & Links, P. S. (2012). Dialectical behavior therapy compared with general psychiatric management for borderline personality disorder: Clinical outcomes and functioning over a 2-year follow-up. *American Journal of Psychiatry, 169*(6), 650–661.

McMain, S. F., Links, P. S., Gnam, W. H., Guimond, T., Cardish, R. J., Korman, L., et al. (2009). A randomized trial of dialectical behavior therapy versus general psychiatric management for borderline personality disorder. *American Journal of Psychiatry, 166*(12), 1365–1374.

Reich, D. B., Zanarini, M. C., & Fitzmaurice, G. (2012). Affective lability in bipolar disorder and borderline personality disorder. *Comprehensive Psychiatry, 53*(3), 230–237.

Staebler, K., Helbing, E., Rosenbach, C., & Renneberg, B. (2011). Rejection sensitivity and borderline personality disorder. *Clinical Psychology and Psychotherapy, 18*(4), 275–283.

Summers, R. F. (2003). The psychodynamic formulation updated. *American Journal of Psychotherapy, 57*(1), 39–51.

Wnuk, S., McMain, S., Links, P. S., Habinski, L., Murray, J., & Guimond, T. (2013). Factors related to dropout from treatment in two outpatient treatments for borderline personality disorder. *Journal of Personality Disorders, 27*(6), 716–726.

Zanarini, M. C., Frankenburg, F. R., Hennen, J., Reich, D. B., & Silk, K. R. (2005). Psychosocial functioning of borderline patients and axis II comparison subjects followed prospectively for six years. *Journal of Personality Disorders, 19*(1), 19–29.

Zanarini, M. C., Frankenburg, F. R., Hennen, J., & Silk, K. R. (2003). The longitudinal course of borderline psychopathology: 6-year prospective follow-up of the phenomenology of borderline personality disorder. *American Journal of Psychiatry, 160*(2), 274–283.

CHAPTER

5

Case Formulation in Schema Therapy: Working With the Mode Model

Eva Fassbinder[1], *Odette Brand-de Wilde*[2], *Arnoud Arntz*[2]

[1]**Department of Psychiatry and Psychotherapy, University of Luebeck, Luebeck, Germany;** [2]**Department of Clinical Psychology, University of Amsterdam, Amsterdam, The Netherlands**

INTRODUCTION

Schema therapy (ST) has developed as one of the major treatments for personality disorders (PD) in the last two decades, especially for the treatment of borderline personality disorder (BPD) and Cluster-C-PD (Arntz & Jacob, 2012; Bamelis, Evers, Spinhoven, & Arntz, 2013; Fassbinder & Arntz, 2018; Jacob & Arntz, 2013; Masley, Gillanders, Simpson, & Taylor, 2012; Sempertegui, Karreman, Arntz, & Bekker, 2013). Case formulation is an integral part of ST. For every patient treated with ST an individual case formulation is worked out at the start of treatment. This individual case formulation helps to understand the patient's current symptoms and interpersonal problems in the light of their developmental context. During the therapy process all arising problems are linked to this individual case formulation and therapeutic interventions are on the basis of the formulation. In this chapter, we first give an introduction to the underlying theory and central concepts related to case formulation in ST, then we provide a methodology for clinicians on how to further specify an individual case formulation by use of the mode model, and we show how case formulation affects the therapeutic strategy and helps to select a treatment focus.

Case Formulation for Personality Disorders
https://doi.org/10.1016/B978-0-12-813521-1.00005-9

Underlying Theory and Central Concepts Related to Case Formulation in Schema Therapy

ST, unlike more traditional cognitive behavioural therapies, places a great emphasis on developmental aspects of patients' current symptoms and problems. ST states that the primary origins of PD pathology are unmet emotional needs (such as secure attachment, protection, love, attention, praise, autonomy, spontaneity, and play) in childhood, especially if traumatization of needs is related to the nuclear family. For young children their nuclear family is the entire world. By their experiences and the feedback they get they try to make sense of this world, to understand who they are and what their position in this world is. If basic childhood needs are met, children normally develop healthy views (schemas) of themselves, their relationships with others, and the world as a whole. On the other hand, if a child experiences trauma and frustration of such core emotional needs – in interaction with genetic, other biological and cultural/social factors – this leads to the development of **early maladaptive schemas.** Early maladaptive schemas are defined as broad pervasive life themes or patterns of information processing compromised of memories, emotions, cognitions, bodily sensations and attention preferences, which were developed during childhood or adolescence and elaborated throughout one's lifetime (Young, Klosko, & Weishaar, 2003).

Eighteen early maladaptive schemas have been described based on clinical observation and theoretical considerations (Young et al., 2003). Everyone has maladaptive and adaptive schemas, however, adaptive schemas have not been described yet.

It should be noted that according to Young's definition behaviours are not necessarily part of schemas. Behaviours might reflect the **coping strategy** with which an individual tries to deal with the schema, since if a schema gets activated it causes high distress to the individual. However, when the behaviours directly express the activated schema, then they are considered as part of the schema (e.g., a person showing clinging behaviour when an abandonment schema is activated). Thus, schemas highly influence behaviours, but behaviours are not always part of schemas.

There are three **coping styles**:

- surrender (giving in to the schema, feeling, thinking, and acting as if the schema is absolutely true),
- avoidance (avoiding activation or awareness of the schema), and
- overcompensation (feeling, thinking, and acting opposite to the schema).

Patients with severe PDs often display many schemas and react to them with varying coping styles. In clinical practice it can in such cases be very difficult to understand from the coping behaviour which schema is underneath and should be targeted by therapeutic interventions. Especially while working with patients with Cluster-B-PDs, Young discovered that the schema concept was too complicated to deal with frequent and rapid mood shifts. Due to this clinical experience he developed the schema-mode model, first for BPD patients and later for narcissistic patients (Young et al., 2003). Later disorder-specific schema-mode models were worked out for most other PDs and forensic patients (Arntz, 2012; Bamelis, Renner, Heidkamp, & Arntz, 2011; Jacob, van Genderen, & Seebauer, 2015; Lobbestael, Van Vreeswijk, & Arntz, 2008; Lobbestael, van Vreeswijk, Spinhoven, Schouten, & Arntz, 2010).

A **schema mode** describes the predominant emotional-cognitive-behavioural state at a particular time point. A schema mode includes a combination of an activated schema and a coping strategy, in that sense that the activation of a schema (e.g., when a specific core need is frustrated) leads to a way of coping, which results in the schema mode (Activated schema → coping → schema mode) (van Wijk-Herbrink et al., 2017). A schema mode is a transient state, which can change quickly in response to external and internal triggers, while a schema is a trait, a stable characteristic of a person (Young et al., 2003).

The schema-mode model is the key part of the case formulation that is shared with patients. To perform a successful ST treatment, it is essential that patients know their own mode model. Since the schema-mode model is a key and unique element in case formulation in ST this chapter will concentrate on the mode model. However, it must always be remembered that schema modes are related to schemas and that when a schema mode is targeted, the associated schema is always also addressed.

As can be seen from Fig. 5.1 there are four main groups of modes:

Maladaptive child modes are characterized by intensive affective states such as feeling lonely, sad, anxious, abandoned, helpless, needy, or unloved (*vulnerable child modes*); angry, defiant, or envious (*angry child modes*); and acting impulsively without thinking to get needs directly met (*impulsive child modes*). The emotions, perceptions, and behaviours resemble those of young children. These modes get activated when emotional core needs are endangered.

Maladaptive parent modes are characterized by internalized negative 'parental or significant other's voices' that criticize harshly and devalue patients (*punitive parent mode*) or pose high demands on them and pushes them to do everything perfect, to strive for achievement and success, or to take perfect care of others at the expense of own needs (*demanding parent mode*). These modes are associated with a lot of pressure, self-contempt, shame, self-hatred, and guilt.

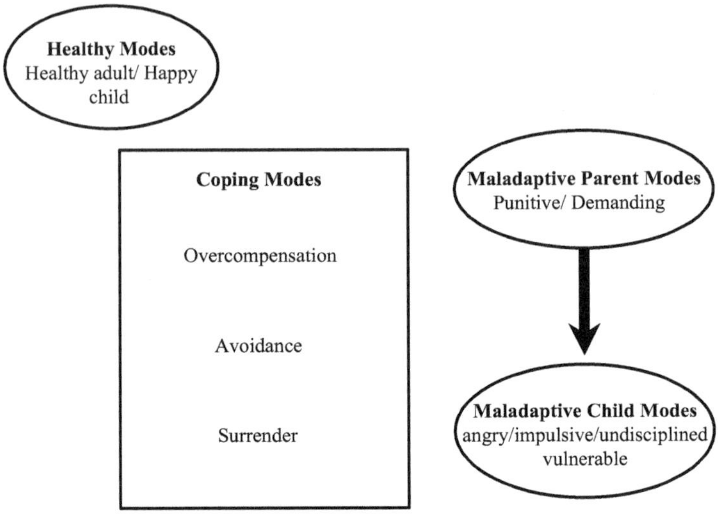

FIGURE 5.1 Basic structure of the mode model. *Adapted from Arntz, A., & Jacob, G. A. (2012).* Schema therapy in practice. *Chichester: Wiley.*

Maladaptive coping modes correspond to the coping styles (*surrender, avoidance, and overcompensation*). They are characterized by an excessive use of these strategies and are acquired early in childhood to adapt to the painful situation and to deal with the frustration of needs and are therefore regarded as 'survival mechanism'. These 'survival strategies' might include very different behaviours associated with only one mode, e.g., in an avoidant coping mode, social withdrawal, drinking, binge eating, or dissociation might be apparent in the same patient, since all these behaviours might serve the function to avoid, reduce, or numb emotional pain. In adult life these modes still protect the person from vulnerable feelings. However, they also block the access to emotions and needs and do not allow individuals to form healthy relationships and to live a life according to their goals and values. Thus, in adult life the needs of the vulnerable child mode are still not fulfilled, as are some (essential) adult emotional needs, leading to a life with low quality and lack of self-fulfillment.

There are two **healthy modes**, which represent functional states and should be strengthened in therapy. The *healthy adult mode* is the part of the self that takes care of the fulfillment of one's needs and can deal with emotions. In this mode individuals make decisions and act in accordance with their needs, goals, and values, even if this might cause anxiety or emotional distress in the short run. They are respectful, supporting, and kind with themselves even if they make mistakes. The *happy child mode* is associated with fun, spontaneity, play, and fulfilment of emotional needs. In this mode people feel happy, accepted, loved, understood, and optimistic. The happy child mode helps to regulate distress and protects from psychiatric diseases. However, in people with PDs this mode is normally very weak.

More information and a detailed description of all modes can be found in the ST manual (Arntz & Jacob, 2012, 2017).

CASE FORMULATION WITH THE MODE MODEL

Transdiagnostic and Disorder-Specific Approach

ST was originally developed as a transdiagnostic approach. In the basic structure as shown in Fig. 5.1 with the four major groups of modes all symptoms and problems as well as healthy behaviours and attitudes can be accommodated. As stated earlier in the chapter, besides the transdiagnostic approach, disorder-specific mode models were developed and tested for most PDs, all but schizotypal and schizoid PD (Bamelis et al., 2011; Lobbestael et al., 2008, 2010). The disorder-specific mode models describe a specific pattern of dysfunctional modes which can be observed in most patients with the respective PD. As an example we describe the mode model of BPD (Arntz & van Genderen, 2009). Treatment based on that model has been evaluated successfully, especially in BPD and Cluster-C-PD, but also in narcissistic, anti-social, and paranoid PD (Bamelis et al., 2013; Jacob & Arntz, 2013; Masley et al., 2012; Sempertegui et al., 2013).

Disorder-Specific Mode Model of Borderline Personality Disorder

Patients with BPD are in a *detached protector mode* most of the time, where they try to avoid feelings and needs. They detach themselves from other people, so that they cannot be hurt or abandoned. In this mode they do not want to talk, feel, or think, and they try to reach this, e.g., by means of avoidance, keeping others at a distance, taking drugs or drinking alcohol, binge eating, self-injury, dissociation, sleeping or staying in bed all day. Patients often feel empty and cold in this mode, however, most of the time they like this better than feeling the emotional turbulences of their child or parent modes. In the *abandoned-abused child mode* patients relive the trauma from childhood, they feel abandoned, sad, hopeless, and helpless, have intensive fears to be left alone, or to be hurt or mistreated. They strongly feel their emotional needs. However, they are desperate to get these needs met and if there was another person to care for them, most of the time they cannot trust this person or their punitive side does not allow them to have their needs fulfilled. In the *angry, impulsive child mode* patients with BPD act impulsively to get needs met and vent feelings in inappropriate ways, e.g., with rage attacks or being very demanding. In the angry child mode, they might accuse others in an inappropriate manner for not caring for them, putting pressure on them, e.g., by suicidal threats. The *punitive parent mode* is most of the times very strong in BPD patients. It shows in self-hatred, harsh self-criticism, shame, guilt, self-denial, and self-punishment (e.g., by self-injury, starving, not caring for the self). *Healthy adult* and *happy child mode* are normally very weak in the beginning of treatment.

Assessment of Relevant Information for Case Formulation

We recommend a structured clinical interview to properly assess syndromal psychiatric diagnoses and PDs (e.g., by means of SCID Interviews) at the start of treatment. With the Young Schema Questionnaire (Young, 1998) and the Schema Mode Inventory (Lobbestael et al., 2010) schemas and modes can be measured via self-report. However, when evaluating these self-report measures it should be kept in mind that there might be biases, since people might lack insight, deny specific aspects, be unwilling to report or answer questions to be socially accepted. Especially for patients with strong overcompensating modes these limitations must be taken into account. Thus, data from these questionnaires is never enough to build a case concept on. Further information is needed as stated later in this chapter.

At the start of treatment therapists assess the current problems and symptoms of a patient as well as their reasons for seeking treatment and their hopes related to treatment. Then the developmental history is carefully taken sometimes accompanied by diagnostic imagery exercises to get a clear view on the patient's learning history. In these exercises the therapist helps the patient to imagine a disturbing situation when they were young, and makes this memory as vivid as possible by asking the patient to close his eyes, speaking in first person and present tense and paying close attention to the child's emotions, cognitions, and needs. It must be noted, that in diagnostic imagery (unlike in imagery rescripting) the therapist does not change the ending of the memory. The primary aim is to better understand and experience the reality of the patient's situation as a child and by this to clarify the origin of dysfunctional schemas and modes. It is, however, important to keep in mind that diagnostic imagery often leads to intense emotions. This can be overwhelming for patients, especially at the start of treatment and for severely ill patients that lack skills to regulate strong emotions and have strong fears of emotions. Thus, e.g., for patients with BPD, solely diagnostic imagery (without rescripting) is not recommend or to be performed with caution. We can especially recommend diagnostic imagery for patients with Cluster-C-PD, since these exercises help to overcome emotional inhibition, although they need some explanation and reassurance (Ten Napel-Schutz, Abma, Bamelis, & Arntz, 2011).

Important Information for Building a Case Formulation

- Primary diagnosis and comorbid psychiatric disorders
- Current symptoms and problems of the patient
- Patient's request for help (what does the patient hope to achieve?)
- Developmental information (if possible supported by diagnostic imagery to get an idea on unmet childhood needs and early coping strategies) including developmental problems, stressful live events, temperament, and (parent) modelling behaviour
- Information on interpersonal interaction patterns (assessment of important interpersonal relationships and problems related to them as well as observation of interaction patterns in the therapeutic relationship)
- Data from Schema Mode Inventory and Young Schema Questionnaire

Linking Symptoms and Problems to the Respective Modes

From the first session on ST therapists pay attention to the patients' modes and try to link the symptoms and problems the patient is presenting to the mode model and to understand relevant emotional-cognitive-behavioural patterns by use of the mode model. Although many symptoms, behaviours, and emotions can belong to different modes, there are some rules of thumb that help to conceptualize the presentations of patients:

- Intense vulnerable feelings like sadness, anxiety, loneliness, or helplessness and emotional needs are most often connected to the vulnerable child modes. Also, behaviours and attitudes that seem childlike often belong to the child modes.
- Self-punishment, self-devaluation, self-hatred, and harsh criticism of the self most often refer to punitive parent modes. While high demands on social behavior (e.g., 'You have to care for others'; 'It is not allowed to feel happy/do something nice, if someone has pain. That is egoistic') or on achievement (e.g., 'You can't allow yourself any weaknesses'; 'You have to be effective'; 'First work, then pleasure') are conceptualized in the demanding parent modes. These modes are often accompanied by feelings of shame and guilt.
- Behaviours that help numbing emotions, needs, and thoughts, like substance abuse, binge eating, dissociation, gambling, watching TV, or cleaning the house all day, keeping away from others or unpleasant situations or not sharing personal information are most often connected with avoidant coping modes, e.g., detached protector mode, while passive, submissive behaviours, trying to do everything the interaction partner wishes, striving for harmony, taking over unpleasant tasks, and problems to say 'no' are typical behaviours of

a compliant surrender mode. Overcompensation is often associated with feelings of power and control. Others often feel dominated by overcompensating modes and pushed into a corner. Here the therapist's feelings are especially important to recognize these modes. Overcompensation might show in quite different behaviours: e.g., very arrogant, overly self-confident behaviour, often discrediting others (self-aggrandizer mode), aggressive and bullying behaviour (bully and attack mode), or overvigilant behaviour (suspicious or perfectionistic overcontroller modes).

- All functional behaviour and attitudes are conceptualized to be part of the healthy adult mode. Keep in mind that every patient is supposed to have at least some healthy adult part, which helps the patient to seek help and maintain the therapeutic relationship.

However, there are many symptoms and emotions that can be related to different modes, even in the very same patient. Self-injury in BPD patients is a good example for that: Self-injury can be used in the punitive parent mode, e.g., to punish the patient for a mistake or for having 'weak' emotions and needs. It can also be part of the detached protector mode to get away from the painful emotional feelings ('It is better to feel that physical pain, it distracts me from my "emotional chaos"'). Sometimes self-injury is connected to the angry-impulsive child mode, if needs were frustrated or endangered and the patient expresses and communicates anger with self-injury ('You know, when you go out with Phil all night and leave me alone, I can't stand that. You must have known before, that I would cut myself!'). Self-injury can also be driven by the vulnerable child mode, e.g., as a cry for help. To correctly conceptualize a symptom or behaviour to the respective mode therapists need to consider the context of the situation, the developmental aspects as well as to ask the patient about the behaviour and its function. If patients are familiar with the mode model, it is often easy for them to say in which mode a specific behaviour in a specific situation took place.

Another example is feelings of anger, which is often connected to the angry child mode. This is especially the case when an important need was frustrated before and the behaviour does not seem like adult behaviour (e.g., patient after therapist did not answer an email: 'I don't want to talk to you today. You should better think about what you have done last week'). But anger can also occur in the angry protector mode. Here the angry behaviour serves to keep other people on a distance or to keep emotions away ('I really do not feel like doing this silly exercise with your stupid chairs!'). While in the angry child mode the therapist can see the need behind the anger and most often feels that the patient wants connection, in the angry protector mode the therapist does not feel the need for close interpersonal contact. Anger can also be part of other coping modes, e.g., of the bully and attack modes. Here the therapist feels attacked and threatened. If anger is directed at the self, it is usually connected to the punitive parent mode. Lastly, of course anger can also be part of the healthy adult mode, e.g., if personal boundaries were crossed. Anger is then expressed in an appropriate manner and helps the individual to get its needs met.

To efficiently conceptualize the mode model and to work out important connections between the modes therapists often ask directly for specific information (e.g., 'You told me that you drink alcohol every day of the week, since your partner is only there on weekends. Does drinking alcohol help you to deal with vulnerable feelings, such as loneliness or sadness? ... Can you tell me how you feel then in your own words?')

Picking the Relevant Modes: Keep It as Simple as Possible

It is the therapist's responsibility to pick the most relevant modes and to keep the case formulation as simple as possible. Since there are many possible modes, this is sometimes a challenging task. The disorder-specific mode concepts support the therapist. Whenever a disorder-specific mode concept is available, the therapist uses this model as a rough frame for case formulation. Thus, if the patient has a BPD, the therapist expects that the patient will show a detached protector mode, a punitive parent mode, an abandoned-abused and angry, impulsive child mode as well as a healthy adult mode. This helps the therapist to pick the right modes with high probability and to concentrate on the most relevant modes. However, it must always be remembered that these concepts just provide a rough estimation. They always have to be adapted to the individual patient. Often, especially in the case of comorbidity, other modes which are not part of the disorder-specific model might be relevant also and need to be integrated in the patient's individual case formulation. Where there is no disorder-specific mode model available the therapist uses the general approach as displayed in Fig. 5.1.

It is recommended not to use more than seven dysfunctional modes, so that therapist and patient do not get lost in detail and concentrate on the most essential problems. This might mean to integrate two modes as one mode, e.g., the angry and the impulsive child mode can be matched to an angry/impulsive child mode (like in the above explained BPD-specific model), or to leave out modes that are not so essential. Especially for the coping modes this might be relevant, since patients often display several coping strategies.

Introduction of the Case Formulation

Introduction of the Mode Model and the Vulnerable Part

After the most important information is assessed, which is normally the case no later than after the first six sessions, the therapist will introduce the mode model to the patient and work out an individual case formulation with the patient. In the following we will illustrate a step-by-step introduction of the mode model with an example of avoidant PD (AVD). The disorder-specific mode model of AVD includes a lonely child mode, a punitive parent mode, an avoidant protector mode and as all models a healthy adult mode. Thus, the therapist expects these modes, but is also open for other aspects.

To introduce the mode model the therapist might say: *'Today I would like to sum up with you, what we have learnt so far. I would like to bring all the problems you told me about into an individual model, which explains us better why the things are the way they are and how you can better deal with them. In ST we work with a model which is called the mode model. Basically it states that each person has different parts or sides of the self. For example everybody has a vulnerable part. This is where people feel very lonely, sad or anxious. And all people have a part that puts pressure on them, devalues them and is very critical. And there are also other parts I will explain to you later ... I would like to start with this vulnerable part. You told me that you often feel very insecure and anxious that someone will criticize you or that you might be attacked for doing something wrong. These fears belong to your vulnerable part, I guess. Do you understand, what I mean? ... Can you tell me how you feel when you are in that vulnerable part?'* The therapist will focus on other important vulnerable emotions and needs and validated them *'You also said that although you are afraid to get in contact with other people, since they might reject you, you often feel very sad and lonely and wish for contact. These feelings of sadness and loneliness and the wish for contact also belong to the vulnerable part of you. It is quite normal that on the one hand there is a part of you who wants to protect yourself from being ashamed and rejected and avoids contact with other, and on the other hand there is this vulnerable part that wishes for contact and feels lonely. We will look at this protecting part later'*.

If possible, the therapist directly makes the connection with the developmental context and educates the patient about needs: *'I think these feelings of your vulnerable part are so intensive, since you were indeed very lonely in childhood. There was nobody to soothe you and nobody with whom you could talk about what was going on in you. And if you said something you did not make good experiences by that, you often were rejected or made ridiculous. I remember the diagnostic imagery we did together, that one with the family dinner, where there was such a cold atmosphere and your dad criticized you for everything you did and made fun of you. And the other one, where you were alone in your room crying and nobody was there. This is not normal for children. Children need a parent, who loves them, holds them and cares for them. A parent that listens to them and soothes them and does not always criticize everything they do. Children need to be accepted the way they are. This way they can learn healthy things about themselves ... As these very basic needs were so harshly frustrated in your childhood, it is quite normal that you still feel so lonely, sad, anxious and insecure when you are in that vulnerable part'*.

To make the case formulation as individual as possible patients choose names for each mode. The therapist introduces this idea and asks the patients directly for a name: *'In ST this vulnerable part is called "the vulnerable child mode". It is important that the mode model we work out today is entirely your model and matching to you individually. Also it is good if we directly have a label for each side, so that we can directly catch it and the two of us know what we are talking about. Thus, it would be great if we can find names for each part of you. Do you have an idea, how we can name that vulnerable part of you? ... In ST we aim to better care for this mode and welcome it, thus it would be great to have a sweet, nice name for it'*. If the patient does not have any idea, the therapist might make a proposal: *'What do you think about "Little Frank"?'*

While working out the individual case formulation with the patient, the therapist directly draws an illustration at the flip chart or on a paper. He draws a circle on the right side at the bottom of the page for the dysfunctional child modes and writes down the feelings the patient names when in this mode. The developmental context should be brought into that model by arrows connecting childhood experiences to specific modes.

Introduction of the Parent Modes

To introduce the parent modes the therapist might say: *'And there is another part in you, where you are very mean with yourself and blame yourself very badly. In ST we call it the punitive part? Do you know what I mean?'* In this example the therapist calls the punitive parent mode only 'punitive mode' and leaves out the 'parent'. This can sometimes be a good strategy to reduce resistance from patients due to feelings of guilt and loyalty. The therapist then explores the parent mode further by asking for associated cognitions, emotions, and behaviours: *'What does this part say to you? ... Wow, these are very harsh messages. How do you feel like, when you hear those messages? ... Is there any behaviour you know from yourself, that is associated with this punitive side of you?'* Then he might again turn to the developmental aspects: *'These punitive modes most often develop if a child was treated badly by important other persons, e.g. when a child is often devaluated, criticized, made ridiculous, or punished harshly for mistakes or for telling how it feels or what it needs. Some people say that they can directly say, whose messages they hear, when they are in that mode. Do you have an idea where this mode has its roots in your development?'* The therapist might also directly share developmental hypotheses (e.g., *'I can imagine that this punitive side developed, since your father was very critical with you and also you told me that you were bullied in school, since you were afraid to talk. What do you think about that?'*) The therapist then again asks for a name and writes the information for the punitive side in another circle above the vulnerable child mode.

Introduction of the Coping Modes

The therapist then educates the patient about the coping modes: *'As we worked out there are many unpleasant emotions in the "Little Frank" mode here (points on the vulnerable child circle in the illustration). He feels very insecure, is afraid to be rejected and the "Devaluer" from above blames him and tells him what a shame he is (points on the punitive side circle). And that was how your reality was every day in childhood, wasn't it? ... If you said something you were criticized and hurt, thus, as a strategy to protect yourself you stopped talking, avoided contact or any attention from others, tried to get invisible, when in contact with others. This is a smart strategy and it was a very healthy choice under these circumstances, we call it a "survival strategy" in ST ... What do you think about that? ... This part is called "Avoidant Protector Mode" in ST. Do you have a name for your protector part?'* As can be seen from the description it is very important to validate the function of this mode throughout. The therapist tries to get more information about this mode and educates the patient further: *'Are there any other behaviours associated with your "Protector"? ... Hmm, you told me, that you often watch TV all night long and spend hours on the internet with gambling and from time to time you smoke pot. I guess, these behaviours are also connected to your "Protector". Maybe this helps you to deal with the sadness and loneliness of "Little Frank"? Maybe it is a safe substitute for the contact he wishes to have? What do you think about that?'* The therapist draws a box on the left side of the illustration and again writes down the most important information.

Introduction of the Healthy Adult Mode

Finally, the healthy adult mode is conceptualized with the patient, which is most of the time pleasant for patients, since it shows that they have a functional side and strengths. The therapist reinforces this side: *'Then there is also a functional side in you. This is the side that said: "It cannot go on like this. I have to change something and get help" and has come to therapy, although you were afraid to come here ... that is the side that tells me openly about all your problems, although you find talking difficult. This is also the side that keeps up the friendship with Steven and which goes to work every day ... This side is called the healthy adult. We might call it "Adult Frank", if this is okay for you?'* The healthy adult side is also added to the illustration to finalize the first version of the mode model (see Fig. 5.2). Patient and therapist will discuss the mode model further.

While educating the patient with the mode model the therapist keeps track and discusses all important issues and modes. Especially the symptoms and problems that have subjectively the highest burden for the patient should be covered. Even if ST therapists are quite direct when introducing the case formulation, it is always a collaborative work of patients and therapists. Therapists give a frame and

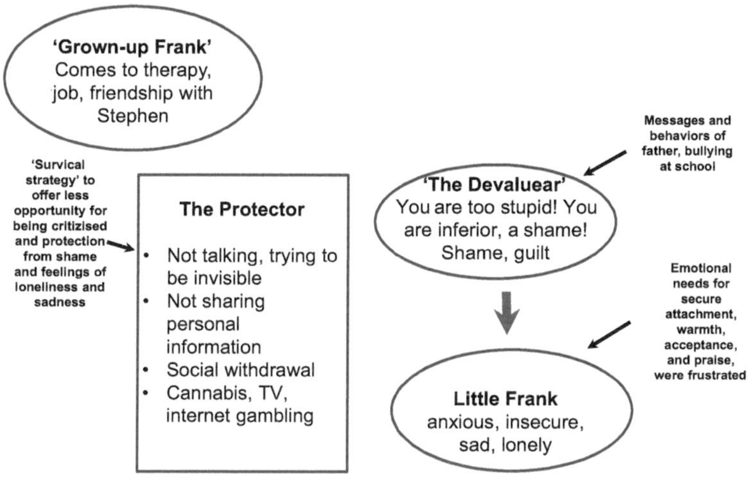

FIGURE 5.2 Frank's mode model.

then discuss everything individually with the patient. Often therapists explain a mode or a group of modes and give some example from people in general or from what the patient has told before (both is validating for patients) to introduce the patient with the mode, they then request feedback, ask the patients what they experience in this mode, and discuss the functions of the mode, e.g., by use of Socratic dialogue. It is important that the model fits for both therapist and patient, thus ST therapists are very open for discussion and different opinions. The therapist does not force the patient to accept a mode or a conceptualization of a symptom but is clear about the model and sticks to important points of it (e.g., everybody has a vulnerable side). If there is a disagreement that cannot be resolved, the therapist proposes to return to this issue later. For example, if narcissistic patients deny their vulnerable child mode, the therapist might leave out the circle for the vulnerable child mode in the illustration in the beginning, but will discuss the mode further later in treatment and will try ways to help the patient accept this mode.

In most cases therapists follow the above shown way for case formulation: First child and parent modes are discussed to validate the emotional suffering of patients, then often as the most severe part the coping modes are introduced as a 'survival strategy' to deal with the suffering. Finally, the healthy adult mode is communicated. However, the therapist might deviate from this order, e.g., if a patient seems not very open for one or another mode, the therapist might pick another order to make the model more acceptable for the patient.

Impact of Case Formulation on the Course of Therapy

In ST the case formulation guides the whole treatment. For each mode there are specific goals and techniques.

Maladaptive coping modes normally dominate in the start of treatment. The therapist's goal is to get through these coping modes. To do so the therapist helps patients to understand why these modes developed and value their adaptive function. They then carefully weigh pros and cons of these modes, make clear that these modes hinder patients to fulfil their emotional needs and empathically confront patients to reduce these modes and teach them healthier strategies.

This opens the door to the *vulnerable child modes*, which are supported and comforted to heal the emotional wounds from childhood. Therapists encourage patients to show their emotions and feel their needs and validate them and help with the fulfilment of needs. The specific design of the therapy relationship as 'limited reparenting', meaning that the therapist behaves – within the professional boundaries of a therapy relationship – as a good parent figure to offer an antidote to traumatization in childhood and to offer corrective emotional experiences. An integral part of healing the child modes is use of experiential techniques such as imagery rescripting and chair dialogues to promote emotional processing of traumatic childhood memories. In Frank's example from earlier in the chapter, the therapist might do an imagery rescripting exercise of the family dinner, where the father was so critical. In the rescripting part the therapist enters the scene, stops the father and tells him that it is poison for children if their parents are emotionally so cold and critical and that Frank needs acceptance and praise instead. Since the father does not stop, the therapist 'performs magic' and shrinks the father so that he is only 10 cm and lets him speak with a 'mickey mouse' voice. Although Little Frank has to laugh a bit, he still feels uncomfortable and lonely. Thus, the therapist brings Frank to his very gentle Grandma who soothes Little Frank and hugs him.

Dysfunctional parent modes should also be reduced, ST therapist even 'combat' these modes to reduce their influence in the patient's life. This is mainly done by means of experiential techniques, e.g., by placing the punitive parent mode in a chair and 'fighting it' or by stopping an abusive parent in an imagery rescripting exercise (like described above).

The *healthy modes* are strengthened throughout the whole therapy process by a variety of techniques.

These goals are made transparent to the patient directly from the beginning. Besides cognitive and behavioural techniques there is a strong emphasis on experiential techniques and the therapy relationship to reach these goals. We refer to the treatment manuals of ST in general (Jacob et al., 2015; Young et al., 2003) and ST for BPD (Arntz & van Genderen, 2009) for further explanation on these goals and techniques. Patients might be

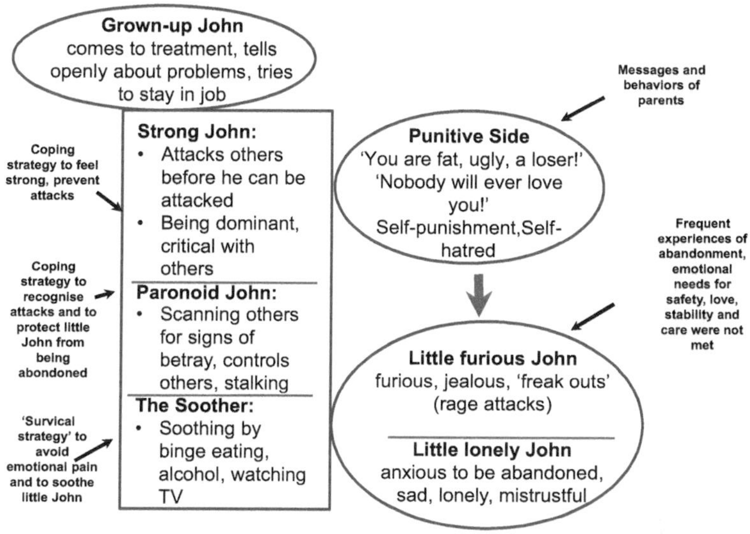

FIGURE 5.3 John's mode model.

educated and supported by *Breaking Negative Thinking Patterns*, a book explaining the mode model and ST to patients and other lay people (Jacob et al., 2015).

ILLUSTRATION OF CASE FORMULATION WITH AN EXAMPLE OF A BORDERLINE PERSONALITY DISORDER (BPD) PATIENT

In this last part we give another example for case formulation. In a patient with BPD we illustrate how to formulate idiosyncratic mode models that deviate from the standard disorder-specific model of BPD. If you as a reader would like to exercise what you have learned so far you might first read the case example and then try to do a case formulation of this case by your own before you look at Fig. 5.3, which shows the final case formulation of that patient. Therapists, especially when they start to learn ST, should prepare the individual case concept of a patient on a piece of paper and discuss it in ST supervision before they educate the patient with the model.

Case Example of a Patient With Borderline Personality Disorder (BPD)

John, a 33-year-old patient, fulfilled the criteria for a BPD, a chronic depression, a binge eating and an alcohol abuse disorder in the diagnostic interviews. In the first appointment he says: *'You should be the person to help me with all that mess in my life. You look pretty young … At least you are a woman, I can't talk to men … Okay, well, I have nothing to lose and nobody wants to work with me, anyway … I guess, you will give up soon, too. I give you five sessions.'* After some therapeutic interventions John calms down a bit and says: *'You want to know my problems, okay I am totally alone and I will always be alone. There is nobody that is interested in me, there never was and there never will be. Every day is awful: I go to work, I have fights with my colleagues and my boss, I go home and come to my lonely apartment and I cannot stand these feelings. I go out to buy alcohol and chips and then I eat, drink and watch TV. Sometimes I cut myself because I hate myself so much, that I am such a loser and so fat.'* Asked for his relationships with women he reports: *'Well, this never worked out. I had so many fights when I was in relationships with women. I guess, I could not believe that they really loved me. I was very jealous, always afraid that they might leave me. If I found out something, that looked like they did not love me or betrayed me, I got so furious. One time I went to a disco, because my ex-girlfriend told me she wanted to go out with her girlfriends and I could not believe that. Well, I was right: I saw her talking to another man and I freaked out and beat him up, so that he ended in hospital.'* Asked for his childhood it turned out that John's father lived with another family and only seldom came to see John. He often told John he would come around and do something with him, but then did not show up. John always felt that his father was not interested in him but that he loved and spent time with his other children. His mother was very young when John was born. She drank alcohol and often went out at nights. He often woke up at night, totally alone and scared to death, not knowing if she would come back. She often screamed at John, blamed him for being stupid, fat, and awful, and gave him the feeling that it was his fault that his father left them. She often used him to try to get his father back. From five years old John was most of the time in foster families, but since 'he was too difficult' nobody really wanted to keep him. In school he was also bullied until 'I trashed up a boy. Then they were silent and had respect. I learnt to be strong so that nobody would dare to attack me again'.

John's mode model is shown in Fig. 5.3. John also chose names for each mode. In the case of conceptualization the therapist uses the disorder-specific mode model for BPD as an orientation and detects as BPD-specific modes an **abandoned-abused child mode** ('Little lonely John'), an **angry child mode** ('Little furious John'), and a **punitive parent mode** ('Punitive Side'). However, the BPD-specific coping mode, the detached protector mode, does not match perfectly with John's 'survival strategies'. John shows two overcompensating modes: a **Bully and Attack mode** ('Strong John'), which he learnt at school to prevent attacks from other pupils, and a **Suspicious Overcontroller Mode** ('Paranoid John'), in which John scans other people for signs of being abandoned or betrayed to protect

'Little John' who has often experienced mistrust and abandonment. As an avoidant coping mode John displays a **Detached Self-Soother Mode** ('The Soother'). In this mode he tries to soothe himself through binge eating, alcohol, and watching TV when he feels lonely and sad. In the **healthy adult mode** ('Grown Up John') John's therapy attendance and that he tries to be open about his problems, even if he feels ashamed, as well as that he tries to keep his job, are conceptualized. The childhood origins are again worked in by use of arrows.

CONCLUSION

The mode model provides a clear structure for the development of an individual case formulation. The case formulation clarifies current symptoms and interpersonal problems and explains them from a developmental perspective. Although the mode model is intended to be transdiagnostic, there are also disorder-specific case concepts for most PDs. These disorder-specific mode concepts support the therapist with a rough frame for building a case formulation together with the patient, however, therapist always need to adapt the model to the individual patient. The case formulation helps patients to better understand their problems and most of the times is perceived as validating and relieving by patients. The case formulation guides the whole treatment process. For each mode there are specific goals directing the therapist's behaviour. Treatment based on the mode model has shown to be effective especially for patients with PD and other chronic conditions. Moreover, this treatment is well accepted by patients and therapists and shows low drop-out rates.

Acknowledgements

Several details of the case descriptions (e.g., age, profession, parts of biography, and symptoms) were changed so as to protect client privacy.

References

Arntz, A. (2012). Schema therapy for cluster C personality disorders. In M. van Vreeswijk, J. Boersen, & M. Nadort (Eds.), *Handbook of schema therapy: theory, research and practice*. Sussex: Wiley.

Arntz, A., & Jacob, G. A. (2012). *Schema therapy in practice*. Chichester: Wiley.

Arntz, A., & Jacob, G. A. (2017). *Schema therapy in practice*. Chichester: Wiley.

Arntz, A., & van Genderen, H. (2009). *Schema therapy for borderline personality disorder*. Sussex: Wiley.

Bamelis, L. L., Evers, S. M., Spinhoven, P., & Arntz, A. (2014). Results of a multicenter randomized controlled trial of the clinical effectiveness of schema therapy for personality disorders. *American Journal of Psychiatry, 171*, 305–322.

Bamelis, L. L., Renner, F., Heidkamp, D., & Arntz, A. (2011). Extended schema mode conceptualizations for specific personality disorders: An empirical study. *Journal of Personality Disorders*, *25*, 41–58.

Fassbinder, E., & Arntz, A. (In preparation). Schema therapy. *In The APA Handbook of CBT*. Washington: APA Books.

Jacob, G. A., & Arntz, A. (2013). Schema therapy for personality disorders-a review. *International Journal of Cognitive Therapy*, *6*, 171–185.

Jacob, G. A., van Genderen, H., & Seebauer, L. (2015). *Breaking negative thinking patterns: A schema therapy self-help and support book*. Sussex: Wiley.

Lobbestael, J., van Vreeswijk, M., Spinhoven, P., Schouten, E., & Arntz, A. (2010). Reliability and validity of the short schema mode inventory (SMI). *Behavioural and Cognitive Psychotherapy*, *38*, 437–458.

Lobbestael, J., Van Vreeswijk, M. F., & Arntz, A. (2008). An empirical test of schema mode conceptualizations in personality disorders. *Behaviour Research and Therapy*, *46*, 854–860.

Masley, S. A., Gillanders, D. T., Simpson, S. G., & Taylor, M. A. (2012). A systematic review of the evidence base for schema therapy. *Cognitive Behavioral Therapy*, *41*, 185–202.

Sempertegui, G. A., Karreman, A., Arntz, A., & Bekker, M. H. (2013). Schema therapy for borderline personality disorder: A comprehensive review of its empirical foundations, effectiveness and implementation possibilities. *Clinical Psychology Review*, *33*, 426–447.

Ten Napel-Schutz, M. C., Abma, T. A., Bamelis, L. L., & Arntz, A. (2011). Personality disorder patients' perspectives on the introduction of imagery within schema therapy: A qualitative study into patients' experiences. *Cognitive and Behavioral Practice*, *18*, 482–490.

van Wijk-Herbrink, M. F., Bernstein, D. P., Broers, N. J., Roelofs, J., Rijkeboer, M. M., & Arntz, A. (2018). Internalizing and Externalizing Behaviors Share a Common Predictor: the Effects of Early Maladaptive Schemas Are Mediated by Coping Responses and Schema Modes. *Journal of Abnormal Child Psychology*, *46*, 907–920.

Young, J. E. (1998). *Young schema questionnaire short form*. New York: Cognitive Therapy Centre.

Young, J. E., Klosko, S., & Weishaar, M. E. (2003). *Schema therapy - a practitioner's guide*. New York: The Guilford Press.

CHAPTER

6

Cognitive Analytic Therapy: A Relational Approach to Young People With Severe Personality Disorder

Louise K. McCutcheon[1,2,3], *Ian B. Kerr*[4], *Andrew M. Chanen*[1,2,3]

[1]Orygen, The National Centre of Excellence in Youth Mental Health, Melbourne, Australia; [2]Centre for Youth Mental Health, The University of Melbourne, Melbourne, Australia; [3]Orygen Youth Health, Northwestern Mental Health, Melbourne, Australia; [4]Department of Psychotherapy, Coathill Hospital, Coatbridge, Scotland

INTRODUCTION

Cognitive Analytic Therapy (CAT) is an integrative model with a strong and central focus on the relational nature of development and psychopathology. It is based on a view of human beings as being fundamentally constituted relationally and socially, and therefore it is particularly focused on understanding the individual's problematic self-management and interpersonal relationship patterns. In CAT, all higher mental activity and behaviour is seen as deriving from these patterns. CAT developed as a time-limited individual psychotherapy that is practical and collaborative in style. A central feature of CAT is the joint (patient–therapist) creation of a shared understanding of the patient's difficulties and their developmental origins, using plain language written and diagrammatic 'reformulations'. These form the basis for understanding self-management and interpersonal problems both within and outside therapy, assisting the patient to recognize and revise their dysfunctional relationship

Case Formulation for Personality Disorders
https://doi.org/10.1016/B978-0-12-813521-1.00006-0

patterns, and assisting the therapist to avoid or recover from collusion with such patterns. One particular advantage of CAT is its integrative and 'transdiagnostic' approach, which can encompass within the overall treatment model the myriad of co-occurring problems that are so often the norm for patients.

WHAT UNIQUE FEATURES CHARACTERIZE COGNITIVE ANALYTIC THERAPY?

As its name implies, CAT arose from an attempt to find a common language for elements from psychoanalytic theory, such as object relations, and cognitive psychology (Ryle, 1985, 1991). CAT has been informed by other models, including Kelly's personal construct theory and Vygotsky's activity theory, evolving into an integrated model of development and psychopathology (Leiman, 1994; Ryle & Kerr, 2003). Fundamentally, CAT is a relational model that invites individuals to consider the ways that they relate to themselves and to others, and to take an active part in observing and understanding their relational patterns and the effects that these might have on their lives and the lives of others. The therapy focuses particularly on relational patterns (often developed early in life) that have led to current self-defeating or problematic thoughts, feelings and behaviours, and to developing a validating and non-blaming description of how and why these developed jointly with the therapist. The process of reflecting together allows the patient to begin to revise, develop and practice alternative and more adaptive relational patterns. CAT is a practical, time-limited intervention that aims to assist patients to develop a conceptual model of their own difficulties, thereby allowing them to become their own therapist in the future.

CAT facilitates three important processes over the course of therapy; 'reformulation', 'recognition' and 'revision'. Reformulation is the first and the most important, and involves the therapist and patient constructing together an explanation that links and reframes the problems and their relational origins. The therapist seeks to engage the patient in a qualitative exploration of current symptoms or problems, in terms of the associated thoughts, feelings, behaviours, and the meaning associated with these, and then links these to current, as well as early, relational experiences.

Early in the therapy, a plain language, written reformulation letter is collaboratively developed, and then read out and discussed with the patient. The letter aims to validate the patient's life narrative, especially any adverse and painful experiences, and to begin to link these to any self-defeating patterns and current problems bringing the patient to therapy. It can be particularly helpful for the patient to discover that the current problems arise from past attempts to solve a difficulty. For example, a man who can reframe his problematic drinking as emerging from his earlier attempt to manage intense loneliness and disconnection as an adolescent, can take a less critical and more compassionate position in relation to himself. Rewriting the patient's past formulation of his difficulties in a non-blaming way opens up a clearer path to change. The reformulation process is central to CAT and guides the rest of the work. Rather than try to capture the patient's whole life story, the reformulation aims to focus on what has led to the current problems, to identify an achievable set of goals for the therapy and to anticipate any problems that might impede the therapy. In contrast to a standard psychiatric formulation, the 'reformulation' is developed jointly with the patient, using the patient's own language. Reading out the reformulation letter together often marks a turning point in the therapy, as the patient feels heard and more deeply understood, and the letter sets out for discussion the subsequent tasks and goals of therapy.

The diagrammatic version of the reformulation tends to focus on the current form of the problematic relational patterns, rather than their developmental origins, which are described in more detail in the letter. The reformulation, especially the diagrammatic formulation, is amended and added to over time, as the joint understanding is enriched and deepened. The letters and diagrams are the tools of reformulation and underpin the subsequent important process of 'recognition' of the problematic patterns, and then 'revision' of these patterns, in which new, alternative, and more adaptive patterns are discovered and practised.

During the middle phase of therapy, much of the focus is on facilitating the patient's capacity to identify patterns that are occurring outside of the therapeutic relationship, and, increasingly, to distinguish what is being enacted within the therapy. The therapist-patient relationship is used to explore, to reflect upon, and to practise more adaptive relational patterns. The experience of enacting more adaptive relational patterns with the therapist provides the patient with an experience of a 'good enough', compassionate and benign carer, an experience that can be used as a model for future relationships. The very process of thinking about, reviewing, and exploring this new kind of relationship with the therapist, itself enhances the reflective skills of the patient. At the end of the therapy, both patient and therapist write each other a final letter that gives an opportunity for both to reflect on the progress, achievements and process of therapy from their own points of view.

CAT is a time-limited model in which the contract for the number of sessions is set at the beginning. The most common contract is for 16 sessions, but smaller contracts of 12 and 8 are often used. Longer contracts of 24 are recommended for complex presentations such as severe personality disorder or anorexia nervosa (Ryle, 2004). Therefore, by the end of the therapy, it is unlikely (and not expected) that all problems will be fully resolved. Rather, it is hoped for and planned that the patient will have developed a clearer understanding of how their problems developed, and how they are being maintained. Ideally, the patient will have some experience of doing things differently while undergoing therapy. These 'exits', such as responding to him/herself in a new way, and responding to others in new ways, are drawn on the map as alternatives to the problematic RRs. This process of identifying and then revising problematic relational patterns aims at allowing the new relational responses ('exits') to become increasingly familiar and automatic, thereby adding to the patient's repertoire of relational patterns. As the end of therapy approaches, the responsibility for continuing the work of therapy is progressively handed over to the patient. The therapist uses the time limit actively to keep the therapy 'on track' and moving. At the same time, the therapist is working on keeping the goals achievable and within the patient's capacities (Leiman, 1994). The therapist must pay attention to how the patient is understanding and using the therapy. In order to be most effective, the therapist must be able to 'tune in' and to maximize their collaboration. By the end of the CAT contract, the aim is for some new and more positive and adaptive relational patterns to have been identified, explored, and added to the diagram.

Sometimes, the patient will not have made as much progress as either he/she, the therapist, or others in the patient's life might have wanted. Many patients, and indeed therapists, can struggle with acceptance of, and readiness for, the end of therapy. CAT is an explicitly time-limited model, and the planned ending allows and promotes exploration of these expectations and the feelings associated with them (e.g., sadness, regret, anger) from the outset. By raising the ending early on, rather than allowing avoidance of the discomfort or pain associated with ending, the patient has an opportunity to plan for it, to explore it, and to experience a tolerable, manageable, and hopefully a 'good enough' ending.

COGNITIVE ANALYTIC THERAPY (CAT) MODEL OF DEVELOPMENT AND PSYCHOPATHOLOGY

CAT has attempted to integrate new and evolving knowledge about the biopsychosocial underpinnings of development and developmental psychopathology. Infants are born with a biological predisposition to seek out social interaction, rather than being a naïve 'blank slate' (Reddy, 2008). The interpersonal and self-management patterns, arising from the interaction of the infant's temperament with its parents' or caregivers' own personality styles, can either facilitate normal development or create difficulties. It is understood that these 'dyadic' early relationships are internalized, and that these shape the way the developing infant relates to others and to themselves. In CAT, these dyadic relationship patterns (called reciprocal roles; RR) are a core concept of the model. Thus, CAT has a radically social view of the self, in which the 'self' is considered to be a collection of internalized reciprocal roles that are acquired throughout early and subsequent development (Ryle, 1985).

Thus, a child who experiences their parents as loving and nurturing, and feels secure and loved in response, will simultaneously internalize the parental or 'other' experience (loving) as well as the child's 'self' experience (loved). Because both poles of this relationship are internalized, this child knows how to enact both, to be loving, and how it is to feel loved. The child also knows how to elicit loving responses from others. As they develop, they will be able to enact similar patterns of being nurturing and caring towards themselves and others. They will also know how to express their needs to elicit care from others. Therefore, the child who has had a range of appropriate and 'good enough' caring experiences during early life is more likely to be able to cope with adverse situations when they arise. Such children are likely to have developed a range of appropriate and adaptive ways to seek help or care when it is needed, which they will enact and revise over time, adapting to new experiences and circumstances.

The number, range and quality of reciprocal roles that an individual experiences and internalizes throughout their life will shape how adaptively they can respond to others and to their own internal experiences. When development is suboptimal, and early care-giving interactions are harsh, critical or punitive, the relationship patterns that are internalized and re-enacted with oneself and others are also likely to be harsh and punitive.

A second key concept in CAT arose from the observation that all goal-directed activity, including behaviours, thoughts, and feelings, can be described in terms of a procedural sequence model (PSM): first, the context one finds oneself in is appraised, the options for action and possible consequences of the action are considered, a plan is selected, and finally the assumptions are either revised or confirmed (Ryle, 1991). Many patients present to therapy with self-defeating or maladaptive patterns of thinking, feeling and acting. The CAT therapist is interested in assisting the patient to notice their maladaptive patterns (procedural sequences), and to identify the interpersonal relationships (the reciprocal roles) that have precipitated them. Together, these patterns are called Reciprocal Role Procedures (RRPs), because they represent the way that reciprocal relationships (RRs) are enacted.

To expand on the previous example, a boy who has experienced appropriate care will be able to cope when he first starts school because, although he feels sad at the separation from his mother, he will be able to elicit caring responses from others (e.g., the teacher, who engages him in an activity as his mother leaves) or he will be able to soothe himself (e.g., by reminding himself that his mother will collect him at the end of the day). In contrast, a boy who has had harsh and punitive developmental experiences might feel abandoned and that nothing can bring his mother back (and so cry inconsolably) or he might become angry with her for leaving (and so act aggressively towards his peers).

In CAT, it is explicitly acknowledged to the patient that the recurring patterns (RRPs) with which they are struggling can be seen as the product of their earlier attempts to manage or cope with difficult developmental experiences. Often, these coping strategies or patterns were somewhat effective, or at least understandable, responses to past experiences but which have now become less effective or frankly maladaptive. Therefore, in CAT, psychopathology is seen to be the result of a lack of revision of these procedural sequences (i.e., despite the evidence, the patient continues to act in a self-defeating way). Having developed these patterns early in our lives, they are usually familiar and automatic, and tend to be re-enacted without much active thought or reflection. Therefore, an explicit aim in CAT is to develop the reflective capacity of the patient and to assist the active review of their problematic patterns.

To assist this process, Ryle described three common types of maladaptive procedures in simple terms that would allow patients to more easily notice and identify them:

- 'Traps' refer to patterns of behaviour that serve to confirm the patient's negative assumptions about him/herself or others – a vicious circle. An example of this is the assumption that one is hopeless and can't do well, which leads to poor motivation, poor performance and self-criticism of one's performance, thus proving the original negative thoughts that one is hopeless and can't do well.
- 'Dilemmas' refer to highly polarized choices, in which the patient believes that their only alternatives for relating to self and others are binary, extreme and/or dysfunctional. For example, either I bottle my feelings up and feel unheard or I explode and hurt others.
- 'Snags' are particularly self-defeating assumptions that lead the patient to abandon his/her appropriate goals. For example, a patient sabotages a positive relationship because he/she does not believe that he/she deserves care.

The process of identifying the most problematic patterns can be facilitated early in the therapy by providing patients with a list of common traps, dilemmas and snags (summarized in the Psychotherapy File (Ryle & Kerr, 2003)), and asking them to endorse those with which they struggle. They are also encouraged to modify the wording or to bring examples of novel patterns to more accurately describe their own experiences. The process of working through this list either together or in between sessions demonstrates to the patient, from the beginning, that therapy will involve a process of reflecting on one's own behaviour, thoughts and feelings, and considering the consequences of these procedural patterns. Modifications and novel patterns also demonstrate that the therapist is interested in the patient's unique (idiographic) experience, rather than entirely a priori assumptions about the nature of relationship patterns.

THE ATTRIBUTES OF COGNITIVE ANALYTIC THERAPY (CAT) FORMULATION OF PERSONALITY DISORDER

The particular aspects of the CAT approach that lend themselves to the formulation and treatment of both personality disorder and young people are summarized here:

- The therapeutic position is one of curiosity and collaboration, in which the therapist aims to 'do with' rather than to 'do to' the patient.
  - The formulation of presenting problems is collaboratively developed, and is based on the patient's descriptions and words, rather than based on a predetermined model.
  - Any links made by the therapist between past and present relational patterns are tentatively presented to the patient for consideration, rather than assumed always to be correct.
  - The patient is considered to be 'doing the best they can', given their context and previous relational experiences.
- CAT is active for both therapist and patient
  - The therapist is more like a partner or coach, rather than an all-knowing expert and the reformulation is a joint articulation of the explanation and setting of goals for the therapy.
  - The therapist aims to provide a 'good enough', compassionate caring relational experience, thus expanding the patient's repertoire of RRs (which constitute the patient's self)
  - A goal of therapy is to foster autonomy and to facilitate a sense of agency in the patient and to enhance reflective capacity.
  - Encouraging 'thinking about thinking' through the process of 'reformulating' and jointly using the tools of CAT in the room.
- The reformulation predicts that some patterns might be enacted during the therapy, thus allowing the therapist to more easily talk about transference and countertransference (in terms of enactments of RRPs).

CAT has particular advantages when working with patients traditionally considered to be challenging or complex, such as those with a personality disorder or intellectual disability, or those with complex co-occurring (comorbid) problems. Its integrative and 'transdiagnostic' approach encompasses the range of difficulties that might be experienced at any time (e.g., psychiatric disorders or psychosocial problems) within the overall treatment model, rather than seeking separate intervention. Also, CAT sees 'psychological mindedness' as a goal of therapy, rather than a prerequisite, allowing it to be used with patients who would traditionally be unlikely to be considered 'therapy ready'. Finally, while CAT is essentially a talking-based therapy, the model can be modified for use with less verbal patients or for those with intellectual/learning difficulties, and can also encompass a range of other approaches (e.g., behavioural (Clayton & Lloyd, 2013)). CAT's relational formulation can also be used indirectly to manage very complex patients, especially helping clinicians avoid colluding with maladaptive and unhelpful relational patterns (Caruso et al., 2013; Kellet et al., 2014; Kerr, 1999).

COGNITIVE ANALYTIC THERAPY (CAT) MODEL OF BORDERLINE PERSONALITY DISORDER

Ryle's **multiple self-states model** describes three specific forms of difficulty in borderline personality disorder (BPD) (Ryle, 2004). Firstly, the person's repertoire of reciprocal roles is likely to be restricted to a small number of particularly harsh, critical, neglecting and punishing roles, resulting in a small number of extreme and inflexible options for relating to both self and others. Secondly, the self-states (each pole of the reciprocal role, e.g., 'abused victim', 'enraged abuser' or 'neglectful carer') are less integrated than in well-functioning individuals. Therefore the patient with BPD is more likely to shift between these states rapidly, unpredictably and dramatically, reporting intense changes in mood and behaviour associated with these states, and feeling less aware of other possible states outside of the one currently being enacted or experienced. This dissociation between the self-states then also leads to the third problem of poor capacity for self-reflection, which in turn results in difficulty learning from experience, and poor revision of maladaptive or self-defeating procedures. CAT's collaborative, integrative and relational approach is well suited to rectifying these issues.

THE PROCESS OF REFORMULATION

The CAT approach to formulation starts with the aim of understanding the patient's current difficulties and the relational patterns underlying them, and by collecting qualitative information about the origins of these patterns. Most commonly, the patient will start by describing the problems or symptoms being experienced currently, and the therapist will start to notice the relational patterns that are maladaptive, self-defeating or maintaining the problems. The therapist suggests and tests out possible links with early relational experiences and attempts to construct with the patient's help, a narrative that explains the likely origins of the problems in a non-blaming way. The therapist must work within the capacities of the patient to achieve optimal change. The therapeutic relationship itself is seen as an opportunity for a reparative relational experience (thus expanding the collection of internalized RRs) and is used as a model to reflect on and to explore what a compassionate and 'good enough' caring experience might feel like. The formulation also includes some anticipation that the self-defeating relational patterns are likely to be enacted at some point in the therapy and can be reflected upon and discussed if and when that occurs.

APPLYING COGNITIVE ANALYTIC THERAPY (CAT) TO A CASE EXAMPLE

Case Example: Laura

Laura was an 18-year-old female university student referred following her presentation to the emergency department with a paracetamol overdose. She was seen the following day for assessment and reported she had been experiencing difficulties on and off since the age of 14. These included episodes of major depression, generalized anxiety symptoms, fluctuating suicidal ideation and a history of intermittent self-harm. She also reported longstanding problems indicative of personality disorder features including extreme perfectionism that got in the way of completing tasks, and a need to keep things ordered (obsessive compulsive personality disorder features), as well as mood instability, relationship instability, self-harm and frantic efforts to avoid abandonment (BPD features).

Laura was able to describe the current patterns occurring but was less clear about the origins of patterns, and therefore this was explored more gradually. She was asked more exploratory questions about events leading up to her referral, particularly what she was thinking, feeling and what she had wanted from others. Laura reported having felt particularly stressed and emotional over the past few weeks since her exams had finished. Without classes to attend, she often felt at a loss. She followed her friends' activities online, but this tended to exacerbate her experience of feeling left out and lonely. She had attended a number of parties, drank a lot more alcohol than usual and had been more confrontational with her friends. She reported a number of incidents in which she had said things that were misinterpreted by others, that led to online fights and her feeling hopeless and completely ostracized by her social group. She was angry with her friends as well as with herself for messing everything up. She had increasing thoughts of suicide and finally acted on her plan to end her life by taking 150 paracetamol tablets (75 g). She had some doubts and sent a text message to her cousin who called the ambulance that took her to hospital. This procedural pattern was able to be mapped onto an early diagram with Laura to help her begin to identify the triggering state, viz. feeling lonely and ignored. She could acknowledge quite clearly that she wanted connection and care from her friends but had not clearly let this be known. By pretending all was fine, she had continued to feel ignored and uncared for. Laura felt a bit surprised to see that what she thought was an appropriate action (to be stoic and to cope alone) kept her feeling stuck and lonely. The therapist observed that it seemed the self-harm was her best effort to cope at that time. She was also interested in whether Laura would immediately become self-critical, or whether she would be able to take a more compassionate stance towards herself at this point. When Laura was silent, the therapist was able to use this opportunity to gently bring herself and their relationship into the room, by reflecting openly about her own feelings of ambivalence about probing too much or too quickly, and her doubts about how to support Laura at this early stage of the therapy.

This openness led to Laura feeling more confident to go on, and to her agreeing that self-criticism was unhelpful. They then began to map the more problematic procedural pattern that led to the overdose. Early on she could report that she believed at the time that she had to 'do something dramatic' to get a response from others to her desperate feelings of loneliness. However, she was unable to identify her self-defeating belief that she did not deserve care, unless she demonstrated she was extremely distressed (by harming herself or attempting suicide). With early mapping work, the therapist is particularly interested in capturing patterns that could potentially interfere with the therapy. In this instance, the therapist was able to begin to talk to Laura about her expectations of care from the therapist. They discussed how Laura might be able to let her know if she felt let down or wanted more from the therapist, without having to resort to doing something dramatic. Laura was able to have this discussion without feeling ashamed and so was able to agree to try to talk about it, should she notice this.

The next step was to begin to try to collect a more qualitative understanding of Laura's history to try to understand how these patterns arose. Laura reported that life had seemed 'fine' until she was about 10 years old. She felt close to her mother, although her mother was often ill, and she got on well with her brother, who was six years older than her and was protective of her. She recalled not having a strong sense of her father being around, reflecting that perhaps he was away a lot for work. With some gentle questioning, Laura was able to talk about her fears about her mother's illness and she recalled an incident in which her mother had been rushed to hospital, and when she arrived home from school the house was empty and she felt terrified and alone. She and her therapist were able to agree that her early experiences were therefore characterized by a sense of feeling 'cared for' by her mother and brother, but that she had also often had an accompanying sense of unease about life being 'unpredictable' and that at any moment she might be left alone and uncared for. This led to a discussion about one of the goals for the remaining therapy. Laura agreed that she wanted to reduce her feelings of anxiety about how much people cared about her, and to identify how she could feel more cared for. The therapy contract was set for 16 sessions and they agreed to revisit this goal regularly, as Laura felt anxious about ending therapy.

The next few sessions were aimed at working towards the reformulation. Together the therapist and Laura explored the possible links between her early relational experiences with her parents, and the procedural patterns she developed as a way to manage uncomfortable feelings, building up a narrative that explained in non-blaming terms, how and why she was feeling stuck now. Laura recalled that by the age of 10, her parents were fighting a lot, and she was aware of the tension in the relationship. She felt she had to tiptoe around the house to avoid setting her father into a rage, therefore her early attempts to manage this stress were aimed at pleasing her parents. Given her parents' own difficulties, it was unlikely that they were able to notice her attempts, leaving her feeling lonely and unloved. Laura found it much easier to seek approval and attention from her teachers and so became very focused on maintaining her academic grades, and on keeping her world in order. These strategies were understood in therapy as attempts to feel in control at a time that often felt very out of her control. The situation deteriorated further, with Laura's parents separating and her brother moving out. Laura attempted to care for her ill and highly distressed mother, however, this also failed and finally Laura was left in the care of her distant and angry father. She did what she could around the house to please and care for him, but she experienced him as always angry and critical, and felt neglected and ignored. She blamed herself for her predicament and began to self-harm as a way of managing her self-loathing. She found her peer relationships complex and difficult to understand, feeling alternately judged and ignored by her friends, and disappointed by their lack of sympathy. She didn't tell anyone about the situation believing it would overwhelm and harm her mother. She felt guilty about having let others down, and believed that she should be able to manage on her own, berating herself when others offered support. At the same time, she desperately wanted care and attention, and became more and more angry when others were not able to respond in the 'right way', or provide enough of the care she hoped for.

In preparation for writing the Reformulation Letter, the therapist and Laura had noticed two strong relational themes, and through the exploration had been able to link the current enactments to the patterns' origins. The first theme that Laura reported often feeing criticized/controlled and punished by others. Initially they observed that this RR had developed in relation to her father. She identified she felt stupid and pathetic and that her life was out of her control in response. The therapist was curious about whether Laura might recognize that she was enacting the same RR (criticizing/punishing) both towards herself and to others. The therapist was careful to take a non-blaming approach, by explaining that the process of modelling from parents would be understandable. Laura was initially somewhat surprised, commenting that she had never thought about her actions in this way. She found the self-to-self enactment of this pattern easier to identify than her being criticizing of others. The therapist was aware that suggesting this in itself might trigger her self-criticism. This allowed them to talk about the aim of therapy being to reflect with less blame and criticism. This focus on the therapeutic relationship also allowed the therapist to be able to bring some personal reflection about her experience of the other end of that pattern (in terms of her feeling the need to avoid Laura's criticism). The use of gentle humour and some normalizing of criticizing patterns was helpful and allowed Laura to feel supported by the discussion rather than further criticized. This was later labelled by Laura as the 'Criticizing/Striving Pattern'. As they started to define the emerging pattern in their discussion together, the therapist started to write/draw the patterns on a blank page. The emerging diagram sat between them on a table during the session, and the therapist gave Laura a copy of the latest version to take away each week.

The second theme that was emerging in Laura's story was one in which she often felt neglected and ignored. Laura could acknowledge she felt highly anxious about the care she received from others and worried a lot about it disappearing. Together they discovered that this pattern had originated as a result of her mother's illness and her perception that her father was disinterested in her. Over time, Laura's expectations of care increased, and she focused more and more on how to find and keep the care she so desperately wanted. She also became more likely to judge care offered as inadequate and reject it (thereby enacting the neglecting/ignoring RR self-to-other). With her therapists' help, she realized that when she pretended she was 'fine' but in fact neglected her own needs (a self-to-self enactment), this led to her blaming herself for being undeserving (back to the first RR). She convinced herself that she could only deserve care if she were spectacularly unwell. She felt she had to self-harm and take large overdoses when she was distressed, rather than to let others know her distress in less dramatic ways. This was later labelled the 'Seeking Care Pattern'.

From the outset, the therapist felt a strong pressure to 'get it right', usually in response to Laura's nonverbal communications of irritation, and occasional overt expression of displeasure when she felt that the therapist had misunderstood her or felt she was taking over. On several occasions at the end of the session, the therapist found herself wondering if she had been too challenging or directive with Laura, and whether this would affect the therapeutic relationship. Initially, Laura had some trouble identifying her feelings. However, as she started to feel less fearful about her therapist exposing her, she was able to allow herself to risk feeling vulnerable and speak more openly.

LAURA'S REFORMULATION LETTER

The reformulation Letter was written to Laura by the therapist and read out at the fifth session.

Dear Laura,

I am writing this letter to check that we have a shared understanding of what we think has contributed to you coming to see me. It would be good to hear your thoughts about this and whether you think I have understood things well enough. This does not have to be the final version, we can change anything I have wrong or you can write back in your own words if you wish.

You have come to see me because you feel stuck. It seems that the last three years have been particularly difficult for you. Increasingly you worry about how much people care for you, and this has led to you harming yourself when overwhelmed. This marks a return to something you had done in the past, and you feel angry with yourself for slipping back, making it even harder to stop. Although you have been involved with psychiatric services on and off over the last four years, you feel let down and angry that things are not better for you.

We have talked about how you grew up in a family in which you had a place with your cousins living nearby and an older brother who protected you. You remember feeling really shocked when your mum and dad decided to separate. Although they had been arguing a lot, you didn't imagine it might lead to them breaking up, so this was understandably a very difficult, confusing time. Your mother was very distressed and was struggling to cope, and at thirteen you often found yourself looking after her by yourself. This must have been a very sad and lonely time, when no one was there for you, and everything felt out of control. Importantly, you felt unable to let others, especially your mum, see this sadness. You were terrified about what would happen if you were to fall apart like your mother, so you pretended you were OK, even when you were not. Perhaps people couldn't respond to your needs because they didn't know how you felt? You have said that secretly, you were longing for someone else to step in and look after you. However, when others do step in, it doesn't feel quite as you had hoped.

We have discovered together that the focus on trying to do things perfectly, began as a way to stay in control of your life. This seemed to work and people, especially teachers, noticed and encouraged you. But it also led to a constant striving and a pervasive fear that their attention would disappear (and perhaps also doubts about whether you were good enough?). You became increasingly critical and angry with yourself, and it eventually developed into a need to punish yourself through cutting your arms. This brought relief but it was short-lived, and the cycle of striving started again. Your distress often felt overwhelming, and you worried it would be too much for others. So you hid your feelings from everyone, partly to protect them, but also perhaps because you felt guilty and weak? You felt you didn't deserve to have needs or emotions. You became an expert at covering things up and locking your emotions away. This left you really stuck, feeling unheard and unloved, and with striving and overworking or self-punishment as the only ways to deal with this. We have started to talk about how you feel trapped in this pattern now.

This has led to us beginning to explore what you want from others. It seems you hope and perhaps even sometimes expect them to be able to guess what you need? However, because you pretend to be OK and perhaps even push away care because it makes you feel pathetic and guilty, the people around you ultimately don't recognize when you are distressed. This confirms your belief that they don't care about you and that you deserve this, leaving you feeling lonely and ignored. It seems that this pattern has led to you continuing to feel unloved and unsupported, and to you needing to do more and more dramatic things in order to deserve care.

So far we have discussed our goal in therapy as being to look out for, and to think about changing, the following patterns.

The seeking care pattern. When feeling lonely and uncared for, it is understandable that you should want care from others, but we have found out that a big problem is that you also believe that you don't deserve it. You feel like you only have two choices: either you bottle your feelings up, 'pretend to cope' and get nothing because no one realizes you need anything; or you feel you can only deserve care if things are very, very bad. So you do something very dramatic, you cut yourself or take an overdose. You hope people will notice and respond in a caring way. Sometimes it works… but perhaps not entirely (the wrong care from the wrong people?) and this can result in you pushing care away. This can also lead to others stepping in and taking over from you. It seems to me that neither of these strategies really gets you what you want. You feel upset and guilty and continue to feel bad. Sadly, sometimes you get the opposite of what you want: criticism, punishment or others controlling you. This leads to the next pattern we have talked about.

The criticizing/striving pattern. When feeling criticized and pathetic, you understandably feel bad, and therefore long for some recognition. You are smart and have learned that people notice hard work. However, it seems striving to be the best has become an empty goal. It doesn't leave you feeling satisfied, but has you criticize yourself more and more harshly. Because you don't believe that you deserve care and attention just for being who you are, it seems it is always conditional. You can only deserve attention/care if you have performed faultlessly, or you are really unwell.

I hope we can think more about these patterns over the remaining weeks, to try and find better ways for you to get what you want. We have already started to notice some moments when you have done something a bit differently, and have not automatically repeated these cycles. I know it is not always easy to talk about these things, but I also know you would like to have relationships in which you feel valued for who you are and you would like to feel less pressured.

I also wonder if we should watch out for these patterns potentially emerging in our work together. For example, you might hope I can anticipate the kind of care you want, and then feel disappointed when I don't get it right.

Laura, I think we have made a good start. I feel confident that with continued discussion, our work together can help you to progress towards these goals.

I look forward to hearing what you think of this.

Kind regards, (Therapist)

REMAINDER OF THE THERAPY

After this session, subsequent work involved refining the diagram (see Fig. 6.1), assisting Laura to recognize unhelpful patterns when interacting with others and then starting to look for alternative ways to respond. The main RR (that of criticizing/controlling/punishing-to-feeling pathetic/stupid/out of control) was explored and Laura was increasingly able to identify examples in which she enacted these patterns with others, or herself through her self-critical thoughts and her self-punishing episodes of cutting. The therapist and Laura were also able to discuss how this 'criticizing/striving pattern' was commonly enacted by the health system. The therapist was able to share how she felt a strong invitation to become controlling at times when Laura was not caring for herself. They were also able to talk about the times when Laura enacted the top pole of the RR by being either criticizing or controlling towards others. After further discussion, the 'seeking care pattern' was added to Laura's diagram, which led to a gradual exploration of her hopes and expectations of care, particularly why she always felt disappointed with others' efforts to care for her.

Each week Laura and her therapist were able to use the examples during the week to further refine their understanding of the patterns, and record this diagrammatically. They explored earlier experiences particularly those that may have shaped Laura's critical beliefs about herself being stupid and pathetic, and the fears associated with the idea that others would leave her. The most self-defeating of these led to self-harm and giving up. Laura was able to use the conversations and reflections in therapy to take a more realistic and compassionate view of how these beliefs had emerged. They were then able to focus increasingly on the alternate relational patterns, and a new RR of accepting/respecting-to-feeling accepted/'good enough' was added to the diagram. This emerged from discussion of her experiences of trying new ways

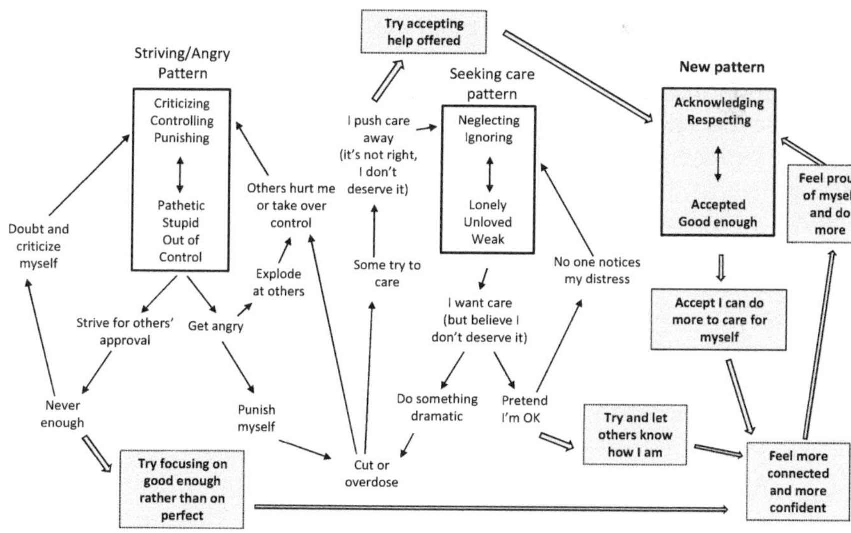

FIGURE 6.1 Laura's final diagrammatic reformulation with new more adaptive ways of relating (exits), *marked in bold.*

of relating in vivo with the therapist, with herself and outside therapy with others. Given some of the more extreme patterns were triggered by Laura's need for care, this was explicitly discussed, and realistic needs for support and love were normalized. More adaptive and effective strategies for seeking care were examined and Laura was able to come up with some on her own.

By the end of the therapy, Laura was pleased with her increased knowledge about herself. She felt calmer about ending the therapy, seeing it as an opportunity to try out her new skills. She acknowledged that she felt some anxiety, but that she also had several follow-up appointments booked and knew how to re-contact if necessary. She had a number of activities in which she was engaged, including a part-time job. She was no longer harming herself and she was feeling more comfortable about asking for help from family and friends. At follow-up, she was feeling happy with her progress and increasing sense of autonomy. She had not harmed herself for almost a year, was dating, had completed the semester at university and was looking for full-time work over the summer.

CONCLUSIONS

CAT is a time-limited psychotherapy in which the therapist invites the patient into a collaborative, non-blaming relationship, from which they then reflect on how internalized harsh and punitive relational patterns are enacted in self-defeating and maladaptive ways. The experience of a realistic, compassionate and 'good enough' therapeutic relationship is internalized by the patient (expanding the relational self) and is used as a model for possible future relationships. The accuracy and validity of the process of reformulation in capturing the core relationship themes has been demonstrated (Bennett & Parry, 1998), as has the impact of reformulation in therapy with patients considered 'difficult to help' (Evans & Parry, 1996). The development of the tools, the reformulation letter and the sequential diagrammatic version of the reformulation allow for modelling of the reflective process, management of enactments of unhelpful patterns and provides an opportunity for therapy to proceed at the patient's pace. This is particularly important when discussing highly sensitive interpersonal patterns, of the sequelae of trauma and abuse and allows the therapy to be grounded and address patients' goals (Chanen et al., 2008; Clarke, 2013; Clarke, Thomas, & James, 2013; Richardson, 2012).

Acknowledgements

A number of details of the case description (specifics about the presenting problems, personal and family history as well as some of the wording in the letter and diagram) were changed so as to protect client privacy.

References

Bennett, D., & Parry, G. (1998). The accuracy of reformulation in cognitive analytic therapy: A validation study. *Psychotherapy Research, 8*(1), 84–103.

Caruso, R., Biancosino, B., Borghi, C., Marmai, L., Kerr, I. B., & Grassi, L. (2013). Working with the "difficult" patient: The use of a contextual cognitive-analytic therapy based training in improving team function in a routine psychiatry service setting. *Community Mental Health Journal, 49*, 722–727.

Chanen, A. M., Jackson, H. J., McCutcheon, L. K., Jovev, M., Dudgeon, P., Yuen, H. P., et al. (2008). Early intervention for adolescents with borderline personality disorder using cognitive analytic therapy: Randomised controlled trial. *British Journal of Psychiatry, 193*(06), 477–484.

Clarke, S. (2013). *A comparison of 24-session cognitive analytic therapy and treatment as usual for participants with a personality disorder*. https://doi.org/10.1186/isrctn79596618. http://isrctn.org.

Clarke, S., Thomas, P., & James, K. (2013). Cognitive analytic therapy for personality disorder: Randomised controlled trial. *British Journal of Psychiatry, 202*(02), 129–134.

Clayton, P., & Lloyd, J. (2013). *Cognitive analytic therapy for people with intellectual disabilities and their carers*. Jessica Kingsley Publishers.

Evans, J., & Parry, G. (1996). The impact of reformulation in cognitive-analytic therapy with difficult to help clients. *Clinical Psychology and Psychotherapy, 3*, 109–117.

Kellett, S., Wilbram, M., Davis, C., & Hardy, G. (2014). Team consultancy using cognitive analytic therapy: A controlled study in assertive outreach. *Journal of Psychiatric and Mental Health Nursing, 21*, 687–697.

Kerr, I. B. (1999). Cognitive-analytic therapy for borderline personality disorder in the context of a community mental health team: Individual and organizational psychodynamic implications. *British Journal of Psychotherapy, 15*(4), 425–438.

Leiman, M. (1994). The development of cognitive analytic therapy. *International Journal of Short-Term Psychotherapy* (2/3), 67–82.

Reddy, V. (2008). *How infants know minds*. Harvard University Press.

Richardson, P. (2012). *A randomised controlled trial (RCT) to assess the incremental costs and clinical benefits of cognitive analytic therapy (CAT) to standard care within community mental health teams in the treatment of severe personality disorder*. https://doi.org/10.1186/isrctn88887622. http://isrctn.org.

Ryle, A. (1985). Cognitive theory, object relations and the self. *The British Journal of Medical Psychology, 58*(1), 1–7.

Ryle, A. (1991). Object relations theory and activity theory: A proposed link by way of the procedural sequence model. *The British Journal of Medical Psychology, 64*(Pt 4), 307–316.

Ryle, A. (2004). The contribution of cognitive analytic therapy to the treatment of borderline personality disorder. *Journal of Personality Disorders, 18*(1), 3–35.

Ryle, A., & Kerr, I. B. (2003). *Introducing cognitive analytic therapy: Principles and practice*. John Wiley & Sons.

Further Reading

Ryle, A. (1997). *Cognitive analytic therapy and borderline personality disorder: The model and the method*. Wiley.

CHAPTER

7

Case Conceptualization in Clarification-Oriented Psychotherapy

Rainer Sachse

IPP, Institut für Psychologische Psychotherapie, Bochum, Germany

WHAT IS CLARIFICATION-ORIENTED PSYCHOTHERAPY?

Clarification-oriented psychotherapy (COP) is a psychologically founded, empirically validated psychotherapy form developed from the process-oriented approach of client-centred psychotherapy (cf. Greenberg, 1984, 2002; Rice, 1974; Rice & Greenberg, 1984; Truax, 1963, 1968) and from cognitive psychotherapy (Beck, Rush, Shaw, & Emery, 1981).

Extensive and detailed process research was carried out within the scope of COP (cf. Sachse, 1990a, 1990b, 1992a, 1998; Sachse & Sachse, 2016a, 2016b, 2016c, 2016d, 2016e) on the basis of which essential therapeutic principles were developed:

1. The processes of clarifying relevant dysfunctional schemas (client's assumptions that are automatically activated and then influence information processing and action regulation) are very important for a successful therapy.
2. Without help, a deep, detailed and comprehensive clarification of schemas is difficult or even impossible for clients.
3. Clients need the expert and constructive guidance by therapists in this clarification process.
4. Therapists can use targeted interventions to control the processes of clients in a well-aimed and specific manner and in this way 'catalyze' the clarification of schemas.
5. Clarification requires a trusting therapist-client relationship.

Case Formulation for Personality Disorders
https://doi.org/10.1016/B978-0-12-813521-1.00007-2

6. This can be built up through a targeted relationship formation adopted by the therapist: the therapist behaves 'complementary', i.e., they systematically 'comply with' and are appreciative of the client's central relationship motives within the framework of the therapeutic rules.
7. However, clarified schemas have to be further processed cognitively and emotionally, with a view to inhibiting dysfunctional schemas and enabling new functional schemas to be developed.
8. A cognitive-emotional technique, the so-called one-person role play, has been developed for this purpose and has proven to be effective.
9. Clients exhibiting specific disorders (e.g., depression, psychosomatic illnesses, personality disorders) need specific types of supplementary interventions as for example building motivation for change, systematic elaboration of avoidance processes, etc.
10. In various empirical studies, the effectiveness of COP could be proven, e.g., for the treatment of depression (Sachse, Sachse, & Diermann, 2018), psychosomatic disorders (Sachse & Sachse, 2016d), and in particular for personality disorders (Sachse & Sachse, 2016a, 2016b, 2016c, 2016d).

An absolutely central element of COP is *clarification*: on the basis of a trustful therapist–client relationship actively established by the therapist, the real motives of the clients they are presently unaware of are clarified with a view to eliminating the client's state of alienation; clarification also aims at representing and clarifying dysfunctional client schemas that are co-determining the problems encountered. Dysfunctional schemas are assumptions/convictions of clients whose activation leads to unfavourable interpretations, emotions and actions.

The second major task of COP deals with processing and modifying these clarified schemas therapeutically which enables the client to behave more constructively and flexibly during daily routines, exhibit less or none disturbing 'symptoms', better face up to everyday situations both cognitively and affectively, and thus lead a more satisfied self-regulative life.

The key objective of COP focuses on (re)establishing a functional *self-regulation* (Baumann & Kuhl, 2005): the client shall be put in a position that enables them access to their motives, appropriately deal with situations, take decisions that both comply with and face reality and are compatible with his/her motives. Moreover, the client shall perform processing and make decisions without disturbances caused by dysfunctional schemas, symptoms and unreasonable behavioural costs (e.g., health costs, interactional crises, dissatisfaction etc.).

To accomplish these objectives, COP is comprised of a number of subdomains that involve tasks the therapists have to accomplish and that require their expertise to be brought to bear in various fields.

Relationship Formation

One expertise domain in COP concerns the therapist's active and well-aimed approach to establish a relationship. For this purpose, a therapist may adopt strategies of the 'general relationship formation' or strategies of the 'complementary relationship formation', which may also be called, with slightly different elaborations, the motive-oriented therapeutic relationship (Caspar, 1986, 2000, 2006, 2007, 2008, 2009). By adopting these strategies, the therapist will build up a trustful therapist–client relationship that forms the basis for all clarification and processing work that follows (Sachse, 1995, 1999a, 2006b).

Clients with narcissistic personality disorder trust the therapist if they are convinced they will never be belittled or depreciated by the therapist. And this the therapist can achieve best by agreeing with and confirming with the client to indicate and make clear they recognize and appreciate the client's resources and success: if they do this, the client will, little by little, arrive at the conclusion the therapist perceives them in a positive way also when the therapist later on addresses 'problems' or 'inadequacies'.

Therefore, the therapist must show agreement with the client in this phase of therapy and this means: 'feed', feed, feed the client (with motive-consistent messages concerning his/her person and relationships)!

If the client demonstrates how 'great' they are, what they have accomplished, that he/she alone has saved his/her company, etc., the therapist appears to be impressed, and shows their great appreciation and agreement.

Creating Motivation for Change

Same as any other personality disorder a narcissistic disorder is 'ego-syntonic': the relevant aspects of the disorder are not at all perceived by the person as disturbing, as having to be changed. And for that reason, clients completely lack the motivation to work on these aspects therapeutically and as a result they do not have a 'working mission'. As much as they want to reduce their costs (e.g., emotional stress, constraints on the scope of action and behaviour, physical discomfort, and the like), they have no intention to change themselves: this is an extremely difficult starting situation for the therapists because costs that a system creates cannot be reduced without making changes to the system.

Therefore, generating the motivation to bring about changes is essential: not only must the client realize they *incur costs*, they must also accept that the *costs are relevant* and, above all, must understand *that they produce the costs themselves*. This is the only way to strengthen the clients' motivation to work on themselves (Sachse & Langens, 2015; Sachse, Langens & Sachse, 2012; Sachse, Sachse, & Fasbender, 2010, 2011, 2016)!

Clarification of Relevant Schemas

In this phase, all relevant schemas of the person contributing to the problem must be clarified, i.e., explicitly represented cognitively (cf. Sachse, 1992a, 1992b, 1993, 2003, 2004a, 2016).

And in doing so, a therapist should observe

- that schemas exist that stem from an assumption level ('I am a failure') and a contingency level ('if you are a failure, you will be rejected'),
- that schemas are complex, that is, they always consist of many interconnected assumptions, and
- that many assumptions the schema includes are not clear to the client or are avoided and that clarification processes must therefore be targeted and controlled.

It is important to clarify all four types of schemas:

- Self-schemas: Both the negative schema assumptions and the unrealistic positive schema assumptions have to be made clear.
- Relationship schemas: Assumptions about relationships that prevent clients from establishing a good relationship (and bond) should be clarified.
- Normative schemas: All normative schemas (and thus avoidance targets) should be clear, as they restrict, drive and put the client under massive pressure, etc.
- Rule schemas: The rules set by the client should also be made explicit and it should become clear what costs they generate.

Processing of Schemas

Once a schema has been sufficiently clarified, it can be systematically *processed*: it will then be questioned, refuted, inhibited and replaced by more constructive alternative schemas. For this purpose, a therapist can use cognitive techniques (Beck, 1979; Beck & Freeman, 1993) as well as emotionally affective techniques (Sachse, Püschel, Fasbender, & Breil, 2008).

We use these techniques as well as motivational techniques mostly within a therapeutic framework, a method called 'one-person role play' based on the different elaborations of the two-chair dialogue in psychotherapy: in this method, the client is instructed to be his or her own therapist and 'discuss' their schema with themselves or develop assumptions of his or her own (cf. Sachse, 1983, 2013, 2014, 2015c; Sachse, Breil, & Fasbender, 2009; Sachse & Fasbender, 2013; Sachse, Fasbender, Breil & Püschel, 2009).

Specific Therapeutic Interventions

Depending on the disturbance and the client, further specific interventions can be implemented at this point, e.g.,

- If clients exhibit a high degree of alienation, i.e., a poor representation of their own motives, a special training can be carried out with a view to reducing alienation.
- If clients show competence deficits, e.g., with respect to social competence or emotional regulation competence, then specific training measures can be adopted (Gross, 1999, 2002; Gross & Munoz, 1995).

Transfer

The clients should then be encouraged to apply everything they have learned in therapy in everyday life: a successful therapy means *that a client can think, feel and act differently in day-to-day life.*

Therefore, the therapist agrees with the client as soon as possible on concrete homework to be done by the client.

THE MODEL OF DUAL-ACTION REGULATION

Based on systematic analyses of clients with personality disorders, a general model of personality disorders has been developed, the Model of Dual-Action Regulation (MDAR); this model has proven to be both practical and empirical (Sachse, 2001, 2002, 2004b, 2006a, 2006b, 2008, 2013; Sachse, Fasbender, Breil & Sachse, 2012; Sachse, Fasbender, & Sachse, 2014; Sachse, Sachse, & Fasbender, 2011), which will serve as the basis of the case formulation in COP.

MDAR specifies which psychological variables play a role for the specific type of information processing and for the specific action regulation of persons suffering from personality disorders. And it also specifies how these variables interact. Characteristic features and peculiarities of individuals with personality disorders as well as basic therapeutic approaches can be derived from the model.

MDAR comprises three levels:

1. the level of the relationship motives or the authentic regulation of actions,
2. the level of the dysfunctional schemas, and
3. the level of nontransparent action, also known as the 'game level' or interactional manoeuvres (Fig. 7.1).

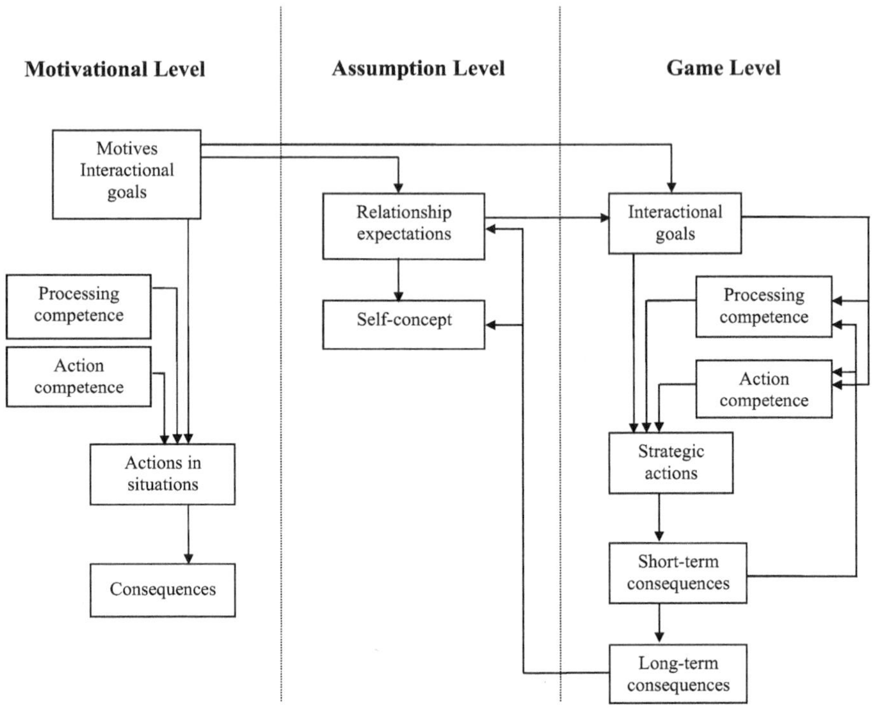

FIGURE 7.1 The model of dual-action regulation (MDAR).

Relationship Motives

The model assumes that a person, already as a child or adolescent, has a number of *central relationship motives,* such as the motive for recognition, importance, reliability, solidarity, autonomy, and boundaries/territoriality (for more information see Langens, 2009; Sachse, 1999b, 2006a; Sachse et al., 2009). These motives form a hierarchy, i.e., one motive is central (high in the hierarchy) for a certain person, others are still important to a certain degree and others are relatively unimportant (which relationship motives are central in each case also characterizes a specific personality disorder).

At the level of interactional goals, these motives are concretized and operationalized by a person in actual, situational goals.

The person now orchestrates his or her actions, in particular their *interactional actions,* with the aim of satisfying the central motives or the interactional goals derived from them, or more precisely: *to get them satisfied by others* (because they are 'motives for relationships', and these can only be satisfied by other persons). For this purpose, the person uses processing and action competences in his or her actions, and depending on how effectively the person acts, they experience positive consequences (the others behave in a motive-consistent manner, i.e., satisfying the motive) or negative consequences (others do not behave in a motive-consistent way or even act in a way that infringes the motive).

Dysfunctional Schemas

At the second level of the model, we assume that there are dysfunctional schemas that strongly determine the information processing and regulation of people's actions. We assume that a distinction can be made between two types of dysfunctional schemas: self-schemas and relationship schemas (cf. Sachse et al., 2009).

Self-schemas are those that contain assumptions of the person about themselves such as 'I am a failure', 'I am not important' as well as relevant contingency assumptions and assessments.

Relationship schemas are those that contain the person's assumptions about relationships, about how relationships work, what to expect in relationships, and again, relevant contingency assumptions and assessments (e.g., 'you are devalued in relationships', 'relationships are unreliable').

These schemas are dysfunctional, because they give rise to negative expectations and particularly also to negative interpretations of situations or negative affects. They determine a fast and highly automated processing of information and lead to what we call 'hyperallergic reactions': trifling situational triggers quickly result in violent (affective) reactions. For example, someone who has been afflicted by the 'I'm not important' schema may react terribly hurt and offended to a minimal inattentiveness of an interaction partner.

Intransparent Action and Behaviour

Persons whose relationship needs are systematically frustrated over a long period of time, i.e., who do not receive any important signals from relevant reference persons despite their high motives for importance, may now develop strategies by means of which they still can persuade important interaction partners to satisfy certain interactional goals: these strategies develop if (and only if!) they are successful, and thus the persons necessarily consider these strategies to be 'good solutions' to face up to difficult situations: therefore, the strategies are certainly perceived as *ego-syntonic*, that is, as part of one's own person, and not as disturbing, dysfunctional or problematic.

The strategies are manipulative (with 'manipulative' *not* being evaluative, but meant only in a psychological sense and in the descriptive sense of intransparent influence by the person of the interaction partner!), because the interaction partner is fundamentally deceived by the person's goal of action. For example, a child who behaves in a funny way does not necessarily do so because he/she fundamentally wants to be a funny person. However, this is exactly what his/her interaction partner (e.g., father) believes. The child behaves in this way to have motive-consistent experiences, like getting attention (which the interaction partner does not know, in general). The child thus pretends something that is not the case and leaves the interaction partner in the dark about the actual intentions. *And this, exactly, is manipulative:* the interaction partner is prompted to do something for reasons that he or she does not really understand. Therefore, the strategic behaviour is also *intransparent*.

Compensatory Schemas

At the level of nontransparent action and behaviour, the game level, there are compensatory schemas; these serve to compensate for dysfunctional schemas (on the schema level) or to ensure that they do not prove to be true.

On the one hand, there are compensatory self-schemas that contain positive or (compensatory) exaggerated self-assumptions; there are compensatory norm schemas that contain (often exaggerated) goals (in the form of 'must do/have' sentences), and there are compensatory rule schemes that contain (also often exaggerated) instructions to others. We (Sachse et al., 2009) have described these schemas as 'compensatory' because their purpose is essentially to 'iron out' the negative contents of the self- and relationship schemas at the schema level or to ensure that the contents and consequences specified therein do not occur.

Compensatory norm schemas contain instructions on how the person should or must be: they thus contain the person's *goals* (in the sense of explicit goals; see Püschel & Sachse, 2009). Normative schemas are therefore interactional goals at the 'game level'.

Norm schemas are those that contain 'instructions' of the person to themselves, e.g., 'be successful', 'be the best', 'be the most important', 'by all means avoid embarrassment', 'avoid all situations in which you could be criticized'.

Normative schemas thus comprise goals in the form of regulations: 'be XY', 'you must do/have XY', 'you must not do/have XY', etc. These instructions can be binding on the person to varying degrees, which in turn depends on how the contingency level of these schemas is defined (cf. Sachse et al., 2008).

Rule schemas do not contain rules that the person should follow, but rules that others, the interaction partners, should follow! Rule schemas thus contain interactional expectations, e.g., 'others have to treat me respectfully', or, 'a partner has to pay attention to me around the clock'.

At the contingency level of such schemas there are no catastrophes that could take place for the person themselves, but rather consequences that threaten the interaction partner of the rule-setting person, e.g., 'if someone does not treat me with respect, I may react angrily', or, 'if my partner doesn't pay attention to me, I'll make a scene'.

Rule schemas compensate in particular for the negative relationship expectations of the dysfunctional relationship schemas: if a person has adopted the schema 'in relationships one is not respected', then he or she develops a (more or less strong) expectation of interaction partners on the game level, which precisely contradicts this assumption: 'my partner has to treat me respectfully – and if not, they'll be sorry!'

The reaction when activating rule schemas is therefore not taking offence, but annoyance, which means that a person may react here with a maximum of fury in the case of a slight 'misdemeanour' on the part of interaction partners.

Interaction Tests

Tests are actions by means of which a person wants to find out something specific about an interaction partner; they want to do this because they hope the interaction partner has certain positive qualities, but at the same time they fear that he or she does not have them.

Tests are thus used centrally to create 'safety' in situations and instances where the person is suspicious.

The test situations are usually quite difficult for the interaction partners, because only through difficult, demanding tests can be determined whether an interaction partner 'really proves themselves'.

Tests are always aimed at *testing the relationship*, they always relate to examine and verify the attitudes or characteristics of the interaction partner with regard to the formation of a relationship. In this context, the interaction partners can be tested for a wide range of different aspects, e.g.,

- whether they remain appreciative in critical situations,
- whether they are really reliable,
- whether they are solidary,
- whether they are competent,
- whether they are strong enough, and
- whether they can assert themselves.

WHAT CHARACTERIZES CLIENTS WITH NARCISSISTIC PERSONALITY DISORDER?

A narcissist is generally understood to be a person who is very performance-oriented, focused on success, strongly convinced of themselves or their abilities but is nevertheless sensitive to criticism, and surrounds themselves with status symbols (Vazire, Naumann, Rentfrow, & Gosling, 2008) and yet remains discontented.

Persons with narcissism show both a positive to grandiose as well as a negative self-concept riddled with self-doubt, so that they alternate between a positive and negative state of mind (see Zeigler-Hill, Myers, & Clark, 2010).

Therefore, from this point of view, the distinction between 'grandiose' and 'vulnerable' is a continuum on which most narcissists move (cf. Miller, Hoffman, Gaughan, Gentile, Maples, & Campbell, 2011; Miller, Price, Gentile, Lynam, & Campbell, 2012; Rohmann, Neumann, Herner, & Bierhoff, 2012).

For the characterization of narcissists, see Emmons (1984), Kernis and Sun (1994), Millon (2000) and Ronningstam (2005, 2011a, 2011b).

Narcissists have a very positive self-schema as well as massive self-doubt (Brown & Zeigler-Hill, 2004; Campbell & Foster, 2002).

They are very egotistic (Emmons, 1987) and want to be recognized and admired (Campbell, 1999).

Sometimes, they tend to overestimate their abilities (Campbell, Rudich, & Sedikides, 2002).

They are highly performance/achievement-oriented, but extrinsically motivated (Crocker, Luhtanen, Cooper, & Bouvrette, 2003).

Like all personality disorders, clients with narcissistic personality disorder range from mild style to severe disorder; as a narcissistic trait, it is rather a resource; as a disorder, it is a burden. As a disorder, the extremely performance-oriented and manipulative behaviour generates extreme costs: interactional problems, psychosomatic disorders (especially cardiovascular problems), burnout, too little time for oneself, chronic dissatisfaction, suicide risk, etc. (Bachar, Hadar, & Shalev, 2005; Morf & Rhodewalt, 2001).

We distinguish between two categories of clients with narcissistic personality disorder: the successful and the unsuccessful narcissist.

The focus of successful narcissists is primarily on performance/achievement and for that reason they are usually successful in their professions; they are autonomous and well organized with a high level of perseverance and self-efficiency expectation; they tend to compete strongly with others, have a keen sense of entitlement and define rules of conduct for others; they are highly egocentric and think they are the most important person in the universe. In spite of this, they have constant feelings of self-doubt and remain highly sensitive to criticism (cf. Sachse, 2007, 2008).

Empirically, there are more than 50 discussed characteristics of successful narcissists such as increased aggression, extraversion, perseverance, high autonomy, bonding problems, competitive behaviour, etc. (Bogart, Benotsch, & Pavlovic, 2004).

In many areas or fields, unsuccessful narcissists have characteristics similar to those of successful narcissists: an exaggerated and unrealistically positive self-schema, a strong rule-setting behaviour, boasting, etc. Unlike successful narcissists, however, they do not have a real performance or achievement record: typically, they drop out of school, abandon several apprenticeships, are unemployed, still live with their mothers and play computer games, etc.; there is an increased risk of developing an alcohol or gambling addiction. Unsuccessful narcissists have a very low self-efficiency expectation, massive self-doubt and a low willingness to exert themselves or work hard. What makes the therapy particularly difficult is a certain concordance between the negative self-schema contents and aspects of reality: facts like 'I haven't achieved anything/I am inefficient' are difficult to work on when it seems that the client has actually achieved little or performs badly. Due to lack of space in this chapter I will concentrate on the successful narcissists.

WHAT DEFINES A NARCISSIST FROM THE PERSPECTIVE OF DUAL-ACTION REGULATION MODEL?

In our opinion (Sachse et al., 2010), it is possible, but not very meaningful, to orientate oneself only to the DSM definitions of narcissistic personality disorder, because the criteria are empirically and theoretically questionable. From a psychologically informed perspective, we assume that narcissists can be defined by the following criteria, whereby we first define successful and then, in contrast, unsuccessful narcissists, that means, narcissists, who do not compensate through achievement (cf. Döring & Sachse, 2008; Sachse, 2005, 2006a, 2006b, 2007, 2008, 2013).

The criteria for successful narcissists are:

1. Strong Appreciation Motive
   Narcissists always have a clear motivation for appreciation and acceptance: primarily, it is all about receiving positive feedback from others about themselves. However, the narcissists often are unaware of this (they consider themselves 'performance-motivated').
2. Strong Autonomy Motivation
   Successful narcissists also have a strong motive for autonomy: they want to determine essential areas of their lives themselves, they do not want to be determined and patronized by others.
3. Negative Self-schema
   Narcissists, even those who are successful, *always* have a negative self-schema that stems from their biography: it contains assumptions such as 'I am not ok as a person, not lovable', 'I am not competent, I am a loser', etc.

   This self-schema may range from slightly negative to extremely negative.

   This schema is activated by criticism, failures, etc., and this is *exactly* what makes narcissists so sensitive to criticism.

4. Positive Self-schema
   Moreover, narcissists always have a (parallel) positive self-schema (among other things to compensate for the negative schema): this schema contains assumptions such as 'I am (highly) competent', 'I have (exceptional) abilities', 'I am (extremely) successful', and so on.
   The assumptions of the scheme range from slightly positive to extremely positive.
   And the assumptions of the scheme (compared to the 'real' resources of the person) are realistic to highly unrealistic.
   The assumptions of successful narcissists are rather very positive, but mostly highly realistic.
5. Swaying between the Schemas
   Narcissists sway between the schemas: sometimes the positive schema dominates and the person is then in a positive state of mind, sometimes the negative schema dominates and the person considers themselves a (complete) failure. As a rule, however, the negative schema of a person is responsible for persistent (more or less strong) self-doubts (even in the case of very successful narcissists). (Swaying between schemas often results in misdiagnoses of a bipolar disorder I; cf. Fulford, Johnson, & Carver, 2008.)
6. Negative Relationship Schemas
   Narcissists have a relationship schema that gives rise to assumptions such as: 'in relationships, one is evaluated, judged, and devalued', 'in relationships, one is patronized, controlled', etc.
7. Normative Schemas
   Successful narcissists usually have strong (compensatory) norm schemas, such as: 'be the best', 'avoid mistakes', 'make yourself invulnerable', but also: 'avoid dependency', 'keep control', and many others.
   From this normative schema results the (high) performance behaviour, which then leads to real successes and real compensations (positive feedback, etc.). In motivation theory, however, 'performance' is an *avoidance target*: the person is not intrinsically performance-motivated.
8. Rule-Setting Behaviour
   The persons set *rules for others* to a large extent, i.e., rules for how they want to be treated or not treated by others: in doing so, they assume that they are legitimated to set such rules, and that they are legitimated to punish rule violators. They set rules such as: 'no one has to interfere with me', 'no one must criticize me', 'I have special rights', 'I'm entitled to preferential treatment', etc.
9. Manipulation
   Narcissists send images and appeals to a high degree: they want to be seen by others as great, competent, successful, intelligent, etc.

(images) and they want others to praise them, confirm them, not criticize them, etc. (appeals). In essence, narcissists use interaction partners to achieve their goals.

10. Tests
Narcissists, especially successful ones, often carry out so-called 'tests': they test the therapists to see whether they are professionally competent enough (for example by asking them what exactly they want to do therapeutically) or they test whether the therapist can appropriately deal with the client (e.g., 'I don't see any diplomas here – are you a psychologist at all?').

THERAPY

A therapy with narcissists can be divided into phases (some of which overlap to some extent and are passed through repeatedly); such a 'phase model' is helpful for orientation:

Phase 1: Building relationships: In the case of narcissistic clients, the therapist should above all behave in a way that is complementary to the appreciation motive, i.e., praise the clients, do not question them, underline their resources, etc.
Phase 2: Development of a working mission: The client should be made aware that they generate the costs of *their own system*, e.g., in the case of narcissists, that they behave manipulatively and thus annoy their interaction partners.
Phase 3: Clarification of schemas: In this phase, the dysfunctional and compensatory schemas are to be constructed systematically so that a psychological model of the disorder can be established.
Phase 4: Processing of schemas: In this phase, the relevant schemas are to be systematically discussed therapeutically and alternative schemas are to be developed.
Phase 5: Transfer: Here the client should try out new schemas and new behavioural ways and attitudes in reality.

CASE CONCEPTUALIZATION OF NARCISSISTIC PERSONALITY DISORDER

For the therapist to be able to develop a psychologically grounded case formulation for clients with narcissistic personality disorder, it is necessary to construct a model for each patient's functioning (Sachse, 2017). For this purpose, therapists must systematically process the information they receive from the client. The therapist thus develops a client model, i.e., a mental model about central psychological aspects of the client.

On the basis of this information, the therapist develops a Dual-Action Regulation Model that is individually tailored to the client in question.

They thus specify:

- The client's central relationship motives.
- The central self- and relationship schemas of the client.
- The compensatory norm and rule schemas of the client.
- The manipulative strategies the client adopts, i.e., which images and appeals the client is implementing towards the therapist and other interaction partners.
- The tests the client conducts.

This results in a specific client model on the basis of which therapeutic strategies and interventions can be derived that are indicated for the respective client.

The following are the main sources of information for the therapist:

- Verbal statements the client makes about their own experiences and actions, about interactions and relationships, about intentions, emotions etc. in relevant everyday situations.
- The concrete behaviour of the client in psychotherapy, e.g., the images and appeals that the client uses with respect to the therapist.
- The client's nonverbal behaviour in the therapy process, i.e., gestures, facial expressions, paraverbal expressions and the like, by means of which the client for example stages 'drama' situations.

A special rating system developed for the analysis of client behaviour allows the therapist to draw specific conclusions from this information with respect to a client model: through their images and appeals and through their concrete interaction behaviour the clients also disclose to the therapist relevant information even if they verbally behave strongly according to social desirability: it is precisely from the interactions with the therapists that conclusions can be drawn (Sachse, 2015a).

Moreover, a special rating system has been developed and validated with the help of which the client's relationship formation, their avoidance level, processing and other process characteristics can be ascertained (cf. Kramer & Sachse, 2013; Sachse, 2015b, 2015d; Sachse & Kramer, 2015a, 2015b, 2015c).

These conclusions lead to hypotheses which are then checked, elaborated, modified or, should it be necessary, discarded and replaced by new hypotheses in further processing steps (Sachse, 2017). In this context a therapist must

- understand the respective contents (problems, constructions, motives etc.);
- assess which diagnosis/diagnoses apply to a client;

- assess how a client works in the clarification process, e.g., whether he/she avoids, is open, tries to understand contents etc.;
- assess how trustful the client's relationship with the therapist is and whether the client is willing to be guided by the therapist, etc.

As a result, elaborate hypotheses about the client are already arrived at during the first two to three sessions, which develop into an elaborate model after four to five sessions. However, with some highly distrustful clients, this process may take longer.

Further information such as questionnaires, anamneses etc. are used to verify and differentiate the hypotheses.

The Case

The client, 'Mr. Alexander', was a 62-year-old head physician who was about to retire. He came into therapy because he had severe relationship problems – with his wife, his children, his subordinates. In addition, he suffered from increasing dissatisfaction, which he could not explain with all his successes, honours etc. He was afraid of retirement because he feared he would be useless and not know what to do.

He tried to do something special in many areas and thus felt himself to be 'rushed and driven': he took on honorary posts and additional tasks, and made extensive and difficult journeys, some of which were even risky. This left him little time for himself and his wife. All these aspects intensified the conflicts between him and his wife.

Conceptualization

During the first therapeutic sessions, a case conceptualization was elaborated and discussed in a collegial supervision group.

The following client model was established:

- *Relationship Motives*
  Clearly, the client was highly motivated and most centrally, he showed a high motivation for autonomy and solidarity.
- *Positive Self-schema*
  The positive self-schema revealed assumptions such as:
  - I am extraordinarily intelligent, efficient, persevering, courageous, prudent.
  - I understand the world better than anyone around me.
  - I make the right decisions quickly and reliably.
  - I can manage risks excellently.
  - I know exactly which actions are effective and which are not.
  - I can trust my judgement.

- *Negative Self-schema*
  Clarification of the negative self-schema was difficult but was possible eventually. There were assumptions like:
  - Basically, I'm weak and incompetent.
  - I can't trust my intelligence and performance.
  - Strictly speaking, I'm essentially inadequate and worthless.
  - All I achieve is a deception package.
- *Relationship Schemas*
  Characteristic relationship schemas were as follows:
  - In relations, you are evaluated and belittled.
  - In relationships, you are not recognized, but criticized.
  - You can't rely on others.
  - Others are trying to criticize me.
- *Norm Schemas*
  In his biography, the client has developed relatively strong compensatory normative schemas:
  - Be the best!
  - Always give the maximum to be recognized!
  - Do something extraordinary, do something special!
  - Avoid criticism and devaluation!
  - Avoid dependence!
- *Rule Schemas*
  The client demonstrated powerful rule schemas that led to major interaction problems:
  - Others have to admire me and find me great!
  - Nobody has to criticize me!
  - Everybody does exactly what I say!
  - My assessment is correct and must not be called into question!
- *Interaction games*
  The client has the impression that his wife has to fulfil all his wishes because he is so successful and earns the money. He forced her to follow his rules and argues that this is necessary.
- *Further Problems*
  As a result of the schemas the following was found to exist:
  - exaggerated opinion of oneself and greatly overtaxing oneself,
  - increased sensitivity to criticism and rage against critics,
  - strong mistrust in relationships, lack of self-opening, attachment problems,
  - great anger over all the actions of others that did not meet his expectations,
  - unwillingness, but *not* inability to empathize: 'you are not empathetic to weakness, incompetence and laziness',
  - extremely strong compensatory action: high performance, but above all extraordinary activities (e.g., dog sledding in winter in the Yukon, alone on the Kilimanjaro, and the like).

In summary, it can be said that the client acts according to the motto 'higher, faster, further': he is never satisfied with the state he has reached, but always sets himself higher goals without really achieving a state of satisfaction.

MEANING OF THE CASE CONCEPTUALIZATION

The case conceptualization, which in COP we call a 'client model', is essential for the therapist, because, based on it, fundamental therapeutic indication decisions can be deduced: it determines the type of complementary relationship formation, the leverage points for confrontational interventions, the schemas to be clarified and worked on, and so on.

Thus, case conceptualization is the central 'control or guiding element' for the therapy: the therapist orientates his or her strategic actions to it. In the course of the therapy, the conception must always be reviewed, elaborated, modified and, due to changes the client experiences, updated again and again (Sachse, 2017).

Therapy

By taking complementary actions, it was relatively quickly possible to establish a trusting relationship with Alexander, especially through a consistent and complementary relationship formation with respect to the appreciation motive. In this way, the client may be well prepared to get involved in clarification processes with the therapist.

Through confronting interventions, the costs were made salient to the client and it was elaborated that the client generated the costs *himself*: even the rule-setting structures and their costs became clear. Repeatedly, the confrontations led to interactional crises in which the client was angry with the therapist and in which the therapist had to realize a high degree of complementarity. After all, it was possible to confront the client without facing crises.

As far as Alexander shows sufficient motivation for change, the process of clarifying schemata is started and continued until a consistent model can be developed on the basis of which the client's problems can be deduced psychologically.

After sufficient clarification of the schemas, Alexander began a phase of

- processing the negative self- and relationship schemas via the one-person role play, which was relatively easy to carry out (e.g., the schema 'I'm a failure');
- disputation of normative schemas and the development of alternative targets – that was considerably more difficult (e.g., the schema 'I have to be the best');

- disputation of the rule schemas (e.g., the schema 'nobody must oppose me') and the development of authentic alternative behaviour (e.g., a higher degree of empathy for the weaknesses of others) – here didactics and training were necessary, since the client was unable to exhibit an alternative behaviour; and
- development of a motivation for empathy, especially towards his wife and children.

During the final therapy phase, the transfer phase, concrete tasks were then agreed upon with the client. The therapy was successful: the client still showed narcissistic traits, but was far less driven, more authentic, more satisfied and was able to deal with interaction partners in a much more constructive way.

The individual therapy was followed by a (successful) couple therapy, which even more improved the quality of the relationship between partners and the client's willingness for empathy and negotiations.

CONCLUSION

A case conceptualization or a client model is of central significance in COP: the therapist forms hypotheses from the very first moment of interaction and examines, elaborates and modifies them continuously in the therapy process; in this way, a first case conceptualization is developed relatively quickly on which therapists can orientate their actions. This case conceptualization will then form the basis of their therapeutic actions and approaches and is also constantly 'put to the test' through therapeutic interventions, so that there is an ongoing feedback between case conceptualization, interventions, effects and renewed hypotheses (Sachse, 2017). In this manner, a valid client model is established which is indispensable for the therapist.

Acknowledgements

Permission of client transcripts (and/or photos) has been received in writing to the author(s).

References

Bachar, E., Hadar, H., & Shalev, A. Y. (2005). Narcissistic vulnerability and the development of PTSD: A prospective study. *The Journal of Nervous and Mental Disease*, *193*, 762–765.

Baumann, N., & Kuhl, J. (2005). Selbstregulation und Selbstkontrolle. In H. Weber, & T. Rammsayer (Eds.), *Handbuch der Persönlichkeitspsychologie und Differentiellen Psychologie* (pp. 362–373). Göttingen: Hogrefe.

Beck, A. T. (1979). *Wahrnehmung der Wirklichkeit und Neurose*. München: Pfeiffer.

Beck, A. T., & Freeman, A. (1993). *Kognitive Therapie der Persönlichkeitsstörungen*. Weinheim: Psychologie Verlags Union.

Beck, A. T., Rush, A. J., Shaw, B. F., & Emery, G. (1981). *Kognitive Therapie der Depression*. München: Urban & Schwarzenberg.
Bogart, L. M., Benotsch, E. G., & Pavlovic, J. D. (2004). Feeling superior but threatened: The relation of narcissism to social comparison. *Basic and Applied Social Psychology, 26*, 34–44.
Brown, R., & Zeigler-Hill, V. (2004). Narcissism and the non-equivalence of self-esteem measures: A matter of dominance? *Journal of Research in Personality, 38*, 585–592.
Campbell, W. K. (1999). Narcissism and romantic attraction. *Journal of Personality and Social Psychology, 77*, 1254–1270.
Campbell, W. K., & Foster, C. A. (2002). Narcissism and commitment in romantic relationships: An investment model analysis. *Personality and Social Psychology Bulletin, 28*(4), 484–495.
Campbell, W. K., Rudich, E. A., & Sedikides, C. (2002). Narcissism, self-esteem, and the positivity of self-views: Two portraits of self-love. *Personality and Social Psychology Bulletin, 28*(3), 358–368.
Caspar, F. (1986). Die Plananalyse als Konzept und Methode. *Verhaltensmodifikation, 4*, 235–256.
Caspar, F. (2000). Therapeutisches Handeln als individueller Konstruktionsprozess. In (2nd ed.) J. Margraf (Ed.), *Lehrbuch der Verhaltenstherapie* (Vol. 1) (pp. 155–166). Berlin: Springer.
Caspar, F. (2006). Theorie und Praxis der Diagnostik, Prognose, Indikationsstellung, Fallkonzeptualisierung und Behandlungsplanung in der Verhaltenstherapie. In B. Strauß, F. Hohagen, & F. Caspar (Eds.), *Lehrbuch Psychotherapie* (pp. 1143–1179). Göttingen: Hogrefe.
Caspar, F. (2007). *Beziehungen und Probleme verstehen. Eine Einführung in die psychotherapeutische Plananalyse* (3rd ed.). Bern: Huber.
Caspar, F. (2008). Motivorientierte Beziehungsgestaltung – Konzept, Voraussetzungen bei den Patienten und Auswirkungen auf Prozess und Ergebnisse. In M. Hermer, & B. Röhrle (Eds.), *Handbuch der therapeutischen Beziehung* (Vol. 1) (pp. 527–557). Tübingen: DGVT-Verlag.
Caspar, F. (2009). Therapeutisches Handeln als individueller Konstruktionsprozess. In J. Margraf, & S. Schneider (Eds.), *Lehrbuch der Verhaltenstherapie* (pp. 213–225). Heidelberg: Springer.
Crocker, J., Luhtanen, R. K., Cooper, M. L., & Bouvrette, S. (2003). Contingencies of self-worth in college students: Theory and measurement. *Journal of Personality and Social Psychology, 85*, 894–908.
Döring, S., & Sachse, R. (2008). Psychotherapie bei Cluster-B-Persönlichkeitsstörungen: Die histrionische und die narzisstische Persönlichkeitsstörung. In S. C. Herpertz, F. Caspar, & C. Mundt (Eds.), *Störungsorientierte Psychotherapie* (pp. 456–463). München: Urban & Fischer Verlag.
Emmons, R. A. (1984). Factor analysis and construct validity of the narcissistic personality inventory. *Journal of Personality Assessment, 48*(3), 291–300.
Emmons, R. A. (1987). Narcissism: Theory and measurement. *Journal of Personality and Social Psychology, 52*, 11–17.
Fulford, D., Johnson, S. L., & Carver, C. S. (2008). Commonalities and differences in characteristics of persons at risk for narcissism and mania. *Journal of Research in Personality, 42*, 1427–1438.
Greenberg, L. S. (1984). Task Analysis: The general approach. In L. N. Rice, & L. S. Greenberg (Eds.), *Patterns of change. Intensive analysis of psychotherapy process* (pp. 124–148). New York: Guilford Press.
Greenberg, L. S. (2002). *Emotion-focused therapy: Coaching clients to work through their feelings*. Washington: American Psychological Association.
Gross, J. J. (1999). Emotion regulation: Past, present, and future. *Cognition and Emotion, 13*, 551–573.
Gross, J. J. (2002). Emotion regulation: Affective, cognitive, and social consequences. *Psychophysiology, 39*, 281–291.

Gross, J. J., & Munoz, R. F. (1995). Emotion regulation and mental health. *Clinical Psychology: Science and Practice*, *2*(2), 151–164.

Kernis, M. H., & Sun, C. (1994). Narcissism and reactions to interpersonal feedback. *Journal of Research in Personality*, *28*, 4–13.

Kramer, U., & Sachse, R. (2013). Early clarification processes in client presenting with borderline personality disorder: Relations with symptom level and change. *Person-Centered and Experiential Psychotherapies*, *12*(2), 157–175.

Langens, T. (2009). Das Motivkonzept: Ein Vergleich zwischen Klärungsorientierter Psychotherapie und allgemeiner Motivationspsychologie. In R. Sachse, J. Fasbender, J. Breil, & O. Püschel (Eds.), *Grundlagen und Konzepte Klärungsorientiener Psychotherapie* (pp. S. 117–141). Göttingen: Hogrefe.

Miller, J. D., Hoffman, B. J., Gaughan, E. T., Gentile, B., Maples, J., & Campbell, W. K. (2011). Grandiose and vulnerable narcissism: A nomological network analysis. *Journal of Personality*, *79*(5), 1013–1042.

Miller, J. D., Price, J., Gentile, B., Lynam, D. R., & Campbell, W. K. (2012). Grandiose and vulnerable narcissism from the perspective of the interpersonal circumplex. *Personality and Individual Differences*, *53*, 507–512.

Millon, T. (2000). DSM narcissistic personality disorder: Historical reflections and future directions. In E. F. Ronningstam (Ed.), *Disorders of narcissism* (pp. 75–91). Northvale: Jason Aronson Inc.

Morf, C. C., & Rhodewalt, F. (2001). Unraveling the paradoxes of narcissism: A dynamic self-regulatory processing model. *Psychological Inquiry*, *12*, 177–196.

Püschel, O., & Sachse, R. (2009). Eine motivationstheoretische Fundierung Klärungsorientierter Psychotherapie. In R. Sachse, J. Fasbender, J. Breil, & O. Püschel (Eds.), *Grundlagen und Konzepte Klärungsorientierter Psychotherapie* (pp. 89–110). Göttingen: Hogrefe.

Rice, L. N. (1974). The evocative function of the therapist. In D. A. Wexler, & L. N. Rice (Eds.), *Innovations in client-centered therapy* (pp. 289–311). New York: Wiley.

Rice, L. N., & Greenberg, L. S. (1984). The new research paradigm. In L. Rice, & L. S. Greenberg (Eds.), *Pattern of change* (pp. 7–25). New York: Guilford.

Rohmann, E., Neumann, E., Herner, M. J., & Bierhoff, H. W. (2012). Grandiose and vulnerable narcissism. *European Psychologist*, *17*(4), 279–290.

Ronningstam, E. F. (2005). *Identifying and understand the narcissistic personality*. New York: Oxford University Press.

Ronningstam, E. F. (2011a). Narcissistic personality disorder in DSM V – in support of retaining a significant diagnosis. *Journal of Personality Disorders*, *25*(2), 248–259.

Ronningstam, E. F. (2011b). Narcissistic personality disorder: A clinical perspective. *Journal of Psychiatric Practive*, *17*(2), 89.

Sachse, R. (1983). Das Ein-Personen-Rollenspiel: Ein integratives Therapieverfahren. *Partnerberatung*, *4*, 187–200.

Sachse, R. (1990a). Acting purposefully in client-centered therapy. In P. J. D. Drenth, J. A. Sergeant, & R.-J. Takens (Eds.), *European perspectives in psychology* (Vol. 1) (pp. 65–80). New York: Wiley.

Sachse, R. (1990b). Concrete interventions are crucial: The influence of therapist's processing proposals on the client's intrapersonal exploration. In G. Lietaer, J. Rombauts, & R. van Balen (Eds.), *Client-centered and experiential psychotherapy towards the nineties* (pp. 295–308). Leuven: University Press.

Sachse, R. (1992a). *Zielorientierte Gesprächspsychotherapie – Eine grundlegende Neukonzeption*. Göttingen: Hogrefe.

Sachse, R. (1992b). Differential effects of processing proposals and content references on the explication process of clients with different starting conditions. *Psychotherapy Research*, *4*, 235.

Sachse, R. (1993). The effects of intervention phrasing of therapist-client communication. *Psychotherapy Research*, *3*(4), 260–277.

Sachse, R. (1995). *Der psychosomatische Klient in der Praxis: Grundlagen einer effektiven Therapie mit "schwierigen" Klienten*. Stuttgart: Kohlhammer.
Sachse, R. (1998). Goal-oriented client-centered psychotherapy of psychosomatic disorders. In L. Greenberg, J. Watson, & G. Lietaer (Eds.), *Handbook of experiential psychotherapy* (pp. 295–327). New York: Guilford.
Sachse, R. (1999a). *Psychotherapie psychosomatischer Magen-Darm-Erkrankungen. Psycho-logische und somatische Veränderungen und Reduktion der Gesundheitskosten*. Ruhr-Universität Bochum, Fakultät für Psychologie.
Sachse, R. (1999b). *Persönlichkeitsstörungen. Psychotherapie dysfunktionaler Interaktionsstile* (2nd ed.). Göttingen: Hogrefe.
Sachse, R. (2001). *Psychologische Psychotherapie der Persönlichkeitsstörungen*. Göttingen: Hogrefe.
Sachse, R. (2002). *Histrionische und narzisstische Persönlichkeitsstörungen*. Göttingen: Hogrefe.
Sachse, R. (2003). *Klärungsorientierte Psychotherapie*. Göttingen: Hogrefe.
Sachse, R. (2004a). From client-centered to clarification-oriented Psychotherapy. *Person-Centered and Experiential Psychotherapies, 3*(1), 19–34.
Sachse, R. (2004b). Histrionische und narzisstische Persönlichkeitsstörungen. In R. Merod (Ed.), *Behandlung von Persönlichkeitsstörungen* (pp. 357–404). Tübingen: DGVT-Verlag.
Sachse, R. (2005). Was wirkt in der Behandlung von Persönlichkeitsstörungen? In N. Saimeh (Ed.), *Was wirkt? Prävention – Behandlung – Rehabilitation* (pp. 222–229). Bonn: Psychiatrie-Verlag.
Sachse, R. (2006a). *Persönlichkeitsstörungen verstehen – Zum Umgang mit schwierigen Klienten*. Bonn: Psychiatrie-Verlag.
Sachse, R. (2006b). Narzisstische Persönlichkeitsstörungen. *Psychotherapie, 11*(2), 241–246.
Sachse, R. (2007). Therapie der narzisstischen und histrionischen Persönlichkeitsstörungen: Zwei Fallberichte. In S. Barnow (Ed.), *Persönlichkeitsstörungen: Ursachen und Behandlungen* (pp. 404–410). Bern: Huber.
Sachse, R. (2008). Histrionische und narzisstische Persönlichkeitsstörung. In M. Hermer, & B. Röhrle (Eds.), *Handbuch der therapeutischen Beziehung* (Vol. 2) (pp. 1105–1125). Tübingen: DGVT-Verlag.
Sachse, R. (2013). *Persönlichkeitsstörungen: Leitfaden für eine psychologische Psychothera-pie*. 2. Überarb. erweiterte Auflage. Göttingen: Hogrefe.
Sachse, R. (2014). Schemata und ihre Relevanz für affektive und emotionale Verarbeitung. In R. Sachse, & T. A. Langens (Eds.), *Emotionen und Affekte in der Psychotherapie* (pp. 56–70). Göttingen: Hogrefe.
Sachse, R. (2015a). Änderungs- und Stabilisierungsmotivation in der Therapie und ihre therapeutische Beeinflussung. In R. Sachse, S. Schirm, & S. Kiszkenow-Bäker (Eds.), *Klärungsorientierte Psychotherapie in der Praxis* (pp. 111–121). Lengerich: Pabst.
Sachse, R. (2015b). Das Persönlichkeitsstörungs-Rating-System. In R. Sachse, S. Schirm, & S. Kiszkenow (Eds.), *Klärungsorientierte Psychotherapie in der Praxis* (pp. 29–52). Lengerich: Pabst.
Sachse, R. (2015c). Die Entwicklung der BIBS: Bearbeitungs-. Inhalts- und Beziehungsskalen. In R. Sachse, S. Schirm, & U. Kramer (Eds.), *Klärungsorientierte Psychotherapie. Systematisch dokumentieren: Die Skala zur Erfassung von Bearbeitung, Inhalt und Beziehung im Therapieprozess* (pp. 21–23). Göttingen: Hogrefe.
Sachse, R. (2015d). Reliabilitäten des BIBS. In R. Sachse, S. Schirm, & U. Kramer (Eds.), *Klärungsorientierte Psychotherapie. Systematisch dokumentieren: Die Skala zur Erfassung von Bearbeitung, Inhalt und Beziehung im Therapieprozess* (pp. 24–25). Göttingen: Hogrefe.
Sachse, R. (2016). Was sind und was sollen Klärungsprozesse? In R. Sachse, & M. Sachse (Eds.), *Klärungsprozesse in der Praxis II* (pp. 15–29). Lengerich: Pabst.
Sachse, R. (2017). *Therapeutische Informationsverarbeitung*. Göttingen: Hogrefe.
Sachse, R., Breil, J., & Fasbender, J. (2009). Beziehungsmotive und Schemata: Eine Heuristik. In R. Sachse, J. Fasbender, J. Breil, & O. Püschel (Eds.), *Grundlagen und Konzepte Klärungsorientierter Psychotherapie* (pp. 66–88). Göttingen: Hogrefe.

Sachse, R., & Fasbender, J. (2013). Interaktionsschwierigkeiten im Therapieprozess bei Klienten mit narzisstischer und histrionischer Persönlichkeitsstörung. In H. W. Hofert, & U. Härter (Eds.), *Schwierige Patienten* (pp. 203–214). Bern: Huber.

Sachse, R., Fasbender, J., & Breil, J. (2009). Klärungsprozesse: Was soll im Therapieprozess wie geklärt werden? In R. Sachse, J. Fasbender, J. Breil, & O. Püschel (Eds.), *Grundlagen und Konzepte Klärungsorientierter Psychotherapie* (pp. 36–64). Göttingen: Hogrefe.

Sachse, R., Fasbender, J., Breil, J., & Püschel, O. (2009). *Grundlagen und Konzepte Klärungsorientierter Psychotherapie*. Göttingen: Hogrefe.

Sachse, R., Fasbender, J., Breil, J., & Sachse, M. (2012). *Klärungsorientierte Psychotherapie der histrionischen Persönlichkeitsstörung*. Göttingen: Hogrefe.

Sachse, R., Fasbender, J., & Sachse, M. (2014). *Klärungsorientierte Psychotherapie der selbstunsicheren Persönlichkeitsstörung*. Göttingen: Hogrefe.

Sachse, R., & Kramer, U. (2015a). Untersuchung der BIBS-Skalen: Korrelationen der PTBS-Variablen untereinander. In R. Sachse, S. Schirm, & U. Kramer (Eds.), *Klärungsorientierte Psychotherapie. Systematisch dokumentieren: Die Skala zur Erfassung von Bearbeitung, Inhalt und Beziehung im Therapieprozess* (pp. 26–33). Göttingen: Hogrefe.

Sachse, R., & Kramer, U. (2015b). Validierung der BIBS-Skalen an Klienten-Erfolgsmaßen. In R. Sachse, S. Schirm, & U. Kramer (Eds.), *Klärungsorientierte Psychotherapie. Systematisch dokumentieren: Die Skala zur Erfassung von Bearbeitung, Inhalt und Beziehung im Therapieprozess* (pp. 39–49). Göttingen: Hogrefe.

Sachse, R., & Kramer, U. (2015c). Veränderungsmessungen mit den BIBS. In R. Sachse, S. Schirm, & U. Kramer (Eds.), *Klärungsorientierte Psychotherapie. Systematisch dokumentieren: Die Skala zur Erfassung von Bearbeitung, Inhalt und Beziehung im Therapieprozess* (pp. 90–104). Göttingen: Hogrefe.

Sachse, R., & Langens, T. A. (2015). Motivierung von Klienten im Therapieprozess: Herstellung und Steigerung von Änderungsmotivation. In R. Sachse, S. Schirm, & S. Kiszkenow-Bäker (Eds.), *Klärungsorientierte Psychotherapie in der Praxis* (pp. 97–110). Lengerich: Pabst.

Sachse, R., Langens, T. A., & Sachse, M. (2012b). *Klienten motivieren – Therapeutische Strategien zur Stärkung der Änderungsbereitschaft*. Bonn: Psychiatrie-Verlag.

Sachse, R., Püschel, O., Fasbender, J., & Breil, J. (2008). *Klärungsorientierte Schema-Bearbeitung – Dysfunktionale Schemata effektiv verändern*. Göttingen: Hogrefe.

Sachse, R., & Sachse, M. (2016a). Effekte Klärungsorientierter Psychotherapie bei Klienten mit narzisstischer Persönlichkeitsstörung. In R. Sachse, & M. Sachse (Eds.), *Forschung in der Klärungsorientierten Psychotherapie* (pp. 76–80). Lengerich: Pabst.

Sachse, R., & Sachse, M. (2016b). Wirksamkeit Klärungsorientierter Psychotherapie bei Klienten mit histrionischer Persönlichkeitsstörung. In R. Sachse, & M. Sachse (Eds.), *Forschung in der Klärungsorientierten Psychotherapie* (pp. 81–84). Lengerich: Pabst.

Sachse, R., & Sachse, M. (2016c). Effekte Klärungsorientierter Psychotherapie bei Klienten mit dependenter Persönlichkeitsstörung. In R. Sachse, & M. Sachse (Eds.), *Forschung in der Klärungsorientierten Psychotherapie* (pp. 85–88). Lengerich: Pabst.

Sachse, R., & Sachse, M. (2016d). Wirksamkeit Klärungsorientierter Psychotherapie bei Klienten mit psychosomatischer Verarbeitungsstruktur. In R. Sachse, & M. Sachse (Eds.), *Forschung in der Klärungsorientierten Psychotherapie* (pp. 89–93). Lengerich: Pabst.

Sachse, R., & Sachse, M. (2016e). Welche Persönlichkeitsstörungen profitieren wie von Klärungsorientierter Psychotherapie? In R. Sachse, & M. Sachse (Eds.), *Forschung in der Klärungsorientierten Psychotherapie* (pp. 97–98). Lengerich: Pabst.

Sachse, R., Sachse, M., & Diermann, E. (2018). Effekte Klärungsorientierter Psychotherapie bei Klienten mit depressiven Störungen. In R. Sachse, & M. Sachse (Eds.), *Forschung in der Klärungsorientierten Psychotherapie II*. Lengerich: Pabst (im Druck).

Sachse, R., Sachse, M., & Fasbender, J. (2010). *Klärungsorientierte Psychotherapie von Persönlichkeitsstörungen*. Göttingen: Hogrefe.

Sachse, R., Sachse, M., & Fasbender, J. (2011). *Klärungsorientierte Psychotherapie der narzisstischen Persönlichkeitsstörung*. Göttingen: Hogrefe.

Sachse, R., Sachse, M., & Fasbender, J. (2016). *Grundlagen Klärungsorientierter Psychotherapie*. Göttingen: Hogrefe.

Truax, C. B. (1963). Effective ingredients in psychotherapy: An approach to unrevealing the patient-therapist-interaction. *Journal of Counseling Psychology, 10*, 256–263.

Truax, C. B. (1968). Therapist interpersonal reinforcement of client self-exploration and therapeutic outcome in group-psychotherapy. *Journal of Counseling Psychology, 15*, 225–231.

Vazire, S., Naumann, L. P., Rentfrow, P. J., & Gosling, S. D. (2008). Portrait of a narcissism in physical appearance. *Journal of Research in Personality, 42*, 1439–1447.

Zeigler-Hill, V., Myers, E. M., & Clark, C. B. (2010). Narcissism and self-esteem reactivity: The role of negative achievement events. *Journal of Research in Personality, 44*, 285–292.

CHAPTER

8

Formulation of Functioning for Avoidant Personality Disorder in Metacognitive Interpersonal Therapy

Giancarlo Dimaggio, Raffaele Popolo, Giampaolo Salvatore

Centro di Terapia Metacognitiva Interpersonale, Rome, Italy

UNDERLYING THEORY

Avoidant Personality Disorder (AvPD) is one of the most severe and disabling conditions among all personality disorders (PD), with an estimated prevalence of 1.7% among the general population and the highest rate in Norway (Torgersen et al., 2001; Weinbrecht, Schulze, Boettcher, & Renneberg, 2016). It co-occurs with symptom disorders, such as social phobia, general anxiety, eating disorders and substance abuse, and involves reduced capacity to work and form stable intimate relationships (Weinbrecht et al., 2016). In spite of its similarities with social phobia, the domains of intimacy and attachment are severely disturbed and patients have diminished capacity to understand mental states (Eikenæs, Pedersen, & Wilberg, 2016; Pellecchia et al., 2018). Key to delivering effective therapies to this problematic population is a fine-grained case formulation, making it possible to pinpoint which mechanisms of change to target. This is best achieved by identifying which domains of psychopathology (Livesley, Dimaggio, & Clarkin, 2016) to focus upon with the aim of devising treatments that are attuned to the actual needs of sufferers.

Metacognitive Interpersonal Therapy (MIT; Dimaggio, Montano, Popolo, & Salvatore, 2015; Dimaggio, Semerari, Carcione, Nicolò, & Procacci, 2007) focuses on four domains: (1) maladaptive schemas for self

Case Formulation for Personality Disorders
https://doi.org/10.1016/B978-0-12-813521-1.00008-4

and others; (2) impaired metacognition, which is the ability to recognize and reflect on mental states, both of oneself and of the others; (3) reduced autobiographical memory; (4) maladaptive emotional regulation and coping, at both extremes, i.e., dysregulation and inhibition. MIT hypothesizes problems are kept going by interaction mechanisms among these domains (Dimaggio, Semerari et al., 2007).

Treatment for AvPD is largely underinvestigated and only a few studies have tried to address it. Outcomes are positive but less than optimal and there is no conclusive proof that one treatment works better than others. There is a significant percentage of dropouts and many do not respond, or only partially. In early cognitive behavioural therapy (CBT) studies, the recovery rate was just 40% when using only the fear of negative evaluation scale (Renneberg, Goldstein, Phillips, & Chambless, 1990). More positive outcomes were achieved by Emmelkamp et al. (2006), who showed that CBT and Brief Dynamic therapies had positive effects on avoidance and social phobia, with CBT being significantly superior. Only 9% of the sample had Avoidant PD after treatment in the CBT group, against 36% in dynamic therapy. Only 15 out of 21 patients were available for follow-up in the CBT group, and outcome regarding PD was only measured as having versus not having AvPD. This means that in theory some may have achieved recovery with a reduction of only one criterion. Strauss et al. (2006) achieved a 21% drop-out rate and a recovery rate between 63% and 67% for AvPD.

In the psychodynamic field, Svartberg, Stiles, and Seltzer (2004) found no superiority of CBT over dynamic therapies; recovery rates were only 40%–52% in terms of symptoms, while PD remission was not calculated. Schema-therapy was found superior to Clarification Oriented Therapy (COT) (Bamelis, Evers, Spinhoven, & Arntz, 2014) for a wide array of non-borderline PDs, though quality of COT is questionable as there was no regular model-consistent supervision. Results were not reported specifically for AvPD. Drop-out rates were 25.8% in Schema-Therapy. A noncontrolled study of Schema-Therapy in groups (Skewes, Samson, Simpson, & van Vreeswijk, 2014) had 35% dropouts and only 36.8% of patients achieved reliable symptom change at termination. Outcome for AvPD was not assessed. In a multiple baseline Schema-Therapy study with older adults (Videlerm et al., 2017), three patients had AvPD at intake and completed treatment, and none had AvPD at the end of therapy. There is room for optimism when treating AvPD. Coming studies need to analyze outcomes in terms of the residual presence of AvPD, number of specific and overall PD criteria met, and symptoms, functioning and quality of life. Drop-out rates can realistically be reduced to around 20% or less, and recovery could increase.

Evidence for the effectiveness of MIT for PD, and AvPD in particular, is appearing. In one single case series (Dimaggio et al., 2017), one client had AvPD and met 23 overall criteria at intake. He achieved remission for

AvPD and met only 10 PD criteria at therapy termination. In a multiple baseline case series (Gordon-King, Schweitzer, & Dimaggio, 2018), three patients had AvPD at intake and none after one year. Reliable change was achieved in symptoms and functioning. In a pilot randomized controlled trial of 16 sessions of group MIT versus TAU + waiting list (Popolo et al., 2018), 10 patients received MIT, six of whom had AvPD. Only two participants out of 10 dropped-out (not reported whether they had AvPD). Reliable change was achieved with large effects on symptoms and functioning and MIT-G substantially outperformed the control group. The capacity to appraise the mental states of self and others significantly improved only in the MIT group.

The larger picture on outcome for AvPD is that there are large margins for improvement and MIT holds realistic promises of being effective and containing dropouts to a very small percentage; possibly the sensitivity of its case formulation is one contributing factor.

MALADAPTIVE SCHEMAS FOR SELF AND OTHERS

PDs endorse dysfunctional views of self and others and their interactions. When thinking about interpersonal relationships, they tend to predict that these will go awry and their needs and wishes will be unmet. For example, when driven by the wish to be appreciated, a patient with AvPD tends to expect others to harshly criticize her, eliciting feelings of shame, humiliation and sadness at the idea of having failed. She is prone to seeing others as judgemental even with minimal cues; when signals are ambiguous, patients rely on negative attributions. A teacher's neutral expression during an examination becomes proof of looming failure. We first describe the social motives that drive the human actions around which schemas are built, and then the typical AvPD schemas.

Interpersonal Motives

Interpersonal schemas are predictions about how others will respond to one's goals. Humans are driven by a set of evolutionarily shaped motives, and suffering stems from expectations these goals will remain unfulfilled (Baumeister & Leary, 1995; Fassone et al., 2016; Gilbert, 1989; Lichtenberg, 1989; Liotti & Gilbert, 2011; Panksepp, 1998; Tomasello, Carpenter, Call, Behne, & Moll, 2005). These motives include: (1) attachment (Bowlby, 1988), which is the need for love, care, nurturing and protection when one feels vulnerable or in need; (2) care-giving, which is the tendency to help persons we feel connected to when they are vulnerable or suffering; (3) the need for autonomy and independence, which is activated to explore the environment and find resources. Curiosity and playfulness are correlates of its activation; (4) social rank, which is triggered when resources are limited and is aimed at deciding who will access them first after a hierarchy has been established. Persons motivated by social rank can experience anger when others challenge them or threaten their status; pride or contempt arise when they feel they are superior or will win a competition. Conversely, shame occurs when they feel like losers or inferiors. Sadness arrives when they lose hope they can restore their rank; (5) group inclusion/affiliation, which refers to the basic need to belong to a society where they share interests, values, rituals, rules and practices; (6) sexuality, which regulates behaviours related to attracting a romantic partner, with the goal of forming long-term bonds where primary sexual drives can be met and which yield erotic pleasure. Finally, (7) cooperation among peers maintains stable bonds. Cooperation happens when we form alliances aimed at putting resources together to meet common goals.

AvPD is guided by maladaptive self–other attributions when driven by these motives. We review evidence about the more dominant interpersonal patterns, while trying to frame them in the context of the earlier-described motives. For the sake of space we focus on social rank, attachment, autonomy and group belonging. In the case formulation paragraph we describe the structure of schemas according to MIT.

Social rank is an area where AvPDs experience some major problems. They tend to feel being criticized for not being up to others' expectations and are afraid of social judgement. Fear of criticism is at the very heart of the DSM definition of AvPD (American Psychiatric Association, 2013). Patients fear shame and ridicule, and feel inadequate, inferior, inept and unappealing. All these elements, with the associated feelings of fear of judgement and shame, can be categorized as happening when social rank is turned on (Gilbert, 1989). AvPDs need to feel considered worthy and are quick to think that others will judge and possibly humiliate them, which evokes shame and social anxiety. Empirically, fear of parental criticism and excessive concern about making mistakes, elements of maladaptive perfectionism, were associated to AvPD traits in both clinical and community samples (Dimaggio, Lysaker et al., 2015; 2018). The punitive and demanding schema modes (Young, Klosko, & Weishaar, 2003) are heightened in AvPD (Bamelis, Renner, Heidkamp, & Arntz, 2011). Avoidance was the most common mode in sessions with AvPD patients, followed by vulnerability – probably attachment-related – and then by the dysfunctional parent mode, which reflects issues of punishment and harsh judgment (Peled, Bar-Kalifa, & Rafaeli, 2017). The compliant/surrender mode was heightened, possibly a sign of the activation of social rank, as AvPDs submit to avoid further criticism. Submissiveness has been found to be the prominent interpersonal problem in AvPD (Wright, Scott, Stepp, Hallquist, & Pilkonis, 2015).

Attachment is disturbed in AvPD. Empirical evidence shows that AvPDs expect others not to meet their requests for care and instead either reject, control or set limits. Alternatively AvPDs can be anxious and alarmed. This pattern corresponds to fearful attachment. AvPDs find intimacy discomforting, and lack confidence in attachment relationships; some found that AvPD features Disorganized/Unresolved attachment (Nakash-Eisikovits, Dutra, & Westen, 2002). This pattern involves confusion about what to expect from others, ranging from rejection to threat, or to care. Individuals with disorganized attachment are unable to form a stable strategy for achieving intimacy and seek care, while being vulnerable to any kind of negative outcome. Their tendency to dismiss attachment may be a strategy for handling the fear and confusion stemming from the construction of others as unpredictable and dangerous. Attachment disturbances distinguish AvPD from social phobia. AvPD had more attachment anxiety and separation frustration than social phobia alone (Eikenæs et al., 2016). AvPDs report stories of childhood physical neglect (Eikenaes, Egeland, Hummelen, & Wilberg, 2015) and feel vulnerable, lonely, abandoned and thus tending to be detached self-soothing (Bamelis et al., 2011).

As regards autonomy/exploration, AvPDs tend to passivity, with low levels of focusing on their goals and a lack of deep-seated desires to drive them. They do not try to overcome obstacles or persevere in tasks aimed at reaching goals (Dimaggio, Montano et al., 2015). They are high in submissive behaviours, or low dominance, as seen from the other pole, which researchers consider a sign of poor agency (Wiggins & Pincus, 1989). AvPDs' symptoms and problems increase when they are less dominant and assertive (Wright et al., 2015), due probably to a hypo-activation of the exploratory system.

As regards group belonging, research has been performed using interpersonal inventories, where many items reflect low group affiliation ability, e.g., 'It is hard for me to join groups' (Pilkonis, Kim, Proietti, & Barkham, 1996). The main aspect of AvPD is social avoidance (Monsen, Hagtvet, Havik, & Eilertsen, 2006). AvPDs' tendency to experience group exclusion is related to both fear of rejection and criticism and to lack of capacity to feel connectedness (Colle et al., 2017). They would like to join, but feel inadequate and inferior. They do not focus on possible shared elements and end up feeling different. AvPDs have difficulties recognizing their own feelings and thoughts and are poor at understanding others' minds (Dimaggio, Procacci et al., 2007; Pellecchia et al., 2018; Semerari et al., 2003). Consequently, they do not form an image of themselves sharing thoughts, values and feelings with others.

MIT identifies schemas according to a very specific structure, largely based on the Core Conflictual Relational Theme (Luborsky & Crits-Christoph, 1998): (1) core self-images underlying the wish, for example *I as unworthy and flawed* as opposed to *worthy and functioning*. Every wish is sustained by at least two core self-images: one positive and one negative; (2) an 'If … then …' procedure (Baldwin, 1992) to fulfil the basic wish; this is an adaptive procedure, of the type: 'If I show my qualities, then the other …'; (3) the other's expected or appraised responses. Again, there is more than one response. For example, when driven by the negative self-image, the other may be construed as harsh, critical or spiteful. When driven by the positive self-image (worthy and functioning), the other can be constructed as either benevolent and praising or as unfairly harsh and critical; (4) the self's responses to the other's responses. These include cognitions, affects and bodily feelings, and typically trigger maladaptive coping. For example, a patient driven by social rank, with an *unworthy* active self-image, can be convinced the other is critical and spiteful. The self's response may be: 'I deserved criticism, I failed, so I feel ashamed and sad'. When the underlying self-image is *worthy*, the reaction will be that criticism is unwarranted; this evokes anger.

IMPAIRED METACOGNITION

Poor metacognition (Semerari et al., 2003), i.e., the capacity to understand mental states both of oneself and the others, and to regulate emotions and social behaviour on the basis of mentalistic knowledge has long identified in AvPD. Metacognition includes operations ranging from being aware of what one feels and thinks to higher order capacities such as forming an integrated view of oneself and the others as situations and mental states change. It includes the ability to see the world from the eyes of the others and to use an increasingly complex reading of mental states to soothe suffering, solve social problems, sustain bonds and alliances and solve conflicts. The metacognitive system is broadly impaired in AvPD. The capacity to recognize what one feels and communicate it to others is poor and taking a critical distance from one's own ideas, i.e., differentiation, is limited (Dimaggio, Procacci et al., 2007; Johansen, Normann-Eide, Normann-Eide, & Wilberg, 2013; Nicolò et al., 2011; Semerari et al., 2014); AvPDs have problems in considering their maladaptive beliefs about self and others to be subjective and not necessarily mirroring reality. A male patient in his 30s in group therapy was so convinced a girl he was dating had no interest in him that he did not pay attention to expressive and behavioural cues and used an excuse to leave quickly. Only after some therapy work did he realize he was not questioning his schema-driven attribution.

The capacity to form a coherent self-image is damaged in AvPD. Patients may hold positive beliefs about self and others, but lack a coherent self in which positive and negative aspects are balanced. They undervalue moments in which they act driven by their positive qualities and switch to negative attributions. Another young male patient noted the girlfriend he was dating seemed distant. He concluded she had no more interest in him and he did not phone her for two days. The girl contacted him and said she had had some difficult moments, but was still interested in him. The patient realized he did not consider discrepant information when he was prey to negative affects evoked by ideas of being uninteresting and unlovable.

AvPDs' narratives display poor capacity to understand the mind of the others and take their perspective (Dimaggio et al., 2009; Pellecchia et al., 2018; Semerari et al., 2014). In laboratory tasks they have problems identifying facial expressions of fear (Rosenthal et al., 2011). Their capacity to use awareness of mental states for effective problem solving, i.e., metacognitive mastery, is limited (Carcione et al., 2011). In treatment-seeking substance abusers, poor capacity to recognize own affects predicted a number of Cluster C PD traits (including avoidant) but the effect was mediated by poor metacognitive mastery. Poor awareness of one's own affects creates social problems, as manifested by a higher number of PD criteria, but only if it is coupled with poor mentalistic problem-solving strategies (Lysaker et al., 2014).

POOR AUTOBIOGRAPHICAL MEMORY

AvPDs are not keen on storytelling. They use generalized statements to report their problems. Their initial sessions are filled with: 'I feel tense when meeting people', 'My workplace is bad'. They express theories for their problems depicting a society they do not belong to, and where it is hard to get along with others. They report suffering often as physical symptoms. They lack the capacity to describe specific aspects of their experience happening during episodes where they interact with others, which is narrative episodes. Research and clinical observations note the existence of overgeneral memories in AvPD (Dimaggio, Montano et al., 2015; Spinhoven, Bamelis, Molendijk, Haringsma, & Arntz, 2009).

MALADAPTIVE EMOTIONAL REGULATION AND COPING

Patients with AvPD expect negative reactions from others, typically criticism and rejection. They also have a bias towards overattribution of negative intentions towards them. A computer programmer in his 50s experienced anxiety at the idea of standing in front of his workgroup. He was easily convinced the others would find him ridiculous because his voice trembled and interpreted any facial expression as a sign of criticism.

This made him feel shame and sadness at the idea of being unworthy, a typical AvPD feature.

When patients with AvPD experience negative emotions, they adopt maladaptive coping procedures, both behavioural and cognitive. These strategies are counterproductive in that they (1) fail to tone emotions down; (2) overregulate emotions (Dimaggio et al., 2018; Popolo et al., 2014) to the point patients become unaware of them and can no longer use them as a reliable guide; (3) include behaviours that hamper the opportunity to meet deep-seated wishes (desires). Massive avoidance prevents, for example, searching for a job, striving for a better work position or courting a potential romantic partner. We lump together here emotion dysregulation and maladaptive coping. The reason is that emotional regulation is about reaching an optimal level of emotional arousal. Sensations linked to hypo- and hyper-arousal are disturbing to people, who then strive to return to a tolerable level of affect experience. Coping involves both managing distress and avoiding the negative consequences of interactions. Coping and emotional regulation tend to go together. For example, a patient might feel ashamed when meeting a critical other, so that she has at the same time to tolerate shame and protect herself from the negative image of self-as-flawed and inept. A patient with AvPD may avoid a potential malevolent judge for two reasons: (1) preventing the experience of shame to not feel pain, and (2) coping with the negative self-image by preventing its surfacing in consciousness.

When analyzed with self-reports, both emotional inhibition and dysregulation are massively present in AvPD. As regards inhibition, patients tend to prevent social displays of feelings and are shy about them (Dimaggio et al., 2018; Popolo et al., 2014). As regards dysregulation, when their arousal mounts they have very limited capacity to tone it down. As a result, emotions spiral out of control and overwhelm them, so that they are unable to form strategies for dealing with them, sustain goal-oriented action or think they can control affects (Dimaggio et al., 2017). We list here some of the most prominent emotional regulation and coping strategies together, trying to identify when they are used for restoring a tolerable level of affect experience and when for dealing with negative self-images.

Avoidance seems the strategy AvPDs adopt most easily and quickly, with a limited thinking effort. Behavioural avoidance involves social withdrawal or resorting to solitary activities. AvPDs use the Internet to get some social contact without intimacy, ranging from sex to online games. They compulsively watch TV series and listen to music or do other activities not involving deep exchanges with others. If they get along with others, this is often restricted to shared interests, and they do not engage in other forms of contact. Performing these activities grants some rewards, makes them feel alive and renders their loneliness easier to bear.

Cognitive avoidance (Borkovec, Alcaine, & Behar, 2004, pp. 77–108) involves acting so as to not think of, or recall, situations that could activate negative images. It may go as far as dissociation or excessive fantasizing. Cognitive avoidance can be used consciously. One patient with AvPD said: 'I don't want to think about painful situations. I don't like emotional suffering. If I put my mind elsewhere I feel better'. However, avoidance did not solve his problems and he suffered from social anxiety and had intense worry. In anxiety disorders, experiential avoidance, including cognitive and behavioural aspects, is a predictor of symptom maintenance (Spinhoven, Drost, de Rooij, van Hemert, & Penninx, 2016). Moreover, it is related to repetitive thinking, such as worry and rumination, in maintaining anxiety. Though research does not explicitly focus on AvPD, but instead on social phobia which overlaps susbtantially with it, we contend these observations can explain part of the problems of AvPD as well. Worrying and ruminating are cognitive strategies used to cope with perceived threats and regulate the associated emotions (Wells, 2008). Both involve negative and positive metacognitive beliefs, that is beliefs about beliefs, about the usefulness of worrying itself. They are divided into (1) positive beliefs: 'Worrying helps me prevent danger' and (2) negative beliefs, e.g., about the uncontrollability of repetitive thinking: 'When I start worrying it's like a train I can't stop'. Repetitive thinking sustains anxiety and depression (Spinhoven et al., 2016), both aspects strongly associated with AvPD. Positive and negative metacognitive beliefs can coexist. In AvPD worry tends to focus on the idea that others represent a threat and is aimed at forestalling harm by acting in ways patients consider more socially acceptable. In this case worry is focused on negative images. Worry and avoidance sustain themselves reciprocally (Spinhoven et al., 2016). A student who has to decide whether to take an exam starts thinking about negative outcomes. He has a positive metacognitive belief about worrying: 'If I worry, I will study harder'. This instead increases anxiety and sense of vulnerability, which in turn foster worry in about preventing failures. Anxiety mounts to the point that avoidance helps soothe it, so that the student decides to not show up to the exam. This cuts arousal in the short-term but sustains the negative self-image. Sense of failure paves the way for further worrying the next time he has to face a challenge. We have noted repetitive thinking in virtually all of our AvPD clients (Ottavi, Passarella, Pasinetti, Salvatore, & Dimaggio, 2016) and we expect research will confirm its presence.

Another coping strategy in AvPD is perfectionism, which is aimed at sustaining a desired self-image. Perfectionism pertains to the activation of the social rank system. It is present in the majority of PDs (Dimaggio, Lysaker et al., 2015; Dimaggio et al., 2018; Dimaggio, Montano et al., 2015). In a first clinical sample (Dimaggio, Lysaker et al., 2015; Dimaggio, Montano et al., 2015), significant correlations of AvPD traits with all the aspects of maladaptive perfectionism emerged (Frost, Marten, Lahart, & Rosenblate, 1990), in particular with excessive concern over mistakes, doubts about actions and also expectations of parental criticism. In a large clinical sample (Dimaggio et al., 2018), perfectionism was highly correlated with AvPD. In an MIT formulation, perfectionism is a coping strategy enacted to try to restore self-esteem after meeting a negative response from a harsh, spiteful or rejecting other. A typical example is: 'I long for approval but I'm convinced that the other will judge me as I feel I am unworthy. When I sense I am criticized I feel ashamed. Only if I improve my performance have I any chance of appreciation'. Raising the bar is an attempt to comply with others' expectations. This strategy is problematic even if conditional acceptance is obtained (which rarely happens). In fact, AvPDs maintain the idea they cannot be appreciated for what they are, but need to improve themselves, given that the core self will be rejected. Perfectionism can be an alternative to avoidance, so that AvPDs force themselves to pursue unrealistic standards. It can also sustain avoidance, when coupled with worry. A person starts thinking about improving her performance. At the beginning she tries practising more but is anxious at the idea of being criticized. Eventually the combination of anxiety, distress and fatigue sustains the negative self-image and makes the cost of perfectionism unbearable, leading to behavioural avoidance.

A last form of coping is resorting to narcissistic functioning (Dimaggio, Procacci et al., 2007; Dimaggio, Semerari et al., 2007; Young et al., 2003). AvPDs harbour grandiose fantasies where they take revenge and reverse roles, passing from subjugated to dominant, from slave to tyrant. This shift can happen in situations where they achieve success and protects them from contact with the negative self-image. Behaviourally, they are dominant and arrogant towards those they see as inferior. At the same time, they keep worrying about flaws being detected, which, on the one hand, fosters anxiety about this and, on the other hand, makes them persist in hyper-compensating and sustains their perfectionism. In sum, AvPDs use many maladaptive coping strategies, which, interacting together, lead to cycles sustaining negative interpersonal schemas, increasing suffering and worsening social performance.

A METACOGNITIVE INTERPERSONAL THERAPY (MIT)-BASED CASE FORMULATION: SELF-SUSTAINING PROCESSES

MIT case formulation is based on an understanding of the schemas shared by patient and therapist. In PD different elements of pathology interact as a system, creating problem-sustaining cycles (Dimaggio, Procacci et al., 2007; Dimaggio, Semerari et al., 2007). In the case of AvPD the elements have a series of toxic interactions which make it very difficult for an individual to escape. Schemas are typically not represented at a conscious level and persons are guided by implicit assumptions they are barely aware of. Patients endorse generalized ideas about themselves and others that they take for granted.

CLINICAL GUIDE TO CASE FORMULATION

There are several tools available for assessing a patient with AvPD (see Table 8.1). MIT prefers to assess schemas with transcript analysis, using methods like the Core Conflictual Relationship Theme (Luborsky & Crits-Christoph, 1998) or Plan Analysis (Caspar & Ecker, 2008), because in their narratives patients report aspects of their current experience which they do not consider when answering questionnaires. Information coming

TABLE 8.1 Assessment of AvPD

Domain	Test	Authors
Schemas for self and others	Young Schema Questionnaire	Young (1998)
	Inventories of Interpersonal problems	Pilkonis et al. (1996)
	Core Conflictual Relationship Theme	Luborsky and Crits-Christoph (1998)
Metacognition	Metacognition Assessment Scale-R	Carcione et al. (2010)
	Toronto Alexithimia Scale – 20	Bagby, Parker, and Taylor (1994)
	Movie for the Assessment of Social Cognition	Dziobek et al. (2006)
	Metacognitive Questionnaire	Wells and Cartwright-Hatton (2004)
Autobiographical memory	Autobiographical Memory Test	Williams and Broadbent (1986)
Emotion regulation and coping	Kellner's Emotional Inhibition Scale	Grandi, Sirri, Wise, Tossani, and Fava (2011)
	Difficulties in Emotion Regulation Scale	Gratz and Roemer (2004)
	Frost Multidimensional Perfectionism Scale	Frost et al. (1990)
	Penn Worry State Questionnaire	Meyer, Miller, Metzger, and Borkovec (1990)

from narratives is richer and provides a picture closer to their actual psychological functioning, though inventories may be useful for a first quick evaluation of schemas.

Metacognition is best evaluated in patients' discourse, e.g., with interviews systematically assessing all its elements (Semerari et al., 2014). Memory specificity can be assessed with the Autobiographical Memory Test (ATM; Williams & Broadbent, 1986), which measures how one tends to use generalized versus specific memories to describe experience. Emotion regulation skills can be analyzed with self-reports, which provide a first-glance view of how patients relate to their affects. Finally, worry and other problematic coping strategies can be assessed with questionnaires, which are a reliable and provide a guide for the beliefs sustaining repetitive thinking. Information coming from all these interviews, tasks and questionnaires provides a clinician with a comprehensive view of patients' problems and malfunctioning, which can be shared with them at therapy outset. Overall, MIT prioritizes information coming from the therapeutic conversation.

METACOGNITIVE INTERPERSONAL THERAPY (MIT)-BASED CASE FORMULATION AND THERAPY PLANNING: MARIO'S STORY

MIT has been manualized on a step-by-step basis (Dimaggio, Montano et al., 2015). Case formulation is mostly based on an evaluation of the initial sessions, in the context of the first major therapy stage, *Shared formulation of functioning*. It starts with eliciting specific and detailed autobiographical memories, with the aim of overcoming the obstacles of reduced emotional awareness, intellectualizing thinking style and avoidance of intimacy with the therapist. Narrative episodes are the basis for promoting awareness of cognitions, affects and their interactions that is improving self-reflection. MIT pays attention to the metacognitive level patients are able to deploy to act within the therapeutic zone of proximal development, avoiding interventions the patient is unable to make use of (Zonzi et al., 2014).

With multiple episodes clinicians and patients can formulate the latter's maladaptive interpersonal schemas. The goal is to plant a seed of differentiation, that is the capacity to understand that suffering comes from one's own construction of interpersonal relationships. Clinicians also foster access to the healthy self and tentatively implement adaptive behaviours consistent with patients' innermost wishes and preferences. They guide patients to grasping that relationships can be seen in ways not predicted by their schemas and that things may appear different when seen from a different perspective. To promote these aspects, MIT adopts many techniques (see Dimaggio, Lysaker et al., 2015; Dimaggio, Montano et al., 2015 for an overview), recently including experiential work, in the form of guided imagery, two-chair technique, role-play and body work. Formulation of functioning includes aspects of early change promotion: (1) symptom decrease; (2) improving metacognition; (3) accessing the healthy self at an experiential level.

True and proper *Change promoting* is the second part, which begins only successfully agreeing on a formulation. AvPDs need to have achieved a capacity for differentiation, even if unstable, and to be aware of healthy self-aspects. We present a clinical case focusing on the *Shared formulation of functioning* aspect. There is also some description of the change process.

Client's History and Presentation of Problem

Mario was a 40-year-old university professor. He asked for therapy because of problems at work and with intimacy. His fear of criticism made him avoid social contact to the point of not having any friends. Thinking about his condition made him feel sad and ruminate about his failures. He had always been shy. He was a perfectionist and imposed unrelenting standards both on himself and others. Of alcohol and benzodiazepines he said, 'They tear down the wall between me and others', but they made him ashamed of what others would think of his abuse. Without alcohol before a social encounter he worried about his defects and about his mind going blank during a conversation. He feared scorn and ridicule. He worried about the outcome of his current romantic relationship, fearing abandonment because of his alleged unworthiness. He was severely depressed to the point of not keeping his house clean.

His father was 'mean, stingy, distant'. His mother was closer and more relaxed. He had only a few short-term romantic relationships, as he never felt like deeply sharing anything. He was married when he was 30 for five years. He hated meeting his wife's family or going out with her friends. He says: 'I faced these situations heroically'. Then his wife asked for divorce. Mario feared he was not achieving what he should, but to avoid criticism he procrastinated and avoided social exposure, with the result that he could not pursue his ambition of being a successful researcher. He felt he had missed opportunities. In the initial sessions he could only describe in a generalized way his core beliefs of self-as-flawed, inferior and socially rejected, with others depicted as spiteful and unaccepting. He wanted to be part of a group and share with others, so that he was driven by the wish for group inclusion, but he expected criticism. Mario suffered from Avoidant PD with subthreshold Obsessive-Compulsive and Depressive PD, as diagnosed with the SCID-II. He met a total of 15 PD criteria. As regards the key elements of an MIT-based case formulation, his narrative was extremely impoverished, and he did not report specific autobiographical memories. This is an excerpt from the initial stages:

> T: So you are anxious: Can you tell me more about what you are afraid of? Is there any situation that provokes anxiety?
> M: I don't know. University in Italy is strange. People are not committed to their work … then … I have this stomach ache and, I don't know, I'm overweight you know. I know I should diet but I'm so weak-willed and so … I should be more self-confident and, I say it to myself every morning. This morning I was browsing through a book. You know it's an author that …

Mario could continue speaking endlessly with a flat tone, without mentioning any specific event and without reporting either emotions or specific facts, or describing any interactions with specific persons. Lack of capacity to describe affects was the prominent aspect of his metacognitive dysfunction, together with the incapacity to differentiate; he did not realize that his perception of self-as-flawed and inferior was an idea that did not necessarily mirror reality. We describe the core aspects of the case formulation during the description of the early therapy stages. As MIT relies marginally on self-reports to assess schemas, we define the schema after the stage in which the therapist elicited specific memories.

Early Treatment Phases and Refinement of the Case Formulation

Mario underwent weekly MIT with one of us (RP). Another psychiatrist gave him Sertraline (100 mg/day) and Lamotrigine (75 mg/day). The initial task was to regulate the therapy relationship and form an alliance. The therapist validated Mario's fears, noting that wanting to be appreciated and fearing criticism is deeply human; Mario 'simply' experienced them too intensely. The therapist had difficulties understanding Mario's cognitions and affects because of his intellectualizing. As a result the therapist had to self-regulate his sense of incapacity. Moreover, given that Mario used avoidance as a coping strategy, by speaking flatly with an inexpressive face, the therapist felt distant, bored and not involved, typical reactions to AvPDs (Dimaggio, Procacci et al., 2007; Dimaggio, Semerari et al., 2007). The therapist had to regulate his tendencies to get distracted, so he looked for common interests, in particular in the university world. He self-disclosed his own fears of social judgement when presenting papers in conferences, which made Mario feel more relaxed and understood. The therapist said continuously that access to specific memories would increase the chances of him understanding Mario. So he asked him to pay attention to events happening in the days after the sessions. In the sixth session he, with some difficulty, obtained an episode from when Mario was teaching.

M: I have not been doing anything lately.
T: What things are you referring to?
M: Don't know. Beginning a diet … I buy junk food and drink alcohol … I should train but don't go to the gym … Luisa (*his partner*) tells me I should walk but I don't …

In this excerpt it is evident that Mario has poor agency, which points to the hypo-activation of the exploratory/autonomy motive. He has difficulties reporting his inner states, which is a key aspect of the metacognitive dysfunction.

M: I have problems at the University. Today I didn't want to teach.
T: Did something happen to provoke this idea?
M: I didn't want to … and the students were too few …
T: Let's keep focusing on this morning. What passed through your mind when you were in the room?
M: I had difficulties in the last lesson.
T: How was it?
M: Bad. I didn't like it.
T: Can you tell me more details about that lesson?
M: It was on Thursday.
T: What kind of lesson?
M: I had to complete a previous lesson …
T: Let's try to reconstruct the scene as if it was happening now. Can you figure it out?
M: A bit.
T: What do you see? What do you note? Were the students there when you arrived?
M: There are students in the classroom, but very few. I don't know why they chose to follow my course.
T: How many hours do you have?
M: Two. But I don't feel good. (*Here Mario has poor metacognitive awareness of affects and cannot articulate the sense of not feeling good using specific emotional language.*) I don't want to stay. (*Poor emotional awareness goes together with maladaptive coping, i.e., behavioural avoidance.*)
T: What happens to make you want to go away?
M: I'm tired. I didn't want to come. Luisa insisted I should work more regularly.
T: Do you feel up to it?
M: Some days I feel better; I don't know why. (*Another moment of poor metacognitive awareness, that is the incapacity to understand the causes evoking an affect.*) That day I was on time, but when I watched the students I felt anxious.

T: Anxious at the idea of what?
M: They were talking and then stopped, waiting for me to lecture.
T: What do you think when seeing these faces?
M: It's hard to begin. I feel awkward.
T: What do you feel?
M: Unease. I go out for a moment and take some pills, but too many. (*Again, poor awareness of affects: he can only say 'unease', followed by maladaptive coping, i.e., inappropriate use of medication for down-regulating affect.*) When I'm back, I stutter. I'm dizzy. It seems they're smiling, as they understand I have problems. Hard for me to bear. I have to go. I say I have a temperature and run away.

With some difficulties, due to his poor awareness of mental states, it is possible to start understanding the structure of the episode in a way consistent with the schema. Note that this is not yet a schema, as schemas require multiple episodes, but the structure of the summary is the same.

Mario's wish involves the social rank motive. He wants to be appreciated; he expects that if he displays his qualities, then the others will be disinterested ('few students') or discover his flaws. As a result, he experiences tension, which he cannot define more because of his poor metacognitive monitoring, and he copes using behavioural avoidance. For a second, a healthier self-image appears 'Sometimes I feel better', but Mario is not aware of what elicited this positive self-state. Moreover, this positive sensation soon fades way without giving him time enough to reflect on it and understand the reasons which made him feel better. The outcome of the episode is that after avoidance and inappropriate self-soothing with medication, Mario's agency drops further. A different episode helps the therapist to formulate Mario's functioning in a shared way:

M: Sunday morning we went out for breakfast and then Luisa asked me to visit her parents, to discuss our wedding plans. (*Mario proposed a few months ago and Luisa accepted.*)
T: How did you feel when Luisa asked you that?
M: Not good. I didn't sleep well … It's hard for me talking with her parents because my mind goes blank and I have nothing to say.
T: What was the emotion at that moment?
M: A bit worried.
T: Worried is similar to?
M: … anxious. It was strange to think about the wedding. I don't know how to join in a conversation about a wedding lunch. (*Mario can report a specific aspect, but cannot be clear about the cognitive antecedent, which is again a sign of poor metacognitive awareness. He also has poor mastery, feels impotent and cannot use knowledge about mental states to confront a social challenge.*)
T: Did you decide to go?

M: I'd have preferred not to (*in absence of knowledge about how to handle social situations, he tends to rely on avoidance*), but Luisa insisted and I said yes. Lessons had been going better and Luisa and I had spent Saturday home talking about the lunch so I felt more relaxed and I could accept it. It would please Luisa and I could show a better side of myself to her parents ...
T: How did the meeting go?
M: I didn't feel good. Luisa and her parents were talking about whom to invite. I could not join in the conversation and felt confused. I ate and drank a lot.
T: You said you wanted to join in the conversation and be appreciated, but then you couldn't.
M: I wanted to... but I was afraid they'd think me strange. I tried to focus on what to say but that made me more and more confused. I shut myself off hoping no one noticed me ...
T: When precisely did you start to disengage from the conversation?
M: Hmm ... Luisa's parents were talking together about episodes I didn't know about and didn't understand. I felt like I couldn't get along with them.
T: What did you think at that moment?
M: ... like they didn't want me there. (*The outcome of the sequence where poor awareness of mental states, poor mastery and tendency is an increase in conviction about the negative self-belief.*) What do they want now?
T: What did you feel then?
M: Don't know. I was so anxious, I was unsure what they thought of me and felt a lot of distress, and then I started drinking. But that worsened things because I imagined they could think I was an alcoholic.
T: And what would be the consequence if they thought so?
M: They would tell Luisa I wouldn't be a good husband and she'd leave me.

The therapist summarized Mario's speech so far. This time he could note a clearer appearance of the healthy self, which he included in his MIT-based formulation.

T: Mario, you wanted to be a part of the conversation, wanted to be included. But mostly your concern was still about performance, being appreciated. You were able to show up because you felt in better shape. This time you were able to feel self-confident for a longer time, which is good. But then during lunch, with closer contact, this part vanished, the negative image of yourself took over and you were dominated by expectations of criticism. Then you could only try to become invisible and drink to sooth your anxiety. This made you feel worse. Your ideas that others dislike you were stronger, to the point of making you fear that your wish to feel loved and accepted by your partner would fail. Is that correct? Does it describe your experience at that moment? (*The therapist come to this conclusion organizing the elements of Mario's discourse consistently with a CCRT structure.*)

Mario nodded and could see himself in this formulation. The therapist asked Mario for remote memories he could associate with the recent ones and with the same structure. Thanks to the past episodes Mario related, it was possible to frame a comprehensive case formulation: Mario is driven by adaptive wishes: to be active, to be cared for and loved and to be part of a group. His basic self-image is *flawed* so that he thinks that when meeting others he expects them to be *critical*. The anticipated or real critical reaction makes him feel ashamed (shame appeared later in the episodes) and sustains his negative self-image. He also has a positive self-image of himself as *capable*, which sustains the hope to be appreciated and included, but it is short-lived. The reaction to the critical other includes feeling anxious. Agency diminishes and Mario resorts to avoidance and drug and alcohol abuse.

Change Promoting

Case formulation is key to treatment planning and achieving change. For the sake of completeness, we describe how the therapist helped Mario make progress by grounding therapy actions in the shared formulation of functioning. After reviewing the episodes and understanding that Mario was driven by maladaptive schemas, the goal was to achieve critical distance from them and sustain the healthy self. Another shared goal was to gain agency over states of suffering and reduce maladaptive coping in the form of avoidance and alcohol abuse. MIT tries to promote change by surfacing aspects of the healthy self. Mario discovered that, beside his oversensitivity to criticism, he was driven by a sincere passion for his work. So they decided to overcome fear of judgement, and he planned to present a paper on a topic he liked to a conference.

M: ... I know I should face the problem seriously, reading a lot for months ... it would be very good to impress the audience at this conference.
T: You feel up to this task?
M: Yes, I can try. Will I be able to deliver something important? Don't know.
T: Do you have memories of successful presentations at conferences?
M: Yes, in the past I did a couple of presentations that created some interest. Though I'm still afraid I could fail.
T: It's very good you can remember you can deliver good talks ... (*The therapist validates Mario's positive state and tries to help him note this aspect and bear it in mind.*) And do you feel capable of tolerating failure?

M: … It sounds painful … maybe I can … it's possible I can do a good job. Just that I'm not sure it's my priority now.
T: Ah! Ok. What is your true priority at this moment?
M: I mean … I am committed to this book I'm writing and … this is very important to me …
T: Is the topic of the conference also of interest to you? (*The goal of this intervention is to make Mario move from the social rank motive to the curiosity/exploration one. Doing things because he likes them, not to be appreciated.*)
M: Yes, I like the ideas. I have to study a lot but it's about things I am curious to learn about …

The conversation began regarding social rank, but the therapist helped Mario passing to curiosity and inner drive. The goal was now of doing something consistent with his own preferences. His mood changed as he focused on the ideas themselves he had to work on. Being criticized, though still eliciting some anxiety, became less significant. Mario now accepted delivering the speech as a behavioural task. The therapist insisted that the task was not about a successful presentation at the conference but facing the idea and trying. With this effort new information about his inner world would surface, and that was the main goal: having a richer understanding of his functioning in the context of trying to interrupt automatic dysfunctional patterns. Thus the risk that patients understand the task on a behavioural level, where performance is at stake, is minimized. In MIT, behavioural exposure and behavioural activation have three goals: (1) promoting agency over one's own goals; (2) fostering metacognition when facing previously unexpected situations; (3) improving access to the healthy self, as usually, even if old patterns arise, new elements are more accessible to consciousness during a task a patient has decided to be engaged in; (4) enriching social life. Mario could tolerate his anxiety and successfully delivered his speech, with a sense of being appreciated.

Outcome

After three years of treatment Mario did not have AvPD anymore and the total number of SCID-II criteria dropped to 6. Anxiety was reduced to a large extent: he no longer took medication and merely had some bouts which he could tolerate. He also recovered from his depression. He stopped his alcohol abuse, which required intensive inpatient treatment to reach detoxification. As regards metacognition, he was more able to identify his emotions. Some tendencies to pessimism and passivity remained, but he acknowledged they were part of his temperament since he was young. Social functioning was improved. He was able to teach regularly, finalized some specialized papers and was finishing writing a book.

He got married to Luisa. He still held tendencies towards social isolation and some sensitivity to criticism. These were considered his *unfinished business*, so that Mario knew he had to try and tackle them as part of his therapy sustaining practices.

CONCLUSIONS

In a moment of confusion about how to best diagnose PD (Livesley et al., 2016) a fine-grained case formulation is key to therapy success. Given that comorbidity among PD is high, it is very difficult that a patient fits neatly into a specific category. Traits merely describe broad features of functioning either described from the observer perspective or based on self-reports. Neither method of assessment grants access to the cognitive-affective functioning of patients, which is the information a clinician needs to plan treatment. To respond to these challenges, MIT focuses specifically on an individualized case formulation, based mostly on the clinical conversation during assessment and early therapy sessions. Clinicians and patients reach a shared understanding of the latter's functioning which helps them to formulate therapy goals they feel committed to and identify with strongly. As noted above, there is initial empirical support for MIT, both in the individual form (Dimaggio et al., 2017; Gordon-King et al., 2018) and in a short-term group format (Popolo et al., 2018), where psychoeducation about human motivation is provided, followed by role-play using episodes concerning the motive (e.g., social rank) at stake in that session. Replication for the group format is underway in Norway and Spain and a multicenter randomized controlled trial is planned. Studies are needed to dismantle treatment and discover the importance of the formulation on effectiveness. There are reasons to think it is relevant. Regarding metacognition, for example, a first study noted that clients with poorer baseline metacognition had worse outcomes (Maillard, Dimaggio, de Roten, Despland, & Kramer, 2017). In parallel, it has been noted that when the therapist makes a CCRT-consistent formulation, the patient perceives it as more empathic and alliance increases (Crits-Christoph et al., 2006). There are good reasons to think that helping clients with PD by recognizing their motives and wishes, identifying the negative responses they expect from others and accessing healthy self-aspects are central elements to achieve change. Overall, if therapists are carefully responsive to patients' functioning, thanks to a fine-grained formulation, there is optimism about the possibility to deliver effective therapies for AvPD.

Acknowledgements

The patient signed a written agreement to use material for his therapy. For the sake of privacy, we altered name, profession, age, and details about his family.

References

American Psychiatric Association (2013). *Diagnostic and Statistical Manual of Mental Disorders, Fifth Edition (Dsm-5).* Arlington, VA: American Psychiatric Publishing.

Bagby, R. M., Parker, J. D. A., & Taylor, G. J. (1994). The twenty-item Toronto alexithymia scale-I. Item selection and cross validation of the factor structure. *Journal of Psychosomatic Research, 38,* 23–32.

Baldwin, M. W. (1992). Relational schemas and the processing of social information. *Psychological Bulletin, 112,* 461–484.

Bamelis, L. L., Evers, S. M., Spinhoven, P., & Arntz, A. (2014). Results of a multicenter randomized controlled trial of the clinical effectiveness of schema therapy for personality disorders. *American Journal of Psychiatry, 171,* 305–322.

Bamelis, L. L. M., Renner, F., Heidkamp, D., & Arntz, A. (2011). Extended schema mode conceptualizations for specific personality disorders: An empirical study. *Journal of Personality Disorders, 25,* 41–58. https://doi.org/10.1521/pedi.2011.25.1.41.

Baumeister, R., & Leary, M. (1995). The need to belong: Desire for interpersonal attachment as a fundamental human motivation. *Psychological Bulletin, 117*(3), 497–529.

Borkovec, T. D., Alcaine, O., & Behar, E. (2004). Avoidance theory of worry and generalized anxiety disorder. In R. G. Heimberg, C. L. Turk, & D. S. Mennin (Eds.), *Generalized anxiety disorder: Advances in research and practice* (pp. 77–108). New York: Guilford Press.

Bowlby, J. (1988). *A secure base: Clinical applications of attachment theory.* London, UK: Routledge.

Carcione, A., Dimaggio, G., Conti, L., Nicolò, G., Fiore, D., Procacci, M., et al. (2010). *Metacognition assessment scale (MAS) V. 4.0 manual.*

Carcione, A., Semerari, A., Nicolò, G., Pedone, R., Popolo, R., Conti, L., et al. (2011). Metacognitive mastery dysfunctions in personality disorder psychotherapy. *Psychiatry Research, 190,* 60–71.

Caspar, F., & Ecker, S. (2008). Treatment of an avoidant patient with comorbid psychopathology: A plan analysis perspective. *Journal of Clinical Psychology, 64,* 139–153. https://doi.org/10.1002/jclp.20448.

Colle, L., Pellecchia, G., Moroni, F., Carcione, A., Nicolò, G., Semerari, A., et al. (2017). Levels of social sharing and clinical implications for severe social withdrawal in patients with personality disorders. *Frontiers in Psychiatry, 8,* 263. https://doi.org/10.3389/fpsyt.2017.00263.

Crits-Christoph, P., Connolly Gibbons, M. B., Crits-Christoph, K., Narducci, J., Schamberger, M., & Gallop, R. (2006). Can therapists be trained to improve their alliances? A preliminary study of alliance-fostering psychotherapy. *Psychotherapy Research, 16,* 268–281. https://doi.org/10.1080/10503300500268557.

Dimaggio, G., Carcione, A., Conti, M. L., Nicolò, G., Fiore, D., Pedone, R., et al. (2009). Impaired decentration in personality disorder: An analysis with the metacognition assessment scale. *Clinical Psychology and Psychotherapy, 16,* 450–462. https://doi.org/10.1002/cpp.619.

Dimaggio, G., Lysaker, P. H., Calarco, T., Pedone, R., Marsigli, N., Riccardi, I., et al. (2015). Perfectionism and personality disorders as predictors of symptoms and interpersonal problems. *American Journal of Psychotherapy, 69,* 317–330.

Dimaggio, G., MacBeth, A., Popolo, R., Salvatore, G., Perrini, F., Raouna, A., et al. (2018). The problem of overcontrol: Perfectionism and emotional inhibition as predictors of personality disorder. *Comprehensive Psychiatry, 83,* 71–78. https://doi.org/10.1016/j.comppsych.2018.03.005.

Dimaggio, G., Montano, A., Popolo, R., & Salvatore, G. (2015). *Metacognitive interpersonal therapy for personality disorders: A treatment manual.* London: Routledge.

Dimaggio, G., Procacci, M., Nicolò, G., Popolo, R., Semerari, A., Carcione, A., et al. (2007). Poor metacognition in narcissistic and avoidant personality Disorders: Analysis of four psychotherapy patients. *Clinical Psychology and Psychotherapy, 14,* 386–401.

Dimaggio, G., Salvatore, G., MacBeth, A., Ottavi, P., Buonocore, L., & Popolo, R. (2017). Metacognitive interpersonal therapy for personality disorders: A case study series. *Journal of Contemporary Psychotherapy*, *47*, 11–21. https://doi.org/10.1007/s10879-016-9342-7.

Dimaggio, G., Semerari, A., Carcione, A., Nicolò, G., & Procacci, M. (2007). *Psychotherapy of personality disorders: Metacognition, states of mind and interpersonal cycles*. London: Routledge.

Dziobek, I., Fleck, S., Kalbe, E., Rogers, K., Hassenstab, J., Brand, M., et al. (2006). Introducing MASC: A movie for the assessment of social cognition. *Journal of Autism and Developmental Disorders*, *36*, 623–636. https://doi.org/10.1007/s10803-006-0107-0.

Eikenaes, I., Egeland, J., Hummelen, B., & Wilberg, T. (2015). Avoidant personality disorder versus social phobia: The significance of childhood neglect. *PLoS One*, *10*(3), e0122846. https://doi.org/10.1371/journal.pone.0122846.

Eikenæs, I., Pedersen, G., & Wilberg, T. (2016). Attachment styles in patients with avoidant personality disorder compared with social phobia. *Psychology and Psychotherapy: Theory, Research and Practice*, *89*, 245–260. https://doi.org/10.1111/papt.12075.

Emmelkamp, P. M., Benner, A., Kuipers, A., Feiertag, G. A., Koster, H. C., & van Apeldoorn, F. J. (2006). Comparison of brief dynamic and cognitive-behavioural therapies in avoidant personality disorder. *British Journal of Psychiatry*, *189*, 60–64.

Fassone, G., Lo Reto, F., Foggetti, P., Santomassimo, C., D'Onofrio, M. R., Ivaldi, A., et al. (2016). A content validity study of AIMIT (assessing interpersonal motivation in transcripts). *Clinical Psychology and Psychotherapy*, *23*, 319–328. https://doi.org/10.1002/cpp.1960.

Frost, R. O., Marten, P., Lahart, C., & Rosenblate, R. (1990). The dimensions of perfectionism. *Cognitive Therapy and Research*, *14*, 449–468. https://doi.org/10.1007/BF01172967.

Gilbert, P. (1989). *Human nature and suffering*. London: Psychology Press.

Gordon-King, K., Schweitzer, R. D., & Dimaggio, G. (2018). Metacognitive interpersonal therapy for personality disorders featuring emotional inhibition: A multiple baseline case series. *The Journal of Nervous and Mental Disease*. https://doi.org/10.1097/NMD.0000000000000789.

Grandi, S. A., Sirri, L., Wise, T. N., Tossani, E., & Fava, G. A. (2011). Kellner's emotional inhibition scale: A clinimetric approach to alexithymia research. *Psychotherapy and Psychosomatics*, *80*, 335–344. https://doi.org/10.1159/000328576.

Gratz, K. L., & Roemer, L. (2004). Multidimensional assessment of emotion regulation and dysregulation: Development, factor structure, and initial validation of the difficulties in emotion regulation scale. *Journal of Psychopathology and Behavioral Assessment*, *26*, 41–45.

Johansen, M. S., Normann-Eide, E., Normann-Eide, T., & Wilberg, T. (2013). Emotional dysfunction in avoidant compared to borderline personality disorder: A study of affect consciousness. *Scandinavian Journal of Psychology*, *54*, 515–521.

Lichtenberg, J. D. (1989). *Psychoanalysis and motivation*. Hillsdale, NJ: The Analytic Press.

Liotti, G., & Gilbert, P. (2011). Mentalizing, motivation, and social mentalities: Theoretical considerations and implications for psychotherapy. *Psychology and Psychotherapy: Theory, Research and Practice*, *84*, 9–25.

Livesley, J. W., Dimaggio, G., & Clarkin, J. F. (2016). Why integrated treatment? General principles of therapeutic change. In J. W. Livesley, G. Dimaggio, & J. F. Clarkin (Eds.), *Integrated treatment for personality disorders: A modular approach*. New York: Guilford.

Luborsky, L., & Crits-Christoph, P. (1998). *Understanding transference: The core conflictual relationship theme method*. New York, NY: Basic Book.

Lysaker, P. H., Olesek, K., Buck, K., Leonhardt, B., Vohs, J., Dimaggio, G., et al. (2014). Metacognitive mastery moderates the relationship of alexithymia with cluster C personality disorder traits in adults with substance use disorders. *Addictive Behaviors*, *39*, 558–561. https://doi.org/10.1016/j.addbeh.2013.11.007.

Maillard, P., Dimaggio, G., de Roten, Y., Despland, J.-N., & Kramer, U. (2017). Metacognitive processes and symptom change in a short-term treatment for borderline personality disorder: A pilot study. *Journal of Psychotherapy Integration*. https://doi.org/10.1037/int0000090.

Meyer, T. J., Miller, M. L., Metzger, R. L., & Borkovec, T. D. (1990). Development and validation of the penn state worry questionnaire. *Behaviour Research and Therapy, 28*, 487–495.

Monsen, J. T., Hagtvet, K. A., Havik, O. E., & Eilertsen, D. E. (2006). Circumplex structure and personality disorder correlates of the interpersonal problems model (IIP-C): Construct validity and clinical implications. *Psychological Assessment, 18*(2), 165–173. https://doi.org/10.1037/1040-3590.18.2.165.

Nakash-Eisikovits, O., Dutra, L., & Westen, D. (2002). Relationship between attachment patterns and personality pathology in adolescents. *Journal of the American Academy of Child and Adolescent Psychiatry, 41*, 1111–1123.

Nicolò, G., Semerari, A., Lysaker, P. H., Dimaggio, G., Conti, L., d'Angerio, S., et al. (2011). Alexithymia in personality disorders. Correlations with symptoms and interpersonal functioning. *Psychiatry Research, 190*, 37–42.

Ottavi, P., Passarella, T., Pasinetti, M., Salvatore, G., & Dimaggio, G. (2016). Mindfulness for anxious and angry worry about interpersonal events in personality disorders. In W. J. Livesley, G. Dimaggio, & J. F. Clarkin (Eds.), *Integrated treatment for personality disorders: A modular approach*. New York: Guilford.

Panksepp, J. (1998). *Affective neuroscience: The foundations of human and animal emotions*. Oxford: Oxford University Press.

Peled, O., Bar-Kalifa, E., & Rafaeli, E. (2017). Stability or instability in avoidant personality disorder: Mode fluctuations within schema therapy sessions. *Journal of Behavior Therapy and Experimental Psychiatry, 57*, 126–134. https://doi.org/10.1016/j.jbtep.2017.05.004.

Pellecchia, G., Moroni, F., Colle, L., Semerari, A., Carcione, A., Fera, T., et al. (2018). Avoidant personality disorder and social phobia: Does mindreading make the difference? *Comprehensive Psychiatry, 80*, 63–169. https://doi.org/10.1016/j.comppsych.2017.09.011.

Pilkonis, P. A., Kim, Y., Proietti, J. M., & Barkham, M. (1996). Scales for personality disorders developed from the inventory of interpersonal problems. *Journal of Personality Disorders, 10*, 355–369. https://doi.org/10.1521/pedi.1996.10.4.355.

Popolo, R., Lysaker, P. H., Salvatore, G., Montano, A., Sirri, L., Buonocore, L., et al. (2014). Emotional inhibition in personality disorders. *Psychotherapy and Psychosomatics, 83*, 377–378. https://doi.org/10.1159/000365110.

Popolo, R., MacBeth, A., Canfora, F., Rebecchi, D., Toselli, C., Salvatore, G., et al. (2018). Metacognitive Interpersonal Therapy in group (MIT-G) for young adults personality disorders. A feasibility, acceptability and clinical significance randomized controlled trial. *Psychology and Psychotherapy: Theory, Research and Practice*. https://doi.org/10.1111/papt.12182.

Renneberg, B., Goldstein, A. J., Phillips, D., & Chambless, D. L. (1990). Intensive behavioral group treatment of avoidant personality-disorder. *The Behavior Therapist, 21*, 363–377. https://doi.org/10.1016/S0005-7894(05)80337-5.

Rosenthal, M. Z., Kim, K., Herr, N. R., Smoski, M. J., Cheavens, J. S., Lynch, T. R., et al. (2011). Speed and accuracy of facial expression classification in avoidant personality disorder: A preliminary study. *Personality Disorders: Theory, Research, and Treatment, 2*, 327–334.

Semerari, A., Carcione, A., Dimaggio, G., Falcone, M., Nicolò, G., Procacci, M., et al. (2003). How to evaluate metacognitive functioning in psychotherapy? The metacognition assessment scale and its applications. *Clinical Psychology and Psychotherapy, 10*, 238–261.

Semerari, A., Colle, L., Pellecchia, G., Buccione, I., Carcione, A., Dimaggio, G., et al. (2014). Metacognition: Severity and styles in personality disorders. *Journal of Personality Disorders, 28*, 751–766. https://doi.org/10.1521/pedi_2014_28_137.

Skewes, S. A., Samson, R. A., Simpson, S. G., & van Vreeswijk, M. (2014). Short-term group schema therapy for mixed personality disorders: A pilot study. *Frontiers in Psychology, 5*, 1592. https://doi.org/10.3389/fpsyg.2014.01592.

Spinhoven, P., Bamelis, L., Molendijk, M., Haringsma, R., & Arntz, A. (2009). Reduced specificity of AM in cluster C personality disorders and the role of depression, worry and experiential avoidance. *Journal of Abnormal Psychology*, *118*, 520–530.

Spinhoven, P., Drost, J., de Rooij, M., van Hemert, A. M., & Penninx, B. W. J.H. (2016). Is experiential avoidance a mediating, moderating, independent, overlapping, or proxy risk factor in the onset, relapse and maintenance of depressive disorders? *Cognitive Therapy and Research*, *40*, 150–163. https://doi.org/10.1007/s10608-015-9747-8.

Strauss, J. L., Hayes, A. M., Johnson, S. L., Newman, C. F., Brown, G. K., Barber, J. P., et al. (2006). Early alliance, alliance ruptures, and symptom change in a nonrandomized trial of cognitive therapy for avoidant and obsessive-compulsive personality disorders. *Journal of Consulting and Clinical Psychology*, *74*, 337–345.

Svartberg, M., Stiles, T. C., & Seltzer, M. H. (2004). Randomized, controlled trial of the effectiveness of short-term dynamic psychotherapy and cognitive therapy for cluster C personality disorders. *American Journal of Psychiatry*, *161*, 810–817.

Tomasello, M., Carpenter, M., Call, J., Behne, T., & Moll, H. (2005). Understanding and sharing intentions: The origin of cultural cognition. *Behavioral and Brain Sciences*, *28*, 675–691.

Torgersen, S., Kringlen, E., & Cramer, V. (2001). The Prevalence of Personality Disorders in a Community Sample. *Archives of General Psychiatry*, *58*, 590–596. https://doi.org/10.1001/archpsyc.58.6.590.

Videlerm, A. C., van Alphen, S. P. J., van Royen, R. J. J., van der Feltz-Cornelis, C. M., Rossi, G., & Arntz, A. (2017). Schema therapy for personality disorders in older adults: A multiple-baseline study. *Aging and Mental Health*. https://doi.org/10.1080/13607863.2017.1318260.

Weinbrecht, A., Schulze, L., Boettcher, J., & Renneberg, B. (2016). Avoidant personality disorder: A current review. *Current Psychiatric Reports*, *18*, 29. https://doi.org/10.1007/s11920-016-0665-6.

Wells, A. (2008). *Metacognitive therapy for and depression*. New York: Guilford Press.

Wells, A., & Cartwright-Hatton, S. (2004). A short form of the metacognitions questionnaire: Properties of the MCQ-30. *Behavior Research and Therapy*, *42*, 385–396.

Wiggins, J. S., & Pincus, A. L. (1989). Conceptions of personality disorders and dimensions of personality. *Psychological Assessment. Journal of Consulting and Clinical Psychology*, *1*, 305–316.

Williams, J. M. G., & Broadbent, K. (1986). Autobiographical memory in suicide attempters. *Journal of Abnormal Psychology*, *95*, 144–149. https://doi.org/10.1037/0021-843X.95.2.144.

Wright, A. G., Scott, L. N., Stepp, S. D., Hallquist, M. N., & Pilkonis, P. A. (2015). Personality pathology and interpersonal problem stability. *Journal of Personality Disorders*, *29*, 684–706. https://doi.org/10.1521/pedi_2014_28_171.

Young, J. E. (1998). *Young schema questionnaire short form*. New York: Cognitive Therapy Centre.

Young, J. E., Klosko, J. S., & Weishaar, M. E. (2003). *Schema therapy: A practitioner's guide*. New York: Guilford Press.

Zonzi, A., Barkham, M., Hardy, G. E., Llewelyn, S. P., Stiles, W. B., & Leiman, M. (2014). Zone of proximal development (ZPD) as an ability to play in psychotherapy: A theory-building case study of very brief therapy. *Psychology and Psychotherapy: Theory, Research and Practice*, *87*, 447–464. https://doi.org/10.1111/papt.12022.

Further Reading

Millon, T. (1999). *Personality-guided therapy*. Chichester: Wiley.

Safran, J. D., & Muran, J. C. (2000). *Negotiating the therapeutic alliance. A relational treatment guide*. New York, NY: Guilford.

CHAPTER

9

What Might Work When Nothing Seems to Work: Case Formulation in the Treatment of Antisocial Personality Disorder in a Forensic Mental Health Setting

I. Franke, St. Nigel, M. Dudeck

Department of Forensic Psychiatry and Psychotherapy, Ulm University, Germany

INTRODUCTION

A case formulation is defined as a 'hypothesis about the causes, precipitants, and maintaining influences of a person's psychological, interpersonal, and behavioural problems' (Eells, 2007 p. 4). It provides an opportunity to apply theory and evidence to a specific case. Given that in antisocial personality disorder (ASPD) antisocial behaviour and offending are considered to be results of dysfunctional psychological processes, this definition is equally applicable to case formulation in the treatment of mentally disordered offenders.

It might not be much of an exaggeration to describe ASPD as one of the most unpopular diagnoses in mental health care and psychotherapy. Lack of empathy, constant rule breaking, egocentricity, and manipulation are among the core features of the disorder; understandably, these features do not seem overly attractive to the majority of clinicians. Nevertheless, with an estimated lifetime prevalence of 1%–4% (Lenzenweger, Lane, Loranger,

https://doi.org/10.1016/B978-0-12-813521-1.00009-6

& Kessler, 2007), ASPD is at least as common as schizophrenia and bipolar disorder. In correctional samples, prevalence rates are especially high and range from 40% to 60% (Fazel & Danesh, 2002). If individuals with ASPD contact mental health care settings, it is not usually to receive treatment for personality issues. They are either voluntarily seeking treatment for a co-occurring axis I disorder (e.g., substance use disorder or affective disorder) or are being referred for mandatory treatment after a court decision or being released on parole. In case of voluntary treatment, treatment usually does not last long and focusses little, if at all, on personality. Patients are often dismissed from services if they break formal or informal rules or commit offences during treatment. Such a dismissal parallels the experience that most of them know from their families and contributes to their attitude of rejecting treatment rather than seeking it (Tyrer, Mitchard, Methuen, & Ranger, 2003). Consequently, patients with ASPD are prone to receive numerous short-term (and probably ineffective) treatments, and their likelihood to become unmotivated and to exploit services increases from one discontinued therapy to the next.

The challenges in working with ASPD patients are even more evident in mandatory treatment settings, where referral to treatment is a result of a decision by a court that represents a normative system that they explicitly reject. Furthermore, the individual patient's treatment goals are subordinated to public safety interests. These aspects have a major impact on patients' motivation, insight, and readiness to change. Nevertheless, if a connection has been established between personality factors and offending behaviour, treatment success (and failure) is directly linked to the risk of reoffending and, subsequently, to decisions about the release of an individual.

So, why is it worth developing, applying, and evaluating strategies for the treatment of ASPD? First, the predominant presence of antisocial behavioural patterns should not obscure the view of the severe psychopathological symptoms and co-occurring disorders that can cause significant distress to the individual. Furthermore, ASPD is a matter of public health and welfare and economics. Direct costs include the expenses for the treatment of mental, substance use, and physical disorders (e.g., infectious diseases), and indirect costs are generated by detention, material and non-material damage caused by crime, and loss of economic productivity. Last, having a mind map of how ASPD symptoms interfere with everyday requirements might help professionals to reduce the workplace risk and help to prevent burnout among staff at forensic mental health care and correctional services.

Because ASPD is highly prevalent in forensic mental health services, case formulation comprises some of the core assumptions of offender treatment. In forensic mental health care, case formulation is specifically recommended for complex cases, for cases that lack an evidence base, and for cases in which previous treatment strategies were unsuccessful or in which there is a need to understand why a therapeutic relationship has broken down (Drake & Ward, 2003, pp. 226–243). These criteria may be fulfilled in most offenders with a diagnosis of personality disorder.

In this chapter, we describe a transtheoretical approach to case formulation that is based mainly on biosocial and cognitive behavioural concepts. However, this does not mean that we consider other concepts to be invalid. We would also like to point out that we do not claim that every patient with ASPD can be treated successfully; nevertheless, all therapeutic efforts should be based on a solid theoretical framework and testable hypotheses.

ANTISOCIAL PERSONALITY DISORDER

Antisocial behaviour can be defined as any violation of a formal or informal social rule that involves criminal or private oppositional acts (Olweus, Block, & Radke-Yarrow, 1986) directed against individuals or society in general. The terms antisocial behaviour, ASPD, psychopathy and violent offending should not be used synonymously, even though these conditions have conceptual overlaps and common pathways. Over the past centuries, the scientific and public view of antisocial behaviour has been affected by various influences. To name but a few, Rush's model of 'the moral alienation of mind' and 'perversion of moral' (Rush, 1812), Prichard's concept of 'moral insanity' (Prichard, 1837), Cleckley's 'The Mask of Sanity' (Cleckley, 1941), and Hare's 'Psychopathy Checklist' (PCL) (Hare, 1980) have essentially contributed to the current understanding of psychopathy and ASPD. The conceptual changes have always affected the law and sentencing as regards the assignment of offenders to treatment or detention and the question of offenders' full legal responsibility. Several issues remain unresolved in ASPD: its classification as a mental disorder; how to assess its severity appropriately; and how to discriminate between antisocial behaviour, ASPD, and psychopathy.

Aetiology

Literature on the heritability of ASPD is rather scarce, and no recent studies have been conducted. Overall, findings suggest a familial aggregation of ASPD and a significant heritable component. In twin studies, nearly 70% of the variance in ASPD was attributed to genetic influences (Brennan & Mednick, 1993; Fu et al., 2002). The current understanding of ASPD is that prenatal or genetic factors interact with adverse environmental influences (Werner, Few, & Bucholz, 2015) (see Fig. 9.1). Regarding disposition, we often find hyperactivity, delayed psychomotor development, and intellectual deficits. Children with Attention Deficit Hyperactivity Disorder (ADHD) are more likely than children without ADHD to exhibit antisocial behaviour in adolescence and adulthood (Barkley, Fischer, Smallish, & Fletcher, 2004).

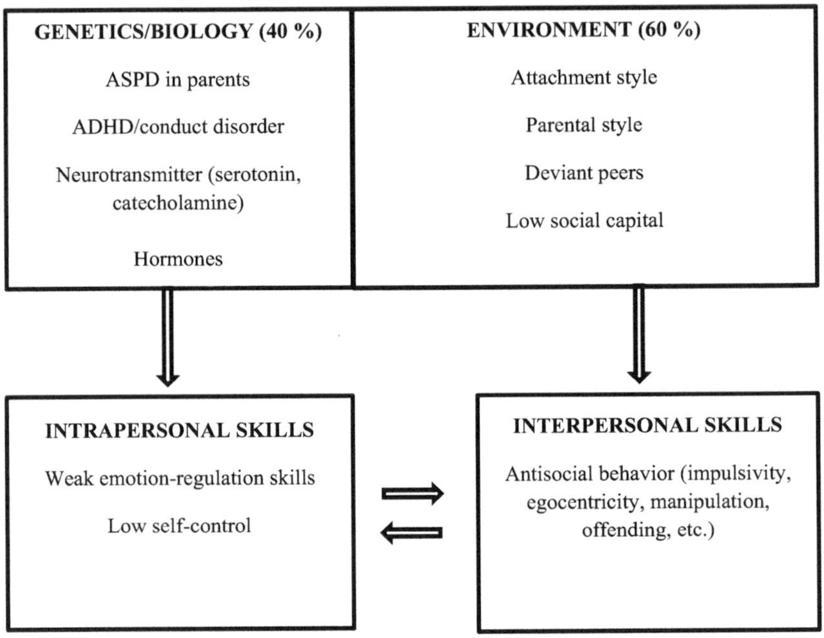

FIGURE 9.1 Biopsychosocial model of antisocial behaviour.

The co-occurrence of ADHD and conduct disorder seems to manifest in more severe antisocial behaviour (Herpertz et al., 2001).

An important biological factor discussed in the context of antisocial or aggressive behaviour is the serotoninergic system, respectively functional polymorphisms of the promotor of the monoamine oxidase (MAO) gene (Caspi et al., 2002; Meyer-Lindenberg et al., 2006; Skondras, Markianos, Botsis, Bistolaki, & Christodoulou, 2004); furthermore, the ratio of testosterone and cortisol seems to be predictive for impulsive and instrumental aggression (Montoya, Terburg, Bos, & Van Honk, 2012).

From the perspectives of developmental psychology and crime theory, low self-control in children – expressed by impulsivity, risk taking and not thinking about consequences – is considered to be a main pathway for antisocial and criminal behaviour (DeLisi & Vaughn, 2008; Gottfredson & Hirschi, 1990). Family variables associated with low self-control in children are low socioeconomic status and a parent-centred parenting style, expressed, for example, by not encouraging the child to have hobbies, using physical punishment and showing indifference towards school attendance (Pulkkinen & Hamalainen, 1995). Individual risk factors for antisocial behaviour have been identified at birth (e.g., low IQ, prenatal exposure to toxins and complications during pregnancy or birth), in early childhood (e.g., developmental delays, language problems, lack of guilt, impulsivity, callous or unemotional behaviour and attention problems), in mid to late childhood (e.g., poor social skills, cognitive attributional bias towards aggression, poor motivation and achievement at school and a positive attitude towards delinquency and substance use) and in adolescence (e.g., heavy substance use, drug dealing, weapon use and victimization) (Loeber, Slot, & Stouthamer-Loeber, 2006, pp. 153–194; Piquero, Moffitt, & Wright, 2007).

Accordingly, reviews and meta-analyses focusing on antisocial behaviour showed evidence of strong genetic effects and of shared and individual-specific environmental influences, with reported estimates of about 40% for the contribution of genetic effects and nearly 60% for the overall contribution of environmental influences (Burt, 2009; Rhee & Waldman, 2002; Torgersen et al., 2008).

The development of offending seems to follow certain patterns. The peak of onset of offending lies between the ages of 8 and 14; and the peak prevalence, between the ages of 15 and 19 (Farrington, 2003). In the theory about antisocial pathways, Moffit discriminates life-course–persistent and adolescence–limited offenders: the majority of crimes are committed by a minority of adolescent offenders, who continue offending throughout most of their lives. The persistent offenders were described as coming from very deprived social backgrounds and being affected by both genetic risk factors (inherited or constitutional neuropsychological difficulties) and harmful parental behaviour (Moffitt, 1993).

Diagnostic Criteria

The diagnostic criteria for ASPD are quite broadly defined and focus on socially abnormal (or at least undesired) behaviour. The diagnosis is given only to persons aged 18 or older, but it is based on a diagnosis of conduct disorder before the age of 15 (Black, 2017). Consequently, the diagnosis has always captured criminal behaviour more than antisocial personality traits. However, the fifth edition of the Diagnostic and Statistical Manual of Mental Disorders (DSM-5) (APA, 2013) places a greater emphasis on such personality traits than previous editions. First, significant impairments in self-functioning (regarding identity or self-direction) and interpersonal functioning (regarding empathy or intimacy) must be present for a diagnosis of a personality disorder. Grouped under the heading of 'antagonism', four traits can be found: manipulativeness, deceitfulness, callousness and hostility. Under 'disinhibition', three behavioural features are listed: irresponsibility, impulsivity and risk taking (APA, 2013). Overall, ASPD is defined by its pattern of self-centred, socially reckless, exploitative and remorseless behaviour that bears a high risk of criminal offences.

ASPD has to be discriminated from psychopathy. The construct of psychopathy is based on the assignment of personality traits to the two factors Interpersonal/Affective and Social Deviance. Nevertheless, psychopathic personality traits do not necessarily lead to criminal behaviour. Because of the overlap between the diagnostic criteria for psychopathy and those for ASPD, mainly in the behavioural symptoms, almost all individuals with psychopathy meet the criteria for ASPD, whereas only a third of the patients with ASPD meet the criteria for psychopathy (Coid, 1998, pp. 431–457). However, offenders who fulfil the criteria for psychopathy assessed with the Psychopathy Checklist-Revised (PCL-R) (Hare & Neumann, 2006, pp. 58–88) are more likely to recidivate and unlikely to respond to conventional treatment approaches (Ogloff, Talevski, Lemphers, Wood, & Simmons, 2015). Consequently, it is useful to assess psychopathy at an early stage of treatment.

Treatment Approaches

The DSM-5 does not specify treatment options for ASPD because the evidence base for effective approaches is insufficient (APA, 2013). Drawing meaningful conclusions from the scientific literature is complicated because of different diagnostic criteria and conceptualizations of the disorder, differences in the definition and measurement of outcomes and difficulties in assessing personality changes. Nevertheless, even though treatment of ASPD is widely considered to be challenging, certain approaches remain promising.

To date, no approved drugs are available that specifically target ASPD. Psychiatric drugs (e.g., mood stabilizers and antipsychotics) can only be prescribed to treat comorbid disorders or used 'off label' to target aggression and impulsivity associated with ASPD (Black, 2017).

As regards psychotherapeutic interventions for ASPD, again few high-quality treatment trials have been performed to date (Black, 2017). Limited evidence exists that treatment models with cognitive behavioural therapy (CBT) are effective in reducing aggressiveness (Davidson et al., 2009; Gibbon et al., 2009).

Patients receiving mentalization-based therapy (MBT) also showed improvements in anger, hostility, paranoia and suicidal and self-harm behaviours (Bateman, O'Connell, Lorenzini, Gardner, & Fonagy, 2016). Because case formulation according to MBT is explained in detail elsewhere in this book, only a brief summary of MBT as it applies to ASPD is given here. One core assumption of MBT is that the ability to mentalize inhibits violence. In individuals with ASPD, this process is disrupted such that they are likely to misinterpret others' motives. Therefore, individuals with ASPD do not experience mental pain associated with another person's state of mind. Antisocial traits stabilize mentalizing by rigidifying relationships within prementalistic ways of functioning (Bateman & Fonagy, 2008). This inflexibility makes a person vulnerable to sudden collapse and feelings of humiliation, especially when the attachment or affiliative system is activated. The arising negative feelings about the self can only be avoided by violence and control of the other person during a momentary inhibition of the capacity for mentalization (Bateman & Fonagy, 2008). The deficits in mentalization ability in ASPD are subtle and may have an adaptive function in maintaining a criminal lifestyle (Dolan & Fullam, 2004). In forensic psychotherapy, MBT is delivered in individual and group settings and is supposed to help patients to maintain mentalizing at times when it is threatened (Bateman & Fonagy, 2008).

Another promising treatment approach is the forensic adaption of dialectic behavioural therapy (DBT-F), which targets individuals with difficulties in affect regulation and impulse control, including those diagnosed with ASPD (McCann, Ball, & Ivanoff, 2000). DBT was developed for the treatment of borderline personality disorder (BPD) (Linehan, 1993). Its adaption for forensic settings follows the rationale that the prevalence of personality disorders (especially BPD and ASPD) is high in forensic psychotherapy and that DBT addresses life-threatening behaviours (both suicidal *and* homicidal) and behaviours that interfere with a treatment programme or with the therapist's motivation to treat (McCann et al., 2000). The original DBT protocol was modified by adding the category of life-threatening behaviours (as are observed in interpersonal violence), paying specific attention to the reinforcement of honest recording of maladaptive behaviours, testing skills acquisition (e.g., with exams), targeting emotional insensitivity and designing a graduate-level skills group to increase empathy for the victims and prevent reoffending (McCann et al., 2000). In a 20-month, nonrandomized pilot study (N=35) in which one third of the participants met the criteria for ASPD, modified DBT-F was compared with treatment as usual (TAU). The DBT group showed a significant decrease in maladaptive coping, a significant increase in adaptive coping and a trend towards significant decreases in depression, hostility, paranoia and psychotic behaviours (McCann et al., 2000). However, a systematic evaluation of these methods is still pending. Hence, for now we must conclude that insufficient data are available to assess the value of psychotherapy in individuals with ASPD. In particular, the effects of therapy on the crucial outcome measures reoffending and violence still have to be proven.

CASE FORMULATION THEORIES

Cognitive Behavioural Theory

Cognitive behavioural theories are the backbone of any current evidence-based method of offender treatment. Because cognitive behavioural models (general and specific) for the case formulation of personality disorders are described in detail elsewhere in this book, this chapter focusses on the specific features of ASPD and offending.

According to classic cognitive theory, personality disorders are the result of maladaptive behavioural and affective strategies to satisfy basic goals. Core beliefs are hypothesized to be the cognitive representation of an individual's life experiences. These core beliefs may have led to maladaptive beliefs which characterize and perpetuate a personality disorder (Beck, Davis, & Freeman, 2015). Individuals with ASPD are characterized by the drive to compete and expand. The strategies to achieve these goals include, for example, deceiving, cheating and robbing. Other individuals are seen as objects for exploitation, physical attack and deprivation. In contrast to narcissistic patients, who are also driven by expansion, patients with ASPD seem to be more independent from social opinion, so they tend to consider other persons' reactions only insofar as they serve their own needs. Their cognitive style is linear, and they have fundamental difficulties in taking on the role or the perspective of another person. The leading affect underlying the behavioural patterns is anger (Beck et al., 2001, 2015) (see Fig. 9.2).

Schema-focused therapy combines the classic cognitive behavioural approach with aspects of experiential, interpersonal and psychoanalytic therapy. Schemas and modes are defined as relatively independent organized patterns of thinking, feeling and behaving that are assumed to underlie the different states of patients with severe personality disorder (Young, Klosko, & Weishaar, 2003). Adding schema theory to the classic

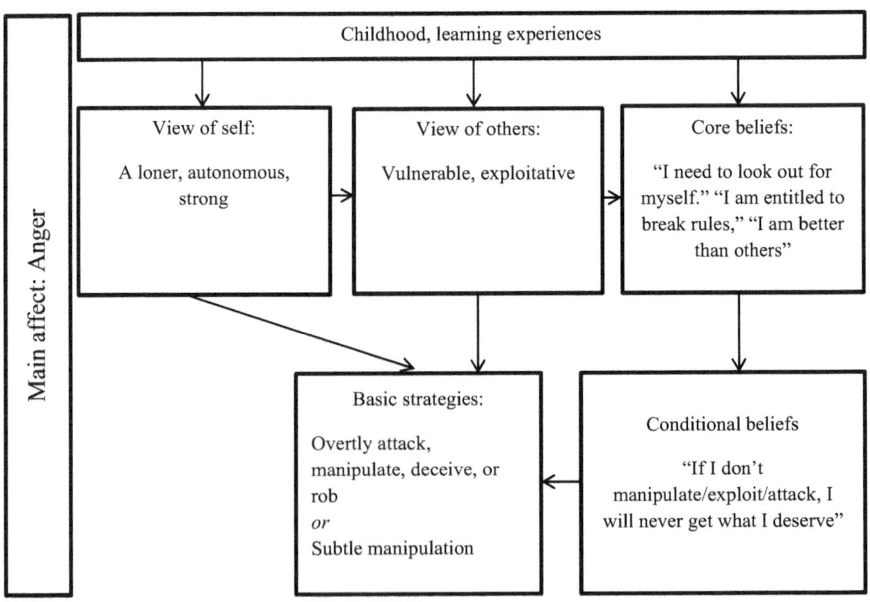

FIGURE 9.2 Cognitive profile of antisocial personality disorder (ASPD), according to Beck, Davis, & Freeman, 2015.

cognitive behavioural approach might improve the understanding of dysfunctional behavioural patterns in ASPD insofar as it emphasizes subjective strain due to early childhood trauma as a conditional and maintaining factor. A detailed explanation of the underlying concepts of schema therapy can be found elsewhere in this book.

Cognitive Behavioural Models of Offending

The formulation of cognitive behavioural hypotheses on offending consists of two steps. First, past offending is assessed by using a decision theory framework. In this framework, (violent) offending is viewed as a choice that has been made, even though it may be inconsiderate; consequently, the offending behaviour is assumed to have been preceded by cognitions (e.g., violence was seen as a valid option under particular circumstances, and positive and negative consequences and potential barriers were weighed against each other). Therefore, the main focus is to understand the function of offending in the individual patient. Second, hypotheses or scenarios of future offending are generated and used to develop management and treatment plans. An important aspect of this formulation is to determine whether an offender has avoidant goals or approach goals: an offender with avoidant goals hopes not to re-offend but makes choices that (could) lead to reoffending, whereas an offender with approach goals seeks or creates situations that provoke reoffending, because he or she sees offending as a desired goal (Ward & Hudson, 2000, pp. 79–101). Each of these pathways requires different strategies and assessment.

A prominent tool is the 'offence cycle', which is based on cognitive behavioural approaches and used to explain offending behaviour and prevent relapse (Laws, 1989). As in the classical functional analysis of problem behaviour, it is assumed that contingencies that were present at the time of the offence can promote reoffending if repeated. Post-offence behaviour, thoughts or feelings are included in the analysis and are used by patients to justify their offending behaviour and make them feel less uncomfortable with the situation. For example, dysfunctional regulation of feelings such as anxiety and depression can trigger craving and substance use which in turn can cause drug-related crime or violent offending. Post-offence behaviour might include further substance use to cope with negative feelings aroused by having committed an offence.

In contrast to general psychotherapy settings, in forensic settings the sources of information usually extend to court files and criminal records. Quite frequently, the information provided by these external sources has to be used to verify or clarify the information given by the patient.

A challenge in forensic case formulation and treatment is that the behaviour to be addressed in treatment (e.g., assault, sexual offending) is usually not evident (Hart, Sturmey, Logan, & McMurran, 2011). One approach to handling this dilemma is based on an analysis of common behaviours that are functionally similar to the offending behaviour: the concept of Offence Paralleling Behaviour (OPB) (Daffern, Jones, & Shine, 2010) aims at identifying current observable behaviour that appears to have the same function as the index offence behaviour. The therapist designs a treatment plan that, according to the concept of OPB, is hypothesized to influence the offending behaviour and reduce the risk of reoffending by treating the proxy behaviour. For example, if patients have a history of violent offending they might be able to control themselves insofar as they would not become directly involved in fights. However, if they are frustrated by staff members they might react impulsively (e.g., by shouting, slamming doors or swearing). In therapy this behaviour would be defined as OPB and addressed by skills training, for instance. The concept of OBP for offenders with severe personality disorders has been modified by including the concept of Lifestyle Paralleling Behaviour (LPB) (Spearing, Wasteney, & Morgan, 2010, pp. 261–273). LPB elements can be observed in the daily routine in forensic environments (e.g., trading of goods with other patients; eating habits and storing of food; inability to maintain a daily structure; and exploitative relationships). Embedding offending behaviour in the individuals' lifestyle (by defining it as an 'occupation') might improve offence-focused work because it feels less threatening to the patient (Spearing et al., 2010, pp. 261–273). Furthermore, it describes problems quite close to the patient's experience, which might also increase motivation and adherence. Paralleling behavioural patterns can also be identified in substance misuse and can support clinical decision making.

To date, there is no empirical evidence for the OPB approach, and its use is somewhat controversial (Hart et al., 2011). The main concerns about OPB are that it is poorly operationally defined and that the identification of behavioural patterns is subject to observer bias. Also unresolved is the question of how situational factors (effects of restrictions) influence an individual's behaviour (Daffern et al., 2007) and how this influence affects the validity of predictions about behaviour outside detainment.

Case Formulation and Risk Assessment

Risk assessment must be integrated into the case formulation for ASPD when there is a history of (especially violent) offending that is linked with the diagnosis. Current risk assessment in forensic mental health is based on the method of Structured Professional Judgement (Webster, Haque, & Hucker, 2013), which is basically a case formulation about the causes, precipitants and maintaining influences of the individual's delinquency combined with instruments based on statistical data ('actuarial risk assessment'). It results in the description of static and dynamic risk factors for reoffending and how the latter might be modified by therapy or monitoring.

For the purposes of this chapter, we chose one of the most established models of forensic case formulation, the Risk-Needs-Responsivity (RNR) model. RNR is based on the Psychology of Criminal Conduct and General Personality and Cognitive Social Learning (Andrews & Bonta, 2010). It assumes that criminal behaviour develops on the basis of personality predisposition and learning and is influenced by the individual's expectations and the consequences of criminal behaviour. The RNR model can be applied to a wide range of offenders and is not specific for personality disorders. The evaluation of treatment according to the RNR model has proven to be effective in lowering recidivism (Dowden, Antonowicz, & Andrews, 2003). One of the main advantages of the RNR model is that it guides therapy by focusing on the risk of reoffending without disregarding each patient's individual characteristics. Therefore, it is a useful approach for case formulation for ASPD in forensic settings, because it helps to identify the primary treatment goals. According to RNR, the treatment of offenders should proceed according to three core principles:

The *Risk* principle addresses the question 'Who should receive treatment?' The amount of treatment delivered to the offender should match his or her risk of reoffending, i.e., offenders with high-risk profiles should receive more intense treatment and management. Risk can be addressed with different evidence-based instruments, so that knowledge of current risk assessment procedures and risk factors is essential for a forensic psychotherapist.

The *Need* principle focusses on 'What should be treated?' Treatment and management should focus on the identified criminogenic needs (i.e., dynamic risk factors that are empirically associated with recidivism). The seven major risk/need factors are antisocial personality pattern, procriminal attitudes, social supports for crime, substance abuse, family/marital relationships, school/work and prosocial recreational activities. The four minor (=non-criminogenic) needs are self-esteem, vague feelings of personal distress, major mental disorder (for example schizophrenia or bipolar disorder) and physical health.

The *Responsivity* principle should answer the question 'What should treatment look like?' Services should be delivered in a way that maximizes their effectiveness, i.e., maximizes the offender's ability to learn from interventions. The therapy focuses on skills acquisition and enhancement and appropriate reinforcement and disapproval; furthermore, the style of delivery should address offenders in a way that matches their learning skills, motivation, abilities and strengths. General responsivity means that approaches that aim to influence behaviour should be based on established cognitive social learning methods. Specific responsivity is described as a 'fine tuning' of cognitive behavioural intervention. Personality is considered to be a responsivity factor; therefore, it might influence an individual's ability to engage in treatment or to benefit from interventions.

Ethical Aspects of Forensic Case Formulation

More than those of other disorders, the diagnostic criteria of ASPD may imply a moral judgement of behaviour. The moral context of human behaviour, i.e., whether something is rated as prosocial or antisocial, depends on culture, society, context and the individual's socialization. Clinicians should base treatment plans and recommendations for risk assessment and lifestyle on the individual's likelihood of reoffending and not on the clinicians' moral and value judgements. The same might apply when assessing behaviour shown by the patient during treatment. Furthermore, it is of utmost importance to put personality-related factors in relation to the situational context of behaviour (Mischel & Shoda, 1999, pp. 197–218). This means that if an offence is the result of an extraordinary life event rather than of a constant theme or trait, the clinician must question whether the behaviour must be addressed in therapy. For instance, the RNR model has been criticized for a lack of conceptual resources to guide therapists and engage offenders because it has a rather reductionist approach to human behaviour, places disproportionally high emphasis on avoidance goals and 'views offenders as disembodied bearers of risk'; furthermore, it does not deal with the question of therapist factors and attitudes of offenders (Ward & Stewart, 2003).

Additionally, clinicians must avoid reducing the understanding and assessing of (violent) offending in ASPD to quantitative analytic methods. This rather technical approach represents a risk in psychotherapeutic work with mentally disordered offenders because it ignores dynamic processes (Hart, Michie, & Cooke, 2007). Nevertheless, the quality of case formulation in ASPD is crucially dependent on the quality of the generated hypotheses. Therefore, the validity of any hypothesis should be tested and the hypothesis should be revised if necessary.

The question whether and how forensic case formulation should be shared with the patient has to be addressed from different perspectives (Davies, Black, Bentley, & Nagi, 2013). First, the concepts of informed consent and shared decision making are the state of the art in (mental) health care. Excluding mentally disordered offenders from the hypotheses that their treatment and risk assessment are built on can be stigmatizing. Second, case formulation can be a valuable tool for promoting insight and change motivation if presented in a way that patients are able to understand. On the other hand, information about the contents of case formulation might activate negative emotions or schemas and cause patients to draw negative conclusions (Johnstone & Dallos, 2013; Pain, Chadwick, & Abba, 2008), e.g., if patients are humiliated or hurt by the description of their behaviour they might feel disregarded and withdraw from the therapeutic process. Furthermore, not all hypotheses that help the therapist to understand a patient's functioning need to be shared with the patient.

EXAMPLE OF CASE FORMULATION FOR ANTISOCIAL PERSONALITY DISORDER (ASPD)

Case Report

Michael was 24 years old when he was admitted to the forensic inpatient service. He was referred through the criminal justice system to receive treatment for a substance use disorder (according to §64 of the German Criminal Code); his conviction was for armed robbery and drug possession and trafficking. The mandatory treatment followed a 14-month imprisonment. Drug screening at intake was positive for synthetic cannabinoids and opioids.

Medical assessments (including MRI of the brain) were normal.

Biography

Michael was born three weeks early by caesarian section. Because of respiratory problems, he received intensive care for four weeks. Together with his two older brothers, he was raised by both his parents and attended nursery and primary and secondary school but did not graduate. He, but not his brothers, was subjected to emotional and physical abuse by his father, who was convinced that Michael was not his biological son. At school, Michael's behaviour was characterized by attention deficits, disorganized behaviour, fidgeting and impulsivity and, from the age of 13 years on, also by increasing antisocial behaviour (absences, smoking cannabis in the school yard, teasing others and forcing others to give him money, shoes or clothes). He stayed away from home and lived with friends or on the streets. Most of his offences were committed with the same group of male adolescents. He was suspended from school when he was arrested for the first time at the age of 15 because of drug offences, repeated theft and robbery. During his stay at a juvenile detention centre, he managed to graduate from secondary school. After release, he started an apprenticeship but was arrested again after eight months. Between the ages of 15 and 24, he spent a total of nearly five years in detention. In the intervals between detentions, he had temporary jobs, which he regularly lost because of substance abuse and aggressive behaviour. Apart from occasional phone calls with his mother, he had no contact with his family. Michael had several casual affairs with women of the same age or younger. He became the father of a son at the age of 17, but child welfare took care of the baby. He had one relationship that lasted nearly two years and was characterized by emotional instability and one reported incident of domestic violence.

Psychiatric History

There was no family history of psychiatric or substance use disorders. At the age of 10, Michael was diagnosed with ADHD by a school psychologist and treated with methylphenidate, which he did not take regularly and stopped completely at age 14. According to the information he provided, after the age of 17 symptoms of a gambling disorder had become evident that resulted in debts of about ₡35,000 (mainly from using slot machines). He reported an attempted suicide (he tried to hang himself while in prison at the age of 21). The only findings in his medical history were several old bone fractures and scars.

History of Substance Use

Michael started smoking cigarettes and cannabis at the age of 12. Two years later, he was smoking regularly and drinking alcohol excessively at the weekend. Additionally, he started using cocaine and other stimulants, followed by sedatives and analgesics (including opioids). He never injected drugs. At the age of 16, he fulfilled the criteria of multiple substance use disorder. In prison, he mainly consumed synthetic cannabinoids and opioids.

Criminal Record

Michael was admitted to the forensic mental health service because of robbery and drug possession and distribution. He was part of a regional drug trafficking ring and used the proceeds to finance his own substance use and gambling and for living expenses. One night, a deal failed and, together with two friends, he consumed some alcohol and cocaine before using a hunting knife to rob a gas station.

His criminal history at the time of admission showed a wide range of persistent offending including arson, bodily harm, assault, theft and traffic offences (driving without a licence).

Psychological Assessments

- Raven's standard progressive matrices (SPM) (Raven, 1998): IQ score of 111.
- NEO Personality Inventory-Revised (NEO-PI-R) (Costa & MacCrae, 1992): the score for the dimension *Neuroticism* was elevated, with an emphasis on the facets 'anxiety' and 'depression'. On the dimension *Extraversion*, Michael described himself as introverted and

self-effacing. The dimensions *Openness to Experience* and *Agreeableness* showed no significant findings. The score for *Conscientiousness* was very low, meaning that Michael described himself as very undisciplined and undutiful and as someone who does not strive for achievement.
- Inventory of Interpersonal Problems (IIP-D) (Horowitz, Rosenberg, Baer, Ureño, & Villaseñor, 1988): Michael's total score was elevated, and he described himself as vindictive and domineering and at the same time as non-assertive and socially inhibited.
- ADHD assessment (WURS-K (Retz-Junginger et al., 2002), ASRS (Kessler et al., 2005): Michael fulfilled the criteria of adult ADHD.
- SCID II (First, Benjamin, Gibbon, Spitzer, & Williams, 1997): Michael met the diagnostic criteria of ASPD. He also fulfilled the criteria of gambling disorder, but the disorder was considered as part of the axis-II disorder rather than an independent comorbidity.
- PCL-R (Hare & Neumann, 2006, pp. 58–88): total score of 22 (cut-off for psychopathy in European samples: 25).

Monitoring on the Forensic Ward

Michael consistently avoided contact with staff during the first weeks of his stay. When actively approached by team members, he stated that it was not his decision to come here therefore he would expect the staff to suggest what he should do. He said he had no idea about the reasons for his offending behaviour – as soon as he had an idea to do something illegal, he would immediately just do it. On the ward, he joined a group of patients who were about the same age and had a similar background. He picked one of the younger patients as his 'best friend', who had to follow his instructions (e.g., buying cigarettes, food and drinks) to receive protection. He and his peer group usually teased weaker patients. On several occasions, Michael was caught stealing food from the food trolley or other patients' lockers. Additionally, he regularly screened new patients for valuable goods (e.g., sneakers or clothes from popular brands, jewellery or clothing) and, if he did not get what he wanted, started either manipulatively persuading or threatening the other patient. In occupational therapy, his efforts and achievement were good and he was also able to do unpleasant parts of the work. After six weeks, he was found to be positive for cocaine and, after three months, synthetic cannabinoids were found in his room. He denied having taken any kind of drug at first and accused the team of having mixed up the samples. He was never involved in physical fights among patients. After a few months, he told his therapist that he felt insecure about how to behave to avoid being judged as strange or weird. He also spoke about concerns about saying the wrong things and consequently not being allowed to continue therapy.

Case Formulation

Michael was born and raised in a family with no known history of mental or substance use disorder. Nevertheless, his further development was influenced by adverse biological and environmental factors (ADHD, parenting style, violence) that caused poor self-control. Neither at home nor at school was he able to develop a functional sense of skill, self-esteem and self-efficacy. The constant feelings of insufficiency and inferiority increasingly turned into feelings of anger that influenced his view of himself and others and his cognition and behaviour in a progressively careless and antisocial manner. He was thereby able to temporarily release his anger. By offending, he gained approval from his peers and obtained material goods, which in turn acted as strong reinforcements. This enabled him to experience self-efficacy and to stabilize his self-esteem. Attacking others served as a strategy to compensate for negative emotions and core beliefs. When using drugs, he became familiar with another strategy to regulate intermittent feelings of guilt and worthlessness (avoidance goals) or to induce or enhance positive emotions (approach goals). During the first few months of his stay, Michael showed plenty of offence-paralleling behaviour, which was used to evaluate the individual hypothesis of offending and other antisocial behaviour.

The risk assessment procedure is not described in detail here. Actuarial risk was assessed with the instrument Violence Risk Appraisal Guide (VRAG) (Harris, Rice, & Cormier, 2002); the total score was 28, meaning that Michael had a high statistical risk of reoffending. The major static risk factor was multiple offending beginning in early adolescence. An antisocial personality pattern (indicated e.g., by the diagnosis of ASPD and offence-paralleling behaviour on the ward), procriminal attitudes (expressed e.g., by core beliefs, such as 'I deserve what belongs to others', and 'I can take what I want immediately and, if necessary, violently'), substance abuse, lack of protective peers and relationships, and antisocial recreational activities (e.g., gambling) were defined as dynamic risk factors. The fact that Michael was able to graduate during youth detention was considered as a potentially protective resource.

Michael had no intellectual disabilities that might have interfered with therapy. The assessments found persistent ADHD symptoms, which might have influenced his ability to benefit from cognitive interventions. Therefore, specific ADHD therapy (psychological and drug therapy) had to be considered early in treatment. The low score for *Conscientiousness* in the NEO-PI-R might have affected his motivation and perseverance in therapy; in such cases, the therapist should consider shortening sessions or formulating short-term goals to create a sense of achievement. The PCL-R score indicated that he did not fulfil the criteria of psychopathy. The major issues that had to be primarily addressed by specific interventions were substance abuse, dysfunctional regulation of emotions, e.g., by dominating others, and being unable to take the perspective of others. The treatment plan comprised definitions of dysfunctional behaviour during treatment and strategies and consequences. After the diagnostic assessment was completed, medical treatment with atomoxetine was initiated, which led to improvements in attention and concentration. Michael joined DBT group therapy to acquire skills for impulse control, and he received specific drug therapy interventions. After 14 months of inpatient treatment he found a job in a carpenter's shop, where he was offered the opportunity to continue his apprenticeship. He was released on probation but had to continue both outpatient therapy and regular drug screening. During the first year of follow-up, he had five positive drug screenings, but he managed to keep his job and flat and did not otherwise offend.

CONCLUSIONS

- Even though treatment of ASPD still lacks long-term evidence, any approach should be based on a theoretical framework that has proven to be feasible. In this chapter we describe one approach of case formulation for ASPD; however, there might be other, equally applicable methods.
- Case formulation is a feasible method to integrate biological, social and psychological theories of ASPD.
- In forensic mental health settings, treatment of ASDP must be combined with risk assessment.
- In case formulation, as in treatment, the moral judgement of a person or his/her behaviour should be avoided.

Acknowledgements

To protect the patient's privacy, we have changed identifying details (sociodemographic data, biography and examples of offence-paralleling behaviour).

References

Andrews, D. A., & Bonta, J. (2010). *The psychology of criminal conduct*. Routledge.

APA. (2013). *Diagnostic and statistical manual of mental disorders (DSM-5®)*. American Psychiatric Publishing.

Barkley, R. A., Fischer, M., Smallish, L., & Fletcher, K. (2004). Young adult follow-up of hyperactive children: Antisocial activities and drug use. *Journal of Child Psychology and Psychiatry*, *45*(2), 195–211.

Bateman, A., & Fonagy, P. (2008). Comorbid antisocial and borderline personality disorders: Mentalization-based treatment. *Journal of Clinical Psychology*, *64*(2), 181–194.

Bateman, A., O'Connell, J., Lorenzini, N., Gardner, T., & Fonagy, P. (2016). A randomised controlled trial of mentalization-based treatment versus structured clinical management for patients with comorbid borderline personality disorder and antisocial personality disorder. *BMC Psychiatry*, *16*(1), 304.

Beck, A. T., Butler, A. C., Brown, G. K., Dahlsgaard, K. K., Newman, C. F., & Beck, J. S. (2001). Dysfunctional beliefs discriminate personality disorders. *Behaviour Research and Therapy*, *39*(10), 1213–1225.

Beck, A. T., Davis, D. D., & Freeman, A. (2015). *Cognitive therapy of personality disorders*. Guilford Publications.

Black, D. W. (2017). The treatment of antisocial personality disorder. *Current Treatment Options in Psychiatry*, *4*(4), 295–302.

Brennan, P. A., & Mednick, S. A. (1993). Genetic perspectives on crime. *Acta Psychiatrica Scandinavica*, *87*(S370), 19–26.

Burt, S. A. (2009). Are there meaningful etiological differences within antisocial behaviour? Results of a meta-analysis. *Clinical Psychology Review*, *29*(2), 163–178.

Caspi, A., McClay, J., Moffitt, T. E., Mill, J., Martin, J., Craig, I. W., et al. (2002). Role of genotype in the cycle of violence in maltreated children. *Science*, *297*(5582), 851–854.

Cleckley, H. (1941). *The mask of sanity; an attempt to reinterpret the so-called psychopathic personality*.

Coid, J. (1998). *The management of dangerous psychopaths in prison. Psychopathy: Antisocial, criminal, and violent behaviour*.

Costa, P. T., & MacCrae, R. R. (1992). *Revised NEO personality inventory (NEO PI-R) and NEO five-factor inventory (NEO-FFI): Professional manual*. Psychological Assessment Resources, Incorporated.

Daffern, M., Jones, L., Howells, K., Shine, J., Mikton, C., & Tunbridge, V. (2007). Refining the definition of offence paralleling behaviour. *Criminal Behaviour and Mental Health*, *17*(5), 265–273.

Daffern, M., Jones, L., & Shine, J. (2010). *Offence paralleling behaviour: A case formulation approach to offender assessment and intervention* (Vol. 48). John Wiley & Sons.

Davidson, K., Tyrer, P., Tata, P., Cooke, D., Gumley, A., Ford, I., et al. (2009). Cognitive behaviour therapy for violent men with antisocial personality disorder in the community: An exploratory randomized controlled trial. *Psychological Medicine*, *39*(4), 569–577.

Davies, J., Black, S., Bentley, N., & Nagi, C. (2013). Forensic case formulation: Theoretical, ethical and practical issues. *Criminal Behaviour and Mental Health*, *23*(4), 304–314.

DeLisi, M., & Vaughn, M. G. (2008). The Gottfredson–Hirschi critiques revisited: Reconciling self-control theory, criminal careers, and career criminals. *International Journal of Offender Therapy and Comparative Criminology*, *52*(5), 520–537.

Dolan, M., & Fullam, R. (2004). Theory of mind and mentalizing ability in antisocial personality disorders with and without psychopathy. *Psychological Medicine*, *34*(6), 1093–1102.

Dowden, C., Antonowicz, D., & Andrews, D. (2003). The effectiveness of relapse prevention with offenders: A meta-analysis. *International Journal of Offender Therapy and Comparative Criminology*, *47*(5), 516–528.

Drake, C., & Ward, T. (2003). *Treatment models for sex offenders: A move toward a formulation-based approach. Sexual deviance: Issues and controversies*.

Eells, T. (2007). *History and current status of psychotherapy case formulation. Handbook of psychotherapy case formulation* (2nd ed.). 4.

Farrington, D. P. (2003). Developmental and life-course criminology: Key theoretical and empirical issues-the 2002 Sutherland Award address. *Criminology*, *41*(2), 221–225.

Fazel, S., & Danesh, J. (2002). Serious mental disorder in 23 000 prisoners: A systematic review of 62 surveys. *The Lancet*, *359*(9306), 545–550.

First, M. B., Benjamin, L. S., Gibbon, M., Spitzer, R. L., & Williams, J. B. (1997). *Structured clinical interview for DSM-IV Axis II personality disorders*. American Psychiatric Press.

Fu, Q., Heath, A. C., Bucholz, K. K., Nelson, E., Goldberg, J., Lyons, M. J., et al. (2002). Shared genetic risk of major depression, alcohol dependence, and marijuana dependence: Contribution of antisocial personality disorder in men. *Archives of General Psychiatry*, *59*(12), 1125–1132.

Gibbon, S., Duggan, C., Stoffers, J. M., Huband, N., Völlm, B. A., Ferriter, M., et al. (2009). *Psychological interventions for antisocial personality disorder. Cochrane database of systematic reviews: Protocols.*

Gottfredson, M. R., & Hirschi, T. (1990). *A general theory of crime*. Stanford University Press.

Hare, R. D. (1980). A research scale for the assessment of psychopathy in criminal populations. *Personality and Individual Differences*, *1*(2), 111–119.

Hare, R. D., & Neumann, C. S. (2006). *The PCL-R assessment of psychopathy. Handbook of psychopathy.*

Harris, G. T., Rice, M. E., & Cormier, C. A. (2002). Prospective replication of the Violence Risk Appraisal Guide in predicting violent recidivism among forensic patients. *Law and Human Behaviour*, *26*(four), 377.

Hart, S. D., Michie, C., & Cooke, D. J. (2007). Precision of actuarial risk assessment instruments: Evaluating the 'margins of error' of group v. individual predictions of violence. *British Journal of Psychiatry - Supplement*, *49*, s60–65. https://doi.org/10.1192/bjp.190.5.s60.

Hart, S. D., Sturmey, P., Logan, C., & McMurran, M. (2011). Forensic case formulation. *International Journal of Forensic Mental Health*, *10*(2), 118–126.

Herpertz, S. C., Wenning, B., Mueller, B., Qunaibi, M., Sass, H., & Herpertz-Dahlmann, B. (2001). Psychophysiological responses in ADHD boys with and without conduct disorder: Implications for adult antisocial behaviour. *Journal of the American Academy of Child and Adolescent Psychiatry*, *40*(10), 1222–1230.

Horowitz, L. M., Rosenberg, S. E., Baer, B. A., Ureño, G., & Villaseñor, V. S. (1988). Inventory of interpersonal problems: Psychometric properties and clinical applications. *Journal of Consulting and Clinical Psychology*, *56*(6), 885.

Johnstone, L., & Dallos, R. (2013). *Formulation in psychology and psychotherapy: Making sense of people's problems*. Routledge.

Kessler, R. C., Adler, L., Ames, M., Demler, O., Faraone, S., Hiripi, E., et al. (2005). The World Health Organization Adult ADHD Self-Report Scale (ASRS): A short screening scale for use in the general population. *Psychological Medicine*, *35*(2), 245–256.

Laws, D. (1989). *Relapse prevention with sex offenders*. Guilford Press.

Lenzenweger, M. F., Lane, M. C., Loranger, A. W., & Kessler, R. C. (2007). DSM-IV personality disorders in the National Comorbidity Survey Replication. *Biological Psychiatry*, *62*(6), 553–564.

Linehan, M. (1993). *Cognitive-behavioural treatment of borderline personality disorder*. Guilford Press.

Loeber, R., Slot, N. W., & Stouthamer-Loeber, M. (2006). *A three-dimensional, cumulative developmental model of serious delinquency. The explanation of crime. Context, mechanisms and development.*

McCann, R. A., Ball, E. M., & Ivanoff, A. (2000). DBT with an inpatient forensic population: The CMHIP forensic model. *Cognitive and Behavioural Practice*, *7*(4), 447–456.

Meyer-Lindenberg, A., Buckholtz, J. W., Kolachana, B., Hariri, A. R., Pezawas, L., Blasi, G., et al. (2006). Neural mechanisms of genetic risk for impulsivity and violence in humans. *Proceedings of the National Academy of Sciences of the United States of America*, *103*(16), 6269–6274.

Mischel, W., & Shoda, Y. (1999). Integrating dispositions and processing dynamics within a unified theory of personality: The cognitive-affective personality system*Handbook of personality: Theory and research* (Vol. 2).

Moffitt, T. E. (1993). Adolescence-limited and life-course-persistent antisocial behaviour: A developmental taxonomy. *Psychological Review*, *100*(4), 674–701.

Montoya, E. R., Terburg, D., Bos, P. A., & Van Honk, J. (2012). Testosterone, cortisol, and serotonin as key regulators of social aggression: A review and theoretical perspective. *Motivation and Emotion*, *36*(1), 65–73.

Ogloff, J. R., Talevski, D., Lemphers, A., Wood, M., & Simmons, M. (2015). Co-occurring mental illness, substance use disorders, and antisocial personality disorder among clients of forensic mental health services. *Psychiatric Rehabilitation Journal*, *38*(1), 16.

Olweus, D., Block, J., & Radke-Yarrow, M. (1986). *Development of antisocial and prosocial behaviour: Research, theories, and issues*. Academic Press.

Pain, C. M., Chadwick, P., & Abba, N. (2008). Clients' experience of case formulation in cognitive behaviour therapy for psychosis. *British Journal of Clinical Psychology*, *47*(2), 127–138.

Piquero, A. R., Moffitt, T. E., & Wright, B. E. (2007). Self-control and criminal career dimensions. *Journal of Contemporary Criminal Justice*, *23*(1), 72–89.

Prichard, J. C. (1837). *A treatise on insanity: And other disorders affecting the mind* (Vol. 1837). Haswell, Barrington, and Haswell.

Pulkkinen, L., & Hamalainen, M. (1995). Low self-control as a precursor to crime and accidents in a Finnish longitudinal study. *Criminal Behaviour and Mental Health*, *5*(4), 424–438.

Raven, J. C. (1998). *Raven's progressive matrices*. Oxford Psychologists Press Oxford.

Retz-Junginger, P., Retz, W., Blocher, D., Weijers, H., Trott, G., Wender, P., et al. (2002). Wender Utah rating scale. The short-version for the assessment of the attention-deficit hyperactivity disorder in adults. *Der Nervenarzt*, *73*(9), 830–838.

Rhee, S. H., & Waldman, I. D. (2002). Genetic and environmental influences on antisocial behaviour: A meta-analysis of twin and adoption studies. *Psychological Bulletin*, *128*(3), 490.

Rush, B. (1812). *Medical inquiries and observations upon the diseases of the mind*. Philadelphia: Kimber, Richardson (New York: Hafner Press, 1962).

Skondras, M., Markianos, M., Botsis, A., Bistolaki, E., & Christodoulou, G. (2004). Platelet monoamine oxidase activity and psychometric correlates in male violent offenders imprisoned for homicide or other violent acts. *European Archives of Psychiatry and Clinical Neuroscience*, *254*(6), 380–386.

Spearing, C., Wasteney, V., & Morgan, P. (2010). *Offenders with severe personality disorder and 'lifestyle paralleling behaviours'. Offence paralleling behaviour: A case formulation approach to offender assessment and intervention*.

Torgersen, S., Czajkowski, N., Jacobson, K., Reichborn-Kjennerud, T., Røysamb, E., Neale, M., et al. (2008). Dimensional representations of DSM-IV cluster B personality disorders in a population-based sample of Norwegian twins: A multivariate study. *Psychological Medicine*, *38*(11), 1617–1625.

Tyrer, P., Mitchard, S., Methuen, C., & Ranger, M. (2003). Treatment rejecting and treatment seeking personality disorders: Type R and Type S. *Journal of Personality Disorders*, *17*(3), 263–268.

Ward, T., & Hudson, S. M. (2000). *A self-regulation model of relapse prevention. Remaking relapse prevention with sex offenders: A sourcebook*.

Ward, T., & Stewart, C. (2003). Criminogenic needs and human needs: A theoretical model. *Psychology, Crime and Law*, *9*(2), 125–143.

Webster, C. D., Haque, Q., & Hucker, S. J. (2013). *Violence risk-assessment and management: Advances through structured professional judgement and sequential redirections*. John Wiley & Sons.

Werner, K. B., Few, L. R., & Bucholz, K. K. (2015). Epidemiology, comorbidity, and behavioural genetics of antisocial personality disorder and psychopathy. *Psychiatric Annals*, *45*(4), 195–199.

Young, J. E., Klosko, J. S., & Weishaar, M. E. (2003). *Schema therapy: A practitioner's guide*. Guilford Press.

CHAPTER

10

Formulating Key Psychosocial Mechanisms of Psychopathology and Change in Interpersonal Reconstructive Therapy

Kenneth L. Critchfield[1], Mariafé T. Panizo[1], Lorna Smith Benjamin[2]

[1]Department of Graduate Psychology, James Madison University, Harrisonburg, VA, United States; [2]University of Utah Neuropsychiatric Institute, University of Utah, Salt Lake City, UT, United States

The challenges involved with treating personality disorders (PD) are well known. Maladaptive patterns that characterize these disorders often result in impairment across multiple areas of life functioning. PD can be marked by repeat hospitalizations, significant self-harm, and suicide attempts. PD is often additionally, associated with poorer response to treatment for symptom disorders (Castonguay & Beutler, 2006; Newton-Howes et al., 2014). High degrees of comorbidity with other psychological disorders, including other PDs, further complicates treatment and defies standardization of approach.

Valiant efforts have been made to develop therapeutic models for PD from diverse theoretical perspectives, as attests the current volume. Treatment research however, has focused on the outcomes of treatment packages that target single disorders (especially borderline personality disorder). Largely left unaddressed by research are basic questions about underlying mechanisms of personality, psychopathology and change, as well as their use to tailor a therapist's approach across the range of PD presentations.

Case Formulation for Personality Disorders
https://doi.org/10.1016/B978-0-12-813521-1.00010-2

Interpersonal Reconstructive Therapy (IRT) theory proposes psychosocial mechanisms, specifically evolved attachment mechanisms that are inherent in natural biology as the basis for treatment tailoring (Benjamin, 2003/2006; 2018). In keeping, the IRT case formulation (CF) focuses on how current patterns with self and others reflect prior learning in the context of important attachment relationships. The CF is essential for the IRT task of first 'learning to recognize what your patterns are, where they came from, and what they are for' (Benjamin, 2003/2006, p. 51), and from there to make choices about more adaptive ways of being.

IRT THEORY

IRT was developed by Lorna Smith Benjamin, and its methods are described elsewhere in book length treatments allowing more depth and illustrative examples than are allowed here (2003/2006; 2018). In brief, IRT operates from the premise that personality pathology 'makes sense'. Most often it reflects the implementation of maladaptive rules and ways of being that were learned and internalized in the context of close attachment relationships. IRT is integrative, incorporating wisdom from attachment and interpersonal theories as well as object-relations psychoanalysis to frame the nature of patient problems. Clinicians may borrow techniques from any approach so long as their methods fit the needs and goals outlined by the IRT CF and help move the patient toward therapy goals. In that sense, IRT represents a 'unified' psychotherapy approach (Magnavita & Anchin, 2014) in that the underlying psychotherapy principles organize and build bridges among CBT, psychodynamic, interpersonal, humanistic/existential, systems, and other therapeutic perspectives (Benjamin, 2003/2006; Critchfield, Mackaronis, & Benjamin, 2017).

According to IRT, the same processes of attachment that lead to healthy, adaptive functioning are also understood to be at the core of personality disorder. In the normative condition, attachment works well from an early age. The normative learning process scaffolds and supports adult functioning that is centred, flexible, and adaptive in normative environments, and includes the ability to effectively address threat and resolve conflict when it occurs. Affect, cognition, and behaviour flow together to support flexible and reality-based ways of being. The personality lends itself to growth, as well as resilience in the face of challenge.

In PD, by contrast, what has often been learned through interaction with loved ones includes severely maladaptive patterns involving hostility, rigidity that defies context, and/or extremes of either enmeshment or differentiation. In PD these internalized messages are at odds with effective recognition and response to both safety and threat. PD patients typically 'come by it honestly' in the sense that learning and participation in these patterns were often adaptive, or even necessary for survival in the original learning environment. Maladaptive settings and relationships that invite re-enactment of the earlier situations are subsequently tolerated or even sought out as 'familiar', or 'deserved', rather than rejected in favour of healthier alternatives.

CENTRALITY OF ATTACHMENT MECHANISMS, LEARNING AND DEVELOPMENT

In IRT, attachment is understood to be more than a past developmental context in which learning was primed and trajectories were set. Attachment to past figures is instead seen as being active across the lifespan. As a mechanism it provides a motivating force that keeps maladaptive personality patterns in place and makes them resistant to change. The experience is that the ways and values of loved ones for the patient 'feel right' or are familiar and bring a sense of closeness and connection to the 'family in the head'. To step outside of the parameters of that learning can feel like a risky betrayal of the family, and/or to risk becoming 'not myself'.

To understand the role of attachment-based learning in maintaining maladaptive patterns, it is important to consider the evolutionary context of the biological functions served by attachment. Consider that it is evolutionarily advantageous, especially while young, to quickly learn and retain messages about what to fear and how to be safe. Our nervous system uses this information in powerful ways from earliest learning. In the context of threat, the nervous system activates powerful negative affect that is adaptive for coping with danger: anger mobilizes the individual and facilitates fighting, chasing, or use of control to neutralize the threat; anxiety activates flight or hide behaviours; and depression shuts down the individual in the face of overwhelm, displaying a submissive or helpless attitude to a perceived dominant force. In the context of safety, the nervous system activates positive affect that is adaptive in conditions of safety: pleasure, relaxation, and curiosity, which in turn support playing, bonding, and nursing.

These sets of behavioural patterns are highly adaptive when appropriately cued so that we learn to fear what is appropriate to fear and to feel safe when it is appropriate to feel safe. Very little of this cuing comes preprogrammed into our genetic code. Instead, we orient from an early age toward a process of embodied, interactive learning with proximal caregivers who facilitate experiential learning and transmit messages about safety and threat. When a secure base pattern is not offered, the proximal caregivers may themselves pose threats, abandon a child to dangers, or shape the conclusions reached by the child about how and why events occur in problematic ways ('you don't deserve to be protected', 'you can't do anything right', 'do as I tell you').

Internalized representations of the main caregivers that carry miscued, maladaptive, or otherwise unhealthy messages of threat and safety have psychiatric symptoms as natural consequences. In other words, the individual experiences anger, anxiety, depression, and so on, in ways that are either (1) out of context, chronically maintained, or out of proportion to actual events (e.g., suicidality in response to a positive evaluation at work), or (2) maintain proximity (consciously or unconsciously) with environments that are themselves toxic, and in which anger, anxiety, or depression would be expectable, normative responses (e.g., chronic anxiety and panic after deciding to return to a relationship with an unpredictable, violent, alcoholic partner).

Benjamin (2008) describes the 'autoimmunity hypothesis of psychiatric disorder' in which ways of being that are recognized as 'me' are approached and maintained; while 'not me' ways are avoided or punished. This situation works well when healthy self-definition is in place, but maintains problem patterns when it is not. It can be seen, for example, in paradoxical patterns often associated with PD such as self-sabotage after success or happiness, or even in response to progress in therapy. This process is often motivated through a desire to receive love and affirmation from (internalized versions of) loved ones – usually, but not limited to, the early proximal caregivers. In essence, their love is to be received in exchange for repeating their roles, rules, and values for the patient. As such, attachment-linked maladaptive behaviour is often referred to in IRT as a 'gift of love' (GOL). The challenge for clinicians is to understand a patient's 'back story' in a way that can make sense of even paradoxical and self-sabotaging scripts, and ultimately uncover putative GOLs that motivate these behaviours.

With regard to PD, in IRT a developmental learning process affects biological, psychological, and social processes to produce predictable, trait-like regularities of behaviour, especially in response to signals of safety and threat in the present. Personality refers to these regularities of interaction with the environment. The PD categories contained in the DSM reflect the more commonly seen and/or clinically salient constellations of problematic interpersonal patterns while the term 'disorder' applies when the attempts to adapt are significantly miscued and cause serious problems.

An outline of the structure and logic of the IRT CF is provided in Fig. 10.1. Where possible, symptoms and problems are understood in terms of associated patterns of relating with self and others that recur across relationships or developmental context. Change in the relational patterns and self-concepts are the ultimate focus of IRT treatment, with symptoms expected to resolve as the associated ways of being that support them shift in healthier directions.

symptoms and problems

↓

(often reflect or derive from)
problematic relational patterns with self and others

↓

(when copied, these patterns suggest internalization of)
specific, key attachment figures

↓

(GOL hypothesis is that patterns are maintained by)
wishes for psychic proximity, love and acceptance from internalized representations

---

(general treatment implications)
enhance awareness of patterns; differentiate from internalizations sufficient to choose differently; block problem patterns; establish new, adaptive ways to be, feel, and think about self and others in the present

FIGURE 10.1 Structure and logic of the Interpersonal Reconstructive Therapy (IRT) case formulation.

DISTINGUISHING BETWEEN ADAPTIVE AND MALADAPTIVE PATTERNS USING SASB

Interactivity and relational context are central to an understanding of adaptive and maladaptive personality patterns in IRT. Affect, cognition, and behaviour are all considered to be important and convergent sources of information. The first two operate together at the subcortical level in service of attempts to respond adaptively to the perceived environment.

Use of a sophisticated interpersonal model to track interpersonal patterns in patient narratives, the Structural Analysis of Social Behaviour (SASB: Benjamin, 1974; 1996), was instrumental to development and articulation of key concepts in IRT. Briefly, SASB is an interpersonal circumplex model that allows for precise description of relational behaviours. As such, it facilitates detection of repeating relational patterns. Clear definition of relational patterns also makes it possible to define adaptive versus maladaptive ways of relating. SASB is a well-validated framework that describes relational behaviours using the three distinctions of Focus, Affiliation, and Interdependence (Fig. 10.2). The first distinction is the attentional focus of a behaviour. In Fig. 10.2, behaviours focused

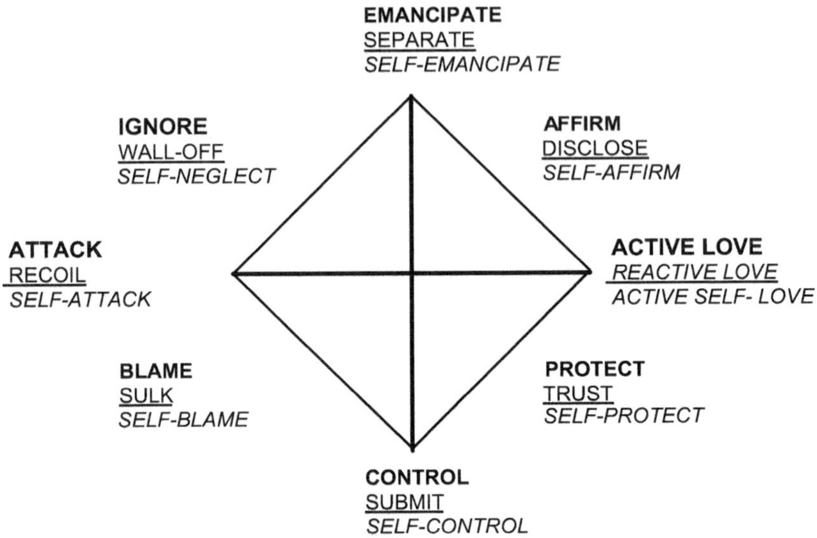

FIGURE 10.2 The one-word cluster model of the structural analysis of social behaviour (SASB). *Fig. 3.9 from Benjamin, L.S. (1996/2003).* Interpersonal diagnosis and treatment of personality disorder. *New York: Copyright Guilford Press. Reprinted with permission of The Guilford Press.*

transitively on others are listed in **bold**. Intransitive behaviours focused on the self are underlined. An Introjective focus (*italics*) represents behaviour directed inward by the self toward the self. Each behavioural focus has a parallel organization by degrees of affiliation (horizontal axis) and interdependence (vertical axis). Affiliation ranges from extremes of hostility (far left) to extremes of friendliness or love (far right). Interdependence ranges from extremes of enmeshment (bottom) to extremes of differentiation or independence (top). Individual behaviours are typically described adequately by appeal to one location on the model that combines focus, affiliation and interdependence. However, human behaviour can also be complex. Such behaviours as mixed messages and double-binds can be described as simultaneous use of multiple positions within the model. Well-meaning advice or support that nonetheless neglects important context could be captured by simultaneous **Protect** plus **Ignore**. For example, offering to buy a drink for a friend known to have a substance abuse problem in an attempt to help him cope with a recent break-up might fit that characterization.

Adaptive personality patterns consistent with internalization of a secure base relationship with caregivers can be defined as a region on the right side of the SASB model. Secure base, adaptive relating involves friendliness in normative settings, along with the ability to be moderately connected/enmeshed or moderately separate/differentiated, and to have a reciprocity of focus on others or the self. Adaptive patterns allow flexible response to circumstance, including the ability to deviate from baseline to address threats and regain safety. This region constitutes the IRT therapy goal, with expectation that centred, pleasant and constructive affects and cognitions will accompany and support adaptive ways of being.

Maladaptive patterns, by contrast involve baseline ways of being marked by deviations away from the secure base region toward any of the following: (1) significant hostility (toward others or the self), (2) extremes (high or low) of enmeshment or differentiation, (3) difficulties maintaining a balanced focus on self or others, or (4) rigidity that prevents healthy adaptation to emergent circumstances (even if the pattern is otherwise friendly and balanced). Predictable affects associated with these ways of being include anger, anxiety, and depression. Expectable cognitions include rigid, binary, 'either/or' thinking, decisions related to fight-or-flight responses, or through disorganization, distraction, or behavioural shut down (Benjamin, 2003/2006; 2018). Research with SASB confirms links between maladaptive patterns, especially hostility, and forms of psychopathology (Benjamin, Rothweiler, & Critchfield, 2006).

Benjamin (1993/1996) offers SASB-based interpersonal definitions of each of the DSM-IV/5 PDs, including the prototypic developmental histories that would lead to specific patterns of functioning in adulthood. These definitions have been operationalized and used to compare each interpersonal PD prototype with copy process patterns observed in patient CF. This method was applied by Critchfield, Benjamin, and Levenick (2015) to a sample of 93 adult inpatients, showing it to have the expected overlap with DSM diagnosis.

While use of the SASB model is not required for effective use of IRT by clinicians, who can often proceed by intuition and 'feel', it is highly recommended to add precision to the recognition and conceptualization of patterns relayed in more complex patient narratives.

IRT CASE FORMULATION METHOD IN FOUR STEPS

The CF interview, described in detail by Benjamin (2003/2006), is guided by the goal of understanding presenting symptoms and problems in terms of their interpersonal origins and reasons to persist in the present. It can be accomplished in an inpatient setting in a relatively short time (e.g., 90 min) because that context assures safety following what can sometimes be a difficult discussion of emotionally laden, traumatic, or 'betraying' (of loved ones) material. In the outpatient context, the same process may need to unfold across 3 to 7 sessions to ensure that the therapeutic relationship is secure and that the depth and pacing of the conversation does not disrupt between-session functioning.

TABLE 10.1 IRT Case Formulation Outline

SECTION 1: PATTERN IN THE PRESENT
Presenting problems
Current stresses
Responses to stresses
Conscious self-concept
Current figures
Summary of Current Pattern(s) in terms of Input > Response > Impact on Self
SECTION 2: DIAGNOSTIC AND CONTEXTUAL FACTORS
Family history of mental disorder
Current diagnoses
Diagnostic criteria for Personality Disorder
Treatment history
SECTION 3: COPY PROCESSES AND GOL
List of Key Figures
Separately describe interactions with, and attributes of each Key Figure
List copy processes for each Key Figure
Links between Key Figures and each symptom
Gift of Love hypothesis (and associated evidence) linking presenting problems and Key Figures
SECTION 4: TREATMENT IMPLICATIONS AND RECOMMENDATIONS
Short-term goals, needs, resources
Long-term therapy goals

The process typically begins with the question 'what do you need help with?' From there, the interviewer creates an empathic and collaborative relationship while filling in the essential elements of the CF outline provided in Table 10.1. The clinician actively seeks to understand how symptoms and problems may reflect ways of relating to self and others that were learned and internalized with loved ones (see Fig. 10.2). If links are established, an additional task is to explore potential GOL motivations that might interfere with change attempts if they are not addressed. To be adherent to IRT, the process must be collaborative, including that the CF is considered valid only if the patient agrees with its content and implications.

STEP ONE: OUTLINE PATTERNS IN THE PRESENT

Symptom-linked relationship narratives are explored with regard to three basic components: (1) input from others or the world, (2) response of the patient to those others, and (3) impact on the self (i.e., on self-concept or self-treatment). Ideally, each of these domains is articulated sufficiently to find a location within the SASB model. Associated affects and cognitions that accompany each relational domain are also tracked.

Once the dominant themes of symptom-linked relational narratives are understood in the present, a transition is made in the interview process to seek earlier precedent. This is done by exploration of prior experiences with important figures in the person's life (e.g., parents, family members, teachers, lovers, abusers). One route commonly taken by IRT clinicians is to reflect back aspects of symptoms and patterns occurring in the present and then asking if the theme is familiar, inviting recollection of earlier times the same themes might have been present. Alternatively, the interviewer might ask directly about the history with important figures in a separate part of the interview, after taking stock of patterns in the present.

STEP TWO: SEEK COPY PROCESS EVIDENCE TO IDENTIFY KEY ATTACHMENT FIGURES

Evidence of internalization is suggested by behavioural repetition of relationship patterns. Three primary types of copy process are emphasized in IRT: (1) identification (be like him/her), (2) introjection (treat yourself as you were treated), and (3) recapitulation (act as if him/her is still there and in control). Identification means that the individual behaves as an important other person did, for example a patient may fearfully avoid contact with others and abuse substances just as an important caregiver did; or launch into a rage over small slights, just as a former lover did. Introjection means that the individual treats him/herself as he/she was treated by an important other person. For example, persistent self-criticism and perfectionism might echo the same critical views received as input from an unpleasable loved one. Recapitulation refers to the tendency to act like or perceive the world as if an important figure is still present and in charge. For example, fear and suspicion may arise with new people as if they are just like a former abuser. Copy processes are not mutually exclusive. They frequently co-occur in a way to suggest internalization of a given relational figure who now contributes to problem maintenance as internalized 'family in the head' (Critchfield & Benjamin, 2008, 2010; Critchfield et al., 2015). In order to qualify as a copy process there must be a high degree of similarity between past and present behaviours. As mentioned before, SASB provides a way to accurately recognize and ensure specificity of patterns consistent with identification, introjection, and recapitulation.

STEP THREE: THE GIFT OF LOVE (GOL) HYPOTHESIS

Once copy process patterns are recognized, the gift of love (GOL) hypothesis can be explored. A key observation of the IRT model isthat maladaptive patterns copied from close attachment relationships often tend to persist due to a yearning desire for love and acceptance from internalized figures. The 'gift of love' speech can be used to discuss the topic and elicit relevant input from patients about their awareness of possible attachment-based motivations.

> So you see that in many ways, you are being faithful to the rules and values that you learned when you were little. The question remains: Why do we do that? Why do we keep on following those old ideas, especially when they don't work so well any more? Well, often it is because without realizing it, we are trying to 'get it right' with [Dad, Mom, brother, etc.]. It is like we do it the way they seemed to want it, in hopes that they will approve and be pleased. It is as if we hope that maybe things could be better after all. Does that make any sense? ***Benjamin* (2003/2006, p. 49).**

Awareness of the GOL motivation can be readily accessed by some patients. For others, the implications are too painful or sensitive to be discussed directly. For these cases the GOL is retained as a hypothesis until they can be further explored as a patient becomes ready to entertain them. The GOL hypothesis must never be imposed or delivered in a confrontational manner. It should also not be approached in a way that suggests the task involves assigning blame to the patient or to others, but only to track patterns in a spirit of 'figuring out how it works'. A confrontational approach could be iatrogenic and profoundly disorganizing for some patients given the nature of the topic.

STEP FOUR: IDENTIFY TREATMENT IMPLICATIONS

Once the formulation of maladaptive copy process patterns is complete, including their links to symptoms and basic understanding of their origins and 'reasons', treatment becomes oriented around the goal of increasing more adaptive ways of being in the present, and to seek differentiation from the messages of internalized figures (or 'family in the head') whenever they block progress toward that goal. Within IRT language, the affects, behaviours, and cognitions that result from maladaptive internalized representations of threat and safety illustrate a 'Regressive Loyalist' (or 'Red') self. By tracing how copy process links and problem patterns explain the presenting symptoms, the IRT CF primarily focuses on Red patterns.

The part of the patient that comes for therapy desiring healthy adaptation, and collaborates toward this goal is called the 'Growth Collaborator' (or 'Green') self. Another term, the 'Birthright Self' refers to the self that would have evolved had secure base conditions existed during the early developmental process (Benjamin, 2008; 2018). Most, perhaps all, people can be seen to have Green and Red to the degree that we all have experience with problematic relationships in ways that inform how we are with ourselves or others. However, people with mental and emotional problems are dominated by Red.

Treatment goals address short-term implications for safety, stability, and reasonable adjustment. They also address longer-term work toward personality reconstruction. In both time frames, the treatment goal of IRT entails deactivating Red and enabling the growth of Green. Change in PD can be a lengthy process that first involves awareness of an individual's symptom-linked patterns, their origins, and the reasons for their persistence. With this awareness, lasting change becomes possible in part via differentiation from internalized attachment figures (upper portions of the SASB model in relation to internalizations), while new patterns that reflect the secure base position on the SASB model (right of Fig. 10.2) appear as a reconstruction of the Birthright self.

APPLICATION OF THE IRT FORMULATION METHOD

John Carlo, is a 29 year old divorced Filipino-American father of one daughter. He was psychiatrically hospitalized on an involuntary basis after an overdose attempt, which he intended to follow with use of a loaded gun. He cited overwhelm, self-criticism and inability to live up to others' expectations. John Carlo had one prior hospitalization for suicidality 10 years earlier that involved serious self injury. Using formal diagnostic methods he qualified for the following DSM-IV diagnoses: Major Depressive Disorder, Psychosis NOS, and post-traumatic stress disorder (PTSD). Underlying these problems, John Carlo qualified for both Obsessive-Compulsive (OCPD) and Passive-Aggressive (PAG) personality disorders on both the formal SCID-II interview, as well as the SASB-based, Wisconsin Personality Inventory (WISPI: Klein et al., 1993). Presenting problems identified by request of the referring inpatient team were depression, suicide attempts, 'lying' (as John Carlo put it), and fears of sexual intimacy.

The process of John Carlo's 90-min consultative interview was remarkable in part due to his scattered and disorganized initial presentation. The interviewer, the third author, responded to this whenever it came up by asking for clarification and offering transparent explanation of her intention to 'see the world as he does'. She also patiently tracked and reflected the interpersonal themes of his nonlinear narrative. Over time, rapport was established and his narrative became comprehensible. The immediate circumstances leading to hospitalization were that John Carlo was alone at his parents' home. He had prepared a suicide note reading: 'Dad. I am sorry I disappointed you, my sisters, my mom, and my daughter'. After taking the pills he called his mother to say goodbye. He remembers dropping the phone and then awakening to the arrival of the police. When asked in interview 'What would he [Dad] say if you had succeeded in killing yourself?' John Carlo said, 'maybe he would feel sorry, upset'.

CURRENT PATTERNS

Highlights of John Carlo's story are as follows: In recent years, John Carlo had been working, making alimony payments, taking part-time college classes in exercise and sport science, and performing at a high level as an Ironman Triathlete. He had been married for 6 years and his daughter is from that marriage. He said that prior to their divorce his ex-wife trashed their home after an argument. She then called the police and presented the house as evidence of his abuse. She also accused him of molesting their daughter. The courts ruled in her favour and John Carlo was ordered to treatment, which he attended. He had supervised visitation rights only. Since the divorce, he says he has spent most of his savings trying to regain custody.

John Carlo has since had intimate relationships with women. However, he is perplexed that after they have sex he switches abruptly from being kind and supportive to pushing them away, becoming hateful, controlling, and critical: 'I am not me'. This also occurred in his marriage. Sex 'takes something away. I feel weak and powerless. I don't like you. I hate you'.

Until recently, John Carlo worked at a packing company, working up to a senior role. He lost that job when the business closed. A new job had much reduced hours and pay. His father, to whom he had long turned for advice, was perceived as offering only criticism: 'You should have not done this, you should have done that'. 'You should be better established by now'. 'You screw everything up'. His father is a coach and sports enthusiast. John Carlo described practicing endlessly and intensely in an attempt to please his father, who values strength and competition. He reported using sport as a way to cope by 'numbing myself' and pushing out all emotion. He has had multiple sport-related accidents that were quite serious, including head injuries.

As he felt increasingly empty and burned out, John Carlo decided there was no hope of getting his father's approval, and that he 'might as well finish it off'. His girlfriend walked in on him as he was preparing to cut himself. Her response was to tell him to move out, and that she did not want to see him anymore. His parents took him in at first, but when John Carlo's father learned why they broke up he told John Carlo he was no longer welcome in the family home. This message precipitated his overdose with a gun at the ready and subsequent involuntary hospitalization.

Table 10.2 provides a summary of John Carlo's current patterns. Symptom-linked themes are based on interpersonal inputs, responses,

TABLE 10.2 Summary of John Carlo's Patterns in the Present

	Input	Response	Impact on Self	Associated Symptoms
Pattern 1	Others, especially father, are critical and reject JC for alleged failures to live up to high demands and expectations for performance.	JC works to please, submitting and working hard to make himself conform to what is wanted and valued for him by others.	When attempts fail and criticism persists, he disciplines and pushes himself to the point of becoming numb. He disallows own feelings. Overwhelmed, he blames and rejects himself.	Depression, Suicidality.
	SASB analysis: **Blame, Attack** after **Control**, and **Control/Ignore.**	SASB analysis: Submit, *Self-Control.*	SASB analysis: *Self-Control* plus *Self-Neglect*; when overwhelmed: *Self-Blame, Self-Attack.*	
Pattern 2	Loving, positive relationship becomes sexual.	JC is initially loving, but after experiencing sexual trauma reminders becomes critical, controlling, distant, rejecting, 'lies' to say he hates his partner.	Becomes 'not me'. JC is angry at himself for self-sabotage and for pushing loved ones away.	'Lying', Intimacy problems, Depression, PTSD.
	SASB analysis: **Active Love.**	SASB analysis: Traumatic script **Blame, Attack, Ignore**, Recoil, Wall-Off.	SASB analysis: *Self-Blame* and *Self-Neglect.*	

and impacts on self as described in the interview. A primary theme is one in which John Carlo works extraordinarily hard to please others, most notably, his father. He repeatedly experiences criticism and rejection due to alleged failures to do what is required. In response, he pushes himself harder (especially physically), suppresses feeling, and when this strategy fails, joins his accusers in blame and rejection of himself even to the point of depression and suicide. A second pattern also emerged, one in which John Carlo dramatically sabotages loving relationships as soon as they become sexual. This pattern appears to originate in triggered memories of abuse, with his response to traumatic reminders being to 'lie' (as he put it), by pushing partners away with cruel and judgemental words.

DEVELOPMENTAL HISTORY AND COPY PROCESS ANALYSIS

John Carlo's family history is replete with trauma, loss, and attempts to please others by 'being strong'. Multiple, gruesome suicides have occurred involving childhood friends and relatives John Carlo knew well. He reports 'becoming numb' while helping clean up the aftermath. Sexual abuse also runs through the family history. John Carlo was raped violently and painfully by his maternal uncle in childhood. Soon after, he decided to start working out in order to defend himself in the future. When the same uncle approached him a few years later, he 'wiped the floor with him'. However, when John Carlo attempted to tell his father about the sexual abuse, he heard 'we don't talk about these kinds of things'. He now feels shame despite his attempts to 'do what I was supposed to do' by being unaffected and defending himself. When younger, his father beat him with a belt for mistakes with any of his many assigned chores. Eventually his father stopped, but verbal criticism escalated as John Carlo entered adolescence.

Table 10.3 shows in SASB-based terms how key aspects of John Carlo's childhood history repeat as copy process. The most salient attachment figure is John Carlo's father, who clearly still plays a major role in his adult life. Introjection of that relationship is evidenced in multiple ways, including self-treatment that involves substantial use of self-control and self-neglect, for example, by 'pushing through' physically while neglecting his feelings. John Carlo often implements these strategies as part of an

TABLE 10.3 Copy Processes for John Carlo in SASB Terms

Person Copied	Copy Processes	Behaviour(s) Copied
Father	Introjection of	**Control** as *Self-Control*
		Neglect as *Self-Neglect*
		Blame as *Self-Blame*
		Attack as *Self-Attack*
	Identification with	**Blame, Attack, Ignore**
	Recapitulation of	Others to Me: **Control, Blame, Attack, Ignore**
		Me to Others: Submit, *Self-Control, Self-Neglect*
Mother	Identification with	Details unclear (relationship less well explored in interview): both are depressed, suicidal, and victims of sexual abuse.

attempt to please unpleasable others who are critical and controlling (e.g., ex-wife), a recapitulation of the relationship with his father. When John Carlo responds to reminders of sexual trauma and rejects his romantic partners after sex, he copies and identifies with father's values, angrily rejecting the perceived threat of sex with the partner. John Carlo's mother may also be important, but less attention was paid to her role in the consultative interview. Identification is suggested based on their shared experience of depression, suicidality, and status as victim of intra-familial sexual abuse. Information subsequently disclosed in therapy sessions would add detail to this part of John Carlo's CF.

The abusive uncle does not appear as a key figure in this formulation. Abusers can be, and often are, attachment figures in their own right, especially when there is evidence of a positive relationship, or hopes of one, along with wishes for acceptance, reunion, or reconciliation. In John Carlo's case, there were few such markers of attachment to the uncle uncovered in the formulation interview. Instead, John Carlo's narrative emphasized his struggles to make sense of the abuse in light of its meaning in relationship to his father, whose values were to be strong, push aside 'weak' feelings, and neutralize perceived threats with control and aggression. Trauma-based repetition of past experience is an important piece of John Carlo's clinical picture. This formulation suggests, however, that addressing it will require focus on how the lessons internalized from John Carlo's father relate to that experience.

COPY PROCESS-BASED DIAGNOSIS OF PERSONALITY DISORDER

The SASB-based interpersonal prototype matching method described earlier was applied to John Carlo's case and showed OCPD to be the best fit. Interpersonally, OCPD involves a baseline position of excessive self-discipline, restraint of feelings, and neglect of the self. There is a strong fear of making a mistake or being accused of being imperfect. Harsh self-criticism can follow even minor mistakes and the quest for correctness lends itself toward inconsiderate control of others (and blame for their failings) as well as blind obedience to authority or principles. John Carlo's themes clearly parallel this description of OCPD. His early developmental inputs involved **Control** paired with **Ignore**, followed by **Blame** for perceived failures. He introjected this input (mostly from father) as *Self-Control* and *Self-Neglect*, followed by *Self-Blame*. He implemented the pattern with romantic partners after sex by angrily rejecting them, becoming like (identifying with) his father. He also recapitulated the complementary pattern of *Submission* by seeking to please others (especially father) and live by their rules.

GIFT OF LOVE

IRT theory suggests that copy process repetitions are motivated by the GOL, that is, the yearning hope and desire to finally be loved, accepted, and/or protected in exchange for living according to the rules and ways endorsed for the individual by loved ones. Lasting change involves lessening this motivation and allowing room to try more adaptive alternatives. The challenge in more severe cases is that the desired love and acceptance from internalized loved ones is at risk of never being realized if the healthier course is pursued. For example, if John Carlo allows himself to follow a treatment programme that in father's eyes requires him to be 'weak' (i.e., tolerate and then understand his own vulnerable, frustrated, and even traumatized feelings) then how will he ever finally gain his father's respect and acceptance for being strong and powerful? This could only happen if the relationship is revisited and significantly reframed. IRT theory suggests that even if family interventions were successful in changing father in the present, the internalized version of him would need to be addressed for change to be lasting.

For John Carlo, the GOL motivation was palpable and readily verified by him in context of the interview. When asked what he would most like to say to his father, his responses were 'Why are you so critical of me?' and then 'Please hug me.' John Carlo described saying to his father at one point, 'I push everyone away because I want you'. He was deeply hurt when his father rolled his eyes in response. The attachment-based yearning for love that is at the core of GOLs is, of course, a topic that should only be addressed with great sensitivity. As noted above, the GOL hypothesis must never be imposed. Instead, copy process offers a behaviourally-anchored way of talking about patterns that have immediate relevance to presenting problems while inviting deeper exploration of internalized relationships as readiness for change develops.

TREATMENT IMPLICATIONS

For John Carlo, a number of treatment suggestions have potential to nurture 'Green', allowing him to discover, listen to, and like himself and his feelings in deeper ways. His romantic relationships may benefit from psychoeducation focused on normative, loving sexuality as distinguished from traumatic or shame-producing experience. Group therapy could offer a setting in which expression of feelings is met with supportive responses that provide antidote to Red expectations. With a new awareness and allowing of feelings, the likelihood of support for Green and secure relationships will be enhanced. John Carlo may also need support and training for how to be a good father. Given the patterns internalized from his own father, therapy might help him become aware of any tendency he may have with his daughter to repeat problem patterns involving tendency to ignore feelings, become critical, or make unrealistic demands for performance. Instead he could learn to simply play, enjoy, and scaffold learning tasks for his daughter in age appropriate ways.

The foregoing treatment implications are fairly generic and 'common sense'. John Carlo had prior treatment attempts with similar goals in mind (e.g., counseling about sexuality and trauma, and parent training). What is less obvious is that none of the above suggestions are likely to take hold at a deep level (and indeed, they didn't) until and unless the persistent yearning to finally be loved and accepted by father is brought into focus. Loyalty to father's ways is at the core of each problem pattern targeted above. If John Carlo continues to hold tightly to father's rules out of a desire to finally be loved by him, then all conversations about sexuality, or about being open and compassionate with others or the self will be blocked. Or, if he does, there may be a heavy price to pay, including a return to disorganization, intense self-criticism, and suicidality.

A full explication of the change process in IRT is beyond the scope of the present chapter. However, it involves use of the CF to navigate several steps of therapy: Collaboration, Learning about Patterns, Blocking Maladaptive Patterns, Enabling the Will to Change, and Learning New Patterns. Throughout, a patient comes to recognize a part of the self that is repeating the old patterns out of a yearning for love and acceptance from the figures with whom they were learned. Awareness of Red patterns and motivations brings about the possibility of choosing healthier, Green ways. An adherent IRT therapist is both patient and active in encouraging awareness and choice. Help on how to navigate the complexities of this process are provided in the treatment manuals offered by Benjamin (2003/2006; 2018).

OUTCOME

John Carlo's treatment spanned 3 years. His two trainee therapists across that time were judged by independent raters to be adherent in implementation of IRT. In other words, the CF was consistently used in conjunction with a core algorithm of empathy, support for Green over Red, and careful tracking of interpersonal patterns and associated affects and cognitions. Fig. 10.3 shows that a dramatic change occurred in John Carlo's ratings of his self-treatment on the SASB-based Intrex self-report questionnaire (Benjamin, 2000). John Carlo started therapy with a self-reported profile involving dangerous levels of *Self-Attack* at worst in a context emphasizing forms of self-discipline (*Self-Protect, Self-Control, Self-Blame*), with little *Self-Love*. Interestingly, John Carlo did not initially

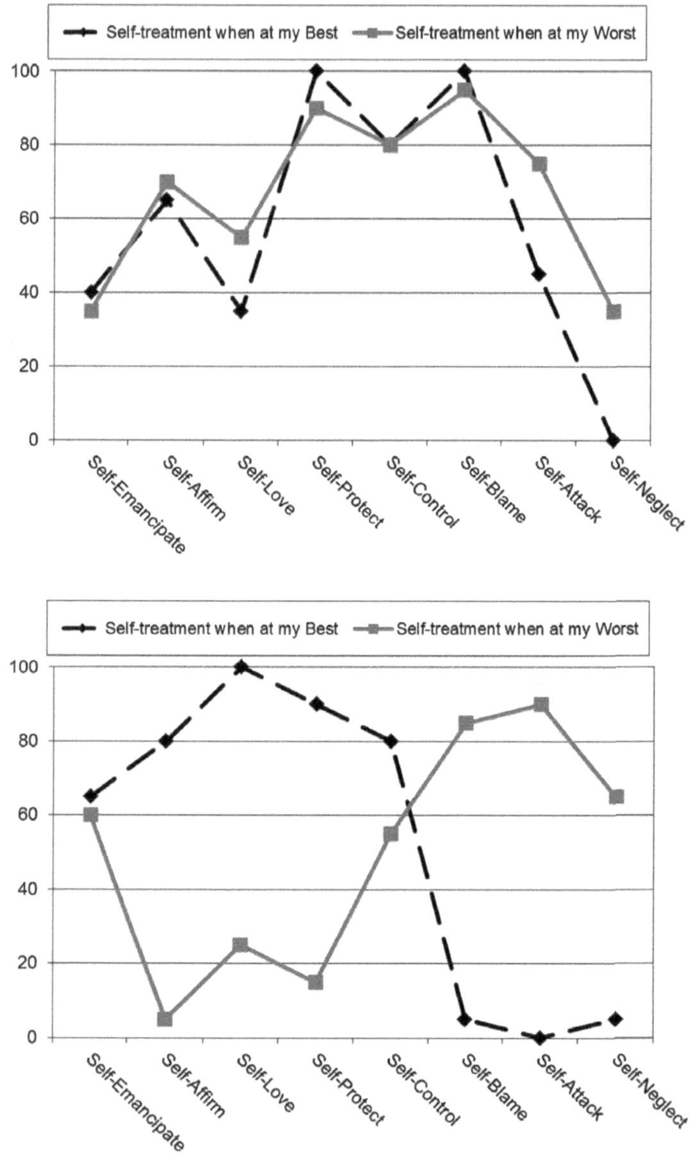

FIGURE 10.3 John Carlo's self-treatment at beginning (top) and end (bottom) of Interpersonal Reconstructive Therapy (IRT).

recognize his 'numbing' and recklessness as *Self-Neglect*, likely adopting his father's view of these behaviours as providing self protection. At the end of therapy (bottom of Fig. 10.3), John Carlo's profile was very different. He was hostile to himself only when at worst, which he estimated to be limited to only 10% of the time. Ninety percent of the time he was in the therapy goal region with a profile containing almost no hostility and peaking on *Self-Love*. This dramatic shift showed that Green ways had taken root. They persisted even in the face of life stressors across the last phase of treatment. At termination of treatment, SCID interviews were again conducted. John Carlo no longer qualified for his list of DSM disorders, including any PD. He had entered into and maintained a loving, sexual relationship. Depression and anxiety levels were below even normative means.

CASE FORMULATION RESEARCH IN IRT

IRT research has focused on attachment-based mechanisms proposed to be at the heart of psychopathology and change. Research efforts by our group show that copy process is nearly ubiquitous and can be detected using the Intrex self-report method in both clinical and non-clinical samples (Critchfield & Benjamin, 2008; 2010). The interview-based formulation method described in this chapter also supports high levels of copy process in PD samples. Additionally, the CF has strong inter-rater reliability and validity evidence (Critchfield, et al., 2015). Estimates of inter-clinician agreement watching the same interview was estimated with Cohen's kappa to range from 0.77 to 0.91 across key figures, copy processes, and their links to symptoms. The method readily distinguished between cases based only on the SASB-defined interpersonal copy process patterns (similar to Table 10.3), confirming that the method is not one-size-fits-all, and can credibly serve as the basis for individual tailoring of treatment. When IRT formulations were used to generate best-fitting PD diagnoses based on interpersonal features (using the method described earlier based on Benjamin's interpersonal translations) the CF yielded similar results to SCID-II PD assessments for the most prominent disorders in the study sample: OCPD and PAG. Good agreement, as well as sensitivity, and specificity were in evidence (Critchfield, et al., 2015).

The attachment-based mechanism of change, the GOL, is at the heart of IRT theory. Research on this topic is currently underway. The primary method is to associate change in levels of awareness and choice about the GOL with outcome among cases referred for demonstrated prior treatment resistance, comorbidity, and high severity (i.e., high base rate of PD). In preliminary analyses, therapist adherent use of the CF predicts retention, symptom change, and reduced rehospitalization (Karpiak, Critchfield, & Benjamin, 2011). Observed links between adherence and outcome appears to be a function of progress differentiating from key attachment figures and relinquishing the GOL (Critchfield, Karpiak, & Benjamin, 2011).

CONCLUSION

At the core of IRT is the observation that problematic behaviours, affects, and cognitions are related to internalized attachment figures, including their perceived rules and values for the individual. The case formulation in IRT tracks these copied behavioural patterns as they relate to current symptoms and helps uncover motivational factors that serve to maintain problem patterns. A treatment approach that effectively brings about differentiation from these internalized relationships appears to be key to the possibility of change for patients characterized by prior treatment nonresponse, diagnostic comorbidity, low functioning, and high severity. However, since the IRT model is rooted in normative, developmental processes of attachment, we have also found wide application of the method in other samples and settings. At lower levels of clinical acuity, patients tend to have internalized less problematic patterns (e.g., it has not been considered disloyal to think for themselves or question the family), or they have been able to internalize a range of relationships that support Green, so that Red is not as powerful overall. Any time patient problems can be understood as echoes of prior experience with loved ones, there is potential for those problems to be maintained by the GOL. In all such cases, the relationship with internalized figures must be factored in to treatment. The IRT CF is the primary tool for ensuring that those relationships are vivid for therapist and patient alike as specific intervention choices are made along the way to treatment goals.

Acknowledgements

Permission for use of disguised clinical data in published work has been received in writing by the authors. Details have been changed so as to protect client privacy.

Conflict of Interest

The University of Utah Conflict of Interest Committee requires that Lorna Smith Benjamin disclose that she is the author of *Structural Analysis of Social Behavior (SASB)* and is eligible for an author's percentage of the sale price if ever *SASB* is sold to a testing company by the University of Utah, the present owner of *SASB*. She is the author of three books for which she receives royalties and three assessment instruments *(Structured Clinical Interview for the diagnosis of Personality Disorder: SCID-II and SCID-PD;* and the *Wisconsin Personality Disorders Inventory: WISPI)* in which she has no financial interest. She also gives workshops to professionals for a fee.

References

Benjamin, L. S. (1974). Structural analysis of social behavior. *Psychological Review, 81*, 392–425.

Benjamin, L. S. (2000). *Intrex User's manual*. Salt Lake City: University of Utah Press.

Benjamin, L. S. (2003/2006). *Interpersonal reconstructive therapy: An integrative, personality-based treatment for complex cases* (paperback ed.). New York: Guilford Press.

Benjamin, L. S. (2008). What is functional about functional autonomy? *Journal of Personality Assessment*, *90*(5), 412–420.

Benjamin, L. S. (2018). *Interpersonal reconstructive therapy for anger, anxiety and depression: it's about broken hearts, not broken brains*. American Psychological Association.

Benjamin, L. S., Rothweiler, J. C., & Critchfield, K. L. (2006). The use of structural analysis of social behavior (SASB) as an assessment tool. *Annual Review of Clinical Psychology*, *2*, 83–109.

Castonguay, L. G., & Beutler, L. E. (2006). *Principles of therapeutic change that work*. New York: Oxford University Press.

Critchfield, K. L., & Benjamin, L. S. (2008). Internalized representations of early interpersonal experience and adult relationships: A test of copy process theory in clinical and nonclinical populations. *Psychiatry: Interpersonal and Biological Processes*, *71*, 71–92.

Critchfield, K. L., & Benjamin, L. S. (2010). Assessment of repeated relational patterns for individual cases using the SASB-based Intrex questionnaire. *Journal of Personality Assessment*, *92*, 480–489.

Critchfield, K. L., Benjamin, L. S., & Levenick, K. (2015). Reliability, sensitivity, and specificity of case formulations for comorbid profiles in interpersonal reconstructive therapy: Addressing mechanisms of psychopathology. *Journal of Personality Disorders*, *29*(4), 547–573.

Critchfield, K. L., Karpiak, C., & Benjamin, L. S. (September 2011). Therapeutic focus on the "gift of love": Preliminary tests of the putative mechanism of change in Interpersonal Reconstructive Therapy. In *Paper presented to the North American chapter of the society for psychotherapy research, Banff, CA*.

Critchfield, K. L., Mackaronis, J. E., & Benjamin, L. S. (2017). Integrative use of CBT and psychodynamic techniques in interpersonal reconstructive therapy. *Journal of Psychotherapy Integration*. https://doi.org/10.1037/int0000092.

Karpiak, C., Critchfield, K. L., & Benjamin, L. S. (June 2011). Empathy, adherence, and outcome in interpersonal reconstructive therapy with treatment-resistant patients. In *Paper presented to the society for psychotherapy research*. Bern: Switzerland.

Klein, M. H., Benjamin, L. S., Rosenfeld, R., Treece, C., Husted, J., & Greist, J. H. (1993). The Wisconsin personality disorders inventory (WISPI): I. Development, reliability, and validity. *Journal of Personality Disorders*, *1*, 285–303.

Magnavita, J. J., & Anchin, J. C. (2014). *Unifying psychotherapy: Principles, methods, and evidence from clinical science*. New York: Springer.

Newton-Howes, G., Tyrer, P., Johnson, T., Mulder, R., Kool, S., Dekker, J., et al. (2014). Influence of personality on the outcome of treatment in depression: Systematic review and meta-analysis. *Journal of Personality Disorders*, *28*(4), 577–593.

CHAPTER

11

Motives, Defences, and Conflicts in the Dynamic Formulation for Psychodynamic Psychotherapy Using the Idiographic Conflict Formulation Method

J. Christopher Perry[1], *Megan Knoll*[2], *Viet Tran*[2]

[1]McGill University at the Jewish General Hospital, Montreal, Quebec, Canada; [2]McGill University, Montreal, Quebec, Canada

Case formulations are idiographic, aiming to describe an individual's psychology and psychopathology with reference to the particulars and life context of the person. Descriptive diagnoses are often not enough to inform treatment, whereas the individualized understanding via case formulation is needed to select and fit treatment to the person better (Macneil, Hasty, Conus, & Berk, 2012). The aim of a dynamic formulation is to summarize the psychodynamic factors operating in the person's life, as evident in his or her history, and to posit their relationship to ongoing experiences, symptoms, relationship patterns and areas of inhibition, avoidance and positive functioning. Formulation is admittedly a series of hypotheses, but should be justified by evidence. To the extent that the formulation is valid, it can serve both as a benchmark of current psychological illness and health, and as a guide to meaningful foci to address in treatment. This chapter describes the Idiographic Conflict Formulation (ICF) method of devising a dynamic formulation (Perry, 1997; Perry, Augusto, & Cooper, 1989). It then applies the ICF method to a woman entering dynamic psychotherapy for recurrent major depression and masochistic (self-defeating) personality disorder.

Case Formulation for Personality Disorders
https://doi.org/10.1016/B978-0-12-813521-1.00011-4

From the inception of psychoanalysis, psychodynamic case formulation was a fundamental aim. David Malan (1976) arguably made the first successful effort to systematize how to construct a dynamic formulation, but his was essentially a relatively short, unitary hypothesis. It's replicability or reliability was largely untested, and one learned largely by reading examples. In recent decades a number of authors have devised systematic formulation methods, usually specifying several components to be included, but leaving the content or descriptive terms largely unsystematized (see Eells, 1997). Despite the clear structure to the formulation methods, this still left an 'anything goes' appearance to the content, leaving the clinician to choose which individual terms to be included in each component category. As a result, it is difficult to compare formulations made by different methods. Nonetheless, comparative research did indicate substantial similarities across some methods (Perry, Luborsky, Silberschatz, and Popp, 1989; Luborsky et al., 1993), although challenges remained. First, each method has different components. For instance, the Core Conflictual Relationship Theme (CCRT) method has 3 components – (1) *Wish,* (2) *Response of the Other,* and (3) *Response of the Self* (Luborsky & Crits-Cristoph, 1990); whereas the Plan Formulation Method has four components – (1) *Goals,* (2). *Pathogenic Beliefs,* (3) *Tests,* and (4) *Insights* (Silberschatz, Fretter, & Curtis, 1986). Second, the content written under each component might use very different terms or describe the same idea differently, further hindering comparison. Third, past comparisons of different formulations on the same patient needed to employ similarity ratings, rather than quantitative methods that could identify shared variance, a qualitative rather than quantitative approach.

The ICF method has been updated for the current chapter and includes the following components, in which section II is new:

I Motives: (1) Wishes, (2) Fears;
II Conflicts and Defences: (1) Conflicts, (2) Defences;
III Resultant Outcomes: (1) Symptomatic Outcomes, (2) Avoidant Outcomes;
IV Stressors and Adaptation: (1) Vulnerability to Specific Stressors, and (2) Best Level of Adaptation.

Inclusion of standardized terms for the motive, conflict and defence components should foster greater reliability in formulating a case. It should also permit direct comparison of single cases to findings from systematic studies. We demonstrate this latter point by comparing the ICF of the case to findings from research the dynamics of depression and masochistic personality which used the same technical terms. The advantage to both clinician and researcher is greater ease in devising the formulation, the ability to detect change over time in some components, and the ability to compare the individual case vis á vis systematic research findings.

STEPS IN CONSTRUCTING A CASE FORMULATION

Information Base

A dynamic formulation requires an information base, usually one or more assessment interviews, or several early therapy sessions in which a history is taken and assessment made. In a research setting, we use two interviews. The first is a dynamic interview, usually about 50 min in duration, which is less structured than other interview types (Beck & Perry, 2008), Guidelines suggest 10 topic areas to explore (Perry, Fowler, & Howe, 2008), and delineate 5 process tasks: frame-setting, offering support, exploring affect, defence interpretations, synthesis (Fowler & Perry, 2005; Perry, Fowler & Smeniuk, 2005). Developing a good alliance in the interview is highly related to its ultimate dynamic adequacy (Perry, Fowler & Howe, 2008). The RAP interview is a semistructured interview eliciting interpersonal vignettes in 3 specific areas (occupation/school, intimate relationships, therapist or other professionals), and also yields dynamic data (Beck & Perry, 2008). It usually takes 20–30 min in duration. The validity of the formulation is dependent on how comprehensive the information base is.

Two sections on *history* and *diagnoses* should precede the dynamic formulation. The ICF itself is then written following the directions for each heading below.

Motives

Describe the subject's conscious and unconscious wishes and fears that have a important influence on his or her life and psychopathology. Include the description and number of the wish or fear (in parentheses) from the Wish and Fear List in Appendix A to provide some standard terms. A wish that is largely disappointed has a prefixed 'd', e.g., d-W3.

There may be some aspects of wishes or fears which are conscious to the subject. However, wishes and fears may operate outside of awareness, giving unconscious meaning to certain experiences, behaviours, and events. Most subjects have from two to four centrally important wishes or sets of wishes, or fears or sets of fears, generally supported by three or more observations from the history or interview, although these do not all have to be mentioned. In addition, there may be other wishes or fears of lesser salience, which may be included or not.

List the sets of wishes or fears in order of their salience in the patient's dynamics. Wishes or fears that often occur together or are thematically linked may be listed together, such as a lower level wish and a related higher level wish or a lower level fear and a related higher level fear. For example, a patient may have both W4, to voice a concern and receive a response, and W 17, to assert oneself to get a specific need met. Within a given set of wishes or fears, list the elements in ascending order of their numbers or levels. This highlights the linkage between lower level and higher level motives.

Wishes: A wish is something that the person wants, strives for, or that leads to approach behaviour. Wishes can be as yet unfulfilled, fulfilled or disappointed. A dynamic wish differs from a simple desire or wish by playing a causal role in a variety of overtly different behaviours, fantasies and experiences.

Fears: Fears are negative beliefs, expectations, or aversive experiences which the subject wishes to avoid. Dynamic fears differ from simple dislikes or phobias because they motivate a variety of behaviours or underlie a variety of experiences which may not appear similar on the surface.

Conflicts and Defences

Conflicts: A psychodynamic conflict is an inferred pattern or constellation of motives, attitudes, beliefs and other cognitions, characteristic interpersonal behaviours, object representations, and ways of handling affects that predispose the subject to having difficulty coping with certain stressors which may occur. The conflict, developed over time and embedded in the subject's personality, gives a particular pathogenic meaning to certain internal and external life stressors. In this view, stressful life events do not directly lead to the development of symptoms; rather, particular life events have a stressful meaning in part because the conflict gives it that meaning. Together, stressor and conflict function somewhat like a lock and key which, mediated by defence mechanisms, lead (1) to the onset of a symptom pattern, such as depression, anxiety or impulsive behaviour, or (2) to attempts to avoid awareness of something related to the conflict. As this view has evolved from ego psychology it also incorporates aspects of object relational and self psychology.

This section list the conflicts that the person has, using the standard list of 14 conflicts in Appendix B. The writer can use just the names of the conflicts or include the description of the conflict with the name. The conflicts can be individualized, if desired, with reference to particular significant persons in the subject's history or specific types of relationships.

Defences: Defence mechanisms are automatic psychological responses to internal and external stressors and conflicts (APA, 1994). As such, they underlie or mediate a wide variety of psychological phenomena both healthy and psychopathological. Clinicians of varied backgrounds often attend to defences in therapy (Banon et al., 2013), especially when they impede awareness of emotional issues and meaningful exploration (Perry & Bond, 2017), hence it is important to include them in the formulation.

This section lists the salient defence mechanisms that the patient uses most commonly to handle motives and affects when conflicts are triggered or engaged. Us the list of 36 defences from the Defence Mechanism Rating Scales in Appendix C. Note that the defences are ordered according to the so-called defence hierarchy of adaptation: lower level defences generally handle stress and conflict less adaptively than mid-level or higher level defences. Defences are listed within defence levels, because the constituent defences have some common aims. For example, all obsessional level defences seek to minimize the distressing experience of affects. While most individuals use 15 or more defences regularly, generally 5 to 7 might be most salient.

Resultants

This part formulates the relationships within constellations of the subject's motives, defences and conflicts which result in symptoms and areas of inhibition and avoidance. Each item consists of one or several sentences that are conditional statements. They may be written in a form like the following: 'whenever … then the subject may …, which results in thinking/feeling/behaving …' These statements are among the most useful for the clinician, because they offer succinct interpretations that link the elements of underlying dynamics to overt experiences, beliefs, symptoms, and behaviours. Therapists may use them as templates or guides for interpretations.

Symptoms and Symptomatic Behaviours: This Resultant component describes the specific psychiatric symptoms and symptomatic behaviours that may be influenced by or result from the subject's wishes and fears, conflicts and defences. The DSM Axis I symptom disorders fit in this section insofar as one can justify a relationship between conflicting motives and the production of symptoms. The meaning and function of a symptom would be described in this section. Symptoms are construed broadly as subjective experiences which cause the individual distress. Common examples are disorders or symptoms like depression or dysthymia, other mood states like irritability, or recurrent negative experiences like often feeling cheated in interactions. Pathological beliefs, negative schemata of self and others, and over-reactions to events are also part of symptomatic outcomes. Symptomatic behaviours are behaviours that are associated with subjective distress and/or impairment. Binge eating, stealing, arguing, procrastination, difficulty in intimate relationships, and trouble holding a job are common examples of symptomatic behaviours. An example follows:

The subject often feels resentful and jealous of others good fortune. This results from his fear of trusting others and being disappointed which conflicts with his wish to communicate his needs and elicit an appropriate response from others. He represses his own wishes and handles disappointments by projection, blaming others.

Avoidant Outcomes: This component describes the characteristic ways by which the subject avoids or mitigates the experience of his or her conflicts. Inferring Avoidant Outcomes requires noticing things that the subject *does not do*, when one would normally expect them to be present. Pathogenic beliefs that protect the subject from awareness of his or her conflicts and inhibit adaptive actions would be described here, as would specific defence mechanisms which the subject uses to avoid awareness of conflicts and the resulting limitations in achievement, intimacy, handling of affect, and so on.

The subject chronically procrastinates finishing his course work. This results from his wish to be seen as a very promising student which conflicts with both his wish to be dependent and his fear that anything he does will be criticized as inadequate (repression, passive aggression). While the procrastination is distressing, it helps him preserve his image as potentially very successful (autistic fantasy, idealization of self).

Specific Stressors and Best Level of Adaptation

Vulnerabiity to Specific Stressors: This section lists the characteristic, specific life stressors which activate or trigger the subject's conflicts. This component captures the specific meanings of those things which are subjectively most threatening. It facilitates the later determination of whether the subject has successfully resolved or adapted to his or her conflicts, as evidenced by handling of these specific stressors with more adaptive defences without avoidant or symptomatic outcomes. An example is:

The subject's fear of being dominated is triggered by disagreements, especially in collaborative work relationships and intimate relationships.

Best Available Level of Adaptation to Conflicts: This section contains a description of the subject's most successful ways of adapting to his conflicts. Delineating the subject's sublimations and best level of adaptation to existing conflicts provides a bench mark of potentially useful solutions currently available to the subject. The therapist should likely support these even if imperfect, as they are temporarily useful adaptations.

CASE EXAMPLE

History. Zofia was a recently separated woman in her mid-40's originally from Europe. She sought psychiatric help when she unexpectedly, lost her job, and finances became a significant stressor. As a diligent worker, she found the reason for her job loss baffling and quickly became depressed. This was her fifth episode of major depression, with two prior suicide attempts. She was referred for treatment to our Depression Research Clinic, where she gave informed consent to participate in a study.

In childhood, Zofia had a difficult relationship with her family. Her father was controlling, demanding and physically and verbally abusive, regularly beating her, her mother and sisters. Her younger sisters were the favoured children, and Zofia had to be very polite and take care of them a lot, as both parents worked. She worked hard to prove her father's denigrations wrong and was successful in school and her early career. She enjoyed being single but gravitated towards men who were disappointing or controlling and then she would break things off.

She married in her mid-20's, and later her husband and she moved to Canada. She had a series of jobs as an assistant, in which she tended to be submissive until she felt abused, and then would suddenly quit. Finally, after getting fed up with her husband's domineering and eventually abusive behaviour, she separated. She later found a part-time boyfriend, after several years, believed that he would never give her what she wanted: commitment, stability and a family. In her friendships, she described herself as 'doing extra for everybody, and getting taken advantage of'. She described herself as isolated and lonely.

Diagnoses. A 3-h Guided Clinical Interview (Perry & Körner, 2011; Perry, 1992) yielded a presenting diagnosis of an acute recurrent major depressive episode, (fifth episode, first onset in her early 30s) and self-defeating PD (DSM-III-R, Appendix A) with significant depressive PD traits (DSM-IV, Appendix B). Whereas her usual Global Assessment of Functioning was 65, her current GAF was 50.

CASE FORMULATION OF ZOFIA

The following is a full formulation, that is, evidence from the interviews is included as justification for the elements of the formulation. This allows the reader to consider how well the formulation fits in with the evidence. In practice, those doing a formulation may choose the expediency of including the elements, but eliminate some or all evidence (Table 11.1). Clinical practice may range between these longer and shorter versions.

TABLE 11.1 The Short Version of the Case Formulation for Zofia

MOTIVES

Wishes	Fears
• To have needs met passively [W3], actively [W4], or assertively [W17] • To be respected for her hard work [W24] • To have a comforting [W5] and loving [W32] relationship	• To be criticized [F14] and failure to perform [W20] • To lose in a competitive situation [F19] with other women

CONFLICTS

Dominant Other
Overall Gratification Inhibition
Competition-Hostility
Ingratiation-Disappointment

DEFENSES

Repression, reaction formation, devaluation of others, help-rejecting complaining, and passive aggression.

RESULTANTS

Symptomatic

- She experiences significant dysphoria and develops a major depressive disorder after being fired from a job, leaving her with a disappointed wish to be respected for her hard work [d-W24]. Her self-esteem is negatively impacted by a lack of praise from her boss (i.e., dominant other) or whenever she becomes aware of her partner's non-committal stance ([d-W32], dominant other). She turns these negative feelings inwards, manifesting at times in the form of suicidality (passive aggression).
- She feels anxious in situations where she feels her performance is being evaluated by her employer, particularly during probation periods and becomes fearful and insecure when her boss does not show her praise ([F14], [F20], dominant other).
- She experiences anger and frustration after going out of her way to work hard and please others, despite feeling like she is being treated unfairly (reaction formation, ingratiation-disappointment conflict).
- She shows hostility in situations where she fears losing to other women ([F19], competition-hostility conflict). She devalues the women against whom she feels competitive to maintain her self-esteem (devaluation).
- She has disappointing romantic relationships, as she pursues men who are unavailable (overall gratification inhibition) or controlling (dominant other). She believes she needs to remain in these relationships to be happy (dominant other). She may avoid asserting her needs, and becomes upset when her needs are left unmet [d-W3]. Occasionally, she does communicate her needs but via help-rejecting complaining.

TABLE 11.1—cont'd

Avoidant

- She avoids looking for other sources of meaning and satisfaction (repression) besides praise for her work performance and being in a loving relationship (overall gratification inhibition and dominant other).
- She avoids expressing her anger directly (repression). Instead, she is over-extends herself (reaction formation, ingratiation-disappointment) or communicates her feelings in an indirect way (passive aggression).
- She is reluctant to engage in psychotherapy with her therapist (passive aggression). She is frustrated with her therapist because of a disappointed wish to be soothed (d-W5), and a discomfort with revealing her problems to another woman (competition-hostility conflict).

VULNERABILITY TO SPECIFIC STRESSORS

- When dominant others act aloof, unavailable, or indifferent, the subject will experience anxiety and fear.
- When she feels powerless to fulfil her wish for admiration and respect for her work, she will feel depressed.
- Women are often experienced as a source competition, which precipitates hostile feelings and a fear of losing recognition from her dominant other to other women.

BEST AVAILABLE LEVEL OF ADAPTATION TO CONFLICTS

- Sometimes, she is able to disagree frankly with significant others without undue reticence or anxiety (dominant other).
- There is little reliance on alcohol, drugs, food, or passive 'intoxicating' experiences as a way to escape from life's obligations (overall gratification inhibition).
- She does not feel guilty when she is successful or terrified of retaliation by others (competition-hostility).
- She has an awareness of the resentment that she feels when her ingratiation is not reciprocated. She experiences an inner struggle over how to express these feelings most effectively (ingratiation-disappointment).

Motives

Wishes

1. The subject has a wish to have her needs met passively at times without having to ask [W3]. At other times, she wishes actively to communicate her needs and elicit some response from others [W4]. In her most adaptive state, she actively asserts herself to get her differentiated needs met [W17].
   a. She wishes for her boss to articulate if she has passed a probation period at work without making an active attempt to communicate her concerns. [W3]
   b. She expresses her wish to be supported by her friend, as she has supported him in the past. [W4]

   c. She confronts her boss for a salary increase and better benefits: 'After, when I asked for it, they said, oh, well, we're not clear; we have to think. At the fourth month when I asked again, they said, oh we're not clear, we have to think about it. Five months. I asked again'. [W17]
2. The subject has a disappointed wish to be respected for her hard work [W24].
   a. When asked how she felt after her boss approved her vacation, she answered, 'Uh because he gave me a chance and he, he saw that I am a very hard worker and he saw me that I was very, very devoted and he saw that all the clients appreciated me and he saw that, and yeah' [W24]
3. The subject has prominent, yet often disappointed wishes to be comforted and soothed by others [W5] and to have a loving relationship [W32].
   a. She feels that in order to recover from her depression, she must have a partner to love and care for her as well as friends, ' … I need love […] I need somebody, a man to take care of me, […] to share a life with him. I don't like to be alone. I like to have friends'. [W32]
   b. She has a disappointed wish for her therapist to be comforting and to make her feel better while she discusses her past negative experiences. [DW5]

Fears

1. She has a strong fear of criticism [F14] and a fear of failure to perform [F20].
   a. 'I was unhappy because I had a very severe father and I didn't have any allowances, anyway I wasn't given allowances. He um he was very severe in a way that uh [pause] everything, I mean my homework, everything what I used to have at that time …' [F14]
   b. When questioned about how she felt about not knowing the status of her employment, she responded 'Very uncomfortable because I didn't know what, what to expect and every single day, I, I thought maybe today is my last day'. It can be inferred that she was afraid of being judged as inadequate and being fired for it. [F20]
2. She also has a fear of losing in a competitive situation against other women. [F19]
   a. She demonstrates competitive urges towards her friend's daughter for his attention, towards the younger woman who took her position at work, as well as towards her younger sisters for her family's inheritance. [F19]

Conflicts and Defences

Conflicts

1. She demonstrates the **Dominant Other Conflict** with romantic partners as well as her superiors at work, which appears to be a repetition of the dynamic she experienced with her father.
   a. 'I'm not ready yet but I wish to meet someone to, to change because I'm very, I'm depending on him. This is the only, as I told you, bad, good [sigh] lover, friend, everything. I don't have anybody else and that's why I'm getting stuck in this relationship'
2. She demonstrates **Overall Gratification Inhibition Conflict**.
   a. She tends to pursue relationships and positions at work that are not sustainable sources of gratification and that are experienced as suffering.
3. She demonstrates **Competition-hostility Conflict**, which may be a function of the resentment she felt for having taken care of her sisters growing up without having felt supported herself.
   a. She demonstrates an urge to outperform other woman, including her friend's daughter, other women at work, her sisters, as well as a general disdain for working with other women.
4. She demonstrates **Ingratiation-disappointment Conflict.**
   a. She feels the need to please and to make concessions to the friends that she shared with her ex-husband, to her sister when she visited her in Canada, to her superiors at work, and to romantic partners; however, she is continuously disappointed and angered when these individuals do not reciprocate with recognition or support.

Defences

1. **Repression**
   a. She is unable to elaborate on certain salient topics such as her recent job loss and sexual desire. When asked about why she was fired from her job, she says, 'I don't know. I don't know exactly. I mean I don't know. I don't know when they fired me, I, I was so upset'.
2. **Reaction formation**
   a. Referring to a time when her sister was visiting, she says, 'I did many, many things for her um I, I uh put out a lot of energy to please and to, to make her a nice vacation and everything. And uh I spent two uh 2 weeks uh it was too much, too much tension between me and her ...'
3. **Devaluation of others**
   a. Referring to a female lawyer she used to work with, she says, 'She is a young, fat and ugly and she has a lots of complexes and I think she was jealous of me'

4. **Help-rejecting complaining**
   a. Referring to how she feels about her friend, she says, 'I can agree but I cannot control my feelings and I cannot control myself from complaining and crying and accusing him that he, he didn't do enough for me'.
5. **Passive aggression**
   a. She passively expresses negative feelings to others in the form of suicidality, ignoring advice from others, and distancing herself from others.

Resultants

Symptomatic Outcomes

1. She experiences significant dysphoria and develops a major depressive disorder after being fired from a job, leaving her with a disappointed wish to be respected for her hard work [dW24]. Her self-esteem is negatively impacted by a lack of praise from her boss (i.e., dominant other) or whenever she becomes aware of her partner's non-committal stance ([dW32], dominant other). She turns these negative feelings inwards, manifesting at times in the form of suicidality (passive aggression).
2. She feels anxious in situations where she feels her performance is being evaluated by her employer, particularly during probation periods and becomes fearful and insecure when her boss does not show her praise ([F14], [F20], dominant other).
3. She experiences anger and frustration after going out of her way to work hard and please others, despite feeling like she is being treated unfairly (reaction formation, ingratiation-disappointment conflict).
4. She shows hostility in situations where she fears losing to other women ([F19], competition-hostility conflict). She devalues the women against whom she feels competitive to maintain her self-esteem (devaluation).
5. She has disappointing romantic relationships as she pursues men who are unavailable (overall gratification inhibition) or controlling (dominant other). She believes she needs to remain in these relationships to be happy (dominant other). She may avoid asserting her need, and becomes upset when her needs are left unmet [dW3]. Occasionally, she does communicate her needs but via help-rejecting complaining.

Avoidant Outcomes

1. She avoids looking for other sources of meaning and satisfaction (repression) besides praise for her work performance and being in a loving relationship (overall gratification inhibition and dominant other).

2. She often avoids expressing her anger directly (repression). Instead, she over-extends herself (reaction formation, ingratiation-disappointment) or communicates her feelings in an indirect way (passive aggression).
3. She is reluctant to engage in psychotherapy with her therapist (passive aggression). She is frustrated with her therapist because of a disappointed wish to be soothed (d-W5), and a discomfort with revealing her problems to another woman (competition-hostility conflict).

Vulnerability/Best Adaptation

Vulnerability to Specific Stressors

1. When dominant others act aloof, unavailable, or indifferent, the subject will experience anxiety and fear (of losing her job, for example).
2. When she feels powerless to fulfil her wish for admiration and respect for her work, she will feel depressed (when unemployed, or after being fired).
3. Women will be experienced as a source competition, which precipitates hostile feelings and a fear of losing recognition by her dominant other to other women.

Best Available Level of Adaptation to Conflicts

1. Sometimes, she is able to disagree frankly with significant others without undue reticence or anxiety (dominant other).
2. There is little reliance on alcohol, drugs, food, or passive 'intoxicating' experiences as a way to escape from life's obligations (overall gratification inhibition).
3. She does not feel guilty when she is successful or terrified of retaliation by others (competition-hostility).
4. She has an awareness of the resentment that she feels when her ingratiation is not reciprocated. She experiences an inner struggle over how to express these feelings most effectively (ingratiation-disappointment).

TREATMENT AND OUTCOME

Zofia was randomly assigned to 18-month of dynamic psychotherapy, receiving 69 therapy sessions. Despite expressing early concerns whether her female therapist could help her, she made substantial improvement during therapy. At 4.5 years, the end of the study, she had made substantial improvement in all outcome measures (range of effect sizes (ESs): 0.91 to 4.57), which changes were greater than the mean ESs for the sample. Nonetheless, the final values for several measures indicated that she had not yet attained healthy cutoff scores. These included defensive functioning, ODF = 4.88, cutoff for healthy-neurotic functioning >5.64; general functioning, GAF = 62.50, cutoff for normal functioning >71; residual depressive symptoms, and HRSD-17 = 9.02, cutoff for minimal depression <6 (American Psychiatric Association, 1994; Frank et al., 1991; Perry, Metzger, & Sigal, 2015). In particular, depressive defenses were still 15.38% of her final defensive functioning, above the cutoff for those at low risk for depression <7.90% (Perry et al., 2015). This suggests that some risk for further depression remained.

DISCUSSION

The ICF method is meant to provide a dynamic formulation that is systematic, valid to the extent that it is backed by evidence, and written in terms that are both standardized and readily understood by the clinician. The ICF provides meaningful elements that could be addressed in therapy. These may even serve as templates for interpretations of defences, motives, conflicts as well as their hypothesized relationship to symptoms, inhibitions and areas of avoidance.

We chose a subject who has masochistic (self-defeating) personality disorder with depressive PD traits, along with recurrent major depression. Previously our team reviewed the clinical-theoretical literature on masochistic personality (Békés, Perry, & Robertson, 2016) employing the same measures used in the ICF. Statistical analyses of the thematic units revealed 3 major dynamic conflicts, two of which were identified in the ICF of Zofia: Overall Gratification Inhibition and Dominant Other conflicts. Both conflicts had originally been described as relating to the psychological organization of depression, as well (Arieti & Bemporad, 1980; Perry, Constantinides, & Simmonds, 2017). Three of Zofia's 6 salient motives were also noted among the thematic units: W3 (28%), W4 (15%), and F14 (17%).

Three of the 5 five defenses noted in her ICF were among the most frequent in the literature on masochism: passive aggression (47%), repression (46%), and reaction formation (39%); while the other two were also noted but less frequently: help-rejecting complaining and devaluation (13% each). Furthermore, 3 (60%) of her defenses, devaluation, passive aggression and help-rejecting complaining, are so-called 'depressive defenses' which studies have identified as important in maintaining depression

(Høglend & Perry, 1998; Perry, Banon, & Bond, 2018). Thus her motive, conflict and defensive profiles are convergent with both depression and masochistic personality, so-called depressive-masochistic personality – which matches her descriptive Axis II diagnoses as well as her recurrent depression.

We have demonstrated the ICF method of case formulation. We have also shown how the ICF directly corresponds to systematic, nomothetic research. Applying the same components – motives, defences, conflicts – and their standardized terms permits one to compare an individual case to relevant research findings, and conversely, to estimate how well the research applies to the individual case. This promotes both clinical accuracy and replicability of the formulation and brings case study and systematic science closer together. Not bad for a days' work (actually 37 years).

Acknowledgements

The Study on which this was based was supported by the *Fund for Psychoanalytic Research.*

The patient on whom the formulation is based gave written permission for use of the study materials for teaching purposes, and some features of the case history were altered to preserve the patient's privacy.

APPENDIX A

The individual 40 Wishes and 40 Fears from the Wish & Fear List, abbreviated[a]

Wishes	**Fears**
VIII INTEGRITY VERSUS DESPAIR	
40 Accept personal limits	40 Loss of hope, faith in ideals
39 Self-assessment & change	39 Selfishness, losing dignity
38 Social disconnection w/age	
VII GENERATIVITY VERSUS STAGNATION	
38 Cope with moral dilemmas	
37 Create, innovate	37 Inability to procreate
36 Be a good mentor, model	36 Lacking creativity, imagination
35 Be a good parent	35 Being poor model, provider
34 To procreate	34 Being uncaring, bad parent

Wishes	Fears
VI INTIMACY VERSUS ISOLATION	
33 Mutually satisfying relationship	33 Not changing relationship patterns
32 Intimacy, love, be loved	32 Sexual relationships
	31 Intimacy, closeness
V IDENTITY VERSUS IDENTITY CONFUSION	
31 Sexual gratification	30 Being unattractive
30 Meaning, purpose	29 Accepting guidance, advice
29 Attract others, have friends	28 No mentor, guide
28 Belong, fit in social group	27 Aimless, no goals
27 Mentor, role model	26 Identity Confusion
26 Relationships develop self	25 Social/gender role failure
25 Attention from opposite sex	
IV INDUSTRY VERSUS INFERIORITY	
24 Gain Esteem for actions	24 Being without friends
23 Succeed, achieve goals	23 Adult responsibilities
III INITIATIVE VERSUS GUILT	
22 Fair treatment, reparation	22 Sexual wishes, acts
21 Cooperate & be helpful	21 Hurting others, guilt
20 Compete and win	20 Failure to achieve
19 Be admired, special	19 Losing in competition
18 Relief from guilt feelings	18 Not being admired, accepted
17 Assert oneself	
II AUTONOMY VERSUS SHAME, DOUBT	
16 Be perfect, avoid shame	17 Being independent, responsible
15 Be spontaneous, carefree	16 Being powerless, helpless
14 Control, dominate others	15 Being dominated, controlled
13 Do whatever one wants	14 Criticism, punishment
12 Retaliate, get revenge	13 Loss of self-control
11 Control one's feelings	12 Becoming fragmented by feelings
10 Have one's privacy respected	
9 Be independent, autonomy	

Wishes	Fears
I TRUST VERSUS MISTRUST	
8 Have others contain me, if out of control	11 Strangers, unfamiliar
7 Be near a significant other	10 Distressing feelings
6 Find others trustworthy, predictable	9 Trusting Others
5 Be comforted, soothed	8 Deprivation
4 Communicate my needs, elicit a response	7 Disappointment or hoping
3 Have my needs met without asking	6 Being dependent upon others
2 Be protected from harm	5 Being unable to communicate my needs
1 To Survive	4 Being alone
	3 Abandonment
	2 Others won't tolerate my feelings
	1 Physical harm, death

[a]*This is an abbreviated version of the Wish and Fear List, the complete version of which is obtainable from the first author (JCP).*

APPENDIX B

Fourteen conflicts from the Psychodynamic Conflict Ratings Scales (PCRS).

1. **Dominant Other** conflict occurs in individuals who require a nurturing and supportive relationship with particular dominant individuals in their lives. They are overly sensitive to criticism and rejection from dominant individuals since they depend on these individuals as a source of self-esteem.
2. **Dominant Goal** conflict is found in individuals who derive their self-esteem largely from areas of achievement with overriding goals. These individuals shun other forms of satisfaction in pursuit of such goals and are particularly vulnerable to setbacks in the goal areas of life.
3. **Counterdependent** conflict characterizes individuals who feel the need to maintain autonomy by disavowing their own dependency needs. Their vulnerabilities lie chiefly in fears of loss of control and autonomy at times when dependency or affection feelings and wishes arise towards others.
4. **Ingratiation-Disappointment** is found in individuals who feel they are less worthy than others but desire recognition and acceptance for being worthy. As a result, they try to please those around them.

They seek approval by making excessive promises, but frequently feel angry and resentful when their promises cost them more than they get in return. They frequently end up disappointing others and themselves as well when failures bring disapproval rather than the approval to which they feel entitled.

5. **Ambition-Achievement** conflict is found in individuals who believe they have special attributes which should lead them to success and other's praise. On the other hand they also may lack the ambition or other requisites for real achievement. To avoid a sense of shame for failure, these individuals often prefer grandiose plans or looking successful to actually working on goals. They thereby often set themselves up to fail, for instance, by self-handicapping, thereby rationalizing failure to achieve.
6. **Competition-Hostility** is found individuals who unconsciously equate competitive strivings with aggressive impulses. Because they feel guilty whenever aggressive feelings arise, they cope in one of two ways. In the first way, they avoid awareness of competitive urges often assuming a meek or deferential demeanour. In the second way, they may counterphobicly act competitively in a wide variety of situations although blind to seeing the degree of associated hostility which later leads to a sense of guilt when successful.
7. **Sexual Pleasure** versus **Guilt** conflict is found in individuals who have a sense of guilt over some aspects of their own sexuality. This leads to blocked awareness of areas of their own sexual interests or behaviour, or it may lead to dividing sexual fantasies and behaviours into idealized 'pure' aspects versus devalued but exciting aspects. This may result in some diminution of interest in relationships where sexuality is deemed permissible. Alternately there may be relationships which are based entirely on sexuality whereas broader intimacy is largely kept away.

   7 Global conflicts: These affect very broad aspects of the patients functioning.
8. **Overall Gratification Inhibition** conflict is found in individuals who believe it wrong to derive satisfaction from their lives and are inhibited from seeking out gratification through the pursuit of goals, relationships, and everyday involvements. They often feel powerless and dysphoric and see life as empty and futile.
9. **Separation–Abandonment Conflict** characterizes individuals who become strongly attached and painfully prone to separation and abandonment feelings. Significant others are experienced as a necessary part of the subject's emotional life. This results in extreme anxiety, bargaining, manipula-tion, and helplessness when rejection is threatened or occurs.

10. **The Global Conflict Over the Experience and Expression of Emotional Needs and Anger** characterizes individuals who are usually inhibited from clearly experiencing their own needs or anger. They generally feel that these are unacceptable vis-a-vis significant others. A pervasive sense of self-loathing, anxiety, and dysphoria commonly arise whenever they become aware of their own needs or anger. In addition, they are generally blocked when expressing themselves except when desperate, in which case they may act in either very entitled or self-destructive ways.
11. **Object Hunger** is found in individuals who experience an emotional void in their lives and believe that their stability is endangered without attachment to some person most of the time. However, this need is not specific to one individual and they are often indiscriminate, so that many attachments are short-lived. The capacity to be alone is very diminished.
12. **Fear of Fusion** is a conflict in which individuals see their wishes for contact with significant others as potentially engulfing and overwhelming. While these individuals desire close relationships, they are overly sensitive to real or imagined threats of others' intrusive-ness and frequently misinterpret others' interest as an attempt to control them. As a result interpersonal closeness is often accompanied by protestation and anxiety over the threat of loss of differentiation between the individual and others.
13. **Rejection of Others** is a conflict experienced by individuals with an underlying negative view of themselves who are unable to regulate their mood or have lasting good feelings about themselves, both of which they desire. As a result they seek a sense of being valuable from others' praise, or they may idealize selected others as if their positive attributes will somehow rub off. Conversely, they may devalue themselves and others when their negative self-view nears awareness.
14. **Resentment Over Being Thwarted by Others** is a conflict in which individuals believe that others have no right to impose limits, controls, or sanctions on them; rather, they believe they should be able to do whatever they want whenever they want. There is often a hidden wish for a strong mentor to step in and help them impose control over their own impulses. The subjects may not be aware of their resentment and covert expression of it. Resentment may show itself in either or both active-aggressive or indirect and passive-aggressive ways.

APPENDIX C

The Hierarchy of Defences and Their Levels of Adaptation

Order	Category	Defence Level	Individual Defences
7	Mature	High adaptive	Affiliation, altruism, anticipation, humour, self-assertion, self-observation, sublimation, suppression
6	Neurotic	Obsessional	Isolation of affect, intellectualization, undoing
5A	Neurotic	Hysterical	Repression, dissociation
5B	Neurotic	Other neurotic	Reaction formation, displacement
4	Immature	Minor image-distorting (narcissistic)	Devaluation of self or object images, idealization of self or object images, omnipotence
3	Immature	Disavowal	Denial, rationalization, projection. Although not a disavowal defence, autistic fantasy is scored at this level
2	Immature	Major image-distorting (borderline)	Splitting of other's images, splitting of self-images, projective identification
1	Immature	Action	Acting out, passive aggression, help-rejecting complaining
0	Psychotic	Defensive dysregulation	Apathetic withdrawal, concretization, delusional projection, distortion, fragmentation, psychotic denial
0 to 7		Overall defensive functioning (ODF)	Aa summary variable consisting of the mean of each defence used, each weighted by its level

References

American Psychiatric Association. (1994). *Diagnostic and statistical manual of mental disorders* (Ed 4). Washington, D.C.: American Psychiatric Press.

Arieti, S., & Bemporad, J. (1980). The psychological organization of depression. *American Journal of Psychiatry, 137*, 1360–1365.

Banon, E., Semeniuk, T., Perry, J. C., Bond, M., Hersoug, A. G., Despland, J.-N., et al. (2013). Therapist interventions using the Psychodynamic Interventions Rating Scale (PIRS) in dynamic interviews and therapy, psychoanalysis and CBT. *Psychotherapy Research, 23*, 121–136.

Beck, S., & Perry, J. C. (2008). The measurement of interview structure in five types of psychiatric and psychotherapeutic interviews. *Psychiatry: Interpersonal and Biological Processes, 71*, 219–233.

Békés, V., Perry, J. C., & Robertson, B. M. (June 6, 2016). (2016). Masochistic personality: A systematic, review of conflicts, defenses, and motives. *Psychotherapy Research*. On line https://doi.org/10.1080/10503307.2016.1189618.

Eells, T. (Ed.). (1997). *Handbook of psychotherapy case formulation*. New York: Guilford Press.

Fowler, J. C., & Perry, J. C. (2005). Clinical techniques of the dynamic interview. *Psychiatry: Interpersonal and Biological Processes, 68*, 316–336.

Frank, A., Prien, R. F., Jarrett, R. B., Keller, M. B., Kupfer, D. J., Lavori, P. W., et al. (1991). Conceptualization and rationale for consensus definitions of terms in major depressive disorder: Remission, recovery, relapse and recurrence. *Arch Gen Psychiatry, 48*, 851–855.

Høglend, P., & Perry, J. C. (1998). Defensive functioning predicts improvement in major depressive episodes. *The Journal of Nervous and Mental Disease, 186*, 238–243.

Luborsky, L. L., Barber, J., Binder, J., Curtis, J., Dahl, H., Horowitz, L. M., Perry, J. C., et al. (1993). Transference-related measures - a new therapy-based class. In N. Miller, L. Luborsky, J. Barber, & J. Docherty (Eds.), *Psychodynamic treatment research: A guide for clinical practice* (pp. 326–341). New York: Basic Books.

Luborsky, L. L., & Crits-Cristoph, P. (1990). *Understanding transference: The CCRT method*. New York: Basic Books.

Macneil, C. A., Hasty, M. K., Conus, P., & Berk, M. (2012). Is diagnosis enough to guide interventions in mental health? Using case formulation in clinical practice. *BMC Medicine, 10*, 111–113. http://www.biomedcentral.com/1741-7015/10/111.

Malan, D. H. (1976). The current position of research in psychotherapy. In D. H. Malan (Ed.), *Toward the validation of dynamic psychotherapy: A replication*. New York: Plenum.

Perry, J. C. (1992). Problems and considerations in the valid assessment of personality disorders. *The American Journal of Psychiatry, 149*, 1645–1653.

Perry, J. C. (1997). The idiographic conflict formulation method. In T. Eells (Ed.), *Handbook of psychotherapy case formulation* (pp. 137–165). New York: Guilford Press.

Perry, J. C., Augusto, F., & Cooper, S. H. (1989). The assessment of psychodynamic conflicts. I: The reliability of an idiographic method. *Psychiatry, 52*, 289–301.

Perry, J. C., Banon, E., & Bond, M. (2018). *Change in defense mechanisms and depression in a pilot study of combined antidepressive medications plus 20-sessions of psychotherapy for recurrent major depression*. In preparation.

Perry, J. C., & Bond, M. (2017). Addressing defense in psychotherapy to improve adaptation. *Psychoanalytic Inquiry, 37*, 153–166.

Perry, J. C., Constantinides, P., & Simmonds, J. (2017). Dynamic conflicts in recurrent major depression: Does combined short-term psychotherapy and medications lead to healthy dynamic functioning? *Psychoanalytic Psychology, 34*(1), 3–12.

Perry, J. C., Fowler, J. C., & Howe, A. G. (2008). Subject and interviewer determinants of the adequacy of the dynamic interview. *The Journal of Nervous and Mental Disease, 196*, 612–619.

Perry, J. C., Fowler, J. C., & Semeniuk, T. T. (2005). An investigation of tasks and techniques associated with dynamic interview adequacy. *The Journal of Nervous and Mental Disease, 193*, 136–139.

Perry, J. C., & Körner, A. (2011). Impulsive phenomena, the impulsive character and personality disorders. *Journal of Personality Disorders, 25*(5), 586–606.

Perry, J. C., Luborsky, L. L., Silberschatz, G., & Popp, C. (1989). An examination of three methods of psychodynamic formulation based on the same videotaped interview. *Psychiatry, 52*, 302–323.

Perry, J. C., Metzger, J., & Sigal, J. J. (2015). Defensive Functioning in women with breast cancer and community controls. *Psychiatry: Interpersonal and Biological Processes, 78*, 156–169.

Silberschatz, G., Fretter, P. B., & Curtis, J. T. (1986). How do interpretations influence the process of psychotherapy. *Journal of Consulting and Clinical Psychology, 54*, 646–652.

Further Reading

Erikson, E. H. (1963). *Childhood and society* (ed. 2). New York: Norton.

Erikson, E. H. (1968). *Identity*. New York, Norton: Youth and Crisis.

Perry, J. C. (2014). Anomalies and specific functions in the clinical identification of defense mechanisms. *Journal of Clinical Psychology: In Session*, *70*(5), 406–418.

Perry, J. C., & Cooper, S. H. (1989). An empirical study of defense mechanisms: I. Clinical interview and life vignette ratings. *Archives of General Psychiatry*, *46*, 444–452.

Perry, J. C., & Despland, J.-N. (2011). A pilot study of wishes and fears among personality disorders. *Canadian Journal of Psychoanalysis*, *19*(1), 3–31.

Perry, J. C., Presniak, M. D., & Olson, T. (2013). Defense mechanisms in borderline schizotypal, antisocial and narcissistic personality disorders. *Psychiatry*, *76*, 32–52.

CHAPTER

12

Case Formulation in Cognitive and Behavioural Therapy

Peter Sturmey[1], *Mary McMurran*[2]

[1]The Graduate Center and Department of Psychology, Queens College, City University of New York, Queens, NY, United States; [2]Institute of Mental Health, University of Nottingham, Nottingham, United Kingdom

INTRODUCTION

Personality disorders are complex developmental disorders associated with persistent and pervasive ways of thinking and feeling about oneself and others and behaving that cause distress or impairment in how an individual functions in many aspects of life. The Diagnostic and Statistical Manual (DSM) of Mental Disorders (American Psychiatric Association, 2013a) lists 10 types of personality disorder in three clusters. Cluster A (odd or eccentric) includes paranoid, schizoid and schizotypal which are characterized respectively by distrust and suspicion, a lack of interest in relationships, and discomfort in social relationships. Cluster B (emotional and erratic) includes antisocial, borderline, histrionic and narcissistic which are characterized by impulsivity, emotional lability, and a limited regard for others. Finally, Cluster C (anxious and fearful) includes avoidant, dependent and obsessive-compulsive, which are characterized respectively by social inhibition, fear of separation in relationships and preoccupation with orderliness.

The DSM-5 also refers to an emerging model of personality disorders based on levels of impairment in functioning and the personality traits related to impaired functioning. Functioning is assessed in two domains: (1) *Self*, which includes Identity and Self-Direction, and (2) *Interpersonal*, which includes Empathy and Intimacy. These elements are assessed using the *Level of Personality Functioning Scale* (American Psychiatric Association, 2013a, p. 775), at five levels of functioning from no impairment (score 0) to extreme impairment (score 5), with an overall score

Case Formulation for Personality Disorders
https://doi.org/10.1016/B978-0-12-813521-1.00012-6

of 2 (moderate impairment) or more indicating a personality disorder. If functional impairment is present, then personality traits are assessed using the *Personality Inventory for DSM-5* (PID-5; American Psychiatric Association, 2013b) which assesses five broad traits: (1) *Negative affectivity* (vs. Emotional Stability): emotional lability, anxiousness, submissiveness, separation insecurity, perseveration, depressivity, and suspiciousness; (2) *Detachment* (vs. Extraversion): withdrawal, restricted affectivity, anhedonia, intimacy avoidance; (3) *Antagonism* (vs. Agreeableness): callousness, manipulativeness, grandiosity, attention seeking, hostility, and deceitfulness; (4) *Disinhibition* (vs. Conscientiousness): Impulsivity, distractibility, risk-taking, irresponsibility, and compulsivity (rigid perfectionism); and (5) *Psychoticism* (vs. Lucidity): Unusual beliefs and experiences, eccentricity, cognitive and perceptual dysregulation. The pattern of functional impairment and traits may match one of six personality disorder types (antisocial, avoidant, borderline, narcissistic, obsessive-compulsive, and schizotypal) and for those who do not fit these criteria there is a 'personality disorder–trait specific' category. Personality disorders may be understood on three levels: (1) the *diagnostic level* summarizes concerns and may be required to access therapeutic services; (2) the *basic trait* level identifies heritable biological characteristics that influence emotional, behavioural, and interpersonal development; and (3) the process level reveals the psychosocial processes by which heritable traits may interact with the social environment over the lifespan to produce personality disorder. Integrating these approaches through case formulation gives a coherent picture that can lead to effective treatment from a range of professionals, including psychiatrists, psychologists and social therapists.

CASE FORMULATION

Case formulation is the abstraction of key features of a clinical case that guide idiographic treatment. It is often rationalized as a reaction to the limits of psychiatric diagnosis whether as an alternative or complementary approach. Andersson and Ghaderi (2006) provided an analysis of five limitations of DSM-IV. (1) DSM reifies behaviour and provides circular explanations for observed behaviour. For example, pathological gambling is inferred from the behaviour of gambling too much and its related problems, and then pathological gambling is used to explain the person's problem. There is no illness of 'pathological gambling', and explaining a person's problem using this diagnostic circularity avoids looking for explanations elsewhere. (2) Psychiatric diagnoses are often non-specific. Diagnosis is based on a person meeting a few of several criteria and so two individuals with the same diagnosis may share little or nothing important in common. There is also overlap between diagnoses, and conversely two individuals with the different diagnoses may share some important features. Although some DSM diagnoses may have moderate to reasonable internal consistency and validity, most do not. (3) Behaviourism is more parsimonious, less stigmatizing and harmful than DSM diagnoses. Human suffering is ubiquitous and partitioning off behaviour as psychiatric diagnoses further stigmatizes and harms people. (4) Although improvements in reliability are often trumpeted as the herald of a scientific DSM, there is little difference between the reliability of DSM-III-R and DSM-IV and most of the hundreds of DSM diagnoses have little data to support their reliability (Kirk & Kutchins, 1992). (5) Finally, DSM is based on a biological model of mental illness in which psychopharmacological interventions that match diagnoses cure underlying illnesses. This is a logical error: a little shyness can be fixed by a drink, but alcohol deprivation is not the cause of shyness. Andersson and Ghaderi (2006) point out that there are more fundamental differences between psychiatric diagnostic and functional approaches to psychopathology. DSM is a deductive, top-down, hypothesis testing approach to science in which hypotheses about diagnoses drive assessment and treatment. In contrast, the functional approach is inductive, bottom up in which scientists start with observations and accumulate replicable data to make limited, cautious generalizations. These two approaches cannot be integrated, but can be used in parallel to inform each other. Hence, a commonly proposed compromise is first to diagnose and then nest functional analyses within diagnostic categories. An alternate approach is to conduct both approaches simultaneously and use them both to inform each other.

Case formulation can be done from many theoretical approaches (Sturmey, 2009). One widely used approach is that of Weerasekera (1996) to assess and integrate information relating to a range of domains, including biological, psychological, familial, social, and cultural. The acronym '5 Ps' is used to structure the process as follows: (1) *Problem*, which refers to a definition of the problem or the constellation of problems and identification of a desired alternative, which will be the therapy end-point; (2) *Precipitating factors*, which are the proximal internal and external factors that trigger the problem(s); (3) *Perpetuating factors*, which are those internal and external factors that maintain the problem(s); (4) *Predisposing factors*, which are the distal internal and external factors that increase the person's vulnerability to the problem(s); and (5) *Protective factors*, which are those internal and external factors that help the person cope with or recover from the problem(s) or prevent relapse. Information about these 5 Ps does not in itself make a case formulation. Rather, case formulation involves integrating the information collected by describing the developmental processes and the functions that the problem behaviours have for the individual, with the ultimate aim being to create an understanding of the individual as s/he is now. An example of a 5P case formulation is given later in this chapter.

APPLICATION OF CASE FORMULATION TO PERSONALITY DISORDERS

Behavioural Approaches

There is a rich history of behavioural approaches to the conceptualization, assessment and formulation of personality disorders (e.g., Nelson-Gray & Farmer, 1999a; Turkat, 1985a,1985b). 'Personality', however, is not a behavioural concept; rather, personality is a kind of everyday shorthand for certain patterns of behaviour, and common reinforcers: '[P]ersonality can be regarded as a complex constellation of learned behaviour that has, at best, an indirect association with C[entral] N[ervous] S[ystem] functioning' (Farmer, 2005, p. 57). Behavioural excesses refer to a broad range of behaviours such as drinking too much, problematic gambling, and promiscuous sex. Farmer (2005) suggested that this pattern of behaviour in part reflects hypersensitivity to reinforcement. This might foreshadow personality disorders also characterized by behavioural excesses and reinforcement sensitivities, such as borderline personality disorder. Behavioural deficits are characterized by insufficient behaviour for a given context. Such a behavioural pattern might reflect environmental impoverishment with lack of opportunities to learn adaptive behaviour due to lack of modelling, lack of reinforcement, or excessive punishment, resulting is slow acquisition of new behavioural repertoires. Thus, individuals who are temperamentally overly sensitive to punishment and extinction might be particularly susceptible to not developing new behavioural repertoires and being overly cautious in novel environments. Again, this behavioural type parallels certain personality disorders such as schizotypal personality disorder. Finally, inhibited and avoidant behavioural patterns are characterized by either freezing, avoidance of fearful stimuli to immediate environmental threats, or avoidance of private experiences, such as bodily sensations and emotions, thoughts, and memories. Individuals who are socially or generally anxious, and who avoid threats through motor behaviour and cognitively through worry, fit this type. Avoidant personality disorder might be an example that fits this behavioural pattern.

Behavioural Assessment and Personality Disorders

There are several good overviews of the behavioural assessment of personality disorders (Farmer, 2000; Nelson-Gray & Farmer, 1999a,b; Nelson-Gray et al., 2009). These authors have proposed that the Stimulus-Organism-Responses-Consequences (SORC) model of assessment of psychopathology (Goldfried & Sprafkin, 1976, pp. 295–321) and Lang's (1968, pp. 90–102) triple response system (motoric, physiologic and cognitive responses) can be used as a framework to structure functional assessment and analysis of personality disorders. The first step in a behavioural assessment is to identify and prioritize responses. For example, in borderline personality disorders motor behaviours might include recurrent suicidal behaviour, physiological responses might include emotional instability and reactivity of mood, and cognitive responses might include an unstable self-image and related self-talk. The second step is to identify specific situations and people that increase and decrease relevant responses. For example, individuals with cluster B personality disorders might show more symptomatic behaviour during interpersonal situations, whereas individuals with obsessive-compulsive personality disorders might show more symptomatic behaviour in situations involving performance and achievement. Thus, situations relevant to the dominant reinforcers for each person might be associated with high level of symptomatic behaviour for the corresponding personality disorder. 'Dominant reinforcers' refers to the class of reinforcer often associated with each personality disorder cluster. For example, the behaviour of individuals with cluster A personalities may often be reinforced by avoidance of warm social relationships; the behaviour of individuals with cluster B personalities may often be reinforced by avoidance of waiting and immediate access to available reinforcers; and the behaviour of cluster C personalities may often be reinforced by avoidance or reduction in fear, anxiety and criticism. A third component is assessment of organismic variables, such as the individual's probable learning history. Individuals with personality disorders often have atypical early childhood learning experiences which may exaggerate certain response classes (e.g., seductiveness across an overly wide range of stimuli), diminish others (e.g., problem solving, learning to tolerate waiting and self-regulation of emotions), potentiate conditioned reinforcers (such as attention) and conditioned punishers (such as being ignored). Thus, behavioural case formulation should infer these histories, and integrate them to the presenting problems and treatment options. Another set of relevant organismic variables are physiological variables, such as under-arousal in individuals with psychopathic personality disorder. Sutker, Bugg, and West (1993, pp. 337–369) concluded that such individuals 'are slow to condition fear to warning signals, less influenced by threats of punishment, less capable of anticipating negative consequences, and inclined to over-respond to unusual or exciting stimuli' (pp. 357–358). A fifth aspect of behavioural assessment is impulsivity – the ability to choose larger, delayed, better quality reinforcers over smaller, immediate, low quality reinforcers (Baum & Rachlin, 1969) – and the ability to regulate one's behaviour in situations where temptations (positive reinforcers) and irritations (negative reinforcers) motivate oneself to engage in behaviour with short-term benefits (e.g., access to sex) and long-term personal harms (e.g., incarceration).

Turkat's (1985a) classic *Behavioural Case Formulation* interestingly, contained three behavioural formulations of personality disorders, one of which was that by Sutker and King (1985, pp. 111–154). They presented a case formulation of an antisocial personality disorder (ASPD) in Mr. V, a 28 year old man initially referred by his family physician because of complaints of back pain following a car wreck with no clear evidence of physical injury, possibly related to seeking pain medication. They conducted a multimodal assessment which included psychometric assessment of intelligence, personality, mood and anxiety; interviews with the patient, including a comprehensive developmental history to identify distal and proximal situations related to his presenting problems; interview with his wife; and self-recording of activities, mood alcohol and drug use.

The authors determined that Mr. V was an intelligent man with ASPD and dysthymic disorder. In his developmental he had few boundaries at home; models for acting out, promiscuity and drug use from his father; encouragement for these and related thrill-seeking behaviour from his peers and teachers; and learned to be superficially charming and social fluent to avoid responsibilities. He did function somewhat better when in the structured environment of being in the military. When he presented, he often engaged in thrill-seeking behaviour, such as flagrant sexual affairs resulting in short-term thrills and avoidance of responsibilities, and long-term depression relieved by alcohol, drug use and abuse of prescription medications. Underlying these problems was someone bored with his unchallenging work (given his intellect) and bored with his wife and family. Both Mr. V and others noticed his exaggerated behaviour, but not his negative mood. His referral was precipitated by legal troubles that portended potential divorce, job loss and were accompanied by his worst periods of depression.

Sutker and King analyzed the problems into four domains: (1) Antisocial psychopathology, such as alcohol and drug misuse, sexual promiscuity and irresponsible behaviour at work, financially and while driving; (2) depression, shown by unhappiness, boredom, reduced work, negative cognitions, thoughts of thrill-seeking, lack of exercise and exaggerations of pain; (3) cognitive and behavioural dyscontrol, as shown by poor judgment, impulsivity, lack of self-discipline, lack of leisure time and inability to tolerate delay of gratification; and (4) social immaturity and dependence, shown by being demanding with his wife, not investing in and lack of satisfaction with personal relationships and childish behaviour. Treatment goals included maintaining a drug and alcohol-free life, finding exciting alternatives to thrill-seeking and promiscuous behaviour, learning to manage his own tension, anger and depression, learning to control his own behaviour, improving his marital relationship or facilitate divorce, and finding vocational and academic goals. Based on this formulation and treatment goals, the treatment plan included: to establish a strong bond with his therapist so that his therapist could work with him on modifying his lifestyle and increase adaptive behaviour; to learn to control his alcohol and substance abuse by identifying situational precipitants for drug and alcohol misuse and might include a period of in-patient treatment with supervised follow-up; and to foster all positive aspects of Mr. V's life including social facility, creativity, physical abilities, sense of humor, including minimizing stimuli associated with thrill-seeking.

CASE FORMULATION OF PERSONALITY DISORDER: TRAITS AND PROCESSES

DSM-5 differentiates between traits, behaviours, and symptoms: *traits* are propensities to behaving in a certain way or experiencing particular symptoms (American Psychiatric Association, 2013a); *behaviours* and *symptoms* are manifestations of traits. Traits are stable, whereas behaviours and symptoms vary with circumstances. That is, even though there are trait propensities, external and internal events trigger trait-related behaviours and symptoms. This understanding opens the door to case formulation in relation to personality disorders since functional impairments relate to personality traits and, if problematic behaviours and emotions can vary with circumstances, what are the processes by which this can happen? In terms of the 5 Ps, traits are predisposing factors, triggering events are precipitating factors, and the processes are contributory perpetuating factors.

An understanding of the processes by which traits influence outcomes in given circumstances requires a developmental model which examines the impact of experiences across the lifespan, such as bonding with parents, parenting styles, family functioning, neighbourhood safety, school context, peer associations, and societal opportunities, with the nature of these experiences identifying them as either risk or protective factors for later personality difficulties. The impact of these experiences differs from one person to another, depending partly on that person's inherent temperament or basic traits and on earlier learning affecting later experiences and learning. The reciprocal interactions between traits and lifespan experiences produce the individual's unique complex of attachment style, core beliefs and schemas, emotion regulation and problem solving capabilities, behavioural repertoires, values, life plans and sense of self that define personality. The perpetuating effect on behavioural symptoms of adult schemas and attachment styles will be illustrated in two common personality disorder types: antisocial and borderline.

Antisocial Personality Disorder

One well-researched pathway is that of early trait impulsivity and adult ASPD (Beauchaine, Zisner, & Sauder, 2017). Impulsivity is associated with a range of externalizing disorders across the lifespan (e.g., attention deficit/hyperactivity disorder) and neuro-developmental delays that compromise emotion regulation and complex problem solving. Understanding impulsivity broadly as a predisposition to excessive approach behaviour, with insensitivity to impending danger or punishment, begins to point to the processes by which these associations may occur. Trait anxiety suppresses approach behaviours and individuals may have elevated trait impulsivity with or without elevated trait anxiety. Impulsive individuals (excessive approach behaviours) who are also low in trait anxiety (low propensity to avoid risk) have even poorer outcomes and may be labelled psychopathic (Frick, Ray, Thornton, & Kahn, 2014).

Tracing the interaction between trait impulsivity and the individual's social environment, there may be adverse impacts across the lifespan. Impulsive and hyperactive children are difficult to manage. Parents who are stressed by factors such as large families, poor housing, or absent partners may rely on parenting styles based largely on chastisement for misbehaviour and ignoring good behaviour, which predict later aggression (Farrington & Hawkins, 1991). Hyperactive children who experience effective parenting are less likely to progress to externalizing problems. When hyperactivity develops into conduct problems in later childhood, this substantially increases the likelihood of persistent problem behaviours (Taylor, Chadwick, Heptinstall, & Danckaerts, 1996). The child who misbehaves in school and is unable to concentrate on schoolwork is neither successful nor popular, which is an unpleasant experience for individual, who may escape through truancy, thus setting the scene for association with antisocial peers, developing problem behaviours such as drinking and drug use, and getting into trouble with authority.

Schemas

One product of the individual's developmental experiences are mental representations of social knowledge and experience (schemas). Early maladaptive schemas derive from early unmet emotional needs and the child develops strategies for coping with life based on these schemas. Schema modes are the emotional states and coping responses employed in the moment, when an internal or external event activates schemas. Young, Klosko, and Weishaar (2003) list 18 early maladaptive schemas in five domains. The five domains are (1) disconnection and rejection, (2) impaired autonomy and performance, (3) impaired limits, (4) other directedness and (5) over-vigilance and inhibition. Examples of schemas from the disconnection and rejection domain include fear of abandonment, feeling unlovable and disconnected from other people and expecting that others will cause hurt. Mode categories, that is the style of response to triggered schemas, are: (1) innate child (vulnerable, angry, impulsive, or contented); (2) maladaptive coping (surrenderer, protector, or overcompensator), and (3) maladaptive parents (punitive, or critical); and (4) health adult.

Using the *PID-5* and *Schema Questionnaire* (Young, 2005) with 662 clinical and non-clinical adults, Bach, Lee, Mortensen, and Simonsen (2016) studied schemas and schema modes in relation to DSM-5 trait domains and facets. Antagonism is one trait domain strongly related to antisocial conduct, and illustrates the processes relating to ASPD. The trait facets related to antagonism were manipulativeness, deceitfulness, attention seeking, grandiosity, hostility, rigid perfectionism, and callousness. These describe behaviours that may be assessed and targeted in interventions. Looking at schemas, those associated with antagonism were entitlement, mistrust, and approval seeking. Such schemas are understandable where childhood needs were unmet and adults were unreliable or punitive and where the child may have resorted to desperate measures to gain approval from carers. Carried into adulthood, these schemas are associated with an attacking schema mode resulting in a self-defeating quest for intimacy, which is one underlying perpetuating factor that explains the continuity of antisocial behaviours.

Attachment

DSM-5 defines intimacy as deep and enduring connections with others, a desire and capacity for closeness, and interpersonal behaviour shows mutuality of regard. The maladaptive intimacy functioning, which may be part of an ASPD, can be understood also in terms of attachment style. Attachment theory holds that early attachments with carers give the child a blueprint for adult relationships (Bowlby, 1969). Bartholomew and Horowitz (1991) have identified two underlying dimensions of attachment and four attachment styles, measured by a simple four-item questionnaire which is described in their research paper. The dimensions, which can be either positive or negative, are how one views oneself (high or low self-worth) and how one views others (supportive or rejecting). Different positions on these dimensions produce four attachment prototypes: (1) *secure attachment* (positive self-model, positive other model) - self-confident, warm, and friendly toward others, have close friendships, and appraise intimate relationships realistically; (2) *fearful attachment* (negative self-model, negative other model) -avoid intimacy for fear of rejection; (3) *preoccupied attachment* (negative self-model, positive other model) - idolize others, and are needing of attention, excessively emotionally expressive, and highly dependent in relationships; and (4) *dismissing attachment* (positive self-model, negative other model) - maladaptive superficial friendships and low-intimacy relationships. ASPD is associated with a dismissing attachment style. Again, a quest for intimacy with an internalized positive self-model and a negative other model is underlying perpetuating factor that explains the continuity of antisocial behaviours.

Borderline Personality Disorder

A second example is an analysis of borderline personality disorder, which is a pervasive pattern of instability of interpersonal relationships, unstable self-image and emotions, and marked impulsivity. Linehan (1993) positioned emotional dysregulation as central to borderline personality disorder, this being a consequence of high emotional reactivity, strong experienced emotional intensity, and a lack of skills for managing strong emotions. The 'hyperbolic' temperament, which is highly heritable, interacts with adverse experiences such as abuse or neglect, and often the invalidation of their experienced emotions, across the life span to produce an adult who responds to triggering events with the behaviours that are symptomatic of borderline personality disorder, including self-harm and suicidal behaviours (Zanarini & Frankenburg, 2007).

In Bach et al.'s (2016) study, negative affectivity, which is strongly related to emotional dysregulation and self-harm, is associated with the trait facets of emotional lability, anxiousness, separation insecurity, rigid perfectionism, and submissiveness, and depressivity. These describe the emotional states that may need to be assessed and targeted in interventions. Looking at schemas, those associated with negative affectivity were abandonment, pessimism, and the associated schema mode was vulnerable child. This schema profile reflects inconsistent childhood attachments and abandonment by carers. Carried into adulthood, these traits and schemas are associated with a preoccupied attachment style, in which the need for intimacy is highly desired and the fear of abandonment leads to emotional dyscontrol. Emotional dyscontrol interferes with intimacy and steady relationships by causing other people to distance themselves, and so the individual's fear of abandonment is perpetuated.

THE CASE OF ARTHUR

To illustrate the construction of case formulations, we now present the case of Arthur, a 31-year old man with problems of anger, aggression, and violence on intimate partners and strangers referred to a forensic psychologist for assessment after an argument with a man in bar that led to an assault. In childhood, he was raised by his alcohol-dependent mother alone and never knew his father. When sober she was caring; when drunk she would often beat him and be fiercely critical of him and tell him he was worthless. He was frequently left to fend for himself, sometimes for days on end, while his mother would binge drink. His mother had several short-term relationships with men, many of whom were also heavy drinkers. He witnessed a number of these men being violent towards his mother. His mother died when he was 10 years old, at which point he was taken into care homes where he displayed emotional and behavioural problems. He was described as 'impulsive and emotionally volatile, with profound difficulties trusting others and a very low sense of self-worth'. His aggressive behaviour left him unpopular with other children and he was bullied. He began to self-harm to relieve distress, repeatedly ran away from his care home and began abusing alcohol. These difficulties disrupted his education and he did not obtain any qualifications.

During adulthood Arthur developed a dependency on alcohol and never sustained meaningful employment, instead funding himself primarily through state benefits and stealing. He has had two long-term intimate relationships, both of which were volatile. At age 22 he received a conviction for an assault against a girlfriend after an alcohol-fuelled row when his partner threatened to leave him. He was also convicted of an assault against a subsequent partner at age 25, when he perceived that she had been flirting with another man in a bar. Subsequently, he threatened to commit suicide. The offence that led to the referral to the psychologist also occurred in a bar. Arthur had been in the bar for several hours drinking and playing pool with a group of men who were regulars. One began to criticize Arthur's pool skills. An argument ensued and he eventually lost his temper and hit this man over the head several times with his pool cue causing serious injury.

During assessment he admitted regular heavy drinking, which he considered mostly to be a habit in that he spent time in bars to fill his day. When intoxicated, he was prone to getting into arguments over very little, and he often lost control of his anger. His relationships were typically with women he met in the bar or in other drinking venues, who were usually also heavy drinkers. Arthur acknowledged a desire for a stable relationship but he reported experiencing persistent abandonment anxiety within his intimate relationships, resulting in jealousy and anger at any perceived threat of infidelity on the part of his partner.

Formulation I: A Behavioural Case Formulation

The first P is **the problem**. Arthur presents many potential problems of which violence resulting in serious injuries to the victim in the bar is the most serious because of the danger to others and the likely restriction in Arthur's life, such as risk of incarceration. Related to that principle problem is a list of other problems. These include: (1) weak adaptive behaviour and lack of goals in the domains of education, work, leisure and interpersonal domains; (2) weak appropriate self-regulation skills related to management of negative emotions, such as anger, jealousy and perhaps depressed mood; (3) emotional regulation using self-harm rather than alternative strategies; (4) excessive drinking; (5) an unstructured lifestyle resulting in spending much time in bars where alcohol predisposes him to violence; (6) lack of models for appropriate behaviour; (7) lack of social support other than from people in the bars he frequents; (8) obtaining money through benefits and stealing, rather than work; (9) inappropriate stimulus control of anger as shown by responding to threats from girlfriends to leave, perceived threats of infidelity and minor criticism of pool skills resulting in anger and violence. Arthur has several strengths, including leisure skills, ability to obtain sufficient money to live on, ability to initiate relationships, some honest reporting of his problems, and goals for a stable relationship. Treatment goals would be that Arthur sustains a happy, loving meaningful relationship that is free of violence or other forms of coercion, has a meaningful, productive and happy lifestyle with work, leisure and friends outside of bars, can manage negative emotions, insults and fear of abandonment adaptively, and has a life which is alcohol-free or does not involve any problematic drinking.

The external **precipitating factors** that trigger the main problem of violence can be summarized using behavioural concepts such as establishing operations (EO), discriminative stimuli (S-Ds), behaviour (B) and consequences (C). Thus, being in the bar, playing pool, and drinking were EOs increasing sensitivity to criticism and increased the reinforcing value of escape from criticism. When others criticized his pool skills (S-D) he hit the other person other the head repeatedly with the pool cue (B) and terminated criticism and the presence of others (C). Likewise, when using alcohol (EO) and his girlfriend threatened to leave him (S-D) he committed an assault (B), which delayed or removed threats his girlfriend threatening to leave him (C). Although based on incomplete information, even this limited sample of his behaviour identifies drinking in bars and perhaps rumination over abandonment as establishing operations that potentiate escape from aversive stimuli such as criticism of his competence, threats of abandonment from his girlfriend, and his girlfriend apparently flirting. The consequences all result in removal of both aversive external stimuli and aversive internal stimuli.

The third P is internal and external **perpetuating factors** that maintain the problem. Arthur's violence is perpetuated by the lack of alternative behaviour, lack of skills in dealing with triggers more effectively and lack of models for appropriate behaviour. Arthur has a low effort lifestyle with weak or absent skills and lack of goals, which give him few easy alternatives to hanging around in bars and drinking. He does not know how to reduce various negative emotions when they occur and replace them with enjoyable activities with positive emotions. Finally, he has few or no immediate models other than other people getting drunk, playing pool and resolving problems through violence.

In Arthur's case, there are many predisposing distal internal and external factors, in which learning early in life sensitized him to certain negative reinforcers, and in which he failed to learn many adaptive behaviours.

The repeated early exposure to punishment likely reduced much appropriate behaviour and he probably learned to avoid his mother, at least when she was drunk, thereby reducing learning opportunities at home. Being raised by a single parent who was also frequently absent also reduced the opportunities to learn a wide array of appropriate behaviours. There were several early models for alcohol abuse and violence and an absence of models of appropriate social behaviour, resulting in the acquisition of violence and drinking to reduce negative emotional states. Extended periods of being alone at home as a child may also have removed social constraints on his behaviour that are typically present and hence may have predisposed him to get into mischief or learn other forms of problematic behaviour.

By the time he was 10 a behavioural repertoire that foreshadowed the presenting problems had been learned. The bullying from other children likely set the occasion to reciprocate in kind, thereby negatively reinforcing aggression through reducing other children's aggression. Learning to regulate his emotions through self-harm was another sentinel event that weakened the likelihood that he might learn appropriate forms of emotional self-regulation. Learning to avoid his peers and staff at his care homes and accessing alcohol further strengthened avoidant strategies as a way to deal with the difficulties he may have had in the care homes. The resulting lack of any educational qualifications left him with a weak repertoire of appropriate vocational skills and likely pushed him toward learning to obtain money through benefits and stealing to pay for alcohol and other necessities.

In the area of the fifth P, **protective factors**, Arthur has a limited number of strengths including being socially motivated, in that he spends time with other people and does have a goal of a stable relationship; some limited leisure skills; and some basic applied problem solving skills, such as obtaining enough money to fund his life.

Treatment Plan

The reliable chain of stimuli and responses which begins with hanging around in bars drunk is a good place to start because intervening earlier in stimulus-response chains will likely produce the greatest response generalization to the later parts of the stimulus-response chain. Merely pointing out this relationship or appealing to him not to engage in this behaviour is unlikely to be sufficient. Rather some low effort, positively reinforcing competing adaptive behaviour is needed. Given his weak adaptive behaviour repertoire, this may take some effort and ingenuity to establish, but might include sampling different leisure activities and structuring his time with short goals for pleasurable activities. Self-monitoring to better understand and describe the relationship between his behaviour and the environment and achieving these short-term goals to himself would probably be helpful.

Similarly, he needs some sober friends in places away from the bars, both to provide alternative social activities and models of better behaviour. Again, this may mean extensive exploration of what interests this man. A later focus of intervention might be to teach him self-management skills to deal more effectively with insults, and angry and jealous feelings which might include a range of simple strategies, like walking away, being assertive, relaxation training, and problem solving to deal with these common situations. To build up a more positive life, it would be helpful to clarify and establish goals and skills in areas of educational, vocation and social behaviour such as finishing some basic high school classes, obtaining training or qualifications in vocational areas of interest and some social skills training.

Formulation II: An Attachment and Schema-Informed Formulation

Arthur meets the criteria for borderline personality disorder with antisocial traits. His personality functioning may be summarized as follows: (1) *Self* – (a) Identity – severely impaired and low self-esteem; poor ability to regulate a range of emotions. (b) Self-direction – severely impaired with few coherent and meaningful short-term and life goals; some antisocial internal standards of behaviour. (2) *Interpersonal* - (a) Empathy – some impairment with restricted comprehension and appreciation of others' experiences and motivations; restricted understanding effects of own behaviour on others. (b) Intimacy – severely impaired with excessive desire and capacity for closeness. He shows traits of high negative affectivity, medium high antagonism, and medium high disinhibition.

Arthur is predisposed to heavy drinking, having learned this from his mother's example. His drinking behaviour developed when he ran away from the controls of the care home and again later in adulthood when he frequented bars to fill his time. He learned that drinking served to help him cope with problems. Arthur's drinking is currently precipitated by boredom and emptiness caused by the lack of life goals and responsibilities and by having partners who also drink to excess.

His early experiences of attachment were insecure, with his mother vacillating between loving and critical and he experienced abandonment by her death when he was a child. Arthur experiences abandonment anxiety, which, given his drinking model and experiences of drinking, predisposes him to drink to cope. He has a *Preoccupied Attachment Style*, typified by idolizing others, needing attention, being excessively emotionally expressive, and being highly dependent in relationships. This has been expressed as violence towards partners who threaten to leave the relationship. Furthermore, alcohol intoxication increases the likelihood of aggression. Arthur is predisposed to aggression as a result of experiences of violent behaviour as a child when his mother hit him, observing violence toward his mother by her partners. In the care home, Arthur developed violent behaviour in response to provocation by bullies. He has learned to respond to perceived insult or injury with aggression. These provocations are likely to be belittlement, given his mother's criticisms of him as worthless and perceived risk of abandonment. His schema modes, activated by disagreements and threatened abandonment, are *Vulnerable Child,* feeling lonely, isolated, sad; and *Angry Child,* feeling angry and impatient because the needs of the vulnerable child are not being met; and *Impulsive/Undisciplined Child,* who acts on impulses in a selfish or uncontrolled manner.

Future problems are likely to arise if he continues to drink heavily, which may persist if he continues to be unemployed and pass his time in bars. Conflict with other drinkers is likely if his self-esteem is challenged through criticism or insults. Arthur's fear of abandonment in relationships is likely to lead to conflict with partners in that there is a risk of him construing a partner's social interactions as a prelude to abandonment, thus triggering the angry child mode. Relationship difficulties are likely to be compounded by one or both parties drinking heavily.

This formulation would be constructed in a co-production with the individual concerned as collaboration may improve treatment outcomes (Tryon & Winograd, 2011). From this formulation, the treatment targets would include: (1) reducing alcohol use or abstaining from alcohol to immediately ameliorate risk of violence; (2) identifying life goals and how to attain them, especially employment and leisure activities; (3) changing maladaptive schema and response modes, with particular reference to attachment styles relating to abandonment and vulnerability; (4) improving relationship choices, particularly seeking partners in non-drinking contexts; (5) improving relationship skills, particularly conflict resolution; and (6) improving emotion regulation through raising self-esteem, as well as reducing drinking and working toward valued life goals. These treatment targets would be organized into a treatment plan in consultation with Arthur concerned in terms of the quickest gains (e.g., immediate reduction in alcohol consumption), then the most understandable and engaging targets (e.g., relationship skills, setting life goals), and then the more long-term therapeutic work to address attachment problems and maladaptive modes of responding to conflict and relationship difficulties (e.g., schema therapy).

Comment

What is striking about the two formulations is their broad agreement in treatment goals: Both agree on reduction in alcohol use, establishing life away from the bar, with better leisure, vocational and social skills, and establishing a life away from drinking and other people who drink. Many of these targets are obvious and there is no need for a full case formulation to identify them. In some cases, a broad lifestyle intervention may be sufficient to bring about change; however, lasting change may require a deeper understanding of the sources and functions of the person's problems.

What each formulation does is bring analysis, theory and logic to the problems presented. This logic gives the individual a framework for understanding his or her problems and hence a sense of hope for change. The theoretical understanding permits the therapist to derive testable hypotheses for change, with these tests being the intervention components. Hypotheses-driven interventions have a better chance of success than best guesses of what might work, and so decrease the likelihood of harm. The matter of which approach is better – behaviour analysis, schemas and attachment or other approaches – needs to be tested empirically. Research into the value and effectiveness of case formulation with personality disorder problems is badly needed.

TRAINING TO MAKE FORMULATIONS OF PERSONALITY DISORDERS

If the skill of formulating personality disorders is to be accurate, complete, and effective in developing idiographic treatments that are superior to treatment as usual and widely disseminated, then training in case formulation must be effective and available on a large scale. Researchers and practitioners have taken some preliminary steps toward this objective. A first step is the agreement as to what constitutes an adequate case formulation. Völlm (2013) reported a Delphi survey of 31 experts with backgrounds in forensic psychiatry or psychology, asking them questions in two rounds concerning case formulation of personality disorders. There was consensus on what constitutes an adequate case formulation: a comprehensive history, including offending history, childhood behavioural problems, and early trauma; personality traits; comprehensive accounts of alcohol and drug abuse, problem behaviours, including premeditated versus impulsive aggression, work and leisure activities; mental health; risk assessment; practical solutions to problems; offence paralleling behaviours; the five Ps; and relationship style.

McMurran, Logan, and Hart (2012) developed a ten-item *Case Formulation Quality Checklist (CFQC)*, simplified later by McMurran and Bruford (2016), whose items cover matters such as coherence, explanatory breadth, simplicity, predictive statements, and action-oriented which has adequate reliability (Minoudis et al., 2013) and validity in that is distinguishes between case formulations from experts and novices and is sensitive to the effects of training (Brown, Beelet, Patel, & Vollm, 2016). Using this checklist, evaluations of training professionals to construct case formulations of personality disorders have had mixed results. Brown et al. (2016) trained 18 probation officers over 5 days to make case formulations of offenders with personality disorders. Evaluation was based on participants' formulation of two cases based on 1000 word written case descriptions, with participants formulating different cases before and after training. An expert rated the quality of the case formulations before and after training using the CFQC. Post-training case formulations were generally better than pre-training vignettes, especially in areas such as factual foundation, breadth of explanation, coherence of explanation over time, generativity and overall quality, although there was no improvement in prioritizing and planning, treatment, consistency with psychological or criminological theory, and simplicity and freedom from unnecessary details. The rater also attempted to identify if the case formulation was a pre- or post-training vignette, with correct identification in 81% of the case formulations. When comparing probation officers' case formulations to those of two experts, the authors noted that probation officers tended to produce long lists of un-prioritized problems rather than abstract out key treatment targets; did not link target problems to underlying causes; and did not identify future desirable behaviours or hypotheses to account for the presenting problems. Clearly, training programmes need to ensure that case formulations are hypothesis driven, particularly in relation to clarifying the underlying causes which are perpetuating factors, and to provide an evidence-based rationale for constructing a treatment plan in which the elements of treatment are ordered and prioritized. In a subsequent study with probation officers, Minoudis et al. (2013) found mixed effects of a 4 × 2-h training followed by 6 months of case formulation consultations in that there was no evidence that training improved case formulations by 20 participants using one vignette and evidence that training did improve case formulations by 13 participants using a second vignette. This suggests that training evaluation and research results are likely to be affected by variability in the vignettes presented for assessment and so standardization of vignettes is important for research in this area. Additionally, there is a question of whether improvements are sustained in the longer term.

Researchers in future might consider defining the skills needed to learn to make case formulations and teaching them sequentially to mastery at an individual pace; providing multiple examples of case formulations as models to follow; requiring practice to competency on multiple cases carefully designed to sample relevant domains of case formulation skills (e.g., different presenting problems, functions or types of case formulations, and differing degrees of difficulty) and application to multiple cases.

CONCLUSION

There is a growing literature on case formulation and related assessment and treatment approaches for personality disorders. This includes case formulations that practitioners can use as the templates for their own cases. There is a modest group of studies suggesting that it is sometimes possible to teach some practitioners case formulation skills. Future research should clarify protocols to conduct case formulations, the role and potential benefits of collaborative case formulation, the relative efficacy of treatment based on standard manualized treatments for personality disorders compared to case formulation-driven treatment and the development of maximally effective and efficient and effective staff training protocols.

Acknowledgements

Some details of the case description such as demographic information were changed so as to protect client privacy.

References

American Psychiatric Association. (2013a). *Diagnostic and statistical manual of mental disorders* (5th ed.). Washington, DC: Author.

American Psychiatric Association. (2013b). *The personality inventory for DSM-5 (PID-5)*. From: http//:www.psychiatry.org/APA_DSM5_The-Personality-Inventory-For-DSM-5-Brief-Form-Adult.pdf.

Andersson, G., & Ghaderi, A. (2006). Overview and analysis of the behaviourist criticism of the *Diagnostic and Statistical Manual of Mental Disorders* (DSM). *Clinical Psychologist, 10*, 67–77.

Bach, B., Lee, C., Mortensen, E. L., & Simonsen, E. (2016). How do DSM-5 personality traits align with schema therapy constructs? *Journal of Personality Disorders, 30*, 502–529.

Bartholomew, K., & Horowitz, L. M. (1991). Attachment styles among young adults: A test of a model. *Journal of Personality and Social Psychology, 61*, 226–244.

Baum, W. M., & Rachlin, H. C. (1969). Choice as time allocation. *Journal of the Experimental Analysis of Behaviour, 12*, 861–874.

Beauchaine, T. P., Zisner, A. R., & Sauder, C. L. (2017). Trait impulsivity and the externalizing spectrum. *Annual Review of Clinical Psychology, 13*, 343–368.

Bowlby, J. (1969). *Attachment. Attachment and loss: Vol. 1. Loss*. New York: Basic Books.

Brown, S., Beelet, C., Patel, G., & Vollm, B. (2016). Training probation officers in case formulation for personality disordered offenders. *Criminal Behaviour and Mental Health, 23*, 236–273.

Farmer, R. F. (2000). Issues in the assessment and conceptualization of personality disorders. *Clinical Psychology Review, 20*, 823–851.

Farmer, R. F. (2005). Temperament, reward and punishment sensitivity, and clinical disorders: Implications for behavioural case formulation and therapy. *International Journal of Behavioural Consultation and Therapy, 1*, 56–76.

Farrington, D. P., & Hawkins, J. D. (1991). Predicting participation, early onset, and later persistence in officially recorded offending. *Criminal Behaviour and Mental Health, 1*, 1–33.

Frick, P. J., Ray, J. V., Thornton, L. C., & Kahn, R. E. (2014). Can callous–unemotional traits enhance the understanding, diagnosis, and treatment of serious conduct problems in children and adolescents? A comprehensive review. *Psychological Bulletin, 140*, 1–57.

Goldfried, M. R., & Sprafkin, J. N. (1976). Behavioural personality assessment. In J. T. Spence, R. C. Carson, & J. W. Thibaut (Eds.), *Behavioural approaches to therapy*. Morristown, NJ: General Learning Press.

Kirk, S. A., & Kutchins, H. (1992). *The selling of DSM: The rhetoric of science in psychiatry*. New Brunswick: Aldine.

Lang, P. J. (1968). Fear reduction and fear behaviour: Problems in treating a construct. In J. M. Schlein (Ed.), *Research in psychotherapy* (Vol. 3). Washington, DC: American Psychological Association.

Linehan, M. M. (1993). *Cognitive-behavioural treatment of borderline personality disorder*. New York: Guildford Press.

McMurran, M., & Bruford, S. (2016). Case formulation quality checklist: A revision based upon clinicians' views. *Journal of Forensic Practice, 18*, 31–38.

McMurran, M., Logan, C., & Hart, S. (2012). *Case formulation quality checklist*. Nottingham: Institute of Mental Health.

Minoudis, P., Craissati, J., Shaw, J., McMurran, M., Freestone, Chuan, S. J., et al. (2013). An evaluation of case formulation training and consultation with probation officers. *Criminal Behaviour and Mental Health, 23*, 252–262.

Nelson-Gray, R. O., & Farmer, R. F. (1999a). Invited essay. Behavioural assessment of personality disorders. *Behaviour, Research and Therapy, 37*, 347–368.

Nelson-Gray, R. O., & Farmer, R. F. (1999b). Functional analysis and response covariation in the assessment of personality disorders: A reply to Staats and to Bissett and Hayes. *Research and Therapy, 37*, 385–394.

Nelson-Gray, R. O., Lootens, C. M., Mitchell, J. T., Robertson, C. D., Hundt, N. E., & Kimbrel, N. A. (2009). Assessment and treatment of personality disorders: A behavioural perspective. *The Behaviour Analyst Today, 10*, 7–46.

Sturmey, P. (2009). *Varieties of case formulation*. 323 p. Chichester: Wiley, UK.

Sutker, P. B., Bugg, F., & West, J. A. (1993). Antisocial personality disorder. In P. B. Sutker, & H. E. Adams (Eds.), *Comprehensive handbook of psychopathology*. New York: Plenum.

Sutker, P. B., & King, A. R. (1985). Antisocial personality disorder. In I. Turkat (Ed.), *Behavioural case formulation*. New York: Plenum. 1985a.

Taylor, E., Chadwick, O., Heptinstall, E., & Danckaerts, M. (1996). Hyperactivity and conduct problems as risk factors for adolescent development. *American Academy of Child Adolescent Psychiatry, 35*, 1213–1226.

Tryon, G. S., & Winograd, G. (2011). Goal consensus and collaboration. *Psychotherapy, 48*, 50–57.

Turkat, I. (1985a). *Behavioural case formulation*. New York: Plenum.

Turkat, I. (1985b). Paranoid personality disorder. In I. Turkat (Ed.), *Behavioural case formulation* (pp. 155–198). New York: Plenum. 1985a.

Völlm, B. (2013). Case formulation in personality disordered offenders – A Delphi survey of professionals. *Criminal Behaviour and Mental Health, 24*, 60–80.

Weerasekera, P. (1996). *Multiperspective case formulation: A step towards treatment integration*. Malabar, Fl: Krieger.

Young, J. E. (2005). *Young schema questionnaire–short form 3 (YSQ-S3)*. New York, NY: Cognitive Therapy Center.

Young, J. E., Klosko, J. S., & Weishaar, M. E. (2003). *Schema therapy: A practitioner's guide*. New York: Guilford Press.

Zanarini, M. C., & Frankenburg, F. R. (2007). The essential nature of borderline psychopathology. *Journal of Personality Disorders, 21*, 518–535.

Further Reading

Brantly, P. J., & Callon, E. B. (1985). Histrionic personality disorder. In I. Turkat (Ed.), *Behavioural case formulation* (pp. 199–252). New York: Plenum. 1985a.

Callaghan, G. M., Summer, J., & Weidman, W. (2003). The treatment of histrionic and narcissistic personality disorder behaviours: A single-subject demonstration of clinical improvement using functional analytic psychotherapy. *Journal of Contemporary Psychotherapy, 3,* 321–339.

Sturmey, P. (1996). *Functional analysis in clinical psychology.* London: Wiley.

Sturmey, P. (2008). *Behavioural case formulation and intervention. A functional analytic approach.* Chichester: Wiley-Blackwell.

CHAPTER

13

Conceptualizing Borderline Personality Disorder Within an Emotional Disorders Framework: Implications for Treatment With the Unified Protocol

Shannon Sauer-Zavala[1], *Kate H. Bentley*[2], *Julianne G. Wilner*[1]

[1]**Department of Psychological and Brain Sciences, Boston University, Boston, MA, United States;** [2]**Department of Psychiatry, Massachusetts General Hospital, Boston, MA, United States**

The term 'emotional disorder' refers to mental health conditions characterized by (1) frequent and intense negative emotions, (2) strong aversive reactions to these experiences, and (3) efforts to escape or avoid them (Barlow, Sauer-Zavala, Carl, Bullis, & Ellard, 2014). The diagnoses most often considered within this larger class include anxiety, depressive, and related disorders (Barlow, 1991), however, borderline personality disorder (BPD) has recently been added to its purview (see: Sauer-Zavala & Barlow, 2014). Although BPD may not appear to share obvious overlap with other emotional disorders at the symptom level, there is growing evidence that these conditions share similar functional processes that underscore their development and maintenance (Sauer-Zavala & Barlow, 2014). In fact, the high rates of co-occurrence amongst BPD and other emotional disorders can largely be accounted for by common vulnerabilities (see: Eaton et al., 2011), and targeting these shared processes in treatment may represent a more efficient approach to addressing comorbid conditions (Barlow et al., 2014). In this chapter, we first review the empirical literature supporting the case for

Case Formulation for Personality Disorders
https://doi.org/10.1016/B978-0-12-813521-1.00013-8

considering BPD a disorder of emotion. Next, we describe the process for conceptualizing BPD within the emotional disorders framework and implications of this approach for treatment. Specifically, we briefly describe the Unified Protocol for the Transdiagnostic Treatment of Emotional Disorders (Barlow et al., 2011), a leading treatment for this class of psychopathology, along with the relevance of its therapeutic strategies for BPD difficulties. A case description using this approach to conceptualization is also provided.

BORDERLINE PERSONALITY DISORDER (BPD) IS AN EMOTIONAL DISORDER

As noted above, BPD is characterized by a similar functional model that has been used to describe emotional disorders (see: Sauer-Zavala & Barlow, 2014): Frequently occurring negative emotions, coupled with aversive reactions to these experiences that lead to reliance on emotionally avoidant coping (see: Barlow et al., 2014). Although avoidant strategies may be effective in the short-term, there is compelling evidence to suggest that suppressed emotions return with greater frequency and intensity (Wegner, Schneider, Carter, & White, 1987), maintaining emotional disorder symptoms in the long-term (Purdon, 1999). The following section summarizes the literature supporting BPD's fit within the emotional disorder framework.

Borderline Personality Disorder (BPD) Is Characterized by Strong Negative Emotions

The hallmark characteristic of emotional disorders is negative emotionality, and a substantial literature suggests that individuals with BPD indeed experience frequent and intense negative emotions. For example, Linehan's construct of emotional vulnerability, an important risk factor in her developmental model of BPD, is defined as high reactivity to emotion-provoking stimuli, strong intensity of emotional responses, and a slow return to baseline levels of emotional functioning following a trigger (Linehan, 1993). Several empirical studies have indeed demonstrated greater levels of negative emotions in BPD compared to nonclinical controls and other personality disorders (e.g., Koenigsberg et al., 2002) and have linked this emotional intensity to severity of BPD symptoms (Rosenthal, Cheavens, Lejuez, & Lynch, 2005). Additional studies utilizing physiological measures also indicate heightened emotional intensity and reactivity in BPD (Austin, Riniolo, & Porges, 2007; Ebner-Priemer et al., 2007). Furthermore, neuroimaging studies suggest that individuals with BPD display reduced hippocampal, orbitofrontal and amygdala volumes and increased amygdala activation in response to emotional cues (see: Rosenthal et al., 2008; Ruocco et al., 2016).

Borderline Personality Disorder (BPD) Is Characterized by Negative Reactions to Strong Emotions

A second important feature of emotional disorders is the tendency to view emotional experiences as aversive. Individuals with BPD demonstrate this negative stance towards emotions across several related constructs. For instance, experiential avoidance, defined as an unwillingness to remain in contact with uncomfortable internal experiences (Hayes, Wilson, Gifford, Follette, & Strosahl, 1996), accounts for significant incremental variance in predicting BPD symptom severity beyond frequency of negative emotions (Iverson, Follette, Pistorello, & Fruzzetti, 2012). Similarly, deficits in mindfulness (approaching emotions with a present-focused, nonjudgmental attitude) explains significant variance in BPD symptom severity even when controlling for heightened negative affectivity (Shorey et al., 2016; Wupperman, Neumann, & Axelrod, 2008). Furthermore, anxiety sensitivity, defined as the belief that emotion-related physiological states will have negative somatic, cognitive, and social consequences (Reiss, 1991), is elevated in individuals with BPD (Lilienfeld & Penna, 2001) and also predicts symptom severity after accounting for the tendency to experience negative affect (Gratz, Tull, & Gunderson, 2008).

Taken together, these findings suggest that BPD and other emotional disorders symptoms are not simply a product of high levels of negative affect; instead, the combination of strong negative emotions *and* how one relates to them when they occur appears to be important for the development of these disorders.

Borderline Personality Disorder (BPD) Is Characterized by Avoidant Coping

Given that individuals with BPD experience high levels of negative emotions and find these experiences aversive, it is not surprising that they engage in efforts to escape or avoid them (Putnam & Silk, 2005). In fact, there is evidence to suggest that the behavioral difficulties associated with BPD serve to suppress intense negative emotion (see: Bijttebier & Vertommen, 1999). For example, there is ample support for the notion that non-suicidal self-injury most often functions to escape unwanted emotional experiences (see: Bentley, Nock, & Barlow, 2014). Likewise, substance users with BPD more frequently describe their drug and alcohol use as serving to escape negative emotions, compared to substance abusers without BPD (Kruedelbach, McCormick, Schulz, & Grueneich, 1993). Further, dissociation and binge eating, also common in BPD, have similarly, been associated with avoidance of negative mood states (Deaver, Miltenberger, Smyth, Meidinger, & Crosby, 2003).

In addition to engaging in behavioural strategies aimed at escaping unwanted emotions, individuals with BPD also engage in cognitive coping motivated by avoidance. For instance, thought suppression, or deliberately attempting to push unpleasant, emotion-inducing cognitions out of awareness, has been shown to mediate the relationship between negative emotionality and BPD symptoms (Rosenthal et al., 2005; Sauer & Baer, 2009). Similarly, rumination, defined as repetitively and passively focusing on negative mood and its possible consequences (Nolen-Hoeksema, 1991), can also be considered an avoidant strategy as passive attention to surface matters may serve to protect individuals from more distressing concerns (Williams & Moulds, 2007). Rumination is common in BPD (Abela, Payne, & Moussaly, 2003), correlated with symptom severity (Baer & Sauer, 2011), and predicts dysregulated behaviour (Sauer & Baer, 2012; Selby, Anestis, Bender, & Joiner, 2009).

Avoidant coping has paradoxically been shown to increase the frequency and intensity of negative emotions (e.g., Muehlenkamp et al., 2009; Wegner et al., 1987), maintaining symptoms across the range of emotional disorders (Abramowitz, Tolin, & Street, 2001; Purdon, 1999). Given the central role that aversive reactions to emotions and corresponding avoidant coping has in the development and maintenance of a wide range of emotional disorders, interventions that target this shared feature may result in promising symptom reduction across diagnoses.

Shared Latent Structure Accounts for Co-occurrence of Borderline Personality Disorder (BPD) and Other Emotional Disorders

In addition to a similar functional, BPD is characterized by a high degree of co-occurrence with other prototypical emotional disorders (e.g., Zanarini et al., 1998). For example, lifetime comorbidity rates for individuals with BPD are as high as 75% for depressive and anxiety disorders (Grant et al., 2008). Furthermore, the combination of a BPD diagnosis with an additional emotional disorder is associated with increased severity and decreased treatment response, for both BPD and the co-occurring condition(s) (e.g., Vignarajah & Links, 2009). One explanation for this pattern of comorbidity is that shared, functional processes (described above) may account for the wide range of emotional disorder symptoms (Barlow et al., 2014). In other words, heterogeneity in the expression of emotional disorders, represented by discrete diagnostic categories, can be considered relatively trivial variations in the manifestation of this broader syndrome. When BPD is included in studies examining the latent structure of emotional disorders, results suggest that its symptoms are largely accounted for by a neuroticism factor, though a small but significant proportion of the variance also loads an externalizing factor (Eaton et al., 2011; James & Taylor, 2008).

UNIFIED, TRANSDIAGNOSTIC CASE CONCEPTUALIZATION FOR EMOTIONAL DISORDERS

The Unified Protocol (UP) for Transdiagnostic Treatment of Emotional Disorders (Barlow et al., 2011, 2018) is a cognitive-behavioural intervention developed to address the range of emotional disorders by targeting shared underlying vulnerabilities, namely, aversive reactions to frequently occurring negative emotions. Specifically, the UP is thought to exert its effects through the systematic extinction of distress in response to strong emotions, resulting in decreased reliance on emotionally avoidant coping strategies, and, in turn, leading to fewer negative emotions overall. Flexible in nature, the UP is delivered over 16–20 sessions and is comprised of eight skills-based treatment modules; five of these modules are considered 'core' meaning they are designed to target the maladaptive responses to emotions described above. The UP has gained empirical support across a range of emotional disorders (Boswell, Anderson, & Barlow, 2014; Ciraulo et al., 2013; Ellard, Deckersbach, Sylvia, Nierenberg, & Barlow, 2012; Gallagher, 2018, pp. 111–128), with the strongest evidence for its use with anxiety disorders (Barlow et al., 2017; Ellard, Fairholme, Boisseau, Farchione, & Barlow, 2010; Farchione et al., 2012). A detailed description of each UP module, along with their application to BPD-related difficulties has been articulated elsewhere (e.g., Sauer-Zavala, Bentley, & Wilner, 2016).

Although there is a strong theoretical basis (described above; for a review, see: Sauer-Zavala & Barlow, 2014), along with preliminary empirical support (Sauer-Zavala, Bentley, & Wilner, 2016), for the application of the UP to individuals with BPD, it is important to conduct a thorough functional assessment to determine whether a particular patient can be conceptualized within this emotional disorders framework, and would thus be more likely respond to treatment with the UP. Procedures for conducting a functional assessment are explicitly incorporated into early sessions with the UP (see: Barlow, Farchione et al, 2018; Boettcher & Conklin, 2018), guided by a Case Formulation Worksheet (see Fig. 13.1 for a completed version).

Generally, the initial session with the UP involves a review of the patient's symptoms, along with an orientation to treatment strategies. Therapists are encouraged to explicitly describe the functional model of emotional disorders and then evaluate the extent to which these features are present in the patient's presentation. UP therapists begin by noting, particularly for patients who meet criteria for more than one disorder, that the co-occurrence of mental health conditions is quite common and that this comorbidity is thought to be the result of shared vulnerabilities. Often, patients will inquire about the nature of these vulnerabilities. First, the

PRESENTING PROBLEMS:

Difficulty performing well and accomplishing tasks promptly at work, trouble getting along with coworkers, strained relationships with friends and family, discontentment with where I am in life

STRONG UNCOMFORTABLE EMOTIONS:

Anxiety, sadness, anger, jealousy, guilt

AVERSIVE REACTIONS:

"I can't handle intense emotions"
"I hate how emotional I am"
"I'm pathetic for feeling this way"

AVOIDANT COPING:

SITUATIONAL AVOIDANCE/ESCAPE: Isolate myself, withdraw, avoid social interactions and dating
SUBTLE BEHAVIOURAL AVOIDANCE: Seek reassurance from friends/family, lash out at others, procrastinate at work, ignore emails, discount my abilities, *talk about people behind their backs*
COGNITIVE AVOIDANCE: Fantasize about moving away or changing jobs, ruminate, compare myself to others

TREATMENT PLAN: FOCUS/APPLICATION OF CORE MODULES:

MODULE 3: Notice when my emotions are building, and bring my attention to the present so I can respond effectively at work and interpersonally

MODULE 4: Think more flexibly and realistically about my abilities at work and in social situations (e.g., how others view me)

MODULE 5: Identify and try alternative actions to my avoidant coping above, especially in relationships and at work

MODULE 6: Identify and practice tolerating physical sensations that make my urges to avoid or lash out stronger

MODULE 7: Practice experiencing my emotions without avoidant coping

FIGURE 13.1 The Unified Protocol Case Conceptualization Worksheet, drawn from the Therapist Guide for this manual (Barlow, Farchione et al., 2018), is used to assist clinicians in understanding their patients within an emotional disorders framework.

tendency to experience frequent, strong negative emotions is described as existing on a continuum and most patients will identify themselves as more prone to intense emotional responses. It can be helpful to reflect that being emotionally sensitive is not necessarily a problem, though individuals who feel their emotions more strongly are more likely to struggle coping with these experiences. Evidence for strong, uncomfortable emotions is recorded on the Case Formulation Worksheet and, given the ample research suggesting the presence of this quality in individuals with BPD (e.g., Linehan, 1993; Rosenthal et al., 2005), this section is often easily completed.

Next, therapists explore the degree to which patients find their emotions unwanted, bad, or dangerous (e.g., shameful, stupid, a sign of weakness) and record their impressions on the aversive reactions section of the Case Formulation Worksheet. This component of the functional model is portrayed as more important for the development of emotional disorders than the tendency to experience strong emotions. Patients may describe aversion to overall emotional experiences or to one part of their experience (e.g., patients with panic disorder may be particularly distressed by physical sessions that accompany emotional responses). Patients with BPD often describe a fear of losing control if they allow themselves to fully feel an emotion, or that these experiences will last forever, consistent with the literature supporting this component of the emotional disorders functional model in BPD described above (see: Sauer-Zavala & Barlow, 2014). In this discussion, as well as throughout treatment with the UP, therapists are encouraged to take note of negative judgements patients make about their emotional experiences or of themselves for having such emotions (e.g., 'This is dangerous', 'I can't handle feeling this bad', 'This means I'm out of control', or 'I'm just being stupid [for feeling this way])'.

Within this framework of emotional disorders, strong emotions, coupled with negative responses to these experiences, often lead to efforts to escape, avoid, or dampen them. UP therapists are encouraged to describe this process to their patients while also investigating whether emotionally avoidant tendencies are present in a particular case. The UP provides guidance for conducting this assessment by explicating various types of avoidant coping that might occur. These include overt situational avoidance (e.g., refusal to enter situations where one might encounter an ex-partner), subtle behavioural avoidance (e.g., text messaging while at a party to avoid looking awkward), cognitive avoidance (e.g., distracting oneself with TV to prevent thoughts about a distressing topic), and emotion-driven behaviours (e.g., engaging in self-injurious behaviour to dampen a strong emotion, yelling at a loved one to avoid sitting with one's anger). Although it is typically not recommended to review these categories with patients at this early stage of treatment, UP therapists can use them as a heuristic to identify patterns of avoidance and record them in the avoidant coping section of the Case Formulation Worksheet. Finally, after the initial session, therapists using the UP consider how each core UP skill (Modules 3–7) can be used to address the difficulties uncovered during the case formulation process – highlighted in the following case presentation.

TREATING BORDERLINE PERSONALITY DISORDER (BPD) WITH THE UNIFIED PROTOCOL: A CONCEPTUALIZATION-FOCUSED CASE PRESENTATION

The following is an illustrative case example depicting the application of the UP case formulation to a patient with BPD, along with how that conceptualization was used to inform key treatment procedures. Specific, potentially identifying details have been altered to protect patient confidentiality. Kim is a 28-year-old, single, Caucasian female who was initially referred for outpatient psychotherapy by her psychiatrist (Dr. S.). Kim had sought psychopharmacological (specifically, stimulant) treatment with Dr. S. about 6 months prior due to 'problems paying attention' that were interfering in her work as an administrative assistant in a veterinary hospital. During their second appointment, Dr. S. provided feedback to Kim that she appeared to be experiencing symptoms consistent with a diagnosis of BPD and referred her for CBT.

Evidence of an Emotional Disorder at Intake

The first psychotherapy session included a thorough diagnostic interview, during which the therapist began to consider how aspects of Kim's presentation may be conceptualized within the UP framework (see Fig. 13.1). Based on the information obtained during this interview, Kim met criteria for both BPD and social anxiety disorder. With regard to BPD symptoms, Kim described longstanding frequent and intense shifts in affect (e.g., 'It feels like I just go from zero to sixty') that negatively impacted her ability to stay on task at work and communicate with others, along with her overall quality of life. Kim described feeling as though intense anxiety (especially at work and in interpersonal situations) and both sadness and 'feeling lonely' would seem to come out of nowhere for her. She also reported often becoming 'irrationally' annoyed or angry at her coworkers, which resulted in making rude comments, rolling her eyes, and ignoring her colleagues; this had been identified as an area for improvement in past performance reviews. Kim's initial descriptions of negative affect – anxiety, sadness, and anger – were conceptualized as frequent and intense negative emotion within the UP conceptualization (Fig. 13.1).

During this initial session, Kim also provided preliminary indications of aversive reactions to the experience of emotion, per the UP framework. For instance, she stated that after Dr. S. told her she met criteria for BPD, she was 'so overwhelmed', and elaborated that she 'couldn't handle how upset I was', which resulted in her not leaving her apartment for several days straight and calling out 'sick' from work (a form of behavioural avoidance, noted in Fig. 13.1). Kim also noted that she 'hates' how emotional she can become. The therapist conceptualized these early statements as themes of aversive reactions to emotion for Kim (see Fig. 13.1).

Kim also endorsed engaging in what she described as 'passive-aggressive' behaviour towards her friends and family; for example, she often said things to make her parents feel guilty for not visiting her more often, despite not necessarily wanting them to come, and that she frequently text messaged her sister and close friends many times in a row to ensure that they still cared about her. The therapist conceptualized these actions as avoidant coping behaviours in the UP case conceptualization; in the short-term, they appeared to provide some relief from the emotions (sadness, anxiety, guilt) and related states (e.g., loneliness), but in the long-term, they potentially were maintaining her negative emotions in the context of her relationships. Additionally, Kim described a pattern of unstable, intense relationships with friends (e.g., picking fights and then ignoring people who she perceived as having wronged her that resulted in having many 'falling outs' with friends from high school and college) and romantic partners; it had been several years since she had been in a serious relationship. Kim reported frequently questioning 'what [she is] doing with her life' and vacillating between wanting to go to graduate school, quit her job to be a dance instructor, and move home to nanny for her sister. The UP therapist also conceptualized Kim's tendency to fantasize about changing courses in life and frequent doubts about her current career path (without making proactive changes or engaging in active problem-solving) as forms of cognitive avoidance (Fig. 13.1) as serving to escape from her anxiety and insecurity in the moment, but maintaining her negative emotions over a longer course of time. Along these lines, she described often feeling jealous (another frequent emotion for Kim, noted in Fig. 13.1) of acquaintances who she perceived as 'knowing who they are' and being better able to effectively handle day-to-day stressors than she.

In terms of her social anxiety diagnosis, Kim endorsed regularly avoiding a variety of social situations (such as parties, small group get-togethers, dating, and participating at meetings, all conceptualized as avoidant coping behaviours within the UP framework) in which others may 'make [her] feel dumb'. Kim offered several examples of how this pattern has interfered with her social life and career advancement, including '*still* being single' – Kim avoided dating out of her fear of being rejected or judged, a form of behavioural avoidance noted in Figure–and feeling 'stuck' in a job for several years that she dislikes. Of note, Kim reported struggling to complete assignments in a prompt fashion at work due to fear of 'not doing a good enough job'. She further recognized that procrastinating (a perfectionistic tendency and per the UP, subtle avoidant behaviour) has prevented her from performing to the best of her ability at work, and thus being promoted. She also reported a subclinical level of depressive symptoms, including occasional low mood, feelings of worthlessness, and infrequent (about once monthly) passive suicidal ideation, with a history of two prior major depressive episodes. At the outset, Kim indicated that her primary goals for CBT were to make new relationships and 'enjoy life more'.

Applying Unified Protocol (UP) Skills to Components of the Emotional Disorder Framework

During the second session, the therapist introduced the transdiagnostic UP framework, which resonated with Kim given her frequent experience of intense negative affect (anxiety, anger, sadness, jealousy, guilt) across many situations. A description of how each UP skill corresponds to aspects of Kim's emotional disorder presentation can be seen in the Treatment Plan section of Fig. 13.1.

During UP Module 1 (motivation enhancement), Kim was open to exploring both the pros (e.g., 'find a more satisfying job') and cons (e.g., less concern from her family if she were to gain more emotional stability) of changing and engaging in treatment. Kim was also able to successfully translate her overall goals of making new relationships into several specific, concrete steps, such as signing up for a weekly hip-hop class, introducing herself to three new people in the class, and initiating social activities, as well as updating her resume, researching job openings and part-time graduate school programmes, and submitting one application per week.

Over the first several sessions, Kim was minimally compliant with completing worksheets outside of session, which she attributed to concerns that her roommate or coworkers would notice her doing so. The therapist viewed this homework non-compliance as a form of emotional avoidance that was unsurprising given both Kim's tendency to avoid situations she feared would result in judgement from others identified during the initial UP case conceptualization and perfectionism with assignments (a more subtle behavioural avoidance). She and her therapist brainstormed several possible solutions to this problem, including completing homework on her iPhone instead of a worksheet (less conspicuous) and scheduling time for homework when she was likely to have more privacy. It also quickly became clear during in-session homework review that when Kim had attempted an assignment, she expected that she had done a 'bad' job or did not understand the workbook readings, despite the fact that her strong grasp of treatment concepts was clear in session. The therapist considered the consequences of Kim's overarching pattern of discounting her abilities (a subtle behavioural avoidance per the UP case formulation) across many life areas, including her career (e.g., doubting that she could obtain another job and be accepted into graduate school preventing her from pursuing either path) and her relationships (e.g., not introducing herself to new people because 'they probably wouldn't like [her] anyway'). In the short-term, this tendency served to reduce her anxiety about the possibility of future failure or rejection, but in the long-term, this behaviour was conceptualized as worsening her self-esteem and preventing her from achieving her goals of pursuing a new career path and having meaningful relationships. During session 4 (Module 2; Understanding Emotions), the therapist worked with Kim to identify these short-term and long-term effects of her emotional responding, which resonated with Kim.

This functional analysis helped facilitate Kim's use of more adaptive emotion management strategies to counter her avoidant coping when distressed at work, including objective recording of upsetting emotional experiences (i.e., 'breaking down an emotion' into cognitions, physical sensations, and behavioural urges in UP Module 2) during periods of downtime and anchoring in the present (UP Module 3; Mindful Emotion Awareness) when an emotion began to build (Fig. 13.1). For example, upon noticing her face flushing and heart beating rapidly after receiving an email from her manager about setting up an individual meeting, Kim described using her breath as a cue to bring her attention back to the present from both past-oriented ruminative thoughts (e.g., 'I must have [messed] up yet again') and negative predictions about the future (e.g., 'my boss will find out'). Anchoring in the present facilitated her ability to resist immediate behavioural urges to send a curt email back or ignore the request for a meeting entirely (both forms of behavioural avoidance, see Fig. 13.1), and instead wait a couple hours to draft her response when feeling calmer. Though Kim struggled to be *nonjudgmental* of her emotions, frequently having aversive, judgemental reactions such as 'this [anxiety] *always* happens to me' and 'I'm pathetic for feeling this way' (noted in Fig. 13.1) her ability to *notice and label* both her primary emotions and secondary (often judgemental) reactions improved.

During UP Module 4 (Cognitive Flexibility), Kim learned to identify her common patterns of automatic negative thinking, including jumping to conclusions about others (family, friends) being upset and/or not wanting to spend time with her, or her coworkers and manager having malicious motives towards her (e.g., 'I always feel like they're talking about me') in neutral situations with little evidence to support these interpretations. These cognitions, of course, intensified her urges to engage in avoidant coping behaviours, such as snapping at others, talking behind peoples' backs, or avoiding interactions entirely (Fig. 13.1). Kim and her therapist also explored possible underlying automatic thoughts that may have been contributing to her surface-level appraisal patterns and emotional responding in key problem areas. Two themes emerged for Kim: beliefs about her lack of competence and worthlessness, both of which played a role in her tendency to catastrophize about 'ending up alone' and never finding career or life satisfaction. Kim was uncharacteristically tearful when discussing these cognitions in session, but able to acknowledge the potential importance of identifying (rather than avoiding) how these global views about herself may be contributing to her distress across many situations. During sessions 8 and 9, Kim learned to generate alternative interpretations for her surface-level negative automatic thoughts and practised applying this cognitive flexibility skill to a recent situation when her roommate asked if she could do Kim a favour by dropping off her clothes at the dry cleaners that evening. Kim's initial automatic thought was 'she must think I can't take care of myself', which contributed to irritability and anger towards her roommate, as well as guilt and frustration with herself. Using challenging questions focused on examining the evidence, Kim was able to generate several alternative and more balanced interpretations, including 'she's probably just being nice' and 'even if she does think I need help, who cares'.

Sessions 10 and 11 (UP Module 5; Countering Emotional Behaviours) transitioned to focusing on identifying and modifying Kim's emotionally avoidant behaviours as identified in the UP case conceptualization to be maintaining her intense and frequent negative emotion (see Fig. 13.1). Kim's idiosyncratic forms of emotion avoidance associated with anxiety (e.g., seeking reassurance that her close family and friends still care about her, avoiding uncomfortable social situations, 'clamming up' with men), anger (e.g., making 'snarky' comments, leaving rude voicemails or sending mean text messages to people she thinks have rejected her, talking about people behind their backs), and intense sadness (e.g., withdrawing, ruminating, comparing herself to others) were conceptualized as providing some immediate relief from the emotions she does not want to experience (because they make her feel vulnerable, weak, out of control, etc.), but are likely maintaining her distress and discontentment over the longer term. The therapist introduced the concept of countering these maladaptive behaviours with alternative actions, which, in contrast to avoidance, tend to feel less comfortable in the moment but lead to less frequent and intense negative emotion over time.

Kim was able to identify a number of adaptive alternative actions that she hoped to try when experiencing urges to avoid, including refraining from seeking reassurance from loved ones, delaying sending a text or email when annoyed, and continuing a conversation with someone she doesn't know well (rather than making up an excuse to cut it short). Given Kim's occasional comments reflecting her continued poor body image (e.g., 'I miss being skinny'), when she offered going to the gym as an alternative action to isolating herself when sad, her therapist encouraged Kim to explore the short-term and long-term consequences of this behaviour in detail. The therapist differentiated between exercising to activate when negative emotions might be driving her to withdraw or not take care of herself (i.e., an adaptive alternative action) and exercising to avoid distressing thoughts (e.g., 'Guys will like me better if I lose weight') and emotions (e.g., guilt, anxiety, sadness) (i.e., a maladaptive, avoidant behaviour). The concept that the same behaviours can serve as both avoidance *and* adaptive alternative actions, depending on the situation and function, appeared to resonate with Kim.

UP Module 6 (Confronting and Tolerating Physical Sensations) included a discussion of the role that physical sensations often play in emotional experiences and how it is usually one's interpretations of uncomfortable physical sensations that serve to intensify negative emotional experiences and lead to urges to engage in problematic responses. Using her previously completed three-component model homework assignments, Kim identified the distressing physical sensations she tends to experience when anxious (heart beating fast, short of breath), angry (feeling hot, tense muscles), sad (weighted down, fatigued), and guilty (pit in stomach). Kim observed how, for example, when her face begins to feel flushed and her fists clench, her urges to say rude things to her coworkers, as well as engage in other forms of avoidant coping across a broader variety of situations, seem to become stronger. During sessions 12 and 13, Kim was willing to engage in systematic interoceptive exposure exercises, including breathing through a thin straw, sitting in front of a space heater while clenching fists, wearing wrist and ankle weights while walking around, with her therapist.

During Module 7 (Emotion Exposure, the final core UP module), Kim and her therapist expanded upon the alternative actions generated during Module 5 to develop a hierarchy of situations and activities that were likely to elicit intense emotion (including anxiety, anger, sadness, guilt, and shame) for her. The rationale of developing such an 'emotion exposure hierarchy' was for Kim to practice experience intense emotion *without aversive reactions and engaging in her avoidant coping behaviours*. By repeatedly experiencing emotions without the distressing, avoidant coping that maintains them, the UP framework posits that the frequency and intensity of patients' negative emotions will reduce over time. Over the next four sessions, Kim applied her newly acquired, non-avoidant emotion management strategies during a variety of emotion exposure tasks, which included (1) waiting until the next morning to respond to an email from her manager (when her initial, avoidant urge was to 'fire back immediately'), (2) undergoing a mock interview with a confederate who criticized her qualifications (while next a space heater to elicit heat-related sensations), (3) complimenting a coworker with whom she recently had conflict, and (4) introducing herself to an attractive man at a social event.

Before each of these exercises, Kim practised challenging any negative predictions about what would happen during the task or her ability to handle the emotions it might elicit, and identifying adaptive alternative actions to counter the emotional avoidance she might be tempted to engage in (e.g., maintaining eye contact instead of averting her eyes). During the exercises, she practised engaging in adaptive alternative actions to her avoidant, emotion-driven urges whenever possible and using her mindful anchoring skills to both remain focused on the present *and* attempt to stay nonjudgmental of her emotional experience. Again, the UP focuses heavily on acting alternatively to emotion avoidance in the later modules as it is behavioural and cognitive avoidance that is thought to maintain emotional disorder pathology per the UP framework. Over the course of completing these emotion exposures, Kim gained new knowledge that even emotions she finds highly distressing tend to reduce in intensity on their own without 'doing something rash' to relieve them, and observed, by repeatedly approaching feared situations, her self-confidence (particularly with regard to managing interpersonal situations that previously made her feel vulnerable) improved. During the final relapse prevention session, Kim noted her long-term goals of continuing to use the UP skills as she pursues other jobs (and possibly graduate school), reconnects with old friends, and goes on dates to keep the possibility of a romantic relationship open.

CONCLUSIONS

The purpose of this chapter was to discuss the theoretical rationale for considering BPD to be an emotional disorder and to discuss the process of conceptualizing a case within this framework. There is ample evidence to suggest that BPD is characterized by frequent, intense emotions and that individuals with this condition find these emotional experiences aversive (see: Sauer-Zavala & Barlow, 2014). As a result, patients with BPD often engage in a host of efforts to avoid strong emotions (e.g., situational avoidance, lashing out at others, rumination, non-suicidal self-injury, binge eating, substance use, other reckless impulsive actions) that provide short-term relief but backfire in the long-run. The conceptualization of BPD as an emotional disorder shares features with other views of BPD. For example, Linehan (1993) also describes emotion dysregulation as the core characteristic of BPD, giving rise to the other diagnostic features.

Given the functional similarities between BPD and other emotional disorders, a leading transdiagnostic treatment for the range of emotional disorders, the UP, was recently applied to small BPD sample; results suggest that this intervention may be a promising, cost-effective approach for individuals with BPD (Sauer-Zavala et al., 2016). However, to ensure that the UP is a good fit for a patient with BPD, or any patient suspected of having an emotional disorder for that matter, it is important to conduct a thorough functional analysis. The UP clearly articulates a process for conducting a case formulation informed by the functional model of emotional disorders, which is described in detail above. BPD is a notoriously heterogeneous disorder (Ellis, Abrams, & Abrams, 2008) and there may be circumstances in which the UP may not be the most appropriate form of care. For instance, some individuals with BPD may present with other, more prominent personality features, beyond the negative emotionality captured in the emotional disorders framework; specifically, disinhibition and antagonism are included in the alternative model of personality disorders in DSM-5 to capture BPD dysfunction. Careful case formulation can help clarify what patients with BPD are likely to benefit from treatment with the UP, or other available treatments.

Acknowledgements

Some details of the case description (i.e., name, profession) were changed so as to protect client privacy.

References

Abela, J. R. Z., Payne, A. V. L., & Moussaly, N. (2003). Cognitive vulnerability to depression in individuals with borderline personality disorder. *Journal of Personality Disorders, 17*(4), 319–329. https://doi.org/10.1521/pedi.17.4.319.23968.

Abramowitz, J. S., Tolin, D. F., & Street, G. P. (2001). Paradoxical effects of thought suppression: A meta-analysis of controlled studies. *Clinical Psychology Review, 21*(5), 683–703. https://doi.org/10.1016/S0272-7358(00)00057-X.

Austin, M. A., Riniolo, T. C., & Porges, S. W. (2007). Borderline personality disorder and emotion regulation: Insights from the polyvagal theory. *Brain and Cognition, 65*(1), 69–76. https://doi.org/10.1016/j.bandc.2006.05.007.

Baer, R. A., & Sauer, S. E. (2011). Relationships between depressive rumination, anger rumination, and borderline personality features. *Personality Disorders: Theory, Research, and Treatment, 2*(2), 142–150. https://doi.org/10.1037/a0019478.

Barlow, D. H. (1991). Disorders of emotion. *Psychological Inquiry, 2*(1), 58–71. https://doi.org/10.1207/s15327965pli0201_15.

Barlow, D. H., & Farchione, T. J. (Eds.). (2018). *Applications of the unified protocol for the transdiagnostic treatment of emotional disorders*. New York, NY: Oxford University Press.

Barlow, D. H., Farchione, T. J., Bullis, J. R., Gallagher, M. W., Murray-Latin, H., Sauer-Zavala, S., et al. (2017). The unified protocol for transdiagnostic treatment of emotional disorders compared with diagnosis-specific protocols for anxiety disorders: A randomized clinical trial. *JAMA Psychiatry, 74*(9), 875–884. https://doi.org/10.1001/jamapsychiatry.2017.2164.

Barlow, D. H., Farchione, T. J., Fairholme, C. P., Ellard, K. K., Boisseau, C. L., Allen, L. B., et al. (2011). *Unified protocol for transdiagnostic treatment of emotional disorders: Therapist guide*. Oxford University Press.

Barlow, D. H., Sauer-Zavala, S., Carl, J. R., Bullis, J. R., & Ellard, K. K. (2014). The nature, diagnosis, and treatment of neuroticism: Back to the future. *Clinical Psychological Science, 2*(3), 344–365. https://doi.org/10.1177/2167702613505532.

Barlow, D. H., Sauer-Zavala, S., Farchione, T. J., Murray Latin, H., Ellard, K. K., Bullis, J. R., et al. (2018). *Unified protocol for the transdiagnostic treatment of emotional disorders: Patient workbook* (2nd ed.). New York, NY: Oxford University Press.

Bentley, K. H., Nock, M. K., & Barlow, D. H. (2014). The four-function model of nonsuicidal self-injury: Key directions for future research. *Clinical Psychological Science*, *2*(5), 638–656. https://doi.org/10.1177/2167702613514563.

Bijttebier, P., & Vertommen, H. (1999). Coping strategies in relation to personality disorders. *Personality and Individual Differences*, *26*(5), 847–856. https://doi.org/10.1016/S0191-8869(98)00187-1.

Boettcher, H. T., & Conklin, L. (2018). Transdiagnostic assessment and case conceptualization: Rationale and application with the Unified Protocol. In D. H. Barlow, & T. J. Farchione (Eds.), *Applications of the Unified Protocol for the Transdiagnostic Treatment of Emotional Disorders* (pp. 111–128). New York, NY: Oxford University Press.

Boswell, J. F., Anderson, L. M., & Barlow, D. H. (2014). An idiographic analysis of change processes in the unified transdiagnostic treatment of depression. *Journal of Consulting and Clinical Psychology*, *82*(6), 1060. https://doi.org/10.1037/a0037403.

Ciraulo, D. A., Barlow, D. H., Gulliver, S. B., Farchione, T., Morissette, S. B., Kamholz, B. W., et al. (2013). The effects of venlafaxine and cognitive behavioral therapy alone and combined in the treatment of co-morbid alcohol use-anxiety disorders. *Behaviour Research and Therapy*, *51*(11), 729–735. https://doi.org/10.1016/j.brat.2013.08.003.

Deaver, C. M., Miltenberger, R. G., Smyth, J., Meidinger, A., & Crosby, R. (2003). An evaluation of affect and binge eating. *Behavior Modification*, *27*(4), 578–599. https://doi.org/10.1177/0145445503255571.

Eaton, N. R., Krueger, R. F., Keyes, K. M., Skodol, A. E., Markon, K. E., Grant, B. F., et al. (2011). Borderline personality disorder co-morbidity: Relationship to the internalizing-externalizing structure of common mental disorders. *Psychological Medicine*, *41*(5), 1041–1050. https://doi.org/10.1017/S0033291710001662.

Ebner-Priemer, U. W., Kuo, J., Kleindienst, N., Welch, S. S., Reisch, T., Reinhard, I., et al. (2007). State affective instability in borderline personality disorder assessed by ambulatory monitoring. *Psychological Medicine*, *37*(7), 961–970. https://doi.org/10.1017/S0033291706009706.

Ellard, K. K., Deckersbach, T., Sylvia, L. G., Nierenberg, A. A., & Barlow, D. H. (2012). Transdiagnostic treatment of bipolar disorder and comorbid anxiety with the unified protocol: A clinical replication series. *Behavior Modification*, *36*(4), 482–508. https://doi.org/10.1177/0145445512451272.

Ellard, K. K., Fairholme, C. P., Boisseau, C. L., Farchione, T. J., & Barlow, D. H. (2010). Unified Protocol for the Transdiagnostic Treatment of Emotional Disorders: Protocol development and initial outcome data. *Cognitive and Behavioral Practice*, *17*(1), 88–101. https://doi.org/10.1016/j.cbpra.2009.06.002.

Ellis, A., Abrams, M., & Abrams, L. (2008). *Personality theories: Critical perspectives*. Los Angeles, CA: SAGE Publications, Inc.

Farchione, T. J., Fairholme, C. P., Ellard, K. K., Boisseau, C. L., Thompson-Hollands, J., Carl, J. R., et al. (2012). Unified protocol for transdiagnostic treatment of emotional disorders: A randomized controlled trial. *Behavior Therapy*, *43*(3), 666–678. https://doi.org/10.1016/j.beth.2012.01.001.

Gallagher, M. W. (2018). The unified protocol for posttraumatic stress disorder. In D. H. Barlow, & T. J. Farchione (Eds.), *Applications of the unified protocol for the transdiagnostic treatment of emotional disorders*. New York, NY: Oxford University Press.

Grant, B. F., Chou, S. P., Goldstein, R. B., Huang, B., Stinson, F. S., Saha, T. D., et al. (2008). Prevalence, correlates, disability, and comorbidity of DSM-IV borderline personality disorder: Results from the wave 2 national epidemiologic survey on alcohol and related conditions. *The Journal of Clinical Psychiatry*, *69*(4), 533–545. https://doi.org/10.4088/JCP.v69n0404.

Gratz, K. L., Tull, M. T., & Gunderson, J. G. (2008). Preliminary data on the relationship between anxiety sensitivity and borderline personality disorder: The role of experiential avoidance. *Journal of Psychiatric Research, 42*(7), 550–559. https://doi.org/10.1016/j.jpsychires.2007.05.011.

Hayes, S. C., Wilson, K. G., Gifford, E. V., Follette, V. M., & Strosahl, K. (1996). Experiential avoidance and behavioral disorders: A functional dimensional approach to diagnosis and treatment. *Journal of Consulting and Clinical Psychology, 64*(6), 1152–1168. https://doi.org/10.1037/0022-006X.64.6.1152.

Iverson, K. M., Follette, V. M., Pistorello, J., & Fruzzetti, A. E. (2012). An investigation of experiential avoidance, emotion dysregulation, and distress tolerance in young adult outpatients with borderline personality disorder symptoms. *Personality Disorders, 3*(4), 415–422. https://doi.org/10.1037/a0023703.

James, L. M., & Taylor, J. (2008). Revisiting the structure of mental disorders: Borderline personality disorder and the internalizing/externalizing spectra. *The British Journal of Clinical Psychology, 47*(4), 361–380. https://doi.org/10.1348/014466508X299691.

Koenigsberg, H. W., Harvey, P. D., Mitropoulou, V., Schmeidler, J., New, A. S., Goodman, M., et al. (2002). Characterizing affective instability in borderline personality disorder. *The American Journal of Psychiatry, 159*(5), 784–788. https://doi.org/10.1176/appi.ajp.159.5.784.

Kruedelbach, N., McCormick, R. A., Schulz, S. C., & Grueneich, R. (1993). Impulsivity, coping styles, and triggers for craving in substance abusers with borderline personality disorder. *Journal of Personality Disorders, 7*(3), 214–222. https://doi.org/10.1521/pedi.1993.7.3.214.

Lilienfeld, S. O., & Penna, S. (2001). Anxiety sensitivity: Relations to psychopathy, DSM-IV personality disorder features, and personality traits. *Journal of Anxiety Disorders, 15*(5), 367–393. https://doi.org/10.1016/S0887-6185(01)00070-6.

Linehan, M. (1993). *Cognitive-behavioral treatment of borderline personality disorder*. Guilford Press.

Muehlenkamp, J. J., Engel, S. G., Wadeson, A., Crosby, R. D., Wonderlich, S. A., Simonich, H., et al. (2009). Emotional states preceding and following acts of non-suicidal self-injury in bulimia nervosa patients. *Behaviour Research and Therapy, 47*(1), 83–87. https://doi.org/10.1016/j.brat.2008.10.011.

Nolen-Hoeksema, S. (1991). Responses to depression and their effects on the duration of depressive episodes. *Journal of Abnormal Psychology, 100*(4), 569–582. https://doi.org/10.1037/0021-843X.100.4.569.

Purdon, C. (1999). Thought suppression and psychopathology. *Behaviour Research and Therapy, 37*(11), 1029–1054. https://doi.org/10.1016/S0005-7967(98)00200-9.

Putnam, K. M., & Silk, K. R. (2005). Emotion dysregulation and the development of borderline personality disorder. *Development and Psychopathology, 17*(4), 899–925. https://doi.org/10.1017/S0954579405050431.

Reiss, S. (1991). Expectancy model of fear, anxiety, and panic. *Clinical Psychology Review, 11*(2), 141–153. https://doi.org/10.1016/0272-7358(91)90092-9.

Rosenthal, M. Z., Cheavens, J., Lejuez, C., & Lynch, T. (2005). Thought suppression mediates the relationship between negative affect and borderline personality disorder symptoms. *Behaviour Research and Therapy, 43*, 1173–1185. https://doi.org/10.1016/j.brat.2004.08.006.

Rosenthal, M. Z., Gratz, K. L., Kosson, D. S., Cheavens, J. S., Lejuez, C. W., & Lynch, T. R. (2008). Borderline personality disorder and emotional responding: A review of the research literature. *Clinical Psychology Review, 28*(1), 75–91. https://doi.org/10.1016/j.cpr.2007.04.001.

Ruocco, A., & Carcone, D. (2016). A Neurobiological Model of Borderline Personality Disorder: Systematic and Integrative Review. *Harvard Review of Psychiatry, 24*(5), 311–329. https://doi.org/10.1097/HRP.0000000000000123.

Sauer-Zavala, S., & Barlow, D. H. (2014). The case for borderline personality disorder as an emotional disorder: Implications for treatment. *Clinical Psychology: Science and Practice, 21*(2), 118–138. https://doi.org/10.1111/cpsp.12063.

Sauer-Zavala, S., Bentley, K. H., & Wilner, J. G. (2016). Transdiagnostic treatment of borderline personality disorder and comorbid disorders: A clinical replication series. *Journal of Personality Disorders, 30*(1), 35–51. https://doi.org/10.1521/pedi_2015_29_179.

Sauer, S. E., & Baer, R. A. (2009). Relationships between thought suppression and symptoms of borderline personality disorder. *Journal of Personality Disorders, 23*(1), 48–61. https://doi.org/10.1521/pedi.2009.23.1.48.

Sauer, S. E., & Baer, R. A. (2012). Ruminative and mindful self-focused attention in borderline personality disorder. *Personality Disorders: Theory, Research, and Treatment, 3*(4), 433–441. https://doi.org/10.1037/a0025465.

Selby, E. A., Anestis, M. D., Bender, T. W., & Joiner, T. E. J. (2009). An exploration of the emotional cascade model in borderline personality disorder. *Journal of Abnormal Psychology, 118*(2), 375–387. https://doi.org/10.1037/a0015711.

Shorey, R. C., Elmquist, J., Wolford-Clevenger, C., Gawrysiak, M. J., Anderson, S., & Stuart, G. L. (2016). The relationship between dispositional mindfulness, borderline personality features, and suicidal ideation in a sample of women in residential substance use treatment. *Psychiatry Research, 238*, 122–128. https://doi.org/10.1016/j.psychres.2016.02.040.

Vignarajah, B., & Links, P. S. (2009). The clinical significance of co-morbid post-traumatic stress disorder and borderline personality disorder: Case study and literature review. *Personality and Mental Health, 3*(3), 217–224. https://doi.org/10.1002/pmh.89.

Wegner, D. M., Schneider, D. J., Carter, S. R., & White, T. L. (1987). Paradoxical effects of thought suppression. *Journal of Personality and Social Psychology, 53*(1), 5–13. https://doi.org/10.1037/0022-3514.53.1.5.

Williams, A. D., & Moulds, M. L. (2007). The impact of ruminative processing on the development of intrusive memories. *Behaviour Change, 24*(2), 55–69. https://doi.org/10.1375/bech.24.2.55.

Wupperman, P., Neumann, C. S., & Axelrod, S. (2008). Do deficits in mindfulness underlie borderline personality features and core difficulties. *Journal of Personality Disorders, 22*(5), 466–482. https://doi.org/10.1521/pedi.2008.22.5.466.

Zanarini, M. C., Frankenburg, F. R., Dubo, E. D., Sickel, A. E., Trikha, A., Levin, A., et al. (1998). Axis I comorbidity of borderline personality disorder. *The American Journal of Psychiatry, 155*(12), 1733–1739. https://doi.org/10.1176/ajp.155.12.1733.

Further Reading

Andrews, G. (1990). Classification of neurotic disorders. *Journal of the Royal Society of Medicine, 83*(10), 606–607.

Andrews, G. (1996). Comorbidity and the general neurotic syndrome. *The British Journal of Psychiatry* (30), 76–84.

Bender, D. S., Dolan, R. T., Skodol, A. E., Sanislow, C. A., Dyck, I. R., McGlashan, T. H., et al. (2001). Treatment utilization by patients with personality disorders. *American Journal of Psychiatry, 158*(2), 295–302. https://doi.org/10.1176/appi.ajp.158.2.295.

Butler, A. C., Brown, G. K., Beck, A. T., & Grisham, J. R. (2002). Assessment of dysfunctional beliefs in borderline personality disorder. *Behaviour Research and Therapy, 40*(10), 1231–1240. https://doi.org/10.1016/S0005-7967(02)00031-1.

De Panfilis, C., Marchesi, C., Cabrino, C., Monici, A., Politi, V., Rossi, M., et al. (2012). Patient factors predicting early dropout from psychiatric outpatient care for borderline personality disorder. *Psychiatry Research, 200*(2–3), 422–429. https://doi.org/10.1016/j.psychres.2012.03.016.

Desrosiers, L., Saint-Jean, M., & Laporte, L. (2016). Model of engagement and dropout for adolescents with borderline personality disorder. *Sante Mentale Au Quebec*, *41*(1), 267–290.

Linehan, M. (2014). *DBT® skills training manual, second edition* (2 edition). New York: The Guilford Press.

Miller, W., & Rollnick, S. (2002). *Motivational interviewing: Preparing people for change* (2nd ed.). New York, NY: Guilford Press.

Miller, W. R., & Rollnick, S. (2012). Meeting in the middle: Motivational interviewing and self-determination theory. *The International Journal of Behavioral Nutrition and Physical Activity*, *9*(25). https://doi.org/10.1186/1479-5868-9-25.

Nock, M. K., & Prinstein, M. J. (2004). A functional approach to the assessment of self-mutilative behavior. *Journal of Consulting and Clinical Psychology*, *72*(5), 885–890. https://doi.org/10.1037/0022-006X.72.5.885.

Selby, E. A., & McHugh, R. K. (2013). Borderline personality disorder symptoms and treatment seeking over the past 12 months: An investigation using the National Comorbidity Survey–Replication (NCS-R). *The Journal of Clinical Psychiatry*, *74*(10), 1026–1028. https://doi.org/10.4088/JCP.12l08232.

Tyrer, P. (1989). *Classification of Neurosis* (1st ed.). Oxford, England: Wiley.

Wnuk, S., McMain, S., Links, P. S., Habinski, L., Murray, J., & Guimond, T. (2013). Factors related to dropout from treatment in two outpatient treatments for borderline personality disorder. *Journal of Personality Disorders*, *27*(6), 716–726. https://doi.org/10.1521/pedi_2013_27_106.

Wupperman, P., Neumann, C. S., Whitman, J. B., & Axelrod, S. R. (2009). The role of mindfulness in borderline personality disorder features. *The Journal of Nervous and Mental Disease*, *197*(10), 766–771. https://doi.org/10.1097/NMD.0b013e3181b97343.

CHAPTER

14

Plan Analysis and the Motive-Oriented Therapeutic Relationship

Franz Caspar

University of Bern, Department of Clinical Psychology and Psychotherapy, Bern, Switzerland

UNDERLYING CONCEPTS

General Position

The basic heuristic assumption of the Plan analysis approach can be formulated as follows: What survives phylo- and ontogenetically must be instrumental (=have an advantage) in the functioning of an individual, or a smaller or larger group of relevance for the individual. Only interpersonal and intrapsychic behaviours with an advantage become part of an individual's repertoire, become a red thread through his or her functioning and are therefore also relevant for a clinical understanding. Not everything is instrumental, but non-instrumental behaviours are rarely so intense, generalized, or persistent that they require special attention. Examples for exceptions can be found in forensic psychology, when for example a person commits manslaughter in an extreme situation, which will never come up again. Even then it is plausible that the behaviour serves an instrumental function, but it does not become part of the repertoire.

The notion of instrumentality must be differentiated though: The advantage may be non-conscious, it may be subjective only, it may be short term, it may exist from a limited perspective only, and it may have existed in the past only. All this may contribute to a situation in which a behaviour or strategy is currently maladaptive and leads or contributes to the problems that bring a patient into therapy or make the interaction with him or her difficult.

Case Formulation for Personality Disorders
https://doi.org/10.1016/B978-0-12-813521-1.00014-X

When carrying through such an instrumental perspective in developing an individual understanding of each case, one encounters a number of concrete challenges and questions. Clinical Plan analysis is primarily a practical approach helping to take an instrumental perspective in a consequent manner that is useful for guiding the therapeutic process. The set of theoretical assumptions on which it is based is deliberately limited to keep the approach slim and compatible with most common approaches of psychotherapy. Nevertheless, Plan analysis builds strongly on some concepts from basic psychology (social and emotion psychology, cognitive science, among others) which have proven their usefulness across subdisciplines of psychology.

Theoretical Concepts of Various Origin

Basic Pillar

The most important historical pillar and theory is the book 'Plans and the Structure of Behaviour', which Miller, Galanter, and Pribram (1960) wrote endeavouring to overcome the limitations of behaviourism. They emphasize the hierarchical structure of instrumental strategies mediating between concrete behaviour and its purpose, with general needs on top of the hierarchy. They also emphasize the non- or only partially conscious nature of most of these strategies: As conscious, deliberate control is slow and uses too much of the limited information processing resources, human functioning would be impossible if pervasive consciousness would be required. Their term 'Plan', which has been adopted for clinical Plan analysis (Grawe & Dziewas, 1978, pp. 27–49; Caspar & Grawe, 1982) is in a way misleading, as its everyday language meaning suggests consciousness and rationality. To underline the difference, Miller et al. (1960) have suggested to capitalize Plan, which is also adopted for clinical Plan analysis. An approach which has a common basis with Miller et al. but is more elaborated as far as the interplay of explicit, conscious and implicit, self-organized functioning (dual-process model) and as far as the adaptation of goals and norms are concerned, is Carver and Scheier's (1998) self-regulation approach.

Additional Basic Concepts

Beyond this, it is more typical for Plan analysis to be open for using theoretical concepts of various origins wherever they can contribute to the clinical understanding of patients, instead of referring to a limited set of theoretical concepts. This openness is in itself part of the conceptual basis of Plan analysis: Grawe has elaborated this mindset as 'General Psychotherapy' (Caspar, 2010a; Grawe, 2002): General psychotherapy means to acknowledge that no approach to psychotherapy is good enough to remain as it is. To have an optimal approach is not something that can actually be reached, but an asymptotic goal. General psychotherapy is therefore not a set of theoretical and practical concepts. It is rather a process in which existing approaches are continually complemented and changed. This should happen in such a way that all concepts and facts (including those which are incompatible with elements in the original approach) are considered that are relevant for the domain, for which an approach claims to be pertinent. This idealistic postulate includes not only using useful elements of all existing sound approaches to psychotherapy, but also the ever developing basis in psychology and other relevant fields. Following the motto of general psychotherapy renders it also more difficult to outline the theoretical base on limited space. To give an idea of the range:

- Classical social psychological models such as Argyle (1969) are used as a basis for social interaction; of course, the classical models such as reactance (Brehm & Brehm, 1981) are referred to in order to avoid reinventing the already known when dealing with resistance, or Nisbett and Wilson (1977) as a basis for implicit processing and the constructivist stance.
- Models from cognitive science deal with information processing on the side of the patient as well as the therapist. While concepts such as Plans, schemas, and scripts that are commonly used in Plan analysis are more traditional, the processes bringing about the phenomena described in these terms are seen in terms of parallel distributed processing, that is, connectionist or neural network models (Caspar, Rothenfluh, & Segal, 1992). Such models work much better than traditional models when it comes to understanding implicit processing, intuition, multiple constraint satisfaction, pattern recognition and completion, or dynamic processes, for example when patients with BPD flip back and forth between incompatible patters of seeking and rejecting closeness. As Plans are seen as largely non-conscious, or not requiring conscious steering, models that conceptualize human information processing as going on in parallel processes without the control of a homunculus-like central unit (like in traditional computers) are particularly attractive. Dual process models (e.g., Carver & Scheier, 2002) illuminate how deliberate, conscious and self-organized, implicit processes work together in the good, adaptive case, and compete with or sabotage each other in the bad, maladaptive case.

The neurobiological perspective helps to understand limitations (for example: the state of the brain of a cocain addict is not suitable for some otherwise useful therapeutic interventions; in some personality disorders, the brain may be impaired by strong interpersonal experiences in the past; Schulze, Schmahl, & Niedtfeld, 2016) and possibilities and requirements for therapy planning (for example that a high number of repetitions is usually needed to build up and strengthen new neuronal connections). In general, Plan analysis has – in line with the general psychotherapy's stance of including what is actually useful for the understanding of a patient and or therapy planning – a positive-critical stance towards neurobiology: It is expected to be useful and should therefore be included, yet an exaggerated optimism to what extent and how fast neurobiology will be useful for psychotherapy is not shared (Caspar, 2015).

Psychotherapeutic Approaches

As far as elements of psychotherapeutic approaches are concerned, it is assumed that different approaches have their strengths in illuminating different aspects of human functioning including the development and maintenance of mental problems. Plan analysis is broadly anchored in the learning theoretical basis of *behaviour therapy*: instrumental conditioning plays a crucial role in developing conscious and non conscious instrumental strategies that are at the heart of Plan analysis, and so does model learning. Classical conditioning is and remains important in the understanding of how emotions, cognitions, physiological sensations and behaviours are triggered, in particular in the implicit, self-organized part of self-regulation. Concepts of cognitive therapy are crucial in the understanding of the cognitive base, that is, premises of the instrumental functioning (for example 'unless I'm perfect, people will reject and abandon me'; 'the closer a relationship gets, the higher the risk of being exploited'), and beliefs may also have an instrumental function (e.g.,: negative assumptions prevent engagement and risk of disappointment).

The *interpersonal* approach (Kiesler, 1982, pp. 3–24; Leary, 1957; Sullivan, 1953) is generally a pillar of Plan analysis emphasizing past and current human relations. It is of particular importance as a basis for understanding how personality disorders develop as maladaptive strategies in malign interpersonal situations. A leading question in Plan analysis case formulations is where in their development of adaptive, flexible interpersonal relations a person got stuck.

The *humanistic approach* helps with understanding human needs and the development and maintenance of the self. For example, it helps to understand in a Plan analysis case formulation for what purpose an individual develops a negative self-image with the purpose of reducing dissonance with the fact that caregivers on which a child depends treat him or her badly.

Although concepts for transference phenomena, intrapsychic conflicts and mechanisms of maintaining consistency (Grawe, 2002) are not necessarily borrowed from the *psychodynamic approach*, it provides a detailed framework for considering such phenomena in the individual case formulation. Modern psychodynamic approaches have contributed specific aspects, for example the Mount-Zion approach the test concept (Silberschatz, 2010).

Finally (and not actually concluding the list of important approaches), the *systemic approach* helps when trying to understand the functioning of an individual in family and other systems. The instrumental perspective of Plan analysis fits very well with the functional perspective of this approach. In all cases, the systemic perspective which includes a transgenerational view, is considered, yet the weight it has varies from patient to patient.

Criteria for the Use of Concepts

Generally, it is the usefulness and not the veridicality of concepts that are the basis for integrating them into the theoretical basis of Plan analysis or for using them in the attempt of developing an individual model of a patient's functioning. This corresponds to the distinction by Foppa (1984) between perspective and explanatory theories: While for the latter empirical 'proofs' of their truth are the main criterion for their acceptance, for the former it is their usefulness, not only for practice but also for goals like theory-building or guiding research. It goes as a matter of course that there is a tendency that empirically false theories are less useful on a long run, but the two criteria are not too closely related.

Empirical evidence is definitely important when it comes to therapy planning: Interventions with good empirical evidence should be preferred, but as it is often unclear to what extent findings in randomized clinical trials are actually relevant for the individual case, it is always the use of the *best available* evidence by an informed clinician that matters in practice (Sackett, Rosenberg, Gray, Haynes, & Richardson, 1996).

METHODOLOGY

The Plan analysis approach includes a case formulation part and a therapy planning and performing part. Essential, in particular for personality disorders, is the concept of the Motive-Oriented Therapeutic Relationship, which builds on Plan analysis but adds essential elements. Plan analysis is clearly not comprehensively conveying how to conduct psychotherapy in general, but a case formulation approach, based on which ideas for therapy that is optimal for the individual case are derived.

How to Conduct Plan Analysis

Introduction

Plan analysis can be seen as a set of rules of how to see and analyze a patient's functioning. To introduce into the full set of rules including the dealing with special questions and problems requires an entire book, and in our experience the learning of using the method reliably takes about

2 weeks including exercises and comparisons with others to establish reliability. When a person eager to learn the method has already developed some of the necessary skills (such as observing nonverbal behaviour), time can be saved. When the goal is not to learn the full approach but just some of the essential heuristics, time needed is also shorter, and this is also the realistic goal for readers of this chapter. Whoever wants to learn more needs to invest more by working through the book (Caspar, 1995; German fourth edition: 2018) or getting access to workshops and supervision.

Procedure in Plan Analysis

The basic question of Plan analysis is 'what purpose, interpersonal or intrapsychic, conscious or not, does a particular behaviour or behavioural aspect serve?', or (looking top down in the instrumental hierarchy) 'what means are used in favour of a particular motive?' For example, on the level of therapeutic relationship, a patient with borderline personality disorder demonstrating a bleeding wrist may do so to get attention, behind a dependent patient's demonstration of helplessness may be the wish of making the therapist take more responsibility. On the level of symptoms and problems brought into therapy, an obsessive-compulsive disorder may have the instrumental function of distracting from traumatizing memories of being painfully bullied in school, or a depression may have the function of preventing a patient of having to make a difficult decision such as coming out versus not.

The patient's self-concept (how s/he sees the own functioning) is important, but the 'real functioning' (in quotation marks because the approach is consequently constructivist, meaning that whatever is inferred is seen as hypothetical) is what really matters. It is only partially represented in the self-concept. This real functioning is inferred from a broad range of sources (observation particularly of non-and paraverbal behaviour in therapy; reports by patient and others; emotional reactions and action tendencies of therapist and others, questionnaires, ...).

Fig. 14.1 shows a schematic Plan Structure, a 2-dimensional representation of hypotheses of a person's functioning. The furcation upwards stands for 'multiple determination', that is a behaviour or Subplan being guided by several superordined Plans. Often one Plan determines *what* is done (*talk to your boss* serves *seek a pay rise*) and another Plan *how* it is done (*talk with low voice, avoid eye contact* serves *avoid tension*), which can be maladaptive (as in this example) or adaptive (*chasing away a person who is trying to steal one's car* serves *prevent the car from being stolen* and *impress your new girlfriend*) which may make his shouting more impressive and effective. An example of multiple determination by three equally important Plans: Make a living, do something meaningful, and seek a profession which allows working half time in favour of the family. A means serving all three plans could be working as a psychotherapist.

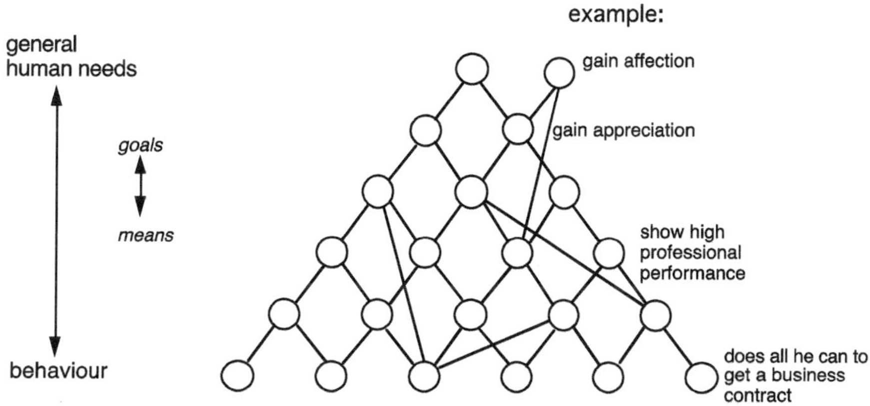

FIGURE 14.1 Two-dimensional Plan structure. The vertical dimension is used to show which elements are sub- versus superordinate, that is means versus purposes or goals. The horizontal dimension can be used freely to depict the elements that are functionally connected as near to each other as possible. The *circles* stand schematically for additional Plans not worked out here.

The downward furcations mean that a Plan includes several Subplans, which can be used in a complementary way, or alternately, depending on the situation. Plans which are important for a particular patient should have several such alternative Subplans to allow for effective, flexible functioning. It is typical though that this is not the case so that when the only or few available means are blocked the motive to which they serve can't be satisfied, and/or the one or few available possibilities are used even when they are not adapted to the situation and therefore ineffective and/or full of negative side effects.

Behaviours are formulated in the indicative form (speaks with a soft voice), Plans are formulated in the imperative form, directed towards oneself ('make the therapist help you', NOT 'help me'). In our experience, the imperative helps avoiding elements like 'anxiety' in the Plan structure of which it is hard to understand how it is instrumentally related to other Plans. 'Stays home' as means for 'avoid anxiety', or 'maintain anxiety' as means for 'prevent your partner from leaving you' expresses much clearer how the instrumentality is meant.

The common and most important way of inferring Plans is bottom up: observing conspicuous behaviour and then inferring what hypothetical purpose it may serve. Instrumental interpretations are always speculative. A decision that has to be made very frequently is whether the content of a patient statement should be taken at face value (e.g.,: patient reports that he takes care of her old mother: take care of your mother→be a good daughter, avoid guilt feelings, or: reports that she takes good care of her mother→make burnout understandable, or: demonstrate to the therapist that you are a good person).

The rule of substantiating each Plan in a structure by multiple observations helps preventing too arbitrary conclusions, and comparing inferences made by others in a group practising Plan analysis is a precious corrective. In research applications we have compared the agreement between persons analyzing the same case, and, while it is hard to imagine how two individuals doing information processing of that complexity could agree 100%, the agreement has most often turned out to be satisfactory (between 60% and 90%; Caspar, 2018). In practice, however, one should not one-sidedly look for confirming but also for disconfirming or differentiating information (e.g., 'avoid tension' is formulated in a general way, but then it becomes evident that the patient does not avoid tension at home. Therefore: modification to 'avoid tension at work').

A very important source of information are emotions. They must be understandable from the perspective of patient Plans, and – the other way round – they provide information about patient Plans. For the most important patient emotions it is recommended to consider four aspects, which don't claim to be original, they rather reflect common concepts for emotion and emotion regulation. After defining the emotion to be analyzed (not too trivial; complex emotions bit by bit), the more narrow or broader situation, foreground as well as background, is described. Then the four aspects follow, which are:

1. Which Plans are *blocked/threatened* in the case of negative, and *furthered* in the case of positive Emotions. The blocking may come from outside, but also be internal, based on conflicts between Plans. Blockages are the more relevant the more important the blocked Plans are and the fewer alternatives are available.
2. Which Plans *determine the kind of the experienced emotion*? Often an emotion that would be plausible based on the situation and the affected Plans is not actually observed or reported. In that case we look for Plans prohibiting or impairing these plausible emotions (e.g., 'avoid being aggressive', more typical for women, or 'avoid weak feelings', more typical for men) and by this render other emotions more probable. In Emotion Focused Therapy (Greenberg, 2012) this process is designated change from primary to secondary emotions. This is an important aspect, as this change of emotions makes them hard to understand and deal with for patients, thus contributing to patient problems.
3. *Coping and avoidance* Plans: Negative Emotions are normally avoided or down regulated in many ways: Solving the problems which cause them, avoiding situations, awareness of problems and emotions, use of substances, intrapsychic regulation (as elaborated by psychodynamic approaches), seeking help including therapy. Actions serving the dealing with emotions can be adaptive or maladaptive

and in the latter case be more problematic than the original emotion. Positive emotions are not avoided but sought – at least in general. But it is not uncommon that also positive emotions have to be coped with, for example avoiding that they develop prematurely or get too strong, in order to avoid disappointment or good feelings one does not believe to deserve.

4. Plans for which the emotion has an instrumental function: Given the instrumental perspective of Plan analysis this is an obvious question to ask, but it comes last to avoid one-sided focus on this question. Instrumental functions of emotions can be interpersonal (binding a partner with an agoraphobia or with the despair of a dependent person) or intrapsychic (avoiding a difficult decision by paralyzing oneself with depressed mood). A general clinical experience is that no emotion is so threatening and painful that it could not prevent an even worse emotion.

After giving the emotion to be analyzed a name and describing the situation, at least the first aspect (blocking/threatening or favouring) needs to be filled. The other three aspects need to be considered but are not necessarily relevant for every emotion. Once one has acquired proficiency in relating emotions to Plans, the ideal is to let a background programme running all the time, which checks also less important emotions continually whether the situation x the so far known Plan structure let the reported or observed emotion appear plausible. Such a background programme does not use a lot of information processing capacity, but raises attention once the check says that the resulting emotion is not as one would expect based on the known factors going into the equation.

The process of gathering information and generating first tentative hypotheses for Plan analysis begins early: knowing that the patient in intake interview next week suffers from anorexia lets me speculate based on default that among her interpersonal motives autonomy and control might dominate. When I see a patient for the first time in the waiting room, bent down, head bowed, I may wonder whether this nonverbal expression is instrumental for making me engaged and sparing at the same time. Explicit hypotheses are typically formed early, but with a high readiness to look for disconfirming and differentiating information as well as alternative interpretations. Plan analysis begins in the back of a therapist's mind already parallel to the first conversation and ideally first tentative conclusions have an impact on the therapist's Motive-Oriented relational behaviour already very early in the contact. A first Plan structure focusing on the therapeutic relationship should be inferred already after the first session, or even before one has met the patient for the first time in case the intake interview has been done by a colleague in an institution, and a video recording is available. After no later than 4–5 sessions a more comprehensive analysis including hypotheses about the development and maintenance of the patient's problems should be done. Such an analysis is usually a basis for much of the therapy, but new information may arise any time, suggesting an adaptation of the analysis.

A therapist very experienced in Plan analysis who observes intensely and generates hypotheses parallel to talking to the patient should not take more than 1h for a patient of medium complexity. A therapist still learning the method will need much more in the beginning, but this is mainly investment into the learning process. An important positive feature of Plan analysis is that it is very flexible in what is focused upon and in what degree of detail various aspects of the patients' functioning are analyzed. As a result, also time invested into an individual case can vary enormously. For a patient with a standard agoraphobia and without major problems in the therapeutic relationship a therapist may need little, for a patient with unique and complex problems and challenging behaviour in the therapeutic relationship it may be wise to invest much more. While experienced therapists become much faster and more efficient, it remains wise to consider a finding in general research on expertise that experienced professionals invest more into analyzing a problem in depth as a basis for effective action (Glaser & Chi, 1988).

The use of prototypical Plan Analyses can speed up individual analysis considerably: For several diagnostic and other groups, analyses have been made and compared for a number of patients and Plans that are very common for the respective group have ben distilled out of these analyses. For example, maintaining and repairing self-esteem is a very typical interpersonal motive with patients suffering from Schizophrenia, and this is also a crucial issue in the therapeutic relationship. For borderline patients a therapist does not need to start over with developing hypotheses about the purpose of cutting herself for every new patient with borderline personality disorder. A therapist has a few defaults, that is expectations (such as getting attention, reducing tension, or punishing herself) based on own experience and/or literature, ideally explicit prototypical Plan Analyses (Caspar, 2018). Such defaults may, of course, not be imposed on a patient, they are hypotheses of which the fit and validity has to be checked carefully for every individual patient. For example getting attention as a motive for cutting is much more plausible when a patient cuts herself on the ward and demonstrates the blood immediately than when she does it at home over the weekend and nobody cares for 2 days.

Model for Psychological Problems

Psychological or mental problems are seen as consequences of maladaptive strategies which were most often learned in an infancy spent under less than ideal conditions. In many cases it is even justified to speak of survival strategies. Different psychopathological models (behavioural, interpersonal, humanistic, psychodynamic, and systemic) are more or less useful in illuminating different aspects of such functioning, which have variable weight depending on the patient and the problem. It is assumed, that, of course, the neurobiological basis plays a role in co-determining abilities, thresholds in emotion regulation, and more. It is, however, hard to imagine, that within the next few years a major part of the premises in a psychotherapist's decision-making in practice would be determined by neurobiological concepts (Caspar, 2015).

Plan analysis is a method for analyzing and representing the current state, that is the resulting instrumental strategies. There are some guiding questions of particular relevance:

- How are the problems related to the Plan structure?
  There are two not mutually excluding possibilities: The problems are side effects of instrumental strategies, or they have themselves an instrumental function. An example for the former are depressive states resulting from an agoraphobic withdrawal with a loss of social contacts and other possibilities of satisfying important needs (withdrawal as coping strategy to prevent anxiety). As far as personality disorders are concerned, it is hard to imagine a problem that is part of a particular disorder and could not be seen as a side effect of instrumental strategies: Anxiety of loss and postponing of needs as a result of desperately trying to please and get care and attention in dependent PD, rejection by others and inefficient way of daily life resulting from sticking to rigid behaviour in obsessive-compulsive PD, isolation and exhausting concerns as side effects of cautionary/protective strategies in paranoid PD, and so on. Often, the strategies have been developed for their short-term positive consequences (which may have lead to a positive balance between positive and negative effects in childhood and youth), but the problems came as long term consequences. Because patients do often explicitly believe to have good reasons for continuing with their instrumental behaviour, or it 'just happens' in a self-organized way, because it has been reinforced so many times, it may be hard to give up the behaviour in spite of the negative consequences.
  The latter possibility, that the problem has itself an instrumental function, is also common in PDs: histrionic patients get attention, dependent patients attention and support, avoidant and obsessive behaviours lead to relief from anxieties, schizoid behaviour helps maintaining a safe distance, passive-aggressive behaviour helps reducing internal tension and taking responsibility for problems, and so on. Also within a PD diagnostic group, variation is possible, it is therefore necessary to analyze each individual case.

- Where and for what reason are the structures rigid?
  This is the second important question, which is based on the belief that unless there are problematic developments or blockades to development in a life, an individual will naturally develop sufficiently rich instrumental interpersonal and intrapsychic strategies to deal with most situations. The typical situation in which patients seek therapy is different: They are stuck because they had a limited repertoire to begin with, they were able to manage more or less, and then change situation blocks the only or few strategies they have for satisfying their most important needs. Sometimes the change is dramatic, such as the loss of a person (or animal) or job. However, nothing dramatic needs to happen: By getting older a person may realize that possibilities he or she has believed to have are diminishing, children get older and leave home. By this, important Plans without much alternatives are blocked, and this leads to negative emotions. Sometimes a person can de-block him- or herself by developing alternatives, sometimes friends or relatives can help, but often the difficult interpersonal behaviour related to PD's leads also to a limited social network, or limited readiness and ability to provide social support in existing networks.

Constructing Therapeutic Action

Plan analysis and its emphasis on differentiated individual case formulations comes along with a strong conviction that optimal psychotherapy – therapy reaching also patients with less than ideal preconditions on all levels, and therapy resulting in a maximum of lasting change – requires an individualized procedure. There are cases with a good fit to standardized programmes, mainly cases without comorbidity and major challenges in the therapeutic relationship. In such cases we should use standardized programmes. More often, however, individualization on the level of intervening with the patient's symptoms and underlying problems as well as on the level of the therapeutic relationship are required. An alternative term for such individualization is responsiveness and it seems that the awareness for the limitations of standardized, manualized procedures is increasing. There has been much debate about this, and space does not allow to go into the debate in detail (Addis, Cardemil, Duncan, & Miller, 2006, pp. 131–160; Caspar, Herpertz, & Lieb, 2016; Norcross, 2002). Instead our favoured model for the construction of therapeutic action will be introduced briefly. A basic assumption is that in reality when individualizing, experienced, good therapists do not use (algorithmically) manualized procedures and then adapt them to the individual patient, on a closer look, they rather construct their behaviour anew in every moment. This does not mean to reinvent the wheel over and over, it is rather a process

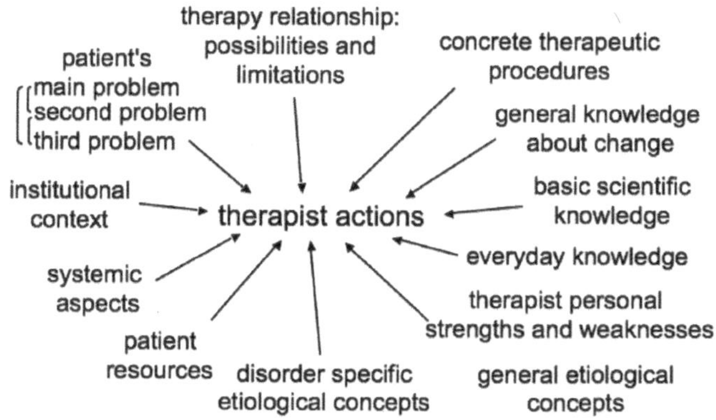

FIGURE 14.2 Constructing therapist action as process of parallel multiple constraint satisfaction: influencing aspects (the brackets connecting the problems indicate that typically problems interact).

of multiple constraint satisfaction resulting in coherent action. Among the constraints may also be larger elements of disorder-specific etiological concepts or even of standardized manuals, but they are not applied but rather utilized and embedded in a heuristic, flexible way.

Fig. 14.2 shows the aspects which are considered, and the list is not necessarily complete.

On the left upper side are the problems, usually several, often interacting, in particular with PD comorbidity. In addition, there are challenges and possibilities in the therapeutic relationship. As far as concrete therapeutic procedures are concerned, even standardized programmes can be used, but only to give ideas, how one could proceed with a particular disorder or type of problem. The left upper side is what is analyzed and described in a case formulation (leaving aside therapy planning if this is part of a case formulation approach). The other aspects, we have to trust, are self explaining.

While the model may look complicated, one has to consider that

- not all aspects are equally important for every patient,
- for therapists in training the supervisor takes some responsibility that no important aspect is neglected, and most importantly,
- experienced therapist perform most of such a construction process in a rather intuitive way, paying (once they have made the case formulation) deliberate attention only to aspects related to which difficulties arise. Multiple constraint satisfaction is actually a task that is performed better in a largely intuitive than in a conscious, step-by-step manner (Betsch & Glöckner, 2010).

The essential idea is that in one intervention all relevant aspects are – to the greatest extent possible – considered simultaneously. Most importantly, mainly for the treatment of PD: Although some interventions may have the sole or dominant purpose in the therapeutic relationship, furthering as opposed to stressing the relationship is a goal (constraint) in all interventions. For example, when introducing into Jacobson muscle relaxation a therapist would not ask a patient with a strong control need to close his/her eyes but to seek a blank spot on the ceiling, the way a homework assignment is given to an autonomy seeking person is different compared to a structure seeking person, when treating a schizoid PD patient, one would intervene with a neutral rather than a too warm/close voice, and so on.

This model of therapist action allows an individual case conceptualization, which should – not necessarily with all details but the essential features – be in a therapist's mind all the time, to have a maximal impact on the therapeutic procedure. Or in other words, such a model makes obvious how much a detailed individual case conceptualization is absolutely essential. Empirically it has been found that psychotherapists using Plan analysis case conceptualizations conduct much richer therapies with a wider range of techniques than others (Grawe, Caspar, & Ambühl, 1990, pp. 294–315). This is particularly relevant for the therapy with PD patients: it has been assumed that technical flexibility is particularly important with these therapies (Fernandez-Alvarez, Clarkin, Del Carmen Salgueiro, & Critchfield, 2006, pp. 203–218; Norcross, 2002).

The Motive-Oriented Therapeutic Relationship (MOTR)

The therapeutic relationship is at the core of the treatment of PD. The concept for deriving prescriptive ideas from Plan analysis case conceptualizations is therefore a particularly precious part of the Plan analysis approach. Historically, Plan analysis has actually developed in the late 70s in an endeavour to make 'difficult patients', of whom many would nowadays get a PD diagnosis, amenable to psychotherapy. 'Prescriptive' is an important word in this context. We all know that the quality of the therapeutic relationship is in solid positive correlation with outcome, but a good relationship quality is not an ingredient, but already a product of an interaction with a patient, in which a therapist must have done something right already. The patient's contribution has received more attention recently (Bohart & Wade, 2013, pp. 219–257) but will not be elaborated here. So the question is: What are the ingredients for a good relationship?

There are only a few empirically supported prescriptive concepts suggesting how to bring about a good relationship, and Motive-Oriented Therapeutic relationship (MOTR) (Caspar, 2008, pp. 527–558) is one of them. The concept is based on two principles:

1. Even problematic behaviour in the therapeutic relationship is guided by unproblematic motives. Unproblematic means in this context: not limiting the therapist unduly in how it would be promising to

intervene with the problems for which the patient seeks help. It also means not requiring the therapist to do something which would be beyond the normal professional limits. Unproblematic refers to the pure motive, nor the problematic means currently used for it. If the motives one could think of are still problematic, one would go higher in the hierarchy of the Plan structure until one arrives at an unproblematic level (but not higher than that, in the interest of been as individual and specific as possible in a hierarchy that gets all the more general the higher one goes).

2. If acceptable motives get satisfied or even over satisfied independent of the (problematic) means used for them, a patient does need to continue to use the problematic strategies. He or she may continue the behaviour to some extent because of being used to it, but usually less frequently and intensely, and often enough, the behaviour stops immediately if the therapist has found a non-contingent way to satisfy the motive. For this, he or she needs to understand the behaviour and its purpose well. Plan analysis is an ideal basis for this. In addition, the therapist needs to find a proactive way for satisfying the underlying motive. Once the functioning is understood, the therapist would not wait until the problem behaviour shows again and then react to it, but figure out ways of satisfying the motive independent of the problem behaviour and as non-contingent to it as possible.

With borderline BPD it can be illustrated that giving attention to a patient can vary much in character. When patients use strategies for getting attention such as cutting themselves, it is hard not to pay attention, for example, to a bleeding wrist. But this is not the pure, honest, deep attention a BPD patient might be desperately looking for. He or she knows that this is blackmailed attention, and as soon as he or she gets it, it has no real value. This prevents the need from really being satisfied and renders the patient insatiable. The contingent relation between problem behaviour and attention reinforces the former nevertheless instrumentally, and the attempt to not reinforce it at least part of the time leads to intermittent reinforcement, which makes the problem behaviour all the more obstinate.

A standard example of dealing with a patient who complains and wines all the time can be found elsewhere (Caspar, 2007, pp. 251–289), here we have an example of hostile behaviour, which may be passive-aggressive critique, staying away from therapy, openly attacking the therapist verbally, or else. How to deal with such behaviour? The MOTR concept tells us to look for plausible motives to which the hostile behaviour may serve. We speculate that it may serve to impede therapy, to keep the therapist in a distance, or to test the therapist's resilience with stress. All these motives will probably still be considered problematic by readers in the sense of making therapy difficult or at least challenging. So the rule is to go a step

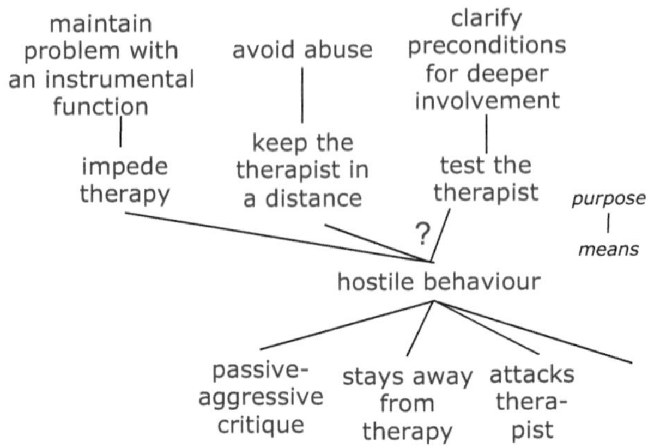

FIGURE 14.3 Plan analysis of patient hostility: multiple forms of appearance, various motives.

higher (see Fig. 14.3). For the hypothetical motive of impeding therapy we may find the superordinate motive of maintaining a problem which has an instrumental function for the patient's balance (for example preventing him from being abandoned by a partner, or being overstrained at work), for keeping the therapist in a distance the motive of avoiding abuse (a patient may have experienced with a previous therapist), and for testing the therapist the motive of clarifying the preconditions for a deeper involvement: 'is this therapist strong and patient enough to accompany me through a deeper, more challenging phase of therapy?'.

It is obvious that there is no universal trick to cope with hostile patient behaviour. Every advice (except for going for a analysis of motives) will be right for some cases and not or dead wrong for others. When the patient has reason to maintain a problem, it may appear as if the hostility is a relationship issue, but originally it is not, and a solution lies in finding alternative means for maintaining the patient's functioning and reassuring the patient that one will not cut the branch on which she or he sits before one has made a ladder available. When a patient wants to prevent being abused by the therapist, this is a relationship issue and the solution is in encouraging an open expression of how much distance feels comfortable, metacommunicating, and, on a longer run, providing corrective experiences. In the case of testing the therapist, hostility certainly does not feel comfortable but can also be as a good sign that the therapist has done so much right so far that the patient considers a deeper involvement. The therapist should show that he is unimpressed, may even show humour, and continues to be a reliable partner in the therapeutic process.

For years – even decades by now, MOTR has proven to be clinically useful. While it is less difficult to find adequate therapist behaviour responding to unproblematic patient behaviour and the motives guiding it, the full power of the MOTR approach shows when it comes to responding to problematic behaviour and the motives guiding it. Impressive pre-post treatment effect sizes, very good ratings of the relationship, and very low drop out rates even with novices in our postgraduate therapist training, can be related to MOTR, and suggest that these concepts can be conveyed also to inexperienced therapists (Wolfer, 2016). How about more rigorous empirical evidence?

In an RCT comparing two forms of broad-spectrum behaviour therapy based on Plan analysis case conceptualisations versus based on a traditional learning theoretical behaviour analysis and client Centred Therapy (Grawe et al., 1990, pp. 294–315) the Plan analysis based therapies were clearly superior in all criteria related to process from both, patient and therapist perspectives, including the therapeutic relationship, and several criteria related to outcome. Although there were several differences between the three forms of therapy, the positive effects have largely been attributed to the complementary therapeutic relationship, a predecessor of MOTR. In a study by Caspar, Grossmann, Unmüssig, and Schramm (2005) the spontaneous, not MOTR-informed, video recorded relational behaviour of psychotherapist treating inpatients with depression has been evaluated for therapist responsiveness in the sense of MOTR. Plan Analyses of the patients have been made and then it has been rated to what extent the interventions were complementary to the patient Plans. Positive correlations have been found between complementarity and outcome assessed by patient rating of improvement (.513 with SCL-90,.386 with BDI; even higher for nonverbal complementarity). Correlations with IIP scales show that therapists behaved more complementarily where it was the easiest: with friendly patients, less with hostile and cold patients.

The most important study on MOTR has been done by Kramer, Kolly et al. (2014): the effects of using MOTR has been shown in an add on design with BPD patients in a 10-session treatment with psychodynamically oriented treatment as usual. When therapists have been trained in MOTR they were able to bring about better outcomes in a number of outcome variables than without using this prescriptive concept for the therapeutic relationship.

More recently, we have been able to demonstrate, that MOTR does not simply mean to be nice with a patient and to avoid tension at any price. Patients do not only have Plans to have a nice relationship with the therapist and to prevent the therapist from threatening interventions, they also want to change with a competent therapist. So it is not a surprise that we found the best outcomes with therapists who did confront patients with important issues thus increasing tension in therapy, while maintaining a sufficiently safe, complementary base in the relationship (Figlioli, Caspar, & Berger, 2013; Möseneder, Figlioli, & Caspar, 2017).

CLINICAL CASE WITH PERSONALITY DISORDER

There are several cases with Plan Analyses reported in the literature, some in English (Caspar, 2010a,b; Kramer, 2009) and some in English and related to personality disorders (Berthoud, Kramer, Caspar, & Pascual-Leone, 2015; Caspar & Ecker, 2008; Kramer, Berthoud, Keller, & Caspar, 2014). As a whole they give a more representative impression of Plan analysis than an individual case report like the following could and are therefore also recommended for complementing reading. Space limitations do not allow to illustrate all relevant aspects of the Plan analysis and MOTR concepts in this single case.

Case Example

Urs is a young IT systems analyst. He comes to our outpatient clinic for the treatment of a social phobia and has also been diagnosed for a comorbid narcissistic personality disorder. He sees the social phobia as disadvantageous not only in private but also in professional contacts, and experiencing himself as avoidant and helpless in contact situations is not compatible with his narcissistic fantasies of being a great entertainer privately and a networking champion in professional contexts.

He had originally planned to fight social phobia with deep brain stimulation, but a psychiatrist he had seen convinced him that this technology would not work with social phobia and is certainly not ready for the market, so he recommended psychotherapy. Urs had accepted this and searched the internet for social phobia and its treatment. He has found a book by a British psychoanalyst which seemed to make a lot of sense to him. Actually, he has contacted the author of that book and asked whether it would be possible to see him for a therapy. The answer was yes, but Urs would have been required to move to GB for at least 2 years. This was not feasible, but he regretted this a lot because, as he said, the author seemed particularly competent for his problems, of which he emphasized how special some features are. He then saw a therapist in Switzerland a couple of times but did not engage in a real therapy, because the therapist did not sufficiently appreciate the concept of this British author. Urs looked for alternatives and so he came to our clinic, actually by a personal recommendation to me as director of the clinic.

In the intake, he took a lot of space verbally (taking a lot of time describing things in detail and looking for special formulations) as well as nonverbally (sitting diagonally in his chair with the right arm over the backrest, head high) and paraverbally (emphasizing, elaborate language including psychological terminology, talking much without letting the therapist in). His problems he describes in many details as 'very special' and mentions also that social phobia is incapacitating. Fig. 14.4 shows a somewhat simplified hypothetical Plan structure.

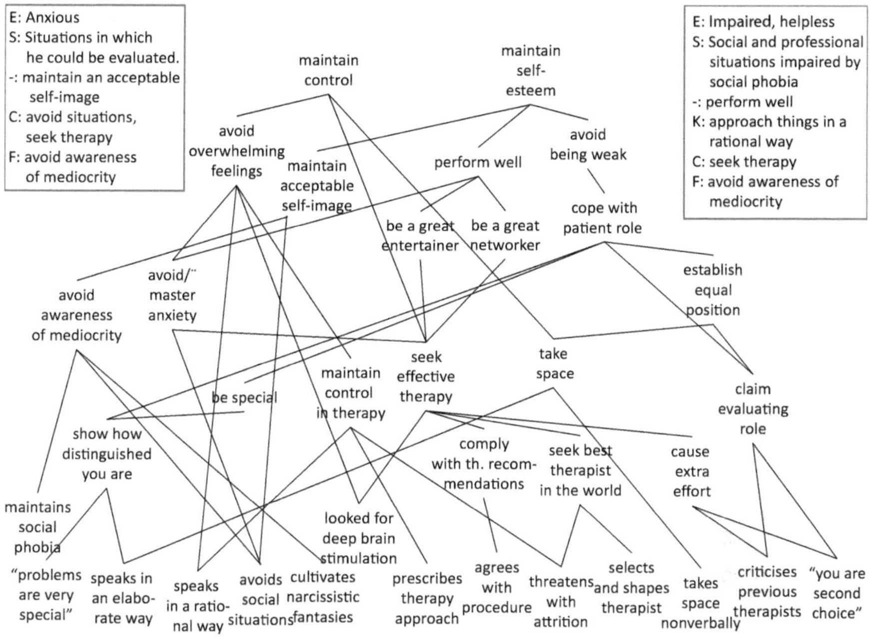

FIGURE 14.4 Plan structure for Urs (Social Phobia and Narcissistic Personality disorder), simplified.

A first impression of such a structure may be that is very complex and hard to get into. It is important to understand that like with EEG curves and X-ray pictures, complexity is much reduced as soon as one gains familiarity with the Plan analysis method, and if one develops such a structure oneself as a therapist step-by-step, it does not seem complex anymore anyway. Generally, you are reminded of our constructivist stance, meaning that all elements of a Plan structure are hypothetical and open to revision.

Urs' dominating needs seem be control and the maintenance of self-esteem. His social phobia results from threats to a fragile self-esteem in situations in which he fears negative evaluations. Here he is confronted with the dilemma that the impairment of his potential performance by his social phobia means additional threat to his self-esteem, but it is also a threat to try to get rid of his social phobia by psychotherapy, as he needs to admit that he has a problem and possibly to take risks related to psychotherapy, such as being exposed to stronger negative emotions. Deep brain stimulation has appeared temporarily as a way of taking a bath without getting wet as far as approaching his problems psychologically is concerned. Once he has decided to engage in psychotherapy he tries to maintain control by setting the stage his way: A rather rational approach in which he determines the concepts; while having to admit that he has problems, he has at least very special problems; he claims an equal position with the therapist; he takes a lot of space in the therapy room verbally as well as nonverbally. One could say that in a very narcissistic way he is as little a 'poor dependent patient' as possible. Experienced colleagues who have seen a video of the intake interview have expressed that they could not work with such a patient.

It may appear clear that a precondition for work with this patient is to embrace the British approach that has impressed him so much, and indeed he offers to lend the book to the therapist. Interestingly, however, when the therapist asked what the patient had particularly liked about the approach, the answer remained pretty vague. This nourished that suspicion that it was rather the wish to control therapy by proposing an approach than the concrete content of the approach which mattered.

Much of the structure, we assume, is understandable while readers go through the structure. One important aspect with a question mark is whether the social phobia –while credibly causing suffering and thus being something he wanted to get rid of – had also to some extent the instrumental function of justifying a lack of professional progress, as its incapacitating effects were also an excuse protecting self-esteem.

Let's quickly turn to emotions: Two of them are briefly analyzed on the upper left and right sides of the Plan Structure (where there is usually some space left; a separate sheet could, of course, be used as well). One is the emotion of **anxiety** in situations (S) in which he could be evaluated, as it is typical for social phobia. The threatened Plan (–) is maintaining an acceptable self-image. As far as Planes determining the kind of emotion (K) are concerned, anxiety is a plausible emotion given his structure and the situation: no need for explanation by Plans determining the resulting emotion. He copes (C) by avoiding situations and more recently by seeking therapy. There is a tentative hypothesis that an instrumental function of social phobia may be to have an excuse for suboptimal performance and thus avoiding an awareness of mediocrity.

A second is the emotion of feeling **impaired**, with some traces of helplessness. He experiences this in social and professional situations (S) when he is impaired by social phobia, for example resulting in missing chances due to avoidance. His Plan of performing well is blocked (–) this way. There is a Plan of approaching things in a rational way which lead usually to a rather cognitive feeling impaired instead of more emotional feeling helpless (which he feels only sometime and only 'a little bit'). Coping (C) is partly maladaptive avoiding (and some drinking), his new, adaptive approach is seeking therapy.

For therapy planning, a crucial question was whether an effort to impress the patient as a competent therapist by explaining and strongly recommending a cbt approach with much exposure might work. At first, there might be the impression that there is no alternative to following his favoured psychoanalytic approach in one way or another. But his structure offers an opening with his wish (determined by narcissistic as well as change-oriented wishes) to have a super competent therapist, a property of whom may be that he dares to counter the patient ideas. This would have to be based, we thought, on an intense nourishing of his narcissistic and control needs by not missing any chance of showing appreciation and giving him control by asking for agreement wish every little step. In addition, a deal was proposed: He was asked to comply with the therapist's – as far as concrete interventions are concerned – cbt-oriented suggestions (arguing also with empirical evidence) but the therapist promised to go into the psychodynamic approach thereafter to the extent that the patient wished.

As far as the planning of the motive-oriented therapeutic relationship is concerned it seems not necessary to list all patient behaviours which would be impeding a therapist or even threatening for an insecure therapist, and certainly wasting a lot of patient attention and energy for his narcissistically coloured and controlling interpersonal behaviour in the therapy situation. However, going up in the hierarchy of motives guiding the problematic behaviours, one would find 'maintain control in therapy', 'maintain an acceptable self-image', 'claim equal position', 'seek effective therapy', and 'be special'. All these motives seem acceptable in that a competent and self-confidential therapist has no major difficulties working with such a patient. If something, it is the patient behaviours that is problematic. According to the second principle of MOTR it was expected that this behaviour would become less intense and possibly even disappear to the extent that the therapist succeeds satisfying the hypothetical motives. This is actually what happened. The patient remained pretty narcissistic, but not in a way that would have made the treatment difficult for the therapist nor distracted the patient too much from the process of change. He agreed with the deal proposed by the therapist and was very compliant and engaged in the therapeutic procedure, nourished by the therapist's appreciation for his engagement and even admiration for his courage in exposing himself to the most difficult sociophobic situations one could imagine. When the therapy resulted in amazing progress with the social phobia, the therapist reminded the patient that now he was ready to deal with this British approach. It turned out that the patient had lost his interest in it. This is –aside from the fact that it was a successful case – the reason why I like this case so much. When asked whether it would be necessary to read and appreciate this book, most therapists who have seen the intake interview said 'of course'. But it was not necessary and this is plausibly because our understanding of this patient's functioning and the resulting MOTR were correct and powerful.

An important issue in therapy planning is always the dealing with a potential instrumental function of the problem. In this case it was the suspicion that offering an excuse for suboptimal functioning may be a factor maintaining the social phobia. This was reason enough to use every occasion to convey to the patient that it is rather the ability to accept one' imperfection than apparent perfection that is admirable. It remained unclear whether it was an effect of this message or whether our tentative hypothesis about this instrumental function was simply wrong: In any case, the was no indication that the patient held to his social phobia in any way.

RESEARCH

Research showing the advantage of using explicit case conceptualizations is generally rare (Eells, Lombart, Kendjelic, Turner, & Lucas, 2005). The study described earlier (Grawe et al., 1990, pp. 294–315) is one of only few experimental studies showing such an advantage. The study by Kramer, Kolly et al. (2014) demonstrates the advantages of Plan analysis based MOTR in the therapy of BPD patients. Therapies based on Plan analysis have repeatedly shown to be effective, but except for the Grawe et al. (1990, pp. 294–315) and the Kramer, Kolly et al. (2014) studies not in experimental designs. Regularly found large pre-post effect sizes and low drop out rates even for novices with unselected, usually (often with PD) comorbid patients (14%; Wolfer, 2016) contribute nevertheless contribute to our confidence that Plan analysis is clinically useful.

As far as reliability is concerned whenever Plan analysis is used as a research tool on the level of master thesis studies and above, a check on interrater agreement is compulsory. Over the years dozens of such comparisons have been made with usually satisfactory results (Caspar, 2018). There were instances, however, with too low agreement in which case Plan Analyses, although time-consuming, were disposed of.

TRAINING

In our own postgraduate psychotherapy training programme, there is great weight on building therapy on a good understanding of the patients' functioning as a basis for an individualized, responsive procedure. Participants learn Plan analysis early in their training, those who have done their master studies in Bern have gradual exposure to the concept already in several lectures and seminars. This can, however, be compensated by those coming from other universities by reading. Normally it takes two 2-day workshops which include small-group exercises to acquire some familiarity with the approach. Such workshops are also conducted as part of postgraduate training programmes in other institutions, and exercises that can be completed by everyone are described in Caspar (1995 in English and 2018 in German).

It is crucial that a number of comprehensive analyses are executed, which is normally done for video recorded cases, so that the interpretations and solutions by several analyzers or subgroups can be compared. As there is never one clearly right solution, such comparisons are at the core of learning Plan analysis. When all others have seen and used conspicuous nonverbal patient behaviour and oneself has not, this is reason to pay more attention to the nonverbal. If one utters often interpretations that the others can't follow, this is reason to become more cautious with interpretations. When an analyzing person always sees narcissistic structures which the others don't see, this is reason to reflect about one's own relation to narcissism. Unless one has built up experience with several Plan Analyses, one does not get into a range of good cost-benefit, because the overall investment of time for each analysis is still determined by investment for learning as opposed of skilled performing. In addition, the overall investment into an individual analysis is largely determined by the degree to which general clinical expertise, for example in observing and interpreting nonverbal behaviour, in utilizing previous cases for developing quick (although always cautious) hypotheses about instrumentality, and so on. It also depends on general expertise in conducting psychotherapy, to what extent a therapist has free information processing resources to begin with Plan analysis based observing, generating of hypothesis, and monitoring of the effects of interventions. On this it depends to a large extent how much extra time a therapist needs outside sessions for Plan Analyses.

Most satisfactory are workshops and supervisions of experienced therapists who have acquired all the regular clinical skills throughout their practice, but are stuck with patients. They know the limits of what they have thought and done so far. When Plan analysis and MOTR helps to find (sometimes surprising) solutions for their cases, this is as convincing as it gets. Colleagues who had some exposure to the concepts in the past without practising it sufficiently, report that it took them a second or third round to develop an in depth understanding of the approach. There are clearly various levels on which the approach can be used. Ideally, the various elements of the approach are integrated in the way therapists' information processing, including implicit, self-organized information processing, works, and interventions are no longer used as explicit techniques.

Acknowledegments

Some details of the case description were changed so as to protect client privacy

Profession, nationality (by choosing a typical Swiss first name while the patient actually was German), the deep brain stimulation, the nationality of the author of the book he liked so much, and many other details have been changed.

References

Addis, M. E., Cardemil, E. V., Duncan, B. L., & Miller, S. D. (2006). Does manualization improve therapy outcomes? In J. C. Norcross, L. E. Beutler, & R. F. Levant (Eds.), *Evidence-based practices in mental health: Debate and dialogue on the fundamental questions*. Washington, DC: American Psychological Association.

Argyle, M. (1969). *Social interaction*. London: Methuen.

Berthoud, L., Kramer, U., Caspar, F., & Pascual-Leone, A. (2015). Complex case – emotional processing in a ten-session general psychiatric treatment for borderline personality disorder: A case study. *Personality and Mental Health*, *9*(1), 73–78. https://doi.org/10.1002/pmh.1287.

Betsch, T., & Glöckner, A. (2010). Intuition in judgment and decision making: Extensive thinking without effort. *Psychological Inquiry*, *21*(4), 279–294.

Bohart, A. C., & Wade, A. G. (2013). The client in psychotherapy. In M. Lambert (Ed.). *Handbook of psychotherapy and behavior change: (Vol. 6)*. Hoboken, NJ: John Wiley & Sons.

Brehm, S. S., & Brehm, J. W. (1981). *Psychological reactance: A theory of freedom and control*. New York, NY: Academic Press.

Carver, C. S., & Scheier, M. F. (1998). *On the self-regulation of behavior*. New York: Cambridge University Press.

Carver, C. S., & Scheier, M. F. (2002). Control processes and self-organization as complementary principles underlying behavior. *Personality and Social Psychology Review*, *6*, 304–315. https://doi.org/10.1207/S15327957PSPR0604_05.

Caspar, F. (1995). *Plan analysis. Towards optimizing psychotherapy*. Seattle: Hogrefe.

Caspar, F. (2007). Plan analysis. In T. Eells (Ed.), *Handbook of psychotherapeutic case formulations* (2nd ed.). New York: Guilford.

Caspar, F. (2008). Motivorientierte Beziehungsgestaltung – Konzept, Voraussetzungen bei den Patienten und Auswirkungen auf Prozess und Ergebnisse. In M. Hermer, & B. Röhrle (Eds.). *Handbuch der therapeutischen Beziehung: (Vol. 1)*. Tübingen: dgvt-Verlag.

Caspar, F. (2010a). How general is Grawe´s "general psychotherapy". *IFP-Newsletter*, 18–26. Retrieved from http://www.ifp.name/newsletter.htm.

Caspar, F. (2010b). A plan analysis view of the case of David. *Journal of Psychotherapy Integration*, *20*(1), 59–71.

Caspar, F. (2015). Psychotherapy research and neurobiology: Challenge, change, or enrichment? In B. Strauss, J. P. Barber, & L. Castonguay (Eds.), *Visions in psychotherapy research and practice: Reflections from the presidents of the society for psychotherapy research*. New York: Routledge.

Caspar, F. (2018). *Beziehungen und Probleme verstehen. Eine Einführung in die psychotherapeutische Plananalyse* (4th ed.). Bern: Hogrefe.

Caspar, F., & Ecker, S. (2008). Treatment of an avoidant patient with comorbid psychopathology: A plan analysis perspective. *Journal of Clinical Psychology*, *64*(2), 139–153. https://doi.org/10.1002/jclp.20448.

Caspar, F., & Grawe, K. (1982). Vertikale Verhaltensanalyse: Analyse des Interaktionsverhaltensals Grundlage für die Problemdefinition und Therapieplanung. Technical Report 1982-5. Institute of Psychology, University of Bern.

Caspar, F., Grossmann, C., Unmüssig, C., & Schramm, E. (2005). Complementary therapeutic relationship: Therapist behavior, interpersonal patterns, and therapeutic effects. *Psychotherapy Research, 15*, 1–10.

Caspar, F., Herpertz, S. C., & Lieb, K. (2016). Was ist psychotherapie? In S. C. Herpertz, F. Caspar, & K. Lieb (Eds.), *Psychotherapie. Funktions- und störungsorientiertes Vorgehen (S. 27–45)*. München: Elsevier.

Caspar, F., Rothenfluh, T., & Segal, Z. V. (1992). The appeal of connectionism for clinical psychology. *Clinical Psychology Review, 12*, 719–762. https://doi.org/10.1016/0272~7358(92)90022~Z.

Eells, T. D., Lombart, K. G., Kendjelic, E. M., Turner, L. C., & Lucas, C. P. (2005). The quality of psychotherapy case formulations: A comparison of expert, experienced, and novice cognitive-behavioral and psychodynamic therapists. *Journal of Consulting and Clinical Psychology, 73*(4), 579.

Fernandez-Alvarez, H., Clarkin, J. F., Del Carmen Salgueiro, M., & Critchfield, K. L. (2006). Participant factors in treating personality disorders. In L. G. Castonguay, & L. E. Beutler (Eds.), *Principles of therapeutic change that work*. Oxford: Oxford University Press.

Figlioli, P., Caspar, F., & Berger, T. (2013). How nice is good for patients and for therapy outcome? The role of confrontation in the process of psychotherapy. In *Paper presented at the 43rd Annual Congress of the European Association for Behavioural and cognitive therapies (EABCT), Marrakech, Marocco*.

Foppa, K. (1984). Operationalisierung und der empirische Gehalt psychologischer Theorien. *Psychologische Beiträge, 26*, 539–551.

Glaser, R., & Chi, M. (1988). Overview. In M. Chi, R. Glaser, & M. Farr (Eds.), *The nature of expertise*. Hillsdale, NJ: Erlbaum.

Grawe, K. (2002). *Psychological therapy*. Toronto: Hogrefe & Huber Publishers.

Grawe, K., Caspar, F., & Ambühl, H. R. (1990). Die Berner Therapievergleichsstudie: Fragestellung und Versuchsplan. In *Differentielle Psychotherapieforschung: Vier Therapieformen im Vergleich. Themenheft der Zeitschrift für Klinische Psychologie* (Vol. 4) 19.

Grawe, K., & Dziewas, H. (1978). *"Interaktionelle Verhaltenstherapie." Mitteilungen der DGVT Sonderheft 1*.

Greenberg, L. S. (2012). Emotions, the great captains of our lives: Their role in the process of change in psychotherapy. *American Psychologist, 67*(8), 697.

Kiesler, D. J. (1982). Interpersonal theory for personality and psychotherapy. In J. C. Anchin, & D. J. Kiesler (Eds.), *Handbook of interpersonal psychotherapy*. New York: Pergamon.

Kramer, U. (2009). Individualizing exposure therapy for PTSD: The case of caroline. *Pragmatic Case Studies in Psychotherapy, 5*(2), 1–24.

Kramer, U., Berthoud, L., Keller, S., & Caspar, F. (2014). Motive-oriented psychotherapeutic relationship facing a patient presenting with narcissistic personality disorder: A case study. *Journal of Contemporary Psychotherapy, 44*(2), 71–82. https://doi.org/10.1007/s10879-013-9249-5.

Kramer, U., Kolly, S., Berthoud, L., Keller, S., Preisig, M., Caspar, F., et al. (2014). Effects of motive-oriented therapeutic relationship in a ten-session general psychiatric treatment of borderline personality disorder: A randomized controlled trial. *Psychotherapy and Psychosomatics, 83*(3), 176–186.

Leary, T. (1957). *Interpersonal diagnosis*. New York: Ronald Press.

Miller, G. A., Galanter, E., & Pribram, K. H. (1960). *Plans and the structure of behavior*. New York: Holt, Rhinehart & Winston.

Möseneder, L., Figlioli, P., & Caspar, F. (2017). Confronting patients: Therapists' model of a responsiveness based approach. *Journal of Contemporary Psychotherapy*, 1–7.

Nisbett, R. E., & Wilson, T. (1977). Telling more than we can know: Verbal reports on mental processes. *Psychological Review, 84*, 231–259.

Norcross, J. C. (2002). *Psychotherapy relationships that work: Therapist contributions and responsiveness to patients*. New York: Oxford University Press.

Sackett, D. L., Rosenberg, W. M., Gray, J. M., Haynes, R. B., & Richardson, W. S. (1996). Evidence based medicine. *British Medical Journal, 313*(7050), 72–73.

Schulze, L., Schmahl, C., & Niedtfeld, I. (2016). Neural correlates of disturbed emotion processing in borderline personality disorder: A multimodal meta-analysis. *Biological Psychiatry, 79*(2), 97–106.

Silberschatz, G. (2010). The control-mastery perspective: A clinical formulation of David's plan. *Journal of Psychotherapy Integration, 20*(1), 81–88.

Sullivan, H. S. (1953). *The interpersonal theory of psychiatry*. New York: Norton Press.

Wolfer, C. (2016). *Therapieabbruch; Eine Untersuchung an der Praxisstelle der Universität Bern*. University of Bern.

Further Reading

Caspar, F., & Berger, T. (2011). Allgemeine Psychotherapie. In B. Dulz, S. C. Herpertz, O. F. Kernberg, & U. Sachse (Eds.), *Handbuch der Borderline-Störungen (2. Aufl., S. 667–680)*. Stuttgart: Schattauer.

CHAPTER

15

Tailored Treatment Planning for Individuals With Personality Disorders: The Operationalized Psychodynamic Diagnosis (OPD) Approach

Johannes C. Ehrenthal[1], *Cord Benecke*[2]

[1]Institute of Medical Psychology, Heidelberg University, Germany;
[2]Department of Psychology, University of Kassel, Kassel, Germany

THE OPERATIONALIZED PSYCHODYNAMIC DIAGNOSIS (OPD) SYSTEM

A key challenge in the assessment of personality disorders is to balance specificity of the diagnostic approach with its usability for everyday clinical practice. Some systems focus on a single personality disorder, while others reflect a single theoretical orientation or psychological model. Although these specific approaches are important to increase precision, often in the context of specific research questions, they may narrow the understanding of a given patient, and restrict communication with colleagues or researchers. An integrative approach that is tried and tested in more than two decades of research, clinical practice and training is provided by the Operationalized Psychodynamic Diagnosis (OPD) system. We will at first describe history and context of the OPD, then provide a brief overview over the system, including research findings, before illustrating how the OPD can be used with a case example.

Case Formulation for Personality Disorders
https://doi.org/10.1016/B978-0-12-813521-1.00015-1

Aims, History and Dissemination of the Operationalized Psychodynamic Diagnosis (OPD) System

The OPD was developed in the early 1990s by psychodynamically oriented specialists in psychosomatic medicine, psychiatry and clinical psychology (Arbeitskreis OPD, 1996). The group was initially motivated by a two-fold critique of the status quo: On the one hand, categorical psychiatric classification as conducted by the Diagnostic and Statistical Manual of Mental Disorders (DSM; American Psychiatric Association, 2013) and International Classification of Diseases (ICD) usually results in a pattern of cut-off scores being reached for specific symptom clusters, which are then labelled as diagnoses. As most patients outside of randomized controlled trials regularly suffer from more than one diagnosis, and some diagnoses share more variance with each other than they differ from each other (Hettema, 2008), the idea of diagnostic entities has been challenged (Insel et al., 2010). Similarly, DSM and ICD diagnoses are not very helpful for individual treatment planning. The mere knowledge about the diagnostic status of a personality disorder does not provide information about aetiology or relevant reinforcing variables in a given case. Lastly, as there are 126 ways to fulfill the minimal criteria for a diagnosis of a borderline personality disorder (BPD), two BPD patients may provide very different symptom profiles (Clarkin, 2006). Dimensional aspects of personality dysfunction have just recently been introduced into the DSM-5 Alternative Model for the Assessment of Personality Disorders (AMPD; Bender, Morey, & Skodol, 2011).

On the other hand, diagnosis from psychoanalytic models is traditionally considered highly complex, with abstract or diffuse wording to describe similar phenomena, or similar words for very different phenomena. For example, the understanding of the Oedipus complex has changed substantially over the last century, with different meanings following specific traditions of the analytic schools (Hartke, 2016). While a non-operationalized case formulation may be good enough for working in a therapeutic dyad, it definitely complicates any clinical or scientific communication.

Therefore, the aim of the OPD was to develop a system that complements DSM or ICD through clinically relevant psychodynamic constructs at a medium level of complexity. By that, it should help clinicians to develop case conceptualizations, and increase communication and interrater-reliability. The OPD thus focuses on observable material as much as possible, provides assessment tools that are in principle teachable, and helps to communicate psychodynamic diagnosis to colleagues, patients, researchers or health-care providers. Consequently, the OPD also developed standardized training courses for interested clinicians.

In 2006, a decade after the publication of the first version of the manual, the OPD task force published a revised version (OPD-2; Arbeitskreis OPD, 2006; Tann & Ristl, 2008). One of the key advancements from OPD-1 to

OPD-2 was the attempt to reformulate the OPD from a mere descriptive tool to a diagnosis system for treatment planning. Its implementations range from short-term and focal outpatient as well as inpatient treatments to long-term psychodynamic and psychoanalytic therapies. Today, the OPD is the most widely used psychodynamically based diagnosis system in German-speaking countries, with literally several thousand therapists trained in basic or advanced courses. The OPD is recognized by health-care providers, and psychodynamically oriented inpatient psychosomatic rehabilitation clinics are required to provide an OPD-based case formulation in their case reports to be reimbursed. Research on the OPD has resulted in more than 250 chapters, articles and books, and the OPD manual has been translated into more than seven languages.

Conceptual Background and Multiaxial Diagnosis

The OPD integrates a variety of interpersonal, psychodynamic and psychiatric theories to provide a coherent model of a patient's psychodynamics in relationship to his or her symptoms. The OPD comprises five axes:

I. Experience of illness and prerequisites for treatment
II. Interpersonal relations
III. Conflict
IV. Structure
V. Psychiatric and psychosomatic symptoms according to DSM or ICD

Definitions, conceptual background and content of these axes will be explained in the following paragraphs. As *Axis V* is self-explanatory, we will not address it any further. *Axis I* captures duration and severity of the problems, the patient's experience of his or her difficulties, including subjective models of aetiology and change regarding somatic, psychological or social factors. This enables the clinician to quickly assess patterns of illness behaviour that may inform necessary therapeutic steps as prerequisites for a certain treatment or adjust treatment options accordingly. For example, a patient with breast cancer who suffers from anxiety and depressive rumination and fulfills the criteria of an avoidant personality disorder sees her cancer as a result of 'being a bad person'. Instead of adapted oncological care, she seeks long-term psychoanalytic therapy to 'battle her cancer'. On the OPD Axis I scoresheet one would see the following pattern: The patient experiences a high level of psychological distress, attributes her cancer to psychological factors and has a primarily psychological change model. As much as this pattern is desirable for individuals with a primarily psychological disorder, the task of a consultation-liaison psychiatrist called to talk to her would be to develop a shared, realistic model of the development of cancer to encourage an appropriate oncological treatment before thinking about any kind of long-term therapy.

Another example would be a patient with an obsessive-compulsive personality disorder who has read about the serotonin hypothesis of depression, and is primarily looking for medication. On the OPD Axis I, he would score high with regard to a somatic disease model, related to a similarly, prominent somatic change model. He may not be ready to invest in a psychotherapy. This would also be true for a narcissistic patient who states that he would lead a happy life if his boss and his neighbours would not treat him unfairly all the time, indicating a high score on the OPD Axis I item for an attribution of his difficulties to social factors. In addition, Axis I assesses personal resources, available social support and internal or external obstacle to change. The latter could also relate to a lack of insurance coverage or absence of a qualified therapist. A separate psychotherapy module helps the clinician to be more precise in assessing what patients expect from and strive for in treatment: Do they primarily look for symptom reduction, do they want to reflect on motives and internal conflicting topics, are they looking for an emotionally supportive relationship, or would they rather prefer guidance and instruction by a therapist? Lastly, the psychotherapy module addresses the individuals' psychological mindedness as well as possible secondary illness gain and other perpetuating behaviour or conditions. To sum up, Axis I is highly relevant for treatment planning, as it helps the clinician to develop an understanding of objective severity, subjective models and wishes, and internal and external barriers to benefiting from a treatment.

Axis II relates to repetitive, maladaptive interpersonal relationship patterns. Drawing on psychodynamic (Johnson, Popp, Schacht, Mellon, & Strupp, 1989; Luborsky & Crits-Christoph, 1998) and interpersonal (Benjamin, 1974; Kiesler, 1983) models, and including transference and countertransference, the OPD proposes four interrelated positions of interpersonal experiencing and behaviour:

1. How the patient experiences others.
2. How the patient perceives his or her own reaction to their behaviour.
3. How others, including the clinician, may perceive the patient's reaction.
4. What kind of interpersonal impulses or behaviour this stimulates in others, including the clinician (i.e., countertransference).

If the counterpart is prone to acting out his or her countertransference, this may be regarded as similar to how the patient repetitively experiences others, and results in maladaptive, self-reinforcing cycles (Schauenburg & Grande, 2011). To capture interpersonal positions in a more precise manner, the OPD Axis II provides clinicians with a list of wordings for interpersonal phenomena derived from interpersonal circumplex models. Axis II of the OPD system is mostly used in a descriptive way (i.e., closely related to the reported and observed material), although circular, self-reinforcing relational dynamics are already visible at this level of analysis. To give an example: A patient talks about unsatisfactory relationships with her partner and superiors at her job and wonders why others always seem to treat her in an unsatisfactory manner. From different relationship episodes, the therapist deducts the following pattern: The patient experiences others as letting her work out issues on her own, while having high expectations, or withdrawing from her. In her own view, she tries to react to this challenge by repeatedly taking care of demands, while trying to hide own needs, or devaluating herself. Others, including the therapist, experience the patient in this effort as rather withdrawing, and subtly controlling and devaluating. This results in two impulses: To either care for her and be especially gentle, but also to become increasingly demanding, to the point of wearily 'throwing in the towel'. If acted out, this may reinforce the patient's experience of others as having high expectations without backing her up if needed (Ehrenthal, 2017).

Axis III captures intrapsychic motivational conflicts. Conflicts form around insecurities regarding specific central themes that develop during childhood. These central themes can be well integrated, and just shape interindividual differences in what one finds important and rewarding in life. If the insecurities run deeper, and regulatory capacities ('ego-functioning') are less developed, these insecurities turn into neurotic conflicts, narrowing and hindering fulfillment of life-goals. The conflicts themselves are usually not consciously experienced but can be identified by specific affects and verified by information from the patient's life history, transference and countertransference. These topics are usually dealt with either in an active or a passive mode. The 'active mode' describes contraphobic attempts, often reaction formation, the 'passive mode' a regressive move, both with the goal of concealing and keeping the underlying insecurities out of conscious experiencing.

The OPD describes seven prototypical conflictual topics:

- *Individuation versus Dependency:* The key insecurity relates to issues of having close relationships. Individuals either strive for autonomy, and become anxious when others get close to them, or they long for closeness, and are challenged existentially whenever there is a real or imagined separation.
- *Submission versus Control:* Here the central insecurity concerns feeling of agency. Individuals either submit to others, but often in a passive-aggressive manner, or they try to dominate any situation where their need to feel in control is challenged.
- *Need for care versus Self-sufficiency:* For this conflict, insecurities about the amount of care in relationships are of central importance. Individuals either view and present themselves as highly needy, or regulate this insecurity by showing no need to be taken care of, but rather take care of everybody else.

- *Self-worth conflict:* Here a basic feeling of worthiness as a person is at stake. Individuals compensate either by devaluating themselves, or by devaluating others.
- *Guilt conflict:* This conflict oscillates around insecurities concerning accountability and guilt and is characterized by either dismissing or taking on any kind of responsibility.
- *Oedipal conflict:* The oedipal conflict according to the OPD is related to insecurities around issues of (gender-related) role-identities. This results in either suppression of any kind of rivalry, attraction, erotic feelings, or an exaggerated rivalry, eroticizing, flirtatious behaviour.
- *Identity conflict:* The identity conflict taps into a narrow area of individuals with conflicting self-images or value-systems. In contrast to structural deficits of identity diffusion, it relates to conflictual tension resulting from dissonance between contrasting inner self-representations (Sandler & Joffe, 1969).

In addition, the OPD provides a category for a stressor-induced conflict, which captures conflicting feelings, thoughts and motives after severe life events, but without biographically salient and persisting motivational life topics. In the rare event that an individual is not able to talk about him- or herself due to very rigid defensive functioning against conflict-related affects and cognitions, this can be also be rated.

Axis IV: Structure. This axis is directly related to personality disorders (PDs), as it assesses basic psychological capacities that are seen as essential for an individual to manage him- or herself in a primarily social world. These capacities usually develop in early childhood by means of social learning processes (Beebe et al., 2010). Early physical, emotional and sexual abuse, as well as neglect, especially if experienced in repeated interactions with significant others, limits the development of an integrated and agentic self. The structure-axis of the OPD integrates clinical models from ego- and self-psychology, object relations theory, and findings from modern developmental psychology (Rudolf, Grande, & Henningsen, 2010).

While 'structure' describes the general organizing principle, its functions comprise abilities in the areas of perception/cognition, regulation, communication and attachment. Those are directed toward the self as well as toward the other, i.e., objects. In other words, the OPD assesses key dimensions of self-perception, self-regulation, internal communication and attachment to internal objects as well as object perception, regulation of relationships, external communication and attachment to external objects. Each of those dimensions consists of three subdimensions, as depicted in Table 15.1.

It is important to keep in mind that the dimensions and subdimensions are an expression of the functioning of what is meant by 'structure'. By that, the selection of the facets is a rational one, based in parts on research,

TABLE 15.1 Axis IV: Structure

Self	Object
PERCEPTION/COGNITION	
Self-perception • Self-reflection • Affect differentiation • Identity	*Object perception* • Self-object differentiation • Whole object perception • Realistic object perception
REGULATION	
Self-regulation • Impulse control • Affect tolerance • Regulation of self-esteem	*Regulation of relationships* • Protecting relationships • Balancing interests • Anticipation
COMMUNICATION	
Internal communication • Experiencing affect • Use of fantasies • Bodily self	*External communication* • Making contact • Communicating affect • Empathy
ATTACHMENT	
Attachment to internal objects • Internalization • Use of introjects • Variability of attachment patterns	*Attachment to external objects* • Capacity for attachment • Accepting help • Detaching from relationships

but also clinical theory and usability for treatment planning. For example, classical psychodynamic defence mechanisms are not a separate dimension of Axis IV, but rather part of the description at different levels of structural integration as well as with regard to the specific ability to make use of more functional, intrapsychic versus interpersonal defences in the dimension of 'protecting relationships'. All the dimensions are framed and formulated in a way that they may serve as direct targets of psychotherapy interventions (see Table 15.2).

Personality Disorders: The Operationalized Psychodynamic Diagnosis (OPD) Levels of Structural Integration Axis (LSIA)

Axis IV ('Structure', or LSIA) and its subdimenions are coded dimensionally with the so-called Levels of Structural Integration Axis (LSIA). Its four levels (1 = high level of integration, 2 = medium level of integration, 3 = low level of integration, 4 = disintegration) can be further differentiated by adding intermediate steps, resulting in a total of seven gradations. Individuals with high levels of structural integration usually have a relatively autonomous self, are able to realistically self-reflect and

TABLE 15.2 Core Capacities of the Subdimensions of Axis IV

PERCEPTION/COGNITION	
Self-perception	
Self-reflection	Ability to focus the perception onto oneself, and benefit from it.
Affect differentiation	Ability to experience and differentiate affects within oneself and understand their meaning.
Identity	Ability to develop and maintain a stable and coherent self-image.
Object perception	
Self-object differentiation	Ability to differentiate between oneself and others, especially with regard to location of the source of affects, intentions, impulses, and thoughts.
Whole object perception	Ability to incorporate positive and negative qualities of others/objects into a single, integrated image or representations.
Realistic object perception	Ability to realistically perceive others within the context of their external situation and intentions.
REGULATION	
Self-regulation	
Impulse control	Ability to regulate and integrate internal impulses.
Affect tolerance	Ability to tolerate and process own affects, especially negative affects.
Regulation of self-esteem	Ability to retrieve a feeling of self-worthiness after a related challenge.
Regulation of relationships	
Protecting relationships	Ability to process internal impulses within oneself without having to act them out in relationships.
Balancing interests	Ability to bring one's own interests to bear while simultaneously take into account the interests of others.
Anticipation	Ability to anticipate others' reactions to one's own behaviour and adequately use this information.
COMMUNICATION	
Internal communication	
Experiencing affect	Abilty to get in a lively contact with one's won emotions.
Use of fantasies	Ability to allow dreams and fantasies, and thereby enrich and think ahead one's own life.
Bodily self	To experience an animated relationship with one's own body.

TABLE 15.2 Core Capacities of the Subdimensions of Axis IV—cont'd

External communication	
Making contact	Ability to adequately and lively establish contact with others.
Communicating affect	Ability to communicate in a lively, reciprocal manner.
Empathy	Ability to emphasize and temporarily identify with the internal world of others.
ATTACHMENT	
Attachment to internal objects	
Internalization	Ability to maintain emotionally positive and stable internal representations of important others.
Use of introjects	Ability to care for oneself, develop confidence, and calm oneself due to positive internal representations.
Variability of attachment patterns	Ability to develop and tolerate qualitatively different internal and external relationship models (i.e., triangulation).
Attachment to external objects	
Capacity for attachment	Ability to generate adequate meaning toward important others.
Accepting help	Ability to adequately utilize others as good objects.
Detaching from relationships	Ability to tolerate separations and withdraw cathexis from important objects.

perceive others, can regulate themselves and their relationships adequately even across longer periods of stress or strain and empathically relate to themselves as well as others, with sufficiently good internal object relations. A central fear of the internal world often relates to losing the objects' love. Individuals at moderate levels of structural integration maintain core structural capacities, but to a lesser degree: they show impairments in the context of their dominating motivational conflicts, which are more burdensome, destructive and less flexible. Self-critical and -devaluating tendencies are common; individuals have difficulties in developing a stable and positive self-image. Regulatory strategies are pressured by conflictual motives, are less flexible and usually tend to over-regulate wishes, impulses, fantasies or emotions. The ability to empathize is reduced, dyadic relationships are preferred and the central fear of the internal world is about losing the object and being left alone. Individuals with low levels of structural integration have a marked reduction of structural capabilities in a sense of habitual underregulation. This refers to perception and general regulatory competence as well as communication skills. Impulses or emotions are highly difficult to process and regulate internally and are regularly acted out in a sense of interpersonal defences. Coherent values and societal norms are rarely guiding behaviour, often accompanied by a lack of real empathy and communicative skills. The central fear of the internal world is to be hurt, damaged or destroyed by malignant objects[1]. Disintegration is characterized by a more or less complete loss of the described capacities, and by decomposition of any borders between self and objects, with a lack of coherence of the self, a flooding by emotions or impulses and strong distortions of reality. Empathic and realistic perception of others is nearly impossible, impulses directly result in behaviour, with individuals feeling nearly no agency any more. The central fear of the internal world at this level is the loss of the self through symbiotic merging of self and object.

Each of the 24 subdimensions are operationalized according to these four levels of structural integration on a checklist. Ratings of the LSIA result in an overall rating as well as a profile on either the eight dimensions or 24 subdimensions. The timeframe of the rating refers to the last two years. Although structure is usually seen as a stable construct, changes of personality integration by aversive or protective experiences, including psychotherapy, are considered. Although individuals with a moderate level of structural integration can also suffer from a PD, especially a higher-order PD, values of 2,5 (between moderate and low levels of integration) are seen as an indicator of marked personality dysfunction; values of three (low levels of integration) or four (disintegration) are a clear indicator of one or more PDs.

A thorough preparation for the assessment and rating of the LSIA is provided within regular basic and advanced OPD training courses, offered in face-to-face as well as online-settings (see www.opd-online.net).

Research on the Operationalized Psychodynamic Diagnosis (OPD) Levels of Structural Integration Axis (LSIA)

The LSIA is one of the axes of the OPD with the strongest research evidence. Interrater-reliability is acceptable with clinically inexperienced raters (Kappa = .65–.70), and good (Kappa = .71–.83; ICC = .79) when trained clinicians perform the ratings (Benecke et al., 2009; Cierpka, Grande, Rudolf, von der Tann, & Staschf, 2007; Cierpka et al., 2001; Doering et al., 2014). In more than 17 independent samples with over 2000 individuals, there is evidence for validity as well. The OPD LSIA scores correlate with other measures of personality integration (Doering et al., 2014). In general, lower levels of LSIA integration are related to higher levels of symptom load, and a higher probability of suffering from at least one PD (for an overview, see Zimmermann et al., 2012). To complement the LSIA expert rating by an individual patient perspective, there is a self-report on the LSIA, the OPD-Structure Questionnaire

[1] The term 'object' refers to significant others as well as their internal representation.

(OPD-SQ) in a long as well as a 12-item screening version. Both versions show good psychometric properties. Higher values representing less self-reported structural capacities are related to attachment insecurity, PDs, neuroticism and less openness to experience, agreeableness, conscientiousness and extraversion, even after controlling for general symptom load (Ehrenthal et al., 2012, 2015). In addition, the OPD-SQ scores correlate with OPD LSIA expert ratings to r = .62 (Dinger et al., 2014), with other questionnaires on personality dysfunction (König, Dahlbender, Holzinger, Topitz, & Doering, 2016; Zimmermann et al., 2015), and differentiate between depressed patients with versus without BPD (Köhling et al., 2016).

Operationalized Psychodynamic Diagnosis (OPD) Levels of Structural Integration Axis (LSIA) and DSM/ICD Dimensional Models of Personality Functioning

The OPD LSIA is of special interest when evaluating the Levels of Personality Functioning Scale (LPFS) of the DSM-5 Alternative Model (AMPD; Bender et al., 2011) and the proposed severity rating for the ICD-11 (Tyrer et al., 2011). OPD LSIA and LPFS ratings are highly related in expert opinion (Zimmermann et al., 2012) and case ratings (Zimmermann et al., 2014), but are different enough for the purpose of cross-validation. In fact, the OPD system may be especially suited for comparison, as it has a strong research base and at the same time more than 20 years of experience in clinical implementation and use.

PRACTICAL APPLICATIONS OF THE OPERATIONALIZED PSYCHODYNAMIC DIAGNOSIS (OPD) SYSTEM

OPD ratings are usually applied to material derived from a 60–90 min clinical assessment interview, which incorporates information on psychopathology, biography, relationships, view of the self and view of important others (Tann & Ristl, 2008). In addition, all other available data can and should be incorporated (Spitzer, 1983).

Assessing Interpersonal Patterns

Maladaptive interpersonal patterns are extracted from at least two to three relationship episodes, where the patient is either instructed to talk about important relationships and exemplify, or the therapist explores spontaneously narrated examples. Here the interviewer invites the patient to elaborate on how he/she usually experiences others in relevant and difficult situations, and how he/she sees his or her reaction to their behaviour.

Some patients are also able to reflect on how their reaction is probably experienced by others, while in other cases this falls to the clinician, which is mostly the case if the patients have lower levels of personality functioning in the areas of, for example, object perception, anticipation or empathy. At the same time, the therapist monitors his or her countertransference to examine what fantasies and impulses the patient may evoke in others. Usually, what is extracted as a formulation of the relational dynamics should at least in part match what can be experienced within the interview. When assessing relationship patterns in patients with PDs it is particularly important to actively clarify, as initially descriptions may appear confusing, or even contradictory. Usually it is possible to extract one or two main patterns, which may relate to very different object relations in patients with PDs.

Assessing Conflictual Motivational Topics

Assessing conflicts is typically performed by looking for patterns and central topics throughout a patient's life history. The interviewer pays close attention to what the patient considers important in life, how he/she differs from others with regard to motives, what are concomitant core affects and of course notable transference-countertransference constellations. In an individual with a neurotic conflict, motivational topics also define predetermined 'breaking points', where individuals with a specific conflictual theme usually experience failure, strain or the development of symptoms. For instance, a patient with a key insecurity in the area of self-worth may experience difficulties throughout his life whenever he is forced to show 'how good he is', for example exams or evaluations. Although the OPD encourages the clinician to decide if the patient's problems are mostly attributable to dynamic motivational conflicts, structural deficits or a mixture of both, it is important to try to evaluate dominant motivational themes in patients with PDs as well. In patients with high or moderate levels of structural integration these topics and their conflictual representation is often clearly visible in the narratives, in dominant affects and countertransference reactions. In patients with low levels of structural integration, however, these motivational topics may be less clear, and serve a different function in the concurrent psychodynamics, as we will point out in more detail later in the chapter.

Assessing Levels of Structural Integration

Levels of personality integration with regard to OPD structural dimensions become visible in relational episodes, but even more so in how successful an individual is in living a relatively stable and fulfilling life. Deficits in structural capabilities usually result in persistent and non-specific difficulties of being able to engage in long-term occupational and personal activities as well as in satisfactory and non-harmful relationships. Specifically, ruptures, split-off representations and affects, regulatory deficits, persistent and harmful interactional patterns, and a feeling of a strong need to co-regulate the relationship and structure the material from the interviewer's side are usually indicators of structural deficits. In addition, patients can be asked directly about structural capabilities, as these and especially the consequences of their absence are usually directly experienced. In the assessment with patients it is important to probe by asking for examples if individuals seem to report structural difficulties, and to determine if these difficulties persist in a variety of situations, or just when facing challenges linked to motivational conflicts. In the latter case, the LSIA may be at a level of moderate integration.

Making Sense of the Interrelatedness of Interpersonal Patterns, Motivational Conflicts and Personality Function

The OPD system puts a special emphasis on the relationship between the three core axes 'relationship patterns', 'conflict' and 'structure'. While Axis II (relationship patterns) usually has a descriptive function ('What is repeatedly happening?'), both Axis III (conflict) and Axis IV (structure) serve as explanatory variables. In other words: After describing maladaptive, repetitive relationship patterns, clinicians examine whether these patterns are driven by motivational conflicts (i.e., wishes and anxieties), structural deficits (i.e., reduced capacities in dealing with internal or external demands) or a mixture of both.

Let's look again at the four positions ((1) how the patient experiences others, (2) how he/she perceives him-/herself reacting to them, (3) how others perceive the patient's reaction and (4) what impulses others feel in response to their perception of the patient's reaction) that are described in Axis II. For understanding relational dynamics it is vital to acknowledge that the patient may see his/her own reaction as nearly inevitable to how others treat him or her, and that this reaction may be perceived very differently by others than initially intended by the patient. From a perspective of the OPD, it is of central diagnostic relevance to explain this key misunderstanding between position one and position three (Ehrenthal & Grande, 2014; Grande, 2007).

There are at least three basic principles in which conflict and structure can fuel maladaptive relational cycles. The first principle is seen in predominantly conflict-based patterns. Here the misunderstanding results from conflicting inner wishes and related defences, which are both stimulating the relational behaviour, resulting in mixed interpersonal signals. Due to this vagueness, others tend to react more to the anxiety than the wish, and thereby reinforce for example an expected rejection. This again raises anxiety, which in turn draws the patient toward evaluating others even more by their own transference-related fears, resulting in a self-reinforcing cycle. For example, the patient mentioned above had a central, conflict-related insecurity around an 'oral' topic, i.e., how much she can rely on being taken care of if needed (OPD conflict 'Need for Care vs. Self-sufficiency'). In her experience, she is doing everything she can for others ('active mode'), with the unconscious wish that others would be there for her as well. However, as she also fears rejections, she simultaneously keeps others at a distance, but puts them in a difficult interpersonal position: If she does not allow others to take care of her, this creates an 'emotional debt' in interaction partners that stimulates uneasiness and ultimately withdrawal.

In patients with lower levels of personality functioning, there are two other patterns. The first one is similar to the conflict-related pattern. However, due to impaired structural capacities, the pattern has a coarsened quality with the interplay between wishes and defences resulting in irritating and inadequate relational behaviour. The counterpart needs to actively co-regulate the relationship as well as own countertransference impulses. For example, a patient with a BPD diagnosis has a similar conflictual theme around wishes for care. However, he perceives others usually as demanding, intrusive or neglecting. In his view, he tries to manage on his own, which others often experience as shutting down, alternated by a strong pressure to help him. This makes it hard for others to regulate their own feelings and impulses, with a mixture of withdrawal or 'taking over' to help the patient, which may increase the patient's paranoid or devaluating view of others.

The second pattern often found in individuals with lower levels of personality integration has a function of protecting the self. If patients are highly fragile, usually in the context of early traumatic, neglecting or highly devaluating experiences, and perceive others (objects) as overwhelmingly powerful and potentially annihilating, relational patterns may be dominated by wishes for closeness as well as seemingly contradictory impulses such as withdrawal, attacking, controlling or devaluating behaviour. In the counterpart, this results in strong impulses to retaliate, devaluate, attack or withdraw themselves. Both distancing from and getting closer to the patient is potentially frightening, leaving just very little tolerance for new interactional experiences. For example, a patient with severe and longstanding emotional and sexual abuse in her childhood sees others as a potential harm. In her own experience, she tries to let other help her as much as she can tolerate but is ultimately ready to run away if needed. Others feel challenged by a seemingly intrusive dominant control of the interpersonal situation, and at other times a strange, but uncomfortable feeling of closeness, resulting in impulses of shielding themselves for a potential attack, while at the same time a guilt-driven attempt to encourage the patient to open up. This again could result in a feeling of being threatened on the side of the patient.

Although it is helpful to differentiate between conflict- versus structure-driven maladaptive patterns, there are also similarities and transitions amongst the two areas. Stable but restricted modes of coping with conflictual insecurities become part of personality, and some conflict-modes are very similar to the phenomenology of specific PDs. For example, the active mode of the self-worth conflict resembles important features of narcissistic PDs, and the active mode of the oedipal conflict reminds of a histrionic PD. As in reality the transitions are fluid, the OPD does not try to artificially distinguish between the two perspectives but provides a model to assess at what level of structural integration the motivational themes are acted out.

To sum up, after describing maladaptive interpersonal patterns, clinicians examine if these patterns result from conflictual motives (wishes, fears and their related defences) or from structural deficits. If the latter is the case, one should decide if the pattern is coarsened due to insufficient structural abilities, or whether it serves as a protection of the highly fragile self.

USING THE OPERATIONALIZED PSYCHODYNAMIC DIAGNOSIS (OPD) SYSTEM AS AN INTEGRATIVE APPROACH TO CASE FORMULATIONS AND TREATMENT PLANNING: A CLINICAL CASE EXAMPLE

Background Information

Carol, a women in her late twenties, suffered from recurrent symptoms of anxiety and panic attacks, recurrent major depressive episodes and self-harming behaviour. In the DSM-IV SCID-II interview, she nearly fulfilled the criteria for BPD, and showed features of Avoidant PD. She started self-harming when she finished high school, and had depressive episodes for two years and suicidal fantasies for several years. She also suffered from intrusive flashbacks and a tendency to quickly dissociate. Previous treatments included two inpatient psychotherapy treatments, one inpatient psychiatric treatment, outpatient psychotherapy as well as medication with escitalopram and lorazepam. Her body-weight was low with a BMI of around 18.5, with some restrictive eating, but not fulfilling criteria for anorexia nervosa.

Carol grew up in a family with two parents and a sibling. She had felt close to her father as a child, until her mother fell ill when she was four and died three years later. On the one hand, she felt lost and alone, and that her father now preferred her sister, who she saw as living up to all his ideals of achievement and intellect. And although she did everything to get her father's love and appreciation, she did not succeed and viewed herself as the black sheep of the family: 'It felt of no importance any more'. On the other hand, she blamed herself for her mother's death, as she used to be a lively child, sometimes angry, and inflicting conflict in the family. During this time, her uncle took care of her in a way that flattered her at first, as he treated her almost like an adult, and made her feel important again. However, this attention gradually developed into physical and sexual abuse, which only stopped when she grew into puberty and had the courage to try to defend herself. During adolescence, she 'forgot' about the abuse, but remembered it during an inpatient treatment at a time when her sibling was pregnant with her first child. Carol started to investigate, and found her sibling confirm her memories, as she had witnessed parts of it but never dared to intervene. Similarly, she found out that her uncle had been convicted for child abuse before.

After finishing school, she wanted to become a nurse, but followed her father's advice that she should rather look for a 'more practical, less intellectual' job. She became successful in the trade she learned, climbed up hierarchies in the companies she worked for, but also switched workplaces when she felt not being taken care of or criticized. When asked about these achievements, she attributed them to 'luck, not skill'. After her second inpatient treatment, she decided to study social work. In addition to her being worried by her sibling having her second baby, she also had an instructor that reminded her of her now deceased uncle.

Carol talked about having been a teenager with very autonomous, but also very 'needy' sides. During her first relationship, she experienced another sexual assault. In her current relationship, which she describes as 'distant, but stable', sexuality is still a problematic topic. Similarly, she described an 'alienated' body-image. Part of what had triggered her latest depressive episode may have been the decision to start living together. She would be highly sensitive to her partner's perceived criticism, but at the same time find him 'too slow', which would sometimes result in angry outbursts from her side. She could see, however, the value of him taking things slowly and not jumping to conclusions as she did.

She had talked things over with her father, and although she started to come to terms with his way of seeing the world – and accepted his apology for not taking care of her – she sometimes still felt very sad and lonely, and missed her mother. Although Carol presented herself as very goal-directed, she was currently unsure of what to do with her life; becoming a social-worker seemed an intermediate step, especially as she had gotten to know her own vulnerability with regard to helping others while rejecting help herself during the last inpatient treatment. When asked about good relationships in her past, she pointed toward her sibling and her mother's sister. However, with her sister having a family, she felt rather alone now.

Self-Report Data and Formal Expert Ratings of Operationalized Psychodynamic Diagnosis (OPD) Axis II, III and IV

Amongst other parameters not reported here, she had a score of 22 in the PHQ-9 depression scale, which is considered in the high range, and a score of 16 in the GAD-7 anxiety scale, which is also in the high range (Kroenke, Spitzer, Williams, & Löwe, 2010). Her scoring in the OPD-SQ can be found in Table 15.3. In all dimensions except for 'Regulation of relationships' she scored higher than a clinical inpatient reference sample, indicating lower levels of personality integration.

The OPD expert rating for Axis II was as follows: Carol experiences others as withdrawing their affection (Axis II item 13), to be very demanding of her (item 10) and to habitually blame her (item 12). In her own view, she reacts to these behaviours by taking care of others (item 7), harmonizing (item 6) and hiding her own needs (item 31). Others, including the interviewer, experience her attempts as controlling (item 10), blaming others (item 12) and losing herself when others show affection (item 21). This could induce two ways of reacting toward her. On the one hand, an interpersonal move toward her: To perceive her as fragile (and devaluate her, item 11), take special care of her (item 7), but then to demand (also as a therapist) change (item 10). The other reaction would be to interpersonally move away from her by distancing oneself (item 32), leaving her a lot of freedom (item 1) and deny any kind of wrongdoing (item 20). Both could be misunderstood as high demands as well as neglect.

The expert rating for Axis III was as follows: The current main conflictual theme was 'Need for care vs. self-sufficiency' in an active mode, the second conflictual theme was 'Self-worth conflict', in a passive mode. However, at other times in the life of the patient the order of the conflictual topics may have been reversed.

The overall rating for Axis IV LSIA was as follows: In between medium-to-low integration (score of 2.5). Regarding the subdimensions, attachment to external objects, external communication and regulation of relationships tended toward medium levels of integration, while self-perception, internal communication and self-regulation showed a rather low level of structural integration. Object perception was in between, with a mixture of projection, but also cognitive abilities to integrate at least some aspects of other persons and internal objects. Attachment to internal objects was somehow split: Parts of her internal world revolved about a central fear of losing the object (medium level of integration), while other parts of her object relations were drawn to a fear of being harmed by the objects (low level of integration).

TABLE 15.3 OPD-SQ Scores of the Patient and Comparison With a Non-clinical Sample From Ehrenthal et al. (2012)

Scale	M of Carol	M (sd) of an Clinical Inpatient Reference Sample (N = 204)
OPD-SQ total	2.46	2.04 (0.57)
OPD-SQ self-perception	2.92	1.94 (0.83)
OPD-SQ object perception	2.54	1.88 (0.66)
OPD-SQ self-regulation	2.97	2.09 (0.70)
OPD-SQ regulation of relationships	0.92	1.76 (0.67)
OPD-SQ internal communication	2.36	1.92 (0.70)
OPD-SQ external communication	2.61	2.00 (0.63)
OPD-SQ attachment to internal objects	2.88	2.28 (0.76)
OPD-SQ attachment to external objects	2.50	2.46 (0.71)

Operationalized Psychodynamic Diagnosis (OPD) Case Formulation

Against a background of early loss, and physical and sexual abuse, we see an interplay between conflictual topics and structural deficits. Carol grew up in a family where she felt closer to her father, and this worked well until her mother fell ill and eventually died. Her death disturbed the developmental task of finding a place and identity in a world full of triangular relationships, which was suddenly reduced to a grieving, unavailable father and a rather typical feeling of guilt. What may have developed into an Oedipal topic under other circumstances now resulted in a regression to more basic insecurity if she would still be loved (need-for-care motive). Carol probably tried to get back her father's emotional attention and affection by developing a high achievement-motive and high self-criticism (self-worth motive). Tragically, her uncle seemed to offer attention and affection, but to a high price of several years of severe abuse, which probably damaged early structural competencies regarding the self and others. While for other teenagers adolescence is an opportunity to catch up on developmental topics and structural capacities, Carol seemed to live in some kind of 'posttraumatic blur', even re-experiencing sexual boundary-violations. At the same time, her father's verdict of her not being smart enough for the job she wanted probably challenged her longing for being loved by him, triggering (together with the boundary-violations) first episodes of self-harm. During that time, her self-worth conflict provided enough motive to try to be as good as possible to pursue a career in her occupation, temporarily stabilizing parts of her life. She decompensates in situations that usually carry a mixture of conflict-related motives (e.g., reinforcing the anxiety of losing her father's affection altogether if he would take care of her sister and her baby), and being confronted with topics of closeness, intimacy and trauma-related cues. At the same time, she cannot rely on structural capacities that would help others find stability, new solutions and ultimately more freedom in dealing with her conflictual insecurities and wishes.

Her maladaptive relational patterns serve a two-fold function. On the one hand, it would be a compromise between keeping the need-for-care motive alive by providing support for others, while at the same time keeping them at a safe distance and avoiding being hurt and rejected. At the same time, this compromise seems coarsened, as her limited structural capacities, especially concerning the self, call for constant co-regulation by the interaction partner.

What would be important in a therapy is to be very mindful of the to-be-expected relational patterns. The clinician should especially strive to find a good balance between leaving the patient enough control to feel in charge, and thereby safe, and eliciting therapeutic tasks and challenges. Trying to be loved and admired for quick progress (self-worth conflict, with the aim of fulfilling a more basic need for care), Carol may appear to be more stable than she actually is. However, apart from the noticeable structural deficits which usually take some time to change, quick progress may also be an interpersonal regulatory move to not become too attached, and therefore to avoid verifying if another person, in this case the therapist, may like her even if she is not always 'the best patient'.

If one would just look at the absence of a regular PD diagnosis, it may be tempting to work with Carol in a very straightforward manner on conflictual motives, dysfunctional cognitions or repressed emotions. However, taking into account the marked deficits in structural capacities, Carol will not be able to deal with the related emotions at first. Therefore, any kind of treatment should address her impaired structural abilities first, especially regarding capacities of the self. Otherwise she may either start to dissociate on a regular basis during sessions or avoid the treatment altogether. Probably a longer-term treatment should be discussed with the patient, keeping in mind that Carol may not be able to consent to this just yet. On the other hand, there is a considerable probability of a good enough long-term outcome, as Carol is clearly motivated, is used to realizing goals in life, and was able to turn at least some parts of her motivational insecurities into career achievements. A future therapeutic challenge is probably to address relationship and intimacy issues, as it is unclear to what extent the relationship in itself is open for change, and what would happen in the case that the couple would split up.

DISCUSSION

In addition to a standardized rating-form used for documentation and research, the OPD holds a variety of possibilities for individualized case formulation and treatment planning. In our view, the OPD has three key advantages for a tailored treatment planning, especially in personality disorders.

First, although developed from a psychodynamic background, the OPD is a truly integrative system. The focus on interpersonal patterns is not only in line with current research (Pincus, 2017), it also opens a window into working with relational patterns (Ehrenthal, 2017; Schauenburg & Grande, 2011). Even when following the assumption that a mature neurotic conflict is very different from motivational topics in PDs, understanding motives is important for working with PD patients as well (Kramer et al., 2014; Levy, Johnson, Clouthier, Scala, & Temes, 2015). Introducing a rating for structural abilities of personality functioning regarding the self and others not only anticipated recent developments in DSM-5 and ICD-11 by more than two decades, but also assists the clinician to make a thorough assessment of what level of intervention the patient is able to work with and process at the beginning of treatment. Although treatments for PDs differ widely in their models and interventions, they all agree on some key elements of good practice. These are for example a focus of working in the present and the centrality of experiences in the session, clear treatment- and change-models and a thorough description of the framework, handling of crisis, a hierarchy of therapy goals and a clear definition of tasks of therapists and patients, and length and frequency of sessions (see Dammann, 2014). In other words, all treatments of PDs take preparations not to overstrain the patients in their perceptual and regulatory capacities, and the OPD LSIA is a tested and tried way of determining the level of what a given patient can tolerate.

Secondly, it is not restricted to a particular psychotherapy model, but leaves room for integration. While other assessment procedures may be highly specific to a single treatment-model, especially the OPD-structure axis is suitable for the development and measuring of change of treatment goals in different psychotherapies. For example, while Dialectic Behaviour Therapy (DBT) may put a strong emphasis on working on experiencing and tolerating affect and controlling impulses, at least in an early phase of treatment, Mentalization-Based Treatment (MBT) would rather focus on self-object differentiation, anticipation and developing empathy. Transference Focused Psychotherapy (TFP) would probably address self-object differentiation, identity and a more integrated use of introjects. Other treatments would be able to frame therapy goals and targets of interventions in the OPD language as well. Thirdly, it is scalable. Patients are not always seen under optimal treatment conditions (Levy,

Ehrenthal, Yeomans, & Caligor, 2014), and sometimes (for example inpatient) treatments need to develop therapy goals that are realistic to work on in a limited amount of time. Treatment goals on the basis of an OPD diagnosis can be adapted to the specific setting in a way that provides a sequence of consecutive sub-goals that are built on each other. Therefore, the OPD helps to adapt to what is possible under individual conditions.

CLOSING REMARKS AND FUTURE PERSPECTIVES

The OPD provides an approach to develop a clinically relevant assessment of individuals with varying levels of personality dysfunction. It helps to quickly determine whether symptoms and dysfunctional relational experiences are fuelled by internal conflicts, structural deficits or a combination of both. This allows the clinician to adapt his or her treatment to what the patient is capable of tolerating, to not avoid challenging those with higher levels of structural integration, but also not to overstrain those with lower levels of structural integration. Hundreds of training courses have shown that the system is applicable to everyday clinical practice. Existing research on the LSIA provides evidence for the usefulness of developing new dimensional models, such as the DSM-5 LPFS. For clinicians, especially, but not exclusively, from a psychodynamic perspective, the OPD provides a single, integrative diagnosis system that can be applied to most patients treated in very different settings. In other words, the clinician does not have to learn new diagnosis systems for new patient population, although an integration of new measures in the logic of the OPD (i.e., relationship patterns, motivational conflicts and structure) is possible. The OPD is suited as a comparison for any new measure of personality functioning. From a clinical perspective, a necessary next step would be to develop and reformulate treatment models along the conceptual lines of the OPD system.

Acknowledgements

Some details of the case description (age, gender, details on life events and relatives) were changed so as to protect client privacy.

References

American Psychiatric Association. (2013). *Diagnostic and statistical manual of mental disorders: DSM-5* (5th ed.). Washington, DC: American Psychiatric Publ.

Arbeitskreis OPD. (1996). *Operationalisierte psychodynamische Diagnostik: Grundlagen und Manual (1. Aufl.).* Bern: Huber.

Arbeitskreis OPD. (2006). In *Operationalisierte Psychodynamische Diagnostik OPD-2: Das Manual für Diagnostik und Therapieplanung (1. Aufl.).* Bern: Huber.

Beebe, B., Jaffe, J., Markese, S., Buck, K., Chen, H., Cohen, P., et al. (2010). The origins of 12-month attachment: A microanalysis of 4-month mother-infant interaction. *Attachment and Human Development*, *12*(1–2), 3–141. https://doi.org/10.1080/14616730903338985.

Bender, D. S., Morey, L. C., & Skodol, A. E. (2011). Toward a model for assessing level of personality functioning in DSM-5, part I: A review of theory and methods. *Journal of Personality Assessment*, *93*(4), 332–346. https://doi.org/10.1080/00223891.2011.583808.

Benecke, C., Koschier, A., Peham, D., Bock, A., Dahlbender, R. W., Biebl, W., et al. (2009). Erste Ergebnisse zu Reliabilität und Validität der OPD-2 Strukturachse [First results on the reliability and validity of the OPD-2 axis structure]. *Zeitschrift fur Psychosomatische Medizin und Psychotherapie*, *55*(1), 84–96. https://doi.org/10.13109/zptm.2009.55.1.84.

Benjamin, L. S. (1974). Structural analysis of social behavior. *Psychological Review*, *81*(5), 392–425. https://doi.org/10.1037/h0037024.

Cierpka, M., Grande, T., Rudolf, G., von der Tann, M., & Staschf, M. (2007). The operationalized psychodynamic diagnostics system: Clinical relevance, reliability and validity. *Psychopathology*, *40*(4), 209–220. https://doi.org/10.1159/000101363.

Cierpka, M., Grande, T., Stasch, M., Oberbracht, C., Schneider, W., Schüssler, G., et al. (2001). Zur Validität der Operationalisierten Psychodynamischen Diagnostik (OPD). *Psychotherapeut*, *46*(2), 122–133. https://doi.org/10.1007/s002780100145.

Clarkin, J. F. (2006). Conceptualization and treatment of personality disorders.

Dammann, G. (2014). Psychotherapeutischer Prozess und Persönlichkeitsstörungen. *Psychotherapeut*, *59*(2), 119–129.

Dinger, U., Schauenburg, H., Hörz, S., Rentrop, M., Komo-Lang, M., Klinkerfuß, M., et al. (2014). Self-report and observer ratings of personality functioning: A study of the OPD system. *Journal of personality assessment*, *96*(2), 220–225. https://doi.org/10.1080/00223891.2013.828065.

Doering, S., Burgmer, M., Heuft, G., Menke, D., Bäumer, B., Lübking, M., et al. (2014). Assessment of personality functioning: Validity of the operationalized psychodynamic diagnosis axis IV (structure). *Psychopathology*, *47*(3), 185–193. https://doi.org/10.1159/000355062.

Ehrenthal, J. (2017). Psychodynamische Psychotherapie – Grundlagen, Wirksamkeit, Methoden, Techniken. *PSYCH up2date*, *11*(03), 267–286. https://doi.org/10.1055/s-0043-103157.

Ehrenthal, J. C., Dinger, U., Horsch, L., Komo-Lang, M., Klinkerfuss, M., Grande, T., et al. (2012). Der OPD-Strukturfragebogen (OPD-SF): Erste Ergebnisse zu Reliabilität und Validität [The OPD Structure Questionnaire (OPD-SQ): first results on reliability and validity]. *Psychotherapie, Psychosomatik, Medizinische Psychologie*, *62*(1), 25–32. https://doi.org/10.1055/s-0031-1295481.

Ehrenthal, J. C., Dinger, U., Schauenburg, H., Horsch, L., Dahlbender, R. W., & Gierk, B. (2015). Entwicklung einer Zwölf-Item-Version des OPD-Strukturfragebogens (OPD-SFK) [Development of a 12-item version of the OPD-Structure Questionnaire (OPD-SQS)]. *Zeitschrift fur Psychosomatische Medizin und Psychotherapie*, *61*(3), 262–274. https://doi.org/10.13109/zptm.2015.61.3.262.

Ehrenthal, J. C., & Grande, T. (2014). Fokusorientierte Beziehungsgestaltung in der Psychotherapie von Persönlichkeitsstörungen. *PiD-Psychotherapie im Dialog*, *15*(03), 80–85. *Psychotherapy Research*, *16*(1), 1–11.

Grande, T. (2007). Wie stellen sich Konflikt und Struktur in Beziehungen dar? *Zeitschrift für psychosomatische Medizin und Psychotherapie*, *53*(2), 144–162.

Hartke, R. (2016). The Oedipus complex: A confrontation at the central cross-roads of psychoanalysis. *The International Journal of Psycho-Analysis*, *97*(3), 893–913. https://doi.org/10.1111/1745-8315.12561.

Hettema, J. M. (2008). The nosologic relationship between generalized anxiety disorder and major depression. *Depression and Anxiety*, *25*(4), 300–316. https://doi.org/10.1002/da.20491.

Insel, T., Cuthbert, B., Garvey, M., Heinssen, R., Pine, D. S., Quinn, K., et al. (2010). Research domain criteria (RDoC): Toward a new classification framework for research on mental disorders. *The American Journal of Psychiatry, 167*(7), 748–751. https://doi.org/10.1176/appi.ajp.2010.09091379.

Johnson, M. E., Popp, C., Schacht, T. E., Mellon, J., & Strupp, H. H. (1989). Converging evidence for identification of recurrent relationship themes: Comparison of two methods. *Psychiatry, 52*(3), 275–288.

Kiesler, D. J. (1983). The 1982 interpersonal circle: A taxonomy for complementarity in human transactions. *Psychological Review, 90*(3), 185–214. https://doi.org/10.1037/0033-295X.90.3.185.

Köhling, J., Moessner, M., Ehrenthal, J. C., Bauer, S., Cierpka, M., Kämmerer, A., et al. (2016). Affective instability and reactivity in depressed patients with and without borderline pathology. *Journal of Personality Disorders, 30*(6), 776–795. https://doi.org/10.1521/pedi_2015_29_230.

König, K., Dahlbender, R. W., Holzinger, A., Topitz, A., & Doering, S. (2016). Kreuzvalidierung von drei Fragebögen zur Strukturdiagnostik: BPI, IPO und OPD-SF [Cross-validation of three questionnaires for structural diagnosis: BPI, IPO, and OPD-SQ]. *Zeitschrift fur Psychosomatische Medizin und Psychotherapie, 62*(2), 177–189. https://doi.org/10.13109/zptm.2016.62.2.177.

Kramer, U., Kolly, S., Berthoud, L., Keller, S., Preisig, M., Caspar, F., et al. (2014). Effects of motive-oriented therapeutic relationship in a ten-session general psychiatric treatment of borderline personality disorder: A randomized controlled trial. *Psychotherapy and Psychosomatics, 83*(3), 176–186. https://doi.org/10.1159/000358528.

Kroenke, K., Spitzer, R. L., Williams, J. B. W., & Löwe, B. (2010). The patient health questionnaire somatic, anxiety, and depressive symptom scales: A systematic review. *General Hospital Psychiatry, 32*(4), 345–359. https://doi.org/10.1016/j.genhosppsych.2010.03.006.

Levy, K. N., Ehrenthal, J. C., Yeomans, F. E., & Caligor, E. (2014). The efficacy of psychotherapy: Focus on psychodynamic psychotherapy as an example. *Psychodynamic Psychiatry, 42*(3), 377–421. https://doi.org/10.1521/pdps.2014.42.3.377.

Levy, K. N., Johnson, B. N., Clouthier, T. L., Scala, J. W., & Temes, C. M. (2015). An attachment theoretical framework for personality disorders. *Canadian Psychology/Psychologie Canadienne, 56*(2), 197–207. https://doi.org/10.1037/cap0000025.

Luborsky, L., & Crits-Christoph, P. (1998). *Understanding transference: The core conflictual relationship theme method* (2nd ed.). Washington: American Psychological Association.

Pincus, A. L. (2017). An interpersonal perspective on criterion a of the DSM-5 alternative model for personality disorders. *Current Opinion in Psychology, 21*, 11–17. https://doi.org/10.1016/j.copsyc.2017.08.035.

Rudolf, G., Grande, T., & Henningsen, P. (2010). In *Die Struktur der Persönlichkeit: Theoretische Grundlagen zur psychodynamischen Therapie struktureller Störungen (2. unveränderter Nachdruck)*. Stuttgart: Schattauer.

Sandler, J., & Joffe, W. G. (1969). Towards a basic psychoanalytic model. *The International Journal of Psycho-analysis, 50*(1), 79–90.

Schauenburg, H., & Grande, T. (2011). Interview measures of interpersonal functioning and quality of object relations. In L. M. Horowitz, & S. Strack (Eds.), *Handbook of interpersonal psychology: Theory, research, assessment and therapeutic interventions* (pp. 343–356). Hoboken, NJ: Wiley.

Spitzer, R. L. (1983). Psychiatric diagnosis: Are clinicians still necessary? *Comprehensive Psychiatry, 24*(5), 399–411.

Tann, M. v. d., & Ristl, E. (Eds.). (2008). *Operationalized psychodynamic diagnosis OPD-2: Manual of diagnosis and treatment planning*. Cambridge, MA, Göttingen, Toronto, Bern: Hogrefe.

Tyrer, P., Crawford, M., Mulder, R., Blashfield, R., Farnam, A., Fossati, A., et al. (2011). The rationale for the reclassification of personality disorder in the 11th revision of the International Classification of Diseases (ICD-11). *Personality and Mental Health, 5*(4), 246–259. https://doi.org/10.1002/pmh.190.

Zimmermann, J., Benecke, C., Bender, D. S., Skodol, A. E., Schauenburg, H., Cierpka, M., et al. (2014). Assessing DSM-5 level of personality functioning from videotaped clinical interviews: A pilot study with untrained and clinically inexperienced students. *Journal of Personality Assessment*, *96*(4), 397–409. https://doi.org/10.1080/00223891.2013.852563.

Zimmermann, J., Dahlbender, R. W., Herbold, W., Krasnow, K., Turrión, C. M., Zika, M., et al. (2015). Der OPD-Strukturfragebogen erfasst die allgemeinen Merkmale einer Persönlichkeitsstörung [The OPD structure questionnaire captures the general features of personality disorder]. *Psychotherapie, Psychosomatik, Medizinische Psychologie*, *65*(2), 81–83. https://doi.org/10.1055/s-0034-1395626.

Zimmermann, J., Ehrenthal, J. C., Cierpka, M., Schauenburg, H., Doering, S., & Benecke, C. (2012). Assessing the level of structural integration using operationalized psychodynamic diagnosis (OPD): Implications for DSM-5. *Journal of Personality Assessment*, *94*(5), 522–532. https://doi.org/10.1080/00223891.2012.700664.

CHAPTER

16

Case Formulation in Interpersonal Defence Theory: A Process Model of Interpersonal Phenomena that Play Key Roles in Psychopathology and Psychotherapy

Michael A. Westerman

New York University, New York, United States

Interpersonal defence theory (e.g., Westerman, 2018a; Westerman & Muran, 2017; Westerman & Steen, 2007) is an interpersonal approach to psychopathology. As such, it is well suited for research and practice with patients with personality disorders. Moreover, the theory's development included research on psychotherapy with patients with personality disorders.

Case formulations play an integral role in the theory. The tenets of the theory are nomothetic, but the particular way in which the processes of interest occur in a given case is idiographic; they depend on specific features of the case identified in a formulation of that case.

The theory and its case formulations provide process models of interpersonal phenomena. They not only identify key features of a case, but they offer accounts of how interpersonal behaviours are organized over time, including causal processes that link interpersonal phenomena together. As a result, the theory and its case formulations provide explanatory models that enhance understanding of problematic processes and have implications for psychotherapy.

In this chapter, I first present interpersonal defence theory, emphasizing how it provides a process model. I then discuss procedures clinicians

Case Formulation for Personality Disorders
https://doi.org/10.1016/B978-0-12-813521-1.00016-3

and researchers can employ for arriving at case formulations based on the theory. The next section of the chapter illustrates the theory's tenets and my remarks about case formulation with a clinical example. I then summarize studies based on interpersonal defence theory that have been conducted of therapy with patients with personality disorders and discuss the theory's implications for psychotherapy.

INTERPERSONAL DEFENCE THEORY

In broad strokes, interpersonal defence theory (1) offers a characterization of problematic interpersonal behaviour patterns that play central roles in many psychological disorders, including, in particular, many cases of personality disorders; (2) explains why people engage in those problematic interpersonal patterns; (3) identifies how other people are likely to respond when an individual behaves in these ways and explains why the problematic patterns lead to those responses; and (4) explains why the responses by others in turn contribute to the persistence of the first person's problematic interpersonal behaviour.

The core of the theory is an interpersonal reconceptualization of defence processes. As the term 'defence' suggests, the theory reflects the influence of psychoanalytic theory, but it also differs significantly from psychoanalytic thinking in a number of ways. According to traditional psychoanalytic notions, defences are intrapsychic processes that modulate inner experiences of anxiety, guilt and self-esteem. By contrast, according to interpersonal defence theory, defences primarily are interpersonal behaviour patterns that attempt to influence the responses of the other person in a relationship. Shortly, I will explain that interpersonal defence theory also includes other psychoanalytic concepts, including conflict, wishes, fears, transference and countertransference. These notions also are reconceptualized in a novel interpersonal framework.

The Theory's Tenets

As one aspect of its emphasis on process, the theory takes as a key guiding idea the view that we should focus on how interaction is organized over time. Instead of conceptualizing interpersonal phenomena as strings of individual behaviours each of which is treated as an isolable building block, we should recognize that any individual interpersonal behaviour is an *incomplete part* of an organized interaction that has to *dovetail,* or *coordinate,* with other behaviours and other aspects of what is taking place to forge the interaction (see Fogel, 1993; Kaye, 1985).

This idea provided the basis for observations that led to the first tenet of interpersonal defence theory: Defensive interpersonal behaviour is characterized by recurring patterns of coordination failures. When people behave defensively, they relate to others in ways that include repeatedly making contributions to interactions that do not mesh with the other person's contributions and their own prior contributions.

For example, I can briefly describe the interpersonal pattern of the patient in the case I will discuss later as follows: She repeatedly put something forward (often as an allusion), but then when the other person tried to engage her in talking about what she put forward, she either trailed off, that is, hesitated and paused as if she did not know what to say and was unable to continue, and/or shifted to another topic (often by alluding to something else). When I turn directly to that case, I will illustrate this non-coordinating pattern concretely with a transcript excerpt from that case. My consideration of the case example also will provide concrete illustrations of the other tenets of interpersonal defence theory that I present in what follows.

Why do people behave in ways characterized by patterns of recurring coordination failures? According to interpersonal defence theory, the answer to this question brings in conflict, wishes and fears, all reconceptualized. In interpersonal defence theory, wishes and fears do not refer to internal processes, but rather to meaningful action patterns. The theory focuses on conflicts between a person's central interpersonal wish and the individual's central interpersonal fear. In conflicts of this kind, the person greatly desires to engage in a pattern of interaction in which he or she acts a certain way (call this X) towards a significant other and the other person then responds in a particular highly salient positive manner, but the person also dreads that if he or she acts towards the significant other in way X, the other person might respond in a particular highly salient negative manner.

The second tenet of the theory is that interpersonal defences are attempts to negotiate these conflicts. They are ways in which people try to pursue interpersonal wishes while they also try to avoid the feared interpersonal outcomes that might result from pursuing that wish. Defensive interpersonal behaviour is characterized by recurring breaches of coordination because parts of those patterns pursue the wish, while other parts attempt to 'cancel out' how doing so opens up the possibility of the fear.

In addition to this tenet about how interpersonal defences are *attempts* at successfully negotiating wish–fear conflicts, the theory also includes several tenets about what I refer to as *'feed-forward effects'*. These tenets concern how defensive behaviour *actually* influences the other person's responses. This is another aspect of why the theory offers a process model – the tenets about feed-forward effects specify causal relationships between behaviours.

According to one of those tenets and in contrast to notions about self-fulfilling prophecies, defensive behaviour typically succeeds at avoiding feared interpersonal responses, even though defensive patterns include efforts to pursue the wish that usually would open up the possibility of the fear. Therefore, in this respect, interpersonal defences 'work'. However, according to other feed-forward tenets, they also influence the other person's responses in several additional ways. Specifically, they make it unlikely that the other person will respond in the individual's wished-for manner, promote positive responses that are distinct from the wish, and promote negative responses distinct from the fear. Later, I will illustrate the feed-forward tenets with the clinical example and explain why interpersonal defences have these effects.

Another tenet of interpersonal defence theory is that the feed-forward effects of an individual's defensive pattern contribute to maintaining that pattern. For one thing, this occurs because the other person does not behave in the feared manner. In addition, the positive responses distinct from the first person's wish support continuation of the defensive pattern. Moreover, the first person can continue to *try* to pursue the wish by acting defensively, even though the pattern does not actually lead to realizing the wish. Finally, although interpersonal defences promote negative outcomes distinct from the fear, which might work against maintaining the pattern in some measure, those relationship outcomes are less salient for the person than his or her central fear, which, again, the pattern successfully avoids.

Another tenet incorporates intrapsychic defence mechanisms in the theory. However, according to that tenet, we should treat those inner mechanisms as nested subprocesses that support defensive interpersonal action patterns.

Interpersonal defence theory explains the relationship between problematic interpersonal processes and symptoms in two ways. Many symptoms, such as being withdrawn or aggressive, are themselves parts of defensive patterns. They play roles in attempts to negotiate conflicts. Symptoms, such as anxiety, and also problematic emotions, like shame, are, in part, consequences of defensive patterns, but quite often such 'responses' also play roles supporting defensive patterns.

Finally, although the tenets of interpersonal defence theory apply to relationships in general, the theory also includes tenets that link the ideas I have presented above with therapeutic relationship processes in particular. According to one of those tenets, we should reconceptualize transference as the appearance of a patient's defensive, noncoordinating pattern in the patient's behaviour towards his or her therapist. According to another tenet, countertransference is the appearance in a therapist's behaviour of the feed-forward effects of the patient's defensive pattern (i.e., negative responses distinct from the patient's fear and positive responses distinct from the patient's wish, and the absence of behaving in the patient's wished-for manner).

CASE FORMULATION

Components

The components of a case formulation based on interpersonal defence theory include (1) a careful description of the patient's defensive, noncoordinating interpersonal behaviour pattern, (2) the patient's central interpersonal wish, (3) the patient's central interpersonal fear, (4) positive responses by others that are distinct from the wish that often occur in the patient's relationships and (5) negative responses by others that are distinct from the fear that often occur in the patient's relationships.

Analytic Methods

Defensive, noncoordinating patterns are identified using discourse-oriented procedures that focus on how interpersonal behaviours are organized over time. These procedures draw on conversation analysis (Drew & Heritage, 2006) and work in developmental sociolinguistics (Keenan & Schieffelin, 1976), which also emphasize sequential features of interaction. However, whereas those approaches try to identify sequential 'devices' employed by members of a culture in general, the patterns of interest in interpersonal defence theory are idiographic. Also, according to interpersonal defence theory, identifying defensive, noncoordinating patterns requires considering the functional role played by aspects of sequential features of exchange with regard to a person's interpersonal wishes and fears (see Westerman, 2011).

Identifying a person's defensive pattern involves examining the unique ways in which that individual's contributions (utterances, gestures, facial expressions, actions) to interactions relate to the other person's contributions and, especially, to his or her own prior contributions. This examination proceeds in a manner that is guided by two considerations: (1) determining whether those aspects of the person's interpersonal behaviour (i.e., how the person relates his or her contributions to the other person's contributions and the person's own prior contributions) are marked by a particular recurring pattern of failures to mesh contributions to the exchange with what is transpiring, and (2) identifying whether, and if so, how, that pattern functions to offer the person ways of pursuing the interpersonal wish while simultaneously trying to cancel out how those efforts might lead to the fear. The case example that appears later illustrates this process.

The Structured Analysis of Social Behavior (SASB; e.g., Benjamin, 1979) provides an excellent framework for the other components of a case formulation based on interpersonal defence theory. Two of the three "surfaces" of the SASB model (the two surfaces depicted in Fig. 16.1) can help researchers and clinicians direct their focus to *interpersonal outcomes* when it comes to identifying a person's wish and fear, positive outcomes distinct from the wish and negative outcomes distinct from the fear. According to interpersonal defence theory, internal experiences, such as anxiety or feeling inadequate, are important, but our primary focus should be on interpersonal behaviours when we consider those components of case formulations.

SASB also is a very useful framework for formulations based on interpersonal defence theory because it provides a basis for making crucial *differentiations* between interpersonal behaviours. All of the behaviours on the right hand sides of the two SASB surfaces shown in Fig. 16.1 are positive in affiliation, but in many cases they differ from each other in degree of positive affiliation, and, more significantly, they all differ from one another on the interdependence (vertical) axis. As a result, the model helps us distinguish between different positive behaviours and, thereby, differentiate between a person's central wish and positive responses that are distinct from that wish. Similarly, the structured

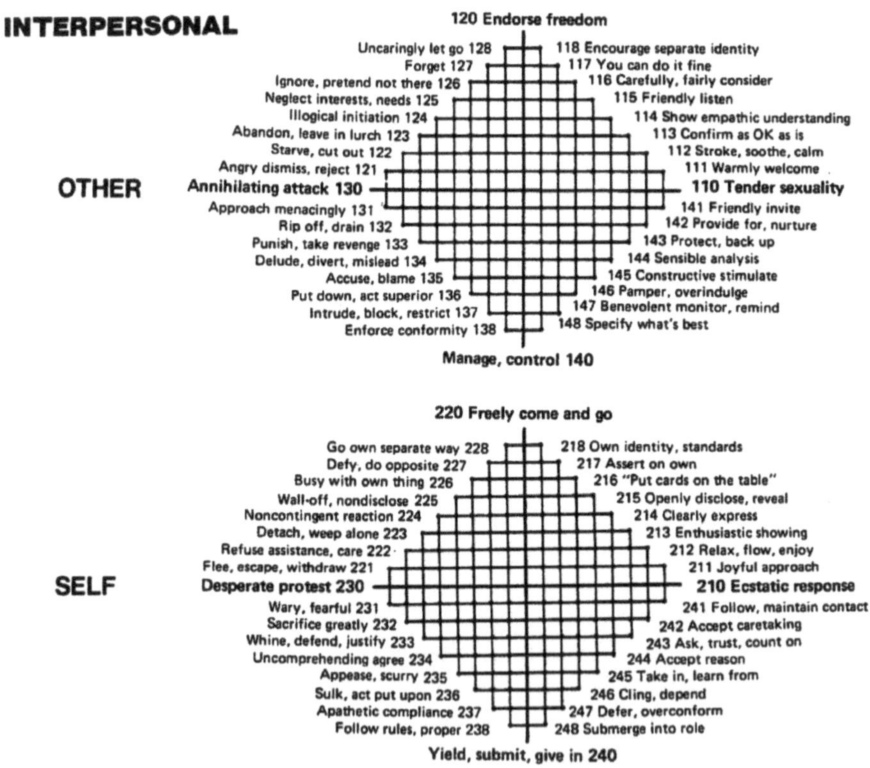

FIGURE 16.1 Structural Analysis of Social Behavior (SASB). The figure omits the introject surface and includes only the two interpersonal surfaces of the SASB model. *From Benjamin, L. S. (1979). Structural analysis of differentiation failure.* Psychiatry: Journal for the Study of Interpersonal Processes, 42, 1–23. *Reprinted with permission of The Guilford Press.*

arrays of behaviours on the left hand sides of the two surfaces make it possible to distinguish between different negative responses and, thereby, differentiate between a central fear and negative responses that are distinct from the fear.

Procedures for Arriving at a Case Formulation

The procedures employed for arriving at these case formulations vary depending on one's purposes. In studies of the theory's tenets, when appropriate, steps can be taken to insure independence in assessments of different components of a formulation. In clinical practice, the tenets can be used to make inferences about certain components of the formulation based on assessments of other components. What follows describes one possible set of procedures that is appropriate in many situations. It can be modified when that is necessary.

The first step is to examine patient-therapist interaction in the first three sessions of a case to make a preliminary identification of the noncoordinating pattern. This involves carefully examining how the patient's contributions to the exchange relate to the therapist's contributions and the patient's own prior contributions and trying to determine what desired outcome parts of the patient's behaviour pursue and what feared outcome aspects of the pattern are attempting to avoid.

Following this, the patient's narratives about events in other relationships (i.e., other than the therapy relationship) during intake interviews (if there were any) and therapy sessions are examined. This part of the analysis should focus especially on narratives about relationships during early childhood. According to ideas about development that are part of interpersonal defence theory, wish–fear conflicts develop as a result of repeated early childhood experiences in which the person pursued a particular interpersonal outcome that was very important to him or her (which becomes the central interpersonal wish) and significant others typically responded in a particular negative manner (which becomes the central fear). At some later point (often at about 10 years of age), the child develops a defensive, noncoordinating pattern to try to successfully negotiate these difficult situations. When that happens, and as I explained earlier, the person's interpersonal behaviour leads to a very different set of outcomes – positive responses that are distinct from the wish and negative outcomes that are distinct from the fear. Therefore, narratives of earlier experiences are especially helpful because the wish and fear appear more clearly. Those narratives may lead a clinician or researcher to revise or refine his or her prior preliminary assessments of the wish and fear components of the formulation.

It also is helpful to consider patients' narratives about contemporaneous relationships outside of therapy. According to interpersonal defence theory, an individual's defensive pattern usually appears in many of the person's important relationships. Researchers and clinicians can consider patients' narratives about those relationships (especially when they include a lot of details about both the patient's and the other person's parts in an interaction) to see if they support ideas based on the other data mentioned earlier about a patient's defensive, noncoordinating pattern and the kind of responses it usually promotes. Here again, this may lead to revising or refining the formulation.

The procedures for arriving at a case formulation also can include another step. Examination of patient–therapist interaction in sessions following the first few sessions provide a very useful opportunity for confirming a formulation. However, here it is important to bear in mind that when treatment is successful, patients' patterns are likely to change at some point during therapy as they begin to behave in a nondefensive manner and pursue their wishes in straightforward ways. Also, others are likely to begin to respond to the patient in new ways. Changes of this kind can offer an important type of confirmation of a formulation if they make it quite clear that the wish was what the researcher or clinician previously thought it was.

CASE EXAMPLE

I now turn to a case example to illustrate many of the ideas that I have presented so far. This section is lengthy because it shows how case formulations based on interpersonal defence theory provide process models that explain clinically important interpersonal phenomena.

The case was part of a large study of psychotherapy for patients with diagnoses based on DSM IIIR of one or more Cluster C personality disorders (avoidant, obsessive-compulsive, dependent and self-defeating, which was one of the Cluster C disorders at the time the study was conducted) and/or Personality Disorder NOS (Muran, Safran, Samstag, & Winston, 2005). Cluster C personality disorders are the most prevalent personality disorder diagnoses.

The patient was a 33-year-old single female. Jane's (pseudonym) diagnosis included dysthymia and social phobia on Axis I and self-defeating personality disorder and PD NOS on Axis II. Her target problems included poor self-esteem, difficulties with relationships, feelings of inadequacy at work and concerns about not making progress in her career. Jane's treatment was short-term (30 once-weekly sessions) psychodynamic psychotherapy. Her therapist was a doctoral level male psychologist with seven years of experience. Outcome of the case was judged to be poor based on pre-established criteria regarding a set of six measures.

Jane's Noncoordinating Pattern

Following the procedures I described earlier, I identified a recurring pattern of coordination breaches in Jane's interpersonal behaviour. As I noted earlier in this chapter, Jane repeatedly put something forward (often as an allusion), but then either trailed off, that is, hesitated and paused as if she did not know what to say and was unable to continue, and/or shifted to another topic (often by alluding to something else). As a result, many of her contributions to interactions did not mesh with the other person's bids or with her own prior contributions.

A transcript excerpt from the 11th session of Jane's therapy illustrates this pattern. In the first turn, Jane refers to a man, David (pseudonym), she met in an adult education class. Following the excerpt, I offer a turn-by-turn analysis of the exchange, pointing out examples of Jane's noncoordinating pattern. Later, I will turn to analyzing the therapist's contributions.

1. Patient: ... don't feel entitled to call him. I feel like I'm going to be disturbing him. (sigh) I'm going off on a tangent ... what was I saying?
2. Therapist: why do you feel it was a tangent ... you were elaborating on – around an issue.
3. Patient: Yeah.
4. Therapist: What happens? Did you get ... come to a dead end? Did you get confused?
5. Patient: I think I ... I got a little confu ... (smiling) I lost sort of my initial point of what I was saying
6. Therapist: (interrupts) Before that happened were you thinking about anything in particular?
7. Patient: (pause) (looking down) Um ... see this is ... this is ... I ... it's like right now I can't even really think.
8. Therapist: (backchannel) Um huh (yes)
9. Patient: It's like, it all feels really jumbled.
10. Therapist: (smug smile) You must think I expect a particular answer.
11. Patient: (smiles) Yeah
12. Therapist: (interrupts) And it's getting you scared.
13. Patient: (laughs) (looks away and down) Yeah, well I'm searching for something ... there is that ... it's like I'm searching for something and I can't find it.

There are several examples of Jane's pattern of putting something forward and then trailing off and/or shifting to another topic in this excerpt. In turn 1, Jane alludes to an important feeling (feeling that she isn't 'entitled' to call David), but then derails this topic by discounting it as just 'a tangent' and asking the therapist to remind her what she had been saying before her allusion to not feeling entitled to call.

In turns 2 and 4, the therapist tries to explore why Jane moved away from her comment about not feeling entitled to call David, inquiring in turn 4 whether she got confused. Jane responds in turn 5 that she got a little confused. By agreeing with the therapist, Jane seems to be putting forward the idea that it would make sense for the two of them to talk about how she got confused. However, note that she accompanies her turn with a smile.

The therapist pursues the idea that she got confused in turn 6, but instead of responding to his question in turns 7 and 9, Jane says that she is unable to continue this thread ('it's like right now I can't even really think ... it's like, it all feels really jumbled'). Jane is making a subtle shift. She cannot say more about how she was confused *a moment ago,* because *right now* she cannot think. The upshot is that she doesn't follow through with her prior comment (turn 5) in which she suggested that it would make sense to talk about how she got confused.

In turns 10 and 12, the therapist suggests that Jane is concerned and scared about his expectations regarding her responses. Jane agrees in turn 11, and she says 'yeah' again near the beginning of turn 13. However, these turns actually make it quite unclear whether she really does agree with the therapist's idea. She offers these contributions while smiling in turn 11 and laughing and looking away and down in turn 13. In addition, in turn 13, she offers a comment that suggests (an allusion) that she may actually see things a different way. The remark 'I'm searching for something and I can't find it' appears to offer a different idea about why she gets lost, an idea that focuses on her inability to follow through, not her concern about expectations.

Explaining Jane's Pattern of Interpersonal Behaviour

The wish and fear components of the formulation for this case provide the basis for understanding why Jane behaved the way she did. Using SASB as a framework and based on examining examples of Jane's in-session behaviour, her narratives about childhood experiences in her family, and her narratives about relationships at subsequent points in her life, I arrived at the following assessments: Jane's central interpersonal wish was to have relationships in which she clearly expressed herself (214, see Fig. 16.1) and enthusiastically showed herself (213) and others responded by showing her empathic understanding (114) and confirming her as OK (113). However, Jane's fear was that if she expressed/showed herself, other people might ignore her (126) and neglect her interests and needs (125).

In the SASB model, clearly expressing oneself (214) and the other person showing empathic understanding (114) are referred to as 'complementary' behaviours. This is also the case for enthusiastically showing oneself (213) and confirming as OK by the other person (113). As such, the behaviours in each of these pairs of behaviours 'pull' for one another. If one person in a relationship behaves a certain way, it becomes somewhat more likely that the other person will respond with the complement of that behaviour. However, it is by no means necessarily the case that this is what will happen. In fact, when as a young child, Jane expressed (214) and showed (213) herself hoping that her parents would respond by empathically understanding her (114) and confirming her as OK (113) (which became her central wish), her parents often responded by ignoring her (126) and neglecting her interests and needs (125) (which became her central fear).

Jane reported that during her childhood, her father ignored and neglected her 'out of disinterest' and that she played a supportive role in her relationship with her mother, rather than vice versa. Her main feeling was that her 'place in the family was in the shadows'. This feeling was augmented by the fact that her brother was a talented musician who 'commanded the attention of the family'.

Returning to Jane's defensive, noncoordinating behaviour pattern: Jane might have pursued her wish by clearly expressing and showing herself, but she was afraid that if she behaved that way, other people might ignore and neglect her. She attempted to negotiate this conflict by behaving in the defensive, noncoordinating manner we saw in the transcript excerpt. If we consider by themselves the many points at which Jane put forward significant matters, we see that her pattern included repeated efforts to express/show herself, which were attempts to pursue her wish. For example, in the first turn of the segment we considered from session 11, Jane said that she did not feel entitled to call David, disclosing (i.e., showing) that she thought she did not have a right to expect much from others and, quite possibly, that she was unsure about her own worth. Taken by itself, this bid might have led Jane's therapist to show Jane empathic understanding and/or confirm her as OK as is. For example, he might have said 'It sounds like it's difficult for you to ask other people for things' (empathic understanding), or 'It's a real strength that you're able to let me see that you feel that way' (confirm as OK as is).

But taken by itself, Jane's comment about not feeling entitled also would open up the possibility that her feared outcome might occur. For example, her therapist might simply have said 'I see' and then switched to talking about a topic he thought they should pursue. Recall, however, that Jane's pattern also included failures at following through and/or shifts of topic, e.g., in her first turn in the excerpt she went on to say 'I'm going off on a tangent .... What was I saying?' These parts of her pattern worked to avoid her fear for two reasons.

One reason hinges on the idea that behaviours have to dovetail with one another over time. Truly expressing/showing oneself not only requires putting forward something significant, it also requires following through by expanding on an initial comment, addressing questions the other person asks and so forth. Jane did not behave in that manner. Instead, she repeatedly derailed her references to significant matters. For example, the second half of Jane's first turn derailed Jane going on to clearly express the feeling that she was unworthy to expect much from others. As a result, Jane's therapist could not ignore or neglect her when she clearly expressed herself and enthusiastically showed herself because she never truly behaved that way.

The second reason Jane's defensive, noncoordinating pattern worked to avoid her fear was that it led others to *respond in other ways instead of her fear,* specifically, with certain negative responses that were distinct from her fear and certain positive responses that were distinct from her wish. I will explain why it had this effect shortly. At this juncture, I will simply point out that Jane's therapist was very actively engaged with Jane in the transcript excerpt we have been considering. He did not neglect or ignore her.

Feed-Forward Effects of Jane's Interpersonal Pattern

As I just explained, Jane's defensive pattern provided her with a way to *attempt* to pursue her wish and also avoid her fear. One upshot of Jane's behaviour was that she *actually succeeded* at avoiding her fear, which conforms to the first tenet about feed-forward effects. However, this case example also illustrates the other three feed-forward tenets.

Jane's defensive pattern also made it almost impossible for other people to respond to her in the manner she wished for. Just as Jane's therapist could not ignore or neglect Jane when she clearly expressed/enthusiastically showed herself (which would have realized her fear) because she never truly behaved that way but rather repeatedly derailed her attempts to put forward significant matters, her therapist also did not have opportunities to show Jane empathic understanding or confirm her as OK when she truly expressed/showed herself (which would have realized her wish). And, in fact, the therapist only very rarely showed empathic understanding or confirmed Jane as OK over the course of treatment.

Although Jane's defensive, noncoordinating interpersonal behaviour made it unlikely that others would respond to her in the ways she feared or wished for, it did promote certain other kinds of responses. Jane's failures to follow through and her topic shifts derailed her efforts to put forward significant matters, but they did not 'cancel out' those attempts to pursue her wish as if they never occurred. Instead, the overall 'package' of her interpersonal pattern led others to treat Jane as someone who was 'holding back from expressing/showing herself'.

As a result, Jane's defensive pattern made it likely that two outcomes would occur. Other people might respond to Jane as if she was 'holding back' in the sense of 'having difficulty expressing herself'. They might try to *help her* let them know who she is, what she thinks and so forth. Along these lines, for example, at one point Jane said that throughout her life people told her that there was something about her that made them want to help her. In SASB terms, we can say that her pattern promoted *benign managing responses* by others, including 'specify what's best' (148), 'benevolently monitor' (147), 'overindulge' (146), 'constructive stimulate' (145) and 'sensible analysis' (144). These were positive outcomes distinct from Jane's wish.

In addition, however, others also responded to Jane as if she was 'holding back' in the sense of 'refusing to go ahead with what she had to say while baiting them to engage her about her allusions'. In these instances, they would try to *get her* to stop holding back by making *hostile controlling responses*, including 'accuse, blame' (135), 'put down, act superior' (136), 'intrude, block, restrict' (137) and 'enforce conformity' (138). These were negative responses distinct from Jane's fear. Along these lines, for example, Jane reported that boyfriends in past relationships and other people she was close to were very controlling and that she had to defer to them, even though she did not want to do that.

The therapist's contributions to the excerpt included examples of both benign managing and hostile controlling behaviours. His response in turn 2 has benign and hostile qualities, but both are controlling. Because he tries to guide her to continue what she was just saying, his response can be described as 'benevolently monitor, remind' (147) and 'specify what's best' (148). However, because the therapist opposes how Jane wants to proceed (to return to what she was saying prior to turn 1) and rejects her view that her remark about not feeling entitled was a tangent, his intervention also can be characterized as 'intrude, block, restrict' (137).

In turn 4, the therapist extends his benign management with questions about whether Jane came to a dead end or got confused. These questions are examples of 'constructively stimulate' (145). In some measure, he continues to 'constructively stimulate' in turn 6, suggesting that Jane consider what she was thinking about before she got confused. However, turn 6 also is marked by hostile control – the therapist interrupts Jane and tries to get her to proceed along the lines he puts forward rather than wait to see what Jane was going to say ('intrude, block, restrict'; 137).

Turns 10 and 12 by the therapist have some aspects of benign management because they suggest a direction for how Jane should think about her confusion (that she must think he expects certain answers and that's getting her scared). In SASB terms, we can describe this as 'constructively stimulate' (145) and also 'pamper, overindulge' (146) (because they take Jane off the hook by providing an answer to the question the therapist asked her in turn 6). However, the hostile controlling aspects of turns 10 and 12 are more prominent. The therapist offers these comments in a smug manner ('put down, act superior'; 136) and presents them ('you must think') as if his view is unquestionable ('enforce conformity'; 138).

Hence, the therapist responded countertransferentially throughout this exchange, as the countertransference concept is understood in interpersonal defence theory. Specifically, his behaviour was characterized by positive responses distinct from Jane's wish and negative responses distinct from her fear. These observations about subtle aspects of the patient's behaviour and the therapist's behaviour at the turn-by-turn, micro-analytic level of analysis have real clinical significance. Taken together, the patient's defensive interpersonal pattern and the therapist's countertransference responses contributed to poor outcome in Jane's case in two ways: (1) the therapy relationship did not provide Jane with corrective emotional experiences in which she pursued her wish in a straightforward manner and the therapist responded in ways that realized her wish, and (2) Jane's noncoordinating pattern of repeatedly putting something forward but then trailing off and/or shifting to another topic (a pattern the therapist's countertransference responses served to maintain) worked against clearly establishing topics of discussion and moving forward on those topics.

Jane's Target Problems and Symptoms

Notwithstanding the fact that interpersonal defence theory focuses a good deal on subtle micro-analytic, turn-by-turn aspects of interpersonal processes, it helps us understand important molar aspects of Jane's case that have clear clinical significance in another way as well. It helps us understand Jane's target problems and symptoms.

Clearly, this is true for 'relationship problems', one of Jane's three target problems. Another example of this sort is that Jane reported that others often viewed her as 'spacey, weak and unintelligent', characteristics that parallel how she got in a 'jumble', as she called it, when interacting with the therapist in the transcript excerpt. Moreover, Jane reported that her pattern of getting in a 'jumble' and trailing off also occurred at meetings at work and in interactions with her boss, and so it may have contributed to her target problem concerning difficulties at work.

Another point here is that it seems quite likely that Jane's defensive pattern affected another one of her target problems, poor self-esteem, and her dysthymia by (a) working against others confirming her as OK and listening empathically to her, (b) sometimes leading other people to treat her as if she needed help, (c) sometimes leading others to behave in hostile controlling ways towards her, (d) contributing to others thinking she was 'spacey' and so forth and (e) contributing to Jane feeling inadequate at work. Note that in addition to resulting from her defensive behaviour, Jane's poor self-esteem also supported that pattern because it increased the likelihood that she would continue to refrain from following through with expressing/showing herself.

Research

Studies have investigated the tenets of interpersonal defence theory and used the theory as a basis for investigating issues about therapy. This research has included nomothetic observational investigations of process and outcome in therapy (e.g., Hartmann, 2001; Westerman, Foote, & Winston, 1995; Westerman, Tanaka, Frankel, & Kahn, 1986), experimental studies with non-clinic samples (Dahmen & Westerman, 2007; Westerman & Prieto, 2006; Westerman & Steen, 2009) and theory-building case studies (Westerman, 2018b; Westerman & de Roten, 2017; Westerman & Muran, 2017). Here, I offer a brief summary of those studies that investigated psychotherapy with patients with personality disorders.

One of those studies (Westerman et al., 1995) investigated relationships between outcome and the extent to which patients' in-session interpersonal behaviour with their therapists was coordinating versus noncoordinating. All patients ($N=16$) in this study had diagnoses on Axis II of DSM III of compulsive, avoidant, dependent, passive-aggressive and/or histrionic personality disorder. Assessments of coordination were made at four time points for each case.

The findings indicated that, for the full sample, coordination averaged across the four phases of therapy was significantly positively related to improvement. This relationship was quite large in magnitude. Average coordination accounted for 31% of the variance in outcome.

Results also showed that *change* in coordination during treatment was differentially related to improvement in the two kinds of brief psychodynamic therapy included in the study. In one treatment condition, which took an insight-oriented approach that focused on identifying patients' maladaptive interpersonal patterns in their relationships, coordination assessed early in treatment was most strongly associated with outcome and there was no relationship between improvement in coordination over time and outcome. In the other condition, which emphasized confronting patients' in-session defensive behaviour, coordination assessed later in treatment was most strongly associated with outcome and there was a positive relationship between improvement in coordination over time and outcome.

Overall, the results suggested that for patients with the types of personality disorders included in this study, the degree to which a patient engages in the therapeutic relationship in a coordinating manner plays a very important role. In addition, the findings offered some support for the view that if a patient with one of those personality disorders relates to his or her therapist in a highly noncoordinating manner early in therapy, it may be best to focus on promoting successful outcome by helping the patient change how he or she relates to the therapist.

However, note that therapist interventions in this study were not examined in terms of case formulations based on interpersonal defence theory.

Any given insight-oriented intervention may or may not have accurately identified key features of a patient's problematic behaviour according to an interpersonal defence formulation and, similarly, a confrontation may or may not have had desirable interpersonal significance when considered in terms of the theory.

The theory-building case studies I referred to earlier went beyond quantitatively assessing extent of coordination failures by carefully examining patient and therapist behaviours in terms of case formulations based on interpersonal defence theory. Two of those studies (Westerman, 2018b; Westerman & Muran, 2017) investigated therapy with patients with personality disorders.

Theory-building case study methodology is well suited for investigating theories in which case formulations play a central role because this method involves intensive qualitative analysis of individual cases. As Stiles (2009) explained, it also offers a way to investigate the validity of theories that is in some respects preferable to hypothesis-testing group studies because in a theory-building case study, a researcher examines whether individual observations simultaneously conform to the multiple tenets of a theory. If they do, this provides compelling incremental support for the theory under investigation.

Westerman and Muran (2017) conducted a theory-building case study of the treatment of a 28-year-old female patient included in the same treatment condition of the umbrella study (Muran et al., 2005) that also included Jane's case. Based on DSM IIIR, she had Axis II diagnoses of avoidant, self-defeating and paranoid personality disorders, and an Axis I diagnosis of anxiety disorder NOS.

The results provided support for the following tenets of interpersonal defence theory: (1) noncoordinating patterns are attempts to pursue wished-for interpersonal outcomes while trying to avoid feared responses, (2) defensive behaviour by patients makes it more likely that therapists will respond countertransferentially (negative responses distinct from the fear and positive response distinct from the wish) and (3) countertransference responses contribute to maintaining patients' defensive patterns. In addition, the study compared the analyses of therapeutic relationship processes in terms of case formulations based on interpersonal defence theory to alliance assessments on the Working Alliance Inventory (Tracey & Kokotovic, 1989). That comparison suggested that the former may provide a better basis for studying the alliance.

I am currently conducting an intensive theory-building multiple case study project (Westerman, 2018b). This project employs a paired-comparison design. It includes four cases, one good outcome case and one poor outcome case treated by the same therapist and another good outcome-poor outcome pair treated by another therapist. Jane's case is part of this project; the case studied by Westerman and Muran (2017) is not. The four cases come from the same treatment condition of the nomothetic umbrella project as Jane's case. The four patients all had diagnoses including one or more Cluster C personality disorder.

Careful analyses of patient and therapist behaviours in terms of case formulations based on interpersonal defence theory provided further support for the tenets of the theory investigated by Westerman and Muran (2017). In addition, the paired-comparison design led to findings about what contributed to positive outcome. In the poor outcome cases, throughout treatment, patient behaviour was noncoordinating and therapist behaviour was characterized by countertransference responses. In the good outcome cases, this was also true for both patient and therapist behaviours up until the middle of treatment. At about that point in both good outcome cases, however, the patients started to behave in a more coordinating manner and therapists' responses became less countertransferential. Preliminary analyses suggest that two changes by the therapists may have played key roles in promoting the good outcomes – making interventions that accurately identified the patients' interpersonal wishes and behaving towards the patients in ways that realized the patients' wishes in the therapeutic exchange.

TREATMENT IMPLICATIONS

I have discussed the treatment implications of interpersonal defence theory at length elsewhere (Westerman, 2018a). Here, I present those implications that are most closely linked to the theory's approach to case formulation.

The key point is that case formulations based on interpersonal defence theory provide ways of understanding clinical situations that are markedly different from how other approaches would lead clinicians to understand those situations. These differences in how therapists understand cases, in turn, have implications for how they try to promote positive change by helping patients come to new ways of understanding themselves, their problems and so forth.

One point along these lines is that if a therapist thinks about a case in terms of interpersonal defence theory, he or she probably will arrive at a different understanding of the patient's fear and, as a result, be in a better position to help the patient recognize that fear than if the therapist does not use interpersonal defence theory as a guide. Very often, therapists guided by other theories focus on patients' internal experiences when they try to identify key fears. For example, in the case example we considered (which, again, had a poor outcome), Jane's therapist thought that Jane was afraid she would fail to live up to the therapist's expectations, a fear that she was inadequate (for a similar example, see Westerman & Muran, 2017). According to interpersonal defence theory, internal experiences of this sort should be considered, but it is especially important to identify the *interpersonal outcome* that a patient most fears, e.g., whether Jane was concerned about being inadequate because she was afraid that the therapist might then respond with hostile control, or instead with attacking behaviour, or instead by neglecting her (see Fig. 16.1).

In addition, when therapists guided by other theories do focus on feared interpersonal outcomes, they are likely to mistake the negative relationship outcomes a patient often experiences as the patient's central interpersonal fear, following the logic of the self-fulfilling prophecy. For example, if Jane's therapist had thought about what interpersonal outcome Jane feared, he might well have misidentified that fear as hostile controlling responses by others because those were the negative responses she frequently encountered and talked about in therapy. The therapist probably would have gone on to conclude that Jane trailed off because she was afraid of evoking that kind of response.

By contrast, according to the formulation of Jane's case based on interpersonal defence theory, Jane actually was afraid of being ignored and neglected, and Jane's manner of trailing off was part of her way of avoiding *that* outcome – in part, by *eliciting* hostile controlling responses from her therapist. If Jane's therapist had been guided by interpersonal defence theory, he might have helped Jane recognize she was afraid that David would simply end the conversation quickly (i.e., ignore/neglect her) if she called and began to talk to him about things that mattered to her.

Interpersonal defence theory also points to the importance of identifying patients' central interpersonal wishes. According to the theory, a therapist's efforts will be limited if he or she does not think about those wishes at all or if the therapist thinks that patients simply wish that their fears will not occur. Jane's case is an example of this problem. Her therapist did not seem to think about Jane's wish and never helped Jane recognize what she really wanted in her relationships. Westerman and Muran's (2017) theory-building case study offers another example of this problem.

In addition, even when therapists consider their patients' wishes, without a formulation based on interpersonal defence theory, they may mistakenly identify a patient's central interpersonal wish as the positive responses the patient often receives. For example, some therapists might have recognized that other people in Jane's life often tried to help her and concluded that she wished for benign managing responses.

As I noted earlier, preliminary analyses from the theory-building multiple case study project I am conducting (Westerman, 2018b) suggest that it may be very important to help patients recognize what they most want in their relationships. If he had been guided by interpersonal defence theory, Jane's therapist might have asked her questions like 'What would it be like if you called David and your conversation went the best way you can imagine?' and then followed up that question with further interventions to help Jane recognize that she hoped David would relate to her in an empathic and confirming manner.

When therapists understand cases in terms of formulations based on interpersonal defence theory, this also leads them to try to *promote positive change by how they themselves relate to their patients.* One point here is that those formulations point away from behaving countertransferentially because they identify the particular kinds of negative responses distinct from the fear and positive responses distinct from the wish that a given patient's defensive pattern pulls for, and they make it clear that behaving in those ways is likely to contribute to maintaining the defensive pattern. This is helpful for limiting those kinds of negative and positive responses (it is not necessary nor probably possible to completely avoid responding in those ways).

As I suggested earlier, therapist responses that realize patients' wishes in the therapy relationship may be especially helpful for promoting overall improvement. Exchanges of this sort lead to corrective emotional experiences. Here, an accurate formulation is crucial because it identifies what the patient's wish is. I am not suggesting that therapists should behave in the manner a patient wishes no matter how the patient behaves. In fact, it is only possible for a therapist to realize a patient's wish when the patient pursues the wish, because interpersonal wishes refer to that sequence, not just the therapist's response. However, therapists do not have to wait to respond in the wished-for manner until their patients pursue their wishes in a fully straightforward manner. Rather, at many moments in therapy it is possible to respond to the part of a patient's pattern that pursues the wish.

For example, recall that I suggested that Jane's therapist could have responded very differently to her comment about not feeling entitled to call David, by saying 'It sounds like it's difficult for you to ask other people for things' (empathic understanding), or 'It's a real strength that you're able to let me see that you feel that way' (confirm as OK as is). To respond in these ways, however, the therapist would have had to respond to the first part of Jane's first turn in which she expressed how she did not feel entitled to call David and not been thrown off track by the second part of Jane's turn ('I'm going off on a tangent … what was I saying?'), which was her attempt at derailing her remark about not feeling entitled.

Note that although interpersonal defence theory offers its own distinct approach to understanding patients and effective therapy, the implications of the theory for treatment that I have presented here can inform how therapists employ a wide variety of types of intervention. In this sense, the theory is integrative in nature. For example, my comments about treatment implications have relevance for interpretive efforts, direct behavioural suggestions and the chair work used in Emotion Focused Therapy (see Westerman, 2018a).

CONCLUDING COMMENTS

Interpersonal defence theory and the case formulations that play an integral role in it offer process models of problematic interpersonal phenomena that lead to novel ways of conceptualizing clinical situations involving patients with personality disorders. The research I have reviewed suggests that this approach holds promise as a guide for psychotherapy and efforts to further advance our understanding of personality disorders.

No doubt, future research and clinical experience will lead to extending, revising and refining the theory, its approach to case formulation and the implications for treatment that follow from the theory and the formulation of a given case. One direction for future research could involve studies that employ nomothetic – idiographic designs, which would investigate hypotheses in groups of patients in terms of unique case formulations for each patient. Another direction to pursue would involve studies with patients with personality disorders other than the categories of personality disorders that have been studied to date from this perspective.

Acknowledgements

Some details of the case description (use of pseudonyms, altering other specific features of the case and limiting the description of specific features of the case) were changed to protect patient privacy.

References

Benjamin, L. S. (1979). Structural analysis of differentiation failure. *Psychiatry: Journal for the Study of Interpersonal Processes, 42*, 1–23.

Dahmen, B. A., & Westerman, M. A. (2007). Expectations about the long-term consequences of recurring defensive interpersonal behavior. *Journal of Research in Personality, 41*, 1073–1090.

Drew, P., & Heritage, J. (Eds.). (2006). *Conversation analysis:* (*Vols. 1–4*). (London, UK: Sage.

Fogel, A. (1993). *Developing through relationships: Origins of communication, self, and culture.* Chicago: University of Chicago Press.

Hartmann, H. A. (2001). Clients' contribution to the alliance and the role it plays in outcome. *Dissertation Abstracts International: Section B, 61*(8), 4406.

Kaye, K. (1985). Toward a developmental psychology of the family. In L. L'AbateL. L'Abate (Ed.), *The handbook of family psychology and therapy* (Vol. 1)(pp. 38–72). Homewood, IL: Dorsey.

Keenan, E. O., & Schieffelin, B. B. (1976). Topic as a discourse notion. In C. Li (Ed.), *Subject and topic* (pp. 337–384). New York, NY: Academic Press.

Muran, J. C., Safran, J. D., Samstag, L. W., & Winston, A. (2005). Evaluating an alliance-focused treatment for personality disorders. *Psychotherapy, 42*, 532–545.

Stiles, W. B. (2009). Logical operations in theory-building case studies. *Pragmatic Case Studies in Psychotherapy, 5*, 9–22. Retrieved from jrul.libraries.rutgers.edu/index.php/pcsp/article/view/973/2384.

Tracey, T. J., & Kokotovic, A. M. (1989). Factor structure of the Working Alliance Inventory. *Psychological Assessment: A Journal of Consulting and Clinical Pyschology, 1*, 207–210.

Westerman, M. A. (2011). Conversation analysis and interpretive quantitative research on psychotherapy process and problematic interpersonal behavior. *Theory & Psychology, 21,* 155–178.

Westerman, M. A. (2018a). Interpersonal defense theory: An integration of philosophical considerations, psychoanalytic concepts, and perspectives on interpersonal processes that provides a guide for a wide range of therapeutic interventions. *Journal of Psychotherapy Integration, 28,* 310–328.

Westerman, M. A. (2018b). *No way out: Interpersonal defenses, psychotherapy, and the participatory philosophical perspective* (Book in preparation).

Westerman, M. A., & de Roten, Y. (2017). Investigating how interpersonal defense theory can augment understanding of alliance ruptures and resolutions: A theory-building case study. *Psychoanalytic Psychology, 34,* 13–25.

Westerman, M. A., Foote, J. P., & Winston, A. (1995). Change in coordination across phases of psychotherapy and outcome: Two mechanisms for the role played by patients' contribution to the alliance. *Journal of Consulting and Clinical Psychology, 63,* 672–675.

Westerman, M. A., & Muran, J. C. (2017). Investigating an approach to the alliance based on interpersonal defense theory. *Psychotherapy Research, 27,* 620–641.

Westerman, M. A., & Prieto, D. M. (2006). Expectations about the short-term functional role played by defensive behavior in interpersonal interactions. *Journal of Research in Personality, 40,* 1015–1037.

Westerman, M. A., & Steen, E. M. (2007). Going beyond the internal–external dichotomy in clinical psychology: The theory of interpersonal defense as an example of a participatory model. *Theory & Psychology, 17,* 323–351.

Westerman, M. A., & Steen, E. M. (2009). Revisiting conflict and defense from an interpersonal perspective: Using structured role plays to investigate the effects of conflict on defensive interpersonal behavior. *Psychoanalytic Psychology, 26,* 379–401.

Westerman, M. A., Tanaka, J. S., Frankel, A. S., & Kahn, J. (1986). The coordinating style construct: An approach to conceptualizing patient interpersonal behavior. *Psychotherapy, 23,* 540–547.

CHAPTER

17

Alliance-Focused Formulation: A Work in Process

Catherine F. Eubanks

Ferkauf Graduate School of Psychology, Yeshiva University, New York, NY, United States

Case formulation typically involves a careful assessment of the patient's background, current circumstances and presenting problems, and the application of theory to arrive at an understanding of what causes and maintains the patient's difficulties (Ingram, 2016). In this chapter, I present a different way of approaching formulation: by focusing on the therapeutic process, with particular attention to the emergence of ruptures in the alliance. Building on Safran and Muran's (2000) seminal work on alliance ruptures, this approach is not only a process formulation in the sense of attending closely to moment-by-moment shifts in the patient–therapist interaction, but it is also a process *of* formulation. With this approach, therapists do not strive to arrive at a definitive understanding of the patient, but rather are continually evolving in their understanding, aware that their experience of the patient is unique and specific to the wishes and needs of both members of this dyad (Muran, 2007).

Due to its close focus on alliance ruptures, this approach is well-suited for patients with personality disorders who are widely recognized as having difficulties in interpersonal functioning (e.g., Benjamin & Karpiak, 2001; Clarkin & Levy, 2004). Patient personality disorder features have been linked to an increased incidence of alliance ruptures (Coutinho, Ribeiro, Fernandes, Sousa, & Safran, 2014; Tufekcioglu, Muran, Safran, & Winston, 2013). With an alliance-focused process formulation, the therapist uses his or her experience of ruptures to work with the patient to develop a better understanding of the patient's interpersonal difficulties. The process of identifying and working through these difficulties together – by repairing alliance ruptures – can be a corrective experience for patients who may be accustomed to being criticized, rejected or feared in relationships (Christian, Safran, & Muran, 2012).

Case Formulation for Personality Disorders
https://doi.org/10.1016/B978-0-12-813521-1.00017-5

DEFINING ALLIANCE RUPTURES

Drawing on Bordin's (1979) conceptualization of the alliance, a rupture can be defined as a deterioration in the alliance, manifested by a lack of collaboration between the patient and therapist on therapy tasks or goals, or a strain in the emotional bond (Eubanks-Carter, Muran, & Safran, 2010; Safran & Muran, 2000). Ruptures have been linked to poor outcome (Muran, et al., 2009), but rupture-repair has a moderate association with positive outcome (Eubanks, Muran, & Safran, 2018a). Thus, while ruptures can be obstacles, if they can be worked through, they become opportunities to enhance the outcome of treatment.

A useful observer-based tool for identifying alliance ruptures is the Rupture Resolution Rating System (3RS: Eubanks, Muran, & Safran, 2018b; see Table 17.1). The 3RS organizes ruptures into two main subtypes: confrontation, in which there is movement against the other, and withdrawal, characterized by movement away from the other. The 3RS operationalizes ruptures in terms of patient behaviours, but ruptures are dyadic phenomena; the therapist is always part of any rupture, and a process formulation should also address how the therapist is moving away from or against the patient. The 3RS also features a set of resolution strategies that therapists may use to repair ruptures.

Research using the 3RS has demonstrated relations between ruptures, repairs and outcome. For example, one study found more confrontation ruptures and less resolution of ruptures in cases that ended treatment prematurely as compared to completer cases (Eubanks, Lubitz, Muran, & Safran, 2018). A study that used the 3RS to compare early sessions of three good and three poor outcome cases of Dialectical Behaviour Therapy for borderline personality disorder found a higher frequency of withdrawal ruptures in poor outcome cases, and also found that these withdrawal ruptures tended to persist across sessions despite therapists' attempts to repair them (Boritz, Barnhart, Eubanks, & McMain, 2018). This finding suggests that withdrawal ruptures in this population may be particularly challenging for therapists.

ALLIANCE-FOCUSED PROCESS FORMULATION METHODOLOGY

The first step in the alliance-focused process formulation is to observe the extent to which the patient and therapist are working together collaboratively. The therapist can use the 3RS codes to identify whether the patient is moving against (confrontation markers) or away from (withdrawal markers) the therapist. Patients may engage in complicated moves that include elements of both confrontation and withdrawal, such as offering a subtly critical remark (confrontation) while smiling in a friendly way to soften the

TABLE 17.1 3RS Rupture Markers and Resolution Strategies

WITHDRAWAL MARKERS	
Denial	The patient withdraws from the therapist or the work of therapy by denying a feeling state that is manifestly evident, or denying the importance of interpersonal relationships or events that seem important and relevant to the work of therapy.
Minimal response	The patient withdraws from the therapist by going silent or by giving minimal responses to questions or statements that are intended to initiate or continue discussion.
Abstract Communication	The patient avoids the work of therapy by using vague, abstract, or intellectualized language.
Avoidant Storytelling and/or Shifting Topic	The patient tells stories and/or shifts the topic in a manner that functions to avoid the work of therapy.
Deferential and appeasing	The patient withdraws from the therapist and/or the work of therapy by being overly compliant and submitting to the therapist in a deferential manner.
Content/Affect split	The patient withdraws from the therapist and/or the work of therapy by exhibiting affect that does not match the content of his/her narrative.
Self-critical/hopeless	The patient withdraws from the therapist and the work of therapy by becoming absorbed in a depressive process of self-criticism and/or hopelessness that seems to shut out the therapist and to close off any possibility that the therapist or the treatment can help the patient.
CONFRONTATION MARKERS	
Complaints/concerns about the therapist	The patient expresses negative feelings about the therapist.
Patient rejects therapist intervention	The patient rejects or dismisses the therapist's intervention.
Complaints/concerns about the activities of therapy	The patient expresses dissatisfaction, discomfort, or disagreement with specific tasks of therapy such as homework assignments or in-session tasks such as empty chair or imaginal exposure.
Complaints/concerns about the parameters of therapy	The patient expresses concerns or complaints about the parameters of treatment, such as the therapy schedule or the research contract.
Complaints/concerns about progress in therapy	The patient expresses complaints, concerns, or doubts about the progress that can be made or has been made in therapy.
Patient defends self against therapist	The patient defends his/her thoughts, feelings, or behaviour against what he/she perceives to be the therapist's criticism or judgement of the patient.
Efforts to control/pressure therapist	The patient attempts to control the therapist and/or the session, or the patient puts pressure on the therapist to fix the patient's problems quickly.

Continued

TABLE 17.1 3RS Rupture Markers and Resolution Strategies—cont'd

RESOLUTION STRATEGIES
The therapist clarifies a misunderstanding.
The therapist changes tasks or goals.
The therapist illustrates tasks or provides a rationale for treatment.
The therapist responds to a rupture by redirecting or refocusing the patient.
Within the context of a rupture, the therapist invites the patient to discuss thoughts or feelings with respect to the therapist or some aspect of therapy.
Within the context of a rupture, the therapist acknowledges his/her contribution to a rupture.
Within the context of a rupture, the therapist discloses his/her internal experience of the patient-therapist interaction.
The therapist links the rupture to larger interpersonal patterns between the patient and the therapist.
The therapist links the rupture to larger interpersonal patterns in the patient's other relationships.
The therapist validates the patient's defensive posture.

blow (withdrawal). In addition, patients with personality disorder diagnoses may have difficulties connecting with others, such that their efforts to engage with the therapist are tangled up in rupture markers. If the therapist is only focusing on the rupture markers, he or she may miss the degree to which the patient is trying, albeit not very successfully, to collaborate.

In addition to observing the patient's behaviour, the therapist needs to pay close attention to his or her own contribution to the alliance. Does the therapist feel connected to the client and engaged in the work? The therapist's own internal experience of feeling tense, irritated or bored may be the first indication that there is a problem in the alliance.

Therapists' responses to patients will not only be reactions to what patients say and do, but will also be shaped by the therapists' own relational wishes and fears. Therapists need to attend to how their own relational patterns complement or clash with the patient's relational patterns. An example of this phenomenon is a systematic case study (Schattner, Tishby, & Wiseman, 2017) that compared good and poor alliance cases seen by the same therapist. In the good alliance case, the therapist's needs for intimacy and closeness met the patient's needs for recognition and support. In the poor alliance case, however, the patient perceived the therapist's pursuit of closeness as intrusive.

Once the therapist has identified how the therapist and patient are moving against and away from each other, the therapist can make inferences about the relational needs and fears that underlie each partner's moves. These inferences serve two important functions. First, they help the therapist to understand what may be contributing to the patient's behaviour in the session. Second, understanding what the patient needs and fears from others helps the therapist to identify ways in which the therapeutic relationship could provide a corrective experience for the patient by meeting the patient's needs for recognition or validation and challenging the patient's fears that others are hostile or neglectful (Christian et al., 2012).

Through a series of task-analytic studies, Safran and Muran (Safran, Crocker, McMain, & Murray, 1990; Safran & Muran, 1996; Safran, Muran, & Samstag, 1994) developed a model of the process of resolving alliance ruptures that offers some guidance on how to identify the fears and needs underlying rupture markers. According to this model, confrontation ruptures are efforts to protect and defend a vulnerable self in order to maintain agency and control. Therefore, confrontation markers give us important information about the patient (or, as we must always keep in mind, the therapist who can also exhibit confrontation markers): (1) the individual who is pushing against the other has an underlying sense of vulnerability, which may be a wish for intimacy or caring; (2) he or she perceives others as dangerous opponents who will exploit this vulnerability; and (3) the individual concludes that the best – or only – way to protect him or herself is to go on the attack and try to maintain agency and control. The therapist can provide a corrective experience for a confrontative patient by tolerating the patient's aggression and responding in a way that neither counterattacks nor capitulates, but rather creates a safe space for the patient to acknowledge and express vulnerability.

According to Safran and Muran's model, withdrawal ruptures are also efforts to protect the self, but through avoidance rather than aggression. The individual who withdraws wants to preserve some kind of connection to the other and is afraid to directly assert his or her needs for fear that this will end the relationship. Therefore, withdrawal markers tell us that (1) the individual who is withdrawing has an underlying need for agency; (2) he or she is afraid to express this need because he or she anticipates that others will respond negatively and it will harm the relationship; and (3) the individual concludes that the best way to protect both him or herself and the relationship is to avoid expressing needs for agency. The therapist can provide a corrective experience for a withdrawn patient by encouraging the patient to assert his or her needs and responding to those needs in a validating and empowering way.

As we draw inferences about our patients' (and our own) underlying needs and fears, we may observe parallels between the therapeutic relationship and past and current relationships in the patient's life. This information can help us to better understand what is contributing to the patient's difficulties, and in fact, the strategy *therapist links the rupture to larger interpersonal patterns in the patient's other relationships* is a 3RS resolution strategy. However, there is a danger in focusing excessively on drawing links: the therapist may miss opportunities for more powerful in vivo experiences. Discussing how a patient felt neglected by a loved one in the past is probably less impactful than exploring how a patient is feeling neglected by the therapist *right now*. Furthermore, therapists' use of links may contribute to ruptures. A therapist may draw links to problems in the patient's other relationships to avoid addressing difficulties in the room. A therapist who is angry with a patient may link to another relationship in an aggressive way – noting that the patient is 'doing something wrong' in both relationships – to keep the focus on the patient's problematic behaviour rather than exploring the therapist's contribution to the rupture.

Given these concerns, therapists should proceed with caution when drawing links between ruptures and other relationships. Perhaps the most useful aspect of these links is to enrich the therapist's understanding of what kind of corrective experience the patient needs. For example, if significant others typically respond to a confrontative patient's aggression by becoming hostile, the therapist might consider validating the patient's concerns and nondefensively acknowledging the therapist's contributions to the rupture. If the patient is accustomed to others fleeing when the patient becomes aggressive, thereby granting the patient a hollow, lonely victory, the therapist might meet the patient's aggression with active engagement and healthy self-assertion, such as reasonable limit-setting.

Similarly, a withdrawn patient who frequently uses long-winded stories to keep others at a distance might benefit from a therapist who gently redirects the patient and thereby shows that she is paying attention rather than perpetuating the benign neglect the patient usually receives. By contrast, if a patient is accustomed to being controlled by domineering others, the therapist might encourage him to elaborate on his experience and might be more cautious about cutting the patient off when the patient has difficulty focusing a rambling narrative.

These discrete examples of confrontation and withdrawal ruptures are simply for ease of presentation; in reality, patients – and therapists – present with complex combinations of confrontation and withdrawal. To demonstrate the knotty intersection of patient and therapist confrontations and withdrawals, I will present a case I saw as part of a research study. Throughout my work with this case, I used the 3RS to help me identify what was taking place in the therapeutic relationship both during the session and while reviewing session videotapes.

CASE EXAMPLE

My patient was a white, heterosexual male in his thirties who worked as a freelance writer. He consented to participate in the research study, which was approved by the institutional review board of the medical centre in which the research programme was located. Specific details about 'Matt' (a pseudonym) have been altered to preserve his privacy. As part of the research protocol, a research assistant administered the Structured Interview for DSM-IV-Axis I & II (SCID I & II: First, Gibbon, Spitzer, & Benjamin, 1997; First, Spitzer, Gibbon, & Williams, 1997) to Matt prior to the beginning of treatment. Matt was diagnosed with dysthymia and generalized anxiety disorder on Axis I, and narcissistic personality disorder (NPD) on Axis II. Matt reported difficulties with his career and with his romantic partner. He was assigned to receive 30 weekly sessions of brief relational therapy (BRT; Safran & Muran, 2000). I am a white, heterosexual, female clinical psychologist, and at the time we worked together, I was 43 years old and 9 years post my doctoral degree. As part of the research protocol, our sessions were videotaped, and both Matt and I completed a post-session questionnaire (PSQ: Muran, Safran, Samstag, & Winston, 1992) after each session. The questionnaire included a 12-item version of the Working Alliance Inventory (WAI: Tracey & Kokotovic, 1989) as well as several single-item indices assessing the presence and intensity of ruptures and the extent to which they were resolved within the session.

Clients with a tendency toward hostile, dominant interpersonal behaviours, characteristic of cluster B personality disorders, have difficulty establishing a good alliance (Muran, Segal, Samstag, & Crawford, 1994). Knowing that Matt had received a diagnosis of NPD, I anticipated that he might engage in confrontative behaviours in an effort to prevent me from seeing and taking advantage of his vulnerabilities. I was also aware that I was putting pressure on myself to perform well, as this was the first research patient I had seen in a few years and I knew that every moment of our interaction would be videotaped and coded by research assistants.

Within the first few minutes of our first session, I observed markers of both confrontation and withdrawal in Matt's engagement with me. After briefly explaining a few logistics related to the research programme, including the fact that the treatment would last 30 sessions, I asked Matt if he had any initial questions.

> Matt: Yeah. Is the hope to, like, work toward something that would be concluded by those 30 sessions?

I experienced Matt's question as simultaneously reflecting a genuine curiosity, as well as the confrontation marker *efforts to control/pressure therapist*, with Matt putting pressure on me to deliver clear results by the end of treatment. As I was already sensitized to pressure due to my own desire to perform well, this question might have been experienced differently by a different therapist. Treatments for personality disorders that have demonstrated efficacy or effectiveness tend to be long-term (Levy & Johnson, 2016). As I knew that patients with a diagnosis of NPD likely need more than 30 sessions of therapy to make substantial progress, I was concerned that Matt might have unrealistic expectations of what therapy – and I – could do for him. In addition to experiencing Matt as pressuring me to some extent, I also felt that Matt was moving away by speaking in an intellectualized manner, an example of the withdrawal marker *abstract communication*. He was not directly asking me how we would work on his particular problems and work toward his specific goals; he framed his question as more of an abstract inquiry into how therapy would proceed.

Catherine: That's a good question. So that's one way to go. Another way to go is to think of it as there are things you could start working on in 30 sessions, and you might decide you then want to get more treatment, and at the end we could talk about options for continuing, like a referral. If you wanted to continue in this programme you would have to take like a six month break.

Matt: OK, yeah. I'm just curious as a person who's never done therapy at all, what the actual function or structure is.

Catherine: Yeah, that's a great question. I don't want to presume that anything can be resolved in 30 sessions, or that anything that can't be resolved in 30 sessions is not an appropriate thing to be talking about. There could be ways of starting to get a better understanding of an issue.

In my convoluted responses, I relied excessively on the resolution strategy of *therapist illustrates tasks or provides a rationale for treatment*. This strategy can be helpful when a patient needs an explanation or psychoeducation, but it can also be a way for the therapist to place herself in the role of dispassionate expert, at a safe remove from complicated emotional responses. I was explaining too much – he had not asked me what would happen if he wanted more than 30 sessions, for example – and I was talking about a hypothetical future rather than taking the opportunity to use his question as a launching point for an exploration of his hopes and concerns about treatment in the here and now. I, like Matt, was also withdrawing by showing some signs of *abstract communication*. Matt's question about the 'actual function or structure' of therapy, and the blasé manner in which he asked it, gave me a growing sense that he was sceptical that therapy could be helpful to him, consistent with the confrontation marker *complaints/concerns about progress in therapy*. The sense of confrontation I perceived likely contributed to my responding in a somewhat *deferential and appeasing* manner with my repeated endorsements of the quality of his questions.

As the session proceeded, the pattern of efforts to engage interspersed with rupture markers continued. Matt put pressure on me by voicing very high hopes for therapy: 'I would like some kind of curveball insight that I'm not even able to anticipate'. He also expressed critical views of treatment in a somewhat intellectualized manner: when I described brief relational therapy (BRT) as 'integrating' elements from psychodynamic, cognitive behavioural, and experiential approaches, he asked, 'Is there a philosophical reason why you guys are using that hybridized approach?' and then proceeded to disparage 'Freudian bulls—t'. Matt's combination of confrontation and withdrawal suggests that he had an underlying sense of vulnerability that he feared I would take advantage of, and simultaneously had a need for agency that he was afraid to express to me because he feared it would harm our relationship. At the same time, I continued to see signs of Matt's interest in collaborating with me. His dogged pursuit of answers about how treatment works suggested a desire to engage. He displayed flashes of wit and humour that I experienced as efforts to connect. I also saw glimpses of his vulnerability, when he turned his critical eye toward himself and spoke about how he was a 'loser'.

It is important to note that my reaction to Matt was very much *my* reaction. My own sense of pressure and my tendency to work hard to please the other person, my tendency to respond to confrontation by placating rather than challenging, and my penchant for escaping uncomfortable emotions through intellectualization all shaped how I experienced and responded to Matt. In addition, I genuinely enjoyed his intelligence and his sense of humour, which helped me feel closer to him; this likely aided in the formation of a bond but may have made it even harder for me to directly address his more hostile moves.

As I learned more about Matt's relational history, I was able to draw links between his past and current relationships and my experience of him. For example, as Matt shared his difficulties with his romantic partner, I could see parallels in our interactions. Matt described conflicts with his partner that appeared to stem from both parties' unwillingness to be vulnerable with each other. Matt did not tell his partner how much he wished to be closer to her; not privy to the depth of his internal experience, she criticized him for being 'emotionally vacant'. Matt's account of growing up poor or 'white trash' and being underestimated by institutions and authority figures provided more context for his intellectualized way of speaking and the wariness he might feel toward a clinical psychologist with a PhD.

These links between our interaction and Matt's other relationships helped me identify how our relationship could serve as a corrective experience for Matt. Matt experienced many people in his life as unreliable, unsupportive and unwilling to understand him. He in turn had difficulty understanding others and was often mystified by the ways in which others would respond to him. I concluded that our relationship could provide a corrective experience if we could create a space where he could express his needs and vulnerabilities, and I could demonstrate understanding and appreciation of him. I also aimed to model transparent ways of communicating, such as *disclosing my internal experience of the patient-therapist interaction,* which I hoped would expand his repertoire of ways to build and strengthen relationships.

However, the risk of drawing links between the therapeutic relationship and other important relationships is that it can take the therapist's focus away from the process. An example of this potential pitfall occurred in our seventh session. On his post-session questionnaire, Matt clearly identified this session as the greatest rupture session of our work together: he rated it the lowest on the WAI, and he also answered the question 'Did you experience any tension or problem, any misunderstanding, conflict or disagreement, in your relationship with your therapist during the session?' with 'constantly'.

Matt began session seven by speaking about a medical problem. He drew a contrast between traditional medical doctors who had been unable to help him, and an alternative medicine practitioner who 'saved my life' a few years ago by performing an intervention that resolved one of his medical problems completely within three weeks. This reminded me of his desire for therapy to resolve his issues within 30 sessions, and I was aware of feeling both *control/pressure* to help him quickly, and an implicit *complaint about progress* – I was yet another unhelpful medical provider.

> Matt: I'm just trapped with my, like, crippling health and, like, existential problems, and just, like, stuck in the cold, like, doing stupid things, trying to, like, reclaim my life, like, bit by bit, and it's pretty exhausting and not, like, ever gratifying.

Matt was withdrawing into *self-criticism and/or hopelessness*. At the same time, I still experienced Matt as critical of the progress he had made thus far, particularly if he was including our work together as one of the 'stupid things' he was doing to try to reclaim his life. When I look back on the videotape now, I am more aware of and empathetic to his despair and hopelessness and the pressure he put on himself to fix his problems. During the session, however, I was more aware of and uncomfortable with his hostility.

> Catherine: Wow. You sound angry today.
> Matt: I guess.

Matt's response was *deferential,* a form of withdrawal; I had missed the mark by focusing on anger, but he did not directly call me on it. I realized that he was being deferential, and I invited him to correct me.

Catherine: Is that the right word?
Matt: More like in despair. I'm not any more angry than I normally am. Like I've only – it's like things are hitting me more, in the sense that when I, like, wake up, I have this, like, I've suddenly started to have this, like, first initial gasping breath of despair, like, as I sort of return to, like, the reality of my existence. Like when I've been sleeping, it's been kind of comfortable and, like, I'm dreaming about things, and I can kind of remember, like, what's nice about living, and then I wake up, and then suddenly I'm like, oh, right *(small smile)*, like I'm back to this.

Matt was sharing his feelings of despair, but at the same time, with the smile – the withdrawal marker of *content/affect split* – he tried to move us away from exploring his despair. Commenting on the smile could have been a way to delve into his despair. Despair can be particularly hard for many therapists to tolerate: for me, despair feeds my sense of pressure that I must *do* something to help. I started trying to gather more information to make sense of why Matt was feeling this way now.

Catherine: Did anything happen in the past few days? I know you're dealing with the health stuff, but romantically, did something happen?

Matt recounted some romantic setbacks, and then returned to the theme of despair.

Matt: It sucks to realize how fragile the little house of cards is that I base my mental stability on.
Catherine: Well, I mean, is it, I mean, a fragile house of cards, that's really fragile. I mean, what about, you're going through a tough time? The end of a multi-year relationship is a big deal. Can you give yourself a little time to mourn that without it meaning that you're weak or fragile or a loser or any of those things?

I was trying to be supportive and encouraging, but in a way that functioned to *shift the topic* (withdrawal marker) away from his despair.

Matt: Yeah, I don't know, I'm not good at that – I'm also not very good at relaxing in general either, I always feel like this pressure to keep going, trying to like make things better and stay motivated because I basically feel like no one is going to help me at all, like, that I'm – that it is entirely up to me, and, like, it has always been ... It's not true that I actually need to just like sit and just watch television for f---ing 12 hours a day (*laughs*) – that's what that literally means for most people, like, 'I'm not going to be too hard on myself', it means that they're going to sit somewhere and do whatever is easiest and most comfortable.

Catherine: But, hold on for a second, the thing I said a couple of minutes ago about giving yourself time, and you were like, yeah, and then you went off very quickly.

I recognized that Matt had *rejected the intervention* (confrontation marker), dismissing my call for self-compassion as advice to watch TV all day. However, I did not fully recognize the elements of confrontation in his response, perhaps because I did not realize how much I had missed by trying to shift the topic away from his despair. Ironically, I framed *his* move as a *topic shift* – 'you went off very quickly'.

Catherine: What happens for you when I say that? What's your internal reaction?
Matt: Well, I think, like, yeah, like, that's actually valid, but when I think about that, I immediately run into all of the reasons why I have not been doing that. Like, it's not like it's a thought that has not occurred to me. And so then it's a matter of, like, explaining what those obstacles are. Not even pretending that those are insurmountable obstacles, but they are just obstacles that exist, that are preventing that from happening. It's not like I could just say, 'cool, I'll try that'.
Catherine: Ok, but I guess I'm also having the experience of, you're – you're lacking support. And your girlfriend is gone, and I guess I'm having this feeling of, maybe, I'm trying to offer you support and you kind of run off. And so I'm wondering, what is it like for you when people try to offer you support? Or maybe I wasn't doing a good job of it?

This response reflects my efforts to facilitate a corrective experience for Matt by demonstrating acceptance and communicating in a more transparent way: I *disclosed my internal experience of the patient-therapist interaction, invited his thoughts and feelings with respect to the therapist or therapy,* and *acknowledged my contribution to a rupture* to some extent ('maybe I wasn't doing a good job of it').

Matt: That's similar to the things – the arguments that I've had with my ex-girlfriend, like I don't really feel like that was support. Like, you know, a suggestion, a thing to do.
Catherine: So what is support? What does that look like?

Unfortunately, by framing the question in the abstract rather than keeping the focus on our process, I opened the door for more *abstract communication*.

Matt: Um, it would be, like, like, uh, an innovative, thoughtful solution that is personalized and that is, like, something I had not considered before. Which I don't think is actually that unrealistic, and it's a thing I've done for people in the past, like, constantly. And, like,

I have a couple of friends who are capable of doing it, and I really appreciate them for doing it. Like one of the things that would happen with my ex-girlfriend is she would say, 'why don't you just work on a new writing project?' and I would say, 'yeah, thanks, I know that, I would love it if I could do that. I can't do that for these reasons, can you help me figure those reasons out? That would be *very* helpful'. (*sarcastic tone*). It's not helpful to say, like, shut up, like, I don't want to hear about this anymore, like, go do something, you're welcome, by the way. It's just useless.
Catherine: Did it feel like that's what I was saying?
Matt: I didn't feel like it was something you considered to be an act of generous support. I thought it was just basically a small inquiry of like, 'oh, it sounds like you are not capable of just like letting this stuff pass over you, so let's talk about why that is'. It didn't feel to me like that was an actual, like an offer I could take seriously.

Matt was now explicitly communicating his *complaints and concerns about the therapist* (confrontation marker). I knew that I needed to explore his concerns further, but I felt wary. Anticipating that he might regard further exploration of our interaction as yet another useless intervention on my part, I preemptively *provided a rationale* for focusing on our relationship.

Catherine: So, so, maybe – and I'm not trying to – I don't mean this to sound like I'm making this all about right here in an unhelpful way. I'm doing this because maybe this will be helpful in understanding the big picture too. So, are you hoping I'll be able to come up with the kind of, the really smart creative idea that you haven't thought about?
Matt: That's the practical hope that I would have for therapy generally … that is like the understanding and the hope that I have, that I volunteer a lot of information and the person is able to make a helpful and objective and somewhat removed assessment, and that is something that I would not be able to provide myself. Like, what I don't want therapy to be is, like, an excuse to allow me to talk to somebody. That is not enough of a service to me. I have people who will listen to me talk. It's not like I'm just so lonely that I don't have that outlet.

Matt was now exhibiting *patient defends self* (confrontation marker). This revealed that he saw my comments about his lack of support as critical or patronizing – that I was suggesting that he was pathetic and lonely.

Catherine: So what I'm wondering about now is – I do think that therapy can provide insight. That's what I would call what you're talking about, like, a new way of seeing things. But I think therapy can also provide a different experience. Um, it can provide an opportunity to try interacting with another person in a different way than you do in your other relationships.

Matt: Why would I interact any differently with you than I would with anybody else?
Catherine: I guess, well, it would be, so, I'm still trying to figure out how much of this is useful or fits your situation, but, like, if, if you were having difficulty being vulnerable with other people, or asserting certain things with other people, then to try to do that with me in therapy is, like, a different kind of experience that can be translated to other relationships.

I again focused too much on how I was conceptualizing his needs and fears in an abstract way that was not anchored in how therapy would benefit him specifically (*abstract communication*). Focusing more on the ways we were moving against and away from each other in that moment would have been a more impactful way to elucidate what Matt needed and feared from me.

Matt: Yeah. I can't tell whether I'm vulnerable or not with people. I feel like I am, but …
Catherine: When you say you're vulnerable with somebody, what does it mean? Do you feel like you've been vulnerable in here?
Matt: Um, I guess, yeah, at the same level that I always am.
Catherine: So what is that? What does that mean to *you*?
Matt: Honest enough about my answers or things that I bring up voluntarily that run the risk of critical disappointment if the response is not positive. Like it's me opening myself up to somebody, responding in a way that might be unflattering to my ego.
Catherine: Like opening yourself up to – they might – the person might be critical or rejecting or something like that?
Matt: Yeah. Which happens, and people have been able to hurt my feelings at times, so I can't pretend that I'm always just so guarded that, you know – I maintain, like, honesty to the extent that it can be offensive to people sometimes.
Catherine: I agree, I think you're very honest, that's for sure. But I wonder about the emotion, how you feel?
Matt: I don't know. I don't know if I'm in touch with it enough to really answer that accurately.

With our *abstract communication*, Matt and I colluded to avoid directly addressing his fears around being vulnerable with me. I also missed an opportunity to ask him directly how much I had disappointed or hurt him; such an exploration could have helped both of us understand his experience better, but it would have required that I make myself vulnerable to hearing more of his criticism of me. It is noteworthy that Matt described vulnerability solely in terms of opening himself up to criticism, with no mention of the possibility that vulnerability can involve opening oneself up to care and support.

We returned to a discussion of our interaction later in treatment, in session 13. In this exchange, we stayed more focused on our interaction. I disclosed to Matt that I sometimes felt that he was trying to keep me at a distance.

Catherine: I don't know, a sense of like, 'don't get too close, don't get – I'm not going to let you in too much'.
Matt: I feel like I'm totally open to that. Even with relative strangers I'm open to that.
Catherine: In here? I mean, let's be specific.
Matt: Yeah, I mean, I don't like when you ask me certain things that don't really make sense to me, um, I'll always try to, like, hear them or respond to them as well as I can.
Catherine: Yeah. I believe that, and I don't want this to sound – I'm not trying to be critical either, and I hope it doesn't sound like that.
Matt: No, no. But I don't think it's a barrier that's like a wall that I'm, like, creating to avoid. It's mainly I don't even understand what the things are. A few weeks ago, you asked me something like, 'do you not let people love you?'. I still don't know what the hell that means. But it's not like, no, we don't discuss that, like that's too close! (*smiling*)
Catherine: Yeah. And you don't feel something – you don't have, like saying that right now, talking about that idea of not letting people love you, that doesn't bring up …
Matt: It feels kind of like what robots get in *Star Trek*, like something more like, it just doesn't actually compute. Like you just have been asked a question that your programming doesn't allow for, and you're, like, trying to understand it by, like, stabbing at it from different angles. But you don't just intuitively know what the hell that means itself, and so it's, like, a little concerning to go, 'oh, is there something I just don't, some basic thing that I just don't actually understand?' That's more the feeling. Like, did I just not learn like a basic human concept?

In contrast to our exchange in session seven, in this discussion there is less confrontation. I am still somewhat cautious and abstract, and Matt may also be somewhat appeasing, but on the whole, we are collaboratively exploring our interaction. By focusing on my experience of how Matt moves against and away from me, I learn that interactions that I perceived to be rejections and evasions were, for Matt, at least in part, efforts to engage, and he blamed himself for some of our difficulties understanding each other.

Session 13 was our next-to-last session. Matt accepted a job that required moving out of state. As the research programme did not collect outcome data on patients who terminated early, I do not know whether

Matt achieved clinically significant improvement on symptoms or interpersonal functioning per our assessment measures. I can say that he ended treatment in a better position professionally, and also in a new relationship with someone whom he described as being more supportive than his previous partner.

FUTURE DIRECTIONS

An important future direction for this alliance-focused approach to process formulation will be to test it empirically. This process formulation approach can continue to be informed by the growing body of research on alliance ruptures. For example, the frequencies of different types of ruptures may vary based on patient and therapist characteristics, such as specific personality features. Awareness of what to look for may aid therapists in identifying rupture processes as they unfold. However, it would be important for therapists to remain attentive to how the process is unique to the interacting wishes and fears of the members of the dyad.

Alliance-focused process formulation is consistent with the tenets of BRT, which was found to be as efficacious as cognitive behavioural therapy (CBT) and short-term dynamic psychotherapy in a sample of patients with Cluster C personality disorders and personality disorder not otherwise specified, and was more successful than the other two treatments with respect to retention (Muran, Safran, Samstag, & Winston, 2005). This approach is also consistent with Alliance-Focused Training (AFT), a form of supervision that trains therapists to attend closely to moments of rupture and their internal experience of them. A recent study (Muran, Safran, Eubanks, & Gorman, 2018) assessed the additive effect of AFT on CBT for personality disorders, and found decreases in patient dependence and therapist blaming and directiveness, and increases in patient and therapist expressiveness and therapist affirmation that could be attributed to AFT; several of these changes were linked to positive treatment outcome.

One interesting thing to observe about the training study (Muran et al., 2018) is that AFT was an adjunct to another treatment: the therapists all began working with their patients in CBT, and then switched from CBT supervision to AFT. The therapists were not asked to abandon their CBT case formulations, but rather to enrich them by attending more closely to the patient–therapist interaction. An alliance-focused process formulation can be integrated with other ways of understanding a therapy case. When the alliance is strong, attending closely to ruptures may not yield much new insight. When the alliance is strained, however, as can happen often in patients with personality disorders, paying close attention to the movements of each partner in the dance can foster greater understanding.

The case example in this chapter also underscores that even when therapists are not perfectly attuned to every move in the dance, they can pursue ever greater awareness and understanding of the therapeutic process. Ruptures are inevitable. The work of recognizing, accepting and addressing ruptures can be a corrective experience for both patient and therapist.

Acknowledgements

The client provided informed consent for information obtained from videotaped recordings of sessions to be used for scientific purposes such as professional publication in transcribed format. In addition, some details of the case description (e.g., name, occupation) were changed so as to protect client privacy.

References

Benjamin, L. S., & Karpiak, C. P. (2001). Personality disorders. *Psychotherapy, 38*, 487–491.

Bordin, E. (1979). The generalizability of the psychoanalytic concept of the working alliance. *Psychotherapy: Theory, Research and Practice, 16*, 252–260.

Boritz, T., Barnhart, R., Eubanks, C. F., & McMain, S. (2018). Alliance rupture and resolution in Dialectical Behavior Therapy for borderline personality disorder. *Journal of Personality Disorders, 32(Special Issue)*, 115–128.

Christian, C., Safran, J. D., & Muran, J. C. (2012). The corrective emotional experience: A relational perspective and critique. In *Transformation in psychotherapy: Corrective experiences across cognitive behavioral, humanistic, and psychodynamic approaches* (pp. 51–67). Washington: American Psychological Association. https://doi.org/10.1037/13747-004.

Clarkin, J. F., & Levy, K. N. (2004). The influence of client variables in psychotherapy. In M. J. Lambert (Ed.), *Bergin and Garfield's handbook of psychotherapy & behavior change* (5th ed.) (pp. 194–226). New York, NY: John Wiley & Sons.

Coutinho, J., Ribeiro, E., Fernandes, C., Sousa, I., & Safran, J. D. (2014). The development of the therapeutic alliance and the emergence of alliance ruptures. *Anales de Psicología, 30*(3), 985–994.

Eubanks-Carter, C., Muran, J. C., & Safran, J. D. (2010). Alliance ruptures and resolution. In J. C. Muran, & J. P. Barber (Eds.), *The therapeutic alliance: An evidence-based approach to practice and training* (pp. 74–94). New York: Guilford Press.

Eubanks, C. F., Lubitz, J., Muran, J. C., & Safran, J. D. (2018). *Rupture resolution rating system (3RS): Development and validation* (Under review).

Eubanks, C. F., Muran, J. C., & Safran, J. D. (2018a). Repairing alliance ruptures. In J. C. Norcross, & M. J. Lambert (Eds.), *Psychotherapy relationships that work* (3rd ed.). New York: Oxford University Press, (in press).

Eubanks, C. F., Muran, J. C., & Safran, J. D. (2018b). *Rupture resolution rating System (3RS): Manual*. New York: Mount Sinai-Beth Israel Medical Center (Unpublished manuscript).

First, M. B., Gibbon, M., Spitzer, R. L., & Benjamin, L. S. (1997). *User's guide for the structured clinical interview for DSM-IV axis II personality disorders: SCID-II*. American Psychiatric Press.

First, M. B., Spitzer, R. L., Gibbon, M., & Williams, J. B. (1997). *User's guide for the structured clinical interview for DSM-IV axis I disorders: SCID-I*. American Psychiatric Press.

Ingram, B. L. (2016). Case formulation and treatment planning. In J. C. Norcross, G. R. VandenBos, D. K. Freedheim, & R. Krishnamurthy (Eds.), *APA handbook of clinical psychology: Applications and methods* (Vol. 3) (pp. 233–249). Washington, DC: American Psychological Association.

Levy, K. N., & Johnson, B. N. (2016). Personality disorders. In J. C. Norcross, G. R. VandenBos, D. K. Freedheim, & N. Pole (Eds.), *APA handbook of clinical psychology: Psychopathology and health* (Vol. 4) (pp. 173–207). https://doi.org/10.1037/14862-006.

Muran, J. C. (2007). A relational turn on thick description. In J. C. Muran (Ed.), *Dialogues on difference: Studies of diversity in the therapeutic relationship*. Washington, DC: American Psychological Association.

Muran, J. C., Safran, J. D., Eubanks, C. F., & Gorman, B. S. (2018). The effect of alliance-focused training on a cognitive-behavioral therapy for personality disorders. *Journal of Consulting and Clinical Psychology, 86*, 384–397. https://doi.org/10.1037/ccp0000284.

Muran, J. C., Safran, J. D., Gorman, B. S., Samstag, L. W., Eubanks-Carter, C., & Winston, A. (2009). The relationships of early alliance ruptures and their resolution to process and outcome in three time-limited psychotherapies for personality disorders. *Psychotherapy: Theory, Research, Practice, Training, 46*, 233–248. https://doi.org/10.1037/a0016085.

Muran, J., Safran, J., Samstag, L., & Winston, A. (1992). *Patient and therapist postsession questionnaires, version 1992*. NY: Beth Israel Medical Center.

Muran, J. C., Safran, J. D., Samstag, L. W., & Winston, A. (2005). Evaluating an alliance-focused treatment for personality disorders. *Psychotherapy: Theory, Research, Practice, Training, 42*, 532–545.

Muran, J. C., Segal, Z. V., Samstag, L. W., & Crawford, C. E. (1994). Patient pretreatment interpersonal problems and therapeutic alliance in short-term cognitive therapy. *Journal of Consulting and Clinical Psychology, 62*, 185–190. https://doi.org/10.1037/0022-006X.62.1.185.

Safran, J. D., Crocker, P., McMain, S., & Murray, P. (1990). The therapeutic alliance rupture as a therapy event for empirical investigation. *Psychotherapy: Theory, Research and Practice, 27*, 154–165.

Safran, J. D., & Muran, J. C. (1996). The resolution of ruptures in the therapeutic alliance. *Journal of Counseling and Clinical Psychology, 64*, 447–458.

Safran, J. D., & Muran, J. C. (2000). *Negotiating the therapeutic alliance: A relational treatment guide*. New York: Guilford Press.

Safran, J. D., Muran, J. C., & Samstag, L. W. (1994). Resolving therapeutic alliance ruptures: A task analytic investigation. *The Working Alliance: Theory, Research, and Practice*, 225–255.

Schattner, E., Tishby, O., & Wiseman, H. (2017). Relational patterns and the development of the alliance: A systematic comparison of two cases. *Clinical Psychology and Psychotherapy, 24*, 555–568. https://doi.org/10.1002/cpp.2019.

Tracey, T. J., & Kokotovic, A. M. (1989). Factor structure of the working alliance inventory. *Psychological Assessment: A Journal of Consulting and Clinical Psychology, 1*, 207–210.

Tufekcioglu, S., Muran, J. C., Safran, J. D., & Winston, A. (2013). Personality disorder and early therapeutic alliance in two time-limited therapies. *Psychotherapy Research, 23*(6), 646–657. https://doi.org/10.1080/10503307.2013.843803.

C H A P T E R

18

Emotion-Based Case Formulation for Personality Disorders

Michael A. Strating, Antonio Pascual-Leone
University of Windsor, Windsor, Ontario, Canada

Personality disorders are characterized by chronic emotional dysfunctions, either as a defining symptom or as a by-product of the disorder. For example, emotion dysregulation is a core feature of borderline personality disorder (Gratz, Moore, & Tull, 2016). As such, a common treatment goal across therapeutic approaches often involves resolution of emotional distress. This requires that clients work through and change their emotions, with the guidance of the therapist who facilitates emotional awareness and expression. Although emotional expression is generally regarded as an important component of good therapeutic process, catharsis on its own is not enough. That is, emotional expression is a necessary, but not sufficient, condition for adaptive emotional change to occur.

So how does a therapist determine whether or not a client's particular moment-by-moment emotional expressions are healthy or productive? Stated another way, how does the therapist determine whether a client is moving forward or merely moving in circles? To answer these questions, the therapist needs a conceptual road map which will allow the therapist to assess the client's current location (i.e., What emotion is the client expressing?) in relation to the destination (i.e., What might be a more adaptive emotion for this client to access?). Armed with this knowledge, the therapist can set a course that will guide the selection and implementation of interventions to facilitate more productive emotional processing. Therapeutic approaches differ in the degree to which working with emotion is an explicit focus of treatment, however, the aim of this chapter is

Case Formulation for Personality Disorders
https://doi.org/10.1016/B978-0-12-813521-1.00018-7

to provide an empirically derived process map that can inform therapist interventions across a variety of modalities.

The current chapter discusses the clinical utility of Pascual-Leone and Greenberg's (2007) sequential model of emotional processing for case formulations of personality disorders. After introducing the theoretical foundation of this model and supporting empirical research, the chapter will describe how the model can be used as a 'process map' to guide clinical case conceptualization and intervention. Clinical applications of this method of emotion-based case conceptualization will then be illustrated using a case example.

EMOTION-BASED CASE CONCEPTUALIZATION: THEORY AND KEY CONCEPTS

To understand what it means to bring about productive changes in emotion, we begin by surveying several models of *emotional processing* that have been proposed in the literature. Behaviourist models have broadly defined emotional processing as reductions in emotional intensity following repeated exposure to emotionally evocative stimuli or through other behavioural down-regulation strategies (Foa & Kosak, 1986; Linehan, 1993). Cognitive models have focussed on changing feelings by reflecting on emotion and changing maladaptive thinking patterns (Beck, Freeman, & Davis, 2004). Whereas, psychodynamic models have emphasized the important role of interpersonal dynamics and insight in bringing about emotional change (Diener & Hilsenroth, 2009).

Although these models appear to conceptualize emotional processing in different ways, these formulations are not necessarily mutually exclusive. Indeed, emotional processing seems to be a multi-faceted construct that involves emotional awareness, affective arousal, down-regulation, cognitive reflection on emotion and emotional transformation (Greenberg & Pascual-Leone, 2006; Pascual-Leone, Paivio, & Harrington, 2016). While acknowledging the importance of each of these components, experiential models also emphasize the role of meaning making in emotional processing. To make sense of an emotion, it is critical to distinguish between categorically distinct emotions (e.g., anger vs. sadness) that are laden with different types of information. Furthermore, the literature suggests that certain qualitative *kinds of* emotional experiences are more productive than others (e.g., one kind of anger may be helpful while another is not; Kennedy-Moore & Watson, 2001). In other words, emotion specificity is key for meaning making and effective emotional processing.

In their seminal book on working with emotion in therapy, Greenberg and Paivio (1997) described a theoretical framework for identifying distinct emotions and their associated meanings towards the goal of transforming problematic emotional experiences. This involves distinguishing between deeper or more fundamental feelings and secondary emotional reactions to those core feelings (e.g., core feelings of shame may be covered up by expressions of hostility). Once secondary emotions are identified and bypassed, clients who engage their core difficulties are in a position to transform maladaptive primary emotions (e.g., chronic feelings of low self-worth) through the assistance of the therapist, who helps them to access adaptive primary emotions (e.g., healthy anger or grief in response to a specific interpersonal violation or loss, respectively). In this way, the client is able to, 'change emotion with emotion'.

This implies that emotional transformation proceeds in a sequential or step-wise fashion. Although this process is influenced by the idiosyncratic meaning which each individual attributes to emotionally evocative experiences and events, there is empirical evidence pointing to prototypic pathways of emotional change and resolution (e.g., Pascual-Leone, 2018).

MAPPING OUT EMOTIONAL CHANGE

Building upon the theoretical framework of Greenberg and Paivio (1997), Pascual-Leone and Greenberg (2007) developed a model of client process which maps out sequential changes in key emotion states that are associated with productive therapeutic work leading to resolution of distress. Because it is not tied to any particular therapeutic modality, Pascual-Leone and Greenberg's (2007) model is trans-theoretical and can be employed within a wide range of therapeutic approaches as a method of case conceptualization based on clients' emerging expressions of emotion in session. As a model of process assessment, clinicians can use this method to make causal arguments about how clients get better at a moment-by-moment level, within sessions (cf. Elliott, 2010). By being attuned to the client's zone of proximal emotional development within this model, clinicians can use the model to meet the client where they are at and to employ interventions to facilitate optimal emotional growth incrementally, moving clients toward positive treatment outcomes.

There are several advantages to using such empirically based process maps for case conceptualization in clinical practice. First, clinicians who make use of systematic methods of case formulation produce better therapeutic outcomes than those who do not (Eells, Lombart, Kendjelic, Turner, & Lucas, 2005; Kramer et al., 2014). Second, other clinical research that is based on global statements about groups of clients, though useful in orientating clinicians, can often be difficult to apply to individual clients. In contrast, process-based models provide concrete and clinically intuitive models of change that are observable by clinicians in session, are 'experience-near' from the perspective of the client (which facilitates alliance-building) and can be easily applied to treatment planning in clinical practice. More specifically, the model we propose allows a therapist to decide which moment-by-moment client processes should be bypassed (i.e., unhelpful emotions) and which should be focussed on (i.e., productive emotions), with an eye to working toward treatment goals. Third, this is a trans-theoretical approach of case formulation that is supported by process research and is applicable across treatment modalities. This ensures that process-based case conceptualizations maximize the potential for tailoring treatment to specific clients across setting and therapist characteristics, including therapists' preferred theoretical orientations. Fourth, because of the concrete and observable nature of these models, these methods can also be useful in training future psychotherapists (Jose & Goldfried, 2008).

We begin with an overview of Pascual-Leone and Greenberg's (2007) model, as presented in Fig. 18.1, followed by an elaboration upon each component of the model as described in the associated coding system. As a sequential model that is ordered in time, emotion categories are

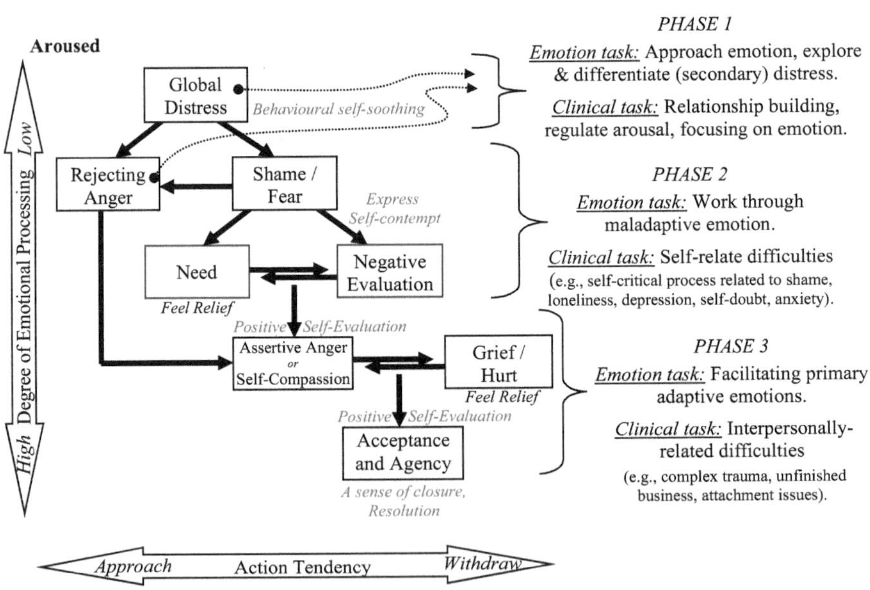

FIGURE 18.1 The sequential model of emotional processing. *Reprinted with permission from Pascual-Leone, A., Greenberg, L.S. (2007). Emotional processing in experiential therapy: Why "the only way out is through".* Journal of Consulting and Clinical Psychology, *75, 875–887 and Pascual-Leone, A. (2018). How client's "change emotion with emotion": A program of research on emotional processing.* Psychotherapy Research, 28 (2), 165–182. *https://doi.org/10.1080/10503307.2017.1349350.*

grouped together according to phases which signal different types of general emotion and clinical tasks as emotional expressions become increasingly advanced or adaptive. The model takes as its starting point (phase 1) global distress and other 'early expressions of distress', the latter of which include rejecting anger and shame/fear (top half of Fig. 18.1). Although these emotions together represent expressions *of distress* rather than expressions of *working through* distress (Kennedy-Moore & Watson, 2001), these initial emotions nevertheless represent a necessary starting point and prerequisite steps to change. The process of emotional differentiation and meaning making begins with a shift from global distress into either 'rejecting anger' or 'shame/fear', which represent two alternative pathways to more adaptive emotional expressions (phase 2). Expressions of 'shame/fear' are transformed through the identification and exploration of core 'negative self-evaluations' and 'unmet existential needs.' This then allows for expressions of assertive anger, self-compassion, and grief/hurt which, together, have been referred to as 'advanced meaning-making states' or 'primary adaptive emotions' (phase 3). Clients sometimes then oscillate between active attempts to meet their own needs (i.e., assertive anger or self-compassion) versus expression of grief over their loss (i.e., hurt or grief), which paves the way for resolution, acceptance, and agency.

Global Distress

In phase 1, the processing of emotion begins with global distress which are expressions of undifferentiated negative feelings and maladaptive secondary emotions such as hurt, confusion, helplessness or self-pity. Global distress is often unspecific and characterized by high arousal with no clear sense of the cause of distress or a direction to resolve the distress. Effective emotional processing, then, must begin by managing and differentiating such vague expressions of emotional pain.

Shame/Fear

Phase 2 in the model involves the differentiation of initial distress into maladaptive emotions of either shame/fear or rejecting anger. Fear and shame are maladaptive primary emotions that are frequently reoccurring feelings of vulnerability in response to some specific autobiographical context (i.e., 'the same old feeling in response to the same old story'). Relative to global distress, these are highly personal states with identifiable causes, typically associated with themes of personal vulnerability due to perceived incompetence, defectiveness, inadequacy or loneliness. Although fear and shame are qualitatively distinct emotions, the model treats them as functionally equivalent since they are both associated with action tendencies of withdrawal and collapse.

Rejecting Anger

There is also a second, alternative pathway, in phase 2, through rejecting anger. Rejecting anger is a secondary emotion characterized by blaming, rejecting and destructive anger that 'pushes away' and creates distance from the source of emotional pain. Although more differentiated than global distress, the meaning underlying rejecting anger is not as well differentiated as more productive forms of anger. Expressions of rejecting anger (i.e., rage, repulsion, hate, blame) have a *fighting against* quality in which there is a clear sense of what one does *not* want, though the needs or wishes being pursued (what one *does* want) are all too often less clear. Nevertheless, expressions of rejecting anger can function as a stepping stone for more productive expressions of assertive anger which occurs when personal needs are identified and engaged (i.e., a *fighting for* quality, discussed later in the chapter).

Existential Needs and Negative Self-Evaluations

A critical middle step in the model is a meaning-making step, the clarification of which propels individuals from less adaptive expressions of shame or fear (phase 2) to more adaptive expressions of assertive anger or self-compassion (phase 3). Further differentiation of personal meaning comes through the articulation of *both* an unmet existential need (e.g., for affiliation or mastery) and a fundamental negative self-evaluation (i.e., a core dysfunctional belief about the self). To achieve more advanced levels of emotional processing, individuals are required to resolve these two seemingly contradictory aspects of experience (i.e., the dialectic or internal conflict) by working through self-critical processes (e.g., shame, self-doubt, etc.). In other words, the bridge between maladaptive and adaptive emotional experiences is in the articulation of one's previously unmet existential needs. This creates a focussed direction and the process of working through produces moments of positive self-evaluation or affirmation where one agentically attends to the fulfilment of existential needs.

Assertive Anger and Self-Compassion

Identifying and resolving the internal conflict between unmet needs and negative self-evaluations ushers in categorically new experiences, marking entry into the third and final phase of the model. At this point, clients have an emerging sense of 'self as deserving'. On the one hand, they may be mobilized to address unmet needs by either fighting for some particular need (i.e., assertive anger) or caring for oneself (i.e., self-compassion and soothing). On the other hand, they may also be confronted with healthy grief over clear and specific losses.

Grief/Hurt

In contrast with assertive anger and self-compassion, grief and hurt do not involve explicit self-affirmations, but are more so characterized by an acknowledgement of pain and loss (without collapsing back into negative self-evaluation, despair, and so forth, as in earlier states). Interpersonal difficulties and painful emotions are resolved via this second dialectical tension (inner conflict) as individuals oscillate between affirming their value and needs (assertion/compassion) on the one hand, and retreating to mourn the loss of damaged relationships or other disappointments (grief) on the other hand.

Acceptance and Agency

The end stage of this model culminates in resolution in the form of acceptance and agency. In short, although the expression and letting go of painful emotions are necessary components in the model, the sequential process described is much more complex than merely exposure or venting. Rather, the central component of this model is the multi-step sequential patterns whereby the core, idiosyncratic meanings of emotional experiences are symbolized and the emotions themselves ultimately transformed, culminating in client acceptance and empowerment as well as resolution of distress.

USING THE PROCESS MAP TO GUIDE CLINICAL PRACTICE

Pascual-Leone and Greenberg's (2007) sequential model of emotional processing highlights concrete markers of emerging emotion that can be used by clinicians as a 'process map' to track in-session change and to guide treatment and intervention. We turn our attention now to the practical application of this model for clinical work with clients presenting with personality disorders. Before examining the specific steps of case formulation, however, it is helpful to first get an overview of the general principles of the model and common trajectories of change in clinical practice.

This model takes a developmental perspective of emotion change. By assessing a client's zone of proximal development, the therapist can use the process map to guide clinical interventions for facilitating emotional development. Building on the work of Vygotsky (1924/1978), the *zone of proximal development* is a key principle that has been applied to therapy to describe the range of task complexity (in this case, the level of emotional processing) that an individual is able to carry out successfully on his or her own or with support and assistance from the therapist (Leiman & Stiles, 2001). As such, therapists can be maximally effective if they match or move slightly beyond clients' presenting levels of emotional differentiation, without going too far ahead of or behind clients' emotional process, either of which may precipitate a collapse (Caro Gabalda & Stiles, 2013).

Much like a road map helps travellers to orientate themselves to (1) their current location in relation to (2) their target destination, the current model serves as a process map to guide therapists in facilitating more advanced and productive levels of client emotional processing and idiosyncratic meaning making. In this way, the model also allows therapists to engage in *process diagnosis* (Goldman & Greenberg, 2015) by assessing clients' dynamic, moment-by-moment, emotional development, answering questions such as 'Where are we in the process?' and 'What is the next step of emotional development that we can plausibly reach in this moment?' Emotion-based case conceptualization allows therapists to stay grounded in present in-session events (*Where are we right now?*), to anticipate immediate changes for growth (*Where do we go from here?*) and to plan interventions (*How do we reach that next step?*) – both within and across sessions – which will bring clients closer to the long-term treatment goals of therapy (*What is the destination*?).

However, emotional growth is not smooth and continuous; trajectories of emotional development typically proceed in a non-linear, 'two steps forward, one step back' fashion (Pascual-Leone, 2009). Indeed, productive emotional processing within session has been found to be characterized not only by more frequent progressions from less-advanced (e.g., global distress) to more advanced (e.g., acceptance and agency) emotional states, but also by greater range and variability in emotion states from the beginning to the end of session. Such variability includes temporary micro-relapses from more advanced to less advanced states, where such collapses decrease in duration over the course of a successful treatment (Pascual-Leone, 2009). In short, productive emotional processing is not a straightforward, linear progression from less advanced to more advanced emotion states. Rather, successful clients often demonstrate a 'saw-toothed' pattern of repeated growth, collapse, and recovery. Much like performing 'emotional push-ups', a single emotional change within session is insufficient to produce long-term, characterological changes, however, repeated cycles of emotional change (i.e., emotional push-ups) over time culminate in larger units of change over the course of therapy (Pascual-Leone, Yeryomenko, Sawashima, & Warwar, 2017). This means that the process model can be used to assess client progress over the course of a session and over the entire course of treatment as therapists attend to clients' expanding emotional range and flexibility over time.

In the hands of clinicians working in session, the model can concretely support the in-session assessment of process as well as treatment planning based on aspects of personality style. It is helpful to first get a sense of the general 'lay of the land' by summarizing the general road map of emotional development, as described in the model earlier (see Fig. 18.1). The model can then be understood as a process map, indicating the moment-by-moment location of a client, as well as the zones of proximal emotional development that may be available in a given moment. In this way, emotion-oriented approaches to treatment will be able to discern potential directions for intervention that are more or less likely to be fruitful in a given moment (e.g., *Given what the client is feeling right now, what kind of process would be most feasible and helpful right now?*). This suggests an *if–then* paradigm for working with emotion in the immediate moment (e.g., *If the client does X, then the therapist could work on Y*). The if–then framework as a platform for administering psychotherapy has been formally discussed and most elaborated as part of emotion-focused therapy (Greenberg & Paivio, 1997), although effective therapists of all stripes must be responsive to moment-by-moment shifts in client process in timing their interventions, something Stiles (2009) identified as *responsivity*.

In addition to identifying and orientating to immediate process (i.e., using a map to follow client process), the model also articulates a range of states that research suggests are required for working through and transforming emotional difficulties. In other words, observing a client's process through this framework also reveals the *emotional repertoire* with which a client typically engages personal difficulties and the range of emotional experiences that client has easily available (or not) to then navigate and work through such difficulties. Clients presenting for treatment usually have restricted emotional ranges and are not as flexible in accessing emotion that may be relevant to their concern, and this rigidity is even more characteristic among clients with personality disorders. Some clients fall into a characteristic despair, while others become enraged at the slightest provocation, and identifying this inflexibility in a client's mode of responding highlights the shortfalls in their emotional ranges. Similarly, making use of healthy assertion, or being able to grieve without becoming overwhelmed and losing the relevant personal meaning related to that feeling, are as much dynamically emerging states as they are achievements in an adult's socio-emotional development. When a clinician observes that a client has a limited emotional range, the model helps identify specifically what emotional states the client can productively make use of and which are most difficult to maintain, and this points the way for treatment planning. Expanding a client's emotional range in some concrete direction, to build and establish some missing affective experience from a client's emotional repertoire, is an important change goal and helps outline treatment planning. Ultimately, developing one's emotional repertoire is not only a way of overcoming some presenting personal difficulty, it is a central form of personality change.

EMPIRICAL SUPPORT FOR EMOTION-BASED CASE FORMULATION

This approach to emotion-orientated case formulation was developed out of the empirical research that was already being establish on the processes of emotional change. To understand how treatment facilitates the modelled emotional processes, it is necessary to demonstrate that interventions can change key processes and that such changes are related to both intermediate outcomes (e.g., within session changes) as well as final treatment outcomes.

The model of emotional processing has been validated in 25 studies to date which have examined micro- and macro-level emotion change processes across a wide range of client populations and treatment approaches (Pascual-Leone, 2018). Eight of these studies have focussed on psychotherapeutic treatments specifically for personality disorders, applying the model to a total of 132 diagnosed cases of personality disorder across those studies. It is worth noting that because process research on the treatment of personality disorders is still in its early years, the amount of research on this model for personality disorders actually represents a sizeable contribution to the field to date. The majority of these studies have investigated emotion change processes in the context of treatments for borderline personality disorder, including dialectical behaviour therapy (Kramer, Pascual-Leone, Berthoud, et al., 2016; Pascual-Leone & Kramer, 2017), motive-orientated therapeutic relationship (Berthoud et al., 2017; Willimann, Berthoud, Pascual-Leone, Grosse Holdforth, & Kramer, 2016), emotion-focussed therapy (Kramer & Pascual-Leone, 2012) and a manualized general psychiatric treatment (Berthoud, Kramer, Caspar, & Pascual-Leone, 2015). Additional research has also examined clarification-orientated therapy among clients who met diagnostic criteria for various personality disorders (Kramer, Pascual-Leone, Rohde, & Sachse, 2016), including a pilot study specifically on narcissistic personality disorder (Kramer, Pascual-Leone, Rohde, & Sachse, 2017).

In a randomized controlled trial, Berthoud et al. (2017) investigated emotional processing over the course of two 10-session treatments for borderline personality disorder; namely, general psychiatric management (GPM) versus GPM augmented with motive-orientated therapeutic relationship (MOTR). Although both treatments showed decreases in early expressions of distress and increases in more adaptive emotions over the course of treatment, relative to GPM clients, MOTR clients displayed greater emotional variability by the end of treatment. In other words, therapists who focussed on responsiveness and the alliance (i.e., MOTR) tended to have clients who showed relatively more movement between different emotional states than GPM clients who spent a greater proportion of time 'stuck' in some emotional states, leaving other states less explored. Furthermore, lower levels of global distress at mid-treatment were predictive of greater reductions in general psychiatric symptoms among MOTR clients, but not GPM clients. This suggests that the enhanced effectiveness of MOTR relative to GPM for borderline personality disorder may be attributed to their differential impact on key emotion change processes posited in Pascual-Leone and Greenberg's (2007) model; and in particularly in the degree to which they facilitate emotional flexibility. As such, clinicians should be mindful not only of the specific types of emotions that are being expressed, but also to the client's emotional variability and capacity to flexibly switch from one state to another, rather than stagnating or getting stuck in the 'same old' states.

Another process study (Kramer, Pascual-Leone, Berthoud, et al., 2016) based on a randomized controlled trial of Dialectical Behaviour Therapy (DBT) skills training for clients with borderline personality disorder also showed support for hypothesized links between emotion processes and treatment outcomes, specifically with regard to expressions of anger. Previous studies had difficulty demonstrating the effectiveness of DBT for anger problems, perhaps because researchers rarely differentiate between different *kinds* of anger, as described by the sequential model. In this study, Kramer and colleagues found that a DBT skills training programme was associated with significantly greater reductions in interpersonal problems than treatment as usual. However, those treatment effects were mediated by *increases* in assertive anger among DBT clients. This was in contrast to the previously dominate expectation that problematic expressions of rejecting anger would decrease with treatment. Instead, the findings are consistent with the sequential processing model, which suggests that some forms of anger are more productive (i.e., assertive) than others (i.e., rejecting) and that more productive expressions of anger can be facilitated by clinical interventions.

As such, clinicians should be aware that not all forms of anger are equal in their usefulness for emotional processing. By way of a case example, a client in emotion-focused therapy (EFT) with borderline personality disorder (Kramer & Pascual-Leone, 2012) engaged in a two-chair dialogue with her dismissive mother. In an imagined conversation between the client's six-year-old self and her mother, the client asserted that, 'It is my right to play here. This is my space and right now I need you to see and respect that'. Expressions of assertive anger such as this tend to be more adaptive than expressions of rejecting anger (e.g., 'I hated you for always barging in on me and telling me not to play here'.). Therefore, this study reinforces the need for clinicians to differentiate between less and more productive kinds of anger to facilitate adaptive processing of anger and resolution of interpersonal difficulties.

Consistent with other case studies supporting the effectiveness of EFT for borderline personality disorder (e.g., Pos & Greenberg, 2012), Kramer and Pascual-Leone (2012) also reported decreases in the client's general psychiatric symptoms and early expressions of distress, as well as greater emotional range/flexibility and more frequent expressions of advanced meaning-making states, over the course of treatment. Likewise, in a study of an unsuccessful client in general psychiatric treatment, Berthoud et al. (2015) reported that the client showed little emotional change and even increases in global distress over time. As such, patterns of individual-level emotional change over time can be used by clinicians to monitor and predict how successful treatment may be for a given client, as well as to adjust the therapist interventions accordingly.

Model-consistent results have also been found among clients engaged in treatment for narcissistic, histrionic, and obsessive-compulsive personality disorders as well (Kramer, Pascual-Leone, Rohde, & Sachse, 2016, 2017). In clarification-orientated psychotherapy, an experiential therapy for personality disorders, Kramer, Pascual-Leone, Berthoud, et al. (2016a) and Kramer, Pascual-Leone, Rohde and Sachse (2016b) showed that both therapist's empathic 'understanding' and 'process directivity' early in a session predicted the extent to which clients subsequently engaged and grappled with experiences of fear and shame later in the same session. Likewise, in a follow-up study (Kramer et al., 2017), clients with narcissistic personality disorder who had reductions in shame across the working phase of therapy (from sessions 25 to 36) also enjoyed an associated decrease in symptoms of depression by the end of therapy. Furthermore, 78% of variance in expressions of self-compassion during session 36 were accounted for by a set of specific therapist interventions which included process-guidance, the therapist's treatment of interactional manoeuvres, and treatment of behaviour-underlying assumptions. The implication of both of these studies is that therapists are able to use empathic skills and specific interventions to guide client process in the exploration of maladaptive emotion and facilitation of adaptive emotion.

CONDUCTING EMOTION-BASED CASE FORMULATIONS

Although informed by EFT theory, this model represents an integrative method of case formulation. This method can be used on its own or it can add a process-experiential layer alongside other theoretical formulations (e.g., cognitive and behavioural formulations based on CBT, DBT, Luborsky's core conflictual relationship theme, etc.). This is because the model highlights *what* emotional processes to target but leaves the question of *how* to facilitate emotional processing open. This means that the model can be flexibly applied and allows for interventions from a variety of therapeutic orientations to facilitate emotional change.

To make use of the empirical support for this model of emotional processing and its potential for application, Pascual-Leone and Kramer (2017) described the formulation of emotion-based case conceptualization as taking place in four steps: (1) assess the client's emotional processes and problems, (2) using the model as a template, populate it with client data and identify the stage at which the client is currently located, (3) identify promising directions for emotional development, and (4) select and employ interventions to facilitate targeted client processes. Each of these steps are elaborated below in the context of the sequential emotional processing model. This method of case conceptualization will also be illustrated concretely using the case example of 'Beth' (pseudonym) who participated in dialectical behavioural therapy for borderline personality disorder (a case previously described in Pascual-Leone & Kramer, 2017).

Step 1: Initial Case Assessment

There are two major components in the initial case assessment. The first component involves identifying the client's presenting problem, narrative and attachment history. The second component involves compiling client affective data.

Beth was a Caucasian woman, in her late thirties, who lived with her partner and two children. She had not completed high school but was starting a college programme and worked part-time doing basic clerical work. Beth arrived at the clinic seeking treatment to address anger problems, suicidal urges and self-harming behaviours, and her unstable housing situation. A structured clinical interview determined that she met DSM-IV-TR diagnostic criteria for borderline personality disorder, alcohol dependence, and partially remittent crack-cocaine dependence. Her symptoms included frantic efforts to avoid abandonment, impulsive substance abuse and dependency-related behaviours. She also reported affective instability for one to three hours at a time, which was often related to problem behaviours such as reckless driving, self-mutilation (i.e., wrist cutting, punching herself in the head) and inappropriately intense fits of anger (i.e., frequent angry temper, recurrent fist fights). When under acute psychosocial stressors she would also sometimes suffer transient episodes of paranoia and dissociation.

With regard to background and attachment history, Beth had been in foster care and was later adopted. She reported that she had experienced both physical and sexual abuse, had distant family relations, and had been homeless at times. She also reported a history of suicide attempts, self-harm and violence (e.g., beating and seriously injuring her partner who had left her for another woman).

When working in session, Beth appeared to be engaged but was highly avoidant and did not readily disclose intimate matters. She was emotionally labile and dysregulated, easily distracted and fidgety in her chair. She fluctuated between playing gravely serious (i.e., holding up her fists threateningly) and joyfully laughing something off. However, she became quiet and increasingly fidgety when the conversation turned to personal difficulties. She often had little insight in her own functioning, but she was motivated to change and understood the rationale for being in a behavioural therapy.

The second component of case assessment entails populating the model with client affective data, using Fig. 18.1 as a lens to organize observations about the client's emotional experience and style. This requires attending to the affective nature of reported difficulties (e.g., client feeling socially disconnected), making in-session observations of emotion and regulation (e.g., client's lack of eye contact, or being easily overwhelmed) and noting the client's capacity to make use of and understand affective experiences (e.g., client's ability to explore and deepen emotional experiencing with the help of the therapist).

Step 2: Tailoring the Case Formulation to Model a Clients' Personal Processes

Following the initial case assessment, the next step is to assess the client's style of processing emotions (i.e., the level of arousal and in-session experiencing), the core content of painful aspects of emotional experience and the issues contributing to emotional experiencing.

Beth generally struggled with emotional dysregulation. The predominant emotion that she expressed in the initial assessment was rejecting anger directed both outwardly at others (i.e., through yelling and violence) and also inwardly at herself (i.e., through self-harm and substance use behaviours). She reported a time when she came home to find her door locked which led to her yelling at her partner's sister and kicking at the door, damaging the deadbolt. In another situation, she became very angry at her partner when they were in a shopping mall. She told him that she 'felt down' due to 'difficult memories related to Christmas', when in actuality, Beth felt ashamed because she had impulsively spent all of her Christmas money on crack-cocaine. As such, her anger at her partner can be understood as a secondary emotion which functioned to displace her core shame related to perceptions of herself as being bad and inadequate. A similar emotional shift was seen in another situation in which she asked her partner for his help on a homework assignment she was working on. He told her that he was tired and declined to help. Beth felt 'stupid' and inadequate for school, as well as feeling uncared for by him (i.e., shame). However, her outward response was to explode and yell at him (i.e., rejecting anger), then isolate herself and engage in self-harm behaviours.

Therapists use the model as a template for describing and locating a client's core affective difficulties, inserting observations from case notes or direct client statements into the boxes in the model. As shown in Fig. 18.2, this is literally using the model as a container to organize client data to create an individualized case formulation (for another example of doing this, see Timulak & Pascual-Leone, 2015). Doing so would unfold over this and the following steps. A client's pattern of emotional processing can then be understood from a variety of theoretical orientations. From a behavioural perspective, Beth's emotional dysregulation can be seen

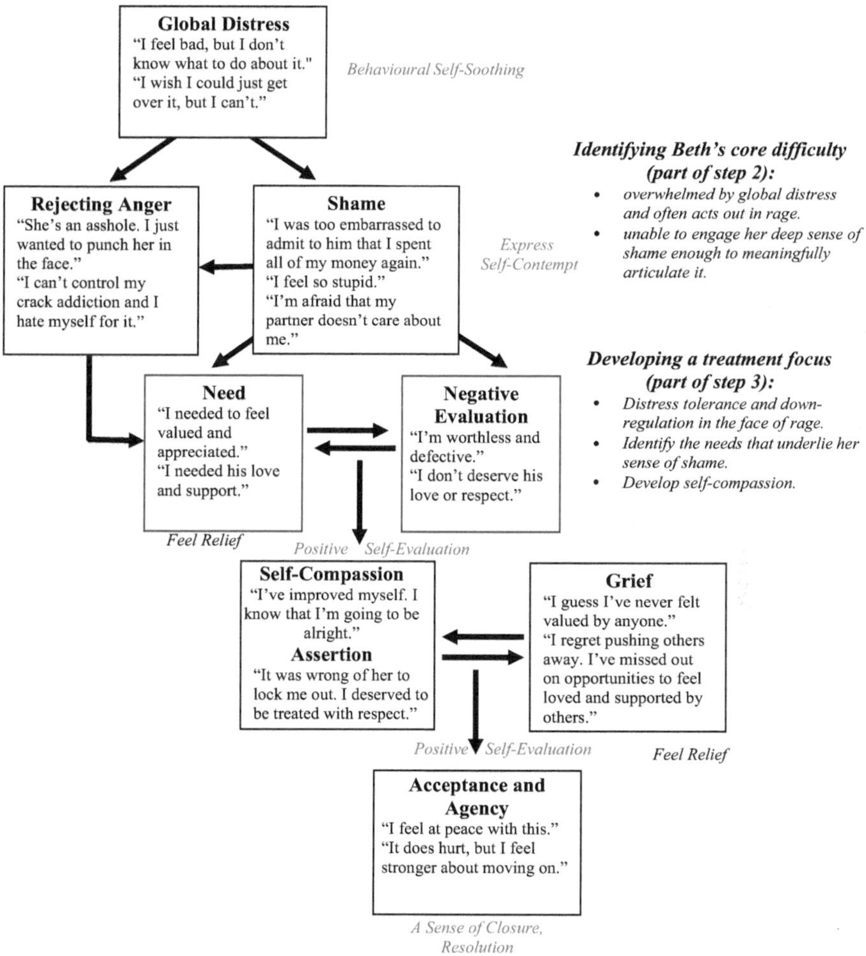

FIGURE 18.2 Populating the model with observations of 'Beth's' emotion. *Adapted with permission from Pascual-Leone, A., Greenberg, L.S. (2007). Emotional processing in experiential therapy: Why "the only way out is through".* Journal of Consulting and Clinical Psychology, *75, 875–887.*

as a learned pattern of negative reinforcement whereby rejecting anger was reinforced by the reduction of shame. Alternatively, from a psychodynamic perspective, rejecting anger may represent a defence mechanism against painful feelings of shame. Whatever the intervention framework being used, the emotional processes at work can be formulated based on client process within a trans-theoretical model.

Step 3: Referring Back to the Model, Making Inferences and Planning Treatment

Once the client's background and affective processes have been formulated, the therapist will have a sense of where the client is currently and most typically positioned on the process map. By referring back to model, the therapist can then identify the client's zone of proximal emotional development as well as *potential* processes that may have not yet been fully explored, pointing the direction for new growth. In this way, the therapist is able to anticipate and target 'good process' before it emerges in session.

Returning to the case of Beth, her core difficulty was with emotional dysregulation. At this point, exploration of more advanced emotional states (i.e., assertive anger, self-compassion, and grief/hurt) was likely to be too evocative and distressing for Beth to be fruitful in the short term. As such, the first objective of treatment was to improve her capacity for emotion regulation and self-soothing before further exploration and transformation of emotion could take place. The therapist used the model to anticipate two potentially helpful pathways, namely, implementing (1) anger management strategies to reduce the intensity of her rejecting anger and (2) distress tolerance skills, particularly in tolerating feelings of shame. Had her dysregulation not placed states of deeper meaning making out of her developmental reach, Beth might have been capable of exploring potentially adaptive experiences of hurt/grief (i.e., acknowledging that she never felt valuable in relationships), assertive anger (i.e., setting personal boundaries without resorting to violence) or agency and acceptance (i.e., admitting the past while keeping focussed on the future). However, activation of these states would not have been helpful or produce lasting change until she first developed self-regulation and distress tolerance skills with substantial support from the therapist.

Step 4: Finding Interventions that Facilitate Targeted Client Processes

In the final step, because the model is integrative, the therapist is able to use his or her chosen treatment approach and associated techniques to facilitate targeted emotion processes. As such, it is up to the therapist to find suitable and effective tasks, implementing and evaluating the impact of different tasks on client emotional development. Thus, it is only at this step where the specific treatment approach begins to shape treatment planning, because although emotion-orientated treatment goals (elaborated in step 3) will be similar, the methods for reaching those goals will obviously vary by treatment approach.

Beth participated in Dialectical Behaviour Therapy (DBT; Linehan, 1993) which emphasizes skills training and behavioural change. This behavioural approach was well-suited to address the core focus of her initial treatment, namely, the development of emotion regulation skills. The general goal for regulating anger was further subdivided into five specific treatment domains; the therapist attempted to (1) facilitate self-soothing and distress tolerance skills through skills groups and homework, (2) create interpersonal experiences of stability and support through empathic but non-evocative validation, (3) regulate anger using behavioural strategies, for example, by disengaging from dialogue when Beth attempted to bully the therapist, (4) regulate shame using behavioural strategies through exposure to and tolerance of personal vulnerability/shame and (5) treat substance abuse using behavioural strategies and psychoeducation.

Beth made a six-month contract to engage in therapy and showed steady improvements in treatment during this time. Self-harm, angry behaviour and substance abuse behaviours were all reduced, though she still felt ashamed about these behaviours. She was ambivalent about making commitments to homework and trying new ways of addressing her difficulties but stated that she looked forward to her sessions. During treatment, she was often in a state of high arousal and undifferentiated global distress. Although she found self-soothing exercises to be comforting, she collapsed back into global distress as soon as she was left without the explicitly structured task and directive support of the therapist. Her initial improvements were promising, but she still had difficulties coping and decided to extend her treatment contract for an additional six months. However, before completing one year of treatment, she reported that she went into a rage while intoxicated, breaking objects in her house. The therapist deemed that her children were at risk and he was legally required to report the incident to authorities, creating a relationship rupture. Consistent with her case formulation, Beth felt ashamed about being a risk for child abuse and responded with rejecting anger and resentment at her therapist and unfortunately, abandoned treatment prematurely.

SUMMARY AND CONCLUSION

Taken together, research in the study of personality disorders provides preliminary support for emotional transformation as a possible causal mechanism of change across different treatment modalities.

While the process model has been examined in relation to a range of treatment problems, up to 43% of that research represents the study of personality disorders. Findings from these studies support the hypothesis that emotional transformation occurs in observable and specific canonical sequences and that these sequences predict positive treatment outcomes among individuals with personality disorders. As such, this model of sequential emotional processing and transformation represents a bridge between clinical research and practice. It provides a promising new and empirically supported foundation for emotion-based case conceptualizations. Regardless of therapeutic orientation, therapists working with clients to treat personality disorders can use this process map for identifying and targeting productive emotional processes to facilitate client emotional growth, character change, and well-being.

Acknowledgements

Some details of the case description (i.e., the client's name, age, race/ethnicity, sexual orientation, and education, as well as some potentially identifying details about the process) were changed so as to protect client privacy.

References

Beck, A. T., Freeman, A., & Davis, D. D. (2004). *Cognitive therapy of personality disorders* (2nd ed.). New York, NY, US: Guilford Press.

Berthoud, L., Kramer, U., Caspar, F., & Pascual-Leone, A. (2015). Emotional processing in a ten-session general psychiatric treatment for borderline personality disorder: A case study. *Personality and Mental Health, 9*, 73–78.

Berthoud, L., Pascual-Leone, A., Caspar, F., Tissot, H., Keller, S., Rohde, K. B., et al. (2017). Leaving distress behind: A randomized controlled study on change in emotional processing in borderline personality disorder. *Psychiatry: Interpersonal and Biological Processes, 80*(2), 139–154.

Caro Gabalda, I., & Stiles, W. B. (2013). Irregular assimilation progress: Reasons for setbacks in the context of linguistic therapy of evaluation. *Psychotherapy Research, 23*, 35–53.

Diener, M. J., & Hilsenroth, M. J. (2009). Affect-focused techniques in psychodynamic psychotherapy. In R. Levy, & S. J. Ablon (Eds.), *Handbook of evidence-based psychodynamic psychotherapy: Bridging the gap between science and practice* (pp. 227–247). Totowa, NJ: Humana Press.

Eells, T. D., Lombart, K. G., Kendjelic, E. M., Turner, L. C., & Lucas, C. P. (2005). The quality of psychotherapy case formulations: A comparison of expert, experienced, and novice cognitive-behavioral and psychodynamic therapists. *Journal of Consulting and Clinical Psychology, 73*, 579–589.

Elliott, R. (2010). Psychotherapy change process research: Realizing the promise. *Psychotherapy Research, 20*, 123–135.

Foa, E. B., & Kosak, M. J. (1986). Emotional processing of fear: Exposure to corrective information. *Psychological Bulletin, 99*, 20–35.

Goldman, R. N., & Greenberg, L. S. (2015). *Case formulation in emotion-focused therapy. Co-creating clinical maps for change*. Washington, DC: American Psychological Association.

Gratz, K. L., Moore, K. E., & Tull, M. T. (2016). The role of emotion dysregulation in the presence, associated difficulties, and treatment of borderline personality disorder. *Personality Disorders: Theory, Research, and Treatment, 7*(4), 344–353. https://doi.org.ezproxy.uwindsor.ca/10.1037/per0000198.

Greenberg, L. S., & Paivio, S. C. (1997). *Working with emotions in psychotherapy*. New York: Guilford Press.

Greenberg, L. S., & Pascual-Leone, A. (2006). Emotion in psychotherapy: A practice-friendly research review. *Journal of Clinical Psychology: In Session, 62*, 611–630.

Jose, A., & Goldfried, M. R. (2008). A transtheoretical approach to case formulation. *Cognitive and Behavioral Practice, 15*, 212–222.

Kennedy-Moore, E., & Watson, J. C. (2001). How and when does emotional expression help? *Review of General Psychology, 5*, 187–212. https://doi.org/10.1037/1089-2680.5.3.187.

Kramer, U., Kolly, S., Berthoud, L., Keller, S., Preisig, M., Caspar, F., et al. (2014). Effects of motive-oriented therapeutic relationship in a ten-session general psychiatric treatment of borderline personality disorder: A randomized controlled trial. *Psychotherapy and Psychosomatics, 83*, 176–186.

Kramer, U., & Pascual-Leone, A. (2012). Emotional processing across long-term psychotherapy in a patient presenting with borderline personality disorder: A case study. In *Presentation at the 42nd EABCT-Congress. Geneva, Switzerland*.

Kramer, U., Pascual-Leone, A., Berthoud, L., de Roten, Y., Marquet, P., Kolly, S., et al. (2016). Assertive anger mediates effects of dialectical behavior-informed skills training for borderline personality disorder: A randomized controlled trial. *Clinical Psychology & Psychotherapy, 23*(3), 189–202.

Kramer, U., Pascual-Leone, A., Rohde, C., & Sachse, R. (2016). Emotional processing, interaction process, and outcome in clarification-oriented psychotherapy for personality disorders: A process-outcome analysis. *Journal of Personality Disorders, 30*(3), 373–394.

Kramer, U., Pascual-Leone, A., Rohde, K. B., & Sachse, R. (2017). The role of shame and self-compassion in psychotherapy for narcissistic personality disorder. *Clinical Psychology & Psychotherapy*. (Advance online publication), https://doi.org.ezproxy.uwindsor.ca/10.1002/cpp.2160.

Leiman, M., & Stiles, W. B. (2001). Dialogical sequence analysis and the zone of proximal development as conceptual enhancements to the assimilation model: The case of Jan revisited. *Psychotherapy Research, 11*, 311–330.

Linehan, M. M. (1993). *Skills training manual for treating borderline personality disorder*. The New York, NY: Guilford Press.

Pascual-Leone, A. (2009). Dynamic emotional processing in experiential therapy: Two steps forward, one step back. *Journal of Consulting and Clinical Psychology, 77*, 113–126.

Pascual-Leone, A. (2018). How client's "change emotion with emotion": A program of research on emotional processing. *Psychotherapy Research, 28*(2), 165–182. https://doi.org/10.1080/10503307.2017.1349350.

Pascual-Leone, A., & Greenberg, L. S. (2007). Emotional processing in experiential therapy: Why "the only way out is through". *Journal of Consulting and Clinical Psychology, 75*, 875–887.

Pascual-Leone, A., & Kramer, U. (2017). Developing emotion-based case formulations: A research-informed method. *Clinical Psychology & Psychotherapy, 24*(1), 212–225.

Pascual-Leone, A., Paivio, S., & Harrington, S. (2016). Emotion in psychotherapy: An experiential-humanistic perspective. In D. Cain, S. Rubin, & K. Keenan (Eds.), *Humanistic psychotherapies: Handbook of research and practice* (2nd ed.) (pp. 147–181). Washington, DC, US: American Psychological Association.

Pascual-Leone, A., Yeryomenko, N., Sawashima, T., & Warwar, S. (2017). Building emotional resilience over 14 sessions of emotion focused therapy: Micro-longitudinal analyses of productive emotional patterns. epub ahead of print *Psychotherapy Research*. https://doi.org/10.1080/10503307.2017.1315779.

Pos, A. E., & Greenberg, L. S. (2012). Organizing awareness and increasing emotion regulation: Revising chair work in emotion-focused therapy for borderline personality disorder. *Journal of Personality Disorders*, *26*(1), 84–107.

Stiles, W. B. (2009). Responsiveness as an obstacle for psychotherapy outcome research: It's worse than you think. *Clinical Psychology: Science and Practice*, *16*, 86–91.

Timulak, L., & Pascual-Leone, A. (2015). New developments for case conceptualization in emotion-focused therapy. *Clinical Psychology & Psychotherapy*, 22, 619–636. https://doi.org/10.1002/cpp.1922.

Vygotsky, L. S. (1924/1978). *Mind and society: The development of higher psychological processes*. Cambridge, MA: Harvard University Press.

Willimann, L., Berthoud, L., Pascual-Leone, A., Grosse Holtforth, M., & Kramer, U. (Jan. 2016). Goodbye global distress – hello what? Sequences of emotional processing in patients with borderline personality disorders. In *Poster presented to the Swiss national science foundation, "mechanisms of change in treatments of personality disorders," Lausanne*.

Individualizing Treatment for Clients With Personality Disorders

Ueli Kramer

As it became evident throughout this volume, there is a great variety in methods of case formulation for describing and explaining problems related to personality disorders (PDs). They vary in focus, underlying theory, complexity, depth and level of differentiation. It might depend both on the type of client and the therapist's preferences which concepts seem useful at which specific moment in therapy. Methods of case formulation have the ambition of treatment planning in clinical practice, but also of explaining, on the level of the individual client, the heterogeneity of the specific disorder. While formulation is pivotal for clinical practice, it may be also indispensable for helping solve complex methodological problems in psychotherapy research.

OCCASIONS TO LEARN FROM THE INDIVIDUAL CLIENT

To demonstrate the articulation between nomothetic databases and the methodologies of idiographic description of the individual case, I have examined all 18 case formulation methods in terms of the initial psychological constraints. Psychological and psychopathological constraints related to PD are understood in the weakest sense possible, as features clients with these disorders may bring into therapy. As such, they become 'occasions to learn from the individual client'. To use a common terminology, I will refer to labels used in the DSM-5 Alternative Model of Personality Disorders (APA, 2013), without assuming that this model be any more useful or empirically based than other approaches to describing the PD pathology. I use the four areas of impairment and the five trait domains (not the specific trait facets).

In Table 1, each case formulation method received a line, in the order of appearance in the present volume; the DSM 5 Alternative Model criteria are in columns. This examination aims at clinical utility. The ratings are based on my own read as editor of this volume and chapter authors were

TABLE 1 How the Different Approaches Address the Constraints on Case Formulation for Personality Disorders

	Identity	Self-direction	Empathy	Intimacy	Neg. Affectivity	Detachment	Antagonism	Disinhibition	Psychoticism
1. McMain	*	**	**	*	***	*	**	***	*
2. Levy	***	**	*	**	**	*	***	**	*
3. Karterud	*	**	***	**	**	*	**	**	*
4. Choi-Kain	**	***	**	**	**	*	**	**	**
5. Fassbinder	**	**	**	*	**	***	**	*	*
6. McCutcheon	*	***	**	**	*	*	*	**	*
7. Sachse	**	**	***	*	**	**	***	*	*
8. Dimaggio	**	**	*	***	*	***	*	*	*
9. Franke	*	**	***	*	**	*	*	***	**
10. Critchfield	***	*	**	***	*	*	**	*	*
11. Perry	**	*	***	***	**	*	**	*	**
12. Sturmey	*	**	**	*	**	*	**	***	**
13. Sauer-Zavala	**	**	*	*	***	**	*	**	*
14. Caspar	**	***	*	**	**	**	***	*	*
15. Ehrenthal	***	*	**	**	**	*	***	*	*
16. Westerman	**	*	**	**	**	***	***	*	*
17. Eubanks	**	**	*	**	*	***	***	*	*
18. Strating	**	*	**	*	***	***	*	*	*

*this constraint is considered in this case formulation method; **this constraint is addressed in detail in this case formulation method; ***this constraint is the core of this case formulation method (1–2 per method).

invited to comment on my rating. The ratings mean the following: one star means that this case formulation method takes this criterion into account, two stars means that this case formulation method addresses this criteria in detail, and three stars means that this case formulation method puts this criterion at the core of its approach. For the latter (rating of three stars), to be useful, only one or two criteria were possible for each method.

This table may be used as a compass to guide clinical decision making to select an appropriate case formulation method and may be interpreted as follows. A client presenting with problems in a domain (in columns) may benefit particularly from certain types of case formulation methods (in rows). A client with problems related to identity may benefit particularly from in-depth understanding according to transference-focused formulation and interpersonal-reconstructive formulations, as well as OPD formulations. A client with problems related to self-direction may particularly benefit from in-depth understanding according to general management formulation, cognitive-analytic formulation and plananalytic formulation. A client with problems related to empathy may particularly benefit from in-depth understanding according to mentalization-based formulation, clarification-oriented formulation, formulations in the forensic setting and psychodynamic formulation. A client with problems in intimacy may particularly benefit from in-depth understanding according to metacognitive interpersonal formulation and interpersonal-reconstructive formulations, as well as psychodynamic formulation. A client with problems related to negative affectivity may particularly benefit from in-depth understanding according to dialectical-behaviour formulation, formulation according the unified protocol and emotion-based formulation. A client with problems related to detachment may particularly benefit from in-depth understanding according to schema-focused formulation, metacognitive interpersonal and interpersonal-defence formulation, alliance-focused formulation and emotion-based formulation. A client with problems related to antagonism may particularly benefit from in-depth understanding according to transference-focused formulation, clarification-oriented formulation, plananalytic formulation, OPD formulation, interpersonal-defence and alliance-focused formulation. A client with problems related to disinhibition may particularly benefit from in-depth understanding according to dialectical-behaviour formulation, formulation in forensic settings and cognitive-behavioural formulation. A client with problems related to psychoticism (no ratings of 3 stars) may particularly benefit from in-depth understanding according to general psychiatric formulation, formulation in forensic settings, cognitive-behavioural and psychodynamic formulations.

The approach taken with this section was to construct an integrative meta-heuristic which may be clinically helpful for decision making. It may assist the clinician to select a case formulation focus, by using one or the other methodology, or by combining case formulation methods, if useful. It may also be useful to explore and appreciate the possible assets and limitations of a case formulation method. For example, a therapist using a case formulation method may be proficient when formulating the corresponding client profile as defined in Table 1, and may struggle with formulating, or understanding, clients with differing profiles. When this therapist works with a client with such differing profiles, or differing trait aspects are presented in a case, it might be advisable to this therapist to try out a complementary case formulation method. This may be a productive, and clinically valid, use of the present meta-heuristic of case formulation methods, with the aim of improving, sharpening and differentiating existing ways of understanding a client.

This meta-approach may be criticized on the grounds of it being quite complex and requiring multiple layers of assessment. Whereas this approach might be necessary in some cases, in some others, a single and readily available methodology may suffice. However, Kahneman (2011) describes such a heuristic as the availability heuristic with an inherent limitation: the more a therapist conceptualizes a particular clinical manifestation as related to a particular cause, as found according to a particular case formulation method, the more this therapist is likely to conceptualize this link in further cases: a false positive relationship may result. This may translate into a potential limitation of any case formulation method: an integrative meta-heuristic may help to compensate for such biases.

In addition, we should acknowledge that the trait dimensions are probably partially overlapping constructs and, in some cases, the (beneficial) effects of case formulation applied to a few central constructs may 'spill over' to several other linked constructs. Thus, it may not be necessary to differentiate between all the different trait dimensions, but only a few, to make this decision, depending on the client.

A COMMON PATHWAY TO UNDERSTANDING A DISRUPTIVE EXPERIENCE: THE SYMBOLIZING PROCESS

Case formulation appears to be an interpersonal process where the therapist uses his/her words to make sense of the client's in-session experiences and manifestations, composed by (1) a mental activity of the therapist – symbolizing the patient's experience on the therapist's mind, or 'in his/her heart' – and (2) an interpersonal activity of using this formulation explicitly to shape an intervention in the therapeutic hour. Putting words to a lived experience may be a common pathway – a sort of common denominator – of any therapist engaging in the activity of case formulation. Symbolizing is the process which puts words – i.e., symbols – to experiences, and by doing so, awareness of these experiences may be sharpened, increased, differentiated and transformed (Stiles, 2017). Much as a parent formulates an experience observed in a child, to help him/her develop a greater nuance in the awareness of these experiences, will the therapist put words to the client's idiosyncratic experience. Such an interaction activity may also serve as guide to the child towards the appreciation of novelty, and the relationship may be strengthened (for more parallels between psychotherapy and the developmental perspective on mother-child interaction, see for example Fonagy, Gergely, Jurist, & Target, 2002; Wallin, 2007; Wiseman, 2017). As such, the activity of formulation builds on a fundamentally human capacity and necessity for survival: the creation of meaning through the means of connections between words and experience (Fogel, 1993; Greenberg & Safran, 1987; Stiles, 2001), in the context of a relationship bond. As such, case formulation is a human process which puts the symbolizing process at its core.

CASE FORMULATIONS AND THE THERAPEUTIC RELATIONSHIP

The therapeutic relationship can be considered as a central ingredient enhancing outcome in treatment for PD (Smith, Barrett, Benjamin, & Barber, 2006). Division 29 Task Force from the American Psychological Association, on the evidence base of the therapeutic relationship (Norcross & Wampold, 2011), concludes that several aspects of the therapeutic relationship are 'demonstrably effective', in particular the therapeutic alliance, empathy and collecting feedback from the client, several aspects of the therapeutic relationship are 'probably effective', in particular positive regard, goal consensus and collaboration, and, finally, as promising features of the therapeutic relationship were described the therapist genuineness (congruence, repairing alliance ruptures and taking into account counter-transference). Whereas all these conclusions apply to clients with PDs, Smith et al. (2006) discuss additionally, specific therapist relationship interventions potentially helpful in the work with clients with PDs, which are therapist self-disclosure and relational interpretations. Based on evidence, for example, that clients with low-level quality of object relations, as it is often the case for clients with PDs, benefit specifically from certain types of interpretations (Hoglend et al., 2011; Piper, Azim, Joyce, & McCallum, 1991), the authors conclude that these relational interventions are particularly powerful when they 'are tailored to certain patient characteristics' (Smith et al., 2006, p. 228). The evidence base of the specific client characteristics which a therapist should attend to is assessed in the second part of Norcross' book (2011) and they encompass client variables such as reactance and resistance, stage of change, preferences, culture, coping and attachment styles, expectations, and religious aspects. In keeping with the integrative approach taken in this volume, these might be generic 'constraints' which any case formulation may consider. As shown in the present volume, the therapist awareness of an occasion to learn from the individual client does not replace the application of an idiosyncratic case formulation to these clinical manifestations. From these elaborations, it becomes clear that the therapeutic relationship encompasses many other aspects than the much-researched, and quite global, variable of the therapeutic alliance. Several aspects concern an interpersonal process (e.g., collaboration), others a therapist stance or behaviour (i.e., empathy). Tailoring relationship interventions to the individual client may enhance the effectiveness of the intervention and the psychotherapy. Case formulation may play a pivotal role in this process.

Reviewing the 18 case formulation methodologies exposed in the present volume regarding their potential of fostering a constructive therapeutic relationship reveals a differentiated picture. First, we assume that there may a 'common' factor related to the process of individualization of a treatment. The effort of making a treatment fit the individual client may impact the therapeutic relationship in the sense of therapist offering a sense to the client that this treatment is for him/for her. The client may feel *he/she is welcome, and personally and uniquely attended to*. This common factor related to individualized case formulation may have an impact per se on the therapeutic collaboration and outcome. Then, more specifically, each author/author group focuses on specific aspects of how to foster the therapeutic relationship, consistent with the underlying theory and the therapist stance advocated by a specific approach.

What are possible implications for the therapeutic relationship for each of the case formulation methodologies? By trying to answer this question in a nutshell, I try to remain as close as possible to the authors' own conclusions from each chapter.

As argued by McMain et al., the precision of the behaviourally based formulation in DBT helps facilitate therapist empathy and compassion for the possibly underlying causes of the presenting behaviour. As argued by Levy et al., the TFP therapist's use of the client's language when formulating, coupled with the 'holding' quality of a deep relational interpretation, may be experienced by the client as validating and accepting, as opposed to an overly warm stance (which may be experienced as invalidating by the client). As argued by Karterud et al., the MBT case formulation, written in plain common-sense language, facilitates both a focus on the individual's needs in the relationship, but also helps the therapist to remain adherent to the specific therapy principles, providing an optimal relationship offer for the client. The case formulation helps facilitate in-session therapist empathy and enlarge the client's self-understanding. As argued by Choi-Kain et al., a psychiatric formulation facilitates rather quickly, by its straight-forward language, a medicalized understanding of the central dynamics in the client. This direct communication may contribute to the increase in the therapeutic alliance and cooperation. As argued by Fassbinder et al., the schema-mode conception may increase the awareness in the client of multiple parts inhabiting it him-/herself and contributing to conflict and problems. This might help focus the client on the core, most vulnerable, part and develop hopefulness in change. As argued by McCutcheon et al., the shared reformulation letter in the context of CAT for youth has both a validating and committing component. It increases collaboration around explicitly formulated goals and strengthens the therapeutic relationship. As argued by Sachse, the clarification-oriented formulation helps the client to become aware of his/her contribution to the interpersonal dynamics and he/she may develop increasingly trust in the therapist as a person, who is behaving complementary to his/her central motives, but not so to his/her interaction problems. As argued by Dimaggio et al., the interpersonal-metacognitive formulation helps the client take a binocular view on him-/herself, in coordination with him-/herself-in-interaction with others. As such, the case formulation may help sharpen the goal of the therapy and engage the client in specific tasks of therapy. As argued by Franke et al., case formulation in forensic settings offers a clear structure helping the client to gain awareness about the precipitant factors of offending behaviours, which may increase collaboration around a specific goal. As argued by Critchfield et al., interpersonal-reconstructive formulation encourages client's awareness of core interpersonal needs and fosters choice in life. As such, clients gain new knowledge about the relationship-underlying motivations. As argued by Perry et al., the psychodynamic formulation helps the therapist to structure a host of information, including unconscious elements, and to intervene along the lines of the formulated content; the client may feel understood on different levels, also the unconscious ones. As argued by Sturmey et al., cognitive-behavioural case formulations help the client to recognize him-/herself in the 'logic' of the proposed content. Such a framework helps creating a new understanding of him-/herself and helps the client to develop a sense of hope for change through therapy. As argued by Sauer-Zavala et al., the unified protocol formulation offers a cogent structure to the client's understanding of his/her emotional problems. The client may feel increasingly confident that emotional competence and skill is within his/her reach, thus, it fosters motivation to change. As argued by Caspar, the motive-oriented therapeutic relationship, based on the plananalytic case formulation, offers the client a corrective relationship experience, mostly on the implicit level, as the therapist works with the complementarity to the behaviour-underlying motives, rather than with the problematic behaviours per se. As argued by Ehrenthal et al., the comprehensiveness of the OPD approach may help the therapist to feel more confident in the therapeutic relationship, as well as more aware of the interpersonal stakes in the here and now. Their explicit sharing may increase the client's relationship awareness and create a treatment focus. As argued by Westerman, the detailed formulation in the context of interpersonal-defence theory fosters therapist responsiveness to client's wishes in therapy, while avoiding maintaining defensive patterns, and novel, corrective interpersonal experiences. As argued by Eubanks, a formulation according to the alliance rupture and repair model explicitly fosters the work on the therapeutic relationship in the here and now, by using therapist self-disclosure, as well as fosters the understanding of its motivational underpinnings. As argued by Strating et al., emotion-based formulations assist the therapist in the awareness of the client's qualities of emotional experience in the here and now, which may be used to encourage deeper and more differentiated experiencing, marked by an even more trusting client-therapist relationship.

From this synthesis, it may appear that relationship variables need to be differentiated on a much more fine-grained and theory-informed level than previously agreed upon in the field (Norcross & Wampold, 2011); case formulation point to the necessity of adopting such an individualized theory-informed perspective. Fine-grained psychotherapy relationship variables may be particularly central for the treatment of PDs, for it was argued that relational and emotional neglect, or abuse, may be one central etiological pathway for the development of any PD (e.g., Herpertz, 2013). As such, the field of psychotherapy may be able to learn from what case formulation methods for PD teach: individualizing treatment may have a major impact – by actively correcting neglectful or traumatic interpersonal experiences – on the very specific healing components of the therapeutic relationship.

In addition, there is still much work to be done to find out how the observed terminological differences translate into in-session practice and whether they represent real conceptual differences, or rather different words for underlying similar concepts and processes. Clinical application, and empirical work, may tell.

INDIVIDUALIZING PSYCHOTHERAPY RESEARCH PARADIGMS

It may not be a coincidence that this book closes with some remarks on possible research paradigms. I know only a few clinicians who may disagree with the importance of individualizing treatments, by using case formulations, for PD. However, the idea of individualizing central variables in psychotherapy research is still in its infancy.

This is somewhat surprising, given that Persons (1991) convincingly pointed out that psychotherapy outcome research fails to study treatments as they are described in the literature, and does not address the core question of which theory-based mechanism is changed by a specific treatment. Indeed, J. Persons was one of the first who made a call to consider the potential gains of individualized psychotherapy research designs, by using case formulations. In his commentary to Persons (1991), Messer (1991) pointed out several obstacles standing in the way of using such idiographic research designs and insisted particularly clearly on issues related to reliability and validity in psychodynamic case formulations. Also commenting on Persons (1991), Garfield (1991), however, disagreed with several points raised, in particular he underlined that very few studies, at the time, actually used standardized procedures and highlighted the limitations of idiographic research, for example the difficulty of reproducing the results in independent settings. Also, the theory-based approach to assessing psychotherapy might be interesting, but it might be even more relevant to observe what therapists *actually do* in session, rather than rely on what they say they do.

Clearly, the use of case formulation in psychotherapy research has potential, but may also imply some risk, which should be attended to. Since the early 1990s, only a few studies have examined the impact of idiographic case formulation on psychotherapeutic change. By change, Persons (1991) understood the impact on specific mechanisms of change: in what follows, we discuss first the impact on psychotherapy outcomes, then address specific questions, before returning to Persons' call to link idiographic research with mechanisms of change.

A few studies have shown an impact of case formulation on outcome parameters in different disorders (Dudley, Ingham, Sowerby, & Freeston, 2015; Eells, Lombart, Kendjelic, Turner, & Lucas, 2005; Emmelkamp, Bouman, & Blaauw, 1994; Ghaderi, 2006; Johansson et al., 2012; Kramer et al., 2014; see also Aston, 2009), In our own study on borderline personality disorder (Kramer et al., 2014), we randomized $N = 85$ clients to two brief versions of psychiatric treatment, one a standard version and one a responsive treatment where the therapists used an idiographic case formulation according to Plan Analysis and implemented the motive-oriented therapeutic relationship. Results were much in line with what was observed by Ghaderi (2006) on a client sample with bulimia: On average, clients in both conditions benefitted – in terms of symptom reduction – from the brief intervention, with small to moderate outcome advantages for general problem load favoring the responsive treatment. So far and to our knowledge, this remains the only experimental demonstration of the impact of a case formulation method for clients with personality disorders, and it demonstrates that the content of Persons' (1991) call has proven to be both inaccurate and accurate: we can conclude today that randomized controlled methodology is compatible with the idiographic formulation approach (which was not predicted by Persons), and there are slight advantages when therapists tailor their interventions to the individual client (which was predicted by Persons; for a discussion, see Eells, 2013a,b; Persons, 2013). Whereas the studies discussed in this paragraph represent an important demonstration of the impact of case formulation, they examined treatment process and outcomes from an evaluative viewpoint, assessing the benefit, added-value, effectiveness, and so forth, of the case formulation applied, rather than being curious about the client's (and therapist's) subjective experiences (Pain, Chadwick, & Abba, 2008), or idiographic changes which may be core to psychotherapy. As pointed out by several authors in this volume, more research is needed on these different levels.

We may summarize that future challenges to the science of case formulation, in particular for clients with PD, may include (1) the establishment of reliability and validity for each of the case formulation methods presented (e.g., Armelius, Sundbom, Fransson, & Kullgren, 1990; Critchfield, Mackaronis, & Benjamin, 2017; Dinger et al., 2014; Ingenhoven et al., 2009; Kuyken, Fothergill, Meyrem, & Chadwick, 2005; Pascual-Leone, 2018; Völlm, 2013); (2) the continued assessment of the impact of idiographic case formulations on process and outcome of psychotherapy, for each of the case formulation methods presented (e.g., Kramer et al., 2014); (3) the tracking of idiographic changes in psychotherapy, as linked to the case formulation; (4) the continued comparison between the idiographic contents of these different case formulation methodologies facing the same case (Perry, Luborsky, Silberschatz, & Popp, 1989); (5) the assessment of feedback loops incorporated in case formulation, with regard to the quality of the formulation; (6) the assessment of the impact of training in case formulation on the quality and differentiation of the case formulation (Minoudis et al., 2013); (7) the assessment of the link between case formulation and development of expertise in psychotherapy (Chi, 2006; Chi, Glaser, & Farr, 1988); (8) the use of novel technologies, including the internet, in the training in case formulation and the clinical applications of case formulations (Caspar, Berger, & Hautle, 2004; Johansson et al., 2012); (9) the use of idiographic case formulation to assess moderators and mechanisms of change explaining the outcome of psychotherapy (Boritz, Barnhart, Eubanks, & McMain, 2018; Crits-Christoph, Barber, & Kurcias, 1993; Silberschatz, Fretter, & Curtis, 1986; Westerman, Foote, & Winston, 1995; Zufferey, Caspar, & Kramer, 2018).

Psychotherapy researchers have called for more studies on explanatory moderators and mechanisms of change of our treatments (Kazdin, 2009; Kraemer, Wilson, Fairburn, & Agras, 2002; Kramer, 2017, 2018; Zilcha-Mano, 2018). Knowing what works for whom addresses the question of treatment moderators, whereas how and why treatments are effective relates to mechanisms of change. Discriminating clients with PD with high scores on psychological mindedness from clients with low scores on psychological mindedness might explain some of the treatment outcome variance, but fundamentally, it does not consider the idiosyncratic nature of the client's experience. It might be advisable, instead, to apply a case formulation method to the clinical material of such cases included in a research study and let emerge, using qualitative methodology, new dimensions and descriptors of a study sample, grounded in the idiosyncratic observations. The methodologies presented in this volume may help, depending on the theoretical framework adopted. Based on the research question and on the specific content, qualitatively anchored variables may be created, for example the level of structural integration of a particular case (based on the TFP approach), the propensity of a case to present an interpersonal hypersensitivity (based on the GPM approach), the specific client's interpersonal agreeableness (based on the Plan Analysis approach; Zufferey et al., 2018) and the client's awareness of an alliance rupture in the process (based on the alliance rupture-repair model). In short, clinically relevant moderator variables may be gained from such qualitatively rooted research.

Whereas the use of information from a case formulation for the clinically valid description and assessment of therapy moderators seems promising, the use of case formulation methodology for explaining how and why psychotherapy works (i.e., the mechanisms of change) seems more complex. Nevertheless, idiosyncratic formulations may help track a specific central process throughout therapy, which may function as the idiosyncratic mechanism of change in a client undergoing treatment. Longitudinal observations based on an idiographic feature require rigorous time-series methodologies: less used approaches may be applied (e.g., Boswell, Anderson, & Barlow, 2014; DeRubeis et al., 2014; Fisher & Boswell, 2016; Ramseyer, Kupper, Caspar, Znoj, & Tschacher, 2014). Also, case study research should not only try to demonstrate that the specific treatment worked, but should also try to explain why and how change occurred (Fishman, Messer, Edwards, & Dattilio, 2017). Such an elaborated theory of a specific case may help better understand the process of therapy and may be anchored in a specific case formulation method, as presented in this volume. Whereas the number of cases in such a study is 1, there are valid methods which help demonstrate how a client process or feature, as observed in a case formulation, changes over the course of psychotherapy. A possible approach is the assimilation model (Stiles, 2001; for an illustration on a case with borderline personality disorder, see Kramer, Meystre, Imesch, & Kolly, 2016), an alternative model is the interpersonal defense theory (Westerman & Muran, 2017); these approaches develop a particular theory based on very detailed case observations – and how they play out in the actual interaction with the therapist.

More globally, case formulation may help addressing a particularly complex question in psychotherapy research: the responsiveness problem

(Kramer & Stiles, 2015; Stiles, Honos-Webb, & Surko, 1998). Therapists not only deliver specific techniques, nor do they formulate a case outside of an interaction context: on the contrary, the emerging interaction context influences the choice of intervention, strategy, planning, but also may influence the case formulation, its focus, depth, differentiation and content. Whereas this problem seems secondary to clinicians, it is particularly thorny for researchers who now need to develop methodologies to capture the interactional nature of psychotherapy and its formulation – the symbolizing process – to produce meaningful conclusions in terms of mechanisms explaining change.

A mindful use of a case formulation method may help here: an appropriate elaboration of the individual client's problem-underlying causal mechanism, as demonstrated in the present volume, may productively use the responsiveness principle in psychotherapy. The activity of symbolizing the interactional dynamics in the session may help the therapist to intervene in a more productive manner, and possibly be more flexible regarding the client's manifestations, while at the same time remain adherent to the prescribed techniques used in the context of an evidence-based treatment for PD. Such hypotheses should be testable with any of the presented case formulation methods. Putting them into action, assessing their immediate impact on process, client's and therapist's subjective experiences, and outcome of psychotherapy for PD, and how it may address some problems created with the therapist's responsiveness may be research perspectives contributing to the science of individualized case formulation.

Acknowledgements

I particularly thank William B. Stiles, and the authors of the chapters, for their comments on an earlier version of this discussion.

References

American Psychiatric Association. (2013). *Diagnostic and Statistical Manual of mental disorders. DSM-5*. Washington, DC: American Psychiatric Publishing.

Armelius, B. A., Sundbom, E., Fransson, P., & Kullgren, G. (1990). Personality organization defined by DMT and the structural interview. *Scandinavian Journal of Psychology*, *31*(2), 81–88.

Aston, R. (2009). A literature review exploring the efficacy of case formulations in clinical practice. What are the themes and pertinent issues? *Cognitive Behaviour Therapist*, *2*, 63–74.

Boritz, T., Barnhart, R., Eubanks, C., & McMain, S. (2018). Alliance rupture and resolution in dialectical behavior therapy for borderline personality disorder. *Journal of Personality Disorders*, *32*(Suppl.), 115–128.

Boswell, J. F., Anderson, L. M., & Barlow, D. H. (2014). An idiographic analysis of change processes in the unified transdiagnostic treatment of depression. *Journal of Consulting and Clinical Psychology*, *82*(2), 1060.

Caspar, F., Berger, T., & Hautle, I. (2004). The right view of your patient: A computer-assisted, individualized module for psychotherapy training. *Psychotherapy: Theory, Research, Practice, Training, 41*(2), 125–135.

Chi, M. T. H. (2006). Two approaches to the study of experts' characteristics. In K. A. Ericsson, N. Charness, P. J. Feltovich, & R. R. Hoffman (Eds.), *The Cambridge handbook of expertise and expert performance* (pp. 21–30). Cambridge: Cambridge University Press.

Chi, M. T. H., Glaser, R., & Farr, M. (Eds.). (1998). *The nature of expertise.* Hillsdale, NJ: Erlsbaum.

Critchfield, K. L., Mackaronis, J. E., & Benjamin, L. S. (2017). Characterizing the integration of CBT and psychodynamic techniques in interpersonal reconstructive therapy for patients with severe and comorbid personality pathology. *Journal of Psychotherapy Integration, 27*(4), 460–475.

Crits-Christoph, P., Barber, J. P., & Kurcias, J. S. (1993). The accuracy of therapists' interpretations and the development of the therapeutic alliance. *Psychotherapy Research, 3*(1), 25–35.

DeRubeis, R. J., Cohen, Z. D., Forand, N. R., Fournier, J. C., Gelfand, L. A., & Lorenzo-Luaces, L. (2014). The personalized advantage index: Translating research on prediction into individualized treatment recommendation. A demonstration. *Plos One, 9*(1), e83875.

Dinger, U., Schauenburg, H., Hörz, S., Rentrop, M., Komo-Lang, M., Klinkerfuss, M., et al. (2014). Self-report and observer-ratings of personality functioning: A study of the OPD system. *Journal of Personality Assessment, 96*(2), 220–225.

Dudley, R., Ingham, B., Sowerby, K., & Freeston, M. (2015). The utility of case formulation in treatment decision making: The effect of experience and expertise. *Journal of Behavior Therapy and Experimental Psychiatry, 48*, 66–74.

Eells, T. D. (2013a). The case formulation approach to psychotherapy research revisited. *Pragmatic Case Studies in Psychotherapy, 9*, 426–447.

Eells, T. D. (2013b). In support of evidence-based case formulation in psychotherapy (from the perspective of a clinician). *Pragmatic Case Studies in Psychotherapy, 9*(4), 457–467.

Eells, T. D., Lombart, K. G., Kendjelic, E. M., Turner, L. C., & Lucas, C. P. (2005). The quality of psychotherapy case formulations: A comparison of expert, experienced, and novice cognitive-behavioral and psychodynamic therapists. *Journal of Consulting and Clinical Psychology, 73*(4), 579–589.

Emmelkamp, P. M. G., Bouman, T. K., & Blaauw, E. (1994). Individualized versus standardized therapy: A comparative evaluation with obsessive-compulsive patients. *Clinical Psychology and Psychotherapy, 1*, 95–100.

Fisher, A. J., & Boswell, J. F. (2016). Enhancing the personalization of psychotherapy with dynamic assessment and modeling. *Assessment, 23*, 496–506.

Fishman, D. B., Messer, S. B., Edwards, D. J. A., & Dattilio, F. M. (2017). Themes and lessons learned. In D. B. Fishman, S. B. Messer, D. J. A. Edwards, & F. M. Dattilio (Eds.), *Case studies within psychotherapy trials. Integrating qualitative and quantitative methods* (pp. 337–362). New York: Oxford University Press.

Fogel, A. (1993). *Developing through relationships: Origins of communication, self, and culture.* Chicago: University of Chicago Press.

Fonagy, P., Gergely, G., Jurist, E. L., & Target, M. (2002). *Affect regulation, mentalization, and the development of the Self.* London: Karnac.

Garfield, S. L. (1991). Psychotherapy models and outcome research. *American Psychologist*, 1350.

Ghaderi, A. (2006). Does individualization matter? A randomized trial of standardized (focused) versus individualized (broad) cognitive behavior therapy for bulimia nervosa. *Behaviour Research and Therapy, 44*, 273–288.

Greenberg, L. S., & Safran, J. D. (1987). *Emotion in psychotherapy.* New York: Guilford Press.

Herpertz, S. C. (2013). The social-cognitive basis of personality disorders. A commentary on the special issue. *Journal of Personality Disorders, 27*(1), 113–124.

Hoglend, P., Hersoug, A. G., Bogwald, K. P., Amlo, S., Marble, A., Sorbye, O., et al. (2011). Effects of transference work in the context of therapeutic alliance and quality of object relations. *Journal of Consulting and Clinical Psychology*, *79*, 697–706.

Ingenhoven, T. J., Duivenvoorden, H. J., Brogtrop, J., Lindenborn, A., van den Brink, W., & Passchier, J. (2009). Interrater reliability for Kernberg's structural interview for assessing personality organization. *Journal of Personality Disorders*, *23*(5), 528–534.

Johansson, R., Sjöberg, E., Sjögren, M., Johnson, E., Carlbring, P., Andersson, T., et al. (2012). Tailored vs standardized internet-based cognitive-behavior therapy for depression and comorbid symptoms: A randomized controlled trial. *Plos Clinical Trials*, *7*(5).

Kahneman, D. (2011). *Thinking, fast and slow*. New York: Farrar, Straus and Giroux.

Kazdin, A. E. (2009). Understanding how and why psychotherapy leads to change. *Psychotherapy Research*, *19*(4–5), 418–428.

Kraemer, H. C., Wilson, G. T., Fairburn, C. G., & Agras, W. S. (2002). Mediators and moderators of treatment effects in randomized controlled trials. *Archives of General Psychiatry*, *59*, 877–883.

Kramer, U. (2017). Personality, personality disorders, and the process of change. *Psychotherapy Research*. https://doi.org/10.1080/10503307.2017.1377358.

Kramer, U. (2018). Mechanisms of change in treatments of personality disorders: Introduction to the special section. *Journal of Personality Disorders*, *32*(Suppl.), 1–11.

Kramer, U., Kolly, S., Berthoud, L., Keller, S., Preisig, M., Caspar, F., et al. (2014). Effects of motive-oriented therapeutic relationship in a ten-session general psychiatric treatment of borderline personality disorder: A randomized controlled trial. *Psychotherapy and Psychosomatics*, *83*, 176–186.

Kramer, U., Meystre, C., Imesch, C., & Kolly, S. (2016). Assimilative processes in a client with borderline personality disorder: Tracking internal multiplicity over the first ten sessions of therapy. *Journal of Psychotherapy Integration*, *26*(2), 144–159.

Kramer, U., & Stiles, W. B. (2015). The responsiveness problem in psychotherapy: A review of proposed solutions. *Clinical Psychology: Science and Practice*, *22*, 276–294.

Kuyken, W., Fothergill, C. D., Meyrem, M., & Chadwick, P. (2005). The reliability and quality of cognitive case formulation. *Behaviour Research and Therapy*, *43*, 1187–1201.

Messer, S. B. (1991). The case formulation approach: Issues of reliability and validity. *American Psychologist*, *46*(12), 1348–1350.

Minoudis, P., Craissati, J., Shaw, J., McMurran, M., Freestone, M., Chuan, S. J., et al. (2013). An evaluation of case formulation training and consultation with probation officers. *Criminal Behavior and Mental Health*, *23*, 252–262.

Norcross, J. C. (Ed.). (2011). *Psychotherapy relationships that work. Evidence-based responsiveness* (2nd ed.) New York: Oxford University Press.

Norcross, J. C., & Wampold, B. E. (2011). Evidence-based therapy relationships: Research conclusions and clinical practices. *Psychotherapy*, *48*(1), 98–102.

Pain, C. M., Chadwick, P., & Abba, N. (2008). Clients' experience of case formulation in cognitive behavior therapy for psychosis. *British Journal of Clinical Psychology*, *47*(2), 127–138.

Pascual-Leone, A. (2018). How clients "change emotion with emotion": A programme of research on emotional processing. *Psychotherapy Research*, *28*(2), 165–182.

Perry, J. C., Luborsky, L. L., Silberschatz, G., & Popp, C. (1989). An examination of three methods of psychodynamic formulation based on the same videotaped interview. *Psychiatry*, *52*, 302–323.

Persons, J. B. (1991). Psychotherapy outcome studies do not accurately represent current models of psychotherapy: A proposed remedy. *American Psychologist*, *46*, 99–106.

Persons, J. B. (2013). Who needs a case formulation and why: Clinicians use the case formulation to guide decision-making. *Paragmatic Case Studies in Psychotherapy*, *9*, 448–456.

Piper, W. E., Azim, H. F. A., Joyce, A. S., & McCallum, M. (1991). Transference interpretations, therapeutic alliance, and outcome in short-term individual psychotherapy. *Archives of General Psychiatry*, *48*, 946–953.

Ramseyer, F., Kupper, Z., Caspar, F., Znoj, H., & Tschacher, W. (2014). Time-series panel analysis (TSPA): Multivariate modeling of temporal associations in psychotherapy process. *Journal of Consulting and Clinical Psychology, 82*, 828–838.

Silberschatz, G., Fretter, P. B., & Curtis, J. T. (1986). How do interpretations influence the process of psychotherap? *Journal of Consulting and Clinical Psychology, 54*, 646–652.

Smith, T. L., Barrett, M. S., Benjamin, L. S., & Barber, J. P. (2006). Relationship factors in treating personality disorders. In L. G. Castonguay, & L. E. Beuter (Eds.), *Principles of therapeutic change that work* (pp. 219–238). New York: Oxford University Press.

Stiles, W. B. (2001). Assimilation of problematic experiences. *Psychotherapy, 38*, 462–465.

Stiles, W. B. (2017). Finding the right words: Symbolizing experience in practice and theory. *Person-Centered and Experiential Psychotherapies, 16*, 1–13.

Stiles, W. B., Honos-Webb, L., & Surko, M. (1998). Responsiveness in psychotherapy. *Clinical Psychology: Science and Practice, 5*, 439–458.

Völlm, B. (2013). Case formulation in personality disordered offenders – a Delphi survey of professionals. *Criminal Behavior and Mental Health, 24*, 60–80.

Wallin, D. J. (2007). *Attachment in psychotherapy*. New York: Guilford Press.

Westerman, M. A., Foote, J. P., & Winston, A. (1995). Change in coordination across phases of psychotherapy and outcome: Two mechanisms for the role played by patients' contribution to the alliance. *Journal of Consulting and Clinical Psychology, 63*, 672–675.

Westerman, M. A., & Muran, J. C. (2017). Investigating an approach to the alliance based on interpersonal defense theory. *Psychotherapy Research, 27*, 620–641.

Wiseman, H. (2017). The quest for connection in interpersonal and therapeutic relationships. *Psychotherapy Research, 27*(4), 469–487.

Zilcha-Mano, S. (2018). Major developments in methods addressing for whom psychotherapy may work and why. *Psychotherapy Research*. https://doi.org/10.1080/10503307.2018.1429691.

Zufferey, P., Caspar, F., & Kramer, U. (2018). The role of interactional agreeableness in responsive treatments for patients with borderline personality disorder. *Journal of Personality Disorders*. (in Press).

Index

Note: 'Page numbers followed by "f" indicate figures and "t" indicate tables'.

A

Abandoned-abused child mode, 91f, 92–93
Active passivity, 8
Alliance-focused formulation
  abstract communication, 343–344, 348, 350
  alliance ruptures, 338
  cognitive behavioural therapy (CBT), 352
  confrontation marker, 348
  content/affect split, 347
  control, 346
  deferential and appeasing, 344
  future directions, 352–353
  hopelessness, 346
  methodology, 338–342
  observer-based tool, 338
  post-session questionnaire (PSQ), 343
  pressure, 346
  rupture resolution rating system (3RS), 338, 339t–340t
  self-criticism, 346
  task-analytic studies, 341
  withdrawal ruptures, 341
  working alliance inventory (WAI), 343
Alliance ruptures, 338
Anger, 84–85
Angry child mode, 91f, 92–93
Antisocial personality disorder (ASPD)
  aetiology, 163–165
  antagonism, 165
  biopsychosocial model, 164f
  borderline personality disorder (BPD), 167
  case formulation, 161
    biography, 173–174
    case report, 173–175
    criminal record, 174
    example, 173–177
    forensic ethical aspects, 172–173
    forensic ward monitoring, 175
    history of substance use, 174
    Inventory of Interpersonal Problems (IIP-D), 175
    PCL-R, 175
    principles, 171
    psychiatric history, 174
    psychological assessments, 174–175
    risk assessment, 170–172
    theories, 167–173
  challenges, 162
  Children with Attention Deficit Hyperactivity Disorder (ADHD), 163–164
  cognitive behavioural models of offending, 169–170
  cognitive behavioural theory, 167–169, 168f
  cognitive behavioural therapy (CBT), 166
  definition, 163–167
  Diagnostic and Statistical Manual of Mental Disorders (DSM-5), 165
  diagnostic criteria, 165–166
  dialectic behavioural therapy, 167
  disinhibition, 165
  individual risk factors, 164–165
  mental health care, 161–162
  mentalization-based therapy (MBT), 166–167
  monoamine oxidase (MAO), 164
  psychopathy checklist-revised (PCL-R), 165–166
  psychotherapy, 161–162
  Rush's model, 163
  treatment approaches, 166–167
Apparent competence, 8
Attachment, 238–239
Avoidant coping, 251–252
Avoidant Personality Disorder (AvPD)
  avoidance, 144
  case formulation refinement, 150–154
  change promoting, 149, 154–155
  clarification oriented therapy (COT), 138
  client's history, 149–150
  clinical guide, 147–148, 147t
  cognitive avoidance, 145

Avoidant Personality Disorder *(Continued)*
cognitive behavioural therapy (CBT) studies, 138
domains, 137–138
early treatment phases, 150–154
impaired metacognition, 142–143
Cluster C PD traits, 143
coherent self-image, 142–143
treatment-seeking substance abusers, 143
maladaptive coping procedures, 143–146
maladaptive emotional regulation, 143–146
maladaptive schemas, 139–142
attachment disturbances, 141
autonomy/exploration, 141
compliant/surrender mode, 140
Core Conflictual Relational Theme, 141–142
curiosity, 139–140
interpersonal motives, 139–142
playfulness, 140
punitive/demanding schema modes, 140
self-other attributions, 140
social avoidance, 141
social rank, 140
submissiveness, 140
Mario's story, 148–156
Metacognitive Interpersonal Therapy (MIT), 137–138
MIT case formulation, 146–147
outcome, 155–156
perfectionism, 145–146
poor autobiographical memory, 143
presentation of problem, 149–150
shared formulation of functioning, 149
treatment, 138

B

Behavioural analysis (BA), 11–12
Behavioural assessment personality disorders, 228–231
Biosocial theory, 4
Borderline personality disorder (BPD), 77, 91–93, 167, 234
BPD. *See* Borderline personality disorder (BPD)
Bully and attack mode, 91f, 92–93

C

Case conceptualization, 125–130
definition, 129–130
therapy, 129–130
Case formulation quality checklist (CFQC), 240–241
Clarification-oriented psychotherapy (COP)
clarification, 114
Model of Dual-Action Regulation (MDAR), 117–121, 118f
behaviour, 119–120
compensatory schemas, 120–121
dysfunctional schemas, 119
interactional actions, 118–119
interaction tests, 121
intransparent action, 119–120
norm schemas, 120
relationship motives, 118–119
relationship schemas, 119
rule schemas, 120
self-schemas, 119
motivation for change, 115
narcissistic personality disorder, 121–123
case, 127
case conceptualization, 125–130
criteria, 123
therapy, 125
process-oriented approach, 113
relationship formation, 115
relevant schemas clarification, 116
schemas processing, 116
self-regulation, 114
specific therapeutic interventions, 117
transfer, 117
Cognitive analytic therapy (CAT)
case example, 103–107
development, 98–101
dilemmas, 100
features, 96–98
Laura's reformulation letter, 107–108
maladaptive ways, 110
multiple self-states model, 102
personality disorder, 101–102
procedural sequence model (PSM), 99
psychopathology, 98–101
reciprocal relationships (RRs), 99
reciprocal role procedures (RRPs), 99
recognition, 96
recurring patterns (RRPs), 100
reformulation, 96, 102–103
revision, 96
self-defeating, 110
snags, 100
therapist-patient relationship, 97
traps, 100
young people, 101

Cognitive avoidance, 251–252
Cognitive behavioural therapy (CBT), 67
Cognitive flexibility, 255–256
Cognitive priming tasks, 65
Competition-hostility conflict, 213
Conceptualization-focused case presentation, 252–258
Conflicts, 208, 213
Coping modes, 88

D

Defence, 208–209, 213
Depressed mood, 32
Detached self-soother mode, 91f, 92–93
Detachment, 225–226
Devaluation, 213
Diagnostic and statistical manual (DSM) of mental disorders
  antagonism, 225–226
  case formulation, 226–227
    diagnosis, 226–227
    5P, 227
  Cluster C, 225
  detachment, 225–226
  disinhibition, 225–226
  functioning, 225–226
  negative affectivity, 225–226
  personality inventory for DSM-5 (PID-5), 225–226
  psychoticism, 225–226
Diagnostic and Statistical Manual of Mental Disorders (DSM-5), 165
Diagnostic impression, 28–31
Dialectical behaviour therapy (DBT), case formulation
  application, 14–15
  behavioural analysis (BA), 11–12
    Beth's case, 12–13, 14t
  biosocial theory, 4
  developmental history, 5
    Beth's case, 5–6
  dialectical philosophy, 4
  emotional vulnerability, 4
  identifying interventions and solutions, 15–16
    Beth's case, 16–17
  invalidating environment, 4
  learning theory, 3
  observing patterns across behaviours, 13–14
    Beth's case, 14–15
  personalizing psychotherapy method, 1
  step-by step approach, 5–17
  steps, 2
  theoretical foundation, 3–4
  treatment targets, identifying/prioritizing, 6–10
    active passivity, 8
    apparent competence, 8
    Beth's case, 10–11
    emotion vulnerability, 8
    inhibited grieving, 9
    macrolevel behaviours, 7–8
    microlevel behaviours, 8–9
    primary treatment targets, 7–8
    secondary treatment targets, 8–9
    self-invalidation, 8
    treatment focus, 9–10
    unrelenting crisis, 9
    vision for life, 7
  wise mind concept, 3
  Zen philosophy, 3
Dialectical philosophy, 4
Diffuse anxiety, 32
Dilemmas, 100
Disinhibition, 225–226
Disorder-specific approach, 81–82
Dysfunctional parent modes, 90

E

Early maladaptive schemas, 78
Emotional disorder
  borderline personality disorder (BPD), 246–248
    avoidant coping, 247–248
    negative emotions, 246
    negative reactions to strong emotions, 247
    shared latent structure accounts, 248
  unified protocol (UP) for transdiagnostic treatment, 249–252, 250f
    avoidant coping, 251–252
    Case Formulation Worksheet, 251
    cognitive avoidance, 251–252
    cognitive flexibility, 255–256
    components, 254–258
    conceptualization-focused case presentation, 252–258
    confronting and tolerating physical sensations, 257
    countering emotional behaviours, 256
    emotion-driven behaviours, 251–252
    emotion exposure, 257–258

Emotional disorder *(Continued)*
evidences, 252–254
flexibility, 249
functional analysis, 255
motivation enhancement, 254
passive-aggressive behaviour, 253
skills-based treatment modules, 249
social anxiety diagnosis, 253–254
subtle behavioural avoidance, 251–252
Emotion-based case formulation
acceptance, 361
agency, 361
anger, 360
anger rejecting, 360
clinical practice, 361–363
clinical research, 357–358
cognitive models, 356
concepts, 356–357
conducting, 366–371
emotional change, 357–361
emotional growth, 362
emotional processing, 358f
empirical support, 364–366
general psychiatric management (GPM), 364–365
global distress, 359
grief/hurt, 361
inferences making, 370
initial case assessment, 367–368
motive-orientated therapeutic relationship (MOTR), 364–365
needs, 360
negative self-evaluations, 360
personal processes, 368–370, 369f
planning treatment, 370
process diagnosis, 362
responsivity, 362–363
self-compassion, 360
shame/fear, 359
targeted client processes, 370–371
theory, 356–357
zone of proximal development, 361–362
Emotion vulnerability, 8
Evidence-based treatments (EBTs), 61
Experiences in Close Relationship questionnaire (ECR), 46

F
Fears, 208, 212
Feed-forward effects, 326–328
Frank's mode model, 88, 89f

G
Generalized anxiety disorder (GAD), 33
General psychiatric management (GPM)
biology and social factors, 61–62
borderline personality disorder (BPD), 61, 63–64
case formulation, 69–74
case vignette, 67–74
cognitive behavioural therapy (CBT), 67
cognitive priming tasks, 64
conceptualization, 61–62, 65
evidence-based treatments (EBTs), 61
experience-sampling diary methods, 65
interpersonal hypersensitivity model, 66
mentalization-based treatment (MBT), 63
psychodynamic formulations, 61–62
psychotherapies randomized controlled trials, 62
self-destructive behaviour, 63–64
transference-focused psychotherapy (TFP), 63
Global assessment of functioning scale (GAF), 41–42

H
Healthy adult mode, 88–89, 91f, 92–93
Humanistic approach, 268

I
Idiographic Conflict Formulation (ICF) method
case example, 210–211
history, 210
case formulation
adaptation to conflicts, 210
avoidant outcomes, 209–210, 214–215
competition-hostility conflict, 213
conflicts, 208, 213
constructing steps, 206–210
defence, 208–209, 213
devaluation, 213
dominant other conflict, 213
fears, 208, 212
help-rejecting complaining, 214
information base, 206–210
ingratiation-disappointment conflict, 213
motives, 207–208, 211–212
outcome, 215–216

overall gratification inhibition conflict, 213
passive aggression, 214
reaction formation, 213
repression, 213
resultants, 209–210, 214–215
specific stressors, 210
specific stressors vulnerabiity, 210
symptomatic behaviours, 209
symptomatic outcomes, 214
symptoms, 209
treatment, 215–216
vulnerability/best adaptation, 215
wishes, 207, 211–212
Zofia, 211–215
components, 204, 205t–206t
Core Conflictual Relationship Theme (CCRT), 203–204
Ingratiation-disappointment conflict, 213
Inhibited grieving, 9
Interpersonal behaviour, 324–326
Interpersonal defence theory
case example, 322–331
feed-forward effects, 326–328
interpersonal behaviour, 324–326
noncoordinating pattern, 323–324
research, 329–331
symptoms, 328–329
target problems, 328–329
case formulation, 315, 319–322
analytic methods, 319–321
components, 319
considerations, 319–320
procedures, 321–322
Structured Analysis of Social Behaviour (SASB), 320, 320f
definition, 316–319
feed-forward effects, 317–318
interpersonal outcome, 332
psychopathology, 315–316
symptoms, 318
theory's tenets, 316–319
treatment implications, 331–334
Interpersonal hypersensitivity model, 66
Interpersonal Reconstructive Therapy (IRT) theory, 182–183
adaptive and maladaptive patterns, 185–187
adaptive personality patterns, 186–187
affect flow, 182
application, 191–192
autoimmunity hypothesis, 184
behavioural patterns, 183–184
behaviour flow, 182
case formulation
research, 199
case formulation method, 187–188
cognition flow, 182
copy process analysis, 194–195, 194t
copy process-based diagnosis, 195
copy process evidence, 189
current patterns, 192–193
developmental history, 194–195
gift of love (GOL), 184, 196
hypothesis, 190
motivations, 187–188
growth collaborator, 190–191
interdependence, 185–186
intransitive behaviours, 185–186
maladaptive patterns, 187
normative learning process, 182
outcome, 197–199
outline patterns, 189
post-traumatic stress disorder (PTSD), 191
psychiatric symptoms, 184
self-treatment, 198f
steps, 187–188
structural analysis of social behaviour (SASB), 185–186, 186f
structure and logic, 185f
subsequent involuntary hospitalization, 192
symptom-linked themes, 192–193
treatment implications, 190–191, 196–197
Wisconsin Personality Inventory (WISPI), 191
Inventory of interpersonal problems (IIP-D), 175

J

John's mode model, 91f

L

Learning theory, 3
Levels of personality functioning scale (LPFS), 41–42

M

Macrolevel behaviours, 7–8
Maladaptive child modes, 79, 80f
Maladaptive coping modes, 80, 80f
Maladaptive parent modes, 79, 80f

Manipulation, 124–125
Mentalization-based treatment (MBT)
Adult Attachment Interview (AAI), 46
borderline personality disorder (BPD)
case formulation 1, 50–54
case formulation 2, 54–56
case formulations, 42–44
epistemic trust, 43–44
global assessment of functioning scale (GAF), 41–42
group therapy, 55
heterogeneity, 41–42
intense temperament, 43
levels of personality functioning scale (LPFS), 41–42
theoretical grid, 42–44
triadic constellation, 43–44
case formulations, 44–45, 50
consequences, 58
difficult patient minding, 57–58
Experiences in Close Relationship questionnaire (ECR), 46
implications, 58
mentalizing attachment relationships, 58
minding minds, 49
needed information, 46
psychoeducational group, 47
reflective functioning (RF), 44–45
reliability and validity, 44–45
technical details, 47–49
therapists mental activity, 49
Mentalizing attachment relationships, 58
Microlevel behaviours, 8–9
Minding minds, 49
Model of Dual-Action Regulation (MDAR), 117–121, 118f
behaviour, 119–120
compensatory schemas, 120–121
dysfunctional schemas, 119
interactional actions, 118–119
interaction tests, 121
intransparent action, 119–120
norm schemas, 120
relationship motives, 118–119
relationship schemas, 119
rule schemas, 120
self-schemas, 119
Monoamine oxidase (MAO), 164
Motivation enhancement, 254
Motive-oriented Therapeutic relationship (MOTR), 278–281
broad-spectrum behaviour therapy, 281
patient hostility, 280f
principles, 278
Multiple self-states model, 102

N
Narcissistic personality disorder (NPD), 27–28, 121–123
Negative affectivity, 225–226
Negative relationship schemas, 124
Negative self-schema, 123
Noncoordinating pattern, 323–324
Normative schemas, 124

O
Object relations theory, 19–21
Operationalized psychodynamic diagnosis (OPD) approach
aims, 292–293
alienated body-image, 306–307
applications, 301–305
assessment of personality disorders (AMPD), 292
axes, 293
structure, 297t–299t
background information, 305–307
case formulation, 308–309
conceptual background, 293–297
conflictual motivational topics, 302
dependency, 295
Diagnostic and Statistical Manual of Mental Disorders (DSM), 292
Dialectic Behaviour Therapy (DBT), 310–311
dissemination, 292–293
formal expert ratings, 307
future perspectives, 311
guilt conflict, 296
history, 292–293
identity conflict, 296
individuation, 295
information, 305–307
integrative approach, 305–309
International Classification of Diseases (ICD), 292
interpersonal patterns, 302–305
interrelated positions, 294
levels of structural integration axis (LSIA), 297–301

DSM/ICD dimensional models of personality functioning, 301
research, 300–301
mentalization-based treatment (MBT), 310–311
motivational conflicts, 303–305
multiaxial diagnosis, 293–297
need for care, 295
oedipal conflict, 296
personality disorders, 297–301
personality function, 303–305
prototypical conflictual topics, 295
psychoanalytic models, 292
self-report data, 307
self-sufficiency, 295
self-worth conflict, 296
stressor-induced conflict, 296
structural integration assessing levels, 303
submission *vs.* control, 295
transference focused psychotherapy (TFP), 310–311
Overall gratification inhibition conflict, 213

P

Parent modes, 87
Passive-aggressive behaviour, 253
Pathological grandiose structure (PGS), 27–28
PCL-R, 175
Personality disorders, 19–21, 101–102
Arthur's case, 234–240
attachment, 238–239
behavioural case formulation, 235–238
case formulation
antisocial personality disorder, 231–233
attachment, 233
attachment prototypes, 233
behavioural approaches, 228–231
behavioural assessment personality disorders, 228–231
behavioural case formulation, 229–230
borderline personality disorder, 234
Case Formulation Quality Checklist (CFQC), 240–241
emotional dyscontrol, 234
hyperbolic temperament, 234
processes, 231–234
schemas, 232–233
training, 240–241
traits, 231–234
comment, 239–240
perpetuating factors, 236
precipitating factors, 236
protective factors, 237
schema-informed formulation, 238–239
treatment plan, 237–238
Personality disorders (PD), 77
Personality inventory for DSM-5 (PID-5), 225–226
Personalizing psychotherapy method, 1
Plan analysis
additional basic concepts, 266–268
basic pillar, 266
behaviour therapy, 268
blocked/threatened plans, 272
classical social psychological models, 267
cognitive science models, 267
conducting, 269–274
coping and avoidance plans, 272–273
criteria, 269
experienced emotion, 272
general position, 265–266
general psychotherapy, 266–267
humanistic approach, 268
instrumentality notion, 265
interpersonal approach, 268
methodology, 269–281
Motive-oriented Therapeutic relationship (MOTR), 278–281
broad-spectrum behaviour therapy, 281
patient hostility, 280f
principles, 278
personality disorder clinical case, 282–286
anxiety, 284
case example, 282–286, 283f
feeling impaired, 284
procedure, 270–274
psychodynamic approach, 268
psychological problems model, 274–276
psychotherapeutic approaches, 268–269
research, 286
systemic approach, 269
theoretical concepts, 266–269
therapeutic action, 276–278, 277f
training, 286–287
two-dimensional plan structure, 271f
Positive self-schema, 124
Post-session questionnaire (PSQ), 343
Procedural sequence model (PSM), 99
Psychoeducational group, 47

Psychopathy checklist-revised (PCL-R), 165–166
Psychoticism, 225–226
Punitive parent mode, 91f, 92–93

R

Reciprocal relationships (RRs), 99
Reciprocal role procedures (RRPs), 99
Recognition, 96
Recurring patterns (RRPs), 100
Reflective functioning (RF), 44–45
Reformulation, 96, 102–103
Revision, 96
3RS. *See* Rupture resolution rating system (3RS)
Rule-setting behaviour, 124
Rupture resolution rating system (3RS), 338, 339t–340t
Rush's model, 163

S

Schema-mode model, 79
Schema therapy (ST)
  anger, 84–85
  borderline personality disorder (BPD), 77, 91–93
    abandoned-abused child mode, 91f, 92–93
    angry child mode, 91f, 92–93
    bully and attack mode, 91f, 92–93
    detached self-soother mode, 91f, 92–93
    example, 91–93
    healthy adult mode, 91f, 92–93
    punitive parent mode, 91f, 92–93
    suspicious overcontroller mode, 91f, 92–93
  case formulation, 83
    coping modes, 88
    healthy adult mode, 88–89
    mode model and vulnerable part, 85–87
    parent modes, 87
  coping strategy, 78
  coping styles, 78
  disorder-specific approach, 81–82
    borderline personality disorder, 81–82
  dysfunctional parent modes, 90
  early maladaptive schemas, 78
  Frank's mode model, 88, 89f
  healthy modes, 80–81, 80f, 90
  information assessment, 82–83
  John's mode model, 91f
  linking symptoms, 83–85
  maladaptive child modes, 79, 80f
  maladaptive coping modes, 80, 80f, 90
  maladaptive parent modes, 79, 80f
  mode model case formulation, 81–91
  personality disorders (PD), 77
  relevant modes, 85
  schema-mode model, 79
  self-injury, 84
  survival strategy, 89
  symptoms and emotions, 84
  theory and central concepts, 78–81
  transdiagnostic approach, 81–82
  vulnerable child modes, 90
Self-defeating, 110
Self-destructive behaviour, 63–64
Self-injury, 84
Self-invalidation, 8
Skills-based treatment modules, 249
Snags, 100
Social anxiety diagnosis, 253–254
STIPO. *See* Structured Interview of Personality Organization (STIPO)
Strong appreciation motive, 123
Strong autonomy motivation, 123
Structured Analysis of Social Behaviour (SASB), 320, 320f
Structured Interview of Personality Organization (STIPO), 37–38
  clinical utility, 38
  reliability, 38
  research, 37–38
  validity, 38
Subtle behavioural avoidance, 251–252
Suspicious overcontroller mode, 91f, 92–93

T

Therapist-patient relationship, 97
Therapists mental activity, 49
Transdiagnostic approach, 81–82
Transference-focused psychotherapy (TFP), 63
  acute organic mental illness, 25–26
  borderline level (BPO), 27
  case example, 31–36
  case formulation, 30–31, 33–36
  client description, 31–33
  depressed mood, 32
  diagnostic formulation, 28–30
  diagnostic impression, 28–31
  diffuse anxiety, 32
  emotional complexity, 21

Generalized Anxiety Disorder (GAD), 33
goals, 25
immature defences, 21–22
information channels, 22
libidinal, 20
mature defences, 21–22
narcissistic personality disorder (NPD), 27–28
nonjudgmental/noncritical stance, 23
object relations theory, 19–21
paranoid-schizoid organization, 20–21
pathological grandiose structure (PGS), 27–28
patient's attitude, 22
patient's sensorium, 24, 26f
personality disorders, 19–21
presenting problem, 31–33
psychiatric attention, 25–26
psychological organization, 21
reality testing assessment, 25–26
research review, 37
structural interview, 21–28, 37–38
  clinical utility, 37
  reliability, 37
  Structured Interview of Personality Organization (STIPO), 37–38
  validity, 37
treatment contract, 29
trigger event, 20–21
unsupportive husband, 32–33
Traps, 100
Treatment plan, 237–238
Two-dimensional plan structure, 271f

U

Unrelenting crisis, 9

V

Vulnerable child modes, 90

W

Wise mind concept, 3
Withdrawal ruptures, 341
Working alliance inventory (WAI), 343

Z

Zen philosophy, 3

FSC
www.fsc.org
MIX
Papier | Fördert
gute Waldnutzung
FSC® C083411

Kolibri 360 GmbH
Ferdinand-Jühlke-Straße 7
99095 Erfurt, Deutschland
produktsicherheit@kolibri360.de